MODERN
CONTINENTAL PLAYWRIGHTS

❧

PLAYS AND PLAYWRIGHTS SERIES

Edited by Arthur Hobson Quinn

*A complete survey of the dramatic field, with books of
selected plays to accompany the compact but authoritative accounts of the drama.*

———

ELIZABETHAN PLAYWRIGHTS
Felix E. Schelling

TYPICAL ELIZABETHAN PLAYS
Felix E. Schelling

MODERN ENGLISH PLAYWRIGHTS
John W. Cunliffe

MODERN CONTINENTAL PLAYWRIGHTS
Frank W. Chandler

MODERN CONTINENTAL PLAYS
S. M. Tucker

MODERN AMERICAN AND BRITISH PLAYS
S. M. Tucker

THE ART OF PLAY PRODUCTION
John Dolman, Jr.

The following volumes are in preparation:

MODERN ENGLISH PLAYS
John W. Cunliffe

THE ART OF PLAYWRITING
Walter Prichard Eaton

(Other volumes to be arranged for)

Harper & Brothers Publishers

MODERN
CONTINENTAL
PLAYWRIGHTS

BY

FRANK W. CHANDLER

*Professor of English and Ropes Professor
of Comparative Literature
in the University of Cincinnati
Author of "The Literature of Roguery,"
"Aspects of Modern Drama,"
"The Contemporary Drama of France," etc.*

HARPER & BROTHERS
NEW YORK AND LONDON
1931

MODERN
CONTINENTAL PLAYWRIGHTS

CONTENTS

v

CONTENTS

vi

CONTENTS

Modern Eng. Playwrig

PREFACE

ON THE continent of Europe since 1880 the drama has flourished as never before except during the Age of Pericles in Greece, of Elizabeth in England, and of the later Renaissance in Spain and France. Those who in the north have contributed most to the art of the theater have been serious souls preoccupied with interpreting life philosophically:—Ibsen and Björnson in Norway; Strindberg in Sweden; Tolstoy, Chekhov, and Andreyev in Russia; Hauptmann and the expressionists in Germany. In France and what was once Austria-Hungary, playwrights, with such notable exceptions as Brieux, Hervieu, and the Čapek brothers, have been less engaged by social and moral issues than by the attempt to offer entertaining representations of "men acting," either idealized, as by Rostand and von Hofmannsthal, or else rendered with poignant or amusing fidelity to fact, as by Lavedan, Donnay, Schnitzler, and Molnár. In the south, interest in drama for its own sake has usually prevailed, although Pirandello in Italy provides a rational counterpoise to the estheticism of d'Annunzio, and Benavente in Spain has been sobered on occasion by northern influence.

Whatever the concern of the playwrights, they have responded, both north and south, to a new surge of creative energy. The most gifted literary artists have been attracted to the theater. Those who once would have written novels in preference to plays have written plays in preference to novels. Both the physical and the spiritual conditions of production have undergone remarkable improvement. Modern stagecraft has become a fine art. Free theaters have arisen to encourage experimentation. The reading of plays has increased a thousandfold. With the spread of education has come the demand for a better class of entertainment. Audiences formerly satisfied with mere pinchbeck have demanded gold of Ophir. Dramatists, responding, have in turn cultivated popular taste, bestowing infinite pains even upon trifles meant only to amuse. The example of a few great writers has demonstrated the possibility of achieving success upon the stage with pieces truly significant, capable of controlling the feelings, thought, and lives of large sections of the public.

From among the ruck of lesser writers for the theater a few in each country emerge supreme. Such representative playwrights are in part made by their opportunities and by the social and literary influences of the moment. But more largely, they themselves will be found, by reason of their native genius, to have shaped these influences, determining the work of lesser men about them. To study the leaders rather than the rank and file who follow or who now and then stray from the main marching column must, of necessity, be the business of this survey. Yet in a few chapters, brief treatment is accorded to a considerable number of those who represent important tendencies. In the main, however, this is a study of prominent playwrights and their plays rather than a history of modern drama.

Acknowledgments are due here to many predecessors in the field of dramatic history and criticism, writers of general surveys of drama, of special surveys of national literatures, of monographs dealing with individual playwrights, and critics whose accounts of separate pieces have appeared in various periodicals and newspapers. For the most part, however, the author has depended upon his first-hand acquaintance with the plays themselves. He has not been content merely to name them or refer to them vaguely in general terms, as is so commonly the practice in histories of literature. He has assumed that it is the reader's desire to be informed as to just what the more important dramas are all about, and he recognizes

PREFACE

that only a specialist could be expected to know the multiple productions in various languages of such an array of playwrights. To interpret is also to criticize. Certainly, in these pages criticism will be found to supplement the careful analysis of individual dramas.

Lest extensive lists of titles in foreign tongues might seem forbidding and pedantic in a volume for the English or American reader, such titles have been rendered into English throughout. Yet where an original is not exactly translated, the foreign title has been added in parenthesis. As a rule, also, dates have been excluded from the text and relegated to the bibliography.

As to personal acknowledgments, the author owes to Professor Arthur Hobson Quinn, editor of the Plays and Playwrights Series, admiration and thanks for wise oversight and the exemplary patience with which he has awaited through the years the completion of a task that has grown increasingly difficult as the dramatists, with greater industry than their critic, have continued to add to their published works. Above all, the author owes to Miss Estelle Hunt, Assistant in Comparative Literature and Secretary of the College of Liberal Arts of the University of Cincinnati, a debt of gratitude for able collaboration in preparing and revising the manuscript, compiling the bibliography and the index, and correcting all the proofs.

F. W. C.

MODERN
CONTINENTAL PLAYWRIGHTS

CHAPTER I

IBSEN—FOUNDER OF MODERN DRAMA

IT IS inevitable that any survey of recent drama in Europe
should start with Ibsen. He stands supreme among the
moderns as the most thoughtful, systematic, and influential
of writers for the stage. Passing from the cultivation of
legendary and romantic plays in verse to that of social and
symbolic plays in prose, he inaugurated a new epoch in the
history of the theater. Through his later work in particular
he powerfully affected his contemporaries and successors. He
united literature with stagecraft; he combined ideas with story;
he brought ethics and sociology out of the closet, challenging
playgoers to think as well as to feel. Having made the drama
unwontedly real by his dealings with the problems of everyday living, he proceeded to make it unreal again, yet true in
a deeper sense, by revealing beneath the surface of common
situations symbolic meanings. In this regard, unwittingly collaborating with Strindberg, Ibsen induced fresh developments
that have eventuated in what is loosely termed expressionism.

Born in 1828, of mixed Norwegian, Danish, Scottish, and
German ancestry, Henrik Ibsen grew up a lonely, solemn boy
in a small town. He served as apprentice to an apothecary
while preparing to study medicine, and, failing to pass his
university examination, scribbled plays, edited a paper, and
for five years acted as literary director of a little theater with
a long name in the city of Bergen. Then, for seven years more,
he was occupied in the same capacity in two theaters at Christiania. During this period of his closest practical connection
with the stage, he not only put on and polished the plays of
others but continued to prepare and produce plays of his own.

1

Of the four that saw the footlights at Bergen, the best were
Lady Inger of Östraat and *The Feast at Solhaug*. These were
followed at Christiania by *The Vikings in Helgeland, Love's
Comedy,* and *The Pretenders*. In substituting a modern theme
and mild satire for romance, *Love's Comedy* differed from
the rest, and, though of less intrinsic merit than *The Pretenders,* it proved prophetic of the new drift in its author's
development. Moreover, written shortly after his marriage,
it seemed to cast doubts upon the institution, implying that
the joy of consummation is likely to be less than that of expectation, and that love can scarcely survive the legal pre-
scriptions and restraints put upon it by society. In all the
romantic pieces which had followed the youthful *Catilina*, Ibsen
showed himself a student of ballad and saga, of the folk songs
collected by Landstad and of the works of Moritz Hansen. It
was evident also that he had read the plays of Scribe and
Hebbel. But, although he owed a debt to such forbears and
especially in technique to Augier and the younger Dumas, he
remained original, the least bookish of dramatists.

In 1864, when Ibsen was thirty-six, he left Norway to
remain abroad for more than quarter of a century, except for
two brief vacation visits at home. He had resented the attitude of his countrymen in refusing to aid Denmark when
Prussia and Austria laid forcible hands upon Schleswig-Hol-
stein. Moreover, he was irritated by the attacks of enemies and
by the national provincialism which later he thrust at in his
social plays. Accepting private aid and finally a state pension,
he lived in Italy and Germany, making Rome, Dresden, and
Munich his headquarters. Here were written those works from
Brand to *Hedda Gabler* which won him European fame. Although his scenes, except in *Emperor and Galilean,* continued
to be Norwegian, his characters and ideals became universal.
Returning from his voluntary exile at the age of sixty-three,
Ibsen spent his last decade and a half in Christiania. During
the first eight years of this final period he composed his four

remaining plays. At his death in 1906, the man who once had been regarded as an iconoclast and a force of evil was hailed as the father of the modern drama and the prophet of a new morality.

Before Ibsen settled down to create that theater of social criticism and individual awakening which is most closely associated with his name, he experimented, not merely with romantic saga plays, but also with the dramatic-epic form made popular by Goethe's *Faust*. In *Emperor and Galilean*, he wrote what he believed to be his masterpiece, an extensive study in ten acts and numerous scenes setting forth through vacillations in the mind of Julian the Apostate the conflict between pagan and Christian ideals, together with the Emperor's failure to reconcile the two and create a Third Empire of the spirit. The Galilean's followers who might have lost their zeal in prosperity now thrive as the result of Julian's persecution. The work is rich in thought, but herein lies its limitation. The thought is not fully incorporated with character and story.

In *Brand* and *Peer Gynt*, however, although the form remains unsatisfactory for acted drama, inasmuch as in each the story is dispersed and told by snatches, yet the characters are sufficiently vital to give interest to the author's parable, and his doctrine is of universal application. Shall the individual succeed by a process of continual adjustments or by pinning faith to a single ideal and refusing compromise? Brand exemplifies the latter attitude. He is a stalwart priest who scorns to do less than his utmost to realize his ideal. That ideal is just one aspect of Christ's teaching exalted to control all others—self-sacrifice. According to Brand, salvation can come only through complete self-abnegation and the imposition of that principle upon others. His child may be threatened with death, but he will not consent to remove from the dark valley where he conceives his duty to lie; his wife may cling to the little mementoes of the dead child, but she must surrender them to a passing beggar lest she grow too soft in her indulgence of grief; his mother may be fatally ill, but he will not visit her unless she promise to give up all that she has treasured. "All or nothing," is Brand's infallible test. Driven from his church because he will not compromise, Brand dies a martyr, startled in his last moments by the thought that perhaps his life has been a failure since God may require of us strength of love as well as strength of will. In his ideal, Brand was mistaken; but in his devotion to it, he was admirable.

Peer Gynt, on the other hand, is thoroughly unworthy, an amusing rogue who, in order to remain himself, would compromise at every turn. The portrait of Brand was inspired in part by such living models as Sören Kierkegaard and his follower, the pastor of Ibsen's native town, Gustav Adolph Lammers. That of Peer Gynt was suggested by Norwegian folklore. Ibsen found in this braggart dreamer an exact antithesis to Brand. Whereas Brand would sacrifice himself, Peer would sacrifice others. Whereas Brand would manfully confront every obstacle, Peer would artfully "go around." He would not despise love; he would profit from it. Throughout his fantastic adventures, Peer, seeking only to save his own soul, is on the road to losing it after all his dodging and turning. What is there left of him finally? Only a poor remnant which Death would toss into the melting pot. Trim yourself daily and hourly to fit into each fresh situation, and ere long nothing will be left of your individual self. Only in Solveig's love which Peer has disdained lies the hope of his survival. Here scenes of satire and grotesquerie mingle with those that are tender and poetic. Important as revealing its author's philosophy, *Peer Gynt* is also memorable as forecasting in part the technique of the later expressionists.

The romantic freedom of invention displayed in these dramas Ibsen proceeded to forego for two decades thereafter, becoming a realist in so far as he fixed attention upon observed actuality. In doing this, however, he was no less busied with ideas. They were merely expounded by persons of the contemporary, middle-class world in which he was living. *The League of Youth*, although in every way inferior to *Peer Gynt*, is of interest as presenting the same theme lowered to the realistic key. Its hero, Stensgård, is a compromiser like Peer who seeks to get on by adapting himself to the exigencies of the instant, turning with amusing facility from sweetheart to sweetheart and from party to party in politics. Though he prates of the public good, he thinks only of private gain. His defeat and exposure are arranged by the dramatist quite after the style of the old bourgeois comedy.

In *The Pillars of Society* Ibsen composed a solider piece of the same sort. Here he was less the satirist than the moralist, denouncing more vehemently, by implication, the hypocrisy and pretense of the respectable. Consul Bernick, who has posed as model man of his community, is in truth a schemer, a philanderer, and by intent a murderer. His assumption of philanthropic motives is mere sham. Essentially dishonest in business, he yet keeps within the law. To account for certain losses, he throws upon a friend suspicion of embezzlement, just as earlier, to escape scandal, he had allowed that friend to accept blame for an intrigue. Bernick has sent away the woman he loved in order to marry another for profit. He sanctions the despatch from his shipyard of a vessel that he knows to be unseaworthy, hoping in his heart that it may carry to the depths the injured friend who has threatened to expose him. But the discovery that on this very vessel his son has embarked as a stowaway brings Bernick to his senses. Moreover, his better nature has been stirred by the reproaches of his former sweetheart—a new woman—who convinces him, and the audience as well, that the pillars of society are truth and freedom. So fully has he mastered the lesson that when his townsmen arrive to hail him as first citizen, he makes a clean breast to them of his sin but already Providence has rewarded him by keeping within the haven the ship that beyond it would have foundered. The piece is almost didactic, and its machinery creaks a trifle. One feels here that the spiritual meaning and the action devised to convey it are not thoroughly fused. Yet *The Pillars of Society*, written during its author's fiftieth year, ushered in those social dramas destined to exert world-wide influence.

The contrast in mental attitude between men and women and especially the deficiencies from the woman's point of view in the institution of marriage engaged Ibsen's attention in *A Doll's House*. This piece, significant only in the last half of its last act so far as doctrine is concerned, adapts the older technique to a new purpose. What could be more conventional than the story of a good wife whom a villain controls through a legal document which she has forged with the best of motives? The villain will expose the wife through a letter. She must keep that letter unread by dancing the tarantella to divert her husband. In the mean time, she has expounded her situation to a confidante, who ultimately calls off the villain by agreeing to marry him. So far, the play is *vieux jeux*. That which gives it an important place in dramatic history is its humanizing of these elements, and its shift in axis from the physical to the spiritual plane when, with the danger past, the wife, confronting her husband, pleads the new individualism for women. Nora, so recently a doll, reads her husband a lecture and leaves. She may return, but only in case the miracle of miracles occurs, each learning apart the meaning of true union. The dialogue in that final scene is capital. Humanly speaking, Nora might have remained to develop herself at home while training her children. Dramatically, her departure was imperative in order to startle the audience into thought. What matter that her development has been unduly rapid? This is a play not of character but of ideas. The ideas seem commonplace now; once they were novel.

When outraged men and even conservative women of an older generation shook their heads at this flouting of the

6

Christian concept of marriage, Ibsen retorted by writing *Ghosts*. Suppose that a less rebellious Nora had remained with a more vicious Torvald, what would have happened? Already in the person of Dr. Rank, Ibsen, the student of medicine, had introduced into *A Doll's House* inherited disease. He would now make it a prime factor in his plot, a curse inflicted upon an innocent son by a profligate father from whom his mother ought to have separated. Mrs. Alving's tragic fault lies far back in her having heeded the advice of Pastor Manders when he bade her return to her wicked lord in accordance with the sacrosanct formula of marriage. Young Oswald, doomed, therefore, from conception, becomes his mother's punishment, and finally he begs her to take the life she has given and save him from threatened idiocy. Her hesitation as the curtain falls is excellent "theater" since it sends the audience home to debate as to what she actually did and how far she was justified.

In *Ghosts* the timorous clergyman Manders, the whining hypocrite Engstrand, the brazen hussy Regina are satirically portrayed and faintly brighten the gloom. With Manders Ibsen almost stooped to caricature; with Mrs. Alving he more subtly suggested the development of a small soul from rigorous conservatism to perplexed radicalism. Oswald, disintegrating bit by bit before our eyes, anticipates the passive hero of naturalism, the victim of a scientific rather than a classic fate. He is the ghost of his dissolute father, and in his scene with Regina at the close of the first act he duplicates his father's scene with Regina's mother years before. The title of the play applies not only to this theatric coincidence; it applies more accurately to those ideas, once living but now dead—spook formulas for conduct—which haunt and enslave us superstitiously. The precise manner in which the orphanage catches fire is left in doubt, but its destruction is ironic, seeming to sweep away the inheritance of the gay chamberlain designed by his wife to blot out the memory of his sins, yet inducing in his son an excitement that culminates in paresis, the father's awful gift to his heir.

As a tragedy of congenital disease, this play is Ibsen's least pleasant and most impressive, although by no means his best. Let those who will, wonder why Regina, who was also the chamberlain's child, should have failed to share the inheritance of her half-brother's illness. The Mendelian law of heredity will explain it, and we may be thankful that only one character lost a mind. Regina had little to lose. The fact remains that everywhere *Ghosts* was hailed by those intent upon breaking with the traditional drama. It became a stock piece on all experimental stages.

From attacking our misconception of marriage as a thing indissoluble, absorbing individual rights, Ibsen turned, in *An Enemy of the People*, to assail our misconception of governmental rule by the compact majority. The one man in a community who would purge it of evil is denounced by every vested interest. He is forbidden to discuss the badly laid water pipes and the pollution of the baths for which the tanneries of his father-in-law are responsible; and at the public meeting packed by his opponents he can only in general terms decry the democratic heresy that right must lie with the many. Right, he asserts, will lie with the few. "The strongest man is he who stands most alone." Here Ibsen, who had not been averse to symbolism in certain features of *A Doll's House* and *Ghosts*, drew a symbolic parallel with his own case. He, the stalwart reformer, had endeavored to cleanse the polluted waters of social life, but society had proclaimed him its enemy, preferring to suppress the truth for the sake of preserving appearances. Tempted, like Dr. Stockmann, to let his fellows poison themselves if they insisted, he had then resolved to fight on, as in this very play, revealing the danger and weakness of the democratic practice of merely counting noses. The piece was written with more vigor than art, employing an unusually large cast, but affording no character analysis, or love, or the customary harking back to an anterior story now brought to its climax. In satire upon compromise and social selfishness, however, and in enunciation of ideas applicable to politics everywhere, *An Enemy of the People* proved effective. Especially clever was its use of dramatic irony, as when the simple-hearted reformer hopes at first that the town will not too greatly honor him for his discovery, or when his friends at last imagine that he has of set purpose depreciated the value of the baths in order to buy their shares at a low figure.

The attack upon formulas for conduct, evident here and in *Ghosts*, *A Doll's House*, and *Brand*, was continued with greater finesse in *The Wild Duck*, which showed the futility of attempting to impose ideals upon others from without, and criticized specifically such formulas as "Sacrifice what is dearest to you," and "Tell the truth, the whole truth, and nothing but the truth." According to Ibsen, sacrifice for the sake of sacrifice is folly, and truth-telling, while desirable in nine hundred and ninety-nine cases, may in the thousandth prove even immoral. He too had preached the necessity of truth and freedom in *The Pillars of Society*, and the wisdom of a marriage of perfect confidence in *A Doll's House*. But in *The Wild Duck* he sought to reprehend those who would deduce from his earlier plays any hard and fast law of conduct to be applied externally to every situation. He would show that circumstances alter cases. Nora and Torvald, no doubt, must speak the truth to each other fully at last, but Gregers Werle, the unintelligent reformer, with his cant about the claim of the ideal, is a fool to expose the past of simple-hearted Mrs. Ekdal to her husband, and a greater fool still to bid Mrs. Ekdal's little girl sacrifice what she holds dearest in order to win back the love of her supposed father. Misery results for all. The child was losing her eyesight in touching up negatives, but she never knew it; nor did she know that she was not the daughter of Hjalmar; nor did he know that she was the child of his benefactor, or that his wife had been that benefactor's mistress. How would a man who has discovered facts like these act in a story-book? That alone is the question in the mind of the poseur who has allowed his wife to manage the house and conduct his business while he lay dreaming of an impossible invention. It is the story-book formula that leads Hjalmar to repulse little Hedwig and to talk of leaving his kindly helpmate, though he be content to stay at least for luncheon. It is the reformer's story-book formula of self-sacrifice that spurs little Hedwig to take her life as something even dearer to her than the pet duck. How absurd! And to the dazed Gregers who contemplates the tragedy he has wrought, a sybaritic physician talks of the crime of killing one's illusions.

In this great and moving play, the richness of characterization and the tender, bitter, humorous, tragic story keep us unaware of the author's doctrine until we have felt it as well as thought it. Here the symbolism of the pet bird wounded by the old reprobate and retrieved from the marsh by his dog is merely insinuated as a parallel to the situation of that strange family in the photographer's gallery, wounded by old Werle, rescued from its comfortable world of self-deception by his foolish son, and but maimed the more.

If, in many respects, *The Wild Duck* is Ibsen's best play for acting, his most subtle is *Rosmersholm*, a study, like its successor, *Hedda Gabler*, of the evil wrought by excessive individualism. Be yourself, first and foremost, Ibsen had urged, but now, lest that counsel be accepted as a justification for utter selfishness, he turned to portray two individualist women—Rebecca and Hedda. They are types contrasted, Rebecca intellectually emancipated but developing a conscience, and Hedda, without intellectual resources or moral restraints, hoist with her own petard. Both dramas are marvels of construction, the past being revealed bit by bit through the action of the present which it wholly determines. Character in both is of prime interest, disclosed with unerring skill; and in *Ros-*

10

mersholm, although what passes upon the stage represents but a few hours, there is suggested a character development which in a novel would have required chapters for its unfolding.

Rebecca West, the adventuress who came to Rosmersholm and by innuendo caused the pastor's wife to fling herself into the mill-race, cannot marry the pastor as she had planned. Once she knew no scruples and stood in awe of no human relationship. Now, having rid herself of her rival, she has lost her sense-intoxicated desire and gained a great self-denying love. Although she has imbued the pastor with something of her own free thought, she has caught from him the spirit of Christian resignation. "The Rosmer view of life ennobles," she says sadly, "but it kills happiness." Even so a pagan might lament his conversion to a creed requiring continence in lieu of bacchanalian self-assertion. When the pastor asks her to marry him, she declines, and that he may again possess his sense of innocence and be able to carry a message of healing to others, she confesses her slaying of his wife and hints also at her doubtful career when earlier she had lived with one now shown to have been her father. The pastor declares that he cannot believe her unless she be willing to do for him as much as his wife had done. Let her, also, efface herself. But he who, under the spell of the Rosmersholm ideal, demands this sacrifice of her, will also sacrifice himself. As they plunge together into the mill-race, the housekeeper remarks, "It is the dead wife who has taken them."

The interest of the piece is wholly subjective. It lies in the exposure of the workings of the moral nature. True, there is evidence here of the older satiric Ibsen in sketches of the conservative schoolmaster, the radical editor, and the enigmatic self-deceiver Ulric Brendel, who affords comic relief and an ironic commentary on the theory of sacrifice. But it is to Rosmer and Rebecca and their spiritual interactions that our attention is drawn. Rebecca is a new woman who submits,

11

in spite of her theories, to the law of love. She who had derided all but self-assertion obeys a preposterous demand that she lay down her life. She yields, not as the result of intellectual conversion, but because a self-denying love has been born out of selfish passion.

A contrasting figure is Hedda Gabler. Equally emancipated, she lacks the emotional and moral nature of Rebecca West. She is the heartless individualist, bored by life, yearning for a thrill, afraid to seek it at first hand, prurient in her curiosity, cowardly in her dread of scandal, unwomanly in everything except her jealousy and her desire for beauty. Aristocratic Hedda, married to the dullest of pedants, despises him and his prosaic aunt, hates her condition as a prospective mother, and seeks relief in scheming to destroy her former lover, the temperamental scholar, Eilert Lövborg. She does this partly because he is her husband's rival for a university position, partly because she would flout his good angel, the stupid Mrs. Elvsted, partly because she would attest her ability to determine the fate of another. When Hedda succeeds in inducing Eilert to drink and sends him off to a gay party where he is likely to be further tempted, her flagging spirits revive. She suggests his suicide when he returns, confessing his fall, the loss of his manuscript, and his arrest at a disreputable resort. No sooner has he departed under her hypnotic suggestion than she burns his manuscript found by her husband, and gloats over its destruction as though it were the child of Eilert and his good angel, Mrs. Elvsted. But swiftly her triumph fades. Eilert dies, shot accidentally through the abdomen in an ugly scuffle instead of shot beautifully through the temple as she had planned, and the pistol he has used, given him by Hedda, is sure to link her with the scandal unless she submit henceforth to the will of a libertine judge. Thus, the free individualist, loving beauty, must become the slave of a bad man in a hideous intrigue. Rather than yield, she uses upon herself the other pistol of the pair inherited from her

father, General Gabler. So, again, excessive individualism de-
feats itself.

But no such moral is obtruded. The play, more than any
other of Ibsen's, is a character study, a sympathetic presentation of the new woman without scruples, a portrait that might
have hung in the gallery of Strindberg. It is difficult to agree
with Edmund Gosse, who maintains that, "In other circumstances, Hedda would have been a power for beauty and good."
Credit her as you will with a yearning for beauty, there is
every evidence that she loves evil for its own sake, and only
lacks the courage of a Lady Macbeth to enact it. The other
folk are types—Eilert and Tesman, contrasted scholars. Tesman is the collector of facts, and Eilert is the creative syn-
thesizer, with the imagination to induce principles and foresee
the future. Judge Brack is the middle-aged libertine, and Mrs.
Elvsted the devoted feminine soul who can find happiness only
in attaching herself to some man. How true and how ironic it
is that, when her idol has been shattered, she should turn with
cheerful facility to his very opposite, the pedant Tesman,
proposing to aid him to reconstitute from notes his brilliant
rival's lost work. That she should have carried about in her
pockets all these notes is as improbable as that Eilert, on his
evenings out, should have borne about with him his precious
manuscript. The use of devices like these and the general's
pistols reminds us that Ibsen was not, after all, so far removed
from his French dramatic models.

It may be fantastic to descry a symbolic analogy between
pistols and the soul of Hedda Gabler, as does one critic, but,
in *The Lady from the Sea*, such an analogy between things
material and spiritual is evident. Here Ellida's yearning for
the sea and her fascination by the freedom-loving Stranger
definitely symbolize her desire for moral freedom. Accorded
such freedom, the mermaid learns that it entails responsibility.
Thereafter, she becomes a land animal, wholly human. The
central story is developed with poetic charm. Ellida, who, for

the sake of a home, has married a sensible physician with grown daughters, languishes for the liberty of her girlhood out at the lighthouse, and recalls the dangerous fascination exerted upon her by the Stranger. Before sailing away he had flung his ring and hers into the sea as a sign of their mystic union. She had forgotten the incident until, expecting her child by Wangel, she began to be haunted by the thought that she had not been true to the Stranger. In one aspect, the play is a study of morbid feminine psychology. But Ibsen uses the states of mind of his heroine for a moral purpose. He brings back the Stranger to contend with the lady's husband, who would forbid her to heed the fellow's absurd demand and would even call in the police, since the Stranger is "wanted" for a murder. Ellida perceives that she is struggling against no external compulsion. "I am not threatened by any outward power. The terror lies deeper. The terror is—the attraction in my own mind." When Wangel accords her freedom of choice, she dismisses the Stranger, who dissolves like a wraith. Henceforth Ellida is in very truth her husband's wife.

Two defects mar this drama. In the first place, its moral receives over-emphasis, the central thought being phrased and rephrased with wearisome insistence. In the second place, its structure is unduly complicated by a secondary action involving the love affairs of Wangel's two daughters and the introduction of persons manifestly forced into the story. That story, moreover, relies too largely upon improbable coincidence and mere melodrama. The Stranger, who is never rationalized, remains little more than the externalization of Ellida's fears and longings.

Ibsen's attempt to combine the natural and the symbolic was continued more effectively in *The Master Builder*. Here again from a realistic story burgeon abstract spiritual significances. The piece, beginning with matter-of-fact scenes, ere long develops into a tenuous fable that suggests much more than it presents. As a drama of ideas, *The Master Builder* expounds two notions: the peril of selfish individualism (already shown in *Rosmersholm* and *Hedda Gabler*) and the struggle of age against youth. Ibsen, conscious of advancing years, felt the inevitable passing of power from the older to the younger generation. He felt both the fear and the fascination of youth, especially in his innocent affair with Emilie Bardach, a girl of eighteen whom, at the age of sixty-one, he had met on a summer visit to the Tyrol. He has universalized these personal sentiments, setting forth the problem of every man who lives long enough to regret what is gone and to strive desperately to hold what is slipping from him. This particular conflict Ibsen associates with that between individualism and altruism.

Solness, the Master Builder, has achieved success at the expense of his wife and his business associates. Grown sick in conscience, he can no longer mount, as once, to the tops of his finished structures. He can no longer build church towers, or even homes for human beings. He has turned to a fantastic type of architecture, uniting the two. He suffers because he has selfishly supplanted old Brovik, and refused to let young Brovik build upon his own account, and because, as a ruse to hold the youth in the office, he has employed the latter's sweetheart and captured her affection. He suffers, too, because, in order to rise, he has willed the destruction of his wife's ancestral mansion, which, burning by chance, has indirectly caused the death of his children. Suspicious and superstitious, even a little mad, he feels that the Higher Powers mock him by furthering his ambition at the cost of his happiness, that his "helpers and servers" are the Lower Powers, and that he himself is something of a troll.

Then, Hilda Wangel, the heedless hoyden of *The Lady from the Sea*, comes knocking at the door. She is the younger generation personified, both his enemy and his friend. She prompts him to loose the bonds of the pair in the office, and to be as valiant as of old. So incited and inspired, Solness ascends the tower that crowns his own new house, but reels to death. Is the Hilda who cries out after his fall that she hears harps in the air just a more ethereal Hedda Gabler, "a little dæmonic wrecker, a bird of prey," as Ibsen once called Emilie Bardach? Or is Hilda the idealistic spirit of youth reanimating one no longer young and so inducing his destruction? Although we may lament here the lack of certain correspondence between the human action and the allegory, we must feel the charm of these autobiographical allusions, the references, for example, to the nineteenth of September and to the three styles of architecture which suggest, respectively, Ibsen's romantic, social, and symbolic dramas. In Aline, the injured wife, Ibsen thrusts again at slavery to a formula, at duty for duty's sake, and in Hilda he seems to create a reflection of the moods of Solness, since at one moment she boasts of indifference to the suffering of others and at the next confesses that she cannot harm one she knows. Historically, *The Master Builder* is of prime importance as having affected the technique of the later symbolists and expressionists. It confirms Ibsen's influence in this direction just as *Ghosts* earlier confirmed his influence upon the naturalists, and *An Enemy of the People* his influence upon the propagandists.

In his three remaining dramas, the great Norwegian continued to reprove excessive individualism. In *Little Eyolf*, a child dies as a result of the selfishness of his parents, who profit from the lesson they have learned by beginning to care for others. In *John Gabriel Borkman*, a would-be superman of finance sacrifices for gold the woman he has loved and dies a witness to the folly of his rejection of spiritual values. In *When We Dead Awaken*, a sculptor, rejecting such values, is made to realize that art is less important than the life which gives it meaning.

These ethical doctrines appear in a fairly natural body in the first two plays. The self-centered scholar, intent upon writing a book on human responsibility yet neglecting or oppressing his own child, and the passionate wife, jealous of that child and of her husband's absorption in his work and his devotion to his supposed half-sister,—these are natural characters, even though the Rat Wife who lures the boy to his death as a female pied piper, be a fantastic abstraction.

Natural, too, is John Gabriel, with his insane ambition for wealth, and his clinging to hope even when, released from prison, he stalks like a sick wolf up and down the gallery of the house belonging to the woman he had loved and jilted for the sake of her wealthy sister. In the acting, this second play is especially effective, since it reveals the character of the mad dreamer and his disillusioned and embittered wife. Both she and the woman he ought to have married—generous Ella Rentheim—are unforgettable figures, the tragedy of their sisterly rivalry being pointed by the disregard for both of Borkman's selfish son.

The symbolism which emerges here but faintly in the suggestion of a metal hand crushing the heart of the gold-worshiping hero, becomes a controlling factor in *When We Dead Awaken*. Indeed, without it, the action would be meaningless. Rubek, who has sculptured a masterpiece, thanks to the devotion of his model, sends her away to pine and die spiritually, thinking only of his art. But this art grows trivial since he has dismissed the ideal, and animal faces leer out from his portrait busts. The earth-loving wife he marries can afford him no inspiration. As his sense of guilt deepens, he alters his statue for the worse, thrusting the figure of Irene to the rear, behind animal forms and faces swarming up from the soil, and setting himself in the foreground bowed low in contrition. So Ibsen would hint at his own loss of esthetic idealism, at his ignoring, for the sake of his art, the claims of love and life. Irene, left empty by her gift to him of her young soul, has wandered distraught, obsessed by the notion that both he and she are already dead. But their love may yet reawaken. "Then let two of the dead—us two—for once live life to the uttermost, before we go down to our graves again!" cries Rubek; and she, released at these words from her madness, replies, "I follow you freely and gladly, my lord and master." What matter now if death from an avalanche overtake them as they climb to the heights?

However interesting in conception, *When We Dead Awaken* is dramatically ineffective, a piece to be read rather than acted. Its meaning is everything, but that meaning is not incorporated in a plausible story. Ibsen's powers were flagging, and, though he lived six years longer, he, too, recognized that his creative account was closed. For this Master Builder to have kept it open would have been to court failure.

Ibsen, it is clear, was notable both as dramatist and as dramatic philosopher. What differentiates his theater from that of his predecessors is his emphasis upon ideas. Expert as he became in stagecraft, he employed such talents to develop a consistent philosophy. Unlike Shakespeare, he did not embroider an ancient story for the sake of the story, or find delight in exhibiting through the interactions of characters the heights and depths of being. Unlike his propagandist disciple Brieux, he did not, on the other hand, attempt to expose social evils and suggest for them specific remedies, thus sacrificing character to doctrine. There came to him, first as a rule, the concept of a moral or social truth, which he would then incorporate in a series of situations, clothing the abstract in the concrete. More and more, latter-day playwrights have followed his example, inspired as was he by the humanitarian and scientific movements of the time. Apostles of the theory of *l'art pour l'art* have struggled vainly against the tendency. Even d'Annunzio, who would denounce the drama of ideas, has written such a drama in *Gioconda*, making eloquent appeal for the artist's right to live his own life in the service of his art.

Ibsen was saved from becoming a mere doctrinaire like Brieux by his esthetic sense. Far better than others, he could unfold upon the stage a stirring story which would illustrate, also, as in a laboratory experiment, some fundamental social or ethical idea. In doing this, he simplified and concentrated the external action, reducing the number of scenes, hushing the bustle on the stage, and avoiding there deaths or violence. He made dialogue more natural and focused attention upon the soul at a crisis, revealing the past of his characters by a process of unveiling. Having picked up a story near its culmination, he by backward glances suggested its beginnings while the play progressed. The artificial, well-made piece of Scribe and Dumas the younger he adapted to a serious use, rejecting, except in Nora and Stockmann, the reliance of Dumas upon the *raisonneur*. Having discarded most devices from the old theatrical bag of tricks, Ibsen won his audience by the fidelity of his representation, by the vitality of his people, by the universality of their problems. Then, with pioneering courage, he supplemented realism by symbolism, combining the two in most unusual fashion.

That Ibsen was a dramatist rather than a philosopher who had condescended to use the theater for doctrinal ends, is proved by the fact that his philosophy is not so novel as to account for the esteem in which he is held. He contends merely that the spiritual life should be preserved at all costs, that hypocrisy and deception should be rejected, that love should not be sacrificed for worldly considerations, that the will should be left free, and that such freedom entails responsibility. He scorns those who refuse to scrap outworn faiths, formulas, and institutions, and those who, professing one thing, do another. Above all, he is concerned to indicate the right relation of the individual to society, stressing the need for self-realization and also setting it proper bounds.

But these beliefs would have attracted little notice had they not been winningly expounded through worthy art. Concerning admirers who esteemed *Peer Gynt* for its thought alone, Ibsen asked, "Why can they not read the book as a poem?" The answer would be that the greatest poems, novels, and plays, so far as they are concerned with character, must involve and stimulate thought. Certainly Ibsen himself, whatever his intention, has successfully married thought and poetry, exerting upon the stage productions of others, in ideas, subject matter, and technique, an influence more potent than that of any save Shakespeare.

CHAPTER II

STRINDBERG—FATHER OF NATURALISM AND EXPRESSIONISM

NEXT to Ibsen and Hauptmann, the most striking figure in the pantheon of European drama at the close of the nineteenth century was August Strindberg. More of a genius than either, he was less understandable. Unbalanced, eccentric, intense, he went his lonely way with little care for tradition or for schools. He was purely individual. He wrote poems, novels, short stories, history, and plays, now singing hymns of hate, and now extolling the redemptive power of love. He expressed with fervid reiteration a few philosophic ideas. He developed in drama the technique of sensational naturalism and also of what was later to be called expressionism. As playwright, he was both realist and idealist, dealing now with sordid actuality, now with fairy lore, and again with dreams and visions. He was violent in his antipathy to woman, ecstatic in his celebration of her virtues, now raging, now crooning, a strange, contradictory, vital, vigorous soul.

Born at Stockholm in 1849, August Strindberg was the son of a cultivated merchant and a servant girl. His parents had been married only after the birth of two children and just before his own. The family, which rapidly increased, lived in poverty and discord. Young August found in school, he says, "a preparation for hell and not for life"; but he read widely, dabbled in science, entered the University of Upsala at eighteen, and remained there, off and on, for five years, restless, dissipated, unhappy. He early felt the urge to write, tried poetry and plays, became a journalist, and from 1874 for eight years, held a place in the Royal Library of his native city. Here he studied history and Chinese, and published

21

several stories, an account of old Stockholm, and a study of the development of the Swedish people. His novel—*The Red Room*—hitting off the artistic and commercial folk he had known at Berns Restaurant, caused a small scandal, and the storm was not allayed by the satirical sketches of *The New Kingdom*, or a volume of *Poems in Verse and Prose*, issued after he had withdrawn from the library to live in Paris. A collection of stories entitled *Married*, written in Switzerland, induced at home the prosecution of the publisher. Although Strindberg returned to defend the case and won a victory, he departed again and remained an exile from Stockholm for some years, residing in Bavaria, Denmark, Berlin, and Paris.

During this period Strindberg's chief contributions to literature lay in the field of drama and of autobiographical fiction. Never since *The Confessions* of Rousseau has there been a franker laying bare of personal life than in that intimate series —*The Son of a Servant, Fermentation Time, The Author*, and *The Confessions of a Fool*. The last, issued in German in 1893, set in the pillory the author's wife, from whom he had been divorced. He described her as a beautiful vampire sucking his heart's blood, and confirming his dread and hatred of woman. In this case the burnt child did not fear the fire, and ere long Strindberg proceeded to marry a fair Austrian, only to be divorced again three years later. Rapt away to the seventh heaven of bliss during courtship, he was promptly plunged to infernal depths after marriage. His genius, moreover, showed the taint of madness. His mental hallucinations and persecution mania reached their height in 1896. The woes of this dreadful time are vividly set forth in the continuation of his self-analysis, *Inferno*.

A visit to the little daughter of his second marriage, coupled with the influence of Swedenborg, calmed the distraught spirit. Faith replaced doubt, a transformation described in the autobiographical *Legends* and *Alone*. But it was a superstitious, mystical faith that he attained, a faith of surrender rather than of triumph, combining elements pseudo-scientific, Catholic, and Buddhistic. Plays of rconciliation and plays of national history followed. Then, in 1901, Strindberg again ventured upon matrimony, having fallen enamored of a young Norwegian actress, Harriet Bosse, who took the leading rôle in his *Easter*. Though she gave him a daughter to whom he grew devoted, the union was legally dissolved three years later. Torn by conflicting emotions, Strindberg continued to write, producing two sardonic novels—*The Gothic Rooms* and *Black Flags*—together with short stories, descriptive sketches, and plays historical and philosophic. By 1910, however, his powers had begun to fail, and he died in 1912 shortly after his townsmen had publicly celebrated his sixty-third birthday.

Although Strindberg has composed voluminously in various genres, the bulk of his work that will survive is dramatic. If he be much more than a playwright, it is as a playwright that he is most distinguished. The stage proved his first and almost his last love. As a youth at the university, he led off with a series of dramas, *The Outlaw* attracting the King's attention with its story of a conflict between Viking and Christian, and *Master Olof* winning the public after several rewritings. This chronicle play depicting the struggles and compromises of a leader of the Swedish Reformation was reminiscent of Shakespeare, Goethe, and Schiller. In the year of its representation appeared *The Secret of the Guild*, and two years later *Sir Bengt's Wife*, both medieval in setting and idealistic in spirit. Next followed *Lucky Peter*, a fantastic trifle in the style of Öhlenschläger's *Aladdin*. Peter, through the aid of an elf and his fairy godmother, leaves the church tower where he has been protected from knowing the world, and goes in quest of truth and happiness. Thanks to a wishing ring, he becomes in turn a wealthy lord, a reformer, and an Eastern caliph. But in each estate he suffers disappointment. Then, out of humor with high society and with nature "red in tooth and claw," he returns, convinced that the fullness of life consists in work and thought for others, a lesson he has learned through his love for a loyal girl of the forest.

Such cheerful beginnings would never have suggested that ere long Strindberg was to be known as the greatest enemy of woman in all literature. But within four years his transformation was complete. Stark, dark, and bitter were the plays produced during the decade from 1887 to 1897. The series opened with *The Father*. Here Strindberg gave unmistakable expression to a philosophy of sexual attraction and repulsion henceforth to be illustrated again and again. Temperamentally erotic, he found in woman a delicious but dangerous excitement. He conceived her to be the insidious enemy of man, inciting his maddest longing and his deepest antipathy.

In *The Father*, a wife, weary and jealous of her husband, contends with him for possession of their daughter. "Now that you have fulfilled your function as father and breadwinner," she tells him, "you are no longer needed and must go." So she insinuates that he is not that daughter's father and that his mind has lost its balance. Distracted by these accusations and the surveillance of an alienist, the man confirms doubts of his sanity by flinging at his wife a lighted lamp. His old nurse, thinking to protect the daughter, lures him into a strait jacket from which he can only impotently rail at women. As he expires of apoplectic rage, the wife clasps her daughter in triumph.

This is not a pretty piece; it is a tense and powerful tragedy of hate in love. The wife affirms that when she loved she did not give herself; she rather took what she wanted. So every woman has warred upon the happiness of the afflicted hero:— his mother, who fought against his birth and atrophied his will prenatally; his sister, who domineered over his childhood; his sweetheart, who repaid his caresses with disease; his daughter, who has turned from him to her mother; his wife, who, having used him to her own ends, would now discard and destroy him fiendishly.

Certain features of the story derive from the *Folly or Saintliness* of José Echegaray, written a decade earlier. But Strindberg applies to a different purpose the situations devised by the Spaniard merely to show how easily a refined sense of honor may be interpreted by the dull world as madness.

Having thus allied himself with the new sensational naturalism just stirring on the stage of the Théâtre Libre in Paris, Strindberg proceeded in *Miss Julie* to contribute to it another play, later improved by reduction from three acts to one. Here the victor in the duel of love is man—a worthless lackey left alone with his master's daughter on Midsummer Eve. The revels of that half-pagan festival offer occasion for the bored and willful lady to tempt Fate by tempting the lackey. She is sick of love in her own class. She has turned off a suitor of rank who declined to jump over her riding whip. From her feminist mother she has learned disdain for men. Yet, out of devilry, she stoops to the lackey and is lost. For their passion of the moment is succeeded by violent revulsion. He who was the servant becomes the master, and Julie in vain begs a kind word even while alleging her hate for him and his sex. She rages at him when he chops off the head of her pet canary lest it encumber their flight to Switzerland, where he will set up a hotel upon the money he forces her to steal from her father. Yet, when he suggests that she cut her throat with his razor, she obeys as if in a trance, defeated in the duel of sex by a mean-spirited drudge.

Again, in the four-act *Comrades*, Strindberg stands revealed as the bitter misogynist, gloating over a woman's defeat. The rivalry between woman and man is here partly professional. Bertha, like her husband, is an artist. From him she exacts every sacrifice that she may create a masterpiece, subduing his will to hers. As she grows more masculine, he becomes effeminate. For her benefit he numbers his superior picture as though it were hers. Yet she, on hearing that his has been rejected at the salon, plans to humiliate him by arranging its return before guests. But the picture rejected proves to be her own. Inferior in talent, petty, mean, spiteful, and a parasite, Bertha is for Strindberg the new woman, a creature to be feared, despised, and chastised. At length the husband turns upon his perfidious wife and, discarding weak chivalry, forces her to her knees. Thereupon, she begs forgiveness, hoping again to rule. But it is too late. The husband drives her out. A mistress will console him for the moment. At home he wishes no rival, no "comrade," but an obedient, old-fashioned wife. Bertha has exploited him, played upon his sympathies, robbed him of strength, gold, time, and talent. Women are insidious feline foes. "Treat 'em rough," is Strindberg's advice.

Another painter who has given his all to an exacting wife is the hero of the short piece *Creditors*. Here the wife has already exploited and deceived a former husband, whom she has pilloried in a scandalous novel. But he turns up to torture his successor, who from concealment sees the lady ready to go back to her first love, and succumbs to epilepsy. The two husbands are contrasted. Adolph, the second, is a weakling, who has belittled himself in order to instil courage into his unworthy mate. Like other women worshipers, he has revered a being actually anemic and of arrested development. It is but natural that he should yield to the hypnotic suggestion of Gustav, an assertive nature strong enough to resist the blandishments of Thekla and cast her off. Gustav is a creditor since his wife and her second husband owe him reparation. Adolph is a creditor who fears that his debtor wife will slay him. The baneful Thekla is debtor to both men. One creditor expires; the other survives to scoff at the tyranny of love.

Such plays, technically adroit, reveal the morbid antipathy to woman engendered in part by Strindberg's experience of marriage. He cannot say enough of the evil of women. He shows them fighting each other, as in *The Stronger*; profiting by the immolation of a father, as in *Facing Death*; destroying the happiness of a daughter, as in *Mother-love*; slaying one man to capture another, as in *Simoom*; playing off a first husband against a second, as in *The Thunderstorm*; and eternally battling with their husbands in marriage. "We love. Yes, and we hate," says to his wife the hero of *To Damascus*. "We hate each other, because we love each other; we hate each other because we are linked together. We hate the link, we hate love; we hate what is most lovable because it is also most bitter; we hate the very best which gives us life."

In the piece called *The Link*, it is not love alone which binds husband and wife; it is the child, the result of their love, for whose sake they would keep secret the causes of their legal separation. But the case being tried in court, they claw each other bloody. Then, when the jury has retired to consider the matter, and the parents of the child seek reconciliation, they recognize that it is God, or nature, which has egged them on to love and to hate. "And why do we not bring to an end these two miserable lives?" asks the husband. "Because the child stays our hands." The wife, who by law will be deprived of her child, can only declaim against God, "Who has put this infernal love into the world as a torment for us human creatures."

Such ideas are most vividly clothed in the elaborate study of marital discord, the two parts of *The Dance of Death*. An artillery captain, stationed on a desolate island, hates his wife, his comrades, and himself. Sick, lonely, frustrated in ambition, he finds his only satisfaction in torturing the woman who bears his name. When she retorts by threatening to disgrace him, he lunges at her with his sabre and suffers an apoplectic stroke. Recovering, and apparently about to be reunited with his wife, the captain again engages in the duel of sex, and now more viciously, since he is jealous of a cousin whom the wife has favored and whose son the captain's daughter would marry. That youth he orders to a remote post, and the daughter he arranges to marry off to an elderly colonel. When she refuses, he ascribes her revolt to her mother's influence, and in the violent scene that ensues he succumbs to a second stroke.

The joy of the wife is boundless, until she realizes that in losing her enemy, she has lost the meaning of her life.

It will be observed that Strindberg, without relaxing his misogyny, has here given to the captain those vampire traits usually assigned to women. The captain is a malignant leech who sucks the life out of his victims of both sexes. Such a male character is less fully shown in the protagonist of *Pariah*, a rascal who vainly attempts to extort blackmail from an archeologist, forcing from him the golden trinkets he has found, after learning that he has once committed an inadvertent murder, and then excusing his own earlier forgery as the result of hypnotic suggestion—an idea stolen from one of the archeologist's books. Another male vampire, more successful, is the scientist of *Debit and Credit*, who has flourished at the expense of brother, friend, and mistress, with Nietzschean disregard of all except himself. The Nietzschean influence is clear, indeed, in several of Strindberg's works, especially in two novels, *Tschandala* and *In the Bond of the Sea*. In the curious monodrama *The Stronger* appears a female vampire who remains triumphantly silent when accused by her married rival. The defeated wife complains, "Your soul crept into mine, like a worm into an apple, and ate and ate, until nothing was left but the rind."

On occasion, Strindberg reinforces his conceptions of the vampire personality and of sex-aversion by his conception of the power of hypnotic suggestion or thought transference. Thus, the hero of *The Father* writhes under his wife's malign intimation that he is insane and that their daughter is not his; in *Miss Julie*, the girl who has sinned obeys, enthralled, the lackey's suggestion of suicide. In *Simoom,* a French soldier expires as a result of the hypnotic control exercised by a baleful Algerine, who makes him think sand to be water, his inability to drink it to be a sign that he is dying of rabies, his wife to be unfaithful, and himself about to be beheaded as a deserter.

In *There Are Crimes and Crimes*, the longest and best play of Strindberg's to develop this theme of thought potency, the evil Henriette, with her mother and her sisters, has willed out of life her father. Now, with her lover, she wills that his child by another shall die since it stands in their way. When the child does actually die, the father is charged with murder on circumstantial evidence. Though eventually exonerated, Maurice awakens to the fact that he is indeed guilty in thought. His rival admits that he too has sinned similarly, and that a friend who has wished the life out of a father has convinced him that no one is really good who has not erred, since, in order to forgive, we must ourselves have been in need of forgiveness. Here sounds an echo of Magda's plea for the necessity of sin and of the Master Builder's declaration that he is guilty in having wished the destruction of his wife's ancestral mansion. The message of Strindberg's play is one of indulgence in view of the fact that our sins are those, not only of deed, but of thought, and that sinning itself may prove a step toward salvation.

Two features distinguish Strindberg from all his contemporaries and his forbears: first, his plays of naturalism which chiefly deliver his anti-feminist attack, and, second, his plays of symbolism which technically prepare the way for expressionism. The pieces thus far considered exemplify his very special stripe of naturalism, which differs from that of Becque, Chekhov, or Hauptmann in being highly sensational. Indeed, he declaimed against the photographic naturalists, demanding a concentration of passion which most ignored. He practised a dynamic concision of plot-arrangement, and a simplicity in scenery quite opposed to the loose structure and the *kleinmalerei* of the Germans. He insisted upon "the true naturalism which seeks out those points in life, where the greatest conflicts occur, which loves to see that which cannot be seen every day, rejoices in the battle of elemental powers . . .; which cares not whether a subject be beautiful or ugly if only it be great." He disdained mediocrity of character, lukewarmness of feeling, and attacked the old theater as "a board school for young people, the half educated, and women." So he proposed a new theater, "where we can be horrified by the horrible, where we can laugh at what is laughable. . . . Let us have a free theater where everything is admitted except the talentless, the hypocritical, and the stupid." As Storm Jameson has said, "His tragedies are the tragedies of exceptional people in conflict with exceptional circumstance."

If Strindberg be an innovator in the field of naturalism, he is also an innovator in the field of imaginative romance. Ordinarily, his romantic dramas are fairly optimistic and intelligible; sometimes, as in *The Dream Play*, he projects upon the stage the wildest imaginings of a mind perturbed. Here, moreover, he gives fantastic expression to his old sex aversion. An Eastern goddess, the Daughter of Indra, descends from heaven to learn if the complaints of mortals be justified. She concludes that the primal Idea, Brahma, having been prevailed upon by the material world-mother, Maya, to propagate himself, produced by union with her an order of human phantasms yearning to enjoy yet destined to free themselves from matter through suffering. Earthly life must be regarded as the material perversion of a spiritual something. Sense obscures pure being. The female principle has conquered spirit and brought sin and sorrow into the cosmos. Man can defeat these only as he wars against love and woman.

In developing such Buddhistic and Platonic notions, Strindberg resorts to the wildest fancies tossed together without coherence. What is the significance of an officer imprisoned in a growing castle surrounded by a forest of giant hollyhocks, a bill poster fishing with a dip net, a girl pasting up every crack in a house until its inmates suffocate, a quarantine officer masquerading as a blackamoor, an academic ceremony conducted by ballet girls, and the organ of a church which turns into Fingal's Cave? Amid this phantasmagoria certain ele-

30

ments are clearly symbolic: a lawyer with hands so black that they can never be cleansed; lovers bound for Fairhaven but detained at Foulstrand; coal heavers lamenting, "This is Hell!" beside a Casino whose occupants retort, "This is Paradise!"; and a door behind which is found only emptiness, although Theology, Philosophy, Medicine, and Jurisprudence have contended to keep it shut. Throughout may be heard the voice of the dramatist, too, declaring mournfully from the lips of his characters: "Nothing ever was as I expected it to be because the thought is more than the deed, more than the thing"; "Duty is everything you dread, sin is what is pleasant, life is nothing but doing things all over, and to die is to have the body subjected to insults"; "At the heart of happiness grows the seed of disaster, happiness devours itself like a flame—it cannot burn forever, but must go out sometime, and this presentiment of the coming end destroys joy in the very hour of its culmination." At length, the Daughter of Indra, shaking the dust of earth from her feet, enters a castle which catches fire as a bud on the roof opens into a great chrysanthemum.

The curious expressionistic technique of this piece is used also in the three parts of *To Damascus*, through which move puppet abstractions. A Stranger rescues a Lady from her werewolf husband, a Physician, and with her suffers subjective ills. They quarrel, are reconciled, and the Stranger, who may represent the soul, after railing at God, learns the power of love, and withdraws repentant to a white monastery on a mountain. It is all madly confused and suggestive, the scenes succeeding one another like chance episodes in a dream. Hugo had remarked that, "Every man, if he be sincere, may tread again for himself the road to Damascus—a journey which must vary with each individual soul." Strindberg here and in *The Great Highway* describes that journey. Of such radical endeavors and of *The Dream Play* he wrote: "Anything may happen; everything is possible and probable. Time and space do not exist; on an insignificant background of reality imagination spins threads and weaves new patterns; a mixture of memories, experiences, free fancies, absurdities, and improvisations. The characters split, double, multiply, evaporate, solidify, diffuse, clarify. But one consciousness reigns above them all—that of the dreamer; it knows no secrets, no incongruities, no scruples, no law." Here may be observed an anticipation of the monodrama of Evreinov, or *The Black Maskers* of Andreyev.

Strindberg is normally skeptical and pessimistic. It is only by exception when a new love has awakened his idealism, in spite of past experience, that he becomes romantic. Yet in a whole series of pieces he reveals this idealism. At worst it is negative, involving resignation in view of our hope for a better world to come. So, in 1910, he wrote: "Only through religion or the hope of something better, and the recognition of the innermost meaning of life as that of an ordeal, a school, or perhaps a penitentiary, will it be possible to bear the burdens of life with sufficient resignation."

Positively, under the spell of Swedenborg, Strindberg was moved to repentance and to faith in a special Providence. Thus, of Swedenborg he says, "He has shown me the only path to salvation: to seek out the demons in their dens within myself, and to kill them . . . through repentance." Like Swedenborg, he felt at times his own powers of clairvoyance and telepathy. He believed that he could see at a distance occurrences that concerned him. He could perceive in the simplest natural phenomena spiritual meanings. His hero in *The Burned Lot* discovers, while gazing upon the ruins of a house gutted by the flames, the sins of those who had lived there. So, for Strindberg, in certain moods, the simplest outward occurrences appear symbolic, every trifle conveying to him some warning or command from the Omnipotent. Most of his romantic dramas are less difficult to understand than *To Damascus* and *The Dream Play*. Some are airy fantasies intended to refute the pessimism of his naturalistic productions. Thus, in *The Keys of Heaven*, St. Peter, seeking his lost keys on earth, finds no aid in the smith bereft of his children by a plague; nor can he be satisfied by the new scientific heaven proposed by a physician, or the heaven of Narcissus in the water's gleam, or that of mere pleasure suggested by the coxcomb Thersites. There must be a nobler heaven of romance, that of Romeo and Don Quixote, or that of religion. But the Pope dismisses Peter as a beggar, and the gate of heaven seen from the earth appears to be just the gate of death. Although those who would capture heaven by rebellion are observed to fail—Icarus, Prometheus, and Jacob—, the smith now discovers that when he remembers his dead children, they reawaken, and that for him the key of heaven is love—a Maeterlinckian conclusion.

Advent continues to preach the redemptive power of love through fantasy, showing the plotting of a judge and his wife against two children who are rescued by a supernatural playmate, while the wicked pair learn in hell to behold themselves truly and to repent. *Swanwhite* is a dramatized fairy tale of a princess enamored of her princely tutor but opposed by a wicked stepmother who would capture him for her own ugly daughter. When the princess summons the aid of her father and declares that, even though her prince appears to be dead, love shall conquer both death and hate, then the prince is revived and the stepmother is released from the spell which had rendered her seemingly evil.

In *The Black Glove* the fantastic and the realistic mingle. Here Saint Nicholas, coming at Christmas to bestow punishments and rewards, will teach a cross-grained wife the lesson of love. He finds her flying into tantrums when opposed in her desires, accusing others of the theft of a ring she has lost, and tyrannizing over her child. But she is duly disciplined by the saint, for her child is taken from her for a day that she may value it as a gift. Then her ring turns up in a discarded glove where she herself had left it, and the kindly taxidermist who had radiated love from his attic dies happy, having seen this temperamental neighbor transformed.

In writing such pieces Strindberg was influenced by Maeterlinck, whom he admired. Similar in sentiment but closer to reality are plays like *Midsummer* and *Easter*. In the former a gardener's son, ungrateful for benefits conferred by a count, suffers the results of his selfishness, on a steamer, at a cake market, and in a churchyard, and then, in two concluding scenes, he begins his right-about-face, after learning that to possess a good conscience and to protect others is the only happiness. *Easter* portrays the sufferings of a family when the head of the house is imprisoned for embezzlement and a creditor threatens. But the creditor proves forgiving at last, having recalled the kindness once done him by the defaulter. In the agreeable trifle, *The Tooth*, Strindberg clears up a husband's misunderstanding with his wife, and in *The Slippers of Abu Casem* he spins an *Arabian Nights* yarn for his little daughter, describing the comic ill luck that befell a miser plagued by the gift of a pair of old slippers placed at his door by Haroun al Raschid.

Most distinctive among these romantic plays, however, are *The Spook Sonata* and *The Crown Bride*. The latter is an imaginative recreation of legend; the former is a curious essay in expressionism. In *The Crown Bride*, Kirsti, though loving a cattle herder, cannot marry him because of the enmity of their families. Their child, accordingly, is born and baptized in secret. When the families agree to the match, Kirsti, who would wear at her wedding the crown, wreath, and veil regarded as symbols of chastity, exchanges her babe for them, tempted and threatened by a witch. But the ceremony about to be performed in a mill is haunted by the babe's apparition. When the pastor would dance with the bride, a water sprite spoils the music, and voices shriek, "Off with the crown!" As the guests rush forth, the voice of a Mocker wails: "Cold is the river; warm is my mother's bosom. Nothing you gave me in life: in death I take what is mine!" The lover, turned against Kirsti by his vindictive sister, bears the drowned babe to burial, saying: "Here is the little one now—as light as the mind of a bad woman. He sleeps, and soon you will be sleeping, too. Kiss his white coffin, kiss it where his small feet are resting—the small, small feet that never had a chance to tread this sinful earth. . . . Now we'll take him into church and play and sing and toll the bells over him, but no clergyman can read him into his grave because of you." Kirsti, convicted, goes to prison, but each Easter is released to do public penance. On one such occasion, as she stands upon the river ice between the embittered families, it gives way and she sinks to the depths. Too late those whose bickering has entailed this tragedy are reconciled and join in singing Luther's Hymn of Praise.

Kirsti is pure at heart, a beautiful soul blighted by the world's evil, but eventually saved by the Child in White symbolizing faith, hope, and charity. Even the water sprite feels a fallen angel's yearning for the good. The midwife witch is the wood nymph as familiar in Norwegian folk-lore as are the Mocker, a disembodied voice supposed to warn women against the temptation of putting to death an unwanted babe, and the Mewler, the ghost of such a babe. Only by heeding the inspiration of the Child in White, says Strindberg, can the world be redeemed.

The best example of Strindberg's free imaginative treatment of reality is *The Spook Sonata,* in which appear the usual friendly enemies, a couple linked by a former love, but now tormented by hate and remorse. Long ago each has been disloyal to the other. The wife, thereafter, has lived apart, a mummy in a closet, revering a statue of herself as a girl, and holding in readiness a screen to be placed before her couch at the approach of death. The man who seduced her had done so because his wife had already been seduced by her husband. That husband invites to a spook banquet of the mad his avenging rival, who has bought up his debts and now exposes the fact that the heroine's daughter is his own and not her husband's. "Here is my mission in this house," he cries, "to tear up the weeds, to expose the crimes, to settle all accounts." But the mummy wife declares him to be even more evil than her husband and commands him to go hang himself in the closet where she has spent twenty years bewailing her one evil deed. As if under a hypnotic spell, the avenger obeys, and she places before the door her death screen.

Though the woman's daughter is to be married to a student, his skepticism blights her soul. "Where are faith and honor to be found?" he asks. "In fairy tales and children's fancies." The hell into which Christ descended was the hell of this world, he asserts. How absurd for the image of Buddha to brood over an earth bulb held in his lap, awaiting its upward growth until it reach heaven! As the student expresses such doubts, the harp which had once responded to the daughter's fingers remains dumb, and the girl herself droops like a sick flower and expires behind the death screen. Then suddenly the student's doubts vanish; he appeals to the gentle Buddha for patience until the earth bulb shall indeed sprout to heaven. He prays, too, for the peace of the departing soul—"child of a world of illusion, guilt, suffering, death, a world of eternal change, disappointment, and pain." Then the harp begins to play of itself "a spook sonata," and he sings from the Poetic Edda verses breathing forgiveness for wrong:

> "Wrong that has wrought in moments of anger
> Never by added wrong can be righted.
> Fear and guilt have their home together;
> Happy indeed is the guiltless man."

When this play was produced in New York at the opening of the Provincetown Playhouse, Eugene O'Neill hailed Strindberg as "the precursor of all modernity in our present theater, just as Ibsen, a lesser man, . . . was the father of the modernity of twenty years or so ago." Said he, "Strindberg still remains among the most modern of moderns, the great interpreter in the theater of the characteristic spiritual conflicts which constitute the drama—the blood of our lives to-day." He continued, "All that is enduring in what we loosely call 'expressionism,' all that is artistically valid and sound theater, can be clearly traced back through Wedekind to Strindberg's *The Dream Play*, *There Are Crimes and Crimes*, and *The Spook Sonata*."

It is through O'Neill that Strindberg's influence has been chiefly exerted in America. At home, Strindberg was subject to violent attacks by the conservatives, among them the secretary of the Swedish Academy, his particular enemy; and as a result his plays were performed with reluctance. Only a few of the historical dramas, together with *Easter* and *There Are Crimes and Crimes*, ran on the regular stage there. *The Father* and *Miss Julie* were acted in Paris fourteen and eighteen years, respectively, before they were given in Stockholm. It was not until the Intimate Theater, his own little playhouse, was opened in 1907 that *The Pelican*, *The Burned Lot*, *The Thunderstorm*, and *The Spook Sonata* were given in the capital. In England recognition came late, also, a few of Strindberg's plays being enacted only with the second decade of the twentieth century. In Germany, however, he gained his first and widest currency in the translations of Emil Schering. To-day his influence is felt in the theater wherever there are those who admire the daring and the original.

Strindberg's achievement in his fifty plays is notable. So far as ideas are concerned, he has recognized, on the one hand, the potency, beneficent or baneful, of hypnotic suggestion and the redeeming efficacy of repentance and love; and, on the other, the threat to man's peace in the new woman, together with the fact that marriage, as Count Keyserling has said, is "an indissoluble bi-polar tension," and that sexual love involves not only attraction but repulsion, the rational nature reproving the sensual after the sensual has triumphed for the moment. As an artist, Strindberg has experimented with rare freedom in various directions. He is an inspired poet, no mere journeyman artificer. In the development of dramatic technique, he has proved an original force, a master in the field of sensational naturalism and at the same time a herald of the new expressionism.

CHAPTER III

Björnson and the Minor Scandinavians

Sigurjonsson, af Geierstam, von Heidenstam, Hedberg, Wied,
Bergström, Wiers-Jenssen, Hamsun, Heiberg

BEFORE 1814, Norway and Denmark had been united,
with their cultural capital at Copenhagen, and the pre-
ponderant language, even for writers of Norwegian birth,
had been Danish. At the separation of the two countries, however, the new generation in Norway favored a literature
nationally distinctive. The radicals followed the lead of Wergeland, whose ardor for reform was fairly Shelleyan. The conservatives found in Welhaven a champion more artistic and
restrained, intent upon continuing the older tradition. For
some time the two schools remained opposed; but, with the
appearance of Ibsen and Björnson in the second half of the
nineteenth century, they were reconciled, and thereafter Norway asserted its supremacy.

As compared with Ibsen, Björnstjerne Björnson was a man
of wider and richer interests and more sympathetic personality. He was not merely a playwright; he was a social and
political leader. By the same token, he was more exclusively
national and less cosmopolitan. Born in 1832, the son of a
clergyman, Björnson removed ere long from that barren north-
land of the Dovre mountains to the more genial Romsdal.
After being trained in the grammar school of Molde and the
high school and the university of Christiania, he proceeded
to try his hand at journalism, fiction, and the drama. He
served as theatrical manager at Bergen and Christiania, edited
a paper for five years, and wrote idyllic tales of the peasantry
under the influence of George Sand, Auerbach, and Blicher,

39

the Dane. He aligned himself with those who, like Wordsworth, appreciated what is natural yet noble among the lowly. He glorified rural life, along with such painters as Knaus and Hübner, Millet, Bastien-Lepage, Dagnan-Bouveret, and Anders Zorn, maintaining an even balance between crass realism and the romantic idealization which falsifies.

For the stage, Björnson began, as did Ibsen, by writing romantic saga dramas—*Between the Battles*, *Halte-Hulda*, *King Sverre*, and *Sigurd Slembe*. The last is a trilogy, its first act in verse followed by eight in prose, describing the efforts of a twelfth-century worthy of illegitimate birth to secure the Norwegian throne. After another saga play—*Sigurd Jorsalfar*—and a drama dealing with Mary Stuart, the attention of Björnson was diverted to the present, and during the 'seventies he composed a new set of dramas. Although to-day they seem old-fashioned in form and conservative in ideas, they were regarded at the moment as daring. For, in them, Björnson exposed contemporary abuses:—in *The Editor*, the unscrupulous press; in *The King*, the weakness of the monarchy; in *The New System*, industrial wrong-headedness; and in *A Bankruptcy*, the tyranny of business. The last piece won especial success, both in and out of Scandinavia, no doubt because it was less specialized in theme and more obviously a lesson in bourgeois morality. Here a captain of commerce who has thriven by sharp practice and by pretending affluence, is confronted with a threat of exposure. The agent sent by Christiania bankers to inspect his accounts reads him a sermon, after he has vainly sought to borrow funds from a visiting magnate and then, in despair, has vowed to shoot either himself or the inquisitor. Abashed by the latter's coolness, and inspired by his cheerful advice, Tjälde accepts bankruptcy, and begins life afresh in all honesty, his wife and daughter now enjoying a happiness they had not known in their days of prosperity. It is all rather dull and trite, with the awkward suitor of one daughter proving his worth in emergency, and the beneficent agent replacing the wealth-hunting suitor of the other daughter.

Domestic problems had already engaged Björnson in *The Newly Married*, an excellent study of a young couple who achieve adjustment to each other only when they revolt against the tyranny of the bride's parents. In *Leonarda*, he depicted a fine-souled woman with a past who renounces the match she would prefer in order that the man she now loves may marry her niece. Thereafter, Björnson continued to produce domestic dramas of one sort and another, compounded of common sense, humor, and morality. The list of such plays includes *Geography and Love*, *Laboremus*, *At Storhove*, *Dayland*, and *When the New Wine Blooms*. Now and then, political controversy colors a work, as in *Paul Lange and Tora Parsberg*, and at least three dramas of ideas stand out,—*A Gauntlet* and the two parts of *Beyond Our Power*. In fiction, after his peasant stories, Björnson grew more realistic, influenced as to method by Zola. The first and best known of his novels of the sort is *Flags are Flying in City and Harbor*, translated into English under the title *The Heritage of the Kurts*.

Among the domestic dramas of Björnson, *Geography and Love* and *When the New Wine Blooms* constitute companion pictures, painted quarter of a century apart. Having shown the difficulties of the recently wedded, the playwright, in these two pieces, exhibits those of couples wedded so long as to become a little weary. In the first, a middle-aged husband resents the interruption of his scholarly pursuits by his wife and daughter, but temporarily left alone, he learns that love is more than professional achievement. In the second play, a middle-aged wife neglects her husband, being a new woman absorbed in her own affairs, and she sets her daughters an example of lack of respect for their father. When he turns for comfort to a young girl and is supposed to have eloped with her, his wife in anguish learns a lesson. Both plays reveal their maker's knowledge of human nature, and both are brightened with humor. The second is far more subtle than the first, and, like *The Master Builder* of Ibsen, it considers the relationship between the older and the younger generation. Just as Arvik, ignored by his immediate family, turns to his wife's young niece, so her father, a widower, turns to Arvik's youngest daughter. "When the new wine blooms, the old ferments." Both men resent the feminism which encourages women to dominate in marriage, setting wifely duties and devotion aside for the sake of unwomanly independence. Since Björnson agrees with them, he portrays Mrs. Arvik as ultimately convinced of her error. It is her example which has caused one daughter to quarrel with her husband, and another to drive off in arrogance her lover. Let women be gracious and affectionate if they would maintain their hold over the hearts of men.

In *Laboremus*, one detects an echo of *Rosmersholm*. Although the heroine, like Ibsen's Rebecca West, has slain by suggestion a sick wife in order to marry the husband, she is cut off from joy by her own past. As in *Rosmersholm*, most of the action has occurred before the rise of the curtain. The unscrupulous Lydia has already wed her man, but she finds her hold upon him relaxing, since he suffers from a sense of disloyalty to the dead Amelia, whose vision has haunted him on the night of his second marriage. Presently he is warned more concretely by a physician of how Amelia died. The second wife so defeated would seek solace in a composer, nephew of the physician, but he too turns from her. He reproves her suggestion of the right of each individual to self-assertion at the expense of all others, and denies that Undine, in the opera he is writing, was justified in luring the wife of a fisherman into the sea in order to possess him for herself. Undine, he affirms, must fail because she has offended against the order of that higher world into which she wished to rise. The vision of the dead wife seems an unnecessarily romantic device. Much better is the scene when the wife's daughter, returning unexpectedly from a long absence, is mistaken by her father for a recurrence of that vision. "Let us work," is the motto of the composer and of Lydia, but the vital urge which in both would result in activity, appears in Lydia as an activity purely animal. To rise to something nobler than the struggle for self-assertion is the business of man.

In *A Gauntlet*, his early drama of ideas, Björnson issued a challenge to women to demand of men in marriage the same chastity which men would expect of them. His heroine is a strong-minded girl who has already withdrawn from one engagement because she found her lover unworthy. Now she discovers that the youth to whom she is betrothed has been involved in an intrigue with the wife of another already dead. In spite of the protests of her family, she dismisses the gay deceiver with a slap in the face from her glove, a gauntlet thrown down to irresponsible men on behalf of a new moral feminism.

First written in Paris in 1883, this play lacked sufficient force since a final act seemed to promise forgiveness to Alf. Four years later, Björnson revised and improved it, stressing the revolt of his heroine. Svava is now a conscious rebel, who declines to prove a passive martyr to man's immemorial inhumanity toward woman. Her attitude is reinforced by that of Alf's aunt, who, having once been taken in by a man, has returned to save Svava from a similar fate, and it is contrasted with that of her mother, who has borne with patience her father's infidelity.

The significance of *A Gauntlet* is less artistic than historical. As a program piece, it is a forerunner of the plays of social criticism, the first of a long line of dramas that constitute what the French call "the useful theater." Here the playwright's contention is everything. He has created a plot and characters possessing little life of their own except as they illustrate and enunciate his doctrine. That doctrine was more directly delivered through a lecture entitled *Polygamy and Monogamy*, given by Björnson in some sixty Scandinavian towns. The fact, however, that he resorted to the stage to popularize his propaganda was later to influence the work of such a dramatist as Eugène Brieux.

A problem less specialized is considered with far greater skill in the first part of *Beyond Our Power*. Here the playwright questions the wisdom of reliance upon a blind faith. He asks whether we do not err in striving to exceed our human limitations, and he indicates through an interesting fable how easy it is to transgress such limitations of faith and also of love. The simple-hearted pastor who works his miracles among the fjords compels the admiration not only of the peasantry but of visitors from far and near. But he cannot heal his devoted wife who lies helpless upon her cot. He loves her the more because she has sacrificed herself for him not merely out of faith. Yet he is determined to wrestle with God and procure the boon of her restoration. For he would demonstrate that what was once possible, according to the Scriptures, may be possible again. Since God must pity the unbeliever as well as the believer, the pastor stakes his all upon a miracle. While he is praying within his church that his wife may rise and walk, an avalanche sweeps down from the mountain, but passes by, sparing him, as if by providential intervention. Then his wife does indeed appear, walking toward him as he emerges from the church. As they meet, she sinks in his embrace. It is love, not faith, that has prompted her, and she has succumbed to the strain. He, too, dies overstrained, exclaiming, "But this was not my intention—or?—or?" According to a bystander he has died of that "or." What the word implies is that Pastor Sang perceives in a flash that he had been wrong from the first in demanding too much of human nature for his wife and for himself. She has walked out of love, as he has striven out of faith, but such efforts wrack us to death, for we are men, not supermen. He has slain his wife by making her, for love of him, attempt more than she can endure.

This commentary on the doctrine of faith cure is enriched by careful character drawing and by satire. The satire cuts at the churchmen, who for professional reasons cannot give credence to the pastor's miracles. The children of the pastor afford an opportunity for suggesting two reasons for unbelief. One is the fact that the truths of Christianity may be found in older religions in the East; the other is the fact that no one save their father is a literal follower of Christ.

It is these children who figure in the second part of *Beyond Our Power*, produced twelve years later. Here, in a piece that is quite inferior, Björnson points the futility of attempting to exceed our human limitations, not in regard to religion and the ministry of healing, but in regard to a social and industrial revolution. Elias and Rachel are the true children of Pastor Sang, but they seek their kingdom of God on the earth. Rachel is sensible and moderate, and with her share of a fortune they have inherited she is supporting a hospital; but Elias, with his, is fomenting a revolt on the part of workers against a capitalist. In his effort to overthrow plutocracy, he joins in a plot to destroy by dynamite a castle in which a certain Holger and his fellow capitalists are meeting. Elias is slain by Holger, who in turn is maimed for life by the explosion. Bratt, the religious enthusiast who had figured in the earlier play, here loses his reason on beholding the ruin that his anarchistic scheming has wrought. An architect, won over to the cause, is distraught and forfeits the love of Elias' sister, and the workers profit nothing from their insurrection. A nephew and a niece of Holger, significantly named Credo and Spero, unite with Rachel in toiling for a happier future to be attained, not through violent self-assertion, but rather through Christian self-abnegation and observance of the Golden Rule. Kindly, genial Björnson! He remains to the last a preacher rather than an artist.

Björnson's conception of his task he stated succinctly: "I am a poet," he said, "not primarily because I can write verse (there are many who can do that); but by virtue of seeing more clearly and feeling more deeply and speaking more truly than the majority of men. All that concerns humanity concerns me. If by my song or my speech I can contribute ever so little toward the betterment of the host of millions of my poorer fellow-creatures, I shall be prouder of that than of the combined laurels of Shakespeare, Milton, and Goethe." Like Tolstoy, he conceived of art as a unifying emotional force, and he defined the true folk-play as one at the performance of which all for the time being would experience the joy of fellow-feeling.

As compared with Björnson, Strindberg, and Ibsen, other Scandinavian playwrights count for little so far as the development of European drama is concerned. Drachmann and Bergström the Danes, Heiberg and Hamsun the Norwegians, Tor Hedberg the Swede, and Sigurjonsson the Icelander are known outside of their respective countries by a few plays, but have done little to determine the main drift of dramatic development. Other men of some note at home are scarcely heard of elsewhere—the Icelander Godmundur Kamban; the Swedes Hjalmar Söderberg, Per Hallström, and Hjalmar Bergman; and the Norwegians Peter Egge, Velte Visle, Gabriel Finne, Anders Stilloff, Alvide Prydz, Alexander Kielland, Arne Norrevang, and Sigurd Ibsen. Kamban's best play, *Hadda Padda*, was produced with success in Copenhagen in 1914. The heroine is a pagan-hearted girl madly enamored of a youth she has played with as a child. But he now prefers her younger sister. In vain, Hadda has given him all in the hope of keeping her hold upon him. Then, by telling him of her having dropped a string of pearls down a gorge, she induces him to lower her over a cliff. As she rests half way down upon a ledge she tugs at the rope that binds her to Ingolf and drags him to the verge of the precipice. Just as he is about to topple over, his brother-in-law saves him by unloosing the end tied round his waist. When the girl, defeated in her jealous design, is drawn up, she cuts the cord that she at least may fall to her death.

More distinctive are Johann Sigurjonsson's plays. Their author, born on an Iceland farm in 1880, attended school at Reykjavik, and then studied veterinary science at Copenhagen. He captured attention there with his pieces written in Danish. *Eyvind of the Hills* is the love story of a widow and an outlaw in her employ, who, being sought by the authorities, flees with her into the wilderness. When his capture is threatened, she consents to marry the pursuing bailiff provided that he refrain from disclosing the outlaw's identity. Then, eluding the bailiff, she makes off to the hills with Eyvind, suffering hardships as they are pushed farther and farther from civilization. She resists the advances of a vagrant laborer who would inform on Eyvind, and sees the two children he has given her perish. The second she even puts to death lest it prove an impediment to their further flight. When the persistent bailiff overtakes them and would claim her, Eyvind slays him. Finally, the pair, driven into the wastes, expire in a snowstorm. Here is no thesis, no plot complication, no analysis of character. Yet the little tragedy proves emotionally effective.

Not so rugged, though redolent of the soil, is *The Hraun Farm*, depicting the attachment to their barren acres of an elderly couple, and the desire of their daughter to marry a stranger rather than the neighbor they have picked out for her. The father has no faith in romantic love. What if he and his wife were scarcely acquainted when they married? Have they not got on well together? The wife had fancied a wandering carpenter, who drowned himself when she wed another. Yet even she reflects that "a man who cannot bear his fate is worth but little." The daughter, hesitant, hears her lover, a geologist, preach the right to be happy. "You think it is your duty to keep your word," he says; "but there is another duty which is far greater, and that is to open your arms to happiness when it comes. There is no greater duty. It is the meaning of our existence. You should understand that, you who have grown like a flower out of the earth." We expect the conflict between the older generation and the new to be irreconcilable, but the girl's mother prevails upon her husband to accept the geologist on condition that the first son of the marriage shall be reared at the farm on the Hraun, or lava field. So, in spite of the wreck of his home by earthquake, and the menace to the family of his daughter's love for a stranger, there still remains hope for the old Icelander. In examining the fallen stones of his house he exclaims: "Yes, they can well be used again—the old stones." What attracts in Sigurjonsson is neither his philosophy nor his technique. It is rather the freshness of his material, and the poetic power with which he bodies forth simple situations and primitive characters.

In turning from Iceland to Sweden, we may chronicle the names of a few who, although engaged chiefly in writing fiction, contribute to drama on occasion. Thus, in the 'eighties, Alexander Kielland, with his *Betty's Guardian*, satirized the new woman and male climbers in politics, and in *The Professor* composed a graver play of real power. In the 'nineties, Gabriel Finne in his spookish *Owl* emulated Maeterlinck's example; and during the first decades of the new century Per Hallström, who like Hamsun returned home disillusioned after visiting America, composed in lighter vein *A Venetia Comedy* and *Erotikon* and in serious mood *The Count of Antwerp*, *Bianca Capello*, *Two Legendary Dramas*, *Two Saga Dramas*, *Charles XI*, and *Gustav III*. In the mean time, Hjalmar Söderberg, a disciple of de Maupassant and Anatole France, had produced *Gertrud* and *The Evening Star*, and in 1922 he added *The Hour of Fate* to voice his resentment at the aloofness of the soul and his yearning to overcome that loneliness through the delights of love. Hjalmar Bergman, a romanticist in *Mary Mother of Jesus* and *Parisina*, has been even more successful as a humorist in his *Marionette* plays and his comedy, *Swedenhielms*. Brutality devoid of poetry marks Gustav af Geierstam's peasant tragedy *Criminals*, in which a wife is slain by her husband and his mistress. Though she has just borne a child, he sends her forth on an errand, declaring that, "It's a cheap sort of cow that can't dance after her first calf." But the wife, already suspicious, peers through a window at her husband embracing their servant girl, and reveals her presence inadvertently by breaking a pane of glass. Later, having bloodied her hands in cleaning a fish, she smears her rival's cheek when striking her, and draws down that rival's threat of retaliation. The vengeance falls quickly, for while singing a plaintive cradle song she is confronted by the servant and her husband, bent on murder. In vain she pleads for mercy. The husband stabs her, and the servant holds a bowl to catch her blood. Then, through the broken window, peers another face, that of a tramping woman who screams and runs to give the alarm. Thereupon the husband, suffering a sudden revulsion, turns upon his temptress and curses her. As the pastor, guided by the tramping woman, appears, the husband, half swooning, asks if he be about to die. "That is for justice to say," responds the pastor, "—and God." Here is nothing of the spiritual uplift that one feels in Tolstoy's *Power of Darkness*.

In complete contrast with this stark little tragedy is Verner von Heidenstam's undramatic plea for mystic faith—*The Birth of God*. At Karnak in Egypt a Swedish merchant, who has surrendered his occupation at home to seek the true deity, encounters an ancient priest of Apollo, awaiting for centuries the moment when he might die after announcing the birth of a new god. All men revere the same religion in spirit, he argues; only they try to understand too much, and are separated by their various phrasings of the creeds. Yes, says the merchant, in the commercialized west, poetry and religion have been stifled. So together the pair of questers after truth climb to a hill top where the merchant immolates himself upon the altar fire they have built, and the priest dies content, declaring that a fresh and universal faith is about to be born.

Between the extremes of mysticism and brutality stand the plays of Tor Hedberg, born in 1862, who keeps his feet upon the earth yet avoids the crudities of naturalism. His *Borga Gard* offers a Swedish parallel to Chekhov's *Cherry Orchard*, its hero a landed proprietor who has seen his estates diminish until only one remains. His sons take little interest in the property or in him, but he marries for second wife a keen-witted peasant girl, who shows him that he possesses hitherto unrecognized water rights, and induces one of the sons to exercise his legal talents in using these rights to the best advantage. Minor characters serve to enrich the simple story, especially the hero's three dependents,—his aunt, his uncle, and his prodigal brother. According to the author, the small aristocracy must look to the peasant class for fresh energy. In *Johan Ulfstjerna*, there is more action, an idealist poet who holds a government post being shocked to find that his son has been selected by conspirators to kill the governor of a Swedish province in Finland. Having resolved to save the boy from becoming an assassin, the poet gains possession of his weapon and takes his place. When the youth exclaims: "Father, what have you done? That was my deed!" Johan the poet answers: "Hush! You see I must die so that you may live!" He has desired that his son shall marry gentle Agda and perpetuate the family. To sacrifice himself to such an end constitutes his last and best poem. He will be delivered from feeling the oppression of a snowy sky and a frozen land. "I, a migrating song-bird, fettered here!" he exclaims, "with snow on my wings till I am no longer able to lift them! Now it's all over."

Of the Danish dramatists, Holger Drachmann, who died in 1908, is recognized as the great avatar of romanticism. He translated Byron's *Don Juan*, wrote fiery poems and novels, and in these and his few plays responded to the spell of folk-lore and Oriental legend. To the theater, he contributed, in the 'eighties and 'nineties, but a fragment of his total work, —the fairy comedy *Once Upon a Time*, the Eastern fantasy *A Thousand and One Nights*, and certain "Melodramas," of which the best is *Völund the Smith*, drawn from the Poetic Edda. In *Honest Fellow* he decks out in medieval trappings his own passional experience with a music hall artist here disguised as Gerd. Through these dramas speaks a Rousseauistic personality that has impressed itself upon the German neoromanticists in particular.

Three Danish dramatists born in the 'sixties are Henri Nathansen, author of *Within the Walls*; Sven Lange, disciple of Ibsen in *A Martyr, A Criminal*, and *Samson and Delilah*; and Johan Skjoldborg of Jutland, chronicler of the deeds of his people in several pieces, the best being *The Race*. Other realists are Gustav Wied and Hjalmar Bergström, both of whom died in 1914. Wied, the elder by a decade, was a self-made man who wrote more than thirty volumes of novels and plays, the latter chiefly satirical. *The Weaker Sex* and *Dancing Mice* are characteristic in their cynicism which still admits of longing for childlike faith and simplicity. In his *Four Satyr Plays*, with their loose-hinged scenes, the stage directions are unusually elaborated. Wied's distinctive quality may be sampled in *The Reckoning*, translated into English as *Autumn Fires*. Here are two inmates of an old men's home, first cousins to the pair in Lady Gregory's *Workhouse Ward*, united by long affection and their common love of quarreling. Each boasts of his strength and derides the other's infirmities. Each insists upon keeping inviolate his part of the room that both occupy. But one prates continually of his little grandson, and the other, a bachelor, grows increasingly wroth, until he can no longer refrain from revealing a secret long hidden. He had been the lover of his friend's wife. Since that wife's daughter was really his, the grandson is his as well. At first the disillusioned rival is horrified; then his anger subsides. "You have made my dead wife a strumpet, and my dead daughter a bastard," he says; "and you have robbed me in my old age of a grandson, all I have in the world. When men are young they see red and kill for that sort of thing. But when they are old, it's different. I can't even be very angry with you, my friend. . . . It is all so far back—in the past—and impersonal." Henceforth, the two, sharing the child between them, will never lack something to talk about. As the curtain falls, they are playing chess together quite amicably.

By the title of his play $2 \times 2 = 5$ Wied would imply that nothing that is so is so if it interfere with our happiness; we are all inclined to adapt the truth to suit ourselves. A liberal schoolmaster has shocked his wife and her father by writing a book designed to make people see themselves as they really are. He is persecuted by the government and sent to jail. When he emerges, he finds his position gone, his father-in-law a renegade to the liberals, who are now in power, his brother-in-law turned conservative and married to a rich widow twice his age, and only a pair of artist friends strong enough to decline a lucrative but compromising job because they would remain true to their higher convictions. The hero has himself earlier refused the editorship of a paper of which he disapproved the policy, but now his wife, learning of the large salary offered him, arrives with affectionate blandishments ready for a reconciliation. So the champion of truth and freedom barters his intellectual honesty for a fat salary, falling a victim to the very weakness he has assailed in others.

Hjalmar Bergström, educated at the University of Copenhagen, and for a dozen years a teacher in the Commercial High School of that city, wrote short stories and three novels, and at thirty-four turned to the stage. His plays, from *Ida's Wedding* to *What People Talk Of*, are studies of observed reality composed in accordance with his dictum that, "One of the main characteristics of all good art lies in its striving to make truth seem probable." He composed one historical drama,

The Golden Fleece, concerned with the sculptor Thorwaldsen, and he dramatized a novel by Pontoppidan, *Thora van Deken*. His more characteristic pieces are faithful pictures of the middle-class life he knew at first hand. *In the Swim* shows a single-tax reformer defying his corrupt opponents but betrayed by his wife. *The Way to God* chronicles the decline from idealism of two friends, eventually convicted of their error and saved. Less ambitious is such a sketch as *Ladies' Tea*, done into English as *The Birthday Party*. This presents the talk of seven old maids assembled to celebrate the fortieth birthday of one of them. Though they boast of their freedom, these bachelor women—artists, singers, secretaries, and trained nurses—would all have forfeited their careers had marriage been possible. Some hint at the men they might have had. One sadly admits that no man has ever looked upon her with passion in his eyes; and one confesses proudly that the child she has adopted is really her own.

It is upon two plays in particular that the reputation of Bergström depends, *Lynggaard and Company* and *Karen Borneman.* The first, a rather drab piece, discusses an industrial problem, but lacks the interest aroused by the sharper conflict between capital and labor set forth in *The Weavers* and *Strife.* Peter Lynggaard, who represents the third generation engaged in a distillery business, has relinquished its control to his Jewish superintendent. The latter, planning to incorporate the concern and to sell it out to a rival trust, is opposed by Mrs. Lynggaard, who summons home from Italy her dilettante son. The latter, a parlor socialist, denounces the inhumanity of corporations which destroy the personal relationship between masters and men. He holds that mere charity has never done anything but harm. Though he would turn the plant over to the workers he is eventually defeated by the wily superintendent, who breaks a threatened strike. Mrs. Lynggaard is a sentimentalist in her sympathy for the toilers; her husband is a weak and incompetent capitalist; and her fa-

ther is an old cynic amused at the moves in the modern industrial game. Her son, who had thought that mere words and
theories would quiet the men, perceives that they wish to win a
victory for themselves, and is glad to make peace with the hard
and efficient Heymann. The author's satire is expended not
only upon Heymann but also upon a violent radical who has
sought to depreciate the currency by counterfeiting and
emerges from prison as a mock reformer more than satisfied to
remain one of the unemployed. There would seem to be little
ground for the condemnation of this play pronounced by the
Russian censor.

The Danish censor had more reason, perhaps, to condemn
Karen Borneman, a much better piece, reproved in the Rigs-
dag by no less a person than the state minister Alberti, shortly
afterwards convicted of embezzlement. Alberti's objection lay
in the fact that the drama expressed too freely the new feminism. Karen indeed represents a new subjective morality for
women, just as her father represents the old objective morality, which demands respect for the institution of marriage, and
the rearing of children as its sole justification. The girl at
home has had a lover in the person of a young novelist who
died. Then she has gone to Paris and cast in her lot with a
sculptor who proved unfaithful. As soon as she learned of his
infidelity to her, she left him. But now he appears in Copenhagen just as she has confessed to a third suitor in all honesty
that she has loved before. This third suitor, a seemingly liberal
physician, withdraws his proposal of marriage on hearing the
truth, and his action awakens the suspicion of her God-fearing
father, a theological professor of the old school. The father
has reproved one son who, because of poverty, declines to beget
children, and he approves and assists another son who begets
children that others must support. With the best of intentions
he has driven one daughter insane by breaking off her match
with a man discovered to have a past. When this rigorous
moralist learns of Karen's alliance with the sculptor, he asserts

that the fellow must marry her. But Karen, like Sudermann's Magda, refuses to unite with one for whom she now feels only contempt, and the professor, informed of her earlier love affair, is shocked both at her and at his wife who has known of his daughter's second liaison. Karen protests that she and others like her have a right to "the most beautiful of the passions bestowed upon man," and declares, "The day will come when we, too, will demand the chance to live our own lives as we choose and as we can, without being held any the worse on that account." She has at least known the fullness of life while there was yet time. The professor can only recall the day of her birth, and his gratitude to God that a new little soul had been entrusted to his care. "At that time," he says, "I didn't think that one day, as an old man, I should have to live through the sorrow of seeing my own child delivered into the hands of Satan." Karen can only answer: "I pity you, father. . . . But how can I help it that I am the child of a time you don't understand? We have never wanted to hurt each other, of course, but I suppose it is the law of life that nothing new can come into the world without pain." She will leave her parents, the broken father and the understanding mother, to return to Paris. Here the father is no bigot, no caricature. He is as honest and sincere in his attitude as is Karen in hers. The censor was justified in regarding the play as symptomatic of the feminism descending from Ibsen's *A Doll's House*. Technically, also, the drama shows the influence of Ibsen, the past being revealed by a process of gradual unveiling through a dialogue simple but suggestive, and the chief characters emerging by degrees.

As exemplifying the lesser Norwegian drama, representative plays by Sigurd Ibsen, Hans Wiers-Jenssen, Knut Hamsun, and Gunnar Heiberg may be noticed. Sigurd Ibsen, son of the great dramatist, is known outside of Scandinavia by a political piece of no special moment, *Robert Frank*. It paints the portrait of a prime minister who opposes a general strike of syndicalists, yet plans to bring workers and employers together by a profit-sharing arrangement as the only safeguard for the modern industrial state. He is unsentimental, honest, determined, a man of iron will who acts as virtual dictator. When the syndicalists' committee calls upon him, he arrests and executes all its members save the leader. This leader he pardons because he believes the fellow to be his rival in the affections of an American girl. But, as a matter of fact, she loves only Frank, and confesses her devotion to him when his political enemies have caused the downfall of his ministry. The proletarian leader, in the mean time, has been rendered suspect to his fellow socialists, who believe that he must have turned traitor since his life is spared. He demands a public explanation from Frank that he may be exonerated, but Frank refuses as he cannot explain without revealing his personal motive involving Julia. Accordingly, the syndicalist shoots him down as his only means of proving that there was no compact between them. In this play by the son of a famous father little survives of the father's subtlety of thought and technique. The personal issue is more important here than any social criticism. Frank is a strong character, less typical, however, than individual.

Hans Wiers-Jenssen, born at Bergen in 1866, has won attention in the English-speaking world through Masefield's version of his *Anne Pedersdotter*, a tragedy of witchcraft laid in the sixteenth century. The youthful Anne, married to an elderly palace chaplain, falls in love with her stepson, and seeks to draw him to her by the occult powers which she believes she has inherited. When she boasts to her husband of her triumph and wills his death, he forthwith succumbs. But at the funeral his mother accuses her, and the bishop demands that, to prove her innocence, she touch the corpse. Attempting to do this, she loses her reason, and in frenzy admits her having bespelled both father and son.

The situation faintly recalls that in d'Annunzio's *Daughter of Jorio*, although the play is less violent. The chaplain has committed a tragic fault in that, out of desire for Anne, he has suppressed the confession of witchcraft made to him by her mother. That mother's companion in the black art, on fleeing to the chaplain's house, has been seized by a pursuing mob and burned, but not before the chaplain has extorted her dying accusation of Anne's mother. It is the chaplain's confession of his sin in concealing this knowledge that prompts his wife to try witchcraft and that enlightens his son as to the nature of the fascination exerted upon him by the girl. Six months later their intrigue has ripened. Whereas the son, ordained as a priest, feels his guilt, Anne revels in her new love and would justify it by the coldness of her husband and the tyranny exercised over her by his mother. Thus each character is carefully motivated. Especially dramatic are three scenes:—that in which Anne, learning that her husband has sinned out of desire for her, seeks to attract him once more, and, being rebuffed, resolves to summon his son to love her instead; that in which she later taunts her husband with the wrongs he has done her, and, boasting of having given herself to his son, wishes him dead; and that in which she goes mad at his funeral. "Yes, I murdered you by witchcraft!" she cries to the corpse. "And I bewitched your son. I got your son into my power by witchcraft. Now you know all." Throughout, however, Wiers-Jenssen is modern enough to let us perceive that Anne's fancied powers are really but natural, love itself being a species of witchcraft.

Knut Hamsun, who received the Nobel Prize for Literature in 1920, was born sixty years earlier in central Norway and came up hit-or-miss, working as cobbler, coalheaver, roadmender, farm-hand, street-car driver, surveyor, journalist, and lecturer. At two different periods he lived in America. Best known as a writer of fiction through such powerful novels as *Hunger* and *Growth of the Soil*, he is much less distinguished in drama. Aside from his play *Tamara*, and a long dramatic poem in eight acts called *Munken Vendt*, he has written but two pieces that have gained currency on the European stage— *At the Gates of the Kingdom*, played in London and New York and translated into French, and *In the Grip of Life*, which was first popularized by being included in the repertory of the Moscow Art Theater. The latter consists of choppy undirected dialogue, which only as the play concludes is seen to tell a story.

Juliana, once a singer courted by the great, has declined, until, in order to retrieve her fortunes, she has married a rich bachelor of seventy. But she loves an antiquary whom she supports by overpaying him for his wares through an agent pledged to secrecy. Although she has hoped thus to keep him from going to the Argentine with a burly adventurer, he is determined to leave her in order to make more money with which to wed a naïve beauty, beloved in turn by the adventurer and by a married lieutenant. The cross-motives of these folk are netted somewhat tenuously through two acts and a half. Then the various strands are drawn tight when, as the adventurer exhibits his pet cobra from South America, Juliana forces Fanny, her rival, down upon the snake. The adventurer, interposing, is bitten by the cobra and dies. The lieutenant, who feels himself responsible because he had removed the adventurer's revolver, commits suicide. Fanny rebuffs the antiquary, who in turn rebuffs Juliana, leaving her to find consolation with the negro servant of the dead adventurer. A silly, ugly play is this, which leaves us asking why such folk are more "in the grip of life" than any others. Various questions remain unanswered. Why should the lieutenant wish to duel with the adventurer on so slight provocation? Why should he be so quick to take his own life? Why should the antiquary, so self-centered, be interested in Fanny? There may be some merit in the pictures of the doddering old husband of the former singer, always complaining of the neglect of the younger generation; of the lady herself, generous to the down-and-out yet cast off by one after another among her lovers;

of the Byronic adventurer Per Bast, commanding his negro boy to shoot off the finger bitten by the cobra; and of the faithless antiquary, supported by the woman he disdains. But the work as a whole possesses little significance.

Far more interesting are the dozen plays of Gunnar Heiberg, born at Christiania in 1857, a theater director at Bergen, and long a newspaper correspondent at Paris. He began his career by writing a Byronic philosophical poem, *The Genesis of Man.* Then he composed a group of lively satirical comedies in complete contrast to his serious plays of sex. He has also issued critical volumes, the best being *The Norwegian Theater.* As a dramatist he represents in his ironic mood a protest against what he regards as the self-righteous attitude of Björnson and those who would harness art to moralistic propaganda. For Heiberg, Björnson and the middle class are anathema. He argues that they fail to recognize the authority of instincts which they would elaborately and hypocritically conceal. In *Aunt Ulrikke,* Heiberg's earliest play, he thrusts good-humoredly at the new woman, selecting as his heroine a kind-hearted eccentric. She moves among amusing folk who include an idealistic girl devoted to the concept of progress, a professor scheming to become a cabinet minister, and a radical politician uttering platitudes to catch the people. Sharper is the lash of satire in the pieces next following. *Love Your Neighbor* assails the sentimental altruists; *Harald Svan's Mother* attacks the improper power of the press; *The Council of the People* pokes fun at democracy; *The Grand Prize* draws the portrait of a leader of the masses suddenly enriched by winning the prize in a lottery; and *King Midas,* the first of this group, laughs at the smugness of Björnson's *A Gauntlet.* Already this had been attacked in Strindberg's story *The Reward of Virtue.* It was now burlesqued by Heiberg's device of making its author in disguise figure as hero. But if Heiberg be a satirist, he is also a poet, who in his graver plays exhibits the Strindberg influence, expressing distrust of love and of woman. It is the nature and business of man to emancipate himself from the thralldom of love; but woman resists his endeavor.

Two pieces will suffice to illustrate Heiberg's conception and his technique. The passionate heroine of *The Balcony* deceives her middle-aged husband and rejoices when he dies in an accident that prevents his discovering her duplicity. Then, having married her lover, and deceived him in turn, she is deserted by him, since he holds that man must work out his destiny alone. Dramatically, the first act is best, and might stand by itself. Here Julie, interrupted in a love scene by the arrival of her husband, sends her lover to the balcony, and then nonchalantly introduces him as a possible purchaser of the house. The husband, in showing off the property, is warned by Julie that the balcony supports are cracked; but, to disprove her words, he jumps upon the flooring, and, at its collapse, falls to his death. Later, when her lover has become her second husband, and regards his work as at least of equal importance with his love, he finds her closeted with a personable youth and realizes that, as once he had deceived his predecessor, so now he has been deceived. For him, however, passion shuts the door on what is best worth while in life. Civilization, as Shaw has said in *Man and Superman*, results from man's endeavors to make of himself something more than the instrument of woman's passion. "Love," says Abel, "has nothing to do with civilization. It is the only natural force that cannot be subdued. A humanity with heart but without love and what goes with it, that is the goal of spiritual progress for the world. Hence we must arm ourselves with all our weapons. For, if love wins, we become mad, foolish, blind, wicked. Love is at home in darkness; it steals our intelligence, our character, our will." Here sound the very accents of the rebellious Strindberg. As for Julie, she despairs, since, to her, passion is everything, and she notes, moreover, that her new lover approves the doctrine uttered by her husband.

BJÖRNSON AND THE MINOR SCANDINAVIANS

As the hero of *The Balcony* finally outgrows the tyranny of passion, so does the hero of *The Tragedy of Love*. He is a dreamy idealist who, for a year, has kept apart from his lady in order that both might test their feelings. Whereas, in absence, Karen's love has declined, Erling's has increased. In his mountain cottage on a stormy night, they meet, and Karen, who might have hesitated, is piqued into claiming him by the taunts of a wandering poet. Love, says the poet, slays, and when one of a pair loves, the other is certain not to do so. Months later, at a railway station, in the momentary absence of her husband, Karen again encounters the poet. His poisoned words have only fortified her, she tells him, and so deeply now does she love that she will ask her husband to prolong their honeymoon. When he declines, she risks death by springing before a train to save a peasant's child. She would prove her readiness to die for him or any other, whereas he will think only of his work.

Two years pass, and in their mountain home we hear Erling reading his wife a lecture. Love, he tells her, must rise from the sensual to the spiritual plane. To him, their home and his career mean everything. To her, love is more important than house and home. No sooner has Erling departed to pursue his tasks as a forester, than the poet reappears. Though Karen, in order to be revenged on her husband, would incite the poet to passion, neither, when brought to the point, can prove unfaithful. As the husband returns unexpectedly, Karen declares to him that she has already given herself to another. Erling rushes forth. But the poet, from his hiding-place on the balcony, has learned that she has sought to use him only to arouse her husband's jealousy and love. Now his own passion turns to hate. As he tosses a knife on a table, Karen follows his hypnotic suggestion. "I could have kept her from it!" he cries to the husband after her death. "It was I who threw the knife on the table so that it rang out." "And you did not stop her?" demands Erling. "No, because I loved her, and she loved you." Then, apostrophizing the stars as the golden tomb where all shall rest who have been slain by love, the poet leaps to death from the balcony. But the husband can only murmur, "Our home!"

This drama, remarkable as a psychological study, is the artistic expression of an idea. Like the couple in Ibsen's *Little Eyolf*, Erling and Karen represent the conflict between sacred and profane love. With Ibsen, there is promise that the conflict will at last be resolved. Here, such resolution is impossible, because woman in her nature differs radically from man. Love is for man a thing apart, but, as Byron said, " 'Tis woman's whole existence." Technically, the play is significant in focusing attention upon mental states rather than action. The dramatist takes no trouble to explain the coincidence of the poet's appearance at the railway station in Germany. He makes no bones about resorting again to the stage device of a balcony, used already in his earlier piece. He bathes his work in poetic glamour, yet depicts truly the behavior of actual personalities of contrasted temperament.

The clear-sighted poet can fathom at once the motives of Karen and the factors that constitute "the tragedy of love"; he would profit from her pique at her husband's lack of response, and yet he is of too fine a nature to stoop to common intrigue. The hungering wife demands all or nothing of her husband's devotion, and remains incredulous of a love that can live and grow in absence from its object. He, on the other hand, relieved of the disturbing hysteria of her presence, cares for her the more, since to him the ideal is more authoritative than the actual, and since a life of creative achievement alone means happiness. "Any pair of sentimental sillies can build themselves a triumphal arch"; he says; "but it takes a rare fortune to build a home like yours and mine." Karen cannot understand him. "I have nothing to do with your trees or your books or your work for other people or the country," she answers, "except in so far as you have loved me." For husband and wife, tragedy arises from the fact that they have nothing in common *except* their love.

The post-War drama is represented in Denmark by B. B. Müller, Sven Clausen, and Johannes Heskiaer; in Norway by Helge Krog, a disciple of Heiberg, and Ronald Fangen, a follower of Strindberg and the Russians; in Sweden, by Pär Lagerkvist, Carl af Ugglas, and Strindberg's daughter Karin Smirnoff. But throughout Scandinavia, of all the literary genres, the drama is least deserving of notice at present. Perhaps it is enough for the Scandinavian North to have produced three such playwrights of the previous generation as Björnson, Strindberg, and Ibsen.

CHAPTER IV

EXPONENTS OF RUSSIAN REALISM

Tolstoy and Gorky

IN RUSSIA, neither poetry nor drama can compare as yet with fiction. But although the novel constitutes the great contribution of the country to letters, the stage has increasingly appealed to the public and to those with ideas to express. The first Russian play dates back to the seventeenth century when Czar Alexis ordered the Protestant pastor of the German suburb of Moscow to prepare a comedy celebrating the birth of the Czarevitch. But it was not until the third decade of the nineteenth century that dramas of any moment appeared. Then, with the chronicle play *Boris Godunov* of Pushkin and the comedies of Griboyedov and Gogol, the foundations of the Russian theater were fairly laid. *The Inspector General* of Gogol remains the most delightful of Russian comedies, one sufficiently intelligible to the foreigner to have proved successful everywhere in later days upon the European stage. Ostrovsky at the middle of the century and up to the 'eighties wrote acceptable domestic and historical dramas, the former dealing with the merchant class in a manner now regarded as somewhat old-fashioned. For the most part, as in *Poverty is no Vice* and *The Thunderstorm*, he was a realist, sober and a trifle dull, fond of depicting the world about him with kindly tolerance, but developing no great social ideals and making little advance in technique, save in such a fairy piece as *Snyegurochka*. More than eight hundred performances of his plays were given during two decades. In 1874 he organized the Society of Dramatic Authors and Composers, and in 1882

64

through his eloquent plea to Alexander III he secured abandonment of the theatrical state monopoly.

Turgenev, in his few early plays, followed the lead of Ostrovsky; and another novelist, Pisemsky, became an actor and wrote many pieces for the theater, his tragedy *Bitter Fate* forecasting Tolstoy's *Power of Darkness*. Another contributor to peasant drama was A. A. Potyekhin whose *Men's Judgment is not God's* has been regarded as the first of the genre. Many playwrights whose names are unfamiliar outside Russia fill in the interval between Ostrovsky and Chekhov. Here are Boborykin, Krylov, the fecund Shpazhinsky, and a dozen others. Count Alexei Tolstoy, who shone as a lyric poet and an historical novelist, wrote dramas which later won European fame when his chaotic pictorial piece of vivid characterization, *Czar Fyodor Ivanovich*, second of an historical trilogy, was used to open the Moscow Art Theater. But it is rather to the plays of Alexei Tolstoy's more distinguished cousin, Leo, that we must look for first light upon the new Russian drama.

Leo Tolstoy was a personality and a prophet rather than a dramatist. Indeed, his plays constitute but a small portion of his total work, six pieces and some fragments now collected in English in a single volume of less than five hundred pages. For him, the theater was a means to an end, and he turned to it only late in his career. He had lost faith in the virtue of art for its own sake, and was seeking a vehicle to propound his ethical doctrines. It is noteworthy that *The Power of Darkness*, written when he was already sixty, should have reinforced the new naturalistic movement at the moment when André Antoine in Paris had just opened his Théâtre Libre. In that Free Theater and in its many offshoots in various lands, *The Power of Darkness* was produced as constituting, along with Ibsen's *Ghosts*, Strindberg's *The Father* and *Miss Julie*, and Hauptmann's *Before Sunrise*, the best exponent of naturalism.

In *The Power of Darkness*, Tolstoy writes one of the most

effective of peasant tragedies, in order to show how easily the ignorant and weak may succumb to evil, and yet how the curse of wickedness may be relaxed by repentance. The hero is a young laborer with a pious father and a scheming mother, who, wishing him to succeed, encourages his master's wife to poison her rich husband. The youth, who has already intrigued with the wife, now marries her. But it is not long before he is making love to his wife's half-witted stepdaughter. The child that she bears, his mother urges him to put out of the way, for then the girl can be got rid of through marriage to a complacent husband. Nikita's wife, too, would have him kill the baby so that, like her, he may be guilty of murder. The scene in which he is egged on by his villainous mother to crush the infant beneath a board and bury it in the cellar where the crime is committed, seems a naturalistic echo of the murder of Duncan by Macbeth. Nikita, who succumbs to the promptings of his mother, suffers imaginary horrors forthwith. Reproached by his God-fearing father and stirred to repentance, he breaks into a confession of all his sins at the wedding-feast of the baby's mother, saying: "My dear father, forgive your accursed son. You warned me at the very beginning. When I first began this wicked life, you told me if one claw is caught, the whole bird is lost." The father in rapture reassures him: "God will forgive you, my dear child. God—God—He is here!"

Tolstoy's method is simple and direct. He does not begin in the midst of things, like Ibsen, and then gradually unveil the past. His first two acts are devoted to the intrigue of Nikita with the wife of his master, and the latter's poisoning. Ibsen would have focused the action at one point, merely telling the story of the poisoning retrospectively. The most powerful act is the fourth, presenting the murder of the infant. In the original version, the audience experiences the thrill of the crime as unseen yet enacted in the shallow cellar beneath the stage, Nikita emerging half-crazed and with his spade threatening those who have incited him to the deed. At the next moment his anger dies. "Mother dear, it's hit me hard. What have you made me do? How those little bones cracked, and how it screamed!" In the second version, more often played, the murder is conveyed to the audience by suggestion through the chatter of a child who tells an old laborer that she has heard a baby's cry and the sound of digging. In vain the laborer tries to divert her with songs and stories. Then from concealment Nikita's voice declares that he still can hear the baby's screams.

Excellent as is all the characterization, that of Nikita's mother, Matriona, stands unrivaled. She is one of the greatest rascals in literature, a jolly soul, sensual and worldly-wise, close to the sixteenth century Spanish anti-heroine, Celestina. She is soft-spoken, plausible, a wheedler, who conceives crimes for others to commit, and consoles their qualms. She is religious, too, and advises giving the dying Piotr extreme unction because "Folk say it's a good thing for the soul." She insists that the baby about to be murdered shall be christened with a cross. To her son who has just done the deed, she says: "Go, my dear, and get a drink. It's rather cruel to do such a thing at night, but after a while, when morning comes and you see the daylight, it will be a different thing." In praising up the deaf and half-witted Akulina to the professional matchmaker, Matriona scouts the idea that the girl is sickly. "The girl's like steel, you can't pinch her. . . . She's a terror at working. She's a bit deaf, that's a fact. But a worm-hole doesn't spoil a red apple."

The vein of humor discernible in the characterization of the villainous Matriona comes fully to the surface in Tolstoy's three comedies—*The Fruits of Enlightenment*, *The First Distiller*, and *The Root of All Evil*. The two latter are slight pieces composed for boys who were giving amateur performances at a country estate. Both are genial temperance tracts. *The First Distiller* is a dramatized folk tale telling how a pious muzhik, when a little devil steals his crust of bread, instead of cursing, blesses the one who has eaten it. Thereupon the little devil complains to his master that he cannot make a muzhik go wrong. Devils who tempt women, merchants, or nobles have a job that is easy, he says; but muzhiks are impeccable; they work from morning till night and in all things rely upon God. Sent back to earth with a flogging, the little devil proceeds upon a new tack, and, hiring out to the muzhik as a laborer, suggests turning the surplus grain in his barns into drink, since everything in nature is meant to give pleasure. Now the muzhik yields, and the devilkin points to his work in triumph: "There he lies in the mud like a boar and grunts. The beast blood was in him always, only it didn't show." Whereupon the master devil remarks: "Well, my clever fellow, you've earned your crust. If only the peasants will keep on drinking liquor, they will always be in our hands."

More realistic, though no less moral, is *The Root of All Evil*, which reads like a leaf out of the Irish comedies of Synge. A tramp quartered for the night in a peasant's *izba* sympathizes with the good wife in that her husband will return tipsy from town and beat her. "Yes," says the tramp, "vodka is 'the root of all evil.'" Yet he succumbs to that evil brought in by the roistering husband, and soon both are swearing maudlin affection for each other and everyone else. But drink makes a thief of the tramp, who runs off with some food. Captured, he is brought back to be given over to the police. Yet the good wife intercedes for him, and the husband in a burst of generosity makes him a gift of the stolen provisions. "If you would lick me like a dog," says the tramp, "it would be easier. I'm a scoundrel. Forgive me, for Christ's sake!" And, sobbing, he flings the tea and sugar on the table. "Thank goodness!" says the wife, "he didn't take 'em, else there wouldn't have been any for our breakfast." The grandmother exclaims, "Indeed, he was a real man!"

Praise of simplicity is to the fore in *The Fruits of Enlightenment*, a longer assault upon the fads and fancies of the rich.

Here the master of an estate, who believes in spiritualism, refuses to accept the terms proposed by certain muzhiks for the purchase of a tract of land. Although the poor fellows can pay only by installments, he insists upon cash. Then his witty chambermaid, in love with the son of one of the muzhiks, makes the latter pose to her master as a spiritualistic medium. The scene when he feigns a trance and extorts the master's signature to the bill of sale following a burlesque lecture by a psychic professor is one of high farce. Though a jealous lackey threatens to expose the chambermaid's trick, her wit prevails, and she departs in triumph with the muzhiks and her bridegroom to live happy ever after in their village.

If the action of Tolstoy's comedy is cluttered by overabundant talk, the characterization is salient and amusing. The master enjoys psychic culture, and his wife delights in scientific twaddle, and his sporting son and his hoyden daughter covet the muzhiks' money. They are only half enlightened. No wonder that the muzhiks shake their heads at these new-fangled notions of spirits and microbes, at the waste of food, time, and effort spent merely on cards and the piano. They hear with astonishment that, in dressing, the lady of the house must have her girths tightened, and that a gentleman was so moved at a dog's funeral that he gave a ruble to his coachman who appeared to be crying when his nose merely ran from a cold. Be simple, be direct, is Tolstoy's dictum.

In addition to some charming dramatic dialogues entitled *The Wisdom of Children*, Tolstoy wrote two serious dramas— *The Living Corpse* and *The Light that Shines in Darkness*. The failure of the law in applying its ready-made formulas to domestic relations is displayed in *The Living Corpse*. Here a husband, knowing his unworthiness and his wife's affection for his friend, disappears in order to allow the pair their freedom. As the husband had foreseen, his wife in due time falls in love with Victor and marries him. Fedya, who had written the couple a letter of farewell and then vanished, leaving his coat on a river bank that the world might think him drowned, wanders with the gypsies and believes that his supposed suicide should at least stand to his credit as a generous action. But he chances in drink to babble his story, and a rascal, overhearing, advises him to blackmail his former wife. Though Fedya repels the suggestion with scorn, the rogue discloses the affair to the police, and Lisa and Victor are accused of having got up the scheme of Fedya's disappearance and committing willful bigamy. When all three are dragged into court, Fedya states the case to the stupid magistrate. But his protests are vain, and when he learns that annulment of the second marriage and deportation or penance in a monastery will be the outcome for Lisa and Victor, he shoots himself. In dying he murmurs: "Forgive me. I could not make you free before. Now it is not for you, it is for my own sake."

The law can do no more than blunder, Tolstoy seems to say, when it attempts to regulate such a subtle, spiritual essence as love. Fedya was indeed unworthy of Lisa and justified in giving her freedom. He recoiled at the thought of providing the evidence which the courts require for divorce. Lacking at first the courage to take his life, he gained that courage at last when he found that only so could his wife and his friend be happy.

This piece under several titles, *The Man Who Was Dead* and *Redemption* among them, has been successful upon the stage. Less dramatic but more subjectively interesting is Tolstoy's five-act drama *The Light that Shines in Darkness*, which expresses his own dilemma as a believer in literal obedience to the precepts of Jesus. To lead the simple life to the full, to give all to the poor, to renounce the gains of civilization in order to quicken the spirit, had become Tolstoy's ideal. In his zeal for the faith, he would strip not only himself but his family of their possessions, yet he realized that to do this would constitute a degree of selfishness incompatible with his

70

theory of love as the guiding spirit. In this work, he wrought out his own inner conflict.

Nikolai, a philosophic landowner imbued with the teachings of Jesus, is shocked at social inequalities and wishes to surrender his property. Though his wife would follow him out of love, she cannot consent to sacrifice the future of her children. She is ambitious for her daughter, who may marry the son of a visiting princess. But Nikolai converts this youth to his theories, showing him the sufferings of the lowly in contrast with the pleasures of the idle rich, preaching to him the doctrine of non-resistance, and leading him to rebel when he is summoned to serve in the army. As a result, the young man, Boris, is first sent to an asylum and then to a disciplinary battalion, while the daughter makes a match more worldly.

In the mean time, Nikolai, troubled by his family's lack of understanding and by the misery that he has brought to the princess and her son, feels that he can no longer live amidst riches while aspiring to Christ-like humility. His sister-in-law thinks him mad, and his wife insists that his Christianity has made him hate her. He replies that though the peasants are dying of starvation there is waste and luxury in his house, and he adds: "I cannot live so. Have pity on me. I am tormented to death. Let me go away." When the princess rails at him for having made of her son a fanatic, he can only reply: "It is not my doing, but God's: God sees how I pity you. Don't oppose the will of God. He desires to test you. Bear it with patience." But, in travail of spirit, he asks himself: "Can it be that I am mistaken—mistaken in my belief in Thee? No! Father, help me."

The last act is given in a few notes found among Tolstoy's papers after his flight from his family and his death from exhaustion at a lonely railway station in 1910. The princess clamors for the release of her son from his military prison, then begs in vain for the Czar's intervention, and finally, in a frenzy, mortally wounds Nikolai as the author of her woes.

But Nikolai avers that the deed was his own, an accident, and he dies rejoicing "that he is clear as to the meaning of his life." What this meaning may have been is suggested by one speech: "It is evident that God does not want me as his servant. He has many other servants and can get along without me. And when I have clearly realized that, calm ensues."

Tolstoy is too great a personality and too inclusive an artist to be confined within the boundaries of any esthetic "ism." Yet his best work in the field of drama is allied with the new naturalistic tendency. Less comprehensive and more intense is the younger naturalist, Maxim Gorky, born in 1868 at Nizhni-Novgorod. His real name was Alexei Maximovich Pyeshkov. His father, a dyer, left him an orphan to make his own way from the age of nine. He served as many masters as Gil Blas, working in a bootshop, helping a surveyor of land, acting as cook on a river steamer, as peddler and laborer, and wandering with tramps. Having educated himself by reading, Gorky secured a position as secretary to a lawyer at Nizhni, met the novelist Korolenko, and by him was inspired to write short stories. His narrative gift as applied to unusual aspects of the actual, freshly observed, stood him in good stead, and in the years from 1892 to 1900 he published four volumes of tales which attracted the attention, not only of his own countrymen, but also of English, French, and German translators. Without a dominating theory of life, Gorky reacted to it emotionally with an intensity that made his stories live. Experience had familiarized him with humble folk, outcasts and delinquents. Like Tolstoy and Dostoyevsky, he was not, however, without idealism. Brutal as much of his work seems, there may be discovered in it a certain faith in humanity and love of men even in their worst moments.

For the stage, Gorky has composed fourteen plays, only one of which stands on the level of his best work in fiction. This is the chaotic yet striking drama *The Lower Depths*, everywhere recognized as the last word in dramatic naturalism.

Less crude are the two plays *The Children of the Sun* and *The Smug Citizen*, both dealing with middle-class society in a more conventional fashion. In his *Children of the Sun*, Gorky writes a domestic drama in which a wife, unhappy because her husband grows too absorbed in his professional researches as a physician, endeavors to provoke his interest by reciprocating the attentions of a painter. The physician has aroused the admiration of a wealthy woman who offers to endow his laboratory if he will but relinquish his wife. In the end, he refuses this offer and responds to his wife's real love for him. Lest the conclusion prove too optimistic, a sub-plot is devised which concludes with the suicide of its hero and the madness of its heroine. "There is so much in life that is rude and cruel, so much that is horrible," laments one of the characters. "But why lie?" retorts another. "People are rude and cruel because such is their nature. Man is a useless and disagreeable creature." This naturalistic assumption is contradicted in part by the statement of another personage to the effect that "Fear of death is all that keeps men from being bold, beautiful, and free; but we—we are the Children of the Sun, radiant source of life; born of the sun, we shall conquer the dark fear of death."

Closer to naturalism in its lack of dramatic structure and its irrelevant talk by disagreeable characters is *The Smug Citizen*, a study of a family group somewhat in the manner of Chekhov. A petty townsman rules his household with a high hand, tyrannizing over his timid wife, his son, his foster son, and his daughter. The daughter, a schoolteacher, is in love with her foster brother, but, discovering that he cares for another, she takes poison and barely escapes dying. Nil, whom she has vainly loved, angers the Smug Citizen by refusing a profitable match in order to marry a little seamstress; and the Citizen's own son Peter, a radical suspended from the university, angers his father by his revolt against their precious provincial society. "Society, that's what I hate," he cries, "constantly increasing its demands upon the individual and constantly putting obstacles in the way of his development. . . . I am an individual, and an individual should be free. . . . We have outgrown your truth," he tells his father, "as we have outgrown the dresses of our childhood. . . . The elements of your life, your whole experience, are of no use to us." At the university he has learned to hate the bourgeois meanness of his home. He departs, accordingly, in company with the widow who has boarded with the family and who declares that when, as the wife of a prison inspector, she lived among convicts, she found their society preferable to that in this self-complacent community. As for Tatiana, the daughter of the Smug Citizen, twitted for her failure to marry, and hurt by the defection of her foster brother, she reflects that, "Nobody declares his love as they write of it in books, and life throughout is not tragic; it flows softly, monotonously by, like a great muddy river, and while you watch it flowing, your eyes become weary, your head becomes dull, and you don't even want to think what the stream is flowing for. . . . Life crushes us," she says, "without noise, without screams or tears, and nobody notices it." The final curtain drops as Tatiana, left alone in the dismal house with the parents whom she cannot respect, flings herself upon the piano keys, whose discordant jangling subsides into awful silence.

In *The Lower Depths*, composed in 1902, a year after *The Smug Citizen*, Gorky made his most distinctive contribution to the stage. It presents in four acts the scattered talk of unfortunates huddled in a cellar kept as a tramp lodging by a receiver of stolen goods. The wife of the proprietor intrigues with a thief among the lodgers. When he chances in a brawl to kill her husband, her sister out of jealousy charges that the pair have plotted the murder, and sends them both to prison. What comes of it all we are never told. There is no central figure and no real action. A pilgrim who has wandered into the night shelter and preached hope to its wretched denizens, disappears. Those who listen to him are left disillusioned, and one of them goes forth and hangs himself. What counts is the portrayal of character in a seemingly artless picture of the underworld. The acts do not move. They are just scenes revealing groups in conversation. The third act, which alone is properly dramatic, passes in a rubbish yard at the rear of the cellar, and concludes with the murder of the proprietor and the arrest of the thief and the proprietor's wife at the instance of the latter's jealous sister.

Among the characters are a morose locksmith; his wife, who is dying of consumption; a baron who has been sent to prison for embezzlement; a street-walker who cries over sentimental novels and fabricates stories of the devotion to her of mythical lovers; an ex-convict embittered by years of prison imposed for his having avenged a wrong done to his sister; a drunken actor who hangs himself; a fur-dyer whose wife has run off with his master; a female vendor of meat pies in love with a policeman; and a Tartar drayman devoted to his Koran. The three figures of the central episode are the keeper of the shelter, a sniveling hypocrite who talks of his love for his poor downtrodden fallen brothers; his wife, a jealous shrew who longs for his death that she may marry the thief; and the thief, already tired of her and preferring her sister.

Most important of all is the pilgrim Luka, with his gentle faith, declaring that a tramp is as worthy as a general, and that even the earth is a tramp in the skies. Luka bids these poor creatures remember that at least they are men. "Gentility," he says, "is like the smallpox; a man may get over it, but it leaves its marks." "We must look," he argues, "for the better man always and everywhere. We must seek him, and respect little children who some day may grow into such better men." He comforts the dying wife of the locksmith; he assures the romantic street-walker that if she believes she has had a real love, then she has had one; and when asked if there be a God, he answers: "If you believe it, there is; if you don't believe it, there is not." Luka's faith in the will to believe is equaled only by his faith in the power of pity. "Christ, He pitied all, and so He ordered us. . . . If you pity a man, then good comes of it." "Courts and prison and Siberia!" he exclaims, "where's the sense? Prison don't teach nothin'—and Siberia don't. . . . But it's the man—'e teaches." The limitation of Luka's idealism is indicated by the locksmith, who, when the old pilgrim has departed, declares, referring to the outcasts, "He pointed 'em someplace, and then never showed 'em the way." Here is indicated the utter woe of life for the many and the necessity of illusion, set forth by the streetwalker and by the baron, who declares that all men have gray souls and they all want to rouge 'em up, and by Natasha, the thief's new fancy, who reflects: "Lies is jollier than the truth. . . . I think to-morrow there will come somebody, something extraordinary. I am always expecting." Yet only the weak need depend on consoling lies to justify the burden that crushes. So Satine declares that truth's the god of the free man. "The weak of spirit, and them that live on the sap of others, it's them that need lying."

If this work were not a slice of life, we should find Luka's Christ-like spirit regenerating each of these dead souls, just as does the mysterious Lodger in Jerome K. Jerome's *Passing of the Third Floor Back*. But since Gorky is a naturalist, Luka achieves no good. Perhaps consumptive Anna dies the more easily because of his advice; the rest, in spite of it, go on deeper into misery.

Gorky's later plays are distinctly inferior, as witness such pieces as *Odd People* and *The Judge*. The former exhibits the freedom in love of a man of letters and the indulgence of his understanding wife. The latter shows the distress of a passionate wretch who, having been imprisoned for eight years on a charge of seducing a minor, emerges suffering from repressions and filled with hatred toward a fellow prisoner who had escaped. The released convict assumes a pilgrim's cassock and with a girl whom he has hypnotized embarks upon his revenge, growing convinced that to wreak it is his mission from on High. This drama, which appeared long after *The Lower Depths*, cannot compare with it in power. That the scenes in the former are not mere fanciful pictures is shown by an account in Gorky's autobiography entitled *In the World*, describing a workman's lodging and the horrors of dirt and vermin and a consumptive's death actually observed. In the same volume may be found an incident from Gorky's youth that throws light on the sort of experience which determined his art and on his reasons for depicting such scenes. He tells how, as a boy, he happened to see the brutal porter of a brothel taking from a cab a drunken girl who had just been driven up. The porter opened the door, seized her feet, and dragging her out, let her head and back strike on the curb. Gorky, incensed, interposed, and by his savage onslaught knocked down the porter. Thereafter, whenever he passed that corner, the porter would threaten him. One day, however, the porter sat stroking a cat which lay on his knees, and asked the boy, pleasantly enough, if he could feel any pity for an animal. "Yes, I should," answered Gorky, and he continues: "When I was three paces from him, he jumped up, seized the cat by the legs, and dashed its head against the stone balustrade, so that I was splashed with its warm blood. He then hurled the cat under my feet and stood by the gate shouting 'What now?'" Again the boy rushed on him and gave him a thrashing, and afterwards, says he, "As I sat on a grassy slope nearly crazy with inexpressible grief, I bit my lips to keep myself from howling." What follows is immensely significant as indicating Gorky's conception of art and of life. He says: "Why do I relate these abominations? So that you may know, kind sirs, that it is not all past and done with! You have a liking for grim fantasies; you are delighted with horrible stories well told; the grotesquely terrible excites you pleasantly. But I know of genuine horrors, everyday terrors, and I have an undeniable right to excite you unpleasantly by telling you about them, in order that you may remember how we live, and under what circumstances. A low and unclean life it is, ours, and that is the truth." Yet he hastens to add: "I am a lover of humanity, and I have no desire to make any one miserable; but one must not be sentimental, nor hide the grim truth with the motley words of beautiful lies. Let us face life as it is!" That is the manifesto of Russian naturalism.

CHAPTER V

CHEKHOV AND THE MOSCOW ART THEATER

DURING the Imperial régime in Russia the two capitals, Petersburg and Moscow, could boast of several theaters maintained by the State—two opera houses, with a third for Italian opera kept up until 1884, and three theaters, one of them devoted to plays in French. These state institutions set the dramatic standard by cultivating the taste of audiences and performers, and presenting the best pieces, both native and exotic. With them, also, was connected a government school of dramatic art. But the censorship tended to hamper free growth. Thus, for example, creators of historical drama were forced to hark back for subjects to the period before 1613, since the Romanovs must not be represented on the boards.

Opera and ballet were furnished by the Great State Theater in Moscow and the Marinsky Theater in Petersburg; classic drama by the Alexandrinsky Theater in Petersburg and the Small State Theater in Moscow. In the latter, during the first half of the nineteenth century, the tragedian Motchalov and the comedian Shchepkin won their laurels, and there in the second half of this century Sadovsky interpreted the plays of Ostrovsky. By degrees, however, this theater became conventional. It needed regeneration, and in 1908 Prince Alexander Ivanovitch Sumbatov was brought in to quicken it to fresh life. He was a Georgian of the older generation, noteworthy as an actor under the stage name of Youzhin, and equally distinguished as a playwright whose dramas had received thousands of representations. Immediately he began to restore the Small State Theater to something of the prestige it had lost by reason of the rise of the Moscow Art Theater ten years before.

More important than these state enterprises, however, were the private ventures that found in the Moscow Art Theater their culmination. Various attempts had been made to establish such private ventures in spite of an ancient law intended to tax them out of existence. In the 'sixties an Artistic Circle gave "general rehearsals" to club members, and an actress of the Small Theater, Madame Brenko, at the opening of the 'eighties furnished literary musical evenings with play readings which were really full-fledged performances. Ostrovsky, most popular of Russian dramatists, and president of the Society of Dramatic Authors and Composers, presented to Alexander III in 1882 an eloquent plea urging the importance of the stage and of a school of dramatic art. Then, with the Czar's approval, he drew up plans for a theater that should provide seats for the masses as well as the aristocrats, and foreign as well as native pieces performed by a trained repertory company. Thereupon, the monopoly of the State theaters being relaxed, F. A. Korsh, a lawyer of Moscow, set up a playhouse in which he gave Tolstoy's *Power of Darkness* and other Russian dramas, and masterpieces, also, by the Norwegians, the Germans, and the French. For Wednesday performances he fixed the admission price so low as to encourage the attendance of the proletariat, and within quarter of a century he had fathered more than five thousand representations. Following his example, others opened private theaters and encouraged a host of rising playwrights. The demands of such critics as Yurev and Veselovsky did much, also, to further the cause of Russian drama.

In 1898 the Moscow Art Theater was started as a result of the collaboration of the actor Stanislavsky and the critic and playwright Nemirovich-Dantchenko. Constantin Stanislavsky, after studying for the stage in Paris, had returned to Moscow in 1888, and assisted in founding the Society of Arts and

80

Letters. With his colleagues of that society, he felt that the Russian theater had hardened into something inflexible and too remote from life. Accordingly, he proceeded to produce plays in a more spontaneous fashion, and was encouraged by the visit to Moscow of the German company of the Duke of Saxe-Meiningen, acting Ibsen and Hauptmann with rare realism.

In the meantime, Vladimir Nemirovich-Dantchenko had been interested, like Stanislavsky, in theatrical reform. Since the age of nineteen he had been writing occasional dramas. He was lecturing on the art of the stage at a conservatory of music and drama known as the Philharmonic Society, and one evening in the late Spring of 1897 he met Stanislavsky in a Moscow café, and together they conceived the plan of the Art Theater. It should engage the best talent to represent in the most natural and effective manner the finest plays. Nemirovich-Dantchenko agreed to raise funds for its launching from among wealthy merchants and to direct its artistic policy, leaving to Stanislavsky supervision of the details of production and a chief rôle among its actors. On March 14, 1898, Alexei Tolstoy's chronicle play, *Czar Fyodor Ivanovich*, was put on, and the favor secured by this brilliant representation was corroborated by the realistic production of *The Sea Gull* by Chekhov which had earlier failed at Petersburg. Thereafter Chekhov became the patron saint of the Art Theater, and the white wings of his sea gull were taken to adorn its curtain and its printed programs.

Since Chekhov's plays require peculiar subtlety and restraint in representation, the Art Theater was influenced the more against the florid exaggeration of the old school, tending to what has been called a style of minimization. It studied to reveal the significance of trifles, laying bare the interplay of souls beneath the surface of what seems utterly commonplace. In time, also, the Art Theater showed the possibilities of fresh scenic effects when staging pieces more or less symbolic, like

The Blue Bird of Maeterlinck, given its initial production here, or *The Life of Man* by Andreyev; and also in a most original presentation of *Hamlet* arranged by Gordon Craig.

During the first twenty years of the existence of the Art Theater, there were acted seventy-one plays, of which twenty-five were foreign in origin. There were included works by such dramatists as Sophocles, Shakespeare, Molière, Goldoni, Ibsen, Maeterlinck, Hauptmann, and Hamsun. Of native playwrights, although Chekhov was most popular, Gorky, Gogol, Pisemsky, Ostrovsky, Pushkin, and the minors were often represented. A studio school, opened in 1912, developed into a trial theater with its own plays which now and then, as in the case of *Twelfth Night* and a dramatization of Dickens' *Cricket on the Hearth*, proved so good as to be transferred to the principal stage.

Until after the outbreak of the War, the Art Theater company visited Petersburg each Spring, and occasionally acted at Kiev, Odessa, and Warsaw. In 1906 the company toured through Germany and Austria; and in 1919 it divided, one part, led by Chekhov's widow, playing in the south of Russia whither all had hoped to go. The northern group, being separated from the southern by the Revolution, staged Byron's *Cain* and a new production of Gogol's *The Inspector General*, and began experiments in the field of music, and Nemirovich-Dantchenko established a Musical Trial Stage for light opera. In 1923 the reunited company made the first of several visits to America.

Now it has usually been held that the Art Theater was responsible for the vogue enjoyed by Chekhov, but Professor Leo Wiener, in his authentic volume *The Contemporary Drama of Russia*, disputes this, asserting that it was Chekhov who made possible the success of the Art Theater. In any case, the playwright, who had begun his career before that theater was founded, became its leading creative support.

Born in 1860 at Taganrog on the Sea of Azov, Anton

CHEKHOV AND THE MOSCOW ART THEATER

Pavlovich Chekhov grew up in humble circumstances. His father was a grocer, and his grandfather had been a serf. After study at a church school, diversified by work in the paternal shop and summers at an estate in the country, where his grandfather was supervisor, Chekhov entered the medical department of the University of Moscow, from which he received his degree in 1884. Two years later appeared his first volume of stories, a collection which discloses the influence upon him of the French. His health was early impaired, however, and he was forced to move to the South. His fiction grew somber, and he began to dally with the drama, which hitherto he had regarded with contempt, having said, "The novel is a lawful wife, but the stage is a noisy, flashy, and insolent mistress." His own full-length plays were anything but flashy and noisy, revealing rather a sedate restraint. In spite of his doubts at their first performance, such pieces as *Ivanov* and *The Sea Gull* were accorded a welcome by the public, but their widest recognition came only when later they were set forth by the Moscow Art Theater, an organization which could understand the author's purposes and give to these artistic being. Of that theater he became the chief provider, and an ardent champion. It was he who incited Gorky to write for the Moscow Art Company *The Smug Citizen* and *The Lower Depths*, and for that company he wrote himself *The Three Sisters* and *The Cherry Orchard*. From his invalid's retreat in the Crimea, he sent word to the manager Nemirovich-Dantchenko: "If I were in Moscow I should try to join your staff, even if it were but in the capacity of a hall porter, so as to help you as best I could and to save you from flagging in that brave young undertaking."

Chekhov married Madame Olga Knipper, leading lady of the Moscow Art Theater, who had taken the principal rôle in *The Sea Gull,* and who has continued to interpret his chief women characters. In 1904, after long suffering from tuberculosis, he died at Badenweiler in the Black Forest. Since then, his work, which he had disparaged as sweet lemonade rather than vodka, has won increasing praise. He is not an inspiring writer of the first class. He is rather a painter of character and manners, faithfully reflecting an unheroic time. In one of his stories he says: "Nature has set in every Russian an inquiring mind, a tendency to speculation, and an extraordinary capacity for belief; but all these are broken into dust against our improvidence, indolence, and fantastic triviality."

A few words will suffice concerning the minor plays of Chekhov. They are stage anecdotes, frequently humorous. Thus, in *The Proposal* the youth who aspires to the hand of his sweetheart cannot refrain from quarreling with her even while proposing. Her joyful acceptance results only in a fresh contention. The situation is analogous to that in Lady Gregory's Irish comedy *The Workhouse Ward*. In his popular hit *The Bear*, a debtor, who demands that a widow pay her late husband's debts, challenges her to a duel which she cheerfully accepts; but he shortly yields to the charms of one so virile, and agrees to become her husband's successor. In *The Jubilee*, the managing director of a bank prepares to receive the congratulations of his employees but is driven distracted, first, by the gossip of his wife, then, by the demands of a comic old woman who mistakes this bank for the army medical department, and, finally, by the despair of his chief clerk suffering nervous prostration in endeavoring to figure up the accounts. The burlesque of this scene finds parallels in *The Tragedian in Spite of Himself* and *The Wedding*. When the bridegroom in the latter insists that a general be invited to attend a wedding supper, there is put off upon him, instead, a deaf naval officer talking in nautical wise like a hero of Smollett, and a jolly mixup ensues.

By contrast, a note of pathos is sounded in *The Swan Song*. Here an old comedian falls asleep in the theater after a benefit performance given to mark his retirement from the stage. On awaking, he confesses to the prompter his disillusionment with life. He has found that the make-believe of the actor affords him no satisfaction. Once at least he had genius, he thinks, in witness whereof he recites tragic passages from Pushkin and Shakespeare. Yet he has never risen to enact such rôles. "I have drained the bottle," he reflects; "only a few drops are left at the bottom." Similarly serious is *That Worthless Fellow Platonov*, an early piece suppressed by the author, but recently published with his own revisions. Here a talkative weak-willed philanderer, caught in various intrigues, is eventually shot by his discarded mistress, the wife of his friend.

Of Chekhov's five major dramas, *Ivanov* was the first. Written in two and a half weeks, it was later revised and improved. The hero is a typical unhappy Russian, out of love with his wife, a frail little Jewess, who, in marrying him, has forfeited the affection of her wealthy parents. Warned that his neglect of her will shorten her life, now threatened by consumption, Ivanov nevertheless spends his evenings with a friend's daughter, who defends him when he is made fun of for his poverty. As she admits to him her love, and they stand locked in each other's arms, there enters his wife. Later, the lovers, blaming themselves, take leave of each other; but Anna, the wife, continues to upbraid her husband, declaring unjustly that he had married her only to secure her parents' wealth, twitting him with trying to take advantage of the girl to whose father he owes money, and charging him with responsibility for the dishonest ruses of his business agent. Stung by her accusations, Ivanov turns upon her, crying, "Hold your tongue, Jewess!" and he adds, with a cruelty for which he at once is sorry: "Know, then, that you—you are dying! The doctor has told me that you are dying!" In the last act a year has elapsed, and the widower Ivanov, about to marry his Sasha, suffers qualms of conscience. When he learns that a busybody physician will denounce him at the wedding, he shoots himself. The piece is characteristic in its portrayal of one without will, overcome by circumstance. "There are so few of us, and there is so much to do!" exclaims Ivanov. "I am a broken man, I am old at thirty. I have submitted myself to old age. With a heavy head and a sluggish mind, weary, used up, discouraged, without faith or love or an object in life, I wander like a shadow among other men, not knowing whether I am alive or what it is that I want. . . . So I carry my sadness with me wherever I go; a cold weariness, a discontent and horror of life. Yes, I am lost forever." Thus the dramatist expresses the discouragement of his countrymen and his own lowered vitality.

In *The Sea Gull*, Chekhov sets forth the woes of a young poet who has written for the actress he loves a symbolic drama to be performed out of doors. Constantin wishes to break with the older formulas of art; but his mother, a conventional actress, brings down the curtain by her ridicule. Disheartened at this and at the faithlessness of his sweetheart, who now prefers the middle-aged author Trigorin, the youth attempts suicide but fails. Although, within two years, his poetry wins him fame, he remains unhappy, for his sweetheart, despite Trigorin's departure with Constantin's mother, had followed the author to Moscow, where she had borne him a child. In the last act, again deserted by Trigorin for her rival, Nina bids Constantin farewell. Cast off by her father, she will go forth into the provinces with a third-rate theatrical company. But she declares that Trigorin's ill-treatment of her has only quickened her passion for him. Constantin in jealous despair sees her vanish; then, having destroyed the manuscript at which he had been working, he shoots himself.

The play is a study of moods and motives in folk rendered unhappy by frustrated ambition. Constantin, who would create a new art to replace the old, is ridiculed at first and, though commanding attention at last, has failed to win the woman he loves. Arkadina, his mother, succeeds only by accepting a low ideal in art and in morals. Trigorin, the publisher poet, though admired by the vulgar, is wearied with his work. Even in his hours of recreation he must seek for fresh material and endure the thrusts of the critics. As for Nina, the sole release she can find from her unhappy love for Trigorin lies in toil, but toil on a lower plane than her youthful dreams had depicted. In the symbolic piece written for her by Constantin, she speaks lines that set forth the emptiness of the life she and her friends have been leading. "The world is dead! Its inhabitants have perished!" she exclaims with Maeterlinckian repetition. "It is cold, cold, cold! It is empty, empty, empty! I am afraid, afraid, afraid! The bodies of the living have fallen into dust, and the eternal Cause has changed them into stones, into water, into clouds." Her fate as a wounded wanderer has been symbolically foretold after Constantin had presented her with the sea gull which lends its title to the play. When she had confessed her inability to divine the meaning of the gift, the facile Trigorin had perceived in it the theme for a story. As the bird loves the water, so will his heroine love the lake beside which she dwells, and as a hunter wantonly shoots the gull, so, wantonly, will a passer-by ruin the girl. Thus, Trigorin had forecast his own relations with Nina.

Superior in its analysis of character and its universality of theme is *The Three Sisters*. Together with their brother, three sisters lead gray lives in a provincial town, hoping some day to return to Moscow, from which their father had brought them eleven years earlier. For the sisters and the brother, Moscow symbolizes romance and opportunity; but their dream of going there is dispelled. Andrei, who would become a professor in the university, remains a petty clerk in the bureaucratic government at home, and is compromised in an intrigue and overruled by the shallow wife for whose sake he has mortgaged the property of his sisters. Olga, the eldest, wears out her life as a school-teacher, unable to realize her ambition of going to the capital, and repressing also her desire to escape from drudgery through marriage. Masha, the second sister, united to a tedious pedagogue, seeks relief from boredom in an affair with an old friend of her father, commander of the local garrison, cursed with a crazy wife. She is left mourning, however, when he is ordered away with the troops. Irina, the youngest sister, who has come to the conclusion that work is the secret of happiness, toils as clerk in a telegraph office and then in the town council, but finds her labors devoid of poetry or ideas. Having consented to marry a baron who has resigned from the army in order to do his industrial bit in a brick yard, she loses him when he falls in a duel with an eccentric rival for her hand. So the three sisters and the brother, beholding their aspirations crumble, lack the strength of character to make them real. They are middle-class people who suffer mentally rather than materially. Defeated in their yearnings, grasping after culture and the higher satisfactions, they are overcome by circumstance and their own weakness.

Here is no plot and no central personage. Instead, Chekhov paints a family and its friends in four scenes distributed over as many years. The portraits are drawn without exaggeration and with perfect distinction. We learn to know patient and pathetic Olga, rebellious Masha, volatile Irina, the mediocre Andrei, his unworthy wife Natasha, Masha's smug pedagogue husband blind to her affair with another, the worldly-wise Vershinin who looks to the law of progress to right present wrongs, the baron with his gospel of work, and the good old army surgeon who has loved the mother of the three sisters and pays them his devotion, though a stoic pessimist. "It's all the same! all the same!" he exclaims at any crisis. When Andrei complains that marriage slays with ennui, the surgeon answers, "Of course; but solitude also is sad, my dear; and then, after all, this or that, what does it matter?"

The sadness of life is not the principal theme of the play, however. For Chekhov brightens the gloom by suggesting the need of faith and of work. Hope in ultimate progress is the balm for present wounds proposed by Vershinin. A time will come, he thinks, when culture will spread, when the three sisters will no longer prove an exception. He believes in work, and so does the baron, who seems to forecast Soviet rule when he says: "Something formidable is threatening us; a strong cleansing storm is gathering; . . . it will soon sweep our world clean of laziness, indifference, prejudice against work, and wretched boredom. I shall soon work, and within twenty-five or thirty years every one will work—every one." Irina, too, declares: "We must work. That is why we are unhappy and look at life so sadly. We don't know what work is. Our parents looked on work with contempt." Yet it is part of the author's irony that those, like Irina and Olga, who work most continue dissatisfied. Chekhov, though he foresaw the new industrial Russia, understood full well that happiness requires something more.

In the year following the production of *The Three Sisters*, Chekhov completed *Uncle Vanya*, revamping his play *The Wood Demon* which had failed eight years before. Here again life is sad but to be lived with fortitude in the hope of heavenly compensation for earthly ills. Uncle Vanya, his mother, and his plain but kindly niece, Sonia, dwell upon the country estate left by his dead sister. Sonia's father, a dried-up professor, has been receiving the proceeds of the estate managed by Vanya, and now, having taken a young and beautiful second wife, he comes down for a visit, and to threaten selling the estate and ousting Vanya and Sonia. So charming is the bride that Vanya is disgusted at not having got ahead of the professor and married her himself; and the district physician, beloved by Sonia, turns from her instantly to the newcomer. Thus Sonia is disdained; and Vanya, distraught by jealousy and the prospect of being pushed out of the only home he knows, shoots at the professor. Though his shot goes wild, and the professor forgives, Vanya is so unnerved that he meditates suicide. But Sonia, who has suffered more than he, bids him bear up under affliction. The professor will leave them in peace. The bride, who knows the mistake she has made in marrying such a man, will hold to her bargain, after bidding the physician a fervent and final farewell. He, too, will depart, indifferent to Sonia but looking to the far future for something better.

The infinite sadness of living is the theme of this play. Not only are the invertebrate Vanya and the patient Sonia exponents of the doctrine of quietistic submission to fate; but most of the others express their belief in life's futility or else illustrate it. The professor admits that he is an old dotard, longing in vain for success and the stir of the world. Helena is also unhappy, for she has married him, dazzled by his learning, only to find herself the wife of a cross-grained invalid, pampered and spoiled, his scholastic achievements a mere bluff. Equally unhappy is the country physician, who enjoys a few bright moments in philandering with Helena. "Life holds nothing for me; my race is run," he complains. "I am old, I am tired, I am trivial; my sensibilities are dead." Once he had been interested in preserving the forests; now he laments the fact that the felling of the woods has not been succeeded by progress. "We have the same swamps and mosquitoes," he says; "the same disease and want; typhoid, diphtheria, burning villages. . . . There's but one hope for us to cherish, the hope that we may be visited by visions,—perhaps by pleasant ones—, as we lie resting in our graves."

If, in *Uncle Vanya*, Chekhov has lost that faith in work and progress which furnishes a background of relief to the sad foreground of *The Three Sisters*, in *The Cherry Orchard*, produced just before his death, he at least contrasts with the dying generation of landed aristocrats the rising generation of the enfranchised and industrious serfs. Once more there is prospect of escape from idle boredom through action, but the dramatist's efforts are expended quite as much in quickening sympathy for the folk of the old order incompetent to cope with the new. The dramatic picture is focused about the sale of an estate enforced by the easy life of its owner in Paris. Madame Ranevskaya and her sentimental, pleasure-loving

brother return from France, where they have idled th
in luxury, to find everything at sixes and sevens.
their property is encumbered with mortgages, they r
scorn the suggestion of a prosperous, self-made neighbor th
they raze the house and cut down the fine old cherry orchard
and lay out the place in villa sites. Then this neighbor buys in
the estate at auction even while they are giving a farewell
dance in the faded ball-room. As he enters to announce his
purchase, the dancers stop in dismay; but the new master,
picking up the house keys flung to the floor by the lady's outraged daughter, bids the musicians resume playing. In the last
act, the house is dismantled. It will be torn down in the Spring.
The family is leaving forever. Madame Ranevskaya will return to Paris and a lover who will squander what little money
remains. Her children and her brother must seek positions in
order to support themselves. Lopakhin, the self-made neighbor, who might have married Madame's daughter, disdains
sentiment. He is far too busy for love. As they all pass out,
only the old footman is left behind, locked in the doomed house,
forgotten by the others. Sick unto death in mind and body,
he will perish there long before the doors are opened for the
final destruction. Already he can catch the sound of axes
felling the cherry orchard outside.

That orchard and the house seem living things, and our
interest is nicely balanced between the setting and the characters. The city is encroaching on the country estates. Trade
is replacing idleness, work is replacing the luxury of art and
pleasure. The aristocrats, corrupt and sentimental, must yield
to the new democracy with its practical common sense. Dreamers and spendthrifts alike pass from the land, which they have
lacked the frugality and the foresight to retain. Those of the
old order recognize their weakness, their maundering inca-
pacity to deal with fresh conditions. The smart young footman
from Paris proves successful in wooing the maid for whose
benefit the poetic clerk can only play the guitar. The peasant

merchant Lopakhin, who once would have jumped at a chance to marry into the aristocracy, is now too much occupied with business affairs. Only those who are ready to adapt themselves to the industrial order can survive and succeed. For the new generation, Russia must be a country of toil, of commercial enterprise. For the student philosopher Peter, the dreamy past is a thing to be disdained. To him, and to Yasha the footman, Russia as yet is a dull, uncivilized country compared with France. Throughout, the tone is steel-gray and somber. As usual, the characters talk at cross purposes, speaking when no one listens, hearing and failing to understand one another, detached spiritually, finding little communion of mind, yet confessing freely their loss of illusions, their imperfections and weakness. As an example of refined realism, *The Cherry Orchard* is unsurpassed.

It should be observed, however, that Chekhov, though he defended his right to seem objective and impersonal in his art, upheld its selective process and was no rigorous naturalist. In writing to the journalist Suvorin he said: "You abuse me for objectivity, calling it indifference to good and evil, lack of ideals and ideas. You would have me, when I describe horse stealers, say: 'Stealing horses is an evil.' But that has been known for an age without my saying so. Let the jury judge them; it's my job simply to show what sort of people they are. . . . You confuse two things," he wrote Suvorin, "solving a problem and stating a problem correctly. It is only the second that is obligatory for the artist." At the same time, he declared for the artist's inevitable reshaping of observed facts. "An artist observes, selects, guesses, combines," said he; "and this in itself presupposes a question: unless he had set himself a question from the very first, there would be nothing to conjecture and nothing to select. . . . If one denies that creative work involves problems and purposes, one must admit that an artist creates without premeditation or intention, in a state of aberration; therefore, if an author boasted to me of having written a novel without a preconceived design, under a sudden inspiration, I should call him mad."

What is the worth of Chekhov's contribution to the theater? His plays are certainly significant. In form they show that absence of the French tradition of the "well-made piece" which Maurice Baring has remarked as distinguishing most Russian drama. They are not carefully shaped to produce a series of climaxes. What counts in them is not a series of catastrophes but the even flow of life revealed as the majority must live it. "What Chekhov desired," says Oliver Sayler, "was to interpret life through its reticences, its nuances, its slender moments." The characters, the action, the speeches all are natural. The style is direct and matter-of-fact except for a chance expression of poetic emotion. Thus a girl laments, "I feel as if I had been in the world a thousand years, and I trail my life behind me like an endless scarf," and another declares, "I used to think so much of love, and I have been thinking about it for so long by day and by night, that my soul is like an expensive piano which is locked and the key lost." In performance the plays are interrupted by long pauses when the people say nothing. In these pauses, as in the undirected talk that breaks them, character is revealed, but what is done counts for less than what is said or left unsaid. So far as plot is concerned, nothing is conventionalized. Servants do not reveal the situation to the audience; confidantes do not elicit secrets from the leading lady; *raisonneurs* do not enunciate the doctrines of the author. Instead, common folk from seventeen to eighty-seven stroll about the scene and talk. Among them there are no villains and no heroes, no magnetic personalities, no strong or willful souls, none torn between compunctions of conscience and burning desire. Chekhov paints a somber world to be tolerated by sensitive creatures without will, hoping perhaps for ultimate improvement, but doing nothing to bring it to pass.

CHAPTER VI

The Little Eccentrics

Artzybashev, Sologub, Evreinov

THE quiet and refined naturalism of Chekhov which displays the crushing of the individual by his environment is not likely to satisfy the self-assertive. For such, Mikhail Petrovich Artzybashev, following the sensational naturalism of Strindberg, provides more thrilling entertainment. A great-grandson of Kosciusko, he was born in 1878 and won fame in fiction by his daring novel *Sanine*. For the stage he has written a few plays of careful structure ringing the changes upon disordered love. Passion he exhibits as the only occupation of woman and the most interesting concern of man. To give free play to instinct he declares to be our duty. Although he distinguishes between physical and spiritual attractions, it is clear that the former are for him dominant. So he depicts what Granville Barker has called "this barnyard world of sex." A cynic in the drama *Jealousy* remarks of his own intrigue that it involves "a concert of amorous tom cats." The same cynic affirms that men foolishly continue to look for Lauras and Beatrices, failing to understand that these ideal ladies never existed except in the minds of their self-deluded lovers. "Not only could a woman never be a Laura;" he remarks, "she could never even invent one," adding that: "When a man and a woman love, we say, 'She gives herself to him'; but that is a pious fraud. The right expression would be, 'She's caught him.'" In illustration of this concept of the seductive and pursuing female, Artzybashev here depicts a wife who strives to fascinate every man she meets, from youthful student to elderly physician and imperious prince. In the last act, however, she is strangled by her jealous husband, warned by a friend of her perfidy and infuriated when she taunts him with the fact that the suspected prince has not been her only lover.

More artistic because more subtle than *Jealousy* is Artzybashev's *Enemies*. Here, without a suicide or a murder to punctuate the play, there is a more elaborate analysis of the difficulties that attend marriage. An elderly professor resents his wife's devotion to housekeeping and her meddling with his studies. Yet, when she dies, he finds himself lonely and conscience-stricken. "I gave her too little care," he says; "I thought only of myself. . . . I imagined that she was in my way, that she was spoiling my life, that she was not worthy of me. . . . I flattered myself that with another wife I might have been different." Now he perceives that, "Nothing is more precious than love, and that there is no punishment more painful than fruitless regret and a tardy repentance." The unhappy marriages of his daughter and his son, added to his own, make the play. The son, a composer deficient in vitality, is wed to a woman who requires it and for that reason takes an officer of the guards, though she recognizes him to be a fool. "Our intimacy shames me like a slap in the face," she admits; "yet while it lasts it makes me forget everything. . . . I have no self-control left, no self-respect."

The professor's daughter suffers because her husband, a physician, insisting that man can love more than one woman at a time, acts upon his theory. "Why must one love necessarily destroy another?" he asks. "We can love both music and painting, Pushkin and Lermontov, the beauty of nature and the beauty of the human body." For her such amorous catholicity is less possible. "I love my love in you," she tells him. "A woman can never forget her first love, while a man rarely even remembers his." To the dashing girl that he has taken for second companion the husband says, "Can't you understand that we can love two, that there is no fraud, nothing low, nothing vile in such a love?" On her declaring that she cannot understand, he retorts, "No woman can, but every man will understand me; it's our nature." The wife in this case, like the husband in the former, forgives. "I shall forget what has happened," she says; "I shall love you again." But there is a tell-tale gleam in her husband's eyes. Can he forget the other woman? A rude old army physician, father of this other, stands as spokesman for Artzybashev's biological theory of love. Karnovich, too, has had his experience with matrimony, and when a lady prays for a good spring rain which will bring everything out of the ground, he exclaims: "God forbid! I have two wives resting there." He holds that a happy marriage is impossible because the interests of men and women are bound to clash. The man who marries can never again feel alone. "Take two of the greatest of friends and put them into one cell," says Karnovich; "they will begin to hate each other. Life together is only possible when there are constant and mutual sacrifices. But where there are sacrifices there can be no happiness." He believes that the soul is but the product of a complicated chemical process, and the purpose of existence is a new product. Love is dependent upon the glands as laughter upon a contraction of the muscles of the throat. Men for him are naturally polygamous. He warns his daughter that: "Every man, including the saintliest of saints, is absolutely capable of loving a thousand women. . . . Woman dreams of some individual, while man dreams of the sex."

In *The Law of the Savage*, these ideas are repeated by a Freudian, who believes that the soul feeds on love, that a man who loves but one woman is either a phenomenon or a cripple. "No matter how strongly a man's love may center on one woman," says Vorosov, "he cannot help feeling attracted when youth and beauty pass his way. He may fight against his instinct; he may crush it. But no such repression goes unpunished." According to the new ethics, repression rather than transgression deserves reproof. The story of the play illustrates the author's conception of the forces that rule humanity, his folk being savages in fine clothes. The central figure is a libertine lawyer, who, like Sanine, is a Nietzschean individualist. As a guest in the house of his friend, he makes love to the friend's wife, with whom he has earlier had an intrigue. Then, though beloved by his own wife, he captures the heart of her younger sister, whom he advises that instinct should be her guide. Discovered by the first lady while embracing the second, he is exposed to his wife, to whom his best excuse for loving her sister lies in the fact that this sister resembles her as she was in days gone by. The outraged wife proceeds to seek revenge by giving herself to a lover, but repents, and tells him that she still loves her Boris. Yet, when the latter appears, she avows her disloyalty in order to wound him. He flies into a rage, arranges to duel with his rival, and then, as his wife kneels to beg his forgiveness, kicks her full in the chest. Such is Artzybashev's application of the double standard. This bounder of a husband, who admits that he has betrayed Zina at every opportunity without any feeling of guilt, makes her the victim of his jealous rage after a single offence on her part. In the last act, though admitting that he has long lived a life of lies, he explains: "I am as you made me and as environment moulded me. I cannot be different, nor do I wish to be. I am a child of my age. I have no faith in anything, and I ask only one thing of life—pleasure, variety." For the law of the duel he would substitute the law of the savage; so, instead of waiting for the signal to fire, he shoots down his rival without allowing him a chance to shoot back in fair play. "This is murder!" cries one of the seconds. "What have you done?" And Boris replies coldly, "What you have seen," and stalks out.

In a later play, *War*, Artzybashev exhibits the life of a family as affected by the great conflict, considering specifically the effect upon women of the loss or maiming of their lovers and husbands. The central figure is a milder matron of Ephesus, devoted to her lord so long as he is whole and sound, able to excite and respond to her passion; yet, during his absence at the front, succumbing in thought to a former admirer, and, upon his return as a cripple, falling into the admirer's embrace. A second woman in the play, when she learns that her lover has died on the field of honor, gives herself to his consumptive rival who has slyly induced the other to enlist. For women the half-living, according to Artzybashev, are better than those who live no longer, just as the strong and the well are better than the maimed. In such matters women, like men, must obey the Life Force. Artzybashev defines his self-assertive doctrine as anarchic individualism. Thus, in his plays there sounds a new note, not only an appeal to sensation, but a challenge to the will. They may mark, as has been alleged, the liberation of the Russian drama from monologue and philosophical discussion, but they exhibit so drastic an individualism that they have fallen under the ban of the Communist régime. Moreover, they are naturalistic, whereas the Communists have turned from the art which transcribes reality to that which suggests meanings through symbols.

This tendency, marked in stage productions before the Revolution of 1917, was induced by the Russian love of stylization in gesture, costume, and scene-setting, revealed also in their dances which create a brilliant and fantastic world of motion against the backgrounds of Bakst. Even before the Moscow Art Theater had swung over to symbolism, its minute realism had incited a revolt on the part of Meyerhold, Kommisarzhevsky, and Alice Koonen. Vsevolod Emilyevich Meyerhold, born of German parents on the Volga, studied law and music and acted with the Moscow Art Theater for four years. After the Russo-Japanese War he left Stanislavsky in order to perform independently in southern Russia, then to serve in Petersburg as director for Vera Kommisarzhevsky, an actress of Polish extraction, and in 1908 to become régisseur of the two imperial theaters, the Marinsky for opera and the Alexandrinsky for drama. Influenced by the Italians and Reinhardt, he regarded the theater as a place of make-believe, no longer darkening the auditorium and throwing the action into a lighted picture frame. Rather, he preferred a stage projecting into the auditorium, and sometimes dispensed with a curtain. Increasingly, too, he favored a bare setting with ladders, flights of steps, platforms at different levels, and machine-like appurtenances.

A second reformer of the stage, Fyodor Kommisarzhevsky, set up a Free School of Scenic Art and in 1914 opened a Memorial Theater named after his sister Vera, who had died four years earlier. The Memorial Theater, seating only a hundred and fifty, introduced foreign novelties such as von Hofmannsthal's *Electra*, Hauptmann's *Hannele*, Wedekind's *Box of Pandora*, Aristophanes' *Lysistrata*, and the English *Everyman*, besides exploiting the minor Russians like Ozyorov, Sologub, Kuzmin, and Remizov. Scenically, Kommisarzhevsky utilized curtains, lights banked at the top of the proscenium, and the softening effect of a film of gauze stretched across the picture. His revolt against realism he explained in a volume *The Art of the Actor and The Theory of Stanislavsky*, affirming that the actor should be "an independent cultural creator, not an imitator or a psychological experimenter." It is worthy of note that, since the Revolution, the Soviet of Workmen's Deputies has secured Kommisarzhevsky to direct performances of opera and ballet at the independent Zimin's Opera House in Moscow, accepting his doctrines in opposition to those of the realists.

The third reformer to secede from the Moscow Art Theater was Alice Koonen, a Swedish actress, who, with her husband, Alexander Yakovlevich Tairov, régisseur of the so-called Free Theater, opened the Kamerny on Christmas Day, 1914. Already she had created the rôle of Mytyl in Maeterlinck's *Blue Bird* and of Anitra in Ibsen's *Peer Gynt* at the Art Theater

and that of Plum Blossom in the *Yellow Jacket* at the Free
Theater. She was thus ready to direct a revolt in favor of
symbolism. Tairov was equally prepared to aid her by his experience as manager of a Petersburg café and a traveling
troop. He proposed now to develop at the Kamerny "the theater theatrical," laying stress upon experiments with lighting
and gesture in such pantomimes as Debussy's *Box of Toys*,
Kuzmin's *The Pentecost at Toledo*, and Donanhy's *The Veil
of Pierrette*; and, after the example of the Art Theater's *Blue
Bird* production, employing music to reinforce the rhythm of
action. The Kamerny proved especially hospitable to the exotic, such pieces as Kalidasa's *Sakuntala*, Calderón's *Life's a
Dream*, Goldoni's *The Fan*, Sem Benelli's *Supper of Pranks*,
Rostand's *Cyrano*, and Wilde's *Salome*. Tairov transferred to
the stage the lines and levels of the auditorium and sought to
make the scene, as he phrased it, "complete the actor as the
snail's shell completes the animal within." He employed in
his settings the geometrical forms of crystals and used costumes highly stylized.

The tendency to depart from realism in stagecraft was
accompanied by a shift toward symbolism and expressionism
in playwriting, illustrated by the work of three writers in particular—Sologub, Evreinov, and Andreyev. Each advanced
critical theories to justify his practice. Thus, Andreyev, in
1913, in an article contributed to the journal *Maski*, discussed
"the theater of the future" which he described as contrasting
with the theater of make-believe. It is to be a "theater pan-
psychic," dependent less upon action and stage trappings than
upon subjective thought and feeling. Like the early Maeterlinck, Andreyev would reveal the life of the soul, "with its
premonitions, its yearnings and searchings," on the ground
that Life has become more and more psychological, that such
primitive emotions as hunger and love are being displaced by
more intellectual cravings, struggles, joys, and sufferings. For

the outward clash of man with man as the result of passion he would substitute the wrestlings of thought.

Fyodor Sologub offers a somewhat different conception of the theater, pointing to it as a temple of religion in which the poet is priest, and the ceremonies are designed to make the worshipers forget for a little the dull round of everyday living. The physical conditions of the theater operate to hamper free communication between the soul of the poet and the soul of his audience. Accordingly, the manager should magnify the poet's importance, says Sologub, and minimize the physical medium. Such an end should be sought by reducing the rôle of the individual actor so far as possible to that of the marionette with slow and beautiful movements and unimpassioned utterance. The picture-frame proscenium should be abolished, together with such devices as footlights and curtain, in order that the poet's creations and the audience may be brought into closer contact. The scenery should be simplified to the last degree, merely suggesting the place of action symbolically. When all these conditions are fulfilled, the ego of the audience will merge with the ego of the poet, who alone for the time being will control actors and spectators.

For Sologub, art is also ideal, the result of imposing beauty upon a world deficient in this respect. Tragedy arises from the clash of the beautiful ideal and the ugly fact, and the greater the art, the more tragic in this sense is it likely to become. The tragic hero, like the poet, seeking to impose the order of beauty upon the chaos of nature, engages in a struggle that leads to his destruction. That such is the nature of every tragic hero, however, is more than doubtful. Evidently, Macbeth, Othello, Lear were not endeavoring to impose order upon a disordered world. Sologub's conception of tragedy is, therefore, limited to a single type, and his illustration of the notion, as presented in his drama *The Triumph of Death*, is not such as to fire disciples with the spirit of emulation.

As for Evreinov, he is equally peculiar in the suggestions

that he offers for theatrical reform. Evreinov stands sponsor for the doctrine of monodrama, which is more comprehensible as theory than when exemplified in his works. In 1909 he issued *An Introduction to Monodrama*, and from 1915 to 1917 he published three volumes of the *Theater for One's Self*. The core of his conception, like that of Andreyev, is the fusion of actor and spectator, of theatrical representation and reality, in the soul of the dramatist. This soul is revealed in the central character of the play into which the audience must enter. Hence other personages upon the stage are for Evreinov mere modifications of the protagonist, or at least his subjective reactions toward things outside him. Thus Evreinov declares, "Only one acting character is possible; in the strict meaning of the word, only one subject of action is thinkable. Only with him do I identify myself, only from his point of view do I perceive the world surrounding him, the people surrounding him. . . . We cannot in monodrama recognize any importance in the other acting characters." As a result, Evreinov would reduce speech to a minimum and exalt gesture and pantomime. He would confine his plots to the simplest.

It will be noted that Evreinov, like Sologub, transgresses the law of psychic distance in his desire to mix audience and actors and to realize their substantial unity. That which constitutes much of the charm of a representation in art is the distinction drawn spontaneously by the mind between reality and esthetic semblance. We know that the representation in the poem, the play, the statue, the picture is not actual, that its material is unlike the material of life, and for that reason we are able to regard it with the mind and feelings as a free presentation of ideas. It is only the naïve and ignorant who, like Partridge at the play in *Tom Jones*, confound the esthetic semblance with actuality. The proposal of Andreyev or Evreinov, therefore, to destroy the line of demarcation between audience and actors is likely to eventuate in nothing more than the comic stepping-out of the scene so common in vaudeville.

A second misconception of the nature of dramatic art on the part of Evreinov would appear to lie in his failure to understand the nature of dramatic confrontation. It is precisely this characteristic, whereby we feel ourselves in several opposing characters simultaneously, that distinguishes drama from other types of art. The co-existence of opposing forces, with all of which we may sympathize, yields the authentic thrill in the theater. To reduce the sense of confrontation by rendering it a conflict only in the soul of the protagonist would be to sacrifice what is perhaps the most significant feature of every great play.

Let us look now at the creative work of these writers, first, at that of Sologub and Evreinov, then at that of Andreyev. Fyodor Sologub, born in 1863, is better known for his tales and his novel *The Little Demon* than for his plays. But the latter are fairly numerous and include *The Triumph of Death*, *Liturgy to Me*, *To Love*, *Night Dances*, *Hostages of Life*, *The Rose Design*, *The Guardian of the Great King*, and *A Stone Cast into Water*, written with Chebotarevsky. Sologub conceives of the hero of comedy as a creature of chance, a bubble floating on the stream of events, and of the hero of tragedy as an exceptional soul of strong will outfaced by circumstance. He beholds the drama passing from realistic play to fantastic spectacle and from spectacle into symbolic mystery, the latest stage of the Russian development. But his own dramas are less imposing than his theory. A description of three will suffice.

In *Vanka the Butler and Page Jean* Sologub writes a comedy of nine scenes, each presented in two versions, one as the incidents would occur in France, and one as they would occur in Russia. A wife begs of her husband the promotion of their servant who has caught her eye, and the servant in turn responds by philandering with the lady in her boudoir, while the maids quarrel among themselves to win his favor, and he succumbs at length to one, thus piquing the jealousy of another. On being exposed, both he and the lady are punished. It is in the harshness of this punishment that the two versions differ. The French count is unrelenting. The Russian prince is less rigorous; he admonishes his princess and forgives her, while the servant escapes, having induced his captors to substitute a beggar at his supposed execution. The French, says the author, are more subtle and refined in vice. The Russians are big, impulsive, kindly children.

In *The Gift of the Wise Bees*, Sologub accords romantic treatment to the story of Laodamia, praying for the return from Hades of her husband Protesilaus, the willing martyr first fallen at Troy. He preaches no lesson of self-control as does Wordsworth in his poem dealing with this subject, but portrays instead the wrath of Laodamia's father that led him to fling into the fire a waxen image of her lord, whereat, as the wax melts, the life of the faithful Laodamia dwindles until she joins her husband in death. In *The Triumph of Death*, Sologub offers the best illustration of his theory of the tragic hero as one who struggles to impose upon resistant nature an ideal of beauty. This conflict is symbolized through a Prologue in which the peasant girl idealized by Don Quixote suggests the poet's mission. She, who appears to the matter-of-fact as no more than a simple wench bearing pails of water on a yoke, is in reality the bearer of potential beauty to men. The water from her pails, regarded by the people as fit only for the task of washing floors, might, if sprinkled, cause life to bloom; but she is scorned by king, page, and poet, and as they settle themselves upon the castle steps as if to witness the play within the play, Aldonza, the peasant girl, exclaims: "Again the spectacle will remain a spectacle, and not become a mystery! . . . But I will not abandon my design. I will now take the form of the slave Malgista, and I will send my daughter

Algista to fulfill my plan. Whether the triumph be life or the triumph be death, the triumph shall be mine."

The plot of the play within the play is taken from the old legend of the daughter of Flor and Blanchefleur destined to wed King Pepin, who believes her beautiful. Fearing lest he slay her on discovering her ugliness, she accedes to the suggestion of a servant, Malgista, that the latter send her daughter, Algista, to the bridal chamber in place of Bertha. The usurper, however, refuses to change places with the princess, and, after wounding herself, accuses the latter of attempting to kill her, and incites the king to banish the princess as an impostor. Eventually he discovers the deception and restores the wronged princess to her rights, even though she be ugly. In Sologub's drama the first act is occupied by the plot of Algista against the veiled bride and the latter's banishment. By the opening of the second act, ten years have elapsed. Algista has turned out to be an excellent queen, but Bertha's brother, in the guise of a minstrel, brings her to court and proves the treachery of the former serving maid. The king in wrath orders Algista and her son to be put to death. At the opening of the third act the two have perished at the hands of the rabble, and their corpses have been thrown into a moat. When the mother of the murdered Algista bears the latter's body back to the castle, and then returns from a second journey with the body of the son, she is amazed to find that the dead Algista has revived and is bidding the inmates of the castle awaken. To the king Algista offers forgiveness on condition that, forsaking the ugly Bertha, he follow her toward a life radiant and free. When the king remains deaf to her pleadings, Algista, again dying with her son, pronounces the king's doom. He shall be transformed into stone. Apparently, the king, although he had plighted his troth to the veiled Bertha, should have continued to honor the beauty who took her place, preferring a projected ideal to the ugly actuality. But the allegory is confused by the fact that Bertha awakens sympathy as a victim of nature in being made ungainly and of injustice in being dispossessed of her place as queen. Moreover, the peasant enchantress of Don Quixote, who in the Prologue here devises the scheme to substitute beauty for ugliness, was of course no schemer, her beauty in the Spanish story lying wholly in the Knight's imagination. An ironical treatment of the central theme by André Rivoire—*Berthe aux Grands Pieds*—may have suggested the play to Sologub. Its presentation by Meyerhold in 1907 was marked by his introduction of flights of steps later so fashionable with the expressionists.

Nikolai Nikolaevich Evreinov, born in 1879, became an enthusiast of the theater at a tender age, wrote a play at seven and a novel at thirteen, and saw life as equilibrist in a traveling circus. After devouring the adventure stories of Mayne Reid and the African travels of Henry M. Stanley, he studied law and music, taught at Libau for two years, and for ten held a clerkship in the Ministry of Ways and Communications. Philosophically, he passed from atheism to simple faith, finding religious comfort, after a period of allegiance to Nietzsche, in the Gospels. Having engaged in amateur theatricals, he tried original writing for the boards, adapted the *Plutus* of Aristophanes, and composed an opera and an opera bouffe and various plays. The latter include *The Rehearsal, Fools as Blind Idols, The Foundation of Happiness, Styopik and Manyourotchka, Grandmother*, and *Such a Woman*. Having determined to give his whole attention to the stage, Evreinov in 1909 organized the Gay Theater for Grown-up Children in Petersburg, and for the first three years of the War directed The Crooked Looking Glass, where he experimented with monodrama. In such monodramas as *The Representation of Love* and *The Theater of the Soul*, he has illustrated his theory but without sufficient success to win many converts.

The Theater of the Soul, played at The Crooked Looking Glass in 1912 and in New York three years later, sets its scene in the soul of a professor, where the action is supposed to last for only half a second. The professor is torn between two loves, that for his wife and that for a dancer. After debating his dilemma, he shoots himself. This is all—an old, old story, rendered novel, however, by its manner of representation. In a Prologue the professor, lecturing on psychology, draws a diagram to symbolize his rational, his emotional, and his psychical selves by the signs $M1$, $M2$, and $M3$ respectively; then he writes a formula that reads $M1 + M2 + M3 = M$, or the integral self. For him the seat of the soul is the heart, and this now becomes the scene lighted by a throbbing red glow in which, out of darkness, appear at different levels three faces, symbolizing his three selves or entities. When the professor shoots himself, ribbons of blood stream from a hole suddenly torn in the heart, and a porter cries out, summoning the psychical self to leave. Yawning, this self takes up its luggage and shuffles off. As a curiosity, *The Theater of the Soul* may have its place, but even so it is less striking than those elaborate moralities of the Spanish stage in the seventeenth century—the *autos sacramentales*. Moreover, Evreinov is easily beaten at his own game by Andreyev in such a piece as *The Black Maskers*. That Evreinov is determined to be original or nothing there can be no doubt. At the Parody Theater in Petrograd he gave *Candida* and, rather than sacrifice Shaw's elaborate and amusing stage directions, had them read aloud by a black boy whose somber color was supposed, in Japanese fashion, to warrant his invisibility; and there also Evreinov produced Gogol's *Inspector General*, exhibiting it on the same evening, first, as it would be done by the Moscow Art Theater, and then by Gordon Craig.

The two trifles of Evreinov best known to English readers are *The Merry Death* and *The Beautiful Despot*. The first is a jaunty harlequinade in the fashion made popular by Lothar's German *King Harlequin*, declared by its author to present symbolically the problem of seeming and being. Evreinov's Harlequin is destined to die at midnight. He has stolen the affections of Pierrot's wife—pretty Columbine—but what of that? How foolish to be jealous! He persuades Pierrot that revenge is puerile, something resorted to only as good manners. He will invite Columbine to dine with them. But Columbine beats Pierrot for suspecting her, and sets him to railing at the audience for having devised such a silly rule as to require an injured husband to wreak revenge. In any case, he has taken his revenge in kind already. So he may as well be jolly and play for Columbine and Harlequin to dance. But the latter has only a few minutes more to live. It has been prophesied that he will expire at midnight of the day on which he sleeps longer than he revels. In vain Pierrot has thrust back the hands of the clock. In vain a physician has told him that he must drink nothing and eat sparingly. "Is a life like that worth living?" asks Harlequin. "That's your affair," says the physician, who then chases his patient three times around the room in order to capture his fee. Yes, Harlequin is dying; the thermometer used for taking his temperature has burst into flame; he breathes like a locomotive, but to the last he will be merry. When Death appears as a charming woman, Harlequin bows, crying, "Honor and place to a beautiful lady!" and hands her a lamp which flickers out. Pierrot in the moonlight remarks, as did the dying Rabelais, "Let down the curtain; the farce is over!" and to the audience he adds that the author will not mind hisses or applause, since he believes that nothing in life is worth taking seriously.

Agreeable as is this fantasy, it scarcely warrants the praise bestowed upon it by the critics, one of whom proclaims it "a technical masterpiece and a fine drama" which "takes its rank with the great Russian comedies"; and another who declares it "the best Russian play since Griboyedov's *Woe from Wit*."

More original, certainly, is Evreinov's *The Beautiful Despot*. Here the dramatist asks whether progress, with its dependence upon machinery, has not spoiled the life of the soul. A gentleman of the old school feels co-existent within him the Liberal and the Despot. In reading the diary of his great-grandfather, he yearns to escape to that time from the ugly present. Accordingly, on his country estate, he dresses his servants in the style of 1808, reads the papers of that year, assumes that railways do not exist and that serfdom has not been abolished. A friend, who calls to ask for an article commending the present for its economic gains, learns that the Beautiful Despot has triumphed over the Liberal in the soul of the Master. "You ask for my articles?" he says; "but that part of me has lost its belief in social ideals and died of sorrow. . . . Have you not noticed how this modern culture is destroying beauty? Can you look on calmly while it prefers the practicality of speech to its imagery, the colorless costume to the picturesque?" So he condemns Americanism, the empire of the machine, the death of art. "Better beautiful and wrong than right and ugly!" he exclaims. As the Master's lady plays Mozart on the harpsichord, the friend feels that he is dangerously dreaming. On the morrow he will ride off as fast as he can and report in Petersburg that the Master is mad.

In his latest work, Evreinov continues to be tormented by perceiving that actual life is less important than the life of illusion. Such is the theme of his drama *The Essential* which has been translated into French by Fernand Nozière and performed at Paris under the title *The Comedy of Happiness*. Here Evreinov, by chance, parallels Pirandello's *Six Characters in Search of an Author*, employing a stage rehearsal to suggest the contrast between reality and make-believe. At the rise of the curtain we behold a succession of visitors to a female seer, who presently proves to be a male philosopher in disguise. This philosopher then induces the actors engaged in a rehearsal of *Quo Vadis* to abandon their stage manager and depict for him a very different scene laid in a bourgeois boarding house, one that helps to smooth out the difficulties of the folk we have met in the first act, who, now that it is Carnival time, assume still other rôles in a harlequinade. The piece is fancifully humorous yet much less likely to be remembered than the playwright's earlier experiments in eccentricity. Neither Evreinov nor Sologub can compare with Andreyev in originality of conception and execution as creators of symbolistic drama. It is to Andreyev, therefore, that we now must turn.

CHAPTER VII

A Major Eccentric—Andreyev

LEONID NIKOLAVICH ANDREYEV was born at Orel, two hundred miles south of Moscow, in August, 1871. After struggling through the school of his native town, he studied law at the University of St. Petersburg, and by the death of his father, an engineer, was left to cope with poverty, and more than once resolved upon suicide. Of his first story concerning a starving student, he says, "I cried when I wrote it, and the editor who returned my manuscript laughed." Nevertheless, he continued to use his pen, and he also tried portrait painting. Then he secured a position with the Moscow *Courier*, publishing sketches which attracted the attention of Maxim Gorky and the critic Merezhkovsky. In the mean time, he read widely, influenced by Poe, by Tolstoy, by the *Bible* (which he termed "the best teacher of all"), and by Nietzsche, whose *Thus Spake Zarathustra* he translated. He wrote imaginative tales of terror like *The Seven Who Were Hanged*, *Thought*, and *Silence*, and in *The Red Laugh* he showed the horror of war, depicting a youth, white of face, who, on saluting his superior officer, is asked if he be afraid, and retorts by opening his mouth to let forth a stream of blood, a toothless laugh, a red laugh. From 1901 forward, Andreyev grew increasingly popular, adding dramas to fiction and becoming one of the best known of Russian writers. His plays sold largely in published form, being in many cases better fitted for reading than for performance.

In addition to writing a score of dramas, Andreyev continued his journalistic labors. With Gorky he opposed the régime of the Czars, founding a daily in Petrograd during the

111

War and sharing at first the hopes of the people at the overthrow of the Romanov dynasty. But soon he became disillusioned, and, with the rise of Bolshevism, assailed the new
movement in his paper *Volga*, while Gorky was upholding it
in his paper *Novaya Zhisn*, the columns of which he had
opened to Lenin when the latter's journal was suppressed by
the Provisional Government. Although after the *coup d'état*
of November, 1917, Gorky turned against the Bolshevists, he
soon accepted their rule and became head of the state publishing department. Andreyev, on the other hand, attacked the
Soviet government in pamphlets entitled *To Thee, O Soldier!
Ruin and Destruction*, and *S. O. S.* Of the Bolshevists he
wrote: "It is horrible to think that Europe for more than a
year could contemplate with equanimity the sight of these
exotic beasts tearing out our hearts, and yet cannot decide
whether this is the vanguard of democracy or of fiends let
loose from hell to destroy our ill-starred world." So he called
to the people of Europe and America for aid as a wireless
telegrapher on a sinking ship might call in the darkness of
night, "Help for the sinking!" Forced out of Russia soon after
the Bolshevists came into power, Andreyev lived on in Finland,
refusing to permit his works to be published by his old friend
Gorky, and still hurling anathemas at his enemies. In 1919,
he died, shot, no one knows how, as he sat in a window.

Andreyev's plays are difficult to classify. He is an imaginative philosopher, a mystic striving to grasp ultimate but not
external reality. "I am not the slave of either symbolism or
realism," he said, "but they are my servants—now the one,
now the other, according to my theme." On the stage he is
rarely realistic. Some of his dramas are but episodes. In one
such, *An Incident*, he betrays the influence of Tolstoy. A merchant, repenting of having murdered a girl long before, is
urged by his wife to make confession, but the police official
to whom he speaks proves to be a legalist pure and simple.
Since the crime has been outlawed for eleven years according

112

to the Russian code, and since the prisons of Siberia are already overcrowded, the official refuses to arrest the conscience-stricken merchant. If the latter insists upon being punished, let him confess to having committed a crime more recent for whose perpetrator the police are now looking.

Irony is again to the fore in *Love of One's Neighbor*, where the proprietor of a mountain hotel, in order to advertise his hostelry, has hired a poor devil to pose upon a cliff as though unable to get either up or down. The guests of the hotel are duly thrilled at the stranger's peril, secretly hoping that he may fall. But the stranger, tied there by day, grows weary of his vigil, and exposes the proprietor's fraud. One lady, proud that she has seen six men drop to death from great heights, has kept asking, "When will this fellow fall?" "To-morrow, lady, to-morrow," answers the proprietor. "I won't tie him so fast, you understand." The implication seems to be that it is only personal acquaintance that engenders sympathy. Let a man be removed from his fellows as one unknown, and the rest of the pack will gather to be in at his death.

The irony displayed in these sketches is stronger in *Savva* and *The Sabine Women*, the first as grim as the second is playful. Savva, a skeptic and nihilist, has been reared in a monastery where an ikon is believed by the peasants to possess divine powers. To rid them of their superstition, Savva would destroy the ikon with a bomb. But his pious sister, learning of his plan, has the bomb turned over to the friars, who permit it to explode after removing the ikon. Thereupon, the crowd that gathers regards the ikon's immunity from destruction as the miracle for which they have prayed. Having slain Savva as author of the outrage, they return to their devotions crying, "Christ is risen!" To Savva death is nothing. "What worse can happen to a man than to be born!" he exclaims. After that, to be asked if one is afraid is "like asking a man who is drowning whether he minds getting wet." Here among the characters are a novice who spends her time chasing butterflies, a drunken brother of the hero who finds pleasure in noting the comic faces of all about him, an ex-seminarist who cannot believe that the world actually exists, and a repentant sinner who in penance for having murdered his son has burned off his arm. Of his fellow men he declares: "Better go to the wolves in the forest. At least, they'll make short work of it, devouring you at once. . . I've seen many evil things, but I've never seen anything worse than Man." Yet he glories in his sacrificial misery. "Here I am with my sorrow; there's no greater upon earth. And yet, if God spoke to me and said, 'I will give you the whole earth if you will give me your grief,' I wouldn't give it away. It is sweeter than honey; it is stronger than the strongest drink. Through it, I have learned the truth."

The bitterness of satire in *Savva* is sweetened in *The Sabine Women*, a jolly burlesque worthy of Bernard Shaw. The Romans, exhausted by the weight and the scratching, screaming, and tickling of their Sabine captives, beg a truce, alleging their desire for peaceful domesticity now that Rome is founded. They would compensate the ladies for the loss of their Sabine children by giving them others, and the ladies are willing. As one expresses it: "I'd rather enjoy having a new husband. The old one was sick of my ménu, but this one will like it." So they all pair off, and the only woman left unmatched seizes upon the sole remaining man, disregarding his protests that she is not his choice. "Never mind!" she exclaims; "that is what my Sabine husband said for thirty years." In the mean time, the bereft husbands practice gymnastic exercises in order to be able to carry enough law books to prove their case for damages against the Romans. As they exercise, they repeat an auto-suggestive formula that forecasts Coué: "Twenty-five minutes' daily drill will banish every pain and ill." Having learned the whereabouts of their abducted wives through the astrologers and an information bureau, they at last advance in pursuit, but with strict legality. Armed only with the justice of their cause, they march two steps forward and one step backward to indicate both the unquenchable fire of their stormy souls and their reliance upon reason and experience. "History makes no leaps," they argue; "and we Sabines, at this great moment, we are history." Encountering the Romans, the Sabine professors, with the precision of a firing squad, set up tables to hold the law books. "What can I do for you?" asks an irreverent Roman. "If this is a circus, I take the liberty of informing you that the Colosseum is not yet finished." The wives, in order to appear in a proper light, announce that they have wept copiously for their former husbands, but charge them with cowardice. "We were abducted; you did not defend us," says a fair one; "you can read about it in any Roman history, to say nothing of the Encyclopædia." Although the women will never freely return to their former lords, they are not averse to another abduction. It would be so romantic. But the good Sabines cannot think of committing illegal violence. "Long live the law!" cries one. "Let them take my wife from me by brute violence; let them ruin my home; let them extinguish my hearth; I shall never prove false to the law!" So off march the legalists in retreat, two steps forward, one step backward, still bending under the weight of their books, and carefully trimming their progress, while the women weep at missing the thrill of a second abduction.

This delicious bit of foolery pokes fun at the Russian situation in 1905 and 1906. The Sabine husbands, representing the Constitutional Democratic party, strive to hold by methods purely legal the Sabine women, who represent the constitutional promises got by force from the government. The Romans are the reactionary administration, not legal but pragmatic. The play points to the inefficiency of the Constitutional Democrats, with their backward step of reliance upon reason and tradition to temper their irresistible advance. In a wider sense, the piece satirizes all those who at a crisis stand upon theory when action is needed.

No greater contrast could be found to these satirical sketches than *The Life of Man*, published in 1906, a modern morality play, showing man in infancy, in love and poverty, in wealth and fame, in misfortune and death. A prologue spoken upon a darkened stage by a Being in Gray forecasts the spectacle to come. The birth of man is suggested by the cry of a mother heard from without and the comments of old women huddled in the foreground. Then a babe's wail sounds faintly, and, as a candle held by the Being in Gray is lighted, he exclaims, "Silence! Man is born." With a shift of scene, years have passed, and man, poor though happy in his love, defies the Being in Gray, in whose hands a third of the candle has burned down. "Ho, you! whatever be your name—Fate, Devil, or Life,—I fling before you my glove. . . . I challenge you to combat." Thus the starving artist challenges Fate, assured of his future success.

That success, in the third scene, has been achieved, for man, grown proud, appears as the host at a ball, attended by admiring friends and embarrassed enemies. But in the fourth scene poverty has overtaken him. His son, the victim of an accident, is dying, and man, bowed with grief, first prays to the Being in Gray, then dreams that his boy is safe, and awakens to find him dead. As the candle of the Being in Gray burns low, man curses him. And now, with the last scene, the hero, ragged and unkempt, surrounded by wretches who warn him of his end, continues defiant to the Being in Gray, whose candle flares and is extinguished. The screaming of the witch-like women who have danced about the hero ceases as the lights are extinguished.

The same year saw the publication of *To the Stars*, based upon the notion that a being sufficiently removed in thought from the earth must regard even the most intimate personal sorrow as trivial. An astronomer, gazing upon the heavens

from his Siberian observatory, cannot realize the significance
of the report that his son, a revolutionist, is imprisoned and
must die. "Do they kill each other yet?" he asks wistfully. "Do
they still have prisons?" But the bride of the condemned man
reports that she has secured a postponement of his execution,
and the hope thus aroused among her friends is maintained
through an act or two until she announces that Nikolai has
been released but that his reason has given way as the result
of his sufferings. "Do you care?" demands the girl, and the
astronomer can only meditate upon the impossibility of any
spirit's being plunged into darkness. What is madness or
death or the reform of a topsy-turvy world to one who looks
only to the stars? When his daughter complains that as-
tronomers waste time in studying the heavens while this earth
needs attention, Sergius replies: "Every second some human
being perishes in the world, and probably every second a whole
world is destroyed in the universe. How, then, can one cry
over the loss of a human being?" When his younger son falls
ill, and is brought to the upper gallery of the observatory, the
astronomer declares: "If anything becomes precious to me,
I like to lift it up here. I think that here among the stars
there can be no suffering and no disease." When his rebellious
son-in-law remarks that only those can afford to scorn earthly
vanities who receive a fat salary to perch in safety on a roof
inspecting the stars, the astronomer retorts: "Not always in
safety:—Galileo died in prison; Giordano Bruno perished at
the stake; the road to the stars has always been sprinkled
with blood."

The acute may here perceive an allegory of the attitude of
the upper-class philosophic Russian toward national disaster.
The rebellion of the few is set against this rational indifference. So the bride of Nikolai burns with the fire of revolutionary fanaticism, and Treitch, a valiant workingman, speaks
with the strength of will of the reformer. "There was talk here
about defeat," he says, "but there is no such thing as defeat.

Earth is but a piece of wax in the hands of man. One must press, knead, mold it into new shapes; one must go forward. Collide against a wall? remove it; collide against a mountain? carry it away; meet a precipice? fly over it; if you have no wings? make them for yourself." Such a spirit of volition contrasts with the more usual submission of the Russian to Fate. Surely, this play is one of the clearest and most effective of Andreyev's dramas of ideas.

In the year following the composition of *The Life of Man*, Andreyev wrote *King Hunger*, a morality play more limited in meaning and less successful. King Hunger, having promised Death and Time to aid the starving, emerges from a blazing furnace before which workingmen have been cursing their toil, and then, at their meeting in a basement, he eggs on the poor to revolt. Disguised as a lackey of the upper classes, King Hunger presides at a mock trial of the proletariat, condemning to death an old man who has stolen a loaf of bread, and a mother who has killed her babe to save it from starvation. The rich, who have been dancing in a great hall above stairs, tremble at blasts from the trumpet of Death as the mob of the hungry rises and threatens them. When an engineer assures the aristocrats that he has invented a projectile to quell the mob of the starving, the dance is resumed, and presently King Hunger appears and announces that the starving have fallen. The rich survey the scene of carnage with satisfaction, but presently King Hunger turns upon them summoning the poor to rebel, and from afar are heard a thousand voices murmuring, "We shall yet come— we shall yet come—woe unto the victorious!"

What does it mean? Is Hunger the friend or the enemy of the poor? He incites them to revolt, yet condemns those driven to crime by his rigor, and then, after the victory of the well-fed, he again calls upon his children to arise. A girl in black represents the more sympathetic impulses of the upper classes; death, like the Being in Gray in *The Life of Man*, remains in-

118

different. As in O'Neill's *Hairy Ape*, so here, expressionism employs effects of sight and sound, the fiery glow of the furnace resembling that of the steamer furnaces in the stokehold, and the beat of the drop hammer resembling the pulsing of machinery in O'Neill's vessel.

A more complex piece of psychological symbolism is *The Black Maskers*, an admirable example of what Evreinov meant by monodrama. Here the hero is the human soul, entrenched within its castle, the body, and yet invaded by maskers who, when it seeks to celebrate a festival, represent its involuntary thoughts of evil. Threatened by these maskers of doubt, despair, and madness, the soul struggles against the nightmare, is overwhelmed, yet dies unyielding. The whole thing seems to be the autobiography of a madman, a pictorial representation of the progress of his conflict against the dark onslaughts of insanity or, morally, the conflict between a soul that yearns for light, and the evil imaginings that besiege it. Literally, Duke Lorenzo is presiding at a masque, to which come guests grotesquely disguised, clad as cripples and corpses, who have entered leering, although the drawbridge protecting his castle has not been lowered. At first, with an assumption of bravado, the duke pretends to take their evil antics in good part, but fear is knocking at his breast; the wine that he serves them proves bewitched; the mirth of his jester is resented with blows; the music that he has composed turns a hellish discord; and he beholds himself represented scoffingly as a babe, half animal, half man, the bastard of a drunken groom. Such in moments of despair are man's doubts as to his origin from the lower beasts. The grinning maskers reveal themselves as the lusts and falsehoods conceived in Lorenzo's brain, his overlords, the veritable masters of his castle. In place of his bride Francesca he confronts only mocking phantasms, one that gazes with her eyes, another that speaks with her voice, a third that rallies him on his attentions to the second, while, in re-

119

sponse to his appeal for his lost love, seven old hags struggle to embrace him.

The song that Lorenzo has composed for the occasion is sung all awry. In vain he disclaims having addressed Satan as the Monarch of the World. The maskers declare him to be but the son of a base groom and, indeed, the vassal of Satan. When Lorenzo would escape to his study tower, he reads there the proof of his mother's sin, and presently his masked double assails him as an impostor. Forced to doubt his identity, he fights and slays this double, and then, retreating to the ballroom, finds it thronged with Black Maskers, "hairy and black from foot to crown, some resembling orang-outangs and others those uncouth hairy insects which in the night-time fly toward the light." They have clambered over the walls, as black thoughts will defy all barriers to invade the haunted mind. For each one that enters, a light has been extinguished, and it is in vain that the first maskers have sought to kindle torches to overcome the gathering gloom. As the cry is raised that murder has been done in the tower, Lorenzo is assailed as the murderer, a masked impostor, and he feels his face stiffening into stone while the Black Maskers trumpet for more of their evil kin, and voices declare him to be mad. In the castle chapel he stands beside the bier of his slain double, beholding those who in life bore him grudges come to pay him their last respects. Then he appears once more in the great hall reënacting the ball in his distraught mind; and singing, against his will, his song to Satan. Cries announce the coming of another guest, one whose eyes are fire, whose locks are gilded smoke, whose voice is the roar of flames. Flames are indeed approaching, for the court jester has fired the castle, and Lorenzo's bride flees, renouncing the happiness of dying with him, for the sake of his unborn son. As the flames swirl about him, Lorenzo cries out: "I greet thee, O Lord! . . . Touch me, O Lord, if I am worthy of Thy accolade." So he expires, declaring with his last breath that there is no serpent in his heart. He has finally triumphed over the powers of evil that assailed him, for, in the flames, the Black Maskers are driven off writhing.

In this play Andreyev attains the apex of his symbolism. No two critics will agree as to the author's meaning. In general, it is clear that a brave soul which insists to the last upon its integrity is besieged by dread questions as to its origin and identity, its guilt, its sanity, its allegiance to God, and that it welcomes death in the flames rather than succumb to the black terror of doubt and madness. The lover of Poe will observe here a resemblance to his poem *The Haunted Palace*, as inspiring the comparison of a mind diseased to a castle that is haunted, and to his stories *The Masque of the Red Death*, as inspiring the notion of horrible guests at a masked ball, and *William Wilson*, as inspiring the duel to the death between a man and his double. Aside from these parallels, which are too close for coincidence, it is obvious that Andreyev's play incorporates to perfection the spirit and the method of Poe.

The last in the series of Andreyev's symbolic plays written from 1906 to 1909 is *Anathema*, which appears to echo in its prologue the Prologue to *Faust*. As Satan wagers with God that he can gain the soul of pious Job if only he be allowed to deprive Job of family, friends, health, and wealth, so here Anathema, turned back by the Guardian of the Gates that shut this world from the Unknown, determines to test the injustice of the Unknown by a human example. To prove his point, he will show the Guardian of the Gates the futility of brotherly love in a special instance. Accordingly, he appears to a poor Jew in the guise of a lawyer bearing the glad tidings that he has inherited a fortune from a brother in America. The wealth which David thus accepts proves no blessing, for his children become engrossed in luxury, and when, at the suggestion of Anathema, he would share his possessions with the poor, his reputation for riches and for more than earthly power proves his bane. No sooner has he given all away, than the crowd, discontented because he can give no more, stones him to death. In an epilogue, Anathema, who may represent blind reason, returns to the inscrutable Guardian of the Gates to boast that goodness has not here been rewarded; but he learns that David in reality survives. Faith and love are superior to reason and cannot die.

In his later work, Andreyev has turned from symbolic to representative drama, leaving the field in which he won distinction for one in which he cannot compete with the masters. Something of symbolism lingers in *He Who Gets Slapped* and *The Sorrows of Belgium,* but the attempt to adhere to life in its externals marks *Samson in Chains, The Waltz of the Dogs,* and *Yekaterina Ivanovna.* A discussion of the last three inferior plays may well precede that of the first two. *Samson in Chains* is a Biblical drama which spoils the old story by trying to present it from a fresh angle. Andreyev's Samson has already fallen, betrayed by Delilah and blinded by her brother Galial, who plans to use his captive's strength in order to win for himself political power. For a little he will curry favor with Samson, releasing him from his task at the treadmill, dressing him richly, and permitting him to return to the arms of Delilah. Though Samson in prison was humble enough, he now grows proud and boastful, cursing all he once held dear. Galial, as they hunt together in the desert, thinks to slay him, but is deterred by a magical storm which he accepts as a warning sign from heaven. Finally, he brings Samson to the temple of Dagon and bids him perform a miracle to astonish the assembled Philistines. Then Samson, threatened with death when he refuses to sacrifice to Dagon, prays to Jehovah to turn to stone the contemptuous Philistines, and instantly in response to his prayer they become transfixed. But Samson, in his moment of triumph, recognizes his own unworthiness as an instrument of Jehovah's will, and, therefore, seizing the pillars of the temple, brings the structure down just to end his own life. Thus Andreyev, shifting the climax of the Biblical drama back from the destruction of the temple to the petrifaction of the crowd within it, makes of Samson's final act no more than a spectacular suicide little motivated. In the Biblical story, the death of Samson was incidental. Only as he perished could his enemies be overcome. According to Andreyev, Samson's strength is psychic as well as physical, and his relations with Delilah, so dramatic and natural in the *Book of Judges* and in Milton's *Samson Agonistes*, are unaccountably altered. That Delilah was responsible for his capture and blinding he scarcely recalls. He regards her still with an affection which she reciprocates. All the interest that might have centered in her character is transferred to her brother, half coward, half blusterer. But even toward him Samson displays little of that resentment which would seem inevitable. Samson, indeed, is a troubled soul, blind in spirit as in body, childlike in his pride and in his humiliation, a story-book magician, goaded into action by the villain Galial and by a woman of his people who yearns to see him a leader and at his fall puts out her own eyes in sympathy. Perhaps from this confused play the author would draw the moral that God can work His constructive purposes only through a pure idealist. Samson is a mental and moral weakling not worthy to become a prophet.

The notion which *The Waltz of the Dogs* and *Yekaterina Ivanovna* are meant to illustrate is that ingratitude or suspicion will render their objects vicious. In the former play the destructive force of ingratitude is the theme. Henry Tile, jilted by his fiancée and intrigued against by his younger brother, goes wrong on his own account, taking to drink and dalliance, planning to embezzle from a bank, and finally committing suicide. Henry is a nonentity whose sweetheart prefers a richer man, and whose brother Carl would rob him of money as well as love. Carl joins with a mean little official in a scheme to murder Henry, after inducing him to insure his life. The official proposes, then, to pocket all the insurance money by murdering Carl in turn. The only use of such melodrama is to show that evil practised against the innocent tends to transform the innocent into the guilty. The title derives from the fact that Henry and his fiancée have enjoyed a musical composition called "The Waltz of the Dogs" which symbolizes their own mechanized conduct. Henry, his brother, and the official who would double-cross them both have been but puppets pulled this way and that in sin like dancing dogs.

In *Yekaterina Ivanovna* it is a woman instead of a man who is turned from innocence to guilt, not by ingratitude but by suspicion. Yekaterina, found by her husband at the rooms of a friend, insists that she had gone there only to reprove the fellow for annoying her with his importunities. Her husband, refusing to believe her, shoots at her blunderingly and drives her from the house with her children. Although six months later he takes her back contritely, he has really slain her soul. She admits that in the interim she had once given herself to his friend, and now she goes from bad to worse, philandering with an artist and with her husband's younger brother. According to Andreyev, Yekaterina, having lost her rhythm in the dance of life owing to her husband's doubt, just whirls about dizzily, an automaton thereafter. She fancies herself to be Salome clamoring for her prophet, and her artist admirer paints her in that rôle, and declares that she is dancing a depraved dance in a dream. Since she has often acknowledged her desire to fling herself from the artist's window, we expect her suicide, but all that happens is her departure with a musician she admires for a motor ride quite approved by her husband, who has now set aside his well warranted suspicions.

No doubt Andreyev was here influenced by the success at the Kamerny Theater in Moscow of Oscar Wilde's *Salome*, but his heroine, though becoming a northern Salome, is, he tells us, more sinned against than sinning. The critics may compare her to Anna Karénina, Emma Bovary, and Manon Lescaut, but Andreyev protests, in his directions to the actress taking

the part, that "the sensual must be subdued and her call for
a prophet must be almost a stern accusation against all around
her." That conception of the character seems perverse. Yekaterina, once her integrity is doubted, loses it completely, becoming lust personified, and there is little ground for her
accusing the world in general. Echegaray, in *The Great
Galeoto*, has developed the idea far better when he shows a
good wife who is unjustly accused developing a single passion
for the one whose name has been unfairly linked with hers.
As for the men in Andreyev's play, they are a contemptible
lot,—the husband an hysterical moron, the first lover a nonentity, the artist a libertine, the husband's brother alone possessing vestiges of will. The psychology is rudimentary, and
the author's grasp on character most uncertain.

No, Andreyev's true field is the symbolic, the portrayal of
the inner life by some outer spectacle. Admirable in *The Black
Maskers*, he is puerile in these attempts at ordinary portraiture. Standing betwixt and between are such semi-realistic and
semi-symbolic plays as *The Sorrows of Belgium* and *He Who
Gets Slapped*. The former is a companion piece to Andreyev's
war novel, *The Confessions of a Little Soul in a Great Time*.
When the Germans invade Belgium, Emil Grelieu, a pacifist
poet, offers himself for service, feeling that he must share the
fate of others. Grelieu stands for Maeterlinck, the soul of
Belgium, just as Count Clairmont, who comes to ask his advice, represents King Albert. "We are the body, we are the
hands, we are the head, while you, Grelieu," he says, "are the
conscience of our people. . . . Let your noble heart tell us
the truth." Although Grelieu and one of his sons are wounded
and another son is slain, he and his gentle wife maintain their
faith in the future. For the present, violence must be met with
violence, the flood-gates must be opened to drive back the
invaders. When the wife, broken in mind, keeps asking for her
dead boy, Grelieu exclaims: "Weep, unfortunate mother! God
weeps with you. But there will be happy mothers here again. I

see a new world; I see a new life." As for the Germans, they cannot understand. They believe themselves invincible. Their methodical nature is suggested in the account given by one officer to another of their commander. "He is a wonderful man! He never sleeps. When he is not listening to reports or issuing orders, he is thinking. He has a German philosophical mind which manages guns as Leibniz managed ideas. Everything is preconceived, everything is prearranged; the movement of our millions has been elaborated into such a remarkable system that Kant himself would have been proud of it. Gentlemen, we are led forward by indomitable logic and by an iron will. We are as inexorable as Fate." Yet the German commander, when the Belgians open the dikes, remains incredulous. "But this is absurd!" he cries, for he has counted only upon resistance by the soldiery in conventional military fashion.

Of all the plays of Andreyev, that which has best succeeded on the stage in this country is *He Who Gets Slapped*, wherein the element of spectacle and the stir of action reinforce a simple story that suggests symbolic meanings. The single scene is the common room of a permanent circus. The leading lady is Consuelo, whose rascally guardian, the manager, is negotiating her marriage with an old roué. She cares nothing for this baron, nor does she care for a youthful acrobat who admires her. The acrobat in turn disdains a female lion-tamer, who adores him in spite of the fact that she is the mistress of the manager.

Into this complex of forces enters a mysterious Stranger of high birth. Defeated in all that he has undertaken, robbed of his wife and his ideas by a rival, he offers to serve as clown, and, when asked his name, answers, "I am He Who Gets Slapped." Achieving success in this rôle, he finds in Consuelo a new inspiration. He declares his love and warns her against the baron. But Consuelo proves as unresponsive to him as to the baron and the acrobat. In the last act, her marriage is about to occur. After a benefit performance she will leave the company. While the actors feast at the baron's expense, the Stranger begs Consuelo to drink one final toast with him. But he has poisoned the draught. As she sinks in death, he too grows weaker. Thereupon the baron, pretending to summon the police, rushes out, and shoots himself. According to Russian superstition, whoever, loving a woman, dies next after her, will possess her in the other world. The baron has beaten the Stranger in death as well as in life. "You loved her so much, baron," murmurs the Stranger with his last breath, "that you want to be ahead of me even there? No! I am coming! We shall prove whose she is to be forever . . ."

Only the final act is effective. Elsewhere, the piece is unreal, confused, and doubtful in motivation. Although the Stranger is represented as heart-broken because his wife forsook him, his attention is focused forthwith upon Consuelo, this girl of the circus. When he shows his card to the manager he is recognized as a high personage, but his identity remains concealed and nothing results from his antagonism to his rival except for one brief scene which recalls the situation in Strindberg's play, *The Stronger*, inasmuch as the rival who has stolen his wife and his philosophy gains nothing thereby, because the wife still extols the Stranger's genius, and his son resembles the Stranger. As for Zinida, the fierce Mænad, all her talk about trying to make her lions love her, and her yearning to be beloved by men, appears unlinked to the story.

Of the twenty-eight characters that crowd the stage, and lend color to its single set, the mysterious Stranger is the chief. According to Stark Young, "He is a philosopher who leaves the world which has never understood him and which has cheapened all his finest thoughts. . . . Under the clown's ridiculous garb, he will say his great thoughts, tell the crowd what wise and beautiful ideas arise in him, and get slapped and laughed at for a fool, when all the while the mockery and jest are at their expense. . . . He loves Consuelo for herself and because she is the image of beauty. He dies with her, following beauty out of the world as he had followed it all of his life." Yet, so far as the Stranger speaks, he displays none of this philosophic wisdom. As for the heroine, she is no more than an idea,—beauty, or the ideal—"she who gets loved," just as the Stranger is "he who gets slapped." That lover she considers only as a clown, and she remains indifferent to Bezano and to the matrimonial bargain by which she is sold to the baron. Although the play seems meant to hint deeper meanings, Andreyev is reported to have said that it was really all on the surface, and that in it he was laughing at the lesson-hunting public. Its closest parallel in recent drama is Hauptmann's *And Pippa Dances*, an allegory setting forth the attitude toward the ideal of a sensualist, an idealist, and a philosopher. In Hauptmann, the sensualist and the idealist contend, but though the heroine dies, the idealist conceives of her as still living, and is assured by the philosopher that this is true. In Andreyev, the sensualist contends directly with the philosopher for the possession of beauty, and all three die, leaving youth in the person of the acrobat to survive.

In general, Andreyev is deficient in mental balance and the sense of fact. The outer world, when he paints it, is too often distorted; the inner world is abnormal. His powers of logic are weak, his inferences are perverse. Yet he is an original genius, just mad enough to fascinate and tantalize, and not so mad as to cause his admirers to suspect that what he says lacks deeper significance. Like Poe, he revels in kaleidoscopic fancies and in contrasts of color, incident, and character, giving rein to his mind to gallop where it will. He is scarcely a dramatist in the older meaning of the term. He admits that his pieces are but presentations, concerned less with deeds than with modifications of the perceiving ego. His hero is the mind rather than a personality complete and reacting with and against other personalities. At his best, as in *The Black Maskers*, he writes monodrama. Usually he makes no attempt to hold the mirror up to outward nature. Instead, he seeks to project into his puppets his personal fears and griefs, his dread of Fate, and his consciousness of life as painful and mysterious. His yearning for union with other souls similarly oppressed is revealed in a letter which he wrote to Herman Bernstein concerning his story *The Seven Who Were Hanged*. Said Andreyev: "The misfortune of all of us is that we know so little about one another—about one another's souls, lives, sufferings, habits, inclinations, and aspirations," and he added, "Literature, which I have the honor to serve, is dear to me just because the noblest task it sets is that of wiping out boundaries and distances." Therein Andreyev shares the belief of Tolstoy that the highest mission of art is the awakening of social sympathy.

CHAPTER VIII

The Soviet Theater and Lunacharsky

IN RUSSIA has arisen a new theatrical development due to
the transfer of power from the aristocracy, bureaucracy,
and bourgeoisie to the workers, soldiers, and peasants. Much
of what is old has been destroyed; but, amid the chaos of the
present, sympathizers with the social upheaval profess to see
a promise for the future. After the Revolution of 1917 the
theater was nationalized, the Communists perceiving its potency for good as well as for evil. According to the figures
quoted by Huntly Carter, chief British apologist for this
development, the Communists increased the number of playhouses from some two hundred in 1914 to nearly six thousand
in 1920. They proceeded, also, to ban from production most
of the plays that had been popular during the later nineteenth
century and the earlier twentieth, and even those of the Free
Theaters, on the ground that they reflected bourgeois life,
being composed by the intelligentsia to exalt individuals rather
than the masses. The Soviet theater, accordingly, became
strongly propagandist, asserting its right to be judged mainly
by its social and political tendencies. It became equally radical
in its methods of stage presentation, departing from the
actualism which had characterized the Moscow Art Theater,
and practising instead free symbolism. It experimented with
all sorts of productions put on in eccentric wise with stylized
scenery or with none. It experimented, too, with plays and
pageants composed and performed for the people by the
people.

At first, in the absence of distinctive Soviet dramas, certain
classics were allowed to remain, chief among them the pieces

of Ostrovsky, since these had satirized shop-keepers and officials. Alexei Tolstoy's *Czar Fyodor* was permitted, also, since
it showed an impotent ruler torn between opposing groups of
the nobility engaged in using him for their own ends. *The Government Inspector* of Gogol was revamped as a satire on bureaucracy, and Griboyedov's *Woe From Wit* as a satire on the
fate of reformers likely to be regarded as half mad. Novels
were dramatized, and the works of Shakespeare, Molière, Lope
de Vega, Goldoni, and Schiller were not forgotten. Of course,
contemporary pieces like Rolland's *Danton*, Verhaeren's *The
Dawn*, Toller's *Machine Wreckers* and *Masses and Man*, and
Kaiser's *Gas* found special favor. Shaw's *Saint Joan* was
played as burlesquing royalty, O'Neill's *Desire Under the
Elms* as representing love up-to-date, and his *Hairy Ape* as
attacking the privileged. Chesterton's *The Man Who Was
Thursday* and Hasenclever's *Antigone* were done with Bolshevik emphasis, the former as expressing the philosophy of
collectivism, the latter as celebrating the first great pacifist.
Authors who had shown Nietzschean individualism, like Artzybashev, or quietistic individualism, like Andreyev, were now
regarded as unfit for the new régime since they voiced ideals
of the intellectual aristocracy rather than those of the revolutionary proletariat. Leo Tolstoy, in spite of his sympathy for
the muzhik, was distrusted as an advocate of Christian submission, and even Gorky's *Lower Depths* was disliked because
of its Tolstoyan pilgrim preaching obedience to the divine will
as the only solace for outcasts. In time, however, antagonism
to Chekhov somewhat relaxed, and his *Cherry Orchard* was
tolerated because of its picture of corrupt landowners ousted
by a self-made man of the new order.

In 1921 a government commission for the theater, which had
been established immediately after the Revolution, was enlarged to include the more conservative like Stanislavsky; but
the preponderance of its support continued to be given to the
radicals led by Meyerhold and the liberals led by Lunacharsky.

The Moscow Art Theater exerted less and less influence except through its tours outside of Russia. Its great period lay in the past between 1898 and 1914. Yet it was reorganized in 1924 and won complete Bolshevik approval when in 1927 Stanislavsky put on *The Armored Train*, by Vsevolod Ivanov, depicting the destruction of Admiral Kolchak's White Soldiers by Siberian peasants. Meyerhold, who had served the Art Theater, early turned to Communism, organizing in 1918 the Theater Department of the People's Commissariat for Education, and conducting at Moscow a Theater of the Revolution. He adapted to Communistic ends plays by Schiller, Verhaeren, and Crommelynck. He proposed a theory of bio-mechanics to govern the gestures of the actor and developed a bare stage ornamented only with the apparatus of a machine shop to express the new industrial civilization. Kommissarzhevsky, who had similarly recoiled against realism, put his theories of revolutionary stagecraft into practice in directing for the Soviets music drama and ballet at Zimin's Opera House in Moscow. Tairov, founder with his wife of the Kamerny, grew more and more fantastic in his productions there, stressing the actor as supreme but, through Cubist costuming in a stiff strange style, making him a dancing puppet. Similar methods have been used at two theaters—the Jewish Kamerny, organized in 1921 by Alexis Granovsky, whose *Sorceress*, written with J. Rabinovich, proved a great success, and the Habima, another Jewish playhouse, first directed by the brilliant Wachtangow. Here the most memorable production has been S. Ansky's *The Dybbuk*, since performed throughout Europe and America. The Jewish Kamerny, developing into the Moscow State Jewish Theater, has sponsored a number of less notable successes, including versions of Jules Romains' two plays on Le Trouhadec, an attack on England called *The Tenth Commandment*, and *A Night in the Old Market*, by I. L. Perez, employing music and pantomime to suggest a parallel between the market and this degenerate world.

132

THE SOVIET THEATER AND LUNACHARSKY

The extreme in dramatic development due to the Revolution is to be found in the theaters for workers and peasants. A Workshop of the Comedy and the Drama was established after the Revolution to receive and revise Communistic plays which poured in from the barely literate. Kerschenezev led an attempt to spread "the creative theater" in all Soviets that it might serve as a living newspaper for those who could not read. A workers' cabaret, the Blue Blouses, was developed, and mass pageants were given, the greatest being that of 1920 at Petrograd in celebration of the storming of the Winter Palace which had occurred there just three years before. The pageant was enacted at night in front of the palace on two great stages joined by a high-arched bridge. The White Stage on the right showed Kerensky's dealings with his money-loving ministers, all eventually put to flight by the rising of workers represented on the Red Stage to the left, where crowds shouted "Lenin!" and sang the International. A fight upon the bridge connecting the two stages precipitated the dash to the palace of Kerensky and his chiefs in automobiles, and presently their further flight across the square and away as regiment upon regiment of Red soldiers advanced from the side streets, and the guns of the battleship "Aurora," anchored in the Neva, began firing just as they had on November 7, 1917. Many of the hundred thousand spectators of the pageant feared that the whole thing might be, not art, but reality, the beginning of a counter revolution.

On a small scale, the theater of the workers had begun in 1905 when five thousand of their number were organized in dramatic circles as a result of the first revolution. Although soon suppressed, these circles were revived in 1917, and ere long every factory had its dramatic club. Peasant theaters also arose, there being nine hundred in the district of Nishni-Novgorod alone. In 1918 V. F. Pletnev established the Proletcult Theater to afford a channel of self-expression for the toilers and to break down theatrical specialization, any man or woman

133

being called upon to play any part from protagonist to scene shifter. In the handsome Villa Morossov, once the home of an aristocrat, the workers set up their circus-like stage, sometimes jazzing such an old success as Ostrovsky's *Enough Stupidity in Every Man*, sometimes adapting stories like Jack London's *The Mexican*, or improvising a piece to explain the meaning of a given picture. They further invented allegories of their emancipation from the tyranny of the rich. Thus, in *The Mangy Dog*, described by Huntly Carter, laborers are bought up for cannon fodder by fat profiteers; they are drilled by officers wearing illuminated death's heads, and subjected to comic examination and rough bartering by Flesh Kings. Then a poet takes his life in despair, and a girl is snatched from the audience and carried off by a procuress to gratify the bourgeoisie. But, as darkness falls, the red star of the Soviet gleams above factory chimneys and to its light is added that of the stock exchange now burning down. Pletnev, himself manager of the Proletcult Theater, has written plays, notably *Over the Top*, a social comedy, and *Lena*, the drama of a strike. This stage of the workers has tended to exalt the power of the machine rather than to assail it as do Čapek's *R. U. R.* and Kaiser's *Gas*.

Although nothing of artistic worth has as yet emerged from such experiments, there have been interesting productions by Meyerhold at the First Theater. He has profited by his long and varied experience in putting on European masterpieces, and has staged at the Zon Theater in Moscow two revolutionary works by Vladimir Maiakovsky, *The Earth Prancing* and *Mysteria-Bouffes*. Both are characteristic. The first starts with an army revolt and the setting up of a socialist government, soon destroyed by Communists. Though their leader is shot, his body is retrieved and elevated for reverence in a red coffin, while his peasant mother harangues the hesitant mob and wins it over to Communism. Then, after a drunken ruler is emptied out of a sack and his officers have grown violently sick, their emancipated soldiers march through the auditorium, and the audience rises to join them in singing the International. *Mysteria-Bouffes* exhibits the effects of a new deluge threatening to drown the earth except for the North Pole, to which come seven proletarians and seven bourgeois to build for their salvation an ark which the bourgeois attempt to seize for themselves. Then the proletarians, on a Dantesque quest, pass through hell to a heaven of machinery. This, when repaired by them, will regenerate the world. In production, the middle aisle was elevated to serve as passageway from the auditorium to the stage, and the fronts of the boxes on either side were removed that actors sitting there might seem also to be part of the audience. At the close, these actor-spectators spoke in turn, each representing some inanimate thing declaring its independence of the rich who once exploited it. In a later piece, *The Bug*, Maiakovsky has endeavored to show Russia of the future, with a reactionary and a bug both reviving in 1979 after an interval of mummification, the reactionary now converted, and the bug exciting curiosity since science has already exterminated all his fellows.

Similarly crude are such topical plays of the proletariat as *Roar China! The Death and Destruction of Europe*, and *Finding Their Place*. The first, by S. Tretiakov, mixes melodrama and propaganda, and employs water in a tank and a revolving stage bearing a ship to express the feelings of the Soviet in regard to their quarrel with the Chinese in Manchuria. The second presents by means of brightly painted wooden screens fifteen aspects of various national capitals and suggests the weakness of each country through action accompanied by insolent jazz. The United States, which is also included, finds representation, for example, in sundry fat financiers taking a rub-down in a Turkish bath while discussing big business. Throughout, the audience shouts derisively at the failings of the Church and the bourgeoisie. In *Finding Their Place* ragged workers are knocked about by the usual stout capitalists and fall into hell, but climb out and are received by angels. Then, growing bored with heavenly ease, they seek their true place of opportunity in a schoolroom. Thereafter, they receive fresh tools from the Soviet officials and lead the audience in singing a song of hopeful refrain to the effect that "The international army shall be the human race." Miss Hallie Flanagan, a visitor to Russia who has described such plays, writes enthusiastically: "In the idea of Communism the theater in Russia has what the Greek Stage had in the gods, what the medieval drama had in the Church—a force outside itself to which it pays tribute with religious ecstasy. The theater of the Revolution pours plays as libations before the altar of its belief. It is a great theater because it is a dedicated theater."

Yet these ventures of the new dispensation are significant less from an artistic than a social point of view. They lack the polish to be seen in the dramas of Lunacharsky, Commissar of Education and of Art, or in that striking play of disillusion, *Red Rust*, by V. Kirchon and A. Ouspensky. This was first produced in 1927 at the Moscow State Proletarian Theater, and has since been seen in Paris and New York. The Red Rust of the title refers to the corrosive skepticism and corruption that has begun to eat into the clean steel of revolution. Faith in the possibility of overturning the world all at once and making it a beautiful place for pure souls is gone, since those revolt in vain who are enslaved by their own passions. The hero is a soldier who would enjoy himself while living upon the glory he has won in the cause of the people. But he declines into selfishness and vice, deserts his peasant wife, and bullies the life out of his gentle mistress after forcing her to undergo successive abortions now legalized by the State. When he kills her, he lets it be understood that she has committed suicide. In his public relations Terekhine is equally a rascal, being endured by his party simply because he is useful as its rough tool in extorting wheat from the peasants. Eventually he is brought to justice, but, before that happens, all the forces of disintegration have been revealed in their various manifestations, all the conflicting ideals and the groups of roughnecks, dreamers, militant students, new women, and passive victims. It is not a picture likely to make Soviet Russia alluring to the foreigner, even though the authors may intend it as a warning to their countrymen to keep the faith and conquer what is evil in their own ranks as once they conquered class tyranny from above.

Less a realist and more a philosopher is Lunacharsky, a man of good family, educated at the University of Zurich. He traveled and studied extensively, became a convert to Marxism, and with Gorky founded a periodical. He was exiled by the Czarist government, but returned at the Revolution to temper its excesses by his culture and common sense. Since the age of twenty he had written plays, beginning with *The Temptation*, a study of a monk dominated by the socialist ideal, and continuing with *The King's Barber*, an attack upon despotism. After the Revolution Lunacharsky revised his *Faust and the City* and produced *The Magi, Vasilisa the Wise, Ivan in Paradise, The Chancellor and the Locksmith, The Deliverance of Don Quixote, The Bear's Wedding*, and two historical pieces, *Oliver Cromwell* and *Thomas Campanella*. He also composed essays on literature, esthetics, and politics, all seen from the Bolshevist point of view. With wide knowledge, he has displayed a certain tolerance, preserving the art treasures of the old régime which the more ruthless would have destroyed. His ideals and his peculiar technique are exemplified in three of his plays recently translated into English.

Faust and the City, written nine years before the Revolution but revamped after it, is a temperate plea for freedom. Faust, holding that a benevolent despot will best ensure the happiness of his people, rules them firmly. But when, by their rising, he is forced from the throne and discovers that they can govern themselves to perfection, he rejoices in their joy. Though he dies, he will continue to live on in spirit in the ideal city.

Lunacharsky's Mephisto is a baron who complicates the action, first by encouraging the daughter of Faust to conceal her love for a man of the people, then by encouraging a son of Faust to carry off a girl of the people and to slay her brother and incite a revolt. When the leader of the revolt, the honorable lover of Faust's daughter, demands of the ruler an equal voice in government, Faust abdicates rather than make such a concession. His son, supported by vested interests, would seize the throne. A rival of the son, a self-seeking tribune of the masses, plots for it also. But in the end the good Gabriel, now married to Faustina, triumphs and then magnanimously resigns his power. Faust himself grows reconciled in love for the child of the pair and in altruistic satisfaction, also, at having constructed a sort of Robot, or Iron Man, to aid humanity's toil. Thus the soul of Faust is saved. He has found his perfect moment, not as with Goethe, in contemplating a future civilization on the site of a drained marsh, but in beholding a Soviet city actually functioning, and in feeling himself at one with all mankind. As he dies, Gabriel exclaims: "Faust is alive in all things! He lives in us! He lives forever!" By comparison with the plays of the Proletcult Theater, this is a cultured drama of ideas poetically phrased. It attacks the old order but does so artistically and without hysterics.

In *The Magi*, Lunacharsky suggests replacing the religion of self-abnegation and repression by a Shelleyan religion of instinct. To this end he unrolls a fantasy in thirteen scenes with symbolic landscape and colors, white representing purity, blue representing wisdom, and red representing passion. He contrasts the celibate monks of a white island with the Magi of a flowery island whose leader advocates full development that each may "perfect the motley manifest of his own soul." At the arrival of the fair Manessa, a white soul turns from her, a blue soul admires her afar, a hunchback is too humble to do more than murmur her name, but a Nietzschean soul would claim her as its own. This Nietzschean is Sempronius,

138

who, to possess her, slays the leader of the Magi, Andromenes. The white soul, shocked at the deed, expires after beholding a vision of Dionysus and his satyrs. But Sempronius, the self-asserter, becoming jealous of the hunchback for whom the lady feels compassion, taunts and shames him, and then broods despondent until the spirit of the slain Andromenes returns to help him, a second David singing to a second Saul. Then the fiery Sempronius, beholding that spirit kiss the lady, kills him a second time, and proceeds once more to assail the hunchback. Presently, all the persons of the earlier scenes are shown struggling up a mountain side. Sempronius, aided in the ascent by the ghostly Andromenes, recognizes in this victim his double. Yes, the slayer and the slain are one, for all that lives partakes of the unity of being. The only God is the sum total of the forces of nature. To will in accordance with such forces is wisdom. No individual can injure another without injuring himself.

More elaborate and fantastic is *Vasilisa the Wise,* a dramatic fairy tale intended to extol the importance of the younger generation. Through our children alone may we gain immortality. Vasilisa, by means of a magic mirror, discovers in the youngest of three sons of a Czar the ideal father for her first child. But after the birth of this son, the father grows restless, weary of being lapped in luxury, and declaring: "I want there to be something lacking. I wish to wish, and my wish is strong, so strong that it makes me unhappy. I am unhappy from happiness." Released by Vasilisa, Ivan sets forth, and, allured by the portrait of the moon-queen, seeks its original, who reciprocates his passion in silence and bears him a daughter. In the meantime, the deserted Vasilisa, beholding his defection in her magic mirror, marries another for the sake of the son that he too will give her. With this second mate she rules the earthly realm left her by Ivan's father, the Czar. But Ivan suffers the loss of his moon-queen through her eating a poisoned apple brought her by Vasilisa's old nurse bent on vengeance. Accordingly, Ivan returns to earth bringing his daughter by the moon-queen, and, after serving in humility as cowherd at Vasilisa's court, he is recognized and reinstated, Vasilisa dismissing her second husband in order to reclaim the first. Her two sons by different men and Ivan's daughter by the moon-queen will all be reared in amity together. "Yes," says Vasilisa, "we must live for children! We must love for children! The race of man will be wise and happy when children live for joy, and the elders live for children. Then we shall go forward! At the height of my earthly wisdom I understand this."

Thus the strange play sets forth symbolically the Soviet attitude toward the family. Love is to be free. An intelligent wife is not to resent her husband's turning to another mate. Let each follow instinct yet remember that children are all important since through them alone do we live on. At the same time, they are not to be regarded with the selfish pride of proprietorship so common among the bourgeoisie. Whatever their origin, they are to be reared together in love. An incidental thrust at proprietorship in goods is given in the conversation of two dwarfs, one upholding the right to hoard bread crumbs, the other asserting man's privilege to enjoy the earth as a common inheritance. Says the first: "To have no property is to have no body. That's why I am a collector. I sleep with my poor treasure by me, and feel all the time that I have something of my very own." Says the other: " 'Mine' and 'Thine,' indeed! I have played at mud pies and laughed at it all; for kings do the same with the kingdoms they call their own—just the same sort of dirt! But to give it all up I escape into the woods and fields. . . . Then I who am so little, I can bestow myself upon the world as well as the biggest giant, and I can say, 'Accept this of me!' " So far as the vacillations of Ivan are symbolical, they seem to signify that man, striving for happiness, cannot rest in it, but seeks action and yet is led astray by visionary aspirations. Then, reclaimed by his power to discern good from evil (if the nurse's apple may be so interpreted), he returns to the common work of the world and finds peace at last. Lunacharsky declares that the message of his play "is expressed not exegetically but artistically." He is indeed a symbolist of perfervid imagination, the natural heir of Andreyev, interested primarily in ideas, and specifically in those controlling the great Russian upheaval.

CHAPTER IX

The Theatric and the Naturalistic in France

Scribe, Dumas *fils*, Sardou, Kistemaeckers, Bernstein,
Becque, Zola, Antoine, Jullien, Ancey

THE harmony of French drama during the last half century is composed of certain strains which, forming a concord, may yet be distinguished as the theatric, represented by Sardou, Bernstein, and Kistemaeckers; the naturalistic, by Becque and the disciples of Antoine; the ironic and realistic, by Lemaître, Capus, Donnay, and Lavedan; the erotic and neurotic, by Porto-Riche and Bataille; the comic, by de Flers and de Caillavet; the moral, by de Curel and Hervieu; the social and reformative, by Fabre, Mirbeau, and Brieux; the romantic, by Richepin, Maeterlinck, and Rostand; and the subjective, by Bernard and Lenormand.

What may be termed the theatric drama harks back to Scribe, who perfected "the well-made play," an entertainment nicely adapted to quicken the pulses and gratify the esthetic instincts of audiences intent upon an exciting escape from reality. Scribe's method for producing such adroit pieces of intrigue stiffened into a formula even in his own practice, since no man can write plays to the number of three hundred and fifty without becoming the monotonous imitator of himself. He had little to say, but he said it so well and so often that his successors, like his contemporaries, acknowledge him as their master in craftsmanship. Emile Augier, accepting the model of Scribe, employed it to different ends, striving to advise and improve his audiences. He was a bourgeois realist, governed by reason, a common-sensible moralist, recommending mar-

142

riage for love instead of money, domestic fidelity, and industrial and political honesty. He upheld the middle classes against the nobility, patriots against cowards, and good wives against unscrupulous courtesans. He assailed pride of wealth and station, abuse of power by the press, and defiance by the individual of conscience and the social order. In a score of plays Augier preached this matter-of-fact doctrine, winning the respect of his countrymen as a creator of character and a painter and satirist of the actual.

That the technique of Scribe and the social criticism of Augier might combine to advantage was perceived by Alexandre Dumas the younger when dramatizing his novel, *The Lady of the Camelias*. Thereafter, with increasing effectiveness, he contributed to what he called "the useful theater," asserting that he was a photographer, instead of a designer like his father, and professing, like Augier, to write with an eye to reforming abuses. Thus he attacked corruption in the family and the state, proclaimed the rights of the natural child and the injured husband, and upheld the need of divorce and, in his later pieces, the duty of indulgence toward those who have erred. But the preacher in Dumas could not spoil the artist, and he refused to sacrifice to doctrine his emotional appeal. Though amplifying the *raisonneur* as a useful mouthpiece to announce his views, and stressing a central thesis, he was equally concerned to demonstrate it in a vital, moving way. Thus, he never lost sight of the theater and the effect his works would produce there. For him a dénouement was not a chance ending but a mathematical total, implying every step in the foregoing process. His dramas, accordingly, were patterns of fine construction, improving upon those of Scribe and Augier since their personages were folk impassioned, descendants of those of an earlier romantic generation. Three plays by Dumas—*The Princess of Bagdad, Denise,* and *Francillon*—were written in the 'eighties, and his ghost still stalks the Gallic stage.

In the field of comedy Labiche satirized the affectations of the bourgeoisie, focusing attention upon single ideas and developing his intrigue according to the Scribe formula by means of mechanical inversions and repetitions. With Meilhac and Halévy, however, comedy became rather a study of incongruity of character; and in *The World of Boredom*, by Pailleron, character portrayal and satire were combined. The influence of "the well-made play" was again evident in the sentimental drama of Octave Feuillet and Jules Sandeau, and in Georges Ohnet's *The Iron Master*; but the theatric drama is best exemplified in the work of Sardou, Kistemaeckers, and Bernstein.

Victorien Sardou was first and last a man of the theater, talented and industrious. He studied the technique of Scribe and applied it for forty-eight years with unrivaled success to subjects domestic and historical, in farce, comedy, operetta, spectacle, tragedy, and melodrama. For a time he inclined to follow the example of Augier and Dumas in reproving folly and vice, but his forte lay in stagecraft rather than social criticism. His distinctive dramas were those of high heroics and intrigue in an historical setting,—plays like *Fatherland*, laid in Spanish Flanders; *Hatred*, in medieval Italy; *Gismonda*, in medieval Greece; *Fédora*, in Imperial Russia; *Théodora*, in the Rome of Justinian; *Thermidor*, *Paméla*, and *Robespierre* in France of the Revolution; and *The Poisons Affair* in France under Louis XIV. A typical melodrama was *The Sorceress*, with its scenes in Spain of the Inquisition; his best historical comedy was the Napoleonic *Madame Sans-Gêne*; and his most elaborate spectacles were *Cleopatra* and *Dante*, composed with Emile Moreau, the first for Bernhardt, the second for Irving. In preparing his varied backgrounds, Sardou made painstaking investigations, proving himself a student of archeology as well as of human reactions. Not that he cared to fathom the mystery of the past for its own sake. He sought merely to secure fresh material for brilliant settings. He was concerned with preparing surprises, twisting the knots of his plot into a tangle that might seem to defy unloosing, startling by some spectacular display or battle of stark passions and imperious wills. He proposed, like Augier and Dumas, to find the kernel of each piece in a central idea, but this was never for him a matter of social or individual reform.

The acknowledged heirs of Sardou, and more remotely of Scribe, are Kistemaeckers and Bernstein, expert contrivers of stage entertainments who make emotion rather than reason their province. Bernstein is a vigorous, brutal talent, gripping the hearts of his spectators. Henry Kistemaeckers, the Belgian, shows an occasional predilection for ideas, as in *Instinct*, which exhibits the triumph at a crisis of spontaneous and primitive responses over cultural restraints, or in *The Occident*, which contrasts the civilizations of France and of Morocco. In these, as in *Marthe*, *The Wound*, and *The Rival*, he develops telling situations that turn upon illicit love, seeming in the last, moreover, to echo d'Annunzio's *La Gioconda* by his study of a sculptor who would subordinate conscience to passion for the sake of his art. Excellent in technique are his comedies *The Merchant of Happiness* and *The Fair Exile* and his melodrama *The Ambuscade*, which repeats a climax still better handled in Bernstein's *Israël*. Especially clever is *The Spy* (*La Flambée*), which successfully omits yet suggests the scenes of decisive action in treating the case of a patriotic murderer defended by his wife, hitherto his enemy. A colonel who has sought financial aid from a foreign banker, rejects with scorn the latter's proposal that he hand over plans of a fortification, and, as they struggle, strangles him. Then he confides to his wife his involuntary crime. Although she had been about to divorce him in order to marry another, his need awakens her protective love. His rival, a minister of state, suspecting the husband, threatens him with exposure to the police, but he defends himself by asking what the minister would have done under similar circumstances. That question elicits the minister's approval. So touched is he indeed that he withdraws forthwith that wife and husband may at last be united. Here, by exception, an attempt is made to analyze the states of mind of the characters. But, as always with Kistemaeckers, plot is to the fore, a plot devised to provide situations rendered striking by vehement language. Such qualities mark, also, *An Evening at the Front*. Here Kistemaeckers in 1918 tells the story of a German long naturalized in France who disappears at the outbreak of the War but returns on occasion to practice espionage in the country of his adoption. When he is apprehended, his wife begs his life of an officer whom she has saved from death. But although the officer yields, the spy is duly punished otherwise.

More effective still as a master of stagecraft is Henri Bernstein who sees what he wants theatrically and never fails to take it. There is no uncertainty in his aim or method. From *The Market*, played by Antoine, to *The Assault*, *The Secret*, and *To the Heights*, Bernstein has captured approval by the strength and directness of his dramaturgy. It little matters what his subject may be, his treatment wins attention. Now he seems cynical, as in *The Detour*, and now almost sentimental, as in *The Fold*; now he is mildly pessimistic, as in *The Tempest*, and now, as in *The Talon*, he is as strident a misogynist as Strindberg, depicting the career of an adventuress who jilts two lovers in order to accept the proposal of a third, thirty years older, and then plots against him with other men as he mounts the political ladder to become senator and minister. In the last act the baneful Antoinette declines to save him from the effects of a compromising letter and smiles grimly as his mind gives way when crowds in the street clamor against him and he is summoned to defend himself in the Chamber. Here are set forth as if for their own sake vanity, lust, and corruption. Similarly in *The Tempest* the people we meet are foolish or vicious, the heroine enthralled by a gambler who embezzles a fortune. Since at her father's instance she has married a man she hates, she now demands that her father provide her with money to rescue the man she loves. When he refuses, she tries to procure the sum by selling herself to a cousin, but all to no purpose, since the gambler commits suicide. Excellent in its emotional scenes, the piece is purely theatric, for the motives of its characters are as questionable as their morals. Hélène may hold attention by reason of her ragings and tearful intercessions, but she is little more than the sum total of the situations in which she figures. Similarly, in *Félix*, situations determine the play, each act affording its special excitement, but the combined situations failing to cohere.

The fact of Bernstein's race adds interest to his studies of Jewish character, *Israël* and *Samson*, although neither play is made by his philosophy of racial prejudice. In both he has built his drama about a thrilling scene. In the first a Catholic youth, having publicly insulted a Jewish banker, is about to respond to the latter's challenge to duel when he learns from his mother that he is the banker's son. Congratulated by his father on being a Jew, he takes his life rather than face his friends of the Anti-Semitic party. That the suicide is far from inevitable matters little to the playwright. In the confrontation and recognition of father and son and the interposition of the woman who unites them as mistress and mother Bernstein repeats with excellent effect a situation employed by Albert Delpit in *The Father of Martial*, by François Coppée in *Severo Torelli*, and by Oscar Wilde in *A Woman of No Importance*. In *Samson* he bespeaks sympathy for a self-made financier, a Jew, whose Gentile wife, forced into marriage, despises him and out of resentment gives herself to a lover. Later she comes to admire the husband who, instead of crossing swords with this rival, invites him to dinner and in a smashing climax informs him that by the forced fall of certain shares they both will be ruined. Thereupon the lady refuses to profit by the freedom she is offered, love for her heroic husband having replaced repugnance in her heart.

Jew-baiters and patriots assailed Bernstein's *After Me*, not on account of the play itself, but because of a letter he had written a decade earlier boasting of his withdrawal from the army. His hero is a captain of industry whose forgery in the past threatens his future. Overwhelmed by financial troubles, Bourgade is about to shoot himself when interrupted by his wife returning from a guilty meeting with his ward. In assailing her and demanding the name of her lover, he abandons his plan of suicide. When the youth confesses and Bourgade bids the lady choose between them, she responds by falling into her husband's arms, reflecting that dishonor has now evened them.

Best known among Bernstein's plays is *The Thief*, a tissue of cleverly wrought situations involving a fair guest at a chateau and the youthful son of the host who, having fallen in love with her, accepts as his own her guilt when certain funds are discovered to be missing. There are telling scenes as a detective accuses Fernand before the whole household and later as the lady, closeted with her husband, is forced step by step into admitting her theft. The husband out of curiosity opens a locked drawer with a knife just as Fernand has professed to have opened one, and, surprised to discover there the missing property, perceives that his wife must be the thief. When he elicits her confession, she professes to have desired to make herself more beautiful for his sake. Though he is placated for a moment, his suspicion flares up as she cannot explain why Fernand has been willing to assume her crime. Eventually she is forgiven by her host, and Fernand is sent to Brazil to recover from his infatuation. In the excitement of witnessing the progress of the action no spectator would be hard-hearted enough to comment upon its improbabilities.

Some of the later plays of Bernstein have exhibited a softening of mood and method. Forgiveness and reconciliation mark their endings. Thus, in *The Assault* a political leader, threatened with the exposure of a youthful error that will bring his downfall, is doubted by his children but upheld in fighting fire with fire by a girl whose faith in him resists even the shock of his admission of guilt. In *The Secret*, an envious woman, meddling with the affairs of others, enjoys the mischief she creates, but at last repents, taking a first step toward regeneration by confessing to her husband, who, during a dozen years of marriage, has never suspected her true character. In *To the Heights* (*l'Elévation*), written while the author lay wounded in a hospital, an unfaithful wife learns from the lips of her soldier lover as he dies the lesson of self-sacrifice and of devotion to a patriotic cause. Increasingly with Bernstein love becomes the dominant theme. His *Judith* contrasts with Aldrich's *Judith of Bethulia* in describing the morbid passion of a Biblical heroine. Giving herself sacrificially to the enemy of her country, Judith feels at last the authentic thrill even though she must straightway slay him. What compared with love are the honors bestowed upon her as the savior of her people? She yearns to see again Holophernes. On returning to the spot where his head is exposed in triumph, and followed by a lover who kills himself because of her indifference, she is horrified to behold in a flash of lightning the longed-for face, its eyes plucked out by crows. In *Mélo*, the rivalry of two friends over the wife of one of them endures after she has meditated poisoning her husband and in remorse has taken her own life. Indeed, only later does the husband discover what has been the reason for her death, and contend openly with his friend over a mere shadow. In all Bernstein's pieces, as in those of Kistemaeckers, there is intensity without depth, dexterity in stagecraft yet a lack of the sweep and splendor—even the tinsel splendor—that Sardou could conjure up. Their methods are the same, but their range, as compared with his, is narrow.

If the first main current in the recent French drama be the wave of influence proceeding from Scribe through Sardou to Kistemaeckers and Bernstein, a second is the counter-current emerging from the Théâtre Libre of André Antoine. Here we have stress upon substance opposed to form, naturalism opposed to romanticism. It was the novelists who early upheld and practiced naturalism—Flaubert, the de Goncourts, and Zola, with Balzac, Daudet, and de Maupassant as contributory forces. On the stage Henry Becque in *The Vultures* and *The Parisian Woman* indicated the possibilities of the new mode. Clotilde in the latter play is a mistress as pious and methodical as any wife, who discovers that the tyranny of a lover is likely to be worse than that of a husband, and settles down in a *ménage à trois* after having been attracted for a little to a second lover less staid and sober than her first. The situations are quietly ironic, as are those in Becque's acrid comedy *Honest Wives* written five years before. *The Vultures* (*Les Corbeaux*) exposes the hypocrisy of professed friends of a well-to-do bourgeois who dies of apoplexy while they are celebrating the betrothal of his daughter. Instantly they turn from fawning upon their patron to plotting against his widow and needy children, and threaten to pluck them bare until another daughter consents to marry her father's unscrupulous partner just to save from disaster those she loves. Here and elsewhere Becque avoids what Sardou most desired—the great *scènes à faire*. By repressing emotion, he heightened it. He recorded soberly his observation of the actual. He drew his pictures without gaiety, pathos, or tragic fervor. He did not moralize or argue; he wrote simply and coldly in the ironic spirit of a disillusioned man of middle age.

Lacking a theory, Becque was far more potent in the theater than Zola, who theorized at length but whose dramas were short-lived. Strangely enough, Zola, who decried the artificiality of the well-made play, produced in such a piece as *Renée* a good old melodrama, with its frail heroine deceived by one man, contracting a white marriage with another, falling in love with the latter's son, and intervening to protect him from his father who would kill him as a rival, and then shooting herself. Zola's theories, indeed, were chiefly applied to the novel, and his only effective plays were dramatizations of his works of fiction. He explained that in preparing *Thérèse Raquin* for the stage he sought to exhibit persons controlled by their bodies, both in their crimes and in their remorse, the latter being but the rebellion of nervous systems strained to the point of breaking. With Taine he argued that vice and virtue are products like vitriol or sugar. His materialistic conception of life he reinforced by reference to the physiological studies of Claude Bernard, Letourneau, and Lucas. It was the aim of all the naturalists to minimize situation and story, and to emphasize temperament, atmosphere, background. They declined to think of character as self-determined. For them it resulted from the shaping stress of natural law—especially the influence of heredity and environment. They aspired to rival the scientists in making art a thing inductive. While anatomizing experience, they fixed their gaze upon the abnormal rather than the typical. With the naturalists came to be associated the Bohemians who found ready hearing for their irreverent witticisms and revolutionary tirades in the cafés of Montmartre. It was in response to the demands of both groups and in recoil against the rising power of the commercial stage that André Antoine established his Free Theater.

Antoine, a clerk by day and an amateur actor by night, conceived the idea of evading the censors and the commercial managers through subscription performances. He would give to a select audience novelties domestic and foreign that otherwise they might never see. On March 30, 1887, his Théâtre Libre opened with four one-act plays, the best being *Jacques Damour*, an adaptation from Zola by Léon Hennique. The performance of a different bill in May and of seven other bills the following season set the venture really going. Long before it was abandoned, in April, 1896, it had made the dramas of Dumas and Sardou seem old-fashioned. It had overturned established traditions; it had given to the French in translation plays by Tolstoy, Ibsen, Hauptmann, Strindberg, Björnson,

Heijermans, Turgenev, and Verga; and it had introduced native writers like Jullien, Courteline, Wolff, Guinon, Fabre, Lavedan, Porto-Riche, de Curel, and Brieux.

Although Antoine inclined to the new naturalism, he did not shut his doors to other tendencies. He even admitted a few dramas that were poetic and romantic. Yet in general he simplified acting and scenery, favored whatever would afford a departure from the *pièce bien faite,* and fostered sensational tragedy and ironic comedy. The tragedy of terror was best exemplified by Oscar Méténier, Fernand Icres, Villiers de l'Isle-Adam, and Louis de Gramont, who wrote in the vein admired by Boulevard idlers savoring strong fare at the Grand Guignol. Their plays were brief and brutal, directing attention to facts rather than causes, avoiding all moralization, and affording by their rough daring a sudden kick of excitement. Thus, in Méténier's *He,* a girl of the streets, bringing home a chance acquaintance, notes that the jewels he empties from his pockets are those of a murdered demi-mondaine, and cunningly sends word to the police while continuing to cajole the doomed murderer. In the versified *Butchers* of Fernand Icres a man whose sister has been violated by a butcher hires a rascal to seduce the butcher's wife and himself takes that rascal's place at her side for one night. Then, when the husband, learning of his shame, would slay the avenger, the latter, after forcing him to gaze upon his wife in the arms of her paramour, slays him instead.

More characteristic of the Théâtre Libre, however, were the drab or cynical comedies of Henry Céard, Romain Coolus, Pierre Wolff, Jean Jullien, and Georges Ancey. Ancey, indeed, carried to its extreme the rudeness of the so-called *comédie rosse,* a slang term derived from the Spanish word for horse. In *M. Lamblin* a wife consents to divide her husband's attentions on specified days with a rival. In *The School of Widowers* a father arranges with his son for so sharing a lady's favors; and in *The Inseparables* a pair of friends come to a similar agreement. In *The Dupe*, however, a wife, forced to endure the infidelity and abuse of her husband, is no longer humorous, for her yielding approaches despair. At her mother's instance she has married him for money. Then, learning to love him, she lets him rob, insult, and knock her down without protest. There is greater restraint in the equally cynical comedies of Jullien, in such a piece, for example, as *The Day of Reckoning* (*l'Echéance*) which exhibits the gratitude of a husband saved by his friend from financial disaster and suicide, and resolved not to inquire too precisely into the relations between his wife and that benefactor. Equally amusing in its worldly satire is *The Serenade*, in which a youth makes love at the same time to the mother and the sister of the boy he is hired to tutor. Though discovered in his double intrigue, he emerges triumphant, assuring the mother that it is her image that he has worshiped in the daughter, and marrying the daughter with her father's consent. At first the father, apprised of his double shame, has thought to slay the blithe tutor. But the daughter intervenes, crying, "Don't kill him, Papa, —think of my child!" Delightful is the scene in which Maxime is invited by his new mother-in-law to sit close to her at luncheon after he has excused his affair with her daughter by saying: "I adored two women in one. Sometimes she was you; sometimes you were she,—you were both one! She was to me the perfume of the flower; you were the fruit." Jullien's *The Master* is a rough peasant play which seems, like Eugène Bourgeois' *The Man Who Was Hanged*, to anticipate the Irish comedies of Synge. It was Jullien, also, who best formulated the doctrine of naturalism, insisting upon the duty of the playwright to cut "a slice of life" from the usual and contemporary, to avoid long expositions and set dénouements, to be as concise as possible in revealing the life of the soul through actual incidents. In production he advocated doing away with footlights and elaborate scenery and stressing pantomime as more effective than speech.

Marked as was the rôle played by the Théâtre Libre, it closed its doors after one hundred and twenty-four plays had been shown. In 1894 Antoine went on tour, leaving a lieutenant to wind up two seasons amounting to eight performances only. Other experimental stages were diverting custom, notably the Théâtre d'Art of Paul Fort, and the Théâtre de l'Œuvre of Lugné-Poë, the former devoted to symbolism, the latter to foreign importations. Naturalism had run its course; Antoine's innovations had been adopted in the regular playhouses, and the authors he had helped to their feet were now able to go their own way. Thus Hennique produced elsewhere chronicle plays less excellent than his early Free Theater success, *The Death of the Duc d'Enghien*. Ancey turned propagandist in *These Messieurs*, and Jullien in *The Scholar* and *The Fist*. Brieux and Fabre, both given a start by Antoine, developed as their specialty the drama of reform. Georges Courteline, whose arch *Boubouroche* had entertained Antoine's patrons, found a larger circle for his fun. Romain Coolus and Pierre Wolff continued to betray in their later comedies something of the better strain encouraged by Antoine, though Wolff tended now and then toward sentiment. Porto-Riche, Lavedan, and de Curel, evolving in accordance with the tendencies they had manifested at the Théâtre Libre, soon outgrew it. As for Antoine, he set up a theater less radical, and eventually, in 1906, became director of the Odéon, remaining in that somewhat conservative office till the outbreak of the War. So the wave of naturalism passed, but not its effects. As a result, the *pièce bien faite* was discredited, and the artist's right to freedom of technique and his duty to hold the mirror up to nature were affirmed. The range of subjects open to him was greatly widened, and, incidentally, room was made for the school of ironic realists, on the one hand, and for that of the moralists and reformers on the other.

CHAPTER X

Ironic Realists

Lemaître, Capus, Donnay, Lavedan

THE French ironic realists are not so brutal or so deliberately artless as the naturalists. Having studied life about them, they pour it into artistic molds in due order and with a purpose, omitting the accidental and superfluous. They are controlled in part by ideas and more largely by a cultivated taste for what is esthetic. They face facts, not so pessimistically as the naturalists, nor so optimistically as the romanticists. They see through hypocrisy, self-delusion, avarice, and ambition, and, not content with painting manners alone, they thrust here and there beneath the surface of abuses with the rapier of satire. The ironic realists include Lavedan, Donnay, Capus, Lemaître, and such lesser men as Gustave Guiches, André Picard, and Albert Guinon, three who continued to write in the style they had used at their first appearance with Antoine, although evincing increasing skill and polish.

Jules Lemaître the critic had read so much that he became a thorough eclectic, possessing no single aim or manner. His plays, accordingly, fall into no one category. Now he works upon a broad canvas, as in *The Kings*, which contrasts democratic and autocratic ideals; now upon a small canvas, as in *The Woman Who Revolted*, *Flipote*, *The Difficult Age*, and *The Princess of Cleves*; and now quite airily in the realm of classical burlesque, as in *The Good Helen* and *The Marriage of Telemachus*, written with Donnay. *Deputy Leveau* assails corruption in politics, its hero a well-intentioned man who goes wrong through ambition. When he is tempted to leave his wife for a marquise, the latter's husband, discovering her infidelity, dismisses her, and she, who had meant to use Leveau as her tool, is obliged to unite with him, although each regards the other with contempt. *The Eldest* treats humorously the plight of the eldest of a family of six daughters forced to stand aside until the others find husbands. Giving herself to a youth at a party and berated by her pastor and most of her relatives, she triumphs, for her lover of the moment offers to become her husband, and all ends cheerfully. *Pardon,* which employs but three characters, is a plea for indulgence toward a sinning wife, rendered more logical by the husband's succumbing in turn when that wife sends her pretty friend to ask his forgiveness. In *White Marriage* the interest centers in a study of morbid psychology. A libertine of fifty, out of curiosity, resolves to make a consumptive girl his wife, but her jealous half sister, tired of sacrificing all to the invalid, turns upon her and then, as she lies fainting, captivates the libertine, whereupon the invalid, reviving, sees enough to hasten her death. *Bertrade* paints the portrait of a broken-down duke at odds with his daughter, who declines to save him financially by making a loveless match, and refuses to allow him to save himself by marrying a former mistress. After he has consumed the daughter's dowry and the fortune of his sister, he snuffs out his life. More agreeable is *The Studio Assistant,* done into English by Jerome K. Jerome as *Poor Little Thing.* Here a middle-aged artist, yearning for lost youth in the person of a charming helper, realizes the depth of his desire for her only when his wife and his son grow jealous. Earlier the wife has objected to the son's making love to the girl, a mere nobody; but now she is won over, not merely by Juliette's graces, but also by the thought that Jacques, in marrying her, will remove a rival. Life in the atelier is admirably drawn, with the affection of the pupils for their master and his dependence upon their adulation. In all these plays Lemaître is a chastened realist who knows and avoids the defects, not only of the conventional drama of Scribe and Sardou, but also of the Théâtre Libre.

Another ironic realist is Alfred Capus who came to Paris from the South in order to enter the ranks of the journalists. Eventually he won fame as editor of the *Figaro*, author of several novels, and member of the French Academy. In his twenty-five dramas Capus regards his fellows with the smile of an amused elderly bystander engaged in reflecting that the fume and fuss of the passing show will subside in time if only the actors trust to luck and common sense, and forgive one another like Christians. Capus is chiefly ironic in his refusal to be fooled by romantic affectations, sorrows, or heroisms. These things cannot last. Ideals are all very well, but men desire realities such as food, clothes, money, and love. Poor things! they succumb to temptation so easily that they should as easily be pardoned. Faith in the benevolence of chance is the guiding motive in comedies like *Brignol and his Daughter, Rosine, The Little Functionary, Luck, The Two Men,* and *The Wounded Bird.* In *Brignol,* for example, a jolly impecunious optimist threatened by a gaming creditor escapes from impending ruin when his daughter marries the creditor's nephew, not out of any preconceived plan but because she chances to fall in love with him. From the first, Brignol, like Mr. Micawber, has been sure that something would turn up. "Why worry?" is his emblem and motto.

Most of these plays are also devoted to drawing the new type of self-dependent heroine, philosophic in facing misfortune. Thus, *The Little Functionary* describes the adventures in love of one reduced to earning her livelihood in a provincial post-office, yet surprising the scornful townsfolk by capturing as husband a nobleman. *Rosine* depicts the struggle for existence of an orphan deserted by her lover, refusing the money he offers, but growing independent as a seamstress and enthralling in spite of herself the husband of one of her customers. When a physician proposes to wed her, his father objects, but at length concludes to assist the young couple with the money he had saved for improving his farm. In *The Wounded Bird*, another deserted heroine makes her way undaunted by the past, and, at the plea of her benefactor's wife, releases that gentleman who has threatened for her sake to sacrifice his diplomatic career.

In spite of Capus' eulogy of woman on her own, he is inclined to satirize feminism so far as it means unscrupulous self-assertion, an attitude revealed in such plays as *An Angel*, *Hélène Ardouin*, and *The Favorites*. In the last he turns to good account his own journalistic experience, poking fun at three fair ones who establish a paper ostensibly to compass social and political reforms but actually to gratify their selfish ambitions. Let women be independent, says Capus, but honestly so, and let men and women in marriage be indulgent. This cheerful matrimonial philosophy is the text of *The Little Minxes*, *The Two Schools*, *The Passersby*, and *The Husbands of Léontine*. Léontine's first husband has divorced her with reason, but, when she returns in distress to claim his protection, he is glad to accord it, for toward one who has lived with you, however unhappily, you still must respond with the feeling of sympathy you might have for a little pet animal that had bitten you. Surely, he says, "you cannot refuse her a piece of sugar." In *The Two Schools* a wife, who sends away her over-susceptible husband, yearns for him again and cashiers his methodical successor, since, after all, of the two schools of husbands she has learned to prefer the lively to the sober. Like her mother, she no longer will inquire too curiously into his conduct. Should Edouard again be untrue, let him keep the affair to himself. In *The Little Minxes* frivolous wives, though disposed to get into mischief, spare their husbands, one because he is about to fight a duel, the other because his jealousy touches her heart. But the husbands themselves are far from impeccable. If they refuse to look for temptation like their consorts, they equally refuse to avoid it.

As for the heroine of *The Passersby*, she belongs to that blessed company of spouses who forgive. Amused by her husband's peccadilloes, she scolds him a little, yet only as a proud mother might reprove a smart but naughty child. No sooner has she excused him for spending too much upon a pretty milliner than she finds him escaping to Havre with the family governess. Although she pursues, it is not in the spirit of vengeance, but merely to claim her own, and to assure him that she will quickly forget. "After all, I am your friend," she says, "your comrade for life." So marital reconciliations are lightly effected by Capus, even if on occasion a wife in his plays turns the tables on her husband by taking a substitute, as is the case in *The Châtelaine*, *Hélène Ardouin*, and *The Adversary*.

The comfortable philosophy of Capus with regard to matrimony finds an echo in his doctrine that the cultivation of happiness is more important than devotion to business. Such is the idea set forth in *Money or Your Life*, *Bourgeois Marriage*, and *Monsieur Piégois*, three plays ironic in their dealings with bankers, promoters, and speculators. In all, a wedding settles the hero's worries of the moment, and in *The Adventurer* a heroine on the verge of committing herself to an unscrupulous deputy is similarly saved by marriage with the cousin to whom she had been betrothed before his departure for Africa in quest of a fortune. Certainly in Capus there is nowhere any depth or notable novelty, but he is a wise worldling, an expert craftsman, a diverting critic of things as they are, amused by the follies and foibles of the human animal. Ashley Dukes has aptly said of him: "He regards life with the heavy eyes of a sophisticated child allowed to sit up too late. If they ever open wide, it is with a twinkle of mischief at the great joke of universal insincerity. There is no fear that France will put him to bed; his comments on the passing show are so amusing."

Another ironic realist who finds love delightful is Maurice Donnay. For him there is nothing morbid, nothing pathological in love, as there is for Bataille. He merely regards it as constituting for the average Frenchman two thirds of life, an incentive, a torment, a satisfaction, something never to be dispensed with since the good God saw fit to create the animals male and female and to save them at the time of the Flood in pairs. Not that Donnay expects love to endure for long; much of its charm lies in the fact that it comes and goes capriciously. The only way to take it is with gallant realism. Let us not be unduly sentimental or romantic or despairing. A sense of humor will save so many love situations. Why be angry if one's wife prove unfaithful? Why talk of duels and law-suits? Face the facts, enjoy as you can and when you can. Know that there are as many good fish in the sea as ever were caught.

The satiric gifts of Donnay were first expended for the benefit of frequenters of the Chat Noir of Montmartre in little dialogues and vaudeville skits. Their author, born in 1859, had reached the early thirties before he set a larger audience laughing by adapting to modern conditions the _Lysistrata_ of Aristophanes, that jolly satire upon war and women performed with such good effect later by the Moscow Art Players. In *The Family Boarding-House* he drew amusing middle-class characters, showing a landlady taking malign pleasure in enlightening a guest concerning the disloyalty of his wife, since that guest had once been the landlady's lover. As for the wife, she will get rid of her husband and marry his rival. In *Lovers*, his first marked success, Donnay shows the mistress of a count making an excursion to Italy with a younger charmer, yet aware that they must part since their life together would soon become as matter-of-fact as marriage. So the pair say farewell, with the deliberate tenderness of those extracting the last drop of emotion from a parting, and later they meet in Paris as excellent friends, Claudine felicitating her ex-lover upon his approaching union with an heiress, and preparing to retire with her count to the country, now that he has loosed the bonds that bound him to his uncongenial wife.

There is a parting less friendly, after a lovers' quarrel, in *The Grief-Stricken Woman*, and an ironical scene as worldlings continue unperturbed in their quest for pleasure when their host has blown out his brains. In *The Emancipated Woman*, a philosopher proclaims his right to cease loving when he will, and advises perfect frankness in breaking with the fair; but he is daunted to find that the widow he still adores has stopped loving him because she prefers an artist. This artist has opposed the philosopher's theory of frankness. He regards it as futile and dangerous to tell women everything, and no wonder, for a mistress, on discovering his infidelity, has wounded him in shooting at her rival. His suffering in the cause of love is what has now captured the fancy of the widow. But, really, women, he asserts, wish always to enact a part. Hence, for them to forego a stormy scene in separating is to forfeit the thrill that makes life interesting. Already, the philosopher has denounced feminism. What need have women for freedom, since already they are masters? Why should they lose their child-like charm by coping with men as creatures of thought and will?

In *Georgette Lemeunier*, Donnay considers the temporary infidelity of a wealthy inventor. Though his wife, outraged, leaves him, she returns when he repents, realizing that he has been schemed against by a promoter who has used his wife as bait to catch the too-susceptible inventor. A sub-plot is devoted to a double intrigue in which each of a married pair finds entertainment elsewhere, while each affinity keeps in touch with the other in order to arrange the best hours for stolen meetings somewhat after the fashion of the underplot in *The Merry Wives of Windsor*.

Often, as here, Donnay's mood is of the lightest. Thus, in *Princely Education*, he shows a queen engaging a clubman of Paris to train her son by passing him from one charmer to another, a process costly to the state but one that the people approve. In *The Scaling* (*l'Escalade*) he laughs at a philosopher who has expounded the psychology of love in a book but knows nothing of it in practice. Two plays, written with Lucien Descaves, satirize radicals. *Birds of Passage* pokes fun at fair Russian revolutionists in Switzerland, and *The Clearing* thrusts at feminists building a little Utopia in France, their society upset, however, by a pretty schoolmistress advised to join them when deserted by her lover. The attack upon feminism is repeated by Donnay alone in *Women Scouts*, its heroine the wife of a manufacturer who separates from her husband in order to direct a salon of the emancipated. When she falls in love with another and then rebuffs him, he complains that she has left him in the embarrassing position of the deserted girl of romance. Since feminism has become fashionable, men have a right to demand redress on being wronged by women. Jeanne, impressed by his reasoning, follows him to his estate, doing so the more readily in view of the fact that she is annoyed by the attentions of a Jewish banker, who has joined the company only to pay court to her. But she finds that she must forfeit social standing in the eyes of her new neighbors unless legally married.

The satire so obvious here is deepened in *Appearances*, which describes a family whose members are determined to be fashionable at all costs. Thus, the respectable father, after forty years of tranquil wedded life, takes a mistress to be in style; his niece takes a lover; and his son-in-law turns to a sister-in-law. Only Juliette, daughter of the house, remains worthy. Her brother, a socialist deputy, eventually shoots her faithless husband, the bourgeois pretentions of all these folk being crowned by unhappiness.

A trifle marked by the mildest satire is *The Seesaw*, in which a husband profits from the absence of his wife to pay court to an actress who had vowed never to accept the attentions of a married man. With the return of the wife, who had gone to a health resort to take the waters and pray for an heir, the husband is drawn back to his duty. But when, at a shift of the seesaw, he yearns again for the actress, she treats him as tyrannously as his wife. Thus the poor devil, drawn now to one and now to the other, is ruled by both.

Three serious plays counterbalance these pieces in lighter vein. Tragedy, in *The Torrent*, results from the retirement to the country of a Parisian who anticipates leading an Arcadian existence as a gentleman farmer. Since the unwonted calm makes him only the more aware of the dullness of his wife, he seeks excitement in the wife of an equally dull neighbor. When the lady discovers that their affair can no longer be concealed, she declines to follow the advice of a priest that she keep silent for the sake of their families. She refuses, also, to permit her husband to accept as his own the babe that is coming. Instead, she leaps into a torrent.

A second serious play is *The Other Danger*, wherein a mother, unhappily wed, finds consolation in a lover. What is her distress to discover at length that her daughter has succumbed to the same fascination! Resisting the temptation to fight in order to retain her hold on the man, the mother yields. Already, reports of her infatuation have troubled the girl, and these can be discredited only if the older woman sacrifice herself. She has remarked, also, the response in her lover to youth in her daughter, that "other danger" before which she must bow.

In *The Return from Jerusalem*, a third serious play, Donnay depicts the incompatibility in love of Gentile and Jew. A Gentile, tired of his wife, seeks change in an intrigue with a pretty Jewess, who is tired in turn of her husband. Then each learns that a gulf yawns between them. The original attraction of the exotic cannot be maintained against the oppositions of race, religion, and tradition. Yet the racial issue is somewhat clouded since the author, instead of showing his hero and heroine forced by such conflicts to break the bonds of marriage, links them only by a liaison.

In one other piece, Donnay has collaborated, writing with

Jules Lemaître an amusing travesty of Greek legend, *The Marriage of Telemachus*. The son of Ulysses, betrothed to Nausicaa, cannot resist the charms of Helen of Troy, who is so thoroughly bored by the conduct of men regarding her that when Telemachus plans to carry her away, she foists upon him Nausicaa instead. "I thought you were going to carry off a married woman," says a boatman to Telemachus. To this the youth retorts, abashed, "So did I."

As a biographer of Molière, Donnay used his knowledge of the great comic master to compose in verse his most ambitious attempt, *Molière's Ménage*. This offers a character study of the hero, who has married at forty but is plagued by the coquetry of his wife, Armande Béjart. Warned by her sister who has loved him, he expresses his bitterness in *The Misanthrope*. He is reconciled at last to Armande by the dying Madeleine, who, while passing her costumes in review, recalls all her famous parts. In every respect this is a beautiful and delicately wrought play.

During the War, Donnay composed several trifles, his *Theater with the Armies* being a one-act skit prepared for a benefit performance, and his *Impromptu* praising the courage of a working girl who marries her fiancé maimed in battle. Since the War, Donnay has scarcely added to his reputation by *The Fair One of Anjou*, written with André Rivoire, or by *The Man Hunt*. Yet the latter is entertaining in depicting the scramble of women for men induced by the male shortage due to the conflict. With an overplus of two million women, each must fight the harder to capture a lover or a husband. Two sisters contend for the attentions of a youth, who disdains them both in order to take their pretty servant. This girl, trained to become a professor, has found since the War that she can make more by becoming a chambermaid. The youth, trained as a lawyer, has found that he can make more by becoming a taxi-chauffeur. Social distinctions have all been overturned. The aristocratic parents of the two sisters rent out seats on their balcony overlooking the Champs Elysées to spectators of the Fête Nationale procession, and a quiet little wife has lost her head in flirting with an American officer.

In spite of the success of an occasional serious play, Donnay has produced nothing philosophic. Yet his work reflects the spirit of his people and his time. With infinite patience he rings the changes upon illicit love, relieving the monotony of that theme by the wit and grace of his dialogue. He raises no moral issues, makes no one ponder a single problem. Having asserted the right to love, he is content to smile at his characters exercising that right in a game of hide-and-seek, and to smile also at whatever is intellectually radical. For the worldly, he concocts smart entertainments touched here and there with just enough sentiment to soften the implied brutality.

Most versatile of the ironic realists is Henri Lavedan, who was born at Orléans in 1859, studied law, but soon turned to letters, and wrote light verse, political prose, and lively dialogues. He was welcomed in the cafés and finally at the Comédie Française, where was produced his first long play, *A Family*. In *Prince d'Aurec*, which followed, he disclosed his ability as a painter of manners and of character, introducing an impoverished nobleman at the mercy of a Jewish banker. The prince is aided by his mother, a sensible woman of the middle class enabled by her money to marry a great name. She perceives that the aristocracy can be saved only by regeneration from without, and secures the promise of amendment from her volatile son who has lost his all at gaming. Amusing, too, are a marquis who serves as adviser to the socially ambitious and a novelist engaged in observing the faults and foibles of the fashionable as material for fiction.

In Lavedan's next play, *The Two Nobilities*, the gay Prince d'Aurec has committed suicide after losing at cards, leaving a son who is reared in America. There he learns the gospel of labor, and develops into a captain of industry. Then the son of this son, back in France, falls in love with the daughter of a marquis, who objects to him as too low in the social scale. But his identity is revealed by a discharged employee of his father, one who has organized a strike to regain his lost position. The story serves merely to point a contrast between the aristocracy of birth and the new aristocracy of service. France is to be saved by those who are not too proud to put their shoulders to the wheel.

Yet Lavedan feels some sympathy for the decadent nobility and even for such an old philanderer as the hero of *The Marquis de Priola*, divorced by his wife but exercising a spell over her still. She interests him as soon as it is necessary to win her back, and he in turn charms her fair intermediary. His protégé, Pierre, hitherto devoted to the marquis, on learning that he is the latter's illegitimate son, rates his father roundly as responsible for his mother's long misery. As Pierre declaims against such injustice and warns him of the revenge that nature is likely to exact for his debauchery, the marquis suffers a stroke. Thenceforth, as a helpless invalid, he must depend upon the care of this son whose disgrace he has caused.

It is the mood of comedy that prevails in a number of plays from Lavedan's pen. In *Gay Livers* and *The Old Stager*, there is cynical bitterness in the picture of folk of the boulevards, restless and disillusioned in their hunt for pleasure. In *The Taste for Vice* the modern ambition to be thought worse than we are is thrust at in the case of a wife who encourages a lover but is saved by one of real honor. Her husband, an author, has tried, likewise, to appear brightly wicked by writing tales of doubtful morality. So reformed is she by her experience that she advises him now to compose a collection to be entitled "The Distaste for Vice."

In *The New Game*, Lavedan depicts the ease with which a worldling takes a wife on a bet, and then drops her for the lady who had piqued him into this marriage. His short-term wife has accepted him merely to be in the mode and, when they quarrel, finds consolation in another. Reproved by the divorce judge for having committed such facile matrimony, the hero explains that marriage resembles spinach—"in order to know if you dislike it, you must first taste it." *Catherine* is a more genial if sentimental comedy in the style of Octave Feuillet. Here a duke, who marries on impulse the music teacher of his sister, resents the tyranny of her middle-class family, and thinks to escape to his fair cousin; whereupon his wife sends for her former admirer, a man of her own class. But he proves to be a virtuous soul who lectures Catherine and shows her that happiness lies only in the pursuit of duty.

Farce replaces sentimental morality in *The Medicis*, which echoes Molière's *Bourgeois Gentilhomme*, not only in its general satire upon commonplace ignorance masquerading as learned elegance, but in one particular scene. The proprietor of a restaurant, having acquired wealth, sets up as a patron of art, names his children Michael Angelo and Euterpe, and falls an easy victim to the flattery of his former chef, now an art critic, who, dressed as an Indian rajah, comes with an interpreter to admire the paintings in the amateur's gallery, and, incidentally, to capture his wife and his wealth. The wife, who paints his portrait, paints also a futurist picture which her husband finds beautiful upside down. It is all excellent fooling, in the vein followed later by Lavedan when he wrote *Pétard*. Here a self-made merchant, whose name is a household word wherever rubber shoes, biscuits, and chocolates are used, would assert his claim to social distinction by purchasing the castle of an aristocrat and winning the hand of a lady betrothed to the aristocrat's son. Through her comes Pétard's defeat, since she has sought to secure from him the deed to the property only in order to restore it to the man she really loves.

Sometimes Lavedan exhibits a bent toward melodrama, relying for the pathetic or the tragic upon situation. This is the case in *Varennes*, written with G. Lenôtre, and in *Sire, The*

King's Dog, and *To Serve*. In *Sire*, an actor, engaged to humor an old countess who imagines that the son of Louis XVI still lives, plays the part so effectively that he himself becomes imbued with royalist zeal and dies in the revolution of 1848. In *The King's Dog*, Madame du Barry, awaiting execution, is torn between terror and hope, but finally rejects the means of escape proffered her by a priest. In *To Serve*, written on the eve of the War, a soldier discovers an explosive so powerful that he resolves to destroy the formula for its manufacture. But his father scoffs at this pacifist in uniform and demands the formula. As the two come to blows, the youth's mother intervenes, threatening to kill herself unless they desist. Already she has lost one son in battle, and at this juncture she learns that another has been killed, and that her husband has undertaken an expedition to avert the menace of invasion at the frontier as soon as hostilities are declared. In the face of such an emergency, she and her surviving son forget their theoretical pacifism. Now every means for the defense of their country seems legitimate.

If this timely play exists largely for the sake of its crucial situation, it also emphasizes an idea. But, in *The Duel*, usually regarded as its author's masterpiece, the interest is essentially moral, and character dominates. A duchess, whose husband has been left but the shadow of a man by his excesses, finds herself beloved by two brothers. One is her spiritual adviser, and the other is her physician. Neither is aware of the other as a rival until the second act, when the abbé, having warned her against disloyalty to her sick husband, finds that the lover he fears is his brother, the physician. Then each assails the other in a rhetorical duel, the physician succeeding in making the abbé doubt his vocation and perceive that his motives have been all too human. When the debauched duke is so accommodating as to take his life, the contention of the brothers becomes more practical. But a missionary bishop, grown philosophic in China, intervenes to prove to the abbé that, although in loving the duchess he has not sinned, he should now relinquish her to his brother and bless them both before departing for Christian service in a leper colony. So Lavedan, the painter of the aristocracy and of Parisian lovers of pleasure, draws portraits of two sympathetic clerics. With considerable skill, also, he suggests the contrast in growth of the two brothers, the pious abbé having once been a skeptical *bon vivant*, and the skeptical physician having once been a devout believer. In time they have shifted rôles. The only defect of the piece is its undue prolixity. These folk talk well, but they talk interminably.

The War, which interrupted Lavedan's production, was echoed in a few minor pieces—*The Sacrifices*, a dramatic poem written with Miguel Zamacoïs, and *War Dialogues* and *Enchanted Portraits*, the last representing the visit of the Kaiser and von Hindenburg to a captured museum and the remarks of the animated portraits at the expense of their distinguished guests. In general, Lavedan is more the moralist than Donnay, Capus, or even Lemaître, but his moods shift with facility. He knows the gay world of the boulevards and the shabby world of pushing parvenus and of aristocrats in decline. He can be satiric or sympathetic, witty or grave. Priding himself upon the variety of his production, he is especially able as a creator of character.

CHAPTER XI

Playwrights of the Erotic and the Comic

Porto-Riche, Bataille, Coolus, Wolff, de Croisset, Bourdet,
Bisson, Tristan Bernard, Guitry, de Flers and de Caillavet

ILLICIT love, which in the theater of Donnay and Capus
bulks so largely, becomes with men of the neurotic and
erotic school an obsession. They are realists, too, and occasionally ironic, but their chief concern is to present on the
boards aspects of morbid passion. Bataille and Porto-Riche,
with some lesser folk, have developed the erotic strain into
a specialty. Georges de Porto-Riche, born at Bordeaux in
1849, is least extreme. He began in the 'seventies with four
romantic plays, their interest focused upon outer action. Then
he turned inward to study vibrations of the heart, and in *The
Luck of Françoise,* produced at the Théâtre Libre, he tempered by humor his portrayal of the maneuvers of a clever
woman to keep her light-o'-love husband from making a fool
of himself with the wife of a friend. She practices the indulgence recommended by Capus, holding him by not seeming to
hold him, forgiving his petty infidelities, inducing the other
lady's husband to forego a duel with him, and accepting his
reversion to her as part of her natural good fortune. Here
the intrigue is nothing, the sentiment is all. Similarly, in *The
Impassioned Wife* (*L'Amoureuse*) Porto-Riche reveals with
scientific impartiality the consuming desire of a woman married to an intellectual husband unwilling and unable to satisfy
her. Having wed her in the hope of securing domestic comfort
and calm, he finds her disturbing to his medical researches and
is glad to purchase peace by handing her over to her former

lover. But, since his very coldness piques her interest, she returns to agitate him afresh. For better or for worse, they are bound together. If the dénouement be ironic here, it is tragic in *The Unfaithful Woman*, a romantic piece with its scene laid in Venice of the seventeenth century and its hero the Doge's secretary. As the secretary is to leave on a mission, he vows fidelity to Vanina, who, learning that already he has deceived her, would excite his interest by letting him suppose her to be wooed by another lover. In male disguise and posing as that lover, she sings a serenade beneath her own window, only to be slain by the jealous Renato. "She was faithful to me," he laments; but a friend who already has sought to make Vanina his own, answers cynically, "She would have deceived you." Deception, indeed, is the normal expectancy of every man or woman in the plays of Porto-Riche. In vain the heroine of *The Past* argues against the necessity of assuming infidelity in her lover. Despite her protests, she is aware that he is dividing his attentions between her and others.

In *The Old Man*, the longest play of Porto-Riche, we behold the rebirth of passion in the breast of a reformed roué living at peace in the country until both he and his son are fired by the charms of a fair visitor. Then the father, at his wife's behest, consents to withdraw, yet only on condition that he be permitted to bid Brigitte a last farewell. Her consequent absence from a rendezvous with the son reveals to the latter the fact of his father's rivalry. So shocked is the youth that he casts himself from a cliff. Though the mother assails the father as responsible, she cannot part from him, since habit as well as love still links them together. To all these folk love has proved a tyrant, nor have they greatly struggled to resist it. So also it excites a husband in *The Merchant of Prints*. He is a lover of engravings, tranquil in his little shop until called to the colors. But the life of the trenches unleashes his primitive instincts, and he returns a changed man to fall in love unworthily with one we never see. Drawn to her against his better judgment and his every interest, he struggles to keep from wronging his wife. Then maddened by the conflict, he and she throw themselves into the Seine. She cannot be separated from him, and he cannot continue to be unfaithful to her. In all these dramas, passion is the principal concern of the playwright. It is not a tranquil, enduring, self-immolating love that he displays, but a stormy, trouble-breeding intoxication, comparable to a disease of body and mind.

So, also, with Henry Bataille, who inclines even more than Porto-Riche to explore erotic abnormalities. Bataille opened his career by writing romantic dramas in verse, striking a characteristic note in *Thy Blood*, where the rivalry of brothers enamored of a blind girl comes to a tragic close as the younger, whom she has saved by blood transfusion, tears the bandages from his arm on learning that she has earlier yielded to the elder. In *The Enchantment*, a love-sick girl infatuated with her sister's bridegroom takes poison on his wedding day, is rescued, and comes to live with the pair and to harass them until they turn her away. In *The Masque* a neglected wife, out of consideration for her husband, justifies their separation by feigning an infidelity of which she is guiltless. Her departure revives his affection, and her continued devotion is confessed when, mistaking him in the dark for the friend who has consented to play the part of her lover, she says enough to ensure their reconciliation. In *Mamma Colibri* a kiss administered to a mother by her son is at first received by her as coming from his friend, whereby her intrigue with the friend is unveiled. Passion, flowering late in Irene, expends itself upon this youth, and renders her at once ridiculous and pathetic. Her husband, an understanding soul, endeavors to save her but in vain. "Woman," he declares, "is not a free and independent being like us; she is subject to laws of nature that no civilization has ever abolished or ever can." When his wife departs to Algiers with her young lover, he awaits the outcome with confidence. Ere long Irene, deserted by the youth for one of his own age, returns exhausted, content to settle down now as a placid grandmother.

The excuse that women are peculiarly the victims of instinct does duty in *The Scandal* when a wife, acting upon impulse, has given herself to a stranger and is threatened with public disgrace. Her husband, a provincial mayor, averts the scandal, partly for his own sake, but chiefly out of compassion for what in her was irresistible. Overmastering instinct accounts for the sudden trespass of the heroine in *The Night Moth* and for the mutual attraction felt by Amaury and Diane in *The Foolish Virgin*, although Diane is less than half the age of Amaury, and the latter is married to a wife so considerate that on two occasions she saves her husband and her rival from the avenging hand of Diane's brother. Diane commits suicide, as does the disillusioned heroine of *The Wedding March*; and, in *Woman Unadorned*, suicide is attempted by the model, little Loulou, when deserted for another by her artist husband. Later she finds consolation in a second artist who had befriended her before her marriage. Certainly the women of Bataille are creatures high strung, neurasthenic, and unmoral. Their sole occupation and interest is love. Only by exception are they as philosophic as the widow in *Poliche*, who parts from her lover after their tender interlude at Fontainebleau, realizing, as does he, that their affair cannot endure, and prepared to replace it by reverting to a former lover.

Triangular love is celebrated in *The Torches* and *The Amazon*, the former seeming faintly to reflect the actual relations of a distinguished scientist and his wife, winners of the Nobel prize. The hero of the play unwittingly discloses the fact that he is enamored of his fair secretary by interposing objections to her marriage with his laboratory chief. The wife, though grieved, offers to the girl as dowry her own share of the prize awarded to the couple for their researches upon cancer. But the master, insisting upon one last meeting with the bride, and interrupted in it by his injured wife and the bridegroom, sees his precious papers burnt in revenge and is mortally wounded in a duel. Then he sends the girl away and, dying, bids his widow and his repentant laboratory chief carry on his scientific labors for the benefit of humanity. In *The Amazon*, Bataille has applied to a situation induced by the War his customary analysis of illicit love. An architect of middle age who had thought to remain comfortably at home during the conflict is prompted to enlist by his admiration for a pretty refugee protected by his wife. It is only after his death at the front that the wife discovers his attachment to the girl and in anger turns her out. The girl, serving gallantly as a hospital nurse, is about to marry an official when the architect's widow, the War being ended, and her jealousy having subsided, perversely challenges Ginette to withdraw from the union that she may remain true to the one whom she had inspired to die for his country. Improbably enough, Ginette accepts the suggestion and unites with her former rival in shedding tears on the grave of their hero.

Fantasy marks *The Dream of an Evening of Love* in which an author finds it impossible to enjoy his lady of the moment because the embodied recollection of a lady of the past intervenes at each juncture. Even when a rival enters to cast off his present fancy, and the hero would take advantage of her situation, he is prevented because the shadow from his past stands between. In *The Child of Love* and *Our Image* realism asserts itself as Bataille deals with intrigue in its effects upon the second generation. A woman of doubtful character, in *Our Image*, must contract a respectable marriage in order to enable her daughter to marry the man who sees in her the image of her mother at an early age; and in *The Child of Love*, a youth is called upon to sacrifice his own romance that his loose-living mother may attain social position with an admirer. In *The Animator*, Bataille depicts the tragedy of a journalist who learns that his wife has been unfaithful, that her daughter is not his, and that the scandal will be made public in a book by an enemy. In *Tenderness* he shows the plight of a middle-aged dramatist whose youthful mistress respects and admires him but requires in addition a lover of her own years. Although the hero sends her away and seeks consolation in another charmer, he comes to the conclusion that love is not merely the tumult of the heart, it is also sentiment; and that sentiment in his case has survived passion, a situation reflecting the actual experience of Bataille with the actress Yvonne de Bray. Another heroine all instinct figures in *Possession*. She is a very Manon Lescaut who runs off with a cousin, abandons him to suicide when he loses at Monte Carlo, gives herself to the son of a duke and then to the duke himself.

In Bataille's last play, *Human Flesh*, interest focuses rather on a man enriched by the War who learns from a mistress long since abandoned that the son she bore him has fallen at the front. Hitherto he has kept his legitimate son out of the fighting, but that youth, on hearing the story, enters the conflict and wins distinction. Then his half-brother, supposedly dead, turns up alive, released from a German prison. Although urged by his mother to claim a share of his father's estate, he declines. He will withdraw with his mother to the country, while the father and the legitimate son will continue to live in town—a comfortable arrangement for any who have chanced to develop two families. In none of these later plays of Bataille, from the *Love Sisters* down, is there anything new. Only his contribution to the Don Juan legend reveals a touch of freshness. This is *The Man With the Rose*, which depicts the Spanish libertine as grown too old to attract the fair any longer, yet seeking vicarious satisfaction by allowing a friend to assume his still potent name in philandering with the wife of a duke. When the duke, surprising the pair, slays the lover, Don Juan claims the body believed to be his, and, to confirm that belief, thrusts into the pocket of the corpse the manuscript of his *Memoirs*. In attending what purports to be his own funeral, he is recognized by only one of his victims, a woman who promises secrecy since he has blessed her with a child. Then Don Juan, forced to retire to a village where he can keep his identity concealed, finds with chagrin that the edition of his *Memoirs* now in circulation is spurious and that he who once broke hearts at a glance can hope to do no more than purchase the favors of a wench at the inn. Let us weep for Don Juan! says Bataille. Let us weep for Bataille! say we. Probably no audience but the French could endure with equanimity such unflagging exploitation of a single passion even by a master like Bataille. For him the theater is a place to represent, not ideas, but emotions, and among emotions he finds just one worthy to excite his efforts. His women, as we have seen, are all daughters of Phædra, love-sick; and his men are love-obsessed. Now and again he turns a little from these people to dwell upon their matter-of-fact surroundings. Pieces like *The Wedding March* and *Poliche*, if written earlier, might, indeed, have been welcomed at the Théâtre Libre as contributions to naturalism.

From that home of the naturalists emerged other playwrights of the neurotic and erotic school, such writers as Romain Coolus (René Weill) and Pierre Wolff. Coolus, in *The Brésile Household*, led off with an astringent dose of cynicism, smiling at the complacence of a husband who decides, after his erring wife has left him for a night, to receive her next morning as though nothing had happened. Such is the spirit displayed in *Raphaël, The Sick Child, Cœurblette, The Cherished Child*, and *Heart to Heart*. In the last, indeed, a husband grows so earnest in reproaching the lover of his wife for being disloyal to her that he even wins back her affection for himself. Coolus is fond of depicting the indulgent hero as equally devoted to his lady and his friend, ready to relinquish the former to the latter out of sheer kindness. In *The Risk*, he varies the situation by showing an aunt who gives over her lover to her niece in the same generous fashion.

As for Pierre Wolff, he has swung between the comedy of

sentiment, in *Fidèle*, *The Secret of Polichinelle*, and *Forbidden Love*, and the *comédie rosse* with which his labors began. In the vein of naturalism are his *Those We Respect*, *What One Loves*, *The Inclination*, *Rascal Léonce*, *The Brook*, *The Lily*, and *Broken Wings*, to mention only a few. Wolff cares nothing for novelty of story or subtle psychological analysis, but he delights in disclosing emotional frailties through skillful dialogue. Occasionally he even lends a touch of heroism to his characters, as in *Forbidden Love*, where the husband, finding his wife enchanted by a rival, determines to disappear, like his self-effacing prototype in Tolstoy's *Living Corpse*.

Many other playwrights have centered attention upon love and not always, as have Bataille and his disciples, upon love disordered. The transition to a less sensational treatment of the tender passion may be seen in the work of Francis de Croisset (Francis Wiener) who evinces sprightly fancy, both in his early experiments in verse and in his graceful comedies in prose, written later. De Croisset's men, as a rule, are creatures highly susceptible, who, after yielding to a variety of fascinations, settle down. This is the case with the jaunty youth in *Chérubin*, with the gay husband in *Happiness, Ladies*, brought to his senses by the tact of his wife, and with the Don Juan in *From One Day to Another*, sobered by the War, and permitting his wife to transfer her allegiance to one more worthy. In *The Borrowed Fire*, on the contrary, the lover is faithful but disdained until his lady's heart is kindled by another. Then he finds that he too may catch warmth from its flame. Obviously, in the contemporary theater of France, the combination of husband, wife, and mistress provides a sure resource, but for dramatists to harp so monotonously upon three strings is unduly to limit their music.

Of late, variations have been played by Lenormand, as we shall see, who plucks a Freudian string, and by Edouard Bourdet, who, in *The Captive*, seeks to exploit disharmonies due to homo-sexual love. Bourdet's drama achieved success at home and abroad partly because, like *The Well of Loneliness*, an English novel, it ventured upon forbidden ground. Yet, if one accepts as representative of a small class of febrile and neurotic persons a heroine struggling against a force too strong for her, there is nothing offensive in the theme and certainly nothing to condemn in the treatment it is accorded here. Bourdet's heroine has conceived for another woman a passion which renders her indifferent to the advances of a male lover. Yet this lover she would keep as a screen to hide her real reason for remaining in Paris against the wishes of her father, a diplomat desirous of taking her to Rome. At first, Jacques accepts her suggestion that he merely pose as her fiancé. Then, in the hope of driving out a morbid passion by one perfectly natural, he marries her. But, although the pair spend a year in travel, Irene returns as mad as ever, and Jacques is forced to recognize the wisdom of the warning earlier given him by a friend who had suffered with a wife similarly infatuated. The play is thoroughly artistic, restrained, and dignified. As in the pieces of Lenormand, its implications are expressed with admirable tact.

What all these neurotic heroes and heroines and the devotees of passional drama in general fail to possess is a sense of humor. Another considerable group of plays and playwrights would furnish comic relief from the stresses of life, whether due to outer adversity or to morbid strains within. They laugh light-heartedly at human folly and conceive a world of grotesquerie. Bourdet himself, author of *The Captive*, who before the War wrote *The Rubicon* and *The Open Cage* and has since produced *The Shepherd's Hour*, *Man Enchained*, and *Just Appeared*, cannot be accused of failure to provoke mirth when he wishes. Indeed, his comedy of manners, *The Weaker Sex*, provided the chief success of the Parisian season of 1930. In similar fashion many a serious dramatist, as we have noted, turns in brighter moments to comedy. This is the case with such masters of stagecraft as Sardou and Kistemaeckers, with the naturalists of the Théâtre Libre, and even with a reformer like Brieux, who, in *The June Bugs*, waxes merry over the tyranny of an imperious coquette exerted upon a poor little pedant. Of course, the ironic realists, men like Hermant, Guinon, Picard, Lavedan, and Capus, have excelled in comedies more or less satiric. But the drama of sheer fun has had its upholders as well, inheritors of the tradition of the joyous farce, manipulators of all the devices that call forth laughter. Alexandre Bisson, who wrote alone and in collaboration piece after piece, carried absurdity to the limit, delighting in confusions of identity, schemes that rebound upon the schemer, concealments and unveilings, with the struggle of husbands to outwit their vigilant wives, and jests at mothers-in-law. Such is the source of mirth in *The Deputy from Bombignac*, *My Governess*, *The Surprises of Divorce*, *The Heroic le Cardunois*, *The Errors of Marriage*, and *The Sleeping Car Conductor*.

The Plautine influence which in part accounts for French farce is supplemented by whimsicalities of character and plot in some of the plays of Courteline, Feydeau, Tristan Bernard, and de Flers and de Caillavet. Absurd hypotheses are at the heart of several of the comedies of Georges Courteline, and a naïve character is at that of his *Boubouroche*, one enraged to discover his mistress unfaithful and yet quickly placated by her assumption of even greater indignation that her virtue should be suspected. With Georges Feydeau, as in *The Lady From Maxim's*, the humor is rendered piquant by an approach to the daring in situation. Comic confusions and indelicacy combine in *The Free Exchange Hotel*, *A Cathartic for Baby*, *Look Out for Amélie*, and *Don't Go About Without Your Clothes*.

Quite as irreverent and hilarious as Feydeau is Tristan Bernard, who builds up his comedies on the model of Plautus, rejoicing in disguises, concealments, mistaken identities, and all sorts of impossible situations that upset any assumption

of dignity. Now he closely follows the *Menæchmi* of Plautus,
as in *The Twins of Brighton*; now he conceives original plots
that hinge upon a husband's taking a thief for his wife's lover,
as in *The Only Bandit of the Village*, or his taking her lover
for a thief, as in *The Gang at Léon*. In *The Ardent Artillery-
man* a female professor of ethics, rebuking her cook for having
hidden a soldier in the kitchen, herself succumbs to his wooing.
In *The Nocturnal Visitors* a sufferer from insomnia is so
pleased to be drugged by robbers that, while they flee for their
lives, supposing her to be bent on vengeance, she pursues
merely to ascertain what opiate they have used so successfully.
In *The Mathieu Case* a lover presents to his lady a trunk in
which he may hide should her husband suddenly appear, but,
being automatically locked within it, he is supposed to have
fled after committing a crime; then, being released by one who
has opened it only to steal, he beholds the pilferer in turn
caught within it. Sometimes Bernard deals with fads like cy-
cling as in *The Ambulant Flirt*, or automobiling as in *The
Touring Club Bride* and *The Soubigou Beacons*, the latter
introducing as heroine the daughter of a duke so devoted to
gasoline as to earn her living in a garage. Sometimes Bernard
allows comic character to dominate, as in *Triplepatte*, whose
hero, being subject to the suggestions of others, cannot decide
whether or not to marry, or *Prince Charming*, whose hero,
though quite irresponsible in money matters, is forgiven by
his friends and his wife. Especially amusing is *The Little
Café*, which shows a waiter inheriting a fortune but pledged
beforehand to forfeit most of it unless he consent to serve his
master for a term of twenty years. Though he feigns madness
to secure his release, he must act quite sanely before witnesses
when threatened with the asylum. Finally, after posing in his
leisure hours as a fine gentleman at a big café, he resigns himself to going on in his humble office at the little café and marrying his master's daughter. The range of Bernard is wider
than that of Feydeau, and of late he has shown a tendency to

become fairly serious, as in *Jeanne Doré*, a melodrama, and *The Force of Lying*, a study in self-abnegation on the part of a general. But it is for his splendid high spirits in comedy that Tristan Bernard will be remembered.

Another maker of mirth who later turned serious is Sacha Guitry, the actor, an audacious and brilliant wit. He laughs at convention and morals in such pieces as *The Key*, *A Fine Marriage*, and *The Night Watchman*. In the last, a professor, discovering that his mistress entertains a second lover, accepts the situation philosophically, assuring her that it is only unfounded suspicion that is abominable, and embarrasses the pair by his generous aid after eliciting sympathy from the audience, already amused by the clever turns of intrigue as a jealous maid servant betrays the lover to her master. An historical comedy seems promised in *The Taking of Berg-op-Zoom*, but the title is soon discovered to refer to the final step in a lover's capture of the wife of another. So *John III, or The Irresistible Vocation of Young Mondoucet*, which appears to be historical, tells rather of the stage aspirations of the son of a shocked bourgeois, a youth called upon in an emergency to play a kingly rôle. With the advent of the War, Guitry waxed graver for a time and developed successfully the biographic drama, a form loosely knit and dependent upon character rather than plot. Such plays as *Jean de La Fontaine*, *Deburau*, *Pasteur*, *Béranger* and *Mozart* exemplify his skill in this direction. He has exposed vicissitudes of the actor's life in *The Comedian*, of his own life in *The Subject for a Novel*, and, lest he be thought to have forgotten his true *métier*, he has continued to write light pieces like *I Love You* and *The White and the Black*, a delicate fantasy like *One Evening When You Are Alone*, a succession of tableaux like *Stories of France*, and a series of smart revues done in collaboration with A. Willemetz.

Among the minor makers of comedy touched more or less with sentiment may be mentioned Albin Valabrègue, Léon

Gandillot, Georges Mitchell, Franz Fonson, Fernand Wicheler, and Jules Renard, whose *Carrot Top* is admirable in its delicate repression. Other minor makers of comedy, from Fernand Nozière to Louis Bénière, have displayed a gift in satire. This satiric vein, and the vein of pure comedy, also, are best exemplified in the works of de Flers and de Caillavet. Here may be found an artistic reserve and polish, a refinement of the brutal, and an appreciation of what is poignantly humorous, sufficient to establish the collaborators as among the masters of French comedy. De Caillavet, who died in 1915, learned his art in producing *revues* and *vaudevilles*, and de Flers, a journalist, learned his in studying the plays of others in order to write dramatic criticisms. From 1900 forward they collaborated, sentiment frequently coloring their plays, as in *The Heart Has Its Reasons*, *The Paths of Virtue*, and *The Angel of the Fireside*—all involving situations calculated to please those of easy morality in that they exhibit not only the frailties of human nature but also its tendernesses. In *Miquette and her Mother*, a little shop girl fascinates a bashful count, then turns actress, and by her talent wins the approval of her lover's uncle, who, improbably enough, marries her mother at the same time that his nephew marries the daughter. Especially delightful is *Love Watches*, popular in many languages, the story of a wife who would get even with her husband by sacrificing her honor to a romantic scholar. In confronting him at his rooms, she loses heart, however, and departs unscathed after he has confessed that all his conquests have been like this, triumphs of the imagination alone. In *The Fan*, a coquette, who has found her satisfaction in alluring and then destroying admirers, succumbs at last to one she has jilted and breaks her fan as a defeated general might break his sword in token of surrender. But since at that moment another fan is presented to her, the daunted lover exclaims, "Already?"

The dramatic censorship having been relaxed, de Flers and

de Caillavet increased the modicum of satire in their works, and in *The King*, *The Sacred Wood*, and *The Green Coat* made merry at the expense of republican worshipers of royalty, and of aspirants for decorations and for the immortality conferred by membership in the French Academy. In such plays they gave free rein to burlesque. Thus, when a count is found kneeling at the feet of a duchess, they are both saved from the wrath of the lady's husband by the quick lie of a smart typist who declares that he was merely imploring the lady to aid his candidacy for the French Academy. Her husband accepts the explanation, and, seeing in the melancholy and obscurity of the count points in his favor for such an honor, secures his election, but is a bit upset when, in reading an address at the ceremony of reception, he happens to quote from a mislaid love letter to his wife caught up by error in his manuscript. Again the typist steps in and caps her former service by agreeing to marry the count, now elevated through her ruse to be one of the Immortals.

Wit, fancy, and sentiment adorn the intricate framework of intrigue in such plays as *Buridan's Ass*, *Papa*, *Primerose*, *Venice*, *The Beautiful Adventure*, and *Monsieur Brotonneau*. Most complicated is *Buridan's Ass*, its hero, like the beast of the proverb perplexed between two bundles of hay, standing irresolute between two ladies. Earlier he has kept four of them in favor but has been dismissed by all four in exactly the same terms, and then has transferred his affections to four others who in turn tire of him and repeat those terms. Everything here, indeed, is either quadrupled or doubled with comic effect, until Georges, who has objected to courting a final heroine on the ground that he can never love what he respects, is enabled to gain happiness with her since she destroys the grounds of that respect deliberately, damaging her fine reputation like Lady Gregory's Hyacinth Halvey. Although satirical comments upon human nature give universality to the work of de Flers and de Caillavet, they charm chiefly by their ingenuity in plot construction, their scintillant dialogue, their good-humored thrusts at fashions of the hour, and their revelation of defects in character. They are adepts at mingling elements as varied as sentiment and burlesque, romance and satire. Among modern French comedies theirs are most likely to be appreciated abroad.

CHAPTER XII

Moralists

Hervieu and de Curel

ALTHOUGH the French drama has shown so pronounced a tendency to deal with passion rather than the restraint of passion by will, yet a counter current may be observed in the plays of the moralists and reformers who would point the necessity for self-control, the evil effects of selfish individualism, and the need of regeneration in various directions. The moralists of the stage differ from the reformers in that they propose no specific remedies for the ills they observe. They are far less didactic. Problems of conduct are their study. If François de Curel be as ready as Henry Bataille to dwell upon the abnormal, his reaction toward it is different. The emotional crises of his characters take on ethical significance. The central thought of each of his plays may be stated as a moral theorem. He is intent upon unfolding the states of mind of strange souls, victims of desire, troubled in conscience, and suggesting by their predicaments nice questions for the casuist to answer.

Other moralists of the French stage have followed in the steps of Hervieu and de Curel. Thus Paul Bourget, the psychological novelist, has developed in *A Divorce* one notion implicit in *The Labyrinth* of Hervieu—the concept of the remarriage of a divorcée as contrary to religion. So, too, in *The Emigré* Bourget has approached *The Fossils* of de Curel in portraying a blue-blooded nobleman out of sympathy with the new skeptical democracy. In *A Case of Conscience*, written with Serge Basset, Bourget seems to borrow a leaf from *The*

Enigma of Hervieu; and in *The Barricade* he evinces an interest in the conflict of capital and labor less propagandist than that in the plays of Hauptmann, Mirbeau, and Fabre. In *The Crisis,* written with André Beaunier, Bourget reveals corruption in politics, and in *The Tribune* he raises the question whether a political theorist who considers himself emancipated from faith in the family will be able to act impartially where the fate of his son is concerned. Such is the theme, also, of *The Apostle* by Paul Hyacinthe Loyson, one of the best ethical studies on the stage. Avoiding the treatment of illicit love for its own sake, Loyson in *The Evangel of Blood, The Right of the Virgins,* and *Enemy Souls* presents struggles of conscience in a world that has lost its traditional bulwarks of loyalty and faith. He believes that a democracy can succeed only as its members are united by their sense of duty. In *The Apostle* he further insists that such a sense may prevail quite independent of religion. An anti-clerical minister of public instruction discovers that his son, a deputy, has been guilty of embezzlement for the sake of an actress, and has further falsely accused his wife and induced the suicide of his secretary. Shall the minister hide the scandal to save his family honor and his political influence? When silence would preserve what most men hold dear, Baudoin speaks out, exposing the infamy of his son and resigning his own position. He is indeed an apostle of truth and freedom. In Loyson there lingers something of Ibsen's doctrine and of Corneille's dramatic reliance upon will.

Prominent among the minor makers of moral drama are Marie Lenéru, Gaston Devore, and Gabriel Trarieux, all engaged in depicting conflicts between instinct and duty. Devore has specialized in displaying matter-of-fact scenes of family life; Trarieux, with greater imagination, invents situations that show character at a crisis. In *The Hostage* he studies free thought in a husband at war with religion in his wife; and in *The Alibi* he discusses a problem of personal honor. In *The Debt* he draws a new Hamlet brooding over the suicide of his father and the speedy remarriage of his mother, and in *An Evening*, a new Ellida Wangel, torn between husband and lover, but cleaving at length to the former when given her freedom to choose.

Most purely abstract of the moralists is Paul Hervieu, born in 1857 and removed by death in 1915. In a series of plays developed with perfect art and logic, he exemplifies the classic tradition, simplifying human experience, eliminating everything that will not reinforce a central thesis. After studying law, and practising journalism, he turned to the theater. A novel later dramatized by Brieux, and pointing to money as the armature which alone binds together a society given over to fashionable frivolity, was followed by a two-act play, *No To-morrow*. This accorded to a fleeting intrigue half-humorous indulgence. A lady who is being conducted by a personable youth from a lover to her bridegroom-to-be, forgets for a few hours the man of the past and the man of the future, and finds happiness with her companion of the present. What of to-morrow? There will be no to-morrow. Sufficient unto the day is the joy thereof.

If Hervieu showed nothing of his characteristic manner in this gently erotic piece, he entered upon the field that he was to make peculiarly his own with his next drama, *Words Remain*. Here he illustrates an old truth, namely, that scandal, however idle, is likely to grow both in volume and in destructive power. Moreover, it may even recoil upon the head of him who has thoughtlessly initiated it. A marquis, seeing the fair Régine parting at her door from a gentleman, hints that she may be in love with him. The suggestion is accepted as an assertion of fact, and leads an elderly suitor to cast the lady off. When the marquis himself, having fallen in love with her, proposes, the man he had slandered objects and wounds him in a duel. Although the marquis might have recovered had he remained quiet, he rises from his sick-bed to protest against others who are exaggerating his original story, and then sinks dying, a victim to his own loose talk. Thus Hervieu has demonstrated that words are not evanescent; they remain and are potent to destroy.

That modern marriage has not greatly relaxed the tyranny of husbands is the dramatist's thesis in several plays. A husband's refusal to grant his wife a divorce sets the action going in *The Nippers* and *The Law of Man*. In the latter, a wife has been wronged. She demands a separation, and threatens to make public the name of her rival. The husband resists, and, since her daughter loves that rival's son, the mother consents to a reconciliation for the sake of the young people. According to French law, her husband was within his rights in declining to give her a divorce. He consents to drop his intrigue and make friends with her out of consideration for the daughter they both love. But the wife has the satisfaction of enlightening the husband of her rival as to that lady's perfidy. As a man, he could readily have divorced an unfaithful wife, but he refuses to do so out of consideration for the son they both love. Thus *The Law of Man* is nicely balanced in plot to show that husbands are unduly favored by the law. But Hervieu, unlike Brieux, proposes no remedy for such legal injustice.

Already, in *The Nippers*, Hervieu had shown a correct and methodical husband declining to allow his wife her freedom. She has bowed to necessity but sought secret comfort from the love of a sympathetic scholar. The husband supposes that he has triumphed, but, when years later they quarrel as to the education of her son, and she blurts out the fact that he is the child of the scholar now dead, her husband is prepared to sue for the divorce he once had denied her. It is her turn, however, to scorn him. She will repudiate the confession she has made to him alone should he proceed at law against her, and he will hesitate to do this out of regard for his honor and for the future of the boy whom he loves as a son. Now that the shoe is on the other foot, the husband perceives that he should have allowed his wife to leave him in the first instance.

He has abused the power given him by "the nippers" of marriage. He is held as securely and unjustly to his wife as earlier she had been held to him.

Symmetry and balance of plot so apparent here are again in evidence in the more melodramatic *Enigma*, wherein two brothers living together on a country estate argue as to what should be done to a disloyal wife. One asserts that such a wife should be slain by her husband outright. The other declares that she should be subjected by him to slow mental torture after her lover has been disposed of. Now each of these advocates of male marital rights suspects his wife of meeting by night a certain gallant. In watching together for a poacher they chance to capture the gay Vivarce, obviously bent on mischief; yet they cannot tell with which lady he has had an assignation. Only his suicide reveals the truth, for at the news one wife remains calm, whereas the other is convulsed with grief. Since it is the husband of the latter who has advocated for female infidelity a punishment of mental torture, we foresee her fate; but shall even a guilty wife, asks the playwright, be permitted by law to suffer such torture from an avenging husband?

In several plays Hervieu has failed to develop the thesis which is to be found at the heart of his most characteristic work. Thus, *Théroigne de Méricourt* is an historical spectacle in six acts belonging to the same class as Rostand's *L'Aiglon*, its heroine a friend of Danton and Robespierre; and *Modestie* and *Bagatelle* are comedies as little didactic as *No To-morrow*. In Hervieu's last play, *Destiny is Master*, given its original production in a Spanish version by Jacinto Benavente in Madrid, the story holds equal interest with the theme of honor. An embezzler who seeks the means to flight is advised by the brother of his wife that duty demands that he either remain and face his accusers or else die by his own hand. Since Gaetan will do neither, the guardian of the family honor acts as judge and executioner.

The tendency toward using a lively external action, evidenced here and in *The Enigma* and *Théroigne de Méricourt*, is apparent also in *The Awakening*, which utilizes a political situation to drive home its moral. Let the value of an illicit love be subjected to the test of death, says Hervieu. Let the woman who believes that she cannot live without her lover suppose him to be suddenly removed. What then? Will she not discover that life even with an unsympathetic husband holds its allurements and its duties? A prince who is willing to sacrifice his hope of a throne for the sake of Thérèse has been warned by his royal father that should she believe him to be dead she will go about her business little moved. He has contended that she will take her life. When he is snatched from her side and reported as slain, Thérèse confirms the king's theory by returning home quietly and presiding at a dinner intended to quiet the scandal about her lest the love match of her daughter be imperiled. To the prince who protests at her forgetting him so soon, she says: "You and I have awakened. When you arise from the dead, you see me allied with the living against you. As for myself, I have learned that you might have disappeared without stopping the course of my life, or even turning it aside for one evening."

In *Know Thyself*, Hervieu counterpoises two triangles with admirable skill in order to prove, first, the folly of exacting a bloody revenge when a wife has compromised herself, and, second, the fact that the code of conduct we so lightly prescribe for others we may reject when the case becomes our own. A general advises a brother officer inclined to forgive his wife that he cannot do so with honor. He must divorce her and duel with his rival. Then the general learns that this rival is his own son, and that his own wife has also had an affair with his ward. Will he apply to himself the advice he has sought to impose upon another? By no means. Blaming now his own neglect, he forgives his wife and her lover, who has after all done his best to separate from the lady, and retracts the counsel he had given the officer. Why should the weakness of an hour destroy the happiness of a lifetime? Blindly we apply traditional formulas for conduct, but let us examine them well and reject those that are not rational, and, above all, let us learn to know ourselves. In structure, this play is a classic masterpiece, wasting not a line, preserving the unities of time and place, moving inevitably toward its culmination, and individualizing its typical characters only enough to make them plausible and interesting. The doctrine, though clear by implication, is not overemphasized.

The two plays of Hervieu best known are *The Labyrinth* and *The Torch Race*. In the former, the dramatist improves upon a situation first employed by *The Cradle* of Brieux. The advisability of second marriage after divorce is questioned on the ground that between the parents of children there is a natural link which no law can break. When a mother, divorced and remarried, is called to watch with her first husband at the bedside of their sick child, it is no wonder that both should forget that they have ever lived apart. Marianne, horrified at what she has done, returns to her parents and confesses her sin. Forgiven by her Catholic mother, who regards any second union to be illegal, she is assailed by her second husband, who threatens death to his rival. Marianne, resolving to see neither husband again, retires to the country, but both follow, each taunts the other, and, as they clench and struggle, they fall from the edge of a cliff into the Rhone. Brieux had avoided this tragic conclusion and raised no churchly objection to remarriage. The play of Hervieu is much more effective, its every detail being calculated to make stronger the situation leading to an emotional dénouement.

Better still as a study in logic is *The Torch Race*, which illustrates, with rare ingenuity, the truth of an almost axiomatic proposition regarding human behavior. Life is like the Athenian torch race in which relay runners endeavor to hand from one to another ahead a flame that must be kept burning.

So, each generation seeks to convey life's flame to the next, and parents instinctively will do more for children than will children for parents. Although most would assent to this notion without requesting a demonstration, it is the demonstration through an experiment in the theatrical laboratory that interests Hervieu. His heroine declares that she would do as much for her mother as for her daughter. A friend denies her contention. What follows proves that he is right.

Sabine is devoted to her daughter whose health and reason are imperiled when her husband suffers financial reverses. In order to save Marie-Jeanne, Sabine begs her mother for a loan, and, being refused, attempts to steal the old lady's securities. She has declined a match for herself out of consideration for the girl, and she has even asked aid of the man she has jilted. Then, when a physician advises that she must go to the mountains for her daughter's health, and her mother insists upon coming too, Sabine yields to a terrible temptation. The physician has implied that the heart of old Madame Fontenais cannot endure such an altitude. It flashes upon Sabine that, should her mother die, she could then pass on the family property to Marie-Jeanne. Accordingly, she encourages Madame Fontenais to accompany her to the Engadine. But the daughter and her husband, on being offered flattering prospects overseas, will forsake Sabine who has done so much for them. Too late the old lady relents; what she can give them counts as nothing compared to what they now expect. So Sabine, deserted by her daughter, looks to her mother as an object of affection. Then the mother, as the physician had foreseen, suffers a heart attack and dies, leaving Sabine to exclaim, "For my daughter, I have killed my mother!" That, at a crisis, any woman would do precisely this, has been the assertion of Sabine's friend, the *raisonneur*, when the piece began. Since men are rationalists, it is left to a man to phrase the doctrine. Since women are instinctive, it is left to the daughter, the mother, and the grandmother to display instinct at work. The failure of the grandmother to respond to requests for aid from her daughter is due to the decline in her of the maternal instinct, which now reacts but slowly. The ingratitude of daughter to mother is illustrated by Marie-Jeanne's turning from Sabine just as Sabine has turned from Madame Fontenais. If the drama leave the heart a little cold, its geometrical construction appeals to the intellect.

Hervieu, indeed, is a modern classicist, intent upon perfection of form in demonstrating moral theorems. He is classical in advocating rational control in life as in art. He is classical in dealing with the universal and abstract. Like Ibsen, he is a deductive dramatist, beginning, not with a story, but with a proposition to be proved and exemplified. His characters are less vital than those of Ibsen, less rich, complex, and human; but his technique commands admiration.

Far more interesting and individual than Hervieu is the vicomte François de Curel. Born in Lorraine in 1854, he was trained in science, but read widely and led the life of an artistic amateur. Having written a novel which failed, he tried his pen at plays, and in 1891 sent to André Antoine three of them signed by three different names. All were accepted. Thus encouraged, de Curel has from time to time interrupted his life of gentlemanly leisure by composing dramas as the spirit moved and without much thought of a popular audience. In spite of his early affiliations with Antoine, his art is romantic rather than naturalistic in tendency and his last plays even dally with the supernatural. A genius of penetrating imagination and dark moods, he has invented unusual situations in which to place more unusual characters.

In his first important piece, *The Other Side of a Saint*, de Curel exhibits the struggle between passion and will in a woman for long years a saint, who nevertheless has earlier sought to murder her rival in love, and who, emerging from her convent, is tempted to visit upon that rival's daughter a resentment still unappeased. The nun would draw Christine from the world, yet, on hearing her speak of her dead father's last message of love, she relents. It is as though she had heard his voice from the tomb. The cup of joy that had been denied her she will encourage Christine to drink. Returning to the convent, she will continue to atone for her murderous attempt so long ago.

In *The Fossils*, a duke, living in a lonely castle in the Ardennes, has found consolation in a secret intrigue with a governess. She, who has yielded chiefly out of fear, has later loved his son to whom she bears a child. The fact that father and son are rivals emerges only when the two quarrel over the education of little Henri. "The child," cries the father, "is ours!" Thereupon the son, shocked at perceiving the truth, declares, "Then one of us must die." Already he is afflicted by consumption. Instead of remaining on the Riviera, whither he has come for his health, he will return to certain death in the bleak north. There he expires after having rendered the boy legitimate by marriage. Both father and son are the fossils of a vanishing aristocracy. The son, however, has foreseen a new aristocracy of service and character, in which his devoted sister and his wife shall rear this child. The play is dreamy, atmospheric, and imaginative, couched in long, poetic speeches that reveal the sufferings of fine-grained souls.

The over-subtle reactions of a neurasthenic pair furnish the théme in *Love Adorns*. One is a widow of wealth, the other is a poor self-doubter, too timid to ask for her hand. When the lady, thinking to bring him to the point of proposing, feigns the need of a husband in order to save her from disgrace, Charles is ready to act out the part expected of him, although he is already aware of her ruse. She, in turn, advises that he rehabilitate his honor, imperiled for her sake, through suicide. She never believes that he will follow her suggestion, nor does he, and yet it is just haunting enough to tease him into doing what often he had meditated. Dissatisfied with this play, which not unnaturally failed, its author twenty-one years later refashioned it completely as *The Dance before the Mirror*, telling again the story of a couple engaged in a game of pretence, each becoming a reflection of the other's desire. But again the public, though more indulgent than before, found the characters perverse and the psychology too difficult to fathom.

In *The Fair Guest* and *The Dancer* (*La Figurante*), feminine minds are explored by de Curel, the first play depicting the awakening of the maternal instinct in the breast of a mother, long absent from her daughters, and the second the resentment of one woman against another whose generosity in love is more maddening than would have been her egotism. With *The Lion's Share* and *The New Idol* de Curel considers the relations of capital and labor and the merits and defects of a devotion to medical science. In the former piece, an aristocrat seeks to atone for his unintentional slaying of a workingman by aiding the cause of the toilers. But he comes to doubt the integrity of his own motives and the possibility of bettering the condition of those he would assist. They cannot understand him, and he dies as the victim of their strike when they have set fire to the ancestral forest which he would keep inviolate. As for *The New Idol*, that title refers to science, a physician believing it to be his duty to sacrifice the individual in experiments calculated to save the many. He has inoculated with the virus of cancer a girl already doomed, as he believes, by tuberculosis. When unexpectedly she recovers from that malady, and learns that she must die as a result of the physician's experiment, she consoles him by accepting cheerfully for the sake of humanity the sacrifice he has imposed. Then, inspired by her faith and courage, he inoculates himself. His wife, who had grown to fear him, perceives at last his true nobility.

In *The Wild Girl* and *The Beat of the Wing*, de Curel lets his fancy stray to remote lands. A savage maiden, captured by hunters and confined in a barbarian's seraglio, is brought to Europe by the French councillor of the tribe and is taught the ways of civilization in a convent. Impressed at first by the new religion, she grows skeptical the more she learns, and is embittered when the man who had rescued her rejects her love. After all, her natural instincts cannot be more than veneered by this foreign culture, and she consents to return to her native land to marry a prince. Even her mother superior approves this course, hoping that through her some of the heathen may be converted. As a matter of fact, the alterations that have occurred within the heart of the wild girl duplicate those bound to occur in the race. Instinct is replaced by religion; then religion, as knowledge grows, is undermined by doubt; and finally doubt is replaced by instinct. In the long run, the return to nature is inevitable.

For one who puts off the restraints of civilization, however, the life of nature holds its dangers. So, in *The Beat of the Wing,* an explorer who has conquered fresh territory for French colonization, after being hailed at home as a hero, has returned to the tropics fortified in pride, believing himself authorized to deal despotically with an inferior race. But his abuse of power awakens such serious protests at home that an expedition is sent to arrest him. In defending himself, he fires upon his countrymen and his flag, and then, being captured by natives in revolt, is tortured and left in the jungle for dead. So mutilated that he can no longer be recognized, save by his brother, the traitor makes his way back to France to horrify that brother, who, being engaged in a political campaign, would deny relationship with one so notorious. The explorer's daughter, brought up in ignorance of her father's identity, and remembering only that her mother had pledged her to hate him, now learns the truth from her uncle, who would use her enmity against this dangerous apparition. But the girl unexpectedly sympathizes with the superman. He has merely striven for glory; he is to be admired rather than condemned. Even his brother, campaigning in a petty way for office, is imbued with this desire for glory, taking care, as he says, of his page in the history of France. In both these plays the exotic is merely suggested, the barbaric incidents being left to the imagination, and the actual scenes taking place at home amid familiar surroundings. So great, however, is de Curel's ability to make real a narrated happening that he loses nothing by this allusive technique.

At the outbreak of the War, de Curel was in Switzerland, and, being past the age of military service, he remained at Lucerne and continued writing. Among his later pieces, two reflect the War—*Inhuman Land*, depicting the conflict directly, and *The Quick and the Dead*, suggesting its after effects. The other plays develop various notions through improbable stories told with a freedom of technique that would have shocked Dumas *fils*. Here are *The Soul in Madness*, *The Comedy of Genius*, *The Intoxication of the Sage*, and *Mystical Storm*.

Least important is *The Intoxication of the Sage*, a curious piece in which the characters are only puppets to emit the author's ideas, their entrances and exits being artificially contrived. A girl, coming to visit her wealthy uncle at his country estate, is informed that she will forthwith inherit it all and that her professor of philosophy from Paris with whom she has fallen in love is about to arrive. Although he has not encouraged her hitherto, he is prompted to propose, admitting, however, that to marry her, now she is rich, may interfere with his studies as much as to marry her poor, his earlier fear. But a rustic baron, a stock-raising neighbor, wins Hortense away from the philosopher. The latter has been giving a beautiful course on the subject "Why do we love?" He has considered the answers to this question of each of the great philosophers without getting farther than Spinoza. To the baron such theorizing is absurd. We love, says he, in order that we may have children. When Hortense goes bathing in the forest, the philosopher withdraws discreetly, his eyes buried in a book. Not so the baron, who pursues the fleeing nymph, her beauties having been described to him by a spying peasant girl. Like de Curel, the baron is a mighty hunter, convinced that the loves of beasts and of men have much in common. He represents the intoxication of love, whereas the sage represents only the intoxication of ideas.

The comparison of human and animal behavior is developed more fully by de Curel in *The Soul in Madness*, which strikes out an amusing character contrast between a skeptical husband and his fundamentalist wife. Justin is occupied with hunting and speculating on evolution, and Blanche is concerned with her symptoms, her religion, and her housework. The niece of this couple, an actress, and her playwright admirer, come down from Paris on a love chase, the lady pretending to flee but leading him on. When at length she succumbs, she provokes the envy of her aunt, still susceptible in spite of her years and her illness. Blanche, indeed, in her attitude toward love, is as matter-of-fact as Juliet's nurse. She is a second Mrs. Shandy, unable to understand a word of her husband's theories. She dies of heart failure while reading an account of the wicked Messalina. She has always feared the skeleton kept in the former studio of her father, a painter. In a scene that externalizes her last delirium, we hear the skeleton talking to her. She had arranged to have the priest bury it, though he objected that it was only a composite affair, made up for commercial purposes of bones from different bodies. Those legs never filled the same pair of trousers, says the priest. But what matter? asks Justin, since each of us inherits features from different ancestors. Justin, indeed, is full of theories of the sort. In observing the conduct of deer during the mating season, he traces the love instinct from the time when it was only a blind attraction in a drop of protoplasm up to the point where in the human soul it can unchain magnificent storms of passion. So the rut of the beast becomes in man the rut of the soul, the soul in madness. But that madness is restrained and directed in the process of human natural selection by reason.

Here the serious and the grotesque are combined as in the last scenes of *The Awakening of Spring*, by Wedekind, and *Liliom*, by Molnár—a feature rare in French drama. There is humor when the dying Blanche learns from the skeleton that her soul is no longer in madness, no longer a cousin of the beast. Now she may enter her celestial Jerusalem an angel among angels. Yet how ironic that her last thoughts should have been, not of the chaste Lucrece, but of Messalina! After all, death alone can kill in us the love impulse.

De Curel's tendency to meddle with the supernatural is given fuller expression in *Mystical Storm*. Here, in the third act, a dead wife appears as a veritable ghost to reassure the husband who has doubted her fidelity. Already, in the first act, we have seen her returning home at night from a rendezvous with a lover, only to find herself locked out by her husband, come back unexpectedly from a journey. With the aid of a passing friend, she has slipped into the house through a ruse, but her exposure to a storm on the heels of a previous illness has resulted in her death. A year later, the husband is strangely agitated, believing that she is about to keep the promise she had made to reappear on the anniversary of her death. Another storm has washed away part of the cemetery, and Clotilde's coffin has been exposed and removed to a chapel, pending its reburial. While her husband is keeping vigil here before the anniversary mass, he is confronted by the specter of Clotilde in bridal attire. She reproaches him for having locked her out that night with a view to letting her suffer a drenching, a relapse, and possible death. But, as he insists that he meant no more than a jest, he sees her ghost transformed into something beautiful, and accepts her declaration of love for him and her assertion of innocence, in witness whereof she breaks a twig above her head and bids him examine it later as proof of her continued existence, and she also bids him interrogate his former rival. No sooner has the spectral Clotilde vanished than the rival appears and protests that, indeed, there was nothing between them. But, since three twigs instead of one are found to be broken, apparently by some passer-by, the skeptical friend of Clotilde, who had assisted her in deceiving her husband, remains unconvinced of the reality of the apparition. Robert, he believes, has merely seen and heard what his imagination desired and dictated. And the audience, it must be admitted, is left in doubt, like the skeptical physician, not of the reality of the apparition, but of the lady's freedom from guilt. Such, in fact, was the playwright's intention.

The power of subjective illusion figures, also, in *The Comedy of Genius,* an unfocused drama in eight scenes, covering many years and involving many characters. A youth, perceiving an actress in a window rehearsing a part, supposes that she is beckoning him in. Their acquaintance thus begun inspires him to become a dramatist and to make her his leading lady and his mistress. His conduct shocks his provincial parents and the sweetheart who had been expecting to marry him. He is perturbed, however, only because he believes that he can never write well until he has included paternity among his experiences. Accordingly, he prevails upon the daughter of a farmer upon his estate to give him a son. But this son grows up to become his rival in art. When the plays of the two are produced on the same day at the Comédie Française, and the father goes to the theater only after the stage is dark, it is to learn that his own piece has failed, and to behold in a vision such notable *dramatis personæ* from the past as Œdipus, Celimène, and Tartuffe. Don Juan, in particular, rallies him on having sought to enrich his genius by fathering a child, who now has defeated him. Genius, says Juan, comes only from God.

Thus inspired, Felix visits a Swiss monastery, and, learning from a monk that the most perfect of all dramatic performances is the mass, recognizes that his own failure has been caused by lack of such love for the world as the mass symbolizes. But his son consoles him by saying that the constant yearning of Felix to make the flowers of his soul blossom for the sake of future generations bears witness to his love of humanity. The piece would have been far better had it stopped with the vision in the theater. That scene in which the creations of past playwrights come to life reminds one of Pirandello's *Six Characters in Search of an Author*, but fails to follow out, as does Pirandello, the philosophic implications of the situation. The chief interest of de Curel's play lies in its autobiographical features. Felix, like de Curel, is condemned by the public as "a difficult author," who leaves cold all but the connoisseurs. "I amuse the intelligent, but I do not touch the heart," he laments. As if to prove the point, *The Comedy of Genius* had to be withdrawn for lack of patronage after only a few performances.

As for the two plays of de Curel which reflect the War, *The Quick and the Dead* is a weak endeavor to exhibit the relaxation of morals after the conflict. It shows the efforts of several to save from suicide an aristocrat, gallant in action, but dissolute in peace and grown disconsolate because he feels that he has caused the death of his fair cousin. She has shot herself as a result of their liaison and his refusal to marry her. Lacking the courage to take his own life at the tomb of the Unknown Soldier, as he had planned, he comes down to die in a family chapel of his country estate. But his salvation is assured by a little novice, who calls out his better nature after he has offended by trying to kiss her. She will withdraw from the religious life to marry and reform him. The characters are as empty as is the plot. Philippe is a flabby hero, a philanderer, who laments the contrast between heroic Paris and Paris after the War, debased by foreigners in quest of pleasure. Intent upon dying theatrically, he is readily restrained by his vision of Jesus raising Lazarus, and by the pleas of a social butterfly who pledges him to use no violence, and of the supposedly vibrant novice—"La Viveuse"—an inspiration to all who have known her as a nurse during the War. On the whole, this is a silly play.

Much better is *Inhuman Land,* which allows us to infer from one incident the brutalizing effect of war. The scene is Lorraine under German occupation. A Prussian princess, come to the front to seek her husband in high command, is quartered upon a French widow, whose son, a spy, chances to arrive from Paris that very day by airplane. Since the princess has already been shown his photograph by the proud mother, she recognizes him in spite of his assumption of a German identity. Between the two a battle of wits ensues, yet both love for the moment and even pass the night together more than amicably, each, however, prepared to slay the other should that other sleep. The novelty of the piece lies in its revelation of basic savagery uncovered by the War.

Here is Paul, who formerly could not endure the sight of a dog harming its quarry, grown insensible to suffering, plotting to kill the fine lady and actually killing without a qualm an inoffensive farmer whose clothes he would don. And here is the elegant princess, ready to give herself for the nonce to her enemy, the son of a peasant, yet equally ready to hand him over to be shot by her compatriots. Discovered signaling from the window, she herself is shot instead by Paul's quiet little mother, once so harmless. The Germans will execute her, of course, but Paul at least will have escaped to Paris, his mission of espionage fulfilled. Such is life in this inhuman territory, where morals and social conventions no longer exist. "Yes, we encounter in this perfidious domain," Paul has told the princess, "like vapors which by night glide over the meadows and melt and mingle in the dim rays of the moon." It is noteworthy that de Curel here evinces no chauvinism. His French folk are no better intrinsically than his Germans.

In general, it may be said of de Curel that, after meditating skeptically yet with tolerant humor upon the problems of life, he writes dramas of thought rather than of feeling. His reflective wisdom is superior to his dramaturgic faculty. Increasingly, he has departed from the technique of the well-made play, permitting his ideas to determine in each case the form he would use. Thus, although *Inhuman Land* observes the unities of time and place, *The Comedy of Genius* defies both, and the supernatural intrudes upon realism in *The Soul in Madness* and *Mystical Storm*. In the playwright's later work, sure of himself as a member of the Academy, he gives free rein to his fancy and his sense of the comic. Naturally drawn to portray unusual folk in novel situations, de Curel centers interest upon a few characters, individual rather than typical. He is no sensualist like Bataille and no mere theorist like Hervieu. Improbable and loose-jointed as are his plots, and diffuse as is often his dialogue, his plays are set apart by their vividness of conception and their poetic verity. They combine real and romantic elements in extraordinary fashion. Back of them you feel a unique personality.

CHAPTER XIII

REFORMERS

Fabre, Mirbeau, Brieux

FROM moralist to reformer the transition is easy. To discuss a question of ethics impartially, to exhibit a character confronted by the necessity of making a decision of conscience, is to prepare the way for urging through art some definite line of conduct. Certain playwrights have taken this step, moved thereto by the example of Augier, the younger Dumas, and Ibsen, and by the desire to benefit their fellow men through the useful theater. Why should the stage be restricted to amusement alone? ask the reformers. The drama is a potent medium for stirring the hearts and moving the wills of those who respond to its spell. Some there are who would isolate art from life, finding its *raison d'être* in the escape it affords from the actual. But in a time when the social conscience is stirring, it tends to criticize life and to appeal to those who have hitherto sought in music, pictures, or drama no more than a momentary diversion. Of the theater Dumas *fils* remarked in the generation that witnessed the birth of Brieux: "We are lost unless we hasten to place this great art at the service of important social reforms and the high hopes of the soul."

The chief exponent of the useful theater, not only in France, but throughout the world, is Eugène Brieux, born in 1858. A Parisian of the middle class, he practised journalism, and ventured upon the stage with a slight farce, *The Divorce Bureau*, written in collaboration with Gaston Salandri. Neither this nor a trifle in verse, *Bernard Palissy*, attracted attention.

Indeed, it was not until the early 'nineties, when Brieux submitted several plays to André Antoine for performance at the Théâtre Libre, that he began to be heard of. His realistic *Artists' Homes* was followed by *Duramé's Daughter, M. de Réboval,* and *Blanchette.* In these he speaks as a moralist and a reformer. Unlike the best dramatists, however, he is intent less upon a study of souls in conflict than upon specific evils and concrete remedies. *Blanchette,* his first marked success, furnishes a case in point, setting forth the misery entailed by educating children of the people beyond their station in life. When a country girl, put through a normal school in the expectation that she will become a teacher, fails to find a position, she must return to her father's inn to serve the customers. She resents this humiliating drudgery, quarrels with her disappointed parent, and, seeking an asylum with a schoolmate, falls a victim, as a result of her romantic training, to the latter's brother. In one version of the play, she goes to the bad. In another, she returns to assist her father with money procured from her lover. In still another, she pockets her shame as well as her pride, and marries a rustic who is ready to forgive her past. So Brieux points out a minor evil in the French social system. By implication he suggests that normal schools should refuse to accept more pupils than can be given teaching positions at graduation.

Corrupt domestic life provokes our reformer's indignation in *The Nest,* and the malign influence of political life, in *Cogwheels.* In the latter, a provincial manufacturer is drawn against his will into the political machine, until, shocked at his enforced dishonesty, he publishes a confession and retires from the dirty business. The defects of institutional philanthropy are considered in *The Benefactors,* and the danger of accepting the new scientific fatalism in *Evasion,* wherein Brieux endeavors to show that a wretched physical inheritance may be overcome by strength of character. In *Racing Results,* he points the disintegrating influence of a passion for gambling; and in *The Substitutes* reproves two classes of mothers, the peasants who forsake their babes in the country in order to hire out as nurses to the rich in town, and the urban ladies of fashion who prefer the social world to the suckling and rearing of offspring.

Divorce is opposed by Brieux, incidentally, in *The Three Daughters of M. Dupont*, along with the marriage of convenience, and directly in *Suzette* and in *The Fair Deserter*, written with Jean Sigaux, both pieces demonstrating the hardships inflicted on children by quarreling parents. The danger of remarriage after divorce is indicated in *The Cradle*, when a mother, confronting again her first husband at the bedside of their sick child, forgets that her second exists. The honor of the national character is upheld against detractors in *The Frenchwoman*, which warns against accepting as an accurate picture the descriptions of family corruption furnished by sensational novelists, and the reports of immorality taken home by foreigners who have disported themselves among the *cocottes* of the capital. The perils for the fair of industrial competition with men are detailed in *Woman On Her Own*, its heroine a girl obliged to earn her living, now as journalist on a feminist paper, and now as factory hand in a bookbindery. She must contend against the love advances of her first employer, and against the jealousy of men who resent her attempt to unionize women workers. To save her second master from a threatened strike, she withdraws, crying out upon the selfish sons of the well-to-do, who, by declining to marry women without a dowry, force them into industry and then fight them as economic rivals. A time will come, she declares, when her sex will be victorious in business, since women waste less than men in debauchery and for smaller pay work more loyally.

Four plays in particular may be considered here as illustrating the methods of Brieux in driving home his theses. In *The Three Daughters of M. Dupont*, the doctrine is least obvious. The conventional marriage for money arranged by parents without regard for the inclination or the spiritual welfare of children is bitterly assailed, two families being shown engaged in deceiving each other in order to win a social and commercial advantage. Julie and Antonin, once they are united, proceed to quarrel. As a husband, Antonin is overbearing and brutal; he refuses to give his wife the child for which she yearns, yet he treats her as a slave to his desires. When she defends herself with her teeth, he threatens divorce. But Julie learns from her sisters that marriage, however unhappy, is better than no marriage at all. For one sister has loved too much, and the other too little. The first, after betrayal, has lapsed into an ancient profession. The second, yearning for affection, has been jilted by the man on whom she had lavished her savings. Both the starved old maid and the surfeited courtesan warn Julie to stick to her husband. In any case, she is better off than they. Julie concludes that she has merely been too romantic in her conception of marriage. A pessimistic satire is this, confused in action, however effective in individual scenes, passing from mordant comedy to a climax almost tragic, and then relaxing tension in a pathetic conclusion.

More definitely militant in its attack upon a particular evil is *The Red Robe*, which arraigns the French system of criminal justice. Men of the law seek and can expect promotion only as they satisfy public opinion by securing convictions for crime. The attorney who is too honest to stoop to browbeating a peasant selected as convenient scapegoat when the author of a murder must be found, will remain without advancement; whereas the unscrupulous prosecutor, masterful in piling up false evidence against his victim, will rise despite his private profligacy. When threatened with exposure, he secures the protection of a member of the Chamber of Deputies, and can snap his fingers at the outraged feelings of the peasant's wife, a knowledge of whose past he has used to

compel her to testify to what has never happened. That finally
she stabs him gratifies the audience, stirred by this spectacle
to denounce the abuse of legal power in high places. Throughout, the cards are stacked at the playwright's pleasure, and
his victory over the minions of the law is no equal battle. His
piece, none the less, is capital melodrama, and its characters,
like those in *The Three Daughters of M. Dupont*, are fairly
vital.

What a contrast appears in the technique of *Maternity*
and *Damaged Goods!* No longer are the characters self-
directed. They are simply puppets set up and manipulated
by Brieux. Plot is also reduced to the lowest terms that doctrine may stand to the fore. In *Maternity* the folly of advocates of an increased birth rate in France is exposed. A sub-
prefect talks glibly of the importance of providing sufficient
human material to stock the garrisons and the factories. He
lives up to his theories at home, demanding a child each year
of his unhappy wife. Yet he is violent in condemning women
unfortunate enough to bear children out of wedlock. So he
sends from the house a servant girl who is to mother a father-
less child, and also his sister-in-law, whose lover declines to
repair the wrong done her since he hopes to marry a girl
with a dowry. When little Annette, grieved to think that she
has brought disgrace upon the family, consults a quack for
relief, she succumbs, and the remainder of the ill-made play
is given over to the trial for murder of the bungling Madame
Thomas. That lady argues adroitly that her services have
been tendered as much out of pity as for pay; and her testi-
mony and that of her other clients lends weight to the author's
belief that birth control is to be preferred to blind obedience
to instinct, that an increase in population is not in itself a
national asset, and that greater indulgence should be shown
the unmarried mother. A later version of the play makes clearer
the inconsistency of the prefect, since now he is shown to be a

dipsomaniac who should have been deterred from fathering more children lest they inherit his predisposition to drink.

In *Damaged Goods*, which achieved notoriety when forbidden by various censors, Brieux reached the limit of what the drama of propaganda can do. With a boldness equaled only by his lack of taste, he proceeded to discuss on the stage venereal disease in relation to marriage. His attitude, as becomes a modern social reformer, is scientific, not ethical. He declines to associate sin with sickness. He assumes that by presenting a particular case of distress caused by the marriage of an innocent girl to a victim of syphilis he can frighten parents into demanding for their children proper prophylaxis before marriage. An unfortunate youth, consulting a medical specialist, is warned against marrying until his health be fully restored. Having disobeyed this explicit advice, he becomes the father of an afflicted child, and again consults the specialist, who advises against permitting a servant to nurse the baby lest she and her own offspring be contaminated. When his wife, through the nurse, learns the truth, she threatens divorce; but the long-suffering specialist intervenes to dissuade her father from demanding such action, and bids him rather encourage legislation requiring a medical certificate for all about to marry. In theme this production owes a manifest debt to Ibsen's *Ghosts*, but characteristically Brieux is concerned only with hygiene, whereas Ibsen was intent upon questioning a social ideal outworn and displaying souls at a tragic crisis. For Brieux the spiritual implications of Ibsen mean nothing. His interest is focused on preventing the transmission of disease. Ibsen's is focused upon substituting a true for a false ideal of marriage.

Although Brieux will undoubtedly be remembered as a dramatic propagandist, it should be noted that he writes on occasion as one interested chiefly in the story he is telling. This is the case in the least doctrinal of his plays, *The June Bugs*, a charming comedy that might have been composed by Capus.

When a kind-hearted schoolmaster, who should have known better, has become involved in an intrigue that wearies and frightens him, he seeks escape from his charmer. But that little minx, making a feint at suicide, leaps into the Seine. Then the schoolmaster must ruefully hand to her rescuer the money he had saved for a holiday. Women, with their whims and theatric poses, are inescapable. Another attempt at writing without a thesis is *The Lavolette Family*. A philandering musician, always in debt, is caught by his wife making love to a pupil, whose husband has loaned him money. In spite of promising amendment, Lavolette is always engaged in these affairs. Yet he is a man of such honor that he protests when his daughter, to save the family from bankruptcy, marries the son of a rich manufacturer. The manufacturer, too, is scandalized, and Cécile's former lover, a violinist, attempts suicide. But all ends happily, for Cécile falls madly in love with her bridegroom and wins the admiration of his father and the approval of her own Bohemian family, thus saved from further financial stress. It is all poor stuff, this domestic comedy, the sort of thing much better done by others. Concerning it Brieux has said that he would show here his repentance for having afflicted the public with thesis dramas. But the writing of such thesis plays constitutes his métier. When he is otherwise occupied, his work is negligible.

In one piece at least—the spectacular *False Gods* (*La Foi*) —Brieux, writing in the abstract manner of Hervieu, has presented a general rather than a specific problem. What, he asks, is the place in life of religion? His answer is that of a tolerant skeptic. Religion may reveal no transcendental truth, yet, as an agency for regulating human conduct, it is essential. As Voltaire remarked, if there were no God, it would be necessary to invent one. To avoid offense, Brieux lays his scene in ancient Egypt. A rationalist deplores the fact that the woman he loves should insist upon offering herself as a sacrifice to Ammon. Thanks to a thunderbolt which appears to intervene at his behest to prevent her sacrifice, he is himself regarded as a god, but he declines the worship offered him and proclaims the folly of idolatry. By becoming a priest he may marry his sweetheart and save her from immolation, but he declines. In the mean time, the people, freed from fear of the supernatural, grow violent, and those deprived of religious hope curse him. But the priests capture the skeptic by showing him a throng of suppliants imploring some sign of forgiveness from Ammon. Out of pity he consents to wield the lever which inclines the head of the temple idol. Thus he relieves the distress of thousands only to discover that their submission has been secured merely to force them into fighting in Pharaoh's wars. When the repentant skeptic confesses the deceit he has practised, he is disbelieved by most. He beholds his sweetheart going to death exalted by her baseless faith, and is himself slain by a dwarf who had expected to be made tall by miracle. Here, then, is an effective parable to show that religion, however delusive, is subjectively necessary to man, and that each believer possesses the kind which he deserves.

In most of the other plays of Brieux, there remains at least a hint of a thesis. Thus in *Little Mistress* the dramatist reproves the owner of a fashion shop so ambitious that he cuts off his son who has fallen in love with a pretty employee, and drives them both to a watery death. Again, in *Simone*, Brieux seems to justify the punishment meted out by a husband to his unfaithful wife, permitting their daughter long afterwards to discover what has happened and forgive her father for his deed. In *Armature*, adapted from Hervieu's novel of the same name, he represents money as the magnetic circuit closer of society, but is more concerned with character study than with the social problem of wealth. In his delightful *Citizen in the Country* there may be a suspicion of self-satire, as though, having attempted to reform the world, he had found how futile were his efforts. Cocatrix, a Parisian who determines to reshape rustic life, is disliked for his pains. When, in discouragement, he would withdraw, the rustics are so relieved that they elect him to parliament, where they will expect him to do the impossible for their benefit giving to each his heart's desire, denouncing in one speech a standing army, arguing in another for the establishment of a fortification and garrison to improve local business.

The tendency to depart from sermonizing is apparent in *The Attorney* (*L'Avocat*), acted in English as *The Accused*, a dull drama of closely knit structure and interminable speeches, considering legal ethics without the melodramatic features of *The Red Robe*. A woman brought to trial for the murder of her husband is defended in court by a friend who, out of love for her, transgresses his professional code since he believes her to be really guilty. When she is acquitted, he learns that she had promised for the sake of family honor to keep silent regarding her husband's brutality, and that she had slain him only to protect the very man who has now protected her. We might suppose that, since her deed was humanly justified, she might give her hand in marriage to her savior, but Brieux, suffering from an attack of conscience, makes her bid him farewell. Like the *Loyalties* of Galsworthy, *The Attorney* is half detective play, half drama of ideas; but here the speeches, instead of being brief and crisp as with Galsworthy, are so extended as to recall the harangues of the old French stage, rhetoric stifling emotion.

A thesis is mildly to the fore in two other plays by Brieux, *Americans in France* and *The Child*. The former contrasts two national temperaments and traces steps in the achievement of a happy accord between them after the Armistice. An impoverished Frenchman is loath to lease part of his estate to a hustling Texan who would improve it according to modern methods. The Frenchman's son would marry an American girl and engage in medical practice in Chicago. The Frenchman's daughter resents his proposed withdrawal and his caring for a foreigner. At length, however, she learns to love the girl he loves, and he in turn learns that his duty lies at home. His sister will marry the genial Texan, and his conservative father will permit the Texan to develop the estate with American efficiency. Here Brieux indicates the matter-of-fact idealism of the Americans, their contempt for tradition, and their readiness to sacrifice personal culture in order to achieve practical results. As for the French, they are sentimental, bound by tradition, and opposed to a division of labor that would deprive their work of its character as art. Smith, the Texan, is superior to Bartlett, the Wyoming ranchman in *The Frenchwoman*. Although the story seems a bit manufactured, the doctrine is not forced. Neither France nor America is overpraised or over-blamed. Each is made intelligible to the other.

In *The Child* Brieux considers the problem of feminism from an angle somewhat different from that assumed in *Woman on Her Own*. The heroine at thirty is economically independent as an hydraulic engineer. But she yearns for some human attachment and specifically for a child. She believes that the time has come for women to assert their right to maternity without marriage. She has declined the proposal of a profiteer, but she gives herself to her cousin on the eve of his departure for Brazil. The members of her family are scandalized to learn that she is to become a mother. She proposes to go abroad and live her own life, but learns in the nick of time that her cousin, stricken in conscience, is returning from Brazil to marry her. After protesting that she will keep her freedom, she yields to family pressure. After all, custom is too strong. This brake upon progress—custom, routine—has long been personified by Pierrette's family under the name "Galaor." It is "Galaor" who forbids, in the name of tradition, your doing what you will. Hence the sub-title of the play, "Pierrette and Galaor."

But Brieux here fails to establish our belief in the love of Pierrette and Henri. He fails to make real to us the scene, merely narrated, of their duel of sex, in which **Pierrette**, having taunted Henri and roused his passion, must yield to force. Hers is therefore not a rational experiment like that of Grant Allen's heroine in his novel *The Woman Who Did.* On the other hand, Brieux has been at pains to render plausible Pierrette's loneliness. She is harried by an ailing mother, deprived of the care of her little niece, moved negatively by the spectacle of an eccentric old maid who dies unloved, and moved positively by the sight of one of her working women, unmarried but happy in her child. According to Pierrette, the War has broken the shackles of woman. No longer need she depend for a livelihood upon the earnings of some man. Is she happier? That is another question. Must she marry the father of her child? Yes, for the present, in most cases.

It has been the service of Brieux to turn the French theater from its monotonous preoccupation with what is frivolous and lightly immoral to the discussion of serious problems. He has made the stage his pulpit and lecture platform, saying frankly, "Had I lived in the seventeenth century I would have been a preacher, but now I write plays." If from the total work of Brieux no more than a few pieces are likely to survive, his name will endure as that of the most competent and distinguished exponent of the useful theater. He has sobered the frivolous, linked the stage with the times, and suggested to playwrights of the new generation fresh fields to conquer.

Brieux is but the leader in a school of reformers to which belong, among others, Emile Fabre and Octave Mirbeau. Fabre, avoiding the passional story of intrigue, has specialized on problems more or less public, particularly those that involve the control of big business and the exercise of political power. Above all, he stresses the part played by greed in the social complex. In *Money,* acted at the Théâtre Libre, he sets forth the sacrifice of happiness for gold. In *Gilded Stomachs* he exhibits "malefactors of great wealth" engaged in manipulating a paper corporation and destroying its one honest director who would oppose them. In *The Clay House* he considers property in its relation to second marriage, depicting the break-up of a family after bickerings over a dowry. In *The Conquerors* he deals with money as an instrument for furthering political ambition, showing a lawyer so eager to enter the ministry of state that he submits to blackmail and consents to raising a loan from the lover of his wife, yet suffers the loss of his son who falls in a duel with a scandalmonger. Thus the hero's political victory is barren and ironic. Even in a drama like *Timon of Athens*, consecrated to the classic misanthrope, Fabre is intent upon exhibiting the improper influence of wealth in determining the approval of others. So, too, in *Public Life*, wealth is involved in the struggle of an upright mayor to secure reëlection. Farrier, like his prototypes in the plays of Daudet, Sardou, Lemaître, and Brieux, is forced to resort to chicanery in order to hold and maintain political office. He rejoices at last in what he had earlier disapproved, intent no longer upon the public weal, but thinking, like his rivals, of his personal fortune alone. Inflexible, however, in honor is the hero of *The Property of Others*, who is suspected of madness when he proves too scrupulous to accept a fortune which he regards as the rightful property of another. In the work of Fabre, the spirit of satire is as potent as that of reform. He is pleased to point the shortcomings of his political characters with the emphasis of a Molière. This is the case in *The Locusts*, which depicts unscrupulous exploitation in the government of a French Asiatic colony, and in *A Great Bourgeois*, which portrays the rise and fall of a family whose acquisition of wealth makes for power. Here three stages in the industrial cycle are defined: that of the honest toiler who establishes the family fortune; that of the tyrannous plutocrat who extends it; and that of the weakling who destroys it through dissipation. In such plays, rather than in his comedies *Like All of Us*, *The Imperishable*, *The Mischief Makers*, and *César Birotteau* is Fabre distinctive. He yields an impression of strength, of burly enmity toward corruption, of downright vigor in recommending the curbing of abuses. His dramas, however, are cluttered with action; he accumulates external obstacles instead of emphasizing inner conflicts; and he is more intent upon building effective scenes than upon affording a consistent and careful study of character.

As for Octave Mirbeau, he shows somewhat the same animus in attacking the power of money in *The Bad Shepherds* and *Business is Business*. The former proves to be as scattering in construction and as crudely theatrical as are the works of Fabre. It aims to enlist sympathy for labor at war with capital, and concludes with a scene of stirring melodrama when the bride of an anarchist is shot by soldiers and dies upon his body. Much more subtle is *Business is Business*, a masterly portrayal of money-lust shriveling the soul of Isidore Lechat and ruining the lives of his wife and children. He is an incarnation of the worship of high finance. He believes that every one has his price, and that the single source of greatness for the individual, the institution, and the nation is money. Capitalist rule has made the people happy with plenty of work and cheap products. He may drive his daughter from home and learn of the tragic end of his gambling son in an automobile smash. But he turns from domestic afflictions to match wits against two business partners. In *The Fireside*, written with Thadée Natanson, Mirbeau directs his attack against a more specialized evil, a mismanaged philanthropy, with orphaned girls starved in a "home" quite after the fashion of a novel by Dickens. The patron of this charity, though a senator and academician, is a rogue seeking credit with the world while helping himself to the funds of the institution. Here the dramatist's tone is one of cynical raillery as it is in *The Portfolio*, which affords brief comment on the woes of the poor and the stupidity of the police.

The drama of reform has been cultivated, also, by those who have written plays of social criticism only on occasion. Thus,

REFORMERS

Donnay, de Curel, Guinon, and Lemaître have contributed their views concerning questions of class and caste. Ancey, Bernède, Lavedan, Rivollet, Loyson, Trarieux, Devore, and Fresquet have discussed matters of religion. Feminism has been debated pro and con by Brieux, Donnay, Bernstein, Madame Roi, and de Rothschild. Divorce has occupied the attention of Hervieu, Paul and Victor Margueritte, Hermant, Brieux, Devore, and Louise Dartigue; and politics have been considered by Claretie, Lemaître, Barrès, Brieux, and others. All sorts of reforms are recommended by these dramatists, from relaxing the rigors of criminal law, to pleading against the reparation of a woman's lost honor by marriage; from railing at mismanagement in children's reformatories, to demanding that physicians prevent the union of the unfit.

That most of these plays with a purpose will vanish along with the special causes they attempt to plead is only too evident. Overweighted with doctrine, they will sink in the stream and be lost. Yet, whenever the freightage is nicely proportioned to the art that conveys it, the drama of reform may come safely to port. That this so seldom happens proves the need of special skill in adventuring upon such a sea.

CHAPTER XIV

ROMANTICISTS

Claudel, Richepin, Maeterlinck, Rostand

AMONG the dramatists who have sought idealistic relief from the burdens of immediate actuality, several groups may be distinguished. Lovers of antiquity have endeavored to revive and to imitate the classic drama. Since 1888, when *Œdipus Rex* was produced in the old Roman theater at Orange, such performances have been popular in the South; but even earlier Leconte de Lisle, Charles Grandmougin, and Anatole France had led the way in reviving ancient legends upon the stage. Paul Mariéton, Alfred Poizat, Georges Rivollet, Achille Richard, Paul Souchon, and Joséphin Péladan are a few among those who have followed in the cultivation of classic drama. Necessarily, they have shown less originality than ingenuity in ringing the changes on old themes, although pieces like *Medea* by Catulle Mendès, *Polyphemus* by Albert Samain, and *The Fury* by Jules Bois, have won admirers.

As a parallel development, the religious drama—Christian and medieval—has enlisted the efforts of some of the same authors, notably Grandmougin and Poizat, and of specialists in this style like Maurice Bouchor, whose mysteries breathe the simple faith of childhood. Dramatists better known in a different field have also resorted to religious material, as witness *The Woman of Samaria*, by Rostand, *Mary Magdalene*, by Maeterlinck, and *The Martyrdom of Saint Sebastian*, by d'Annunzio; but the finest incarnation of the Catholic spirit of pious self-abnegation is to be seen in the dramas of Paul Claudel, diplomatist and mystic. Claudel is all on the side of the angels, of self-mastery and self-abnegation. Two of his plays in particular will survive as perfect expressions of a noble spirit, *The Hostage* and *The Tidings Brought to Mary*. The former, setting its scene in post-Revolutionary days, introduces as heroine the devoted Sygne into whose keeping is committed Napoleon's hostage, Pope Pius VII. She can save God's Vicar from death only by breaking her promise of marriage to a cousin worthy of her love and by uniting with a villain who has slain her parents and the monks of the abbey where she has sought refuge. When the outraged cousin would shoot her wicked husband, she steps between, protecting the latter at the price of her life. Thus Sygne is a more moral and religious Monna Vanna, her tragedy all the greater in that the motives of her sacrifice are never revealed to the man she loves. A less poetic sequel, *Bitter Bread*, at least provides gratifying retribution for the villain of the earlier play. History in both pieces is unhistorical, facts being manipulated to suit the playwright's idealistic purpose. So, too, in *The Tidings Brought to Mary*, Jeanne d'Arc moves in the background, and the heroine's father is doing pilgrimage to the Holy Land. But interest centers upon the character of Violaine, another injured martyr, contracting leprosy from the kiss of forgiveness she has given to the wretch who wounded her when she rebuffed him. Calumniated by a sister who would take her lover, Violaine withdraws to the forest, to live there a life of devotion, and long after to perform a miracle in raising from the dead her sister's child into which she breathes her own pure spirit. Only as she dies does the child's father, her former lover, learn the truth regarding her innocence and continued devotion. In these dreamy plays, the beauty of the moral substance is given beauty of form in free verse and cadenced prose.

Excursions from the present to the medieval, Biblical, and classical past have had their counterpart in the attempt of many other playwrights to revive the drama of Victor Hugo

219

or Théodore de Banville,—romanticism of the heroic or the fantastic stripe. The fairy fantasy and the light romantic play of de Musset have served as models for Maurice Bouchor, André Rivoire, and Miguel Zamacoïs. More serious has been the work of Edouard Grenier, Edmond Haraucourt, Albert du Bois, and Jean Aicard, who draw their subjects chiefly from legend. With Henri de Bornier, Paul Déroulède, Alexandre Parodi, and François Coppée, the inspiration of Hugo is prepotent, history furnishing a background for tragic conflicts. In the plays of Déroulède veiled allusions in the account of past events to matters contemporary reinforce a burning plea for patriotism. Most striking among the Hugoesque pieces are Coppée's *Severo Torelli* and *For the Crown*, and Catulle Mendès' *Queen Fiammette*. These are heroic in sentiment and complicated in intrigue, depending for their thrills upon the surprise, antithesis, concealments, eavesdroppings, and disguise so essential to the romantic theater. Mendès proves a better craftsman in *Scarron* and *Glatigny*, but relapses into melodrama in *The Virgin of Avila*. Representative, also, of the spectacular and sensuous vein is d'Annunzio's flamboyant drama in French verse, *The Pisan Woman*.

A talent distinctive among the romancers is Jean Richepin, who began his career as the singer of jaunty vagabonds. His versatility he exhibits by writing for the stage an adaptation of *Macbeth*; a pastoral comedy, *Towards Joy*; sentimental peasant comedies, *The Filibuster* and *Vagabond*; a musical comedy, *Mademoiselle Napoléon*; a lyrical fairy play, *Beauty in the Sleeping Wood*; and various melodramas, the rural *Bird Lime*, the military *Watch Dog*, the medieval *Truands*, and the early Roman *Fair Martyr*. He has further sponsored a French version of Sem Benelli's sensational *Supper of Pranks*, known in English as *The Jest*. He has dramatized both *Don Quixote* and, in *The Emerald Way*, a novel by Eugène Demolder with its scene laid in Holland. In his dramas of dark intrigue and violent villainy Richepin is less excellent than in his comedies.

These paint fanciful pictures of rustic life, introducing a prince who falls enamored of a countryman's daughter, or a sea wanderer who catches the fancy of a peasant girl half persuaded that he is her betrothed cousin long absent, or a jaunty tramper of the roads who loves a maid in passing and returns years afterwards to set straight what is wrong in her household before faring forth again as a beloved vagabond. Facile in his procedure, Richepin is as airy and nonchalant as his own Chemineau; he is a poet without profundity, but one to be cherished for his ability to charm.

Towering above the swarm of minor poets and romancers stand two—Maeterlinck and Rostand. Maurice Maeterlinck, the Belgian, may claim a place in the French theater from the language in which he writes and the welcome accorded to his plays by French readers and spectators. As time passes, his dramatic contribution tends to depreciate in value and significance; but, from the appearance of *Princess Maleine* in 1889 to that of *The Blue Bird* in 1908, his was a name to conjure with. Born at Ghent in 1862, Maeterlinck studied law at home, responded to the spell of the symbolist school in Paris, and, being summoned back to Belgium by the death of his father, began to write curious little "plays for marionettes." In these he gave imaginative interpretation to our secret fears and impulses. Something of the glamour of Arthurian romance mingles with the terror of the Elizabethan tragedy of blood in *Princess Maleine, Alladine and Palomides,* and *The Death of Tintagiles.* Here youthful innocence is outraged by crime: Maleine is strangled, and Tintagiles is poisoned behind locked doors by wicked queens; and Alladine and Palomides are shut within a subterranean vault by a mad king. Insanity, conspiracy, murder; a sense of impending doom to be averted by no human forethought or virtue; impressionistic backgrounds, dim yet pictorial; an atmosphere heavy with romance; a dialogue naïve and repetitious to the point of inanity: —such are the elements with which Maeterlinck contrives his peculiar effects. The story in *Princess Maleine* is delivered in broken scenes slightly related and never wrought out. Yet the murder of the heroine is accompanied by every theatric device likely to thrill—a crashing thunderstorm, a madman grinning in at a window, a senile king bungling his attempt to aid the villainous queen, a dog whining at the door, and nuns chanting the Miserere.

In other plays the approach of death is more quietly considered; in *Home* and *The Intruder* with admirable restraint and fair realism; in *The Seven Princesses* with decorative symbolism; and in *The Blind* with a philosophic symbolism that tempts yet teases the imagination. Death enters a family circle unseen in *The Intruder*, apprehended only by a blind grandsire, resisted in vain by others, who hope against hope, and by the husband of the dying mother who seeks to keep shut a door that opens of itself. Here again the dramatist uses adroitly every detail that can imply the coming of death, until the cry of the new-born child and a scurrying of feet in the adjacent sick-chamber relieve our nervous tension. Similar in craftsmanship but more tranquil and static is *Home*, with another grandsire already informed of the death by drowning of his granddaughter and obliged to bring the tidings to her family, seen happily ignorant in the lamplight behind barred windows. "They have shut the doors, and the windows have iron bars," says the old man. "They do not suspect that I hold here, two steps from their door, all their little happiness, like a sick bird, in my old hands which I do not dare to open."

The Seven Princesses is a leaf from a fairy tale, with its sleeping beauties reclining in decorative pattern on steps behind glass doors in a hall of marble. They are weary of waiting seven years for a prince who finally disembarks from a toy man-of-war and proceeds to enter the hall through a subterranean passage, only to find that she who lies in the midst is dead. Bit by bit, the audience has come to be sure of that fact and to share in the hesitation of a queen and a king who stand without, wishing yet dreading to waken the sleepers.

More purely sculpturesque is *The Blind*, with its six sightless men and six sightless women in a forest on either side of an ancient priest, their guide, revealed by degrees as having expired, leaving them lost and groping for help. False is their reliance placed, now upon the misty vision of faded asphodels just glimpsed by one who can see a little, and now upon instinct in a dog that can only lead them to the dead priest, and now upon the babbling of a mad woman deemed prophetic, and now upon the wailing of a child, the new generation, which must surely see something if it cries. Although the sound of footsteps comes among them, nothing is there, and it is futile for these helpless souls to ask for pity. Just as the expression of a mood, this piece is remarkably effective, and it gains when considered as symbolizing the blindness of each of us, for we also can truly say: "We have never seen each other. We ask and we reply; we live together; we are always together; but we know not what we are." More specifically, the symbolism has been thought to refer to gradations in the soul's emancipation from slavery to sense, and to our present failure to find guidance in religion.

Two longer dramas which vary the triangular plot are concerned with folk of the fairy-tale world inhabited by Tintagiles, Alladine, and Maleine. The first is *Pelléas and Mélisande*, a tenuous tragedy of the imagination transposing the story of Francesca da Rimini into the land of nowhere. Little Mélisande, found beside a fountain in the forest, and wed by the elderly Golaud, drifts into a dream-like intrigue with his half-brother Pelléas. Fate leads them on, innocent as they are, to a doom inevitable. The suspicions of Golaud deepen. He misses Mélisande's wedding ring that she has dropped in a pool while entranced by Pelléas. He sends her with Pelléas to seek it, aware of the lie that she has told as to the place of its loss. He comes upon them making love in the moonlight, Pelléas bathed in her hair. He later holds up to a window his child to spy upon them, and then, as they are taking a last farewell, he interposes, sword in hand. Pelléas is slain, and Mélisande expires after giving birth to a child. Throughout, the action is conveyed suggestively in many loose scenes, some of them symbolic. A complementary triangular play, less vague, is *Aglavaine and Sélysette*, wherein two women love the same man. Sélysette, the wife, is a gentle, self-effacing soul, who ultimately throws herself from a tower that her lord may enjoy felicity with the more assertive Aglavaine; but the rivals have known no enmity. Each has thought only of benefiting the other and the man beloved. The sentimentalism grows cloying here, and the movement is unduly slow.

From 1896 forward, Maeterlinck lived in France, either at Paris, or near Grasse in the South, or at Saint Wandrille, his reconstituted Benedictine abbey in Normandy. For some years his work was influenced by his talented wife, the actress Georgette Leblanc, from whom later he separated. A most striking change in style was exhibited in *Monna Vanna*, a firmly modeled study of Renaissance Italy, presenting, with the conventional technique of the older stage, two ethical problems. May a wife be justified in selling her honor to save a starving city? And may that wife, when the nobility of her motive is doubted by her husband, leave him for one who understands? Without becoming didactic, Maeterlinck propounds these questions and implies in both cases an affirmative answer. His story is admirably contrived, and to the clearly painted portraits of the three principal characters he adds a fourth, that of the garrulous but idealistic father of the husband, as one who fathoms the depths of the heroine's soul and upholds her decision. Vanna consents to rescue Pisa on the nefarious terms proposed by the enemy general, but when she goes to his tent he proves to be no villain. Instead, he is a romantic lover quite willing to forego the bargain he has driven. When, to save him from the treachery of the Florentines, Vanna brings

him home, her jealous lord insists that she has done so only
to wreak revenge upon him, and by sheer skepticism drives her
into the lover's arms. Now, for the first time with Maeterlinck,
character conquers fate, the folk are real, their motives are
fully analyzed, and their speeches are in the old rhetorical
tradition. The dilemma of the heroine is as ancient as a story
by Bandello and the plot of Shakespeare's *Measure for Measure*.
It precipitates the crisis in Sardou's *La Tosca*, in Stephen
Phillips' *Pietro of Siena*, and in Clemence Dane's *The Way
Things Happen*. But Maeterlinck's handling of the episode is
altogether the most interesting.

In spite of the stage success of *Monna Vanna*, its author
was not wholly weaned from his land of make-believe. In *Joyzelle* he produced once more a misty pastel. Patterned after
Shakespeare's *Tempest*, it altered and thinned the play, omitting its comic features, transposing the parts of Ferdinand
and Miranda, retaining Ariel, and turning Prospero into Merlin, a victim of fate rather than its master. Again the bargain
of honor is used by Merlin in order to test the heroine's love
for his son, and again, as in all the treatments of the theme
except Miss Dane's, the lady is exempted from paying the
price.

The same situation was reverted to later in Maeterlinck's
well-rounded Biblical play, *Mary Magdalene*, in which the
Magdalene's dilemma is precisely that of Vanna and Joyzelle.
A Roman tribune offers to save Jesus from execution provided
that the converted Magdalene yield him what before she would
have gladly given. But to consent now would belie all that the
Master has taught her. When she refuses, He smiles and passes
satisfied to His doom. The scene of the Magdalene's temptation
and victory in the room of the Last Supper amid the frightened disciples is one of the best in the dramatist's theater.

In the meantime, Maeterlinck had composed, in his more
imaginative manner, two librettos. The first, *Ariane and Bluebeard*, is touched with humor in its satire upon the adoring

wives of the fairy-tale hero, released by his sixth spouse, a new woman, yet loath to leave him. The second piece, *Sister Beatrice*, is a grave poetic rendering of the old legend of the nun who violates her vows for love, and, returning to the convent long after, discovers that, since her place has been taken by the Virgin, she may still die in the odor of sanctity. "Who sins for love sins not," says Maeterlinck with questionable ethics. An unacknowledged trifle, *The Miracle of Saint Anthony*, resembles nothing else from its author's pen and might even have been written by the Irishman Synge. It shows a family group scandalized when Saint Anthony offers to raise from the dead their rich relative. They would drive him away. As he resuscitates the corpse for a moment, they are horrified, but it drops back, to the satisfaction of the legacy hunters, and only a scrubwoman will believe that a miracle has occurred.

Most popular as a stage spectacle is Maeterlinck's *Blue Bird*, a fanciful allegory for children and about children, presenting the hunt for the blue bird of happiness by Mytyl and Tyltyl, and leading them through the realms of memory, night, the future, to a forest and a graveyard. Again and again the blue bird, almost within their grasp, proves elusive. But, when Tyltyl, returned, consents to give his pet dove to a sick girl, the dove turns blue, for happiness is to be found at home in an act of unselfish love. Yet, since it is something to be striven for rather than possessed, the bird flies away again. The girl's mother proves to be the good fairy of the vision whose gift of a magic diamond had enabled the children to pursue their quest, and the girl herself turns out to be Light, who had figured in the dream along with such story-book folk as Fire, Bread, Sugar, Milk, a faithful Dog, and a treacherous Cat. Fancy, poetry, humor, and bright scenic effects combine to make this a charming entertainment. A sequel, *The Betrothal*, was less successful, partly because its eugenic thesis lacked general appeal. Now Tyltyl, grown older, is seeking an ideal mate through regions fantastic, beckoned on by six who will later claim him as father, and guided by ancestors good and bad, until he awakens at home to discover in the girl to whom he had once given the bird the original of the Veiled Lady of his vision, his bride-to-be. In the mean time, the figure of Destiny, large at first, has dwindled from scene to scene, and is ultimately turned out, as love and character replace fate.

A later play, *The Power of the Dead*, develops an idea suggested in *The Blue Bird*, namely, that our ancestors live again only as we think of them. Here, however, Maeterlinck shapes the notion to read: "They are alive in us as we are alive in and through them. . . . The good that we do, it is they alone who do it, and when we act otherwise than they would have us, it is only then that they die in our souls and abandon us forever." A youth who has dissipated his fortune permits the death of a money-lender whom he owes. Thereupon, he beholds doors opening and shutting of their own accord, busts of his ancestors moved about, and the statue of his father driving him forth. Having struggled to escape detection, he is confronted by the necessity of confessing his deed, lest his sweetheart's brother be convicted for it on circumstantial evidence. Then he awakens to find his experience a dream, yet to have learned through that dream to be worthy of his ancestors. Apparently, it never occurs to the playwright that in us may live our evil ancestors as well as the virtuous. So the romanticists romanticize heredity. Rostand, in *L'Aiglon*, shows it to be poetically potent in determining the fate of Napoleon's son; Maeterlinck here and in *The Betrothal* makes of it something sentimentally potent only for good. Alas! if this were but true, how much trouble would moralists, sociologists, and criminologists be spared!

An excellent War play, *The Burgomaster of Stilemonde*, contrasts national ideals of self-assertion and self-abnegation with as little chauvinism as could be expected under the circumstances. When a German lieutenant is shot from ambush in an occupied Belgian village, and the gardener of the mayor is accused, the mayor insists upon taking his place. It is he who has been chosen as hostage for the good behaviour of his people, and he knows the gardener to be innocent. By the long arm of coincidence it happens that the mayor's son-in-law, a German youth whom he has trained here in horticulture, is to command the firing squad. Although he does his best to persuade his father-in-law to forego this sacrifice, the stubborn idealist will not budge. Then the Prussian major, who has thus tested his subordinate's loyalty, relieves him of the necessity of supervising the execution. But the execution proceeds none the less. What strange fellows are these Belgians with their talk of honor! Surely they must be mad. So, too, the young Prussian cannot understand his bride's repulsing him after she has heard the shots that slew her gallant father. Yet the enemy is not caricatured, and the mayor is not unduly exalted. He is even surprised to find that such a simple man should be called upon to play hero.

This drama and *Monna Vanna*, moving entirely within the realm of the actual, find a companion piece in *The Cloud that Lifted*, which depends less upon idea than upon the study of a morbid mind suffering from repression. A youth, in self-defence, shooting blindly, has slain the father of his sweetheart, who swears vengeance upon the unknown assassin. Only her friend, Tatiana, who loves him and is madly jealous, has witnessed the deed. Having advised him to conceal it, she herself reveals it to Sonia and threatens to inform upon him when he shall be brought face to face with a detective. But, at the critical moment, Tatiana, overcome by a sudden impulse of generosity, denies that she has ever seen him before. For her "the cloud has lifted." Withdrawing, she turns upon herself the pistol Sonia had intended to use against her, and completes her sacrifice by assuming Axel's guilt as she dies. "It was I," she murmurs, referring to the murder. "You are not to search farther." Here, with unwonted realism, Maeterlinck has indicated as background the political conflict between

Finns and Russians. But his interest centers in drawing the character of Tatiana. With her, as with the heroines of Benavente's *Passion Flower* and Pirandello's *Each in His Own Way*, hatred serves as a mask to love, and love as a mask to hatred, and it is only by degrees that we learn her true motives. Through the first act, she appears to be Sonia's guardian angel, her "harmless little sister"; in the second she weeps as if with contrition on being detected in intriguing against her friend; and only in the last act is she fully revealed as ready to destroy that friend and the man they both desire.

An English reviewer, lamenting the fact that Maeterlinck here bids fair to depart from his early style, remarks: "We are left with a sense of disappointment and pain, a sense we should experience if we were suddenly to discover that Burne-Jones, in his later years, drew the figures in fashion-plates, or that Watts was still alive and had been covering our lamp posts with aluminum paint." No doubt it is the earlier plays of Maeterlinck for which he will be chiefly remembered. In these, he developed a special technique for rendering through suggestion certain moods, and turned attention inward to those states of mind that are more important than external deeds. "I have grown to believe," he once wrote, "that an old man, seated in his armchair, . . . giving unconscious ear to all the eternal laws that reign about his house, interpreting without comprehending the silence of doors and windows and the quivering voice of the light, submitting with bent head to the presence of his soul and his destiny, . . . motionless as he is, does yet live in reality a deeper, more human, and more universal life than the lover who strangles his mistress, the captain who conquers in battle, or the husband who avenges his honor."

To the world in general, romanticism on the modern stage is best represented in France by Edmond Rostand, who combines humor and idealism in his lyrical plays. He was born in 1869 at Marseilles, attended the Lycée Stanislas in Paris, and studied law. In 1890 he published a volume of verse, *Les*

Musardises, and then turned to the theater, beginning as a disciple of de Banville and Hugo. After such ineffectual experiments as *The Red Glove* and *The Two Pierrots*, he presented at the Comédie Française a delightful trifle, *The Romancers*. This turns upon the self-importance in love of a couple whose fathers pretend to be enemies in order to foster the passion of the precious pair, and presently feign a reconciliation when the lady is saved by the youth from a bravo hired to threaten her. Since the lovers quarrel on finding that they have been but the puppets of their fathers, fresh complications arise, Percinet again saving Sylvette from the bravo. It is all light as thistledown, a dainty cobweb spun of filmy verse.

Less humorous and more sentimental is *The Princess Faraway*, which embroiders a fantastic legend of the troubadour Joffroy Rudel, enamored of a princess whom he has seen only in her picture, yet voyaging to Tripoli in a pirate galley to gaze upon her face ere he die. His friend, sent ashore to summon the lady to the ship, is smitten by her beauty and tempted to disloyalty. She too responds to Bertrand, until both, believing that Rudel has expired, are shocked into consciousness of sin, and hasten to the roadstead, where Rudel breathes his last in the lady's arms. Despite the scoffing of a realist merchant and a cynical physician, Rudel has finally attained his ideal. Although, humanly speaking, Bertrand might have married the lady after a proper period of mourning, he departs for the Crusades, and she withdraws to a nunnery. Again sentiment is to the fore in *The Woman of Samaria*, acted, as was the former play, by Sarah Bernhardt. Here Jesus, converting the woman at the well, scandalizes His disciples yet wins them over as they behold her bringing priests and soldiers to hear His message, delivered in flowing Alexandrines.

To judge from such merely agreeable beginnings, no one could have foreseen that Rostand, in the very year of this Biblical play, was destined to achieve a triumph with the rollicking *Cyrano de Bergerac*. All at once, his sentiment was tempered and brightened by humor of the liveliest, and his action and characters became robust. He found inspiration in the career of an actual soldier, philosopher, and man of letters, born in 1619, distinguished alike for his great nose, his feats of valor, and his discipleship in skepticism to Gassendi, Campanella, and Descartes. The historical Cyrano had written a comedy, *The Pedant Tricked*, and two brilliant fantastic fictions, *The Comic History of the States and Empires of the Moon* and its sequel *The States and Empires of the Sun*. As the latter two had contributed to Swift's *Gulliver's Travels*, so the comedy had provided Molière with a scene in his *Rogueries of Scapin*. It had been Cyrano's rôle to assist others without profiting himself, and Rostand was attracted by his unselfishness in love so at variance with his arrant egotism in other relations, as well as by his beauty of soul at variance with his grotesqueness of feature. Rostand, further, caught a hint as to this latter antithesis from an old farce by de Leuven, de Livry, and Lhérie, entitled *Roquelaure, or the Ugliest Man in France*. From such elements, by the transforming power of genius, he created an altogether original play. Cyrano loves his cousin Roxane, but, since his nose blinds her to the charms of his mind and personality, he will unselfishly aid her to defeat the scheming de Guiches and to secure for a husband the dull Christian whom she loves. Not only does he perform Christian's wooing, but, when the latter has fallen at the siege of Arras, he keeps up for Roxane's benefit the fiction of Christian's devotion and cleverness, and even when dying fourteen years later he declines to admit his own deep devotion lest he disillusion the lady. Laughter and tears alternate, as do the violently theatric and the delicately poetic. The improbabilities of the action are rendered temporarily credible, and all but the cynics are bound to rejoice in this liberal outpouring of wit, fancy, and sentiment. What matter if Cyrano die from the treacherous blow of an unseen enemy?

He has fought and triumphed over enemies more potent—hatred, hypocrisy, avarice. To the champions of common sense he may seem absurd; yet he holds sway over the hearts of all who are romantically inclined, since he unites so effectively the charms of d'Artagnan and Don Quixote.

In *The Eaglet* (*L'Aiglon*) Rostand is less spontaneous and more the consciously reflective craftsman engaged in developing a philosophic idea derived in part from *Hamlet* and in part from the preoccupation of the naturalists with heredity and environment as determining factors in the fate of the individual. Why not apply such conceptions to the Napoleonic legend? Why not exhibit the failure of the Eaglet, Napoleon's son, to measure up to the greatness of his father? The boy who inherits that father's ambition is the heir as well of Austrian frailty, through his foolish mother, the Archduchess Marie Louise. Detained at the Austrian court as a virtual prisoner, surrounded by spies in the service of Metternich, he contrives nevertheless to learn the history of his father's achievements through counter-conspirators and prepares by their aid to regain his lost throne. But, weak in body, and a noble coward through conscience, the Eaglet refuses to jeopardize a fair cousin who would render possible his escape. Already he has assented to Metternich's suggestion that he is unable to play the superman. In vain the romantic grenadier Flambeau has sought to awaken in him the soul of Napoleon. On the battlefield of Wagram, where Napoleon once fought, the youth beholds in a vision the spectral victims of his father's ambition demanding his atonement. Perceiving in his own malady such expiation for their sufferings, he succumbs to the inevitable. His tragedy is already complete. That he should die surrounded by the court in a sixth act of calculated pathos is but Rostand's concession to the sentimentalists.

Brilliant in its dramaturgy, a fabric cleverly wrought of materials historical, traditional, and imagined, *The Eaglet* somehow misses greatness. It is too obviously the result of ingenuity, a glorified melodrama bristling with coincidences, surprises, antitheses. Here the unexpected always happens, the principles of climax and contrast are exploited to the limit, and sincerity is sacrificed for the sake of theatrical effect. Yet one must recognize the capital stagecraft,—the use, for example, of such properties as the toy soldiers, Napoleon's three-cornered hat, and his cradle placed beside his death-bed, and of such scenes as the masquerading by Flambeau in his old grenadier's uniform, his pretense that the blood-stain on his breast is the ribbon of the Legion, the hero's confrontation of his grandfather, the Emperor, interrupted by Metternich, and his dashing the candelabrum into the mirror when Metternich has shown him there his Austrian features as evidence of his inherited weakness. In the Eaglet and in Flambeau the playwright's poetic imagination creates characters that live apart from the artificially devised episodes in which they figure.

A decade passed before Rostand gratified his admirers with another drama. This was his *tour de force, Chantecler,* in which the romantic trappings of the costume play are achieved by dressing human actors in the feathers and hide of the barnyard. Rostand, with the satire of the fabulist La Fontaine, thrust at Parisian high society through describing the antics of birds and beasts. More fundamentally, also, he was here smiling at the egotism of the individual who conceives that he is essential to the process of the universe, and at the desire of woman to absorb all of man's attention. Chantecler is devoted to his daily task of summoning the sun to rise. Without his eloquent cockcrow life would cease, he believes. What if the blackbirds scorn him, and the birds of night plot against him as their foe? What if the cynics, the snobs, the fops, and scoffers disdain his inelegant manners? At the guinea-fowl's five o'clock tea, he saves from a hovering hawk those who would snub him, conquers a treacherous cock set on to kill him with steel spurs, and wins the heart of the beautiful hen pheasant. Though she leads him away to the forest, he cannot forget his work. When the pheasant, to show him his futility, soothes him to slumber beneath her wing while the sun comes up of itself, Chantecler is daunted indeed. But so thorough an egotist must speedily recover. At least it is he who announces, if he does not create, the day. He will return to his farm and continue that task. The disconsolate pheasant, to save him from the gun of a hunter, flies before him, then is caught in a trap, and, awaiting death, hears afar Chantecler's *co-co-ri-co* as he returns to his work. At once selfish and unselfish, the pheasant is a very woman, jealous of her lover's interest in his business, yet content to die to make him happy. He is the modern man, exalted by faith in himself, absurdly conceited, performing a task of supererogation which he assumes to be essential. The piece is Aristophanic in its satire, scintillating in its witty and poetic verse which attains lyric heights and drops to local *argot* with exuberant facility. As played by Bernhardt and in America by Maude Adams, it piqued curiosity but failed to interest for long. It could appeal alone to the intelligentsia, and in production the actors were unduly cramped by their animal trappings.

Chantecler was followed by *The Sacred Wood*, an antique parody of no consequence, and by *The Last Night of Don Juan*, completed in 1911 but postponed in performance until 1922. In the mean time, the War had intervened, and Rostand had died at its close, after passing some years of ill health at his château in the South. His final play accords ideal treatment to the famous Spanish legend first popularized for the stage by Tirso de Molina.

As depicted by Rostand, Don Juan the libertine has committed Ethan Brand's unpardonable sin: he has hardened his heart to marble. Having slain the father of one of his long line of ladies, and challenged the statue of the dead man to dine with him, he is about to be consigned to hell by the animated statue and the Devil when his bravado secures him a reprieve for ten years. At the close of that decade we see him

proposing to celebrate his last night with a ball and one
more conquest, but interrupted by the Devil, who appears as
a puppet showman to make clear with jaunty humor that
Juan, in seeking to possess many women, has failed to capture
any. As the Devil conjures them all up, Juan cannot recognize
a single one, for he has never known their souls. "You have
seen nothing; you have known nothing; you have had nothing!" declares the Devil. When Juan boasts that at least he
has corrupted the ladies, they retort in Shavian wise that the
will to love was theirs, not his. He did not even please them,
and, least of all, was he free. He fled from one to another,
trying with each new love to make a rampart against an old
one. When he maintains that at least he has had no rivals, the
women cry: "Romeo! Tristan! Even when we loved you, it was
they who were our gods." "But," says he, "I have made you
suffer." At this remark, the Devil proves that they have sought
voluntarily to enjoy the luxury of grief. One only—the White
Ghost—has pitied him. She is the Ideal that was in each
woman if only he had tried to find it. At length, Juan perceives with chagrin that he has possessed nothing and created
nothing and will leave nothing to survive him. When, swaggering still, he offers to descend to the material hell of flame, he is
warned by the Devil that no such fate awaits him. He has made
of himself just a puppet instead of a vital self-determined
character. To all eternity he must remain the puppet Punch
in the marionette theater of the infernal Showman. "At least
I shall make the girls laugh," retorts the irrepressible Juan,
whereupon the one tear of the White Ghost is dried, and she
murmurs, as Juan is changed into a puppet, "What a pity!"

Thus Rostand transforms the villain voluptuary of Spanish
legend into a sentimental idealist, self-defeated. He is neither
the hardened rascal of Shadwell nor the shameless hypocrite
of Molière. Like Ibsen's Peer Gynt, to whom he owes much,
he has sought to be emperor of himself; yet he fails because
he refuses allegiance to any one cause or person. Allowed, like

Faust, a definite lease of life to use or abuse, he has wasted his time. Instead of the old braggadocio sensualist, punished from without by a claptrap statue, we have here an esthetic sentimentalist for whom the pursuit of the fair but symbolizes the pursuit of the ideal, yet a pursuit misconceived and accordingly futile.

As for Rostand, his fame will rest chiefly upon the delectable *Cyrano* which appeared at a fortunate moment, to refresh romantically a public wearied of naturalism. Charming, brilliant, adroit, Rostand stands apart as an individual figure somewhat less regarded to-day than at the turn of the century. He is an expert playwright, a graceful poet, and a noble idealist.

CHAPTER XV

Post-War Playwrights in France

Porché, Rolland, Pagnol and Nivoix, Raynal, Giraudoux,
Romains, Savoir, Sarment, J.-J. Bernard, Vildrac,
Lenormand

WITH the outbreak of the War in 1914 the French theater lost its hold upon the hearts of the people except
as affording relief from the great menace, or as suggesting,
through pieces that reflected the conflict, ideals of patriotism
to encourage national effort. Older plays that might seem to
bear upon the problem of the moment were revived, from
Erckmann-Chatrian's *Friend Fritz* and Sardou's *Fatherland*
and *Dora*, to the de Goncourts' *The Country in Danger* and
Bornier's *Daughter of Roland*. Popular upon the stage, also,
were more recent works dealing with the relations between
France and Germany, plays like *French Woman's Heart*, by
Bernède and Bruant; *Alsace*, by Leroux and Camille; *The
Oberlé Family*, by Bazin and Haraucourt; *To Serve*, by Lave-
dan; and *The Spy* (*La Flambée*) and *An Evening at the
Front*, by Kistemaeckers.

For such as sought forgetfulness in the theater, there were
performances of recognized masterpieces, from the classics of
Corneille and Racine to the major works of Hervieu and Rostand. The alliance with England stimulated the importation
of many British dramas. Of the few native pieces that were
new, half avoided reference to the struggle. Although, from
1915 onward, plays of the War increased, few were of permanent interest. For the most part, they were written rapidly
in order to catch attention by their appeal to the passions of
the time; and, however successful from this point of view, they

lacked enduring qualities. Better than the average were Bataille's *The Amazon*, Fonson's *La Kommandantur*, Frondaie's *Colette Baudoche*, d'Ambra's *Frontier*, Soulié's *1914-1937*, André Couvreur's *Higher than Love*, Marcel l'Herbier's *Child of Death*, Vernet and Delamarre's *Other Combat*, and Claude Farrère and Louis Népoty's *Vigil of Arms*. In the last, the wife of the captain of a cruiser sunk by a German submarine, wishing to save her husband on trial for the loss of his ship, must disclose the fact that she had been aboard concealed in the cabin of a lieutenant. Though she thus reveals her dishonor, her husband is acquitted and forgives. Some of the more eminent dramatists, like de Croisset, Maeterlinck, and Bernstein, endeavored to make the most of the crisis as an incentive to spiritual regeneration. Especially effective were Maeterlinck's *Burgomaster of Stilemonde*, Bernstein's *To the Heights*, Porché's *The Ruffians and Finette*, and Raynal's *The Tomb Beneath the Arc de Triomphe*.

Maeterlinck's piece, already discussed here, contrasts two ideals, efficient force and passive integrity. As for Henri Bernstein's *To the Heights* (*L'Elévation*), it derives significance from the fresh way in which it adapts to war conditions the old triangular plot. Suzanne, the young wife of a sober professor of medicine, has found happiness in her affair with a dashing officer. The professor suspects nothing until Suzanne's distress at the officer's departure for the front makes clear her infatuation. Then, having elicited her confession, he forgives, for the need of rallying to the national defense blots out all private wrongs and revenges. Together, husband and wife succor the wounded until word comes that the officer, dying at a distance, would speak with Suzanne. The husband, after a struggle with himself, bids her go. To the lover, stricken down, she offers to die. But he begs her to live for the sake of the cause. As he hears his fellow soldiers released from the hospital singing as they return to the trenches, he declares that the War, however horrible, has lifted men out of their selfishness. "It has raised them to spiritual heights, and we who have found our love in this world calamity, we must be worthy of it." The mood of the piece is more in keeping with the time of its writing—the year before the Armistice—than with that of the subsequent period of disillusion. Although Bernstein be an expert playwright rather than a moralist, here for once he has struck a deeper note.

As for François Porché's symbolic play, *The Ruffians and Finette*, it suggests obvious war parallels in narrating the story of a queen whose generosity is abused by certain ruffians. The Queen is France; the Ruffians are the Germans, who would substitute for culture their *Kultur*, first by peaceful penetration, then by blood and iron. They have succeeded in providing her with a steward intent upon preventing her opening the dikes to repel their invasion. She regrets that she had not listened to the warnings of the older generation who once before (presumably in 1870) had suffered from the Ruffians. Now she must seek refuge in her palace from the plotting of their marshal. But her subjects open the sluices in her defence, and her faithful architect—the National Destiny—will wed her, and together they will inaugurate a new era. Although during war time such a drama could find an echo in patriotic bosoms, it is to-day of interest chiefly as an example of a rare stage species—political allegory. Such allegory Porché endeavored to continue in *The Girl With the Rosy Cheeks*, suggesting reforms to be made after the War by an energetic heroine who marries the prince of a land of pale-faced conventional folk.

Pacifism and internationalism had been the notes sounded by Romain Rolland long before 1914. A professor of art at the Sorbonne, he had published studies of opera and Italian painting, and biographies of various painters and musicians and of Tolstoy, whose plea for art as a socializing function he sought to apply to drama in a critical volume, *The Theater of the People*. Although best known as a novelist, thanks to his epic

Jean-Christophe, Rolland has written a series of chronicle plays dealing with the era of the Revolution. Here belong *The Wolves, The Triumph of Reason, Danton,* and *The Fourteenth of July.* The last two have found enthusiastic reception in post-War Germany, Rolland having always manifested an affection for the Germans which they have been glad to reciprocate. His own countrymen he alienated by his essays, *Above the Conflict,* issued from Geneva where he remained in philosophic safety while the fighting continued. Since the War he has written novels and pamphlets in the same vein and a pacifist play *Liluli,* and still other dramas connected with the Revolutionary cycle,—*Shooting Stars (Les Léonides), The Game of Love and Death,* and *Palm Sunday.* The last, which serves as a prologue to all the others, harks back to the days of Rousseau and the slaying of the son of a Bourbon prince by a peasant whose daughter he has seduced. These dramas are propagandist in idea and old-fashioned in technique, the author's spokesman indulging in long flamboyant speeches. Thus a count announces his plan to seek refuge in America. "There are still free horizons over there. The earth and men's thoughts are new; they do not bear the weight of the bloody centuries of Europe. There one stands face to face with Nature, like Adam in the dawn of the world. There we shall try to found anew a race who will lay their claims to nobility, not on the past, but on the future." It is in such Shelleyan sentimental rhetoric that Rolland delights. His characters exist to debate, not as a result of anything happening within them during the course of the play, but because through them sounds their master's voice.

Very different in quality is the pacifism of such a piece as *Merchants of Glory,* by Marcel Pagnol and Paul Nivoix. Here are satirized the profiteers who capitalize the heroism of the fallen. A father about whose son has grown a legend of his having died in driving back single-handed two battalions of Germans is far from pleased when a decade later that son turns up alive. For the father is running for the Chamber of Deputies on the strength of the son's reputation, and the latter's wife is happily remarried. Although the returned sergeant consents to keep out of the way until the election is over, he later demands to be recognized, and then is prevailed upon to remain dead for the sake of others. He will assume a different identity and serve as secretary to his father, now a cabinet minister. In each act has appeared a portrait of the heroic sergeant, each portrait larger and more idealized than its predecessor. At the close of the play all bow in reverence before one that is truly colossal, unaware of the fact that the humble original stands among them. When he is rebuked for failing to doff his hat like the rest, he murmurs: "Excuse me! . . . my emotion! . . . I knew him well." As a contrast to the father whose career has been founded upon exploiting a war-lie is that other father broken by the loss of his son in battle, declining the pension offered him and fulminating against the whole bad business of war, with its propaganda of nationalism, preparedness, and hate toward the hereditary enemy. Pagnol is still better known through his comedies, *Marius* and *Topaze*, the former celebrating a bartender of Marseilles kept from seeing the world by love of a girl at home, and the latter depicting the progress of a schoolmaster from simplicity to self-interested sophistication.

One of the best of War plays composed since the Armistice is that of Paul Raynal, author of such delicate psychological pieces as *The Master of his Heart*, *To the Sun of Instinct*, *La Francerie*, and *The Apotheosis of Life*. Raynal's *The Tomb Beneath the Arc de Triomphe* has been warmly welcomed even in Germany. Dedicated to the French Unknown Soldier, it professes to give a last chapter in his career, and to indicate the sorrow involved in every victory. By implication it assails war and those who glory in it at home. Here a tenuous story is upheld through three acts by only three characters, their speeches either unduly long or else spoken line by line in rapid give and take. A soldier, appearing unexpectedly to his father and his sweetheart, reveals to them bit by bit that he must return to the front in four hours since he has volunteered to undertake a mission certain to prove fatal. Then, since there is no time for ceremonials, the lovers withdraw and sink into each other's arms. When presently the father of the soldier discovers what has happened and reproaches him for having taken advantage of the girl, the youth retorts, accusing him of jealousy. He would retain for himself the girl's devotion. He can safely glory in the War since age renders him exempt from conscription. As the two engage in a wordy duel, the girl interposes and effects their reconciliation, after which the youth departs to die. Here the very brevity of life enhances its value, and its flower is love—a love to be plucked even in the shadow of death. To the girl, the soldier is brother, husband, child, the sum of all that is worthy of adoration. In yielding to him she feels a sacrificial thrill. What signify laws and institutions on the edge of the abyss? Especially vigorous is the portrayal of the resentment of youth against selfish age. What do these parents who have subsisted quietly for two thirds of a century know of war? War, but for the romance in which it has been draped by poets, is terrible and absurd. Yet those who die in the struggle may perhaps take war with them into the grave. May not war, like human sacrifice and slavery, be abolished? There is nothing of propaganda in Raynal's play. The ideas are kept subordinate to emotional situations rendered with rare beauty and restraint.

A different use of the War is made in *Siegfried* by Jean Giraudoux, a drama in four acts drawn from the author's novel *Siegfried and the Limousin*. Here the conflict lies in the background. A French soldier, rescued from death by a German woman but suffering amnesia as the result of a wound, recovers all his powers save memory and develops a German personality. Improbably enough, within seven years, his freshly acquired talents enable him to become minister in the new

German state, while his French identity remains unsuspected by others or himself. Then, by degrees, he is brought back to a recollection of his French self through the plotting of a German revolutionist, who unravels his past and finally summons his former fiancée, a French girl, to confront him. At the sight of Geneviève, Siegfried's sleeping memories awaken. Again he is Jacques Forestier. But what shall he do? Shall he remain to rule the German state or return to France, despite the pleading of his loyal generals, to resume his place as a private citizen, a mere man of letters? In the mean time, Zelten, the schemer, has been seized and sent into exile. The power of the minister will therefore be secure. But, born a Frenchman, he resolves to remain a Frenchman. So, having begged the German generals to conceal what has become of him, he crosses the frontier. The play is characteristic of the new spirit in its tolerant attitude toward the former enemy and in its study of double personality.

The trend toward fantasy may be seen in the satirical burlesques of Jules Romains and Alfred Savoir and in the Pirandellian analyses of personality and madness of Jean Sarment. In such pieces as *Dr. Knock* and *M. Trouhadec Seized by Dissipation* and *The Marriage of le Trouhadec*, the gaiety of Romains knows no bounds. He distorts reality to poke fun at it, showing Dr. Knock gloating over having put a whole village to bed and taught its citizens to employ rectal thermometers all at a given moment with the precision of soldiers engaged in some military evolution. He presents Le Trouhadec, the comic geographer and politician, drilling his constituents to repeat in chorus, "We are the honest folk," and to say over and over with increasing tempo the irresistible catch phrases, "Progress in order and peace in dignity." Similarly, Alfred Savoir, in *The Tamer, or English as it is Eaten*, waxes merry concerning the ridiculous contrast between a brutal lion tamer who believes in absolute discipline and a philosophic Englishman who upholds the freedom of the will. It is the lion tamer whose tyranny wins the circus lady they both love, and the philosopher who is eaten by the animals he pities. In vain he has followed about the show expecting the tamer to be killed by his angry beasts. Now his son will take up the father's task, still hoping for the tamer's downfall, but himself destined some day to be eaten like his father.

Fantasy with its basis in psychology is the forte of Jean Sarment, a pupil of Pirandello, who pricks the illusions of life with a bitter smile. Like his master, he is always asking what is pose and what is authentic personality, and how far we are determined by what others think and expect of us. In *The Pasteboard Crown*, for example, a prince, endeavoring to become what an actress believes him to be, departs in conduct from his inner self. Because she insists upon regarding him as a commoner merely masquerading as a noble in stage properties, he assumes the rôle. She thinks him to be but jesting when he expresses his grief at the reported death of the king, his father, or asserts his knowledge of the whereabouts of the missing heir to the throne. She laughs at his protestations of love in his own person, yet responds when he has her brought to his kingdom and pays court to her as a comedy clown. But that response affords him no satisfaction since her affection is bestowed upon his mocking rather than his kingly self. In short, to please her, he has created a rival personality of which he becomes jealous. He can be rid of this other self only by sending the lady away.

The question of where sanity stops and madness begins renders fantastic *The Shadow Fisher* in which the "shadows" referred to are a species of trout angled for by a harmless madman. He has lost his mental balance on being jilted in love. His mother, hoping that he may be cured by again meeting the girl, brings her home on a visit. Though the youth succumbs, he supposes her to be a different lady, and when the past gradually revives and he recalls her identity, he is again confused by the malice of his brother. This brother, wish-

ing the girl for himself, assures the invalid that she is merely
a second person, a substitute for the beloved original, hired
by his mother to play the part of the first. That explanation
the invalid is disposed to accept since his present fancy is so
much more generous and tender than the first had been. Is the
object of his affections a new flame or is she the old? And is
he sane or mad? Really, of course, he is sane, and yet, restored to reason, he is distressed, whereas when a "shadow
fisher" he had been happy. Since it is better to be mad than
rational, and better to die than to be mad, he dies. Resemblances here to the ideas and situations in Pirandello's *Henry
IV* and *Right You Are* (*If You Think So*) are only too
obvious.

By contrast, in *The Marriage of Hamlet*, Sarment implies
that the serene life which we all profess to desire would not be
so gratifying as the life of tragic excitement which so many
deplore. The tragic hero who complains of his lot would not
be pleased to settle down to domestic bliss. Let Hamlet, his
friends and his foes, live again, and let him be given no
grounds for melancholy,—will he then be cheerful? By no
means! For Hamlet in his character is incurably romantic, and
though, with no father to avenge, he may wed Ophelia, he will
tire of her quickly, noting defects in her person, and shuddering at the prospect of years of placid love-making ahead.
When, for his relief, a ghost is devised to set him doing a
burlesque of the good old story, a servant maid takes the part
of the Shakespearean Ophelia, and her father proves a sturdy
fellow who declines to be stabbed. As for the real Ophelia left
at home, instead of losing her mind, she casts in her lot with
a captain, while Polonius turns justice of the peace. This scintillant parody is introduced by a Faustian Prologue in which
Abraham explains to God the Father that after a lapse of
years three characters out of Shakespeare's masterpiece are
still awaiting judgment, certain that, if their lives could be
relived, they would act very differently. Polonius would eschew

politics; Ophelia would serve as Hamlet's devoted cook; and Hamlet would forget his royal parent's fate. Yes, says Abraham; knowing what they know now, they will live like saints. Although the Almighty is skeptical, He agrees to give the three another chance, saying: "We shall see, Abraham. You will lean out of the golden windows. I will offer you a spectacle. . . . Who knows if I too have not my hours of sly mischief?" Perhaps Barrie's *Dear Brutus* may have afforded just a hint for the central idea of this play. In any case, something of Barrie's fondness for fantasy colors all the pieces of Sarment, who rejoices in setting off against a background of reality his droll Quixotic idealists. The title of one of his dramas—*I Am Too Great for Myself*—might well be the motto of all.

It was the tradition of the Comédie Française and the disinclination of Frenchmen to import foreign novelties that kept the Parisian theater fairly conservative in technique and methods of production up to the War. While Germany and Russia were indulging in a rich variety of experiments, France had looked mainly to her classics, to her well-made plays, to many an escape from reality in the romantic style, and to an even greater number of pieces fostered by Antoine and his group. Antoine, indeed, had been a reformer of stagecraft and drama, potent in his influence, and Paul Fort, Lugné-Poë, and Jacques Copeau had proved fairly adventurous, the first with his Théâtre d'Art, the second with his Théâtre de l'Œuvre, and the third with his Théâtre du Vieux Colombier., But it was only after the War that the French stage advanced its methods up to those already employed in Germany and Russia. And this transformation was effected largely through the efforts of such producers as Charles Dullin, Georges Pitoëff, and Gaston Baty. The drift from literalism in production has corresponded to the drift from naturalism in the plays themselves. Firmin Gémier at the Odéon has been sympathetic to the new movement in both respects. Older play-

wrights like de Curel have not hesitated to resort to
natural; and of the serious newer dramatists, Je
Bernard and Henri-René Lenormand have sough
themes and methods of presentation hitherto unus
has developed the so-called play of silence, and Leno......
developed the Freudian play of instinct. The achievement of
both deserves special attention.

Jean-Jacques, the son of Tristan Bernard, fecund writer of
lively farces, is the complete antithesis of his father, composing subtle dramas which avoid both action and rhetoric, and
reducing plot and dialogue to their lowest terms. The word, he
declares, is only a weak instrument for what we seek to express.
Its value is that of a violin string in repose. But with it what
resonances are possible! And the implications of the silences
between words may be eloquent. Such silences Maeterlinck had
stressed, and a later dramatist, Denys Amiel, in the preface
to his printed plays, had followed Maeterlinck in commenting
on the fact that beneath apparent calm may lie poignant
depths, and that most lives are made up of impulses, thoughts,
and feelings that fail to eventuate in speech. Bernard enunciates the same doctrine. "The theater is above all the art of
the unexpressed. It is less by replies than by the shock of
replies that the deepest sentiments reveal themselves. Beneath
the heard dialogue is an underlying dialogue to be rendered
sensible. The theater has no worse enemy than literature, for
literature expresses what should be merely suggested. . . . A
sentiment commented on loses force. The logic of the theater
will not admit any sentiments that the situation does not impose. And if the situation imposes them, there is no need of
expressing them. That is why less is said by a well-rounded
poetic couplet than by some apparently casual remark."

Yet Bernard does not overwork this doctrine of silence. He
simply advocates the minimizing of talk, and so arranges his
plays that the crises are prepared for beforehand to deliver
themselves through gesture, facial expression, or a few mono-

ables. The situations he selects are those to be conveyed most quietly. Such is the case in his two early plays, *The Fire Slow to Rekindle* and *Martine*. In the former, the relations of husband and wife are set forth with perfect delicacy. The husband, a schoolmaster, long absent at the front, returns after the Armistice to learn that an American officer billeted upon Blanche has departed only that day. As his jealousy grows, fed by trifles, it divides him more and more from his wife who had kept her loyalty intact for four years. He has heard a dying comrade confess to having been the secret lover of Blanche's best friend. May not Blanche as well have had and kept such a secret? These doubts render Blanche so unhappy that at length she is ready to throw in her lot with the American and warns her husband of her design. When he threatens to restrain her by force, she dissuades him by asking what sort of life they would lead together should she yield against her will. As her father-in-law describes the loneliness from which she has suffered while awaiting André's return, the latter is touched, and she hesitates as she pictures him left equally desolate. "You will live here?" she asks. "You will spend your Sundays alone among these furnishings that have witnessed our love?"

"Be merciful!" he pleads.

"But I, too, I have known this loneliness. It is terrible," she admits. "How can I go?" So pity restrains her and the fire that was hard to rekindle will burn again.

In *Martine*, the conclusion is less cheerful, but the dramatist's methods are the same. Another soldier, at the end of the War, seeking in a village the house of his grandmother, is guided thither by a peasant girl who lives next door. He and she have met under an apple tree in the fields and fallen promptly in love. But a lady of culture to whom the soldier had earlier been attentive reappears and wins him for a husband. The inexpressive Martine utters no protest. Awkwardly she stands by as the couple embrace after separation. Bash-

fully she listens when the other woman speaks of her hope of
an heir. Mutely she sees the two leave for Paris. Months later,
when Martine has been forced to marry a rustic admirer, her
soldier comes down to the funeral of his grandmother. "Are
you happy, Martine?" he asks. "Do you ever recall those
hours together?" Silent at first, she is finally goaded into
speech. "What is the use of recalling? Why say all this to me
now? Is it not enough what you have done to me?" That simple
protest reveals the wound in the peasant girl's heart. No
sooner has her soldier taken his leave than her husband remarks that the grandmother's house next door has just been
sold to a stranger. So, even the scene of her little romance
will be taken from her.

To discover, in matters slight as these, emotional depths is
the aim of Bernard, an aim that determines his choice of subject and treatment in every play. In none is there any stir of
action. How little happens in *The Secret of Arvers*, or *The
Springtime of Others*, or *Invitation to Travel!* The first is
just a single scene depicting with the lightest touch the unre-
quited love of a minor poet for the daughter of a famous man,
Charles Nodier. When she asks that the poet write in her
album, he inscribes there a sonnet declaring his passion. Then
he waits for her to read it aloud. But her mind is wandering,
and she recites the sonnet brokenly, line by line, without thinking, and admitting a hundred interruptions. As the poet withdraws disheartened, she starts humming some of his phrases.
"What are you singing?" asks her father. "I? singing!" she
exclaims in surprise.

Similar restraint is to the fore in *The Springtime of Others*,
which, like Donnay's *Other Danger*, shows a woman discovering a rival in her daughter. Only here the mother is scarcely
aware of her motives at first. While idling among the Italian
lakes she has been approached by a man whose attentions she
supposed to be designed for herself. He had come, however,
to ask her permission to pay court to her daughter. A year

later, when the young people have married, she insists upon sharing their lives, objecting to their calling her "Mamma," and declaring that they three shall be comrades together. Her inability to leave them alone arises from an unrecognized jealousy which makes her interpose no end of obstacles between them and leads even to her suggesting that she carry off her daughter to Spain.

"But do you hate Maurice?" asks the puzzled daughter. "If not, what then?" In the silence that follows the question, the two women face each other like enemies, until the elder steps back horrified. For the first time she sees herself truly. Yes, she has been in love with her daughter's husband. She will beat a hasty retreat.

Less tense is the situation in Bernard's *Invitation to Travel*, its heroine a romantic wife dreaming of a youth who has gone to the Argentine. In leaving, he had given her a fan and a volume of Baudelaire, things she professes to scorn, thus screening from herself her real liking for the donor. She may tear up his photograph, yet his image is impressed upon her heart. Why is it that in teaching her little boy his geography lesson, she dwells so poetically upon the Argentine? Why is it that she plays on the piano the traveler's favorite piece, Duparc's *L'Invitation au Voyage*? On learning that Philippe has returned, she is all of a flutter and contrives to meet him. In the older drama, the scene of her reunion would have been regarded as a sure *scène à faire*, but here it is merely reported. In the last act, the romantic wife has come home disillusioned. Her idol has proved to be only a bore. He would talk of nothing but the output of his Argentine factory and his eminence as vice-president of the Chamber of Commerce. Indeed, he was much less alluring than the husband she regarded as so methodical. After putting the fan and the Baudelaire aside, she sits down to play that husband's favorite nocturne while he stoops to kiss her hair.

More original in conception are *The Soul in Distress* and

Denise Marette. In the former a married woman yearns for
her alter ego, that other soul which, according to the Platonic
philosophy, was divided from hers at birth and goes seeking
reunion with it. But though she meets her affinity now and
again, they scarcely speak. Once, having interrupted a journey
in response to an irresistible impulse, she catches sight of him
leaving her hotel, and again at a pond in the Tuilleries where
he has just quarreled with a mistress and she has debated following a drug addict to his rooms, she touches the hand of her
alter ego when together they rush to save a child from falling
into the water. Years later, still failing to find satisfaction
either in dissipation or in hospital service, she is tempted to
leave her husband, yet begs him to prevent her doing so, and
adds, "I have such need of love"; to which he retorts, "But
not from me." Therein lies her difficulty. And even now her
old yearning reawakens. She feels her other self to be near.
As, obeying her impulse, she opens a door, she beholds him
lying dead, frozen on the threshold in his abortive effort to
reach her. So in life we struggle in vain to find those with
whom alone our happiness lies. But the idea of this play is
too fantastic to carry conviction save to the sentimental.

Fantasy of a different sort marks *Denise Marette,* which
introduces a ghost in the final act. Denise is the gifted daughter of a painter in decline. When he can no longer wield the
brush, she passes off her work as his own, and the critics acclaim the charm of the master's second manner. To salve her
conscience for such deceit, Denise resolves to expend her earnings in her father's name on a home for artists to be erected
after his death. In the mean time, a lover, reproaching her
for having forsaken their studio, marries another. Thus she
sacrifices love, leisure, even her identity for the sake of her
father. Yet after he has died and appears to her in his studio
as a phantom, it is to charge her unjustly with having failed
to maintain his glory. He talks only of himself until suddenly he seems transformed into the less selfish father of her

childhood, one who would play with her at hide and seek as they used to in the old days. As though hiding from her now, the phantom begins to fade out, and Denise, calling after him, is aroused by the entrance of a maid, who finds her rubbing her eyes, wondering, as do we, whether what she has seen was but a subjective delusion. This resort to the supernatural is in keeping with the new expressionistic tendency in the theater, although that which transcends reality be less expertly handled than in Wedekind's *The Awakening of Spring*, Molnár's *Liliom*, or the later plays of de Curel.

Not only does Bernard react against the naturalism of an older school; he reacts also against the technique of the well-made play. Instead of focusing his scenes, he scatters them over considerable periods of time and deliberately avoids those confrontations which his predecessors have deemed essential. He even keeps off the stage important characters, letting their existence be simply spoken of and inferred. Thus the American officer in *The Fire Slow to Rekindle* and the Argentine lover in *Invitation to Travel* are heroes unseen by the audience, and to others, like the painter in *Denise Marette* and the lady's alter ego in *The Soul in Distress*, he accords only a speech or two. Bernard's drama, in short, is one of nuances and intentions. In this regard it carries forward the purposes of Maeterlinck in a world more real.

Another playwright of the same school is Charles Vildrac, author of *The Pilgrim* and *Madame Béliard*, and of *The Steamship "Tenacity"* and *Michel Auclair*, the latter two adapted in English by Sidney Howard. Vildrac excels as a refined and restrained realist who renders very simply spontaneous feeling suggested by a natural situation. In *Michel Auclair*, for example, he reveals the self-sacrificing love of a bookseller in a little town, one who finds, after a year's absence in Paris, that his former sweetheart has married a swaggering soldier as dishonest as he is stupid. Instead of taking advantage of the plight into which this rival is drawn, Michel studies his character in order to regenerate it for the sake of Suzanne. Once only is he tempted to strike the fellow down. Then, repentant, he goes about the task of creating a worthy husband for the girl and opportunities for both to ensure her future happiness.

This piece, acted by the Provincetown Players, is less excellent than *The Steamship "Tenacity"*, which ran for long at Copeau's Vieux Colombier. Here two former soldiers preparing to seek their fortunes in Canada are detained at a French port while their vessel is being repaired. Both fall in love with a pretty waitress at the inn. The more assertive of the two, who has planned the journey, elopes with her whom his dreamy friend lacks the decision to carry off. Then, since the girl prefers to remain in France, the dreamer fares forth alone. The very name of his ship—"Tenacity"—is ironic. As an old sailor has remarked, there are people who are corks on the tide of life, and there are others of apparent will, folk like proud weathercocks firmly pivoted though also obedient to a force without them. Whether you be temperamentally assertive or passive, you will find your share of sadness and of gaiety in life, and you may as well recognize that your future is determined for you by trifles, little accidents; but accept that future with cheerful stoicism. Vildrac charms by the chastened simplicity, the pure beauty, of his work.

The originality of Bernard and to a less degree of Vildrac is a matter of technique; that of Henri-René Lenormand is a matter of thought and theme. Born at Paris in 1882, Lenormand, son of a musical composer, traveled, wrote a volume of verse, *Landscapes of the Soul*, and provided the Grand Guignol in 1905 with a two-act thriller, *White Madness*. Here, forecasting the subtlety he was to exhibit in all his later work, he suggested the malign influence of a Swiss mountain which attracts yet punishes with death those who would conquer it. The scene passes on the terrace of a hotel from which what occurs on the heights is described by one of the characters, who observes it through a telescope. A pair of lovers, the day before, have debated what each would do in case they slipped in the ascent. The girl has admitted that she would cut the rope joining them should Marc bid fair to drag her down in his fall, but he has retorted that, were the case reversed, he would die rather than cut the cord. Next day, the parents of the two, overcome with anxiety because there has been a storm during the night, learn that the lovers, already half-way up the mountain, have foolishly gone on; and then hear their returned guide, as he gazes upward through the telescope, hint at the tragedy above,—the lover's cutting of the rope to save himself. As the girl's father assails the father of the youth at this act of cowardice, the guide by a further sign indicates that Marc also has plunged to the depths.

After writing *The Possessed* and *Dust*, Lenormand came into his own in the play *Time Is A Dream*, produced in 1919. An introspective youth just returned to Holland from Java broods over the thought that space and time are phantasmal. "Within eternity we are at the same instant about to be, and living, and dead. To die is to awaken, to know, perhaps to attain that point in eternity where time is no longer a dream, the frontier where all things are coexistent. . . . It isn't the dreaming that matters, it's knowing that there's no solid earth under your feet; stretching out your arms and realizing that they can never reach reality because all things are phantoms and the shadows of phantoms." The fiancée of this musing skeptic, on arriving to visit his sister, thinks that she sees a green boat on a pond, with a man's face beside it in the water. At first she supposes this to be a ghostly reminiscence of a past drowning at this very place. Then she becomes convinced that it is rather the presage of something to come. When her lover confesses having attempted suicide ten years before, she asks if it were by leaping into this pond, and learns that in-stead he sought death by hanging. But now, as though her question regarding the pond had suggested the thought to him, Nico buys a green boat from which presently he does drown himself. The girl has thus unwittingly helped to make real what she had only imagined. In such fashion do coming events cast their shadows before. Nico the dreamer is the least dramatic of characters, a passive pessimist who admits that his mind is as choked with doubts as is the pond with weeds. Love can afford him no solace, for, as he tells his sweetheart, each soul is fearfully solitary. Moreover, time is illusory. "Man walks in Time as in a garden; behind him there goes one spreading a veil so that he may not behold the flowers of the past; before him goes one spreading a veil so that he may not behold the flowers of the future. But all these flowers bloom at once behind the two veils, and the eyes of the initiate contemplate them continually."

Much closer to the realm of the real is Lenormand's drama *The Failures*, in which a couple succumb to the power of evil through the pressure of adversity, each compromising with worthy ambitions and ideals in order to gain a momentary advantage, and each believing that such violation of the sanctities may be indulged in with impunity. Both, however, sink lower and lower until the man in drunken madness slays the woman and then himself. He is a playwright and she an actress, their high hopes fallen as they tour the provinces in a third-rate company. When she slips from virtue to keep body and soul together, he forgives; yet, to show that he is not afraid to drop to her level, he duplicates her fall by one of his own. At first they seem drawn even closer together by these violations of the self. But their mutual infidelities grow, and jealousy awakens in the man, who charges her with mocking at his failure. Since both have survived their lives, he shoots her and then, to avoid arrest, shoots himself. These fourteen conversations conducted with a minimum of action and words sound a crescendo of despair in sick souls.

Lenormand, who made the acquaintance of the work of Freud only in 1917, had already fixed his interest in two Freudian elements, the influence of the unconscious, especially as manifested through dreams, and the psychology of sex. Regarding the first he has confessed: "All my plays tend toward the elucidation of the mystery of the inner life, toward solving the enigma that man presents to himself. My theater offers a conflict between the conscious and the unconscious." It goes without saying that he finds a dominant phase of the unconscious in the sexual urge. So, in *Simoom*, he reveals bit by bit the perturbations of a father in love with his daughter yet scarcely aware of what troubles him. A French trader after years of isolation in the desert has sent for his daughter, and at her coming beholds in her the image of her dead mother, whose infidelity had driven him to seek forgetfulness in the African wilds. The source of his suffering he will scarcely admit to himself, yet his incestuous love prompts his refusal to permit a young Arab to marry Clotilde. That refusal incites the father of the Arab to take revenge by seizing the French messengers sent to the coast in a simoom. In the meantime, the mistress of the Frenchman, a violent half-breed, in jealousy slays Clotilde, using a poisoned knife concealed in a fan. She does this just as the girl, for the first time divining her father's passion for her, is about to flee with the Arab. As Laurency gazes on the face of his daughter, thus sacrificed, his features exhibit sudden relief. For the future, he will be exempt from the torment of his evil love, like the hero of d'Annunzio's *Dead City*, who for the same reason slew his sister.

Lenormand's *Man and his Phantoms* and *A Secret Life* study the devastating effects upon the soul of hypertrophied sex instincts. In the latter, a musician has put into his work the wild force of nature as he has experienced it in the Far East, but his music lacks humanity, for he has given free play to his passions irrespective of the harm done to others, and at home he is leading a life of secret indulgence. A girl whom his wife had redeemed from her addiction to drugs he deliberately lures back to vice, and when his patient wife, having traced him to the den he maintains in a remote district of Paris, reproaches him for his conduct toward Vera, he justifies his sensual abandon as needful to supply the emotion for his art. But Vera, driven distraught, commits suicide, and the shock of her deed at last stirs the conscience of the musician. As he goes to the piano and improvises, the human sympathy hitherto lacking in his work rings out, and the wife in gratitude exclaims, "He is saved!"

If here Don Juan scarcely atones for his ruthless following of instinct, it is his well-deserved sufferings that make the play *Man and his Phantoms*, in which the hero is haunted by the specters of his victims, and dies in a paroxysm of fear, if not of remorse. The Man, as he is called in expressionistic wise, has conquered no end of fair women of every class and condition, driven on by desire for the infinite. No sooner has he mastered one than he thirsts for another. Now it is a peasant girl in her cabin on the Alps; now it is a Parisian girl who thrusts into the flames the child she bears him; now it is an hysterical wife in Algeria, to whom he frankly says: "Expect neither goodness, kindness, nor lies from me. It is as impossible for me to pity you as to love you. All I can do is to lend myself to your madness." From his dealings with those who are decent he sinks to the lowest professionals. A psycho-analyst assures him that in his endeavor to possess many, he has never possessed even one, that while pursuing he has fled. Seeking joyous companionship, he has found only more absolute solitude; for, behold a paradox!—"Don Juan is a solitary." His may be the body of a man, but his is also the soul of a woman. At the same time, in woman he is looking for the phantom of man, hence each of his victories is destined to prove a defeat. To a youth, called merely The Friend, he declares that, "When a man makes love, he is groping vainly for his own skeleton, . . . the bony framework which the sexes have in common." When he accuses the youth of supplanting him with one of his victims, the youth retorts that what he has done the Man has but taught him to do. "You have formed me; you have imbued me with your thoughts and desires, and you are surprised to find me in your image. If Don Juan had a son, he could not resemble his father more than I resemble you."

The remainder of the play shows the retribution that falls upon Don Juan. The peasant girl, who, following him to Paris, has died in misery, appears at a spiritualistic séance to warn him that he too will die within the month of May. The medium who conducts the séance sniffs the smell of something burning, —a mystical recollection of the death by burning of his unwanted child, and a forecast, further, of the fire that half consumes his room on the last day of May. As he lies dying in that room, the phantoms of his various victims emerge above the charred rubbish crying, "We are dead because you willed it!" and accusing him, also, of undue intimacy with The Friend. But the phantom of his mother dismisses the others as the inventors of spiteful lies, for, mother-like, she still believes in her son. A strange and terrible play is this, an attempt, in seventeen dislocated scenes of staccato dialogue, to treat the old Spanish legend in accordance with modern psycho-analysis. The piece is to be contrasted with Rostand's *Last Night of Don Juan*. The central notion in both is the same, but Rostand handles the theme with poetry and humor, Lenormand with psychological insight and grim seriousness.

The psycho-analyst of *Man and his Phantoms* becomes the hero of *The Devourer of Dreams*. De Bronte admits that he is obsessed by a wish to read the cryptogram engraved upon each soul. He, too, is "a mock Don Juan," one in whom for love has been substituted scientific curiosity leading him to anatomize and incidentally to corrupt or destroy all the women who care for him. In one he discovers an unsuspected talent for fraud, and moves her to become an international crook. In another he discovers an unsuspected source of her hypochondriac dreams and suicidal mania, and discloses to her bit by bit the childish deed that has affected her whole life. At the

age of six she had suffered an instinctive sex love of her father
and a corresponding sex jealousy of her mother. That mother
she had actually betrayed to pursuing tribesmen by waving a
scarf as signal to them from the mouth of a cave wherein the
mother and she had taken refuge. When years afterward she is
brought back by de Bronte to the scene of that infantile crime,
she fully recalls it for the first time and is overwhelmed with
remorse. From that remote Freudian impulse all her dreams
and delusions have developed, and it needs only the prompting now of the other woman, her Nietzschean rival, to incite
Jeannine to shoot herself. "It is quite dark," says the rival,
handing her a pistol. "Don't go out unarmed." As for the
psycho-analyst, even though he has lost Jeannine as the result
of his experiment, he feels a certain elation in having fathomed
the secret of that subconscious mind. But the other woman in
whom he has unleashed the powers of evil claims him for her
own, perhaps a fitting punishment for any Devourer of
Dreams.

With *The Red Tooth* Lenormand reverts to the idea set
forth in his *White Madness*, writing a piece twice as long to
expose the fatal fascination exerted by a mountain upon the
minds of superstitious peasants. A youth with a passion for
climbing promises the girl he loves that he will cease his
attempts to conquer the Dent Rouge, but he pines away at
the restriction. She is looked upon askance in the village as a
stranger, although for the sake of Pierre she has given up a
luxurious life to become the drudge of his jealous mother and
his ailing grandsire. Her father, conquered by her lover in
a wrestling bout, has cursed her and confessed that her mother
was a creature of low caste and worse morals. Thereafter, as
Pierre languishes deprived of his mountain, Claire languishes
deprived of her freedom. Then her husband, accusing her of
having bewitched him, breaks his vow and climbs the Dent
Rouge to outstrip a rival. But even as the village bells are
ringing his triumph, he falls to his death; and Claire, who

once when he beat her had willed that he fall and in dreams has seen him do so, accepts the fiction of her guilt, a situation not unlike that in Wiers-Jenssen's *Anne Pedersdotter*, and remotely resembling also the conclusion of d'Annunzio's *Daughter of Jorio*. In the background rises the baleful mountain luring the hero to his doom; in the foreground are the ignorant country-folk resenting the intrusion of the stranger from the Argentine. That stranger's loneliness deepens in the dark winter as they bury in the snow on the roof above her head the body of her husband's dead grandsire, and as they steal upon her when they think her sleeping in order to prick her with needles to test the strength of her witchcraft. Is it any wonder that at last she feels, like Ibsen's Master Builder, that she controls malign powers and by black magic can compass what she wills?

The Coward, another play with its scene laid in Switzerland, affords an interesting picture of war-time slackers behind the lines pretending illness and haunted by multiple fears. According to Lenormand, war may be brutal and absurd, but those who decline to take part in it when their fellows are engaged may endure even worse madness. In a sanitarium are gathered imaginary invalids gossiping and backbiting as they recline tucked up in steamer-chairs on a terrace overlooking the eternal snows. Jacques, a constitutional coward, feigns weakness and a cough, and at night dreams in terror of a soldier pursuing him with fixed bayonet. Although it is his wife who has kept him out of the War, he smarts now from her contempt. In vain he reasons with himself that to the universe as a whole it cannot matter whether he, a speck of dust, accepts or refuses a law laid down by his fellows. Yet, cringing with fear, he falls an easy victim to a blackmailing libertine who makes him spy upon his fellow patient, a German professor. As the latter catches Jacques endeavoring to entrap him and abstract certain papers, he, in turn, uses blackmail upon the coward and extorts from him information which results months later in the death of several Frenchmen. Though by now Jacques has withdrawn from the sanitarium, he is followed by a committee of his countrymen bent on vengeance. They invite him politely to ride with them to the German frontier, and the scene is ironic as he yields to their flattery and promises his wife to return ere long bringing a little butter now so difficult to procure. We know that he is riding to his death.

So Lenormand demonstrates that the life of slackers is even less desirable than that of soldiers in the trenches. These dissipated, selfish creatures scheming to take advantage of one another, each fearful of his neighbors as well as of the War, are victims of dreams and repressions that threaten to break through their self-imposed calm, as in the case of a Russian who, in shooting at bottles, talks of the wine he spills as blood.

In *The Red Tooth* had figured a half-wit Swiss girl whose counterpart becomes the heroine of *The Innocent*, a piece in one act. Plagued by the village children, the Innocent is shielded by her little sister. But a scheming couple try to make her their cat's-paw by prompting her to push into a torrent as though in play a child who stands between them and an inheritance. They even promise her as bribe a wedding gown when a burly mill worker jokes her into believing herself beloved by him. But half-wit though she be, she turns from her tempters, for love has awakened in her the will to resist evil.

This pretty and idyllic play is less characteristic of its author's vein than *Mixture* or *In the Shadow of Evil*, the former concerned with the rivalry of mother and daughter, and the latter with the power of injustice to breed injustice. At a remote post in the African interior a French official treats the natives with unreasoning cruelty. Whereas a chieftain wrongfully accused by another is shamefully whipped at the official's orders, the man who is guilty goes free. The victim's bewilderment is shared by the audience. Why, we ask, is the official so perversely unjust? In the answer to that question lies the significance of the play. Long years before, the official had himself been the victim of wanton injustice from a superior on the coast who had taken malicious delight in choking off his supplies and sending him stuff that could not be used. As a result, his nature has been warped. Thereafter he has found malign pleasure in passing on injustice to others. But his superior, having repented, chances now upon the victim he had never seen before and begs forgiveness. Yet evil once planted is bound to grow, and it is as likely to destroy the innocent as the guilty. The whipped chieftain has been pitied by the only white woman in the place, the wife of the official's assistant. She, going fearlessly to dress his wounds, is slain out of revenge by his mistress. Thus injustice propagates itself. Moreover, the law of justice is purely a human invention. In the jungle it is each for himself, and the devil take the hindmost. The play is rich in exotic atmosphere, charged with the currents of elemental passion.

Nowhere in Lenormand's work is his interest in the power of evil better shown. That power Poe and Baudelaire had both accentuated. Baudelaire had protested against the notion, dear to the sentimentalists and humanitarians, that we are all born good. And Poe, in his *Black Cat* and *Imp of the Perverse*, had pointed to our primitive impulse to do evil for the sake of evil. "Who has not," asks Poe, "a hundred times found himself committing a vile or stupid action for no other reason than because he knows he should not? Have we not a perpetual inclination, in the teeth of our best judgment, to violate that which is Law, merely because we understand it to be such?" Of Lenormand and his fellows of this generation John Palmer has said that they are "quite involuntarily obsessed with a sense of the positive, active, and creative power of evil. The old defense of discord as a necessary preliminary to harmony, the old recognition of blemishes in detail which emphasize the beauty of the whole, the old defense of ugliness as an essential element in beauty," these have disappeared. "The evil in modern art is evil for its own sake, a positive and not a negative element, an independent and prevailing force, not an indirect process or discipline toward good." In his recognition of evil as coexistent with good, Lenormand breathes the new spirit. He is modern, also, in defining man, not by his actions controlled by the will, but by those which reveal a subconscious will. His restless and perturbed heroes act by secret impulses which they cannot dominate. "All my plays," he confesses, "tend toward the elucidation of the mystery of the inner life, toward solving the enigma that man presents to himself. My theater is a dialogue, a combat, between the conscious and the unconscious." So Lenormand, like Pirandello, seeks the true self beneath the surface selves and finds it whenever the personality fails to maintain a proper balance, as in dreams or sickness or a shift from familiar conditions to those exotic and enervating. He adopts a loose and direct technique that will most readily serve his purpose, revealing most simply the life of the individual rather than the social life, and activity that is mental and emotional rather than external.

CHAPTER XVI

Hauptmann—Master of Central European Drama

IN THE history of German drama, except for a few great names, the period from 1830 to 1885 is peculiarly drab. During this period, according to one chronicler: "All forceful progressive movements seem to have died away; the old worn-out fields are cultivated with ever decreasing profit; the petrified forms resist every attempt at improvement. To develop conventional beauty is the highest aim." Even after the national victory of 1870, the situation was no better, hopes for improvement in the theater being dashed, says Georg Witkowski, by "the low condition of artistic education, the preponderance of coarse materialism, which celebrated its orgies in the years immediately following the war, the complete exhaustion which after the great commercial crisis of 1873 lamed every effort, and, above all, the demoralization of the actor's art. . . . Hardly ever has there been, in a highly civilized nation, in an epoch of great national triumphs, a stage so degenerate as the German of the 'seventies."

Among the few who kept alive dramatic art during the first portion of this period, Franz Grillparzer and Christian Friedrich Hebbel were the chief. The former, who began his career in 1817 and died in 1872 long after he had ceased to produce, is now recognized as the master of Austrian drama. He was an idealist inspired by Greek and Spanish examples in his handling of classic and romantic themes, a troubled soul of high poetic gifts expressing his countrymen's disillusion in the years between the Napoleonic wars and the revolution of 1848. Hebbel, the North German, whose *Judith* was first played in 1840, continued to draw upon the Scriptures, legend, and history in such works as *Herod and Mariamne*, *Genoveva*, *Gyges and his Ring*, *Agnes Bernauer*, and the eleven acts of his *Nibelungen* trilogy. In *Mary Magdalene*, he foreshadowed the methods later employed by Ibsen, finding his tragic conflict in a social situation which he criticizes, and also picking up his story close to its climax and then casting back to explain, bit by bit, its antecedents.

Among lesser playwrights there were Karl Gutzkow, who urged contemporary life as the subject for drama but actually exploited history, and Otto Ludwig, who gave his hesitant attention to embroidering for the stage the story of the Maccabees and the tragic revenge of a forester who slays his own daughter in mistake for the son of his master. Ludwig was capital in his use of detail, but he added nothing to dramatic development. He was far more able as a writer of fiction, as were Gustav Freytag and Paul Heyse, both of whom contributed to the theater, the first with his striking play *The Journalists*, the second with a series written through more than three decades and including tragic pieces in one act and, at the end of his career, a much discussed Biblical work, *Mary of Magdala*. In Austria the peasant drama was persistently cultivated by Ludwig Anzengruber, who wrote in dialect and with absolute knowledge of the life he set forth.

Unquestionably, the most original manifestation on the German stage during the mid-century was the music drama of Richard Wagner, composed on the theory that the music should be not an end in itself as in Italian opera, but an interpretative aid in a work combining the various arts after the fashion of Greek tragedy. The establishment at Bayreuth of Wagner's Festspielhaus in 1876 affected the regular theater, but already an experiment in stage production at another provincial center had begun to exert extraordinary influence. This was the development at the court theater of Duke Georg of Saxe-Meiningen of an unusual company engaged in the presentation of classics in the very best style. The Duke had married a protégée of Frau Cosima Wagner, the accomplished actress Helen Franz, who confirmed his taste in matters theatrical. As a beneficent despot, he trained the company of his court theater, supervising every detail of production that could enhance artistic unity and a stage picture correct in local color. Then he sent his troop on successful tours through Germany and to other lands—Austria, Hungary, England, the Low Countries, Scandinavia, Russia, and the United States. During the seventeen seasons between 1874 and 1890, his players gave more than twenty-five hundred guest performances, favoring such classics as Shakespeare's *Julius Cæsar* and *A Winter's Tale*, Schiller's *Robbers*, *Wilhelm Tell*, and *Wallenstein*, and occasional dramas by Lindner, Fitger, Kleist, von Wildenbruch, Molière, and the youthful Ibsen and Björnson. The plays chosen were chiefly heroic and romantic, and in setting them forth the Meiningen emphasis fell upon clearness of speech, historic accuracy, perfection of the ensemble, effectiveness in crowd scenes, and whatever of stagecraft, costuming, and acting would conduce to completeness of illusion. Production at the many other court theaters had developed since Goethe's efforts at Weimar a tradition in the acting of native classics and of Shakespeare which tended to harden into convention. It was against such convention that the "Meininger" protested.

The influence of the "Meininger" performances proved potent, and imitators good and bad sprang up on all sides. In Vienna, during the 'seventies, the Burgtheater accomplished much in the same direction under Franz Dingelstedt, who was followed in 1881 by Adolf Wilbrandt, himself a dramatist. In Vienna, too, Heinrich Laube, who had written many plays and had earlier functioned at the Burgtheater, sought to rival the Burg performances at the Stadttheater. Munich and Hamburg contributed their share. In Berlin, the Prussian Court Theater, directed by an ex-army officer, Botho von Hülsen, held to the old and empty tradition, but in 1883

Adolf L'Arronge opened his Deutsches Theater, designed to emulate the methods of the "Meininger." Here were performed the classics—Lessing, Goethe, Schiller, Kleist, Grillparzer, Hebbel, Molière, and Shakespeare—together with plays by such moderns as von Wolzogen, Fulda, Blumenthal and Gustav von Moser, author of *War in Peace* and *Reif Reiflingen*, dramas exalting the military ideal.

But the Meiningen style in turn became a convention, and against it eventually reacted a fresh theatrical impulse, that of the upholders of naturalism. New plays and new methods of production were desired when those of a former day had begun to weary. The younger generation looked to Scandinavia and to France for inspiration. Ibsen from the North and Antoine from the South afforded something novel. The introduction of Ibsen's social dramas began with *The Pillars of Society*, acted first in Germany at Berlin in 1878. *A Doll's House* appeared at Hamburg with a happy ending, and then, as originally written, at Munich. *Ghosts* was performed at Augsburg and presently at Meiningen, where the Duke himself put it on against the will of the townsfolk, and was forced to give tickets away in order to fill his theater. Then followed productions of *An Enemy of the People* and *The Wild Duck*. It was with *Ghosts* that the Freie Bühne of Berlin opened its career, September 29, 1889.

This German Free Stage was due, not only to the influence of writers like Ibsen, Tolstoy, and Strindberg, but, above all, to the Parisian venture of André Antoine, whose Théâtre Libre, already described, had been started two years before. Antoine and his company had visited Berlin, and in April, 1889, at the Schiller Café, a group of ten enthusiasts met to consider the possibility of emulating Antoine's example. The members of this group were Harden the journalist, Fischer the publisher, Jonas the jurist, Stockhauser who later translated Maeterlinck, Wolff, Schlenther, Brahm, and the brothers Heinrich and Julius Hart,—the last four representing critical theory. Although Harden and Wolff withdrew, their places were taken by Mauthner and Fulda, and Otto Brahm was chosen Director. Besides the ten active members there were to be a thousand contributors subscribing to performances relieved of all censorship. Two years before the establishment of the Freie Bühne, Arno Holz and Johannes Schlaf had proposed a reform tending toward naturalism, in accordance with which they issued under a Norwegian pen name certain sketches and then wrote a play, *The Selicke Family*. This paints a minute picture of a single household presided over by a tipsy bookseller whose daughter, in attempting to hold the afflicted family together, refuses the escape offered her through marriage with their lodger, a theological student. There was nothing spectacular or even dramatic about this rather dull piece. The family instead of the individual was the center of interest, and the scenes and the subjects were drawn from everyday life. The work was read in manuscript by the youthful Hauptmann, whose faith in naturalism it corroborated, and it appeared, along with Hauptmann's own maiden efforts, *Before Sunrise* and *The Festival of Peace*, during the opening season of the Freie Bühne. Other selections for that year included Fitger's *By God's Grace*, Anzengruber's *The Fourth Commandment*, and translations of such foreign dramas as the de Goncourts' *Henriette Maréchal*, Björnson's *A Gauntlet*, Tolstoy's *The Power of Darkness*, and Alexander Kielland's *Homeward Bound*. In the second season there were five performances and among them Hartleben's *Angèle* and Hauptmann's *Lonely Lives*, and in the third season but one—Strindberg's *Miss Julie*. Obviously, it was Hauptmann whose conversion to naturalism and dominance as a playwright of the Freie Bühne won success for the enterprise.

Born in 1862 in the Silesian village of Obersalzbrunn, Gerhart Hauptmann was the son of an innkeeper, whose father, in turn, had been innkeeper and weaver. After schooling at

Breslau, he was confided to a pious uncle in the country to learn farming, but two and a half years later returned to Breslau to enroll in the Royal College of Art. Ere long he matriculated at Jena, where he heard the lectures of Haeckel and Eucken and applied himself to history and music. At twenty-one he made a Mediterranean cruise, studied sculpture at Rome, and later settled in Berlin to devote himself to drama. The naturalistic theory which he accepted was based, as we have seen, upon the new faith in the determinism of heredity and environment and the freshly awakened interest in the fourth estate as a result of the social democratic movement. In place of aristocratic heroes of tragedy, creatures of dominant will, the naturalists employed middle-class and low-class folk, more sinned against than sinning, molded by the pressure of their social situation and their biological inheritance. Gone were the well-made stories of the romanticists, beautifully balanced; gone were the conventional character types, and the polished dialogue, brightened by the give and take of repartee and rendered ornate by tirades rhetorical and poetic. Instead, naturalism favored the simplest and roughest language, the dialect speech spoken in the fields and the slums. It favored characters in representative groups or carefully individualized, set forth in relation to a milieu minutely observed. It favored "kleinmalerei," or miniature painting, and the emergence of background and local color rather than plot. Show us life as it is, said the naturalists, spare nothing, fear nothing. For the masses life is hard, since human institutions embody the selfishness of the fortunate and individuals are engaged in bitter competition wherein only the fittest survive. Moreover, men are beasts, subject to the control of instinct, driven by passions that they cannot resist. Assailed from without and within, they struggle, foredoomed for the most part to failure.

In *Before Sunrise*, Hauptmann may have thought that he was exposing a bloody slice of life, without selection or arrangement, but no program piece for the stage was ever more deliberately ordered to prove its author's contention. He would demonstrate that an evil heritage and environment will operate to destroy the individual as effectively as any classic Fate. To prove his point, he depicts a degenerate family of Silesian farmer folk enriched and corrupted by the discovery of coal on their land. Krause has taken to drink. His second wife is intriguing with the depraved son of a neighbor whom she would nevertheless marry off to her younger stepdaughter. The elder is a dipsomaniac, whose first child has died of alcoholism at three, whose second is born dead, and whose husband is assailing the virtue of his sister-in-law, a gentle girl, reared apart in a Moravian convent, but now come home to be sickened at the spectacle of such vice. Is it any wonder that Helene should fall in love with the only other decent person here, an idealist reformer bent upon improving the life of the miners? If only Alfred Loth would marry and take her away! But, when he learns from the family physician that the Krause stock is corrupt, he beats a retreat. He who would benefit the world at large lacks courage to save one creature in need. What if his unborn children inherit corruption? When Helene reads his note of farewell, she snatches a hunting knife from the wall and takes her life just as her father comes reeling in from the tavern chanting a lewd song about his handsome daughters.

In writing this piece, Hauptmann was bound to show man as the victim of heredity and environment. There must burn no faintest gleam of light "before sunrise." Esthetically, his play was revolting. Only Helene and Loth were allowed to retain any virtue, and both were the passive folk of naturalism. The rest were evil in motive—even the physician seeking merely to fill his pockets by exploiting the dissipated miners. Yet the critic must recognize here the stark sincerity of the dramatist, the precision of observation evidenced even in his stage directions, and the tragic power engendered by a perception of life as controlled by natural laws destructive of the individual who happens to be born of bad protoplasm and into a situation inimical to his healthy development.

A year later Hauptmann painted a drab but less repellent picture in *The Festival of Peace*. The irritable son of a couple mismated has quarreled with his father, and both have wandered unhappy for years until, on a Christmas Eve, they meet at home to be reconciled. But bickering breaks out afresh. The tipsy father, fancying that another son is about to thrash him as Wilhelm had once done, suffers an apoplectic stroke; the shrewish maiden sister of the brothers taunts Wilhelm as a parricide; and the festival of peace ends in death for the old man and mutual recriminations for the living. But Wilhelm's sweetheart, though aware of his miserable heritage, evinces greater courage than her male counterpart in *Before Sunrise*. By her love she will save him in spite of his brother's jealousy, his own shattered will, and even her mother's rivalry. Only from without can salvation come to those of bad environment and defective inheritance. Here the social level has been raised, and the study of character is more subtle, the playwright drawing without exaggeration a gallery of distinctive if disagreeable family portraits.

Better still as a drama was *Lonely Lives*, suggested by Ibsen's *Rosmersholm* and by the playwright's own experience. For Hauptmann, who six years before had married the daughter of a prosperous merchant, was now disillusioned, feeling his art to be cramped by her failure to share his esthetic aspirations. Through this piece he gave voice to his loneliness and that of his wife, from whom ere long he separated. Again the hero is passive, a scholar intent upon the creation of a great work, but misunderstood by his kindly Käthe, who can think only of household affairs, and by his parents, shocked at what they regard as his decline into free thought. Johannes Vockerat is sorry for those he would love, and sorry for himself, and sorry also for Anna Mahr, a Russian student, who arrives to afford him the authentic thrill which his wife cannot give. Anna is brilliant and emancipated. She dreams, as does he, of the possibility of a Platonic union. But his wife and his parents object and suffer, and a friend of the family bids the new woman depart. Once she goes, but only to return, and then, convinced of her feminine weakness which would crave more than intellectual satisfaction, she departs forever. The scholar, unable to live without her, and lacking the strength to break his domestic bonds and follow, takes his life. No one is at fault. All are lonely.

For his next play—*Colleague Crampton*—Hauptmann drew upon recollections of his life at the Art Academy to body forth a Micawberish character, a painter grown dissipated, ousted from his professorship, forsaken by his wealthy wife, and thrown upon the charity of his daughter and his pupil, her lover. In spite of their kindness, the old Bohemian will not change. He accepts their gifts as his due and will continue to regard the genial Max Strähler as a duffer in art. Thus, Hauptmann had passed from tragedy to comedy, narrowing each succeeding canvas and resorting to more delicate effects. But forthwith, in *The Weavers*, he broadened his picture to include typical groups rather than individuals, and a social rather than a domestic situation. Applying the technique of naturalism, he produced in the Silesian dialect the first powerful play to represent the battle between labor and capital. His paternal grandfather had been a weaver in Silesia, where the suffering of the toilers had led to their futile revolt in 1844. Hauptmann had heard of this rising from his father. He had also read of it in Alfred Zimmermann's treatise on the linen industry. His imagination had been stirred by a painting of Silesian weavers by Karl Hübner. Accordingly, instead of reproducing some contemporary struggle of masters and men, he harked back to a conflict historical and local. But his interest lay in the universal features of the clash. As a naturalist, he was inclined to focus attention upon a condition rather than a hero; hence his hero became the crowd.

On the one side are ranged those attached to the capitalist Dreissiger, and on the other are the weavers in two different families, together with a revolutionary pair, Becker and Jaeger, who stir them to revolt. Betwixt and between, figure still others—a tutor, an innkeeper, a joiner, a smith, a surgeon, and a rag dealer. These forty characters move through five acts largely pictorial and but loosely united. In the first, poor creatures are bringing the product of their home weavings to be examined and paid for at Dreissiger's office. Most are bullied by the manager and denied more than a pittance until one, braver than his fellows, protests, and a child faints, overcome by hunger. Whose is the fault? Not Dreissiger's. He at least offers to those out of work a chance for earning a little. Then the scene shifts to a weaver's household, where spin in the fading light old Mother Baumert, with her skeleton face, her watery red eyes, and her goiter neck, and, beside her, two starved daughters and a half-wit son with his spider-like arms and legs. In comes her husband staggering under a bundle of yarn and bringing Jaeger, his nephew, fresh from army service in the great world, a cocky fellow who has learned enough to chide these wretches for their easy subservience, and to assail the rich in a song—"Bloody Justice." That song he presently teaches, in spite of threats from the police, to the weavers at the inn and then leads them off to Dreissiger's, where the capitalist has him arrested, but soon must flee as the mob breaks in and vents its rage upon the luxurious furnishings. With the last act appears a new family group, the godly Hilse, his wife, his pacifist son, his militant daughter-in-law, and his granddaughter who has brought home, to the old man's grief, a spoon as trophy from the sack of Dreissiger's house. The mob is coming to destroy the power looms that ruin the hand-loom weavers. Hilse must join them. But he refuses. "You have your good things in this world;—I'll have mine in the next. . . . My heavenly Father has placed me here," he declares. "Isn't that so, mother? Here we'll sit, an' do our bounden duty—aye, though the snow was to go on fire." But, amid the hubbub, as he continues work at his loom, he is shot through the window by a chance bullet. The uproar passes. The soldiers are being driven out of the village by the weavers, and still his deaf and blind wife, unaware of his fate, pleads, "Come, now, father; can't you say something? You're frightenin' me."

Throughout, Hauptmann has sought to present only the sufferings of those who must toil unceasingly for less than a living wage. Here labor is not organized. There is no question of a union or a strike. Tortured animals turn at bay when incited by a force from without. Their distress is depicted with an undue accumulation of horrors, as when Baumert succumbs to nausea on eating his dog after two years of fasting from flesh. Unlike Galsworthy's *Strife*, which this piece inspired, the capitalist is allowed no adequate voice. He is here to be satirized only, as is the Pastor, who holds that nothing can be expected from measures of reform. It should be noted, however, that Hauptmann advances no socialistic ideas. His appeal is not intellectual, like Galsworthy's, but emotional. He simply portrays the evil results of an industrial system fatal to the life and happiness of the workers. The death of Hilse is ironic, since he alone refuses to leave his loom to disturb an order that he regards as ordained of heaven. No longer is such resignation possible in the new era of self-assertive labor contending with capital.

The Junkers and the Kaiser were shocked by this play. In the Prussian Diet, a speaker, affirming that "Hauptmann has degraded the stage to the intellectual level of a brothel," advocated his imprisonment. The Kaiser, who had threatened to withdraw his patronage of the Deutsches Theater if the piece were performed there, later confessed, "I know that Hauptmann is the most eminent German poet, but I cannot forgive him his *Weavers*." Prince Ludwig Hohenlohe Schillingsfuerst wrote in his diary of a more innocent drama: "We saw Hauptmann's *Hannele* this evening, a horrible play! Socialism and realism mixed with a morbid sentimental mysticism. Afterwards we went to Borchard's to revive our spirits with champagne and caviar." Evidently, if Hauptmann were caviar to the vulgar, he was anything but that to princes. Writers of the old school, too, regarded his exaltation of the lower classes as indefensible. Such folk, they argued, should appear upon the stage only in the capacity of servants and never as the principal characters.

But naturalism would not down. In *The Beaver Coat* and its sequel, *The Conflagration* (*Der rote Hahn*) of the next decade, Hauptmann composed comedies of low life centered about a woman thief, an innocent-seeming washerwoman, wife of a poacher. Like Autolycus, she is a snapper-up of unconsidered trifles. On the point of falling a victim to the law, she escapes by her easy audacity and pretends to be so scandalized at conditions in her town that she will move away unless local morals improve. But, in the sequel, having lived longer and remarried, she grows less whimsical and more hardened in crime, turning from petty thievery to arson. When the imbecile son of a neighbor is falsely accused of burning the heroine's house, which she has destroyed for the insurance money, the neighbor vows revenge. In danger of exposure, she dies just as her son-in-law, an architect, has dedicated a new house erected on the ruins of the old, which she has burned down in order to afford him scope for his talents. "People like us," she reflects, "has to turn their hands to anythin'. An' they tells you, Be good, be good! How? What chanct has we got?" Her husband, ignoring her passing, thinks only of his own as he gazes into a mirror at the reflection of his fixed pupils, a symptom that his time is short.

Both plays were detailed and prolix, however remarkable as the revelation of small and disreputable souls. But Hauptmann could by no means be confined to such low-life genre painting. In *The Journey to Heaven of Hannele* he united fantasy with naturalism, and in the more ambitious *Florian Geyer*, he extended naturalism to embrace an historical study on the grand scale, bestowing upon the Peasants' War of the early sixteenth century the same sympathetic treatment he had already given to the minor revolt of nineteenth-century weavers.

At the moment, *Florian Geyer* proved a failure, but the whirligig of time has brought in his revenges. Since the War it has been hailed as an expression of the best in the national spirit, President Ebert praising its author as a poet of the children of poverty. Again, the conflict set forth is that of groups and classes. The peasants and the Free Knights are allied against the reforms proposed by the Diet of Worms, both jealous of the rising wealth and power of the towns. But the Knights soon desert the peasants, who, under Florian Geyer, lay siege to the stronghold of the Bishop of Würzburg. While Florian is away seeking guns sufficient to breach the walls, his followers, forgetting their promise to make no attack, suffer defeat. Götz von Berlichingen, who had joined them from selfish motives, proves a traitor. Florian, warned of disaster, declines to take refuge in France. Wounded and concealed in the castle of his brother-in-law, he is betrayed by the latter's wife. When the gypsy camp-follower who loves him is stabbed, Florian leaps from hiding, waves in the face of the carousing Knights the torn banner of the peasants, and is shot down by a fellow who would avenge a personal affront and capture the reward laid upon Florian's head. Admirable in conception, the play lacks coherence in execution. It involves more than sixty speaking parts; its scenes are confused and overcrowded, only the reflex of the main movement appearing before the last act; and its archaic language, though an achievement for a modern, renders it difficult to understand. Amid the cross currents of a muddled conflict Florian battles for humanity. But attention is held less by him than by these currents, and dissertations upon politics and religion block the dramatic progress. For once, the poet would seem to have attempted more than he could well achieve, or at least to have erred in adapting to a theme appropriate for romantic handling the methods of naturalism.

In the earlier *Hannele*, however, Hauptmann, by contrast, restricted his endeavor to setting forth a single character in one situation. A child, in attempting to escape the brutality of her stepfather, has thrown herself into a pool. Her dream of death and her triumphant preparation for Heaven make the play, in which the projection of her delirium is set off by a preliminary scene as she is carried into an almshouse among grotesque paupers by the schoolmaster and the woodcutter who have rescued her. She is examined by a policeman and a magistrate, and attended by a nurse and a physician. In her vision Hannele is protected from the dark Angel of Death by her dead mother who bears the semblance of the nurse. Then she beholds the village tailor come to array her as Heaven's bride, and the schoolmaster, who leads his pupils in a hymn and makes them apologize for their harsh treatment, and rebukes her wicked stepfather for declaring that he has never harmed her. Presently the schoolmaster's shabby cloak drops away, revealing him resplendent as the good Jesus, who describes for her in lilting verse the beauties of Heaven and charges angels strewing flowers to care for her tenderly. For a moment the light fades, and then, as it brightens again, the physician, bending over her, is saying to the nurse, "She is dead."

Nothing could be simpler than this static dream play, realistic in its humorous presentation of the paupers, then fanciful yet naturalistic, too, in so far as it reflects a child's morbid states of mind. Is it any wonder that little Hannele confuses the Frau Holle of folk-lore who lures children into the waves with what she has heard of the Christ, or that Heaven for her is the realization of those material joys of which she has been deprived on earth? Spectacular and sentimental, the piece was welcomed as a novelty, and its vogue was enhanced by the absurd ban put upon it by British and American censors, who detected irreverence in the dying girl's identification of the schoolmaster with Jesus.

Up to this point, Hauptmann had exemplified in unusual variety the tenets of naturalism. But in *Hannele* he had shown fine fancy, and in *Florian Geyer* ample historical imagination. It was clear that, when he chose, he could lift from the earth and fly free in the realms of romance. Such a flight he proceeded to accomplish in *The Sunken Bell*, producing a drama in verse, fascinating as a story and significant in its implied philosophy. When the bell which its founder had hoped would sound the glory of God from the heights is sent careening down the mountainside into a mere by a mischievous wood sprite, its maker staggers after in despair. Sinking exhausted, he is comforted by the blonde nymph Rautendelein. Though she draws about him a magic circle to keep mortals away, a witch gives anxious villagers permission to bear him back to his wife in the valley. Then Rautendelein, weeping her first tear, and warned by a water sprite against fixing affections upon a mortal, follows after. Down in the valley, where Heinrich has been lamenting her loss, she appears, makes him hers by an incantation, and leads him back to the free glad life of the forest. There they are happy while Heinrich fashions bells for a joyous sun worship and scorns the Vicar come to summon him to a life of duty. That old life no more frets him now than does the bell, its voice hushed forever in the mere. But the Vicar threatens him. "That bell shall toll again! Then think of me!" Henceforth Heinrich is perturbed, taunted by the sprites, and finding his dwarfs no longer obedient. Though he repulses the villagers ascending the heights to burn his pagan temple, he beholds his children mounting with an urn containing their mother's tears, and is startled by the deep clang of the sunken bell tolled from the mere by the hand of that wife who has drowned herself in despair. Then, cursing Rautendelein, he flees. But in the valley he is no longer at home, for he has lived too long upon the heights. Back he comes, accordingly, in quest of his nymph, yet only to find her withdrawn to the well of her lover, the water sprite. The life of instinct in the forest can no more be his than the life of duty in the village. He is a creature now of neither world. He should have dared to be a superman living beyond good and evil, says the witch. Failing in this, he can only die. So she sets before him three goblets. That of white wine will restore his vanished power, that of red will reveal his vanished nymph, and that of yellow, which brings death, he must quaff if he takes the other two. Gladly Heinrich pays the penalty in order to conjure up even for a moment from the Nicklemann's well the fair Rautendelein. Combing her golden locks, she rises to kiss and bid him an eternal farewell; and, dying, he fancies that he hears the sun bells' song.

Delightful as a fairy tale, this drama possesses the added attraction of suggesting deeper meanings. Here may be heard the echo of a struggle between the sense of domestic duty and the yearning for a free artistic career which Hauptmann himself had experienced in his first marriage. Here, also, may be observed a personal esthetic allegory not unlike that to be discerned in Shakespeare's *Tempest* or in Ibsen's *Master Builder* and *When We Dead Awaken*. The playwright, in *Florian Geyer*, had fashioned a naturalistic work upon which he had staked his hopes. But it had failed and fallen. Then, finding refuge on the heights in this very play, deserting the valley of naturalism, Hauptmann had dreamed a dream gloriously romantic. But the old naturalism had summoned him back to the valley of reality, and his new helpers and servers—the demigod dwarfs of imagination—had seemed loath to obey him. Haunted by doubts of his ability to create according to the new fashion, though unable to return to the old naturalism, he here laments the failure of his naturalistic *Florian Geyer* yet questions his power to succeed with the idealistic *Sunken Bell*. But the latter itself constitutes a refutation of his doubts.

More important, however, than any personal or artistic allegory is the ethical symbolism of the piece. In its universal aspect, it represents the world-old conflict between impulse and control, between nature and the moral life. The artist, like every other man, though in higher degree, yearns to escape the thralldom of humble responsibilities in the valley. He aspires to the individual freedom of the heights. Yet he finds that, to a social being, such freedom is impossible. The sunken bell of conscience will toll. Social duties are imperious. Perhaps the greatest artist—the superman—may ignore them. But none save the greatest can do so with impunity. Let us be thankful that the doctrine is nowhere crystallized into any trite aphorism, that it is held in the play merely in solution. And let us be grateful, also, that this work of art may be enjoyed just as a lovely poetic creation, rendering more sympathetically than any other drama since *A Midsummer Night's Dream* the mood of fairy folk-lore.

It might have been inferred that Hauptmann, abjuring naturalism in *The Sunken Bell*, would thereafter devote himself exclusively to the romantic; but such was not the case. Of the dozen and a half plays that followed from his pen, ten were idealistic, and eight were naturalistic. As the spirit moved him, he wrought upon the heights or in the valley, his mood in both regions varying at will from gay to somber. For convenience we may neglect chronology and consider together, first, the graver realistic dramas, then those of lighter cast, and finally the romances—symbolic, legendary, and ideal.

Of the five tragedies of naturalism that followed *The Sunken Bell*, three were devoted to setting forth the tyranny of love, one exhibited the compelling power of the maternal instinct, and one—*Michael Kramer*—pointed the failure of a humdrum father to understand his temperamental son. Kramer, though a teacher of art in the Royal Academy, is only a good Philistine, preaching the virtues of sobriety and industry to the boy who yearns to live his own life joyously. Such talent as Arnold might have developed in different surroundings is repressed. His mother, though at heart a stranger to her husband, holds over him always that father's disapproval. His sister, disillusioned because the man she loves has married another, blames her parents for their lack of sympathy with each other and for their children. When Arnold, infatuated with a café keeper's daughter, is rebuked by his father, rebuffed by the girl, and mocked in her presence by the café hangers-on, he takes his life. The father whose hopes are thus shattered finds his only comfort in the thought that now at least he has suffered the worst. With the very accents of the stricken mother in Synge's *Riders to the Sea*, he says, "Whatever lies before me in the future cannot give me joy, cannot cause me dread; the world holds no threat for me any longer."

Naturalistic is the absence of dramatic spectacle in this play. The café heckling is merely overheard; Arnold's suicide is merely reported. Nobody is at fault. The fate of each proceeds from his character under the pressure of environment. Life is like that. The older generation, with the best of intentions, crushes the younger; parents and children have little in common. As in the plays of Chekhov, so here one feels the stoicism of despair. According to Ludwig Lewisohn, "It is the union of unerring observation of the actual with philosophic largeness of vision that renders *Michael Kramer* one of the most satisfying achievements of the modern drama."

Of the tragedies expounding the tyranny of love, two are dramas of the peasantry—*Teamster Henschel* and *Rose Bernd*—and one—*The Flight of Gabriel Schilling*—is a play of the upper middle class. Henschel is a fellow of powerful body and simple mind destroyed by a temptress. He has given his word to his dying wife never to marry their servant. But Hanne Schäl is a schemer prompt to exert her wiles upon the teamster as soon as his wife breathes her last. Shall he break his vow? In vain he looks for a guiding sign at the grave of his wife. Then, assuming that silence gives consent, he weds Hanne, professing to do so for the sake of his child. But Hanne by neglect causes the death of that child and rages at him for bringing home to take its place one of her own. She intrigues with the waiter and the guests of the inn beneath which they lodge. Though she laughs at every charge laid against her, Henschel can guess her perfidy. The misfortunes which dog his steps he regards as a supernatural rebuke for his broken promise. The fault is his; he must atone. So he dies by his own hand. Unlike the men victimized by women in the plays of Strindberg, he feels no rancor against his destroyer. Perfect is the picture here of life in the Silesian hostelry, as Hauptmann had seen it in youth, and perfect also is the skill with which he paints these people.

The influence of Strindberg in determining both situation and central idea is more obvious in *The Flight of Gabriel Schilling*, where, for the unsophisticated peasant frenzied by his infidelity to a dead mate, is substituted as hero a supersensitive artist distracted by the claims of two women, his wife and his mistress. When they follow him to an island of refuge, so distraught does he become that to elude them he plunges into the sea. In healthful contrast to the neurotic Gabriel stands his host, the sculptor, for whom love is only an incident, however delightful; and, in contrast to Gabriel's selfish and possessive wife and mistress, stands the sculptor's lady, content to take what he offers, recognizing that the surest means for holding a man is to yield him his freedom. As for Gabriel, he drowns himself less from conscience than the desire to escape feminine thralldom. Love he has found to be only a torment of opposed attractions and repulsions.

Passion on the part of others which drives both Schilling and Henschel to death brings tragedy also to the peasant heroine of *Rose Bernd*, a motherless girl whose charms attract three admirers. One is an honest bookbinder convinced, like

Hilse in *The Weavers,* that suffering in this life is but the path to joy in the next. His suit, distasteful to Rose, is favored by her equally pious father. Already, however, she has succumbed to the warmer advances of a landowner of middle age, unhappy at home and tempted to find compensation by toying with this ward of his invalid wife. When he and Rose are detected together by a rough machinist, the latter proceeds to use his knowledge to force the girl to his will. Not satisfied with completing her ruin, he fights and maims her inoffensive lover and, being sued for slander by Rose's father, lays bare to the court her shame. Thereupon, the jealous landowner also turns upon her, glad to be relieved of the onus of causing her fall. Though the bookbinder still would marry her, she refuses, and, like Hetty Sorrell, strangles her new-born child in the fields that it may escape the martyrdom of love. Rose is a passive heroine, doomed by her environment and the lust of man. To her narrow-minded yet generous lover she cannot respond. The landowner fascinates her; the machinist frightens her; so-called justice destroys her. A stirring tragedy is this, graphic in its use of external detail, and, above all, gripping in its emotional rendering of inner stresses and strains.

Much less effective is Hauptmann's late play *Dorothea Angermann,* which repeats in lower key the theme of *Rose Bernd.* Again we have a heroine more sinned against than sinning. She is the daughter of a pastor who favors her match with his friend. This careful friend has waited to propose until he could secure a professorship. But by that time Dorothea has been victimized by a worthless fellow, chef at the village inn, and she feels in duty bound to refuse the professor whom she really loves. Her father, playing a variation upon the famous scene in Sudermann's *Magda,* summons in the chef and warns him that he shall not leave the room alive unless he sign a promise to marry Dorothea and sail with her for America at once. Since the chef will gain Dorothea's inheritance from an uncle, he consents. The remainder of the play shows the misery that results from the narrow-minded pastor's demand.

For two acts the scene shifts to Meriden, Connecticut, where Dorothea, deserted by her wretched husband, seeks refuge with her worthy suitor's brother, and is eventually saved from destitution and death by that suitor himself, who has come to America on a visit. He still would claim her, overlooking the blot on her past; but, as they embrace in happy reconciliation, the chef turns up, and, asserting his legal rights, carries her off since she pities him when the others assail him. Ere long he dies from an overdose of morphine that she has administered, and Dorothea returns to Germany only to find her honorable lover already wed to another. Nobody wants her, least of all her hypocritical father. Accusing him of again wishing to be rid of her because she imperils his respectability, she calls him her murderer, and through morphine finds rest from her woes. The background of the first two acts at the Silesian inn is carefully done, and the characters throughout are well drawn, but the bourgeois tragedy lacks authentic fire. Its central scenes depend too much upon the long arm of coincidence.

Lust of man for woman is the force that wrecks the life of Rose Bernd and incidentally of Dorothea Angermann, and lust of woman for man is that which wrecks the lives of Gabriel Schilling and Teamster Henschel. But mother-love is a potent instinct, also; and this, operating among folk of the fourth estate in the city slums, induces the tragedy of *The Rats*. Frau John, who lives in a cavalry barracks transformed into a tenement, yearns to replace her dead child, and passes off as her own the babe of a girl betrayed. The girl has been only too glad to agree to its sale before birth, but no sooner is the bargain closed than she, too, reacts to the maternal instinct, hitherto repressed by fear. In endeavoring to get back her child, she creates a disturbance; and Frau John, alarmed lest her husband learn of her trick, implores the aid of her rascally brother. He responds by luring the girl into the suburbs, and returns with a sprig of lilac in his cap torn from the bush beneath which he has killed her. The horrified Frau John must hide him in the tenement among the other rats, animal and human. When her husband protests against the presence of Bruno as likely to corrupt the child and threatens to take it away, the woman lets slip the truth which she has striven to suppress. The babe is not his. As the man snatches it from her, she runs forth in despair to fling herself beneath the wheels of a dray, the victim of a noble instinct turned awry.

The crucial situation at the last resembles that in Strindberg's *The Father*, but the play of Hauptmann remains markedly original in conception, observation, and execution. Lest the scenes of urban low life shock or weary his audience, the dramatist, grown somewhat mellow with age, has relieved their rough realism by introducing a humorous sub-plot concerning an old-fashioned actor who trains his pupils and stores his stage properties in the tenement. He seeks to conceal from his daughter his flirtation with an actress, but rates that daughter for flirting in turn with his pupil, a former theological student, son of a rustic clergyman. These people and their affairs are important, first, as they brighten by contrast the sordid story of Frau John, and, second, as they afford a striking comment within the play upon the play itself. Here, through the discussions of the actor-manager and his pupil, Hauptmann justifies naturalism. The teacher is scandalized that young Spitta should disdain idealism, poetic justice, and bombastic elocution; that he should maintain that "before art, as before the law, all men are equal," and assert that a barber or a scrubwoman might compare as tragic protagonist with Macbeth or King Lear. Such doctrine, the old conservative denounces as symptomatic of modernism with its rats gnawing in politics to undermine the German Empire and in the garden of art to destroy the very roots of the tree of beauty. But after the story of Frau John has unrolled before their eyes, and young Spitta demands, "Won't you admit that a genuine tragic fatality has been at work here?" Hassenreuter, converted, answers: "Tragedy is not confined to any class of society. I always told you that."

The gift of humor disclosed in *The Rats* is allowed free play by Hauptmann in three less important comedies of modified naturalism—*Schluck and Jau, The Maidens of Bischofsberg,* and *Peter Brauer.* The last, appearing only in 1921 but written before the War, is to be associated with *Colleague Crampton* as the portrait of a whimsical and incompetent artist. For Peter is the prince of cheerful liars, deluding and self-deluded, lazy, blithe and boastful. Having hired and equipped on credit a fine apartment in Berlin, he preens himself upon this act of kindness toward his family, from whom he begs enough to buy a ticket to Silesia, where he is engaged to decorate a garden chapel for a nobleman. His relatives think him on the high road to success, since he writes them that he has been as busy as a hare in the lettuce. So they follow after and pose proudly with him for a photograph of "The Master and his Family." But when the proprietor arrives to inspect the work and finds that it consists of gnomes and dwarfs fit only for a café, he dismisses Peter; and the old pretender, deserted by his family, is left to complain of the harsh treatment of the world. Yet we know that ere long he will regain his spirits, since by temperament he is a confirmed illusionist.

Less farcical is the gentle comedy, *Maidens of Bischofsberg,* into which Hauptmann has woven recollections of a time when he and his brothers fell in love for a season with three sisters living in a former monastery. The heroine, forced to accept as suitor her chill and methodical cousin, a professor of classics, is eventually saved from him by the negligent but fascinating wanderer, who, for her sake, has disappeared to seek a fortune in South America. As for the pedant, he has aroused the just antagonism of a jolly pupil, and by this boy is set to futile treasure hunting in the monastery yet loses the best treasure of all—charming Agatha. The plot here is nothing. The loves of the heroine's sisters lead nowhere. Only the characters count. But Hauptmann with unwonted optimism now praises passion as the flower of life, declaring that from it springs everything which stirs and glorifies the heights and depths of earth.

Better than either of these slight comedies is *Schluck and Jau*, Hauptmann's version of a theme treated by Shakespeare in the Induction to *The Taming of the Shrew*, by Calderón in *Life's a Dream*, by Holberg in *Jeppe of the Hills*, and by Grillparzer in *The Dream, a Life*. Hauptmann, however, has rendered the situation more complex by doubling the hero, with a desire perhaps to emulate certain comic contrasts struck out by Sancho and Don Quixote in their visit to the Duke. Upon two ragamuffins found by huntsmen stretched asleep at the gate of their master's lodge, a jest is played. While Schluck, the village buffoon, is sent to jail for the night, the sleeping "rough-neck" Jau is put to bed in style and cajoled on awaking into believing himself to be the prince, recovered from long illness. Then kindly Schluck, who has once acted a woman's part in a play, is prevailed upon to assume the rôle of Jau's princess. The scenes that ensue are Aristophanic in their fun, Schluck simpering and curtsying in petticoats, and Jau boasting of his prowess, singing to the court, and raging at the ugliness of his spouse. But the trick threatens to turn against its perpetrators when the servants disregard their old master in favor of the new, and the prince, who has posed as physician, is commanded to poison Princess Schluck that Jau may possess instead a lady-in-waiting. Jau, in short, is the beggar set on horseback, grown a tyrant. There is nothing for it but to return him to his humble estate by means of a sleeping potion. As he awakens, before the lodge, his interlude of princely life seems to him to have been but a dream, and when the chancellor assures him that even princes are only dreaming, he shrugs his shoulders and makes for the nearest tavern. Schluck is a character masterpiece, a happy rogue, fond of make-believe like Falstaff, warm of heart, grateful for the smallest favors, and bound to admire and protect his unworthy companion. Here broods a philosophic melancholy to set off the laughter, a feeling that yesterday and to-morrow are two phantoms, that death is behind and ahead, with only the fleeting present between, and that all men—princes and beggars alike—are but dreamers.

But what of Hauptmann's romantic plays—successors to *The Sunken Bell?* Not one has equaled that performance in merit. *Elga* and *The Commemoration Masque* are too slight and incidental. The legendary dramas, *Griselda, The Bow of Odysseus,* and *Veland,* scarcely justify their author's effort to modernize old stories. Of his attempt to present *Hamlet* in rewritten form at Dresden, the less said the better. It is merely curious as making Laertes head the rebellion against Claudius, giving some of his speeches to the hero on the theory that they originally belonged to Hamlet, moving the "To be or not to be" soliloquy from the third to the fifth act, revising the fourth act in particular, and offering six new scenes as an improvement upon the original. As for Hauptmann's semi-historical plays—*Poor Heinrich, Charlemagne's Hostage,* and *The White Redeemer,* though the first be excellent, they fail to reach the level of *The Sunken Bell* in poetry or conception. *Indipohdi* is altogether too fantastic for great art. Only *And Pippa Dances* and *A Winter Ballad* stand out distinctive among the romantic dramas, the former as an unusual example of symbolism, the latter as a subtle study in criminal psychology. In short, Hauptmann's achievement lies principally in the realistic field; yet a review of these idealistic dramas will show at least the breadth and variety of his genius.

In *Elga,* drawn from Grillparzer's *Cloister of Sendomir,* a knight lodged in the haunted chamber of a castle beholds enacted in his dream one tragic chapter in the history of that very room—the revenge upon a faithless wife and her lover by an outraged husband.

The Commemoration Masque, written for the centenary celebration of German emancipation from the Napoleonic yoke, disappointed the militarists. They had expected their foremost poet to glorify his country at the expense of the French, who, under Louis XIV, had seized Strasburg. What was it, they argued, but the recoil against the French that had heartened the Germans for the victory of Leipzig and for Blücher's success with Wellington at Waterloo? But Hauptmann, to the particular disgust of the Crown Prince, composed a puppet play ironically decrying war and glorifying peace, an in genious but inconsequential pageant.

Least successful of the master's legendary dramas is the versified *Veland*, acted in 1925 at the jubilee of the Hamburg Playhouse. It had appeared in fragmentary form three years earlier in his Collected Works. As completed now in haste, it recounted the old tale of Wayland the Smith who wreaks vengeance on a king, his rival in love of a swan maiden. He betrays the king's daughter, apparently slays the king's sons, and then flies away on wings of his own manufacture. But when a shepherd, baptized as Christian, converts him to the belief that love is better than hate, Veland reveals the fact that the princes are alive and that the princess will bear him a son to bring in the new dispensation of charity.

Teutonic legend gives way to Greek in *The Bow of Odysseus*, a romantic revamping of Homer. When Odysseus returns to Ithaca he is distraught from suffering, then recovers his reason by degrees, and yet for protection feigns that he still is mad. His son Telemachus has been saved from the plotting of Penelope's suitors by the granddaughter of a faithful swineherd, the fair Leukone, at times identified with the goddess Pallas Athene. Four acts are given over to the ravings of the hero, and his defensive schemes. In the last act, he sweeps to his revenge in the traditional fashion. Assuring the weak

Telemachus that the latter's weapon shall in turn find work to do, Odysseus asks, "But what will your mother say, now that I have destroyed her charming playthings?" Just what mother said, Hauptmann fails to disclose. For he never shows us Penelope, and he further forfeits half the charm of the Homeric story by leaving her fidelity suspect. Stephen Phillips, in *Ulysses*, had similarly sought to paint the lily, but he did so more attractively. Hauptmann, perhaps for the sake of greater unity, has bent all his efforts toward developing the character of his hero in whom may be detected echoes— very faint—of Hamlet and Lear.

Somewhat better is the legendary *Griselda*, an adaptation of the famous medieval story told by Boccaccio and Chaucer. But instead of eulogizing the willingness of a country girl to obey without question the behests of her lord, Hauptmann rather extols her love. He humanizes her motives and those of her husband, who, wearied of the court, has gone among his people in disguise and fallen enamored of the simple maiden. Ulrich marries her, not to spite his subjects demanding an heir, but out of pure affection. When later he tests her wifely obedience, he does so, not from idle curiosity but because he has waxed jealous of her devotion to their child. Deprived of that child, Griselda retires to her peasant home, not because he sends her there, but voluntarily, feeling that she is no longer needed at the court from which her troubled husband has withdrawn. Later, she returns at his command, ready to console him even as his servant. Here is no apologue recommending the slave-like submission of wives. Yet Hauptmann has found it difficult to reconcile medieval and modern conceptions of marriage. The old story proves but resistant material at best.

The saving power of unselfish love on the part of a woman is exalted in another medieval drama, *Poor Heinrich*, Hauptmann's reworking of a story familiar to Americans through Longfellow's *Golden Legend*. The peasant girl Ottegebe, learning that Prince Heinrich has contracted leprosy during his wanderings in the East, resolves to save him even at the price of her life. He can be cured only if a virgin die for his sake. After due hesitation, the prince, driven forth by his people, accepts her offer; but as they journey together to the scene of her proposed immolation, his heart is moved by the calm beauty of her spirit, and he refuses to profit by her sacrifice. Then she, who has trembled lest her love for him be all too earthly, perceives at last that it is also divine. What is more to the point, her devotion makes him whole; they will marry and be happy.

Very different is the love portrayed in *Charlemagne's Hostage*, a tyrannous passion that destroys even the aged and the wise. The great Emperor falls beneath the spell of a Saxon girl, the personification of all that is sensuously alluring and unmoral. He may denounce little Gersuind as a wanton to please the Churchmen, but he commands her release from her convent prison and listens enthralled as she boasts that, unlike the descendants of Adam and Eve, she does not know the difference between good and evil. Since Charlemagne's love-madness imperils the State, his Chancellor poisons the girl, who submits to drinking the fatal draught because it is given her by one wearing a white beard like her beloved Emperor. From the first she has wooed death at the Emperor's hands, warning him, as she pilfers his ring of seven circlets, that he can never recover it until he has taken her life—a symbolic hint that, until he is freed of the spell of pagan passion, his understanding of the distinction between the seven deadly sins and the seven heavenly virtues cannot be restored. With the death of Gersuind, Charlemagne is again ready to mix with action. Earlier he has struggled between his longing for lost youth, apparently to be realized in this slip of a hoyden, and his desire to choke her that her accursed soul may no longer wrong so beautiful a body. It is the old, old conflict depicted afresh; but Gersuind is no charming child of nature like Rautendelein. Rather, she is all that is most baneful in woman, the typical anti-heroine of Strindberg and Wedekind, representing a power coeternal with God, condemned by Him yet defiant, destined, like another Prometheus, says Hauptmann, "to rise to new passions and torments old."

The conception of love as evil, wrought out on the romantic plane in *Charlemagne's Hostage*, is the same exhibited by Hauptmann on the naturalistic plane in *Teamster Henschel*, *Rose Bernd*, and *The Flight of Gabriel Schilling*. To Montezuma, also, in *The White Redeemer*, love proves fatal, for it is his mistress who betrays him to Cortez in revealing to the Spaniard her lord's faith in the prophecy of a white savior destined to bear him and his race in flaming chariots to the sun. Though Montezuma seeks at first to turn back the invading Spaniards by diplomacy, he presently entertains them as messengers divine. When seized and disillusioned, he and his son refuse to obey the Spaniards' mandate that they curb the revolt of their subjects. The son is dragged to execution, and Montezuma, exposed from a house-top, is stoned by his own people. Dying, he declines the last sacrament proffered him by his pious captors, tears off the bandages that bind his wounds, and with his last breath curses the white brood that has stooped to such cupidity and violence.

Here may be heard a protest against the horrors perpetrated by the belligerent and intolerant white race even in Europe. What to the mystic like Montezuma can this world offer but unmerited suffering? Like so many of Hauptmann's heroes, he is passive, but in the telling of his story, romance and poetry replace photographic realism. The characters are less individual than typical, from the considerate Las Casas and the cruel Alvarado to the churchly Gomara, justifying the slaughter of the Aztecs if only one soul be saved for Christ.

The episodic technique of expressionism employed in this semi-historical romance is used again in another Mexican fantasy—the dreamy *Indipohdi*—whose protagonist, by his name and situation, recalls the hero of Shakespeare's *Tempest*. Prospero, driven from his European throne by an ambitious son, and shipwrecked on an island overseas, is hailed by the Toltecs as a god. For eleven years he serves as their priestly ruler, until, upon that very isle, is cast away his rebel son. This youth, struck by love on encountering his own sister, conspires with a disaffected chieftain against his still unrecognized father. Defeated by that father's magic, he is condemned to a ceremonial death, it being the custom each year thus to propitiate the god of a neighboring volcano as a means to averting its eruption. But the girl, to save Ormann, turns against her father. The latter, like the original Prospero, is magnanimous or nothing. Having sufficiently tested the devotion to each other of his children, he ascends the volcano and in his son's place leaps down its crater, another Empedocles on Ætna. To his children and their future offspring he leaves the island sovereignty.

It would have been simple to obviate here the unpleasant suggestion of incest had Hauptmann but followed Shakespeare in making the lover Prospero's nephew rather than his son. Yet such consanguinity scarcely offends in a plot compacted of the stuff that dreams are made of. There is charm in Ormann's reported meeting with the huntress Pyrrha, his sister, first seen by him as his own fairer double poised upon a crag and bringing down with her arrow a soaring eagle. There is beauty, also, in the love that unites Prospero and his Tehura who alone can understand his noble motives. This is a play of forgiveness and self-abnegation, yet too remote from life to challenge interest. The strange title "Indipohdi" is explained by Tehura as having been originally applied to a Toltec king who sprang out of nothing and returned to nothing. Prospero, seizing upon the word she has used, proclaims himself to be an "Indipohdi" also, descended from that very king.

Of Hauptmann's eleven romantic plays following *The Sunken Bell*, two alone, as has been said, possess qualities that make them noteworthy. *A Winter Ballad* affords imaginative treatment of the workings of conscience. The earlier *And Pippa Dances* pushes to the extreme the sort of symbolism used so effectively in *The Sunken Bell*, combining it with realism in a way to forecast expressionism. Here fantastic features bud out of a natural story and are to be interpreted as allegory.

While Pippa, an Italian dancer, performs in a mountain tavern for the entertainment of glass-workers, her supposed father, detected in cheating at cards, is driven out and slain. During the brawl, Pippa is carried off by a red-bearded giant who has tried to caper with her to the amusement of the rest. Storm-bound in his hut, she shudders with fear, but when he goes forth to ascertain the source of a noise, she is joined by the poet, who has played the ocarina for her dancing and who now makes love to her and leads her away to safety. Through the forest they wander to the cabin of a magician, to whom already has come the manager of the glass works demanding aid in his quest for Pippa. He would pay to see her dance again, and, as if in answer to the magician's summons, she appears at the door with the fainting poet and is accorded refuge from the storm. The manager, perceiving that her affection is already given to the poet, withdraws, cured of his longing for her. But the rude old giant has followed her in. When he rages, the magician renders him motionless under a spell; but Pippa pities and intercedes for him, warming his chilled heart with her hand and dancing again to please him. As for Huhn, the giant, he cannot enjoy beauty without wishing to possess it. When, in glee, he lifts aloft a wine glass and crushes it in his fingers, Pippa expires, as though the glass had held her soul; and the poet, struck suddenly blind, imagines her still dancing her way to Venice, his city of dreams in the South. "And Pippa dances?" he asks. "And Pippa dances," answers the magician.

The first act of the curious play is realistic. Thereafter, all that occurs must be understood symbolically or not at all. The giant Huhn is lust; the magician is intellect controlling lust but tempted to make beauty, or the ideal, its own. Pippa is that ideal ever dancing before man and affecting each beholder differently. Lust would possess and destroy her. Capital—the manager—would buy her. The intellect would protect her from capital and lust, and preserve her for the poet who alone can appreciate her. That poet, by reason of his idealism, still may see and love her, though he be blind and she, in fact, exist no longer. Thus, double and treble meanings are insinuated into a dramatic *märchen*, which, like Pippa herself, will affect each spectator according to his nature. When the piece appeared it provoked adverse criticism on account of its tantalizing technique. But to-day it can more readily be accepted, since the expressionists have accustomed us to the use of exactly these means in the theater. Indeed, *And Pippa Dances*, if it be less satisfying than *The Sunken Bell*, is historically important as marking the advance of the foremost German dramatist toward a phase of art destined for a time to rival and replace naturalism.

Something of the same technique is employed also in *A Winter Ballad*, Hauptmann's most significant play produced since the War. Here, character is the principal concern rather than the hinting of abstract doctrine. Three Scottish mercenaries who have fought in the Swedish wars of the sixteenth century, while awaiting the spring thaw in order to sail home, rob and murder an old pastor, his wife, and his granddaughter. Thereafter their leader, Sir Archie, who has stabbed little Berghild when she flung herself into his arms for protection, is haunted by her spirit. He fancies himself to have been mystically wedded to her in that dreadful moment, and perceives in her foster sister, who had escaped, the dead girl herself. His madness grows, and the living Elsalil seems to him more and more to be the dead girl's double. She follows him as if in a trance, sniffing blood, tempting him to embrace her, protecting him from those who would seize him, and yet appearing jealous that he loves her only because he identifies her with his victim.

Much of the drama passes in Sir Archie's mind. To him, Elsalil's yellow tresses seem to be the murdered pastor's golden treasure; he fears the poisonous bite of her kiss, recalling the kiss which his victim gave him in dying. He implores her to declare that she is Berghild, to swear that his knife did not do the murder. He feels that she and the dead girl by turns drain the hot blood out of him, and strive to win his body's warmth like freezing corpses. When Elsalil, in jealousy, bites his hand, asking whether it be she or her dead rival who inflicts this wound, he cries: "Bleed me, until I am cold as ice, drawing away with my infected blood all the infected madness of my brain, thy image and that other one forever!" Then, fancying that he is pursued across the ice by Elsalil, he hurls back at her imaginary missiles, shouting: "Thou she-cur! I felled her dead. But there she is again. She betrayed me, and betrayed Berghild, too."

In truth, Sir Archie in his delirium slays Elsalil, also, thus sinking from crime to crime. Yet Hauptmann, through this character, would preach the possibility of redemption. When Archie, who has promised to meet the avenging son of the slain pastor on the ice, is advised by his fellow miscreants to join them in escaping to Scotland, his better nature suddenly asserts itself. "No! No!" he protests. And, with that unexpected refusal, says Hauptmann, "he collapses as if struck by lightning, and dies." The pastor's son, perceiving the moral meaning of that death, explains: "It was not God, the Avenger's lightning, that so struck him down! How wonderful! It was his own 'No! No!' with which he checked forever his own step and that of destiny as well. . . . Here lies a conqueror; here lies a man redeemed; . . . and where is my foe?"

So Hauptmann would indicate that the human avenger has lost his enemy with that enemy's conversion to the good will.

Arneson, despite his faith in Christ's law of love, had lived only for revenge since the murder of his parents and his daughter. Archie, suffering torments for his crime, has finally expressed the good within him by at least refusing to persist in evil. Even though in madness he has slain Elsalil as well, he at last is willing to atone. The moral is precisely that set forth at the close of Stevenson's *Markheim*. Though the sinner cannot undo his deed, he may cease further to act. Therein lies his first step toward redemption.

It is interesting to observe that Hauptmann has transformed Selma Lagerlöf's simple and objective *märchen—Herr Arne's Treasure*—into a Hawthornesque study of a guilty soul. What in the Swedish is external, Hauptmann makes subjective. Berghild's material ghost becomes Archie's own identification of the dead girl with the living. Nature, which figured as an avenging protagonist, is reduced to a sympathetic background. And the pastor's son is invented as a seeker of vengeance, himself redeemed from hate when his enemy is so redeemed.

Elsalil, in the tale, fell in love with Sir Archie without knowing of his crime, but, on being apprised of it by the ghost of her foster sister, she slew herself in order that he, who was bearing her off, might be freely struck down by his pursuers; whereupon, "all the women folk wept over the young maid who had loved an evil doer and had given her life to destroying him she loved." This situation, fundamental for Selma Lagerlöf, is discarded by Hauptmann because he would focus attention upon Archie; and Archie, who, in the story, was the most savage of the murderers, and was seized unrepentant aboard ship while attempting to escape, becomes with Hauptmann the least savage of the three,—a sinner of vivid imagination like Macbeth, suffering agonies in conscience, but saving his soul through repentance.

In Hauptmann we must recognize one of the most distinguished dramatists of our time, the initiator of German naturalism, a revealer of experience among the middle classes and the lowly, and at the same time a poet more effective as an idealist because of his comprehension of the real. Pity for the suffering and oppressed, sympathy for those unable to make adjustment to others and to the world, a yearning for self-expression on the heights, and a deepening sense of man's inability to remold "this sorry scheme of things entire" mark the work of Hauptmann. Yet he is no pessimist. He is a master of humor as well as of pathos. For him Pippa dances still, and Sir Archie, sinning as he may, can yet repent. Though the Spaniards bring death to Montezuma, he retains his nobility of soul, and the wronged Prospero for the sake of his children gladly immolates himself in the flames of the volcano.

Increasingly, Hauptmann exhibits an appreciation of quietism. Although, like other lovers of his country, he signed the statement of the ninety-three scholars and men of letters after the outbreak of the Great War, he was at heart a man of peace, passive as his own heroes, dreaming beyond the conflict. Having, in his art, run the whole gamut from naturalism to symbolism and expressionism, looking with acute vision not only outward but inward, he has fashioned an extraordinarily rich and varied fabric to adorn the theater.

CHAPTER XVII

Sudermann—Theatrical Opportunist

REMARKABLY facile as a dramatist, Hermann Sudermann, once regarded as a rival to Hauptmann, has long
suffered depreciation. Yet his war studies in the trilogy entitled *German Destiny* did much to reinstate him in public
esteem before his death in 1928. In the field of the novel his
achievements have been more notable than those of Hauptmann, and in the field of drama he is not to be scorned. For
years, his fame abroad was especially great. Even yet, he is
recognized as at least a leader of the second rank.

Sudermann was the son of a brewer, born in 1857 in a village of East Prussia. Like Ibsen he knew poverty and was for
a time apprenticed to an apothecary. After graduation from
the Gymnasium at Tilsit, he studied philosophy and history
at the University of Königsberg, and then came to Berlin at
the age of twenty. There he responded to the new movement
just beginning in the theater, and in 1889, the year that
Hauptmann issued his naturalistic challenge *Before Sunrise*,
Sudermann presented at the Lessing Theater his thesis play
Honor, directed against the tyranny of a military and commercial ideal, and depicting, also, with naturalistic art, the
members of a lower middle-class family set off against those
of a family of the upper middle class.

In technique, the play showed the influence of Ibsen, Augier,
and the younger Dumas. It was a well-made piece, excellent
in its turnings of plot. At the same time, Sudermann profited
by the new interest in minute observation of the lowly to introduce scenes that would meet the approval of converts to naturalism. Contemporaries who could not stomach the strong meat

of *Before Sunrise* were gratified by *Honor*. Its doctrine seemed to align Sudermann with the young radicals who were ready to pick flaws in the manners and ideals of their elders. His attitude toward naturalism was characteristic. He realized its advantages and disadvantages. Too close an adherence to it would mean the discarding of plot, situation, rhetoric, the painting of a pleasant background, and the enunciation of some edifying moral. On the other hand, in naturalism lay fresh material and novel technical resources for the dramatist. Although Sudermann did not wish to pose as an uncompromising champion of the new, he certainly desired to profit by the fashion. So he told the story of a rich youth in the house on the avenue intriguing with a poor girl in the house on the courtyard. Her brother, returned from long absence, thinks to break up the evil alliance or to punish the seducer. This brother is himself in love with the seducer's sister. Eventually, when he finds that he cannot imbue silly Alma or his parents with his own ideal of honor, he is deterred from taking revenge by a philosophic friend and benefactor, an old-fashioned *raisonneur*, who points out that the code of the duel is absurd, and that there are as many conceptions of honor as there are classes in society. The hero, accordingly, resolves to abandon his low-class family, to marry the heroine, and make for them both "a new home, a new duty, and a new honor."

In his second drama—*The Destruction of Sodom*—Sudermann focused attention upon the upper middle class of Berlin, a corrupt society of financiers and artists. When the wife of a speculator takes under her protection a young painter, his creative powers decline. He consents to cloak their intrigue by marrying her niece. But, in the mean time, he has seduced his foster sister, beloved by his best friend. Ironically tragic is the scene in which he goes into the girl's room while this unsuspecting friend walks across the stage reading a eulogy of his betrayer. When the girl drowns herself, Willy is smitten in conscience and confesses his sin. He begs his friend for punishment, and then dies, suffering a sudden hemorrhage. Thus a vicious environment has been responsible for destroying a youth of talent. Sudermann, however, has failed to impress us with Willy's charm or ability, even though three women adore him, and the public accords him fame for his painting, "The Destruction of Sodom," a picture which suggests the sins and the doom that threaten wicked Berlin.

Naturalistic influence may be noted here in the use of detail and in the presentation of a passive hero who expires at just the right moment. Such a fortuitous death again cuts the knot of intrigue at the conclusion of Sudermann's *Magda* (*Die Heimat*), his third and most popular piece. Although to-day it seems commonplace in doctrine and dramaturgy, once it was regarded in both respects as the last word. Even yet in depicting the struggle between the older and the younger generation it contains much that is universal. A daughter leaves her home when her father demands that she shall marry a certain pastor. In Berlin she leads a free life and bears a child to one who deserts her. Years later she returns to her home as soloist at a music festival. The pastor prevails upon her proud father to receive her, but she has grown too independent to respect his authority. She pokes fun at the provincial ladies who would patronize her, and, encountering her former lover, rallies him on his cowardice in having decamped. Then, her father, the retired colonel, learning of the injury done her by Councillor von Keller, demands that it be repaired by marriage. But Magda, when the councillor refuses to permit their child to join them, rejects his proposal. The colonel, feeling his family to be disgraced, threatens to take her life and his own unless she consent. But before he can shoot her, he is smitten by an apoplectic stroke.

Both plot and characterization are excellent. The father, an officer of the old school, is controlled by the German tradition of paternal authority and the ideal of honor held by his caste. Shocked to discover her intrigue, he assumes that there can be but two remedies for the situation—either he must duel with her betrayer, or her betrayer must marry her. As for von Keller, he is an amusing hypocrite, willing to make amends, because he fears even the paralytic colonel and because Magda, after all, has become a person of note whose talents may aid his political advancement. The child of whose existence he had known nothing heretofore, he would keep in hiding lest the severely disposed be alienated. The pastor is a generous soul without cant or bigotry, respecting Magda's decision against him, loving her still, and doing his best to make her father forgive her. Magda is the new woman, self-made and self-sustaining, temperamental, ironical, impulsive. She declares her gratitude to von Keller for having taught her through love the whole scale of passions that bring women to maturity. Though scarcely true to type in agreeing to marry him out of regard for her father's wishes, she appeals to the gallery in refusing to do so finally. Her statement that "we must sin if we wish to grow," and her hint to her father that she has had other lovers, may offend the moralists. Perhaps, in speaking thus, she may have sought merely to terminate a disagreeable interview, but she may also be telling the truth. At all events, Sudermann would have us sympathize both with his heroine and with her father from whom she inherits her self-assertion and obstinacy. It is only a shift of environment that has differentiated the two. In this use of the determining force of heredity and environment, and in the exaltation of a militant feminist, the influence of naturalism may still be discerned; yet the play is so artificial in technique that it might have flowed from the pen of the younger Dumas.

Henceforth Sudermann, in his realistic dramas, was less concerned with a thesis than with general social satire—now merely amusing as in *The Battle of the Butterflies* and *Storm Brother Socrates*, and now lyrical as in *The Flower Boat* or serious as in *The Joy of Living*. *The Battle of the Butterflies* celebrates the ultimate success of a Cinderella, who, with her two sisters, paints butterflies upon fans in order to keep body and soul together. Their mother, an officer's widow, is bent upon retaining her position by getting her daughters well married. One aspires to capture a count. Another, a merry widow who has procured a husband by deception and then driven him to suicide, has set her cap to marry a millionaire's son. Little Rose, in order to save this flirt, assumes the blame of the latter's affair with a lodger in their house. But eventually her innocence is proved, and she accepts the millionaire's son as Heaven's reward for unselfish virtue. The youth has been reared by his philosophic father as a child of the people, destined to marry a poor girl. Henceforth, no doubt, that father will provide for him and for the three sisters and their foolish mamma.

Here sentiment mingles with humor, and in *Storm Brother Socrates* it mingles with farce in a light-hearted satire upon veterans of the Liberal movement of 1848, still meeting in secret and believing themselves to be radical. Their sons consent, as a matter of tact, to joining the Club, but, when one of the boys operates on the tooth of a dog belonging to the chief of police, there is trouble. What are the old men to think of this aiding and abetting the government? Since a prince sends the father of the dentist an iron cross, the veteran's vanity is touched, and he concludes that bygones should be bygones, that Bismarck has made Germany flourish, and that there is no resisting the march of progress. As he looks from the window at soldiers celebrating the victory of Sedan, he cries, "I am coming to join you!"

The cynical *Flower Boat* of Sudermann recalls the angry satire of *The Destruction of Sodom*, describing corruption among commercial folk and the lesser nobility. The widow of a merchant weds a baron who has been her lover, and later, for gain, contrives the marriage of her elder daughter to the prosaic manager of the family firm. Then she incites this daughter to prove unfaithful. Eventually, the girl's husband, having followed his wife to a flower boat, murders there the man she has come to meet. Thus destructively works the influence of the evil baroness. Her younger daughter, too, in emulating her example, breaks off her betrothal to a worthy suitor in order to marry a wild cousin on condition that each shall remain free. But the dramatist sees to it that Thea and her Fred, wearied of wickedness, shall reform, and Fred be given the management of the firm resigned by his brother-in-law. Virtue, even when deferred, really pays. The regeneration of Thea and her husband remains too improbable to counteract the impression left by this spectacle of vice.

Superior to such pieces is *The Joy of Living*. Here the problem of honor, already discussed in the play of that name and in *Magda*, finds incidental notice. But interest is focused on character. The Countess Beata is a new woman less outspokenly individual than Magda, though more complex. In love with the husband of another, she has checked her intrigue when her lover and her husband became friends. Still devoted to Baron Richard, she would marry her son to his daughter, and prevail upon her good-natured lord to withdraw from the Reichstag that Richard may take his seat. During the campaign the opponent of Richard airs the old scandal. Though Richard is elected, his friend will sue the slanderer; but, on inquiring if he may safely do so, he learns that the story is true. According to the code of honor, the husband and the lover should cross swords, yet to duel will confirm suspicion. When the case is submitted hypothetically to the son of Richard, he declares that any man of honor under such conditions would be more eager to give his life to the husband he has injured than that husband would be to take it. Richard, accepting this decision, promises Count Michael to efface himself after two days. In the mean time he will set his affairs in order and deliver in the Reichstag a speech upholding the sanctity of the home.

The scandalmonger is so touched by the speech that improbably he returns to Richard the letters that have compromised him. Then Beata, in order to protect him and save from the shadow of gossip her daughter and Richard's son, gives a luncheon at which her two men drink toasts to each other. As for Beata, she drinks to the joy of living, and asks: "Which of us is really alive? Which of us dares really to live?" When she sinks dying, the guests suppose that she has succumbed to heart failure, but in truth she has taken poison. In a letter left for her husband, she has written: "I see that some one must pay the penalty:—better I than he. He has his work before him—I have lived my life. . . . He cannot die now without causing the scandal you have been so anxious to avert. I have always loved happiness, and I find happiness now in doing this for his sake, and the children's, and yours."

Although the story is artificial and its ethical issues are confused, Beata is fairly sympathetic, a flawed heroine whose emancipation is tentative only, yet one unselfishly devoted to her lover, believing in the importance of his political future. She deceives her husband for his own good. To his rival she says, "You felt that you were sinning;—I felt that I had risen above myself, that I had attained the harmony nature meant me to attain." She talks of refusing to be crushed by conventional laws, yet she fears appearances. Obviously Sudermann would justify her. She indeed deserves credit for her long withdrawal from intimacy with Richard. Of the fact that he, too, was married, little is made. Presumably Beata's death will release him from the necessity of taking his life as he had promised. He may win political victories but scarcely our admiration. The piece is an excellent picture of folk of the upper class concerned with manners rather than morals.

The implied problem as to which should rule—individualism or altruism—Sudermann had already considered in two other plays, *Happiness in a Corner* and *The Fires of St. John.* In both, altruism conquers. The first is a realistic echo of Ibsen's *Lady from the Sea.* The young wife of a middle-aged schoolmaster cannot forget the freer existence she had known before marriage, when, in visiting a girl friend, she had felt the fascination of the latter's husband. Now he comes in quest of her, declaring that he will claim her as his own. In resisting his suggestion that she visit at his castle, she lets him read her heart. She had accepted the tutor there in a moment of depression due to her hopeless love for the baron. The baron, thus encouraged, grows imperious, and vows that he will demand her release of her husband. Begging that he delay until the morrow, Elizabeth plans to take her life; but her husband, guessing the truth, generously bids her go or stay. Elizabeth, accorded her freedom, reacts as did Ibsen's Ellida Wangel. She no longer yearns to go. She realizes that when she chose to marry him, she was free. "You came in a sad hour, and I said 'yes.' In a happy hour, I would have said 'no.' That I admit. But, after all, it was of my own free will, at least such freedom as one in drowning might exhibit in reaching for the hand stretched out to help. . . . I fled then from the very man from whom I flee to-day." So, her feeling for the Baron, like Ellida's for the Stranger, has been largely compounded of fear. As soon as the schoolmaster understands this fact and that she would cleave to him still, he promises that on the morrow the baron shall depart. "But why do you look at me so?" he asks, and she answers, "It is as though I now saw you for the first time." As he has said, her longing for the great world will subside; and she may yet find happiness in their corner. Ethically this constitutes the most satisfying of Sudermann's dramas. Although deficient in action, it is charged with feeling, and presents a winning plea for an indulgent love based on freedom and a sense of responsibility. It should be compared with *The Lady from the Sea* and Shaw's *Candida*, the first symbolic, and the last brilliantly humorous.

Less effective on the whole, if more dramatic, is *The Fires of St. John*, wherein the hero and the heroine renounce marriage out of gratitude to their common benefactor. George has been reared, since his father's suicide, by an uncle; and Marikke, by that uncle, has been rescued from the clutches of her gipsy mother tramping the roads. As children the pair have played at love, but Marikke learns, after George's betrothal to the daughter of their benefactor, that his passion for her has all along been serious. Is it too late? Must they respect the feelings of childlike Trude and her father? Impulse at war with control is here symbolized by the conflict between unbridled pagan joy and Christian self restraint displayed on Midsummer Night, when the Fires of St. John are allowed to burn through the countryside and for once in the year folk may revel freely. Again, as in *The Joy of Living*, there is here a toast-drinking scene. George lifts his glass to the Pagan Spirit, and later obeys it in action when he and Marikke are left together by chance. Then she, more assertive than he, claims him as her own. Her mother stole; and she too will steal, not pelf, but love. Yet next morning consideration for others reasserts its sway. Marikke bids her lover keep his vow to Trude, and he, after a weak threat of escape through suicide, will assent. The dramatist, however, fails to evoke approval since the duty that conquers passion is here so little justified. By this blind obedience George can bring to Trude or to his uncle no lasting happiness. If the decision of Marikke and the assent to it by George be conventional, the characters are at least made real. Marikke is an interesting figure. We like her best, not in her repentance but in her revolt, when she is conscious of heredity as her fate. George is the passive hero of the naturalists, fearful of his uncle, and following the line of least resistance.

Three inferior realistic plays remain to be considered together—*Stone Among Stones*, half a melodrama of industrial life; *A Good Reputation*, another picture of the corrupt upper middle class; and *The Raschoffs*, a study of father and son enthralled by a siren. In the first, when the philanthropic head of a stone-dressing plant engages as night watchman a convict fresh from prison, the other workers resent his choice, and the man whose job he has taken plots with a bully against him. But the ousted watchman's daughter has been wronged by the bully, and the noble-hearted convict arouses the workmen to demand that the injury done to her shall be repaired by marriage. When the bully would stab him, the hero shows his mettle, and later saves the girl from a death designed for himself. Thereupon the father repents, the seducer flees, and Lore and the crippled daughter of the master of the works are left to contend as to which shall marry this Teutonic Jean Valjean. No mid-Victorian melodrama was ever more trite and conventional. The satirist of high society has here grown bourgeois, sentimental, and moral, affirming that if employers will but treat their workmen with love, this love will in turn provoke loyalty. Lore, when victimized by the bully, has complained of the lot of the workers, saying: "We have become as soulless as stones. We let ourselves be kicked like stones. We are indifferent to everything like stones." Yet these toilers are anything but "stones among stones." Their master, Zarucke, is consideration itself, strangely combining sensibility and stoicism. When his daughter despairs because the bully has rebuffed her, he comforts her, saying that, slowly or quickly, sorrows as well as joys will pass, and that: "Those who are silent are the wise ones. Only he who is far, far apart from the world, can possess it completely."

In *A Good Reputation*, Sudermann returned to his more usual field of social satire, reproving those who intrigue under the cloak of respectability, and asking our sympathy for a heroine unconventional but sound at heart. Dorrit von Tanna has repaid her husband's neglect by open philandering; yet she protects her less moral friend Karla, and prevails upon her to permit the man they both love to attain happiness in marrying still another, his ward. Thus, she restrains Karla from deserting husband and children, and, though earlier condemned by Karla's husband, is finally accorded his praise.

SUDERMANN—THEATRICAL OPPORTUNIST

Reputation means little. Dorrit, who lost it through frankness, was better than Karla, who kept it through subterfuge. In general, this piece, however accurate in its drawing of the upper middle classes, is so confused in exposition and uncertain in moral emphasis as to merit small approval for its technique or its criticism of life.

The curious moral obliquity sometimes evidenced by Sudermann reappears in his late comedy, *The Raschoffs*. On a country estate live father and son, the son neglecting his wife for a siren from Berlin, and the father, to save him, proposing a curious remedy. Let Bernhard bring his charmer to the estate incognito, and ere long he will weary of her. Once the father had tried such a cure with success. Only too pleased to accept this advice, Bernhard summons his affinity to pose as niece of the manager's wife; and presently, as the father had foreseen, she and Bernhard fall out. She contrives a meeting with his wife to vent her spite upon one who, to her, typifies feminine scorn for the déclassé. But finding the wife to be charming in her grief for the recent loss of a child, Wally is moved to pity. So she sets her cap at the elder Raschoff, agreeing to leave the estate and his son only on condition that he accompany her. Shall the father, who is not insensible to the charms of the lady, thus sacrifice himself for the sake of his son? When the son, growing jealous, threatens a duel, the father is pleased to observe such spirit in the weakling, and the two are reconciled. Then each offers to surrender to the other the lady. But she, having received a proposal of marriage from a merchant in Berlin, leaves them both. The elder Raschoff waves her farewell from the window and heaves a sigh of relief. For neither father nor son is there any reproach from the dramatist. Men will be men—even old ones. The father, in fact, is upheld as a model of paternal devotion. Had he fought with his son, the play would have gained as drama; but Sudermann wished to produce, not tragedy, but a cynical comedy. The father alone is thoroughly characterized. Vivid as are the rural scenes, they remain subordinated to the playwright's attempt to answer the question, "How far will a father go, in love for his son?"

In general, the romantic dramas of Sudermann, like those of Hauptmann, are less interesting than his plays of realistic observation. One is Biblical, one fantastic, and three are semihistorical. The Biblical drama *Johannes* retells elaborately the story of John the Baptist. Like Oscar Wilde's *Salome*, it represents the evil heroine as infatuated with the prophet. She even slays her maid whom she hates as a possible rival. Yet she is less the nymphomaniac than Wilde's protagonist, and when, after dancing before Herod, she claims as her fee the head of the Prophet, it is at the prompting of her mother Herodias, and not, as with Wilde, on her own initiative. To the last, Sudermann's Salome would have relented had Johannes but asked of her his life. The German poet shifts our interest from the temptress to the prophet and exhibits his gradual conversion to Jesus' doctrine of love as entailing nonresistance to violence. Accordingly, the crucial scene here is not that of the dance but rather of the refusal of Johannes to save his own life when, by flinging a stone at Herod, he could readily have started a revolt. Instead, letting fall the missile, he submits, saying, "In the name of Him Who bids me love thee."

Romanticism more tenuous marks Sudermann's *Three Heron Feathers*, a symbolic fairy tale. The prince who goes in quest of his ideal, incarnate in a beautiful woman, must burn three feathers in succession, the first in order to behold her, the second to possess her, the third to destroy her. Advised by a witch, he secures the three feathers and burns the first. But the apparition of his ideal fades. Fevered with desire to recapture it, he wanders on and, winning a victory over the suitors of a widowed queen, accepts the hand she proffers in reward. Still intent upon the ideal, the prince burns the second feather, but fails to understand, when his queen comes to comfort him, that she incarnates the ideal. He looks for it, instead, far away. Returning after a dozen years to find his queen still faithful, he perceives that it is she alone whom he loves. To destroy the vision which has so misled him, he burns the third feather. But forthwith the queen sinks dying, for she was his ideal incorporate in the real. Clasping her, he expires of grief, united in death with his ideal. A pretty fable is this, faintly resembling Rostand's *Far-away Princess* and suggested in part by Hauptmann's *Sunken Bell.* The witch—or Burial Woman—is half sister to Ibsen's Rat Wife, and Prince Witte's servant, as contrasting the real with the ideal, is first cousin to Sancho Panza.

Of Sudermann's semi-historical plays in romantic vein, *The Children of the Strand* is in subject late medieval, *The Beggar of Syracuse* and *Claudian's Songs of Praise* are post-classical. The first tells a lively story of the rivalry in love of two brothers, the murder by one of the father of the girl they both adore, the girl's marriage to the other, her lapse into the arms of the murderer, her attempt with his aid to wreck the ship of her husband, the drowning of the guilty pair after the good brother has been saved by a fair captive, and his eventual marriage with that captive, who proves to be a princess. The *Vikings* of Ibsen may have inspired this piece, which could have served Sir Walter as plot for a novel. The scene is the Baltic shore of East Prussia when knighthood was in flower, and the leading characters are half-pagan pirates, rebellious at first to the control of Christian knights, but eventually converted to submission. It is all vigorous and stirring, a dramatized tale of passion and adventure in a picturesque setting. Especially vivid is the portrayal of Brigolla's inner conflict when she and Gregor are thrown together after her marriage to his brother, and when in vain she struggles against the temptation to prove disloyal to her husband and to the memory of her murdered father.

Even more complicated in intrigue is *The Beggar of Syra-*

cuse, which involves, like the *Odyssey*, the return of a ruler supposed to be dead, and the punishment he inflicts upon those who have betrayed him. Lykon, blinded in battle and driven out, has lost his wife and his city to a traitor, but he has been promised by a heavenly messenger that he shall fight as long as night endures, meaning that in blindness he shall fight his country's foe until he die. Although the business of the oracle might have been dispensed with to advantage, and although the play lacks inevitability throughout, it contains excellent scenes, as when the wife of Lykon, reproved for forgetting him, protests that to her he has never died, or when at a banquet Lykon in rags fires his countrymen with patriotic ardor and spurs on a wrestler to fell the blatant Mago who has drunk a lying toast to the welfare of Syracuse.

In *Claudian's Songs of Praise*, Sudermann attempts to recreate the fifth century after Christ. Honorius, Emperor of the West, is a Christian weakling, seldom seen. His Empire is defended against Alaric the Goth by the noble Stilicho, himself the son of a barbarian. Stilicho's devoted friend, the poet Claudian, would make his master ruler of the Romans. To this end Claudian plots to lure Alaric into the Roman camp on a promise of safe-conduct and then to slay him in order that with his fall Stilicho may triumph over the enemies of Rome. But Stilicho is too honorable to profit by such treachery. Having rescued Alaric and led him to safety beyond the Roman lines, he returns to dismiss in wrath his over-zealous poet and to brave the resentment of Roman leaders envious of his power. Although he has married off two daughters in succession to the Emperor, Stilicho's life is now in danger. He retreats from Milan to Rimini, where he is sought out by the still devoted Claudian. Emissaries of the Senate pursue, and after striking down the poet, convey to Stilicho sentence of death. "So shall it be," they cry, "to all the friends of Alaric!" The piece is long, rhetorical, and spectacular. Love bears no part in it. Against the background of a troubled time Sudermann sets in action two interesting characters—the ambitious warrior and the devoted poet—the latter humorous, boastful, now a jester, now heroic, finally a martyr in devotion to his master.

Before passing to the latest realistic plays of Sudermann, something must be said of his pieces in one act, presented in two series—three in *Morituri* and four in *Roses*. The earlier group derives external unity from the fact that in each the central figure is one presumably about to die; the later group by the fact that in each there figure roses. *Teja* of the first group shows the farewell to his bride of a Gothic chieftain who has fought the forces of Byzantium, not for love of carnage, but as the sole hope of safety for his friends. Now, since the ships designed to aid him have gone over to the enemy, his doom is sealed. Yet, heartened by her understanding of his motives, he will enter his last battle bravely. In *Fritzchen*, a youth, disgraced by his affair with the wife of an officer, comes before he duels with the lady's husband, an unerring shot, to take farewell of his parents and his betrothed. The women know nothing of his peril. "My fault!" moans the father, who has incited the youth to philandering. "How handsome he looks!" exclaims the mother, who recounts proudly her dream of seeing him summoned before the Emperor to receive high honors.

Death is merely threatened and not imminent in *The Eternal Masculine*, a light parody in rhyming couplets on the theme of the other two plays. Here an artist presumes upon a queen's admiration of his genius to make love to her while painting her portrait. Incensed, she calls her marshal to punish the insult, knowing that he will be more ready to do so since he loves her. But the artist wheedles the marshal into feigning death in order to hear what the courtiers and the queen really think of him. When the marshal has heard enough, he rises up as if from a swoon and departs with the artist to seek freedom in the camp. The queen, who will plot revenge for the trick played upon her, turns to her valet as the next representative of "The Eternal Masculine" so necessary to the fair.

The mood of the four brief pieces assembled in *Roses* a decade later is again that of Vienna rather than Berlin. In *Streaks of Light* a wife of the people, promised by a count that their affair shall endure so long as the roses bloom, is already weary of her enforced retirement in his darkened pavilion, when a moving shadow blots out the streaks of light that filter through the shutters. In comes her husband, ironic at first, then violent as he stabs her. More sentimental is *Margot*, its heroine a girl betrayed by a baron but now in love with the lawyer who would force the baron to marry her. When she refuses, the lawyer perceives the reason. He is ready to forgive her past. To be worthy of him she will manifest her reform by hard work. As she holds out her hands for him to kiss, she exclaims, "When we see each other again, they'll be red and ugly!" In the mean time, she will send him roses as before. Like a page out of Schnitzler is *The Last Visit*, wherein a countess, for whose sake a captain has given his life in a duel, calls at the house of mourning to retrieve the letters she had written him. Failing to find them, she assails his memory, but is rebuked by a girl, who remarks, in handing back the roses brought by the countess: "Your flowers no longer belong upon his coffin. . . . The night before he died, I became his wife." Finally, in *The Far-Away Princess*, Sudermann exalts the romantic idealism of a student, who, chancing to meet the princess he has idolized, confides to her his devotion. To his pupils, when he becomes a teacher, he will say, "Young men, if you want to be happy as long as you live, create gods for yourselves in your own image; they will care for your happiness." As for the princess, she gazes wistfully after her retreating admirer and will send him roses. Clever and polished as are these "one-acters" they are not especially memorable. Sudermann's forte lay elsewhere, in developing full-length canvases rather than miniatures.

SUDERMANN—THEATRICAL OPPORTUNIST

The later dramas of Sudermann reveal an unsuspected power when, stirred by the War, he presents a realistic reflection of parlous times in two groups of full-length plays. The former, entitled *The Godless World*, comprises *The Woman Friend*, *The Desirable Corner*, and *The Higher Life*, all concerned with self-centered worldliness characteristic of the period just prior to the conflict. The second and more important series, entitled *German Destiny*, comprises *Holy Time*, *Sacrifice*, and *Cry of Need*, important studies of the effect of the War behind the lines at three critical moments—its beginning, its height, and its close.

The first group is of little significance, yet it indicates the unsettled condition of a society in which individualism and skepticism have replaced faith and *gemüthlichkeit*. In *The Desirable Corner*, for example, a publisher who wishes for the general good to erect upon a corner lot a people's theater is opposed by a selfish art collector, who would build such a theater elsewhere merely to gratify the whim of an actress. The contention of the two ends in the publisher's defeat. Forced to resign from the town council, he is saved from melancholia by marrying a sympathetic young woman. His daughter is a dilettante artist; his son declaims against the cult of immoral estheticism, yet is moved in so doing by self-interest; and his niece, an unscrupulous feminist, trifles now with the publisher's son, now with his son-in-law, and now with the art collector. Only the publisher and his young wife possess the integrity without which society is bound to decay. Individualism more immoral figures in *The Woman Friend*, whose heroine is a second Hedda Gabler, bored by her humdrum life, and bent, for wanton amusement, on setting the suitors of a widow at cross-purposes, inducing the suicide of one and the desertion by the widow of her child. Juliane is the new woman malevolently asserting herself, a vampire not only of men but of her own sex as well. Largely comic is *The Rabbit Skin Dealer*, written at the end of the playwright's career, a poor piece that adds nothing to his reputation.

Very different from these inconsequential miniatures depicting the petty conflicts of small souls are the great vivid frescoes of Sudermann's war trilogy. No artist has ever painted more vigorous scenes of what is universal in war hysteria. In a German setting he describes phenomena to be observed in any country at such a crisis.

The first of the group—*Holy Time*—shows the outbreak of hostilities. A merchant, an aristocrat, a socialist, a free-thinking teacher, and a fiery patriot all agree, even after the assassination of the Austrian Archduke, that war is unlikely. It could never be financed; the prosperity of the country forbids; in any case, war is now outlawed, and workingmen would join hands in every capital, refusing to fight, and mothers would sing "The Watch of Peace" rather than "The Watch on the Rhine." A son of the socialist, on the other hand, believes the nation to be too divided to fight for any common cause, the workers hating the bourgeoisie, the men of middle class hating the Junkers, the Gentiles hating the Jews, and the soldiers hating their officers. The teacher asserts that freedom in the schools has been stifled and the State can expect no loyalty there.

But the logic of events proves too strong for these doubters. Confronted by a common danger, all factions unite. Gentiles and Jews, aristocrats and socialists fraternize. The people's leader who had proclaimed "war against war" is now ready to defend the Fatherland by force of arms. He becomes reconciled to the wife with whom he had quarreled. His son, rejected by the army as an invalid, takes his life, feeling that he owes it to the State. The skeptical teacher will enlist after marrying the girl he had been about to jilt, believing now in duty to God and loyalty to his vows. So he marches forth to fall in battle, while she makes use of her feminist freedom only to serve as nurse.

In *Sacrifice*, three years have passed. Discouragement has come, and with it the need for illusion. A youth, returning home for a few days of furlough, brings with him three fellow lieutenants. One, a jaunty aviator, fascinates Walter's sisters and his sweetheart, and she in turn responds to his charm, but, rather than make unhappy her betrothed, sends him back to the trenches believing her still loyal. He and the aviator and the other young fellows all die. The father of the family, reunited for an hour with his wife, brings her a body which he professes to be that of her son, merely to afford her comfort. Throughout is suggested that ironic necessity for illusion proclaimed by Dr. Relling in Ibsen's *Wild Duck*. And for what is the world thus suffering? For what are these youths fighting and dying, but for an illusion?

In *Cry of Need*, the third of the trilogy, another year has passed, bringing defeat. The army is undisciplined and broken, and corruption has wrought havoc at home. Against the maelstrom of dishonesty and incompetency, here and there a strong figure stands out. One is a gallant lieutenant colonel, undaunted by the misery of the nation and the evil beneath his own roof. He will not cringe even though his wife has proved disloyal, and his son, turning a Red, has been slain in a street battle. Another emancipated soul is the nurse of the first play. Confirmed in her feminism, she refuses the proposal of a monarchist adjutant who has resented the rivalry of other nations, declaring: "They have trampled us under foot, us Germans who were once kind and peace-loving, until we have become the terror and the outcasts of mankind; . . . We shall prove ourselves worthy of this new dignity thrust upon us." Yet Sudermann shows the adjutant to be as futile as the young radical, dying a suicide by unsealing a flask of poisoned gas. His master's wife, who is saved from following him by the same path, is forgiven by her husband, the lieutenant colonel. She must live, he tells her, and forget their alienation. "We have much to do, we two. What falls, falls. He who can show himself strong enough answers the Cry of Need."

One other fine figure emerges from the chaos, a lieutenant sent with supplies to Lithuania, forced to battle against rascality on every hand, yet, with his sweetheart, ready to face disaster unafraid. "The whole unhappiness just cannot get inside of me," he says. "Like a poodle, I shake it off. Life, life! the Fatherland and life!" For him and for the lieutenant colonel there is now something more to fight for than the twenty-two crowns and kingdoms of the German rulers. Honest men may serve the people as once they served the Kaiser. Is Germany's defeat expiation for sin? Who knows? Truth will prevail eventually. In the mean time, let the Germans keep faith in their country's honor and respond courageously to her Cry of Need.

From first to last, Sudermann has shown himself to be an accomplished man of the theater, conscious always of dramatic technique, with one eye fixed upon his audience and one on his play, more artificial, therefore, than Hauptmann, more satirical also and less sympathetic. He lacks the philosophical profundity of Ibsen. Interested, to begin with, in questions of honor and duty, he exhibits no deep sincerity of conviction in presenting any situation. You feel that what happens in his plays is determined less by inner necessity than by his desire to produce a telling effect. He is a painter of manners among the upper classes rather than a reformer burning to expound his philosophy of life. He is a keen-witted observer who knows society thoroughly, a realist and an ironist, revealing his characters through a dialogue lively, forcible, flexible, yet too often rhetorical. Still under the spell of the well-made play until the outbreak of the War, Sudermann thereafter adopted the freer forms of the moderns, ready to profit by the fashion of the moment as he had been earlier to take what he could from naturalism. As talented as Pinero, he seems less so, because overshadowed by the more original Hauptmann.

CHAPTER XVIII

LESSER GERMAN PLAYWRIGHTS AND THE NEW STAGECRAFT

Fulda, C. Hauptmann, Halbe, Hirschfeld, Hartleben, Thoma,
Dreyer, O. Ernst, Sternheim, the Romantics, P. Ernst,
Widmann, Reinhardt, Jessner, Piscator

SUDERMANN, however disparaged by the Germans, must
rank high as a practical playwright by reason of his skill
and the extent of his work. But the tale of his fellow dramatists
is large, and something should be said here of such others as
have preceded the recent movement toward expressionism, men
with less originality than Wedekind or Kaiser, yet popular in
their day as providing stage entertainments of merit. They
must be accorded brief treatment that attention may focus
upon a few significant figures.

The closest analogue to Sudermann is Ludwig Fulda, who
has responded even more easily to every gust of fashion. He
began in the 'eighties as a disciple of Paul Heyse, writing *Beneath Four Eyes* and *The Wild Chase*, satirical comedies intended to reprove those who would seek happiness as social
climbers. Then he felt the spell of naturalism, and in *The Lost
Paradise* described a struggle of the classes brought to an
agreeable outcome in the love of a capitalist's daughter for a
reformer. The new woman next engaged his attention in *The
Female Slave*, depicting the revolt of a wife against her brutal
husband. Presently he turned to romance, and, in his *märchen*
drama, *The Talisman*, composed a delightful satire upon the
divine right of kings, wherein enemies of Wilhelm II found
veiled allusions to that monarch's self-complacency and his
dismissal of Bismarck. The play was based upon Anderson's

319

fairy tale of the royal garments warranted to be visible only to the wise and therefore loudly praised by sycophants and the king until an honest maiden dares to speak the truth regarding their non-existence. A later *märchen* drama—*The Son of the Caliph*—was less effective, although skillfully expanding the notion of a tyrant who, being obliged to feel an exact reflex of what he does to others, learns to do to them only as he would be done by, and finds in a faithful woman his guide to a nobler life. Fulda's comedies of the 'nineties included *Comrades*, laughing pleasantly at the new woman, *Youthful Friends*, laughing more farcically at the submission of certain bachelors to their brides, *Lubberland*, a humorous trifle, and *Robinson's Island*, which, like *The Admirable Crichton* of Barrie that followed it, points the contrast between society folk when at home and when shipwrecked upon a desert island. The youth who, in default of birth, wealth, and station, was a nobody in Berlin, becomes on the island the captain of his fate and the ruler of his fellows.

Fulda's most ambitious work is *Herostrat*, a tragedy in verse, its scene ancient Greece, its protagonist the unknown who in order to perpetuate his name set fire to the temple of Diana at Ephesus. The piece died, however, smothered in its rhetoric; but Fulda, nothing daunted, continued to compose serious dramas such as *The Novella of Andrea* and *The Secret King*, one-act plays like *The Dream of the Fortunate*, translations of Ibsen and of Rostand, and comedies such as *The Twin Sisters*, *Coldwater*, *Chance*, *Masquerade*, *The Blockhead*, and *The Example*. The best of these are *The Blockhead*, celebrating the wisdom of a little clerk who in the eyes of the world is only a fool, and *The Twin Sisters*, a light and graceful bit of intrigue, reproving the husband who, thinking to escape from duty to his wife, promptly falls in love with her all over again when, with woman's wit, she appears to him disguised as her own twin sister. Like Sudermann, Fulda has displayed from first to last great industry, ingenuity, and talent. He has combined fidelity of observation with free fancy, continuing the tradition of Grillparzer. He is an agreeable moralist and a facile poet. Although by no means an imposing figure, he is at least one of the most winsome.

The drift from naturalism toward romanticism, already remarked in Fulda, Sudermann, and Hauptmann, may be observed as well in the plays of Carl Hauptmann, Gerhart's younger brother. Originally a philosopher, he retained his fondness for the subtleties of soul, whether dealing with peasants or with heroes. Sexual passion and love of the soil are the themes of his naturalistic dramas. Thus in *Ephraim's Heiress* (*Ephraims Breite*) an old farmer objects to his daughter's marrying an outlander likely to dissipate the family property; she persists, and then, on finding her husband disloyal, drives him forth from the soil that is hers. In *The Expulsion*, a peasant, attached to his mountain acres, marries for second wife a loose woman who longs for the tavern she has left in the valley. He yields to her coaxing that he sell his farm and descend to the town, but when he detects her meeting a lover at the smug new house in the village, he slays his rival. In *Tall Jule* a father and a daughter are united in devotion to their property. To keep it intact, each has vowed that the other shall not marry. But the man, taking a second wife, incurs his daughter's enmity, and, when he dies, the feud descends to his widow, who must contend with the half-crazed Jule until the homestead is lost to both through fire.

These peasant dramas of Carl Hauptmann are counterbalanced by pieces more romantic, curious chronicle plays—*Moses and Napoleon Bonaparte*, one-act experiments collected under the title *Panspiele*, and poetical tales—*The Poor Broombinder* and *The King's Harp*, the last telling of the quest for a lost monarch who reappears as a hermit after having learned that his true happiness is to be found in the joy of his people. A group of one-act plays, *From the Great War*, reflects the spirit of the conflict, which a year earlier the author had

sought to express symbolically in his spectral phantasmagoria
War—a Te Deum. This strange drama shifts its allegorical
scenes bewilderingly, exhibiting the European powers as animals seated about a council board; an archangel slaying their
presiding officer, the wizened Master-Accountant of Europe;
rat-faced phantoms slinking by with drawn stilettos; soldiers
carousing or in flight; a Napoleonic State-Visionary in rags
and chains, escaped from his ocean rock to proclaim himself
the murderer as he rolls through blood in a golden chariot,
wielding a golden scourge; a black and desolate world peopled
by cripples who dig for jewels interred with the dead; the
mistress of the slain Prince Enoch, who has precipitated the
War, praying that her child may learn to love the beautiful
earth, but saluted by the cries of the cripples that he is Enoch,
the son of Cain. In its riot of imagination this piece almost
rivals *The Dream Play* of Strindberg and the symbolic night-
mares of Andreyev.

The year that saw the first theatrical success of Hauptmann
and Sudermann witnessed also the appearance of the maiden
effort of Max Halbe, a young West Prussian. With less artificiality than Sudermann and a greater feeling for structural
form than Hauptmann, he proceeded to produce play after
play depicting individuals struggling, not only with conditions, but with one another. Although his heroes commonly
resort to suicide, or perish in a futile contention with Fate,
they are stronger than the folk of Hauptmann, and the dramatic crises of their lives are rarely sacrificed to a passive
naturalism.

Thus Halbe's first piece, *The Self-Made Man* (*Empor-
kömmling*), shows a stiff-necked father striving to determine
the career of his son and eventually driving the youth to suicide. *The Ice Drift* contrasts a father of the old school, worn
out with trying to control his unruly employees and the river
that inundates his farm; and the son, imbued with ideals of
social justice that lead him to treat his workmen as equals,

with the ironic result that they desert him to carouse in the tavern when the dikes need protection, and he is overwhelmed in the flood. Halbe in his best-known drama, *Youth*, approaches more nearly to naturalism by drawing a family group affected by heredity and environment. A girl born out of wedlock is reared along with her legitimate but half-wit brother by their uncle, a kindly priest. She has inherited her mother's passionate nature and too readily responds when a boy, who visits at the house on his way to the university, confesses his love. Her yielding is further induced by the fact that she has just been threatened with seclusion in a convent by her uncle's clerical assistant, a fanatic who at heart would like Annchen for himself. Having spied upon her meetings with Hans, the fanatic finds a mean satisfaction in reporting her fall to her uncle. But the latter proves to be wisely tolerant. He rebukes and sends away the informer, diagnosing his case correctly. He forgives the girl, and bids the boy complete his university studies before atoning for his fault by marriage. The lovers are about to part with hope of future reunion when the half-wit, insanely jealous, shoots at Hans, but slays Annchen instead as she steps between to save her lover's life. Heredity determines not only Annchen's fall but also the philandering of Hans, who is the son of a coquette with whom the good priest had been in love before she jilted and drove him into the Church. Moreover, heredity is responsible for the mental defects of Annchen's brother, crippled in brain prenatally by his mother's earlier worry over the girl's illegitimacy. Fairly Freudian is the study of the fanatic young priest, fighting in others that which he fears in himself, his repressed instincts turned into zeal for reform,—a forecast of the missionary hero in *Rain*. Although its tragic dénouement be far from inevitable, *Youth* is a moving drama, redolent of springtime and of adolescent love in the country.

Halbe's next plays fell below the level of *Youth*, yet *A Village Tale—Frau Mesick* is of interest as a Strindbergian sketch of the superwife married to a fellow five decades her junior and worrying him into a suicide's grave. The new woman, introduced thus grotesquely, is accorded more sympathy in the Hella of *Mother Earth*, a radical female who edits a journal advocating the emancipation of her sex and enters into a trial marriage with the son of a conservative landowner. When Paul returns home to attend his father's funeral, he succumbs to the spell of mother earth and regrets that he had not married the girl of his father's choice. Although she is now wed to another, early memories revive, and he grows so infatuated with her that he severs his relations with his radical mate, who must concede his right to do so according to their compact. Then he and Antoinette die after a mad hour together. The environment of his rustic boyhood has reasserted its sway; he must atone for the conservative laws he has broken.

The radical woman is again the subject of treatment in Halbe's *The Homeless Ones* contrasting the dependent type with that which is naturally self-directive. The latter, weathering the gale of a love affair, lives secure as a bachelor-maid in Berlin. Her cousin, seeking to emulate her example, but unable to steer a straight course, loses her heart to a libertine and, being deserted, commits suicide rather than return disgraced to her home in the provinces.

In *The Millennium* Halbe expends his efforts less upon a social condition than upon a single character, that of a sinister blacksmith who, consenting to marry the mistress of a baron, is tormented by the arrangement from which in feudal days he would have suffered no disgrace. Becoming a religious fanatic, he believes the millennium at hand, worries his wife into the grave, sees in the burning of his smithy through a thunderbolt a sign of heaven's displeasure, plots against the baron, and then, after Halbe's favorite fashion, dies by his own hand.

In the field of historical drama Halbe has produced *The*

Conqueror and *The True Countenance*, the former dealing
with the period of the Renaissance, the latter more effectively
with East Prussia under the Poles. Woman as temptress here
figures again in the person of Cordula, who leads her husband
a dance, and is seen in her "true countenance" as his evil
angel only after her suicide. The romantic influence observable
in these plays appears also in three comedies that trace the
effect of environment upon the artist. In *May Day*, a poet,
discouraged by popular approval of the commonplace, is ready
to renounce his craft, until he is inspired by love to sing a
great song. In *The Island of the Blest* the founder of a community established for the promotion of art discovers that it
merely fosters corruption, and similarly in *The Blue Mountains* the worshiper of beauty who seeks inspiration in free-
living learns that sensuality debases art.

But it is less for these imaginative moralities than for his
naturalist plays that Halbe merits recognition. In *The Rosenhagens* and *The Stream* he depicts, like Carl Hauptmann, the
attachment of man for his holdings in nature. In *The Rosenhagens* a grasping old fellow is resisted in his desire to acquire
more land by only one neighbor whom accordingly he hates.
At his death, the quarrel descends to his son, who would rear
on this meadow a fine house for the fickle lady of his heart.
Although in the end she jilts him rather than settle on a
country estate among peasants, Karl Egon threatens the
owner of the meadow with expulsion, and is shot for his threat.
He dies in the arms of his pretty cousin, a quiet and submissive
girl of the people, who has helped to foment the quarrel in the
hope of detaching him from her flighty rival, an assertive and
roving new woman.

More picturesque and elemental in quality is *The Stream*,
which appears to be a late echo of Halbe's play *The Ice Drift*.
Here three sons of a landowner contend over his estate which
has been left to them equally, although the eldest has destroyed
the will so devising it in order to retain it entire. When his

children are accidentally drowned in the stream that flows through the farm, he is shocked into confessing his usurpation. His wife, who alone hears his story, demands that he make amends to his brothers, one of whom she would have preferred in marriage, had he but possessed his rightful share and been able to support her. When her husband refuses, she reveals the secret to his rival. But this brother, although defrauded of his bride and his land, recognizes the virtue of keeping the estate intact. The youngest brother, however, is a rebel who, on getting wind of the wrong, will open the river dike and ruin the property. Intercepted by the eldest, he struggles until both are swept to death in the stream, which has proved in a sense as important as any human factor in the tragedy.

The contemporary German drama is rich, not only in playwrights of importance like the two Hauptmanns, Sudermann, Fulda, and Halbe, but also in minor craftsmen distinguished for some special service. Thus Georg Hirschfeld is a disciple of naturalism who applied its methods in depicting the middle classes of Berlin. His earlier pieces—*At Home*, *The Mothers*, and *Agnes Jordan*—are superior to those written later, when, as in *Pauline* and *Late Spring*, he attempted comedy, or turned to the *märchen* drama in *The Way Toward the Light*. Hirschfeld's tendency to weaken his conflicts and to dwell upon resignation rather than will has earned him the title of the German Chekhov, but there is in his work a largeness and a depth which is lacking in that of the Russian. *At Home* sketches effectively in one act the sense of discouragement felt by the head of a household who returns after his day of toil in the city to confront conditions against which he has struggled in vain. His little girl is ill; his younger son is spoiled and unresponsive. His wife is a frivolous creature who thinks only of the money he may bring her. Yet he takes fresh courage when his older son appears after long absence and is shocked to discover the situation that has developed "at home." In *The Mothers*, the characters are wrought out through a full-length story leading to the sacrifice of a girl of the people, who allows her prosperous, middle-class lover to return to his family from which he has fled when forbidden by his father to live his life as a musician. The father has now died, and Robert's sister and mother receive him with open arms. They are kind, also, to Marie, the little silver burnisher, with whom he has found happiness for two years. She, who has been rated for folly by her own mother, hastens after to reclaim him, but is made to realize that, if Robert is to achieve great things in his art, she must give him up. Accordingly, she will return to her tenement to bear his child without letting Robert know,— a somewhat sentimental and improbable conclusion for a naturalistic play. As Marie's mother has pointed out, "We can't mean nothin' to a man of that kind of family. If he's a scamp, the ruin is yours; if he's decent, the ruin is his"—words that prove prophetic. In *Agnes Jordan* Hirschfeld has expanded the horizon of naturalism by presenting his heroine at four widely separated stages of her development through a period of thirty years, the device later employed in *Milestones* by Arnold Bennett and Edward Knoblauch in depicting a family and its ideals that change with the lapse of time. Here interest centers, also, in the playwright's endeavor to show the change that comes over a Jewish group attaining refinement in the younger members, made to suffer in consequence by the elder who cannot understand. Agnes, like Marie, achieves the nobility of renunciation.

Two Bavarians, Ludwig Thoma and Otto Erich Hartleben, are worthy of mention among these minor German dramatists. Otto Erich, whose death in 1905 cut short a promising career, indulges in piquant dialogue and good-natured satire, and sometimes strikes a serious note, as in his pieces concerned with things military—*Departure from the Regiment* and *The Month of Roses*. The latter, with masterly stagecraft, reveals the ruin wrought by a false conception of honor still prevalent among soldiers. An officer, separated by the guile of his regimental comrades from the burgher's daughter he would marry, goes to the dogs and kills both her and himself. Analogous in its attack upon the conventional standards of honor in civil life is *Education for Marriage*. Here a youth of wealth, whose ambitious mother breaks off his match with a poor but worthy girl, leaves her to be betrayed by a libertine and transfers his attention to a servant maid. Such is the effect of worldly meddling with a pure affection, says the playwright. Less satirical but equally serious is Otto Erich's portrait of the new woman in *Hanna Jagert*. Hanna, a girl of the people, experiments first with Socialism and then with individualism, but, finding small satisfaction in either, relinquishes the independence she has won in conducting a garment shop. Then, despite her earlier scorn of marriage, she weds a baron, perceiving in the institution an arrangement of value since it accords to woman a fair degree of freedom within the law. Frequently Hartleben is merely merry, as in *Angèle*, when a father and a son quarrel in rivalry over the same mistress but are reconciled after she discards both in favor of a third, —a situation anticipating that in *The Raschoffs* of Sudermann. Again Hartleben mingles the serious and the comic as in *The Moral Demand*, where the heroine, like Sudermann's Magda, having defied convention and attained independence through her talents as a singer, is offered social respectability by a former admirer, but laughs to scorn his "moral demand."

More vigorous and bitter is the muse of Ludwig Thoma, whose three-act comedy *Moral* created a sensation in 1909. Thoma punctures the Philistine hypocrisy that would cloak a village scandal. A lady of light virtue who has entertained too freely is arrested. The president of the Society for the Prevention of Vice would suppress the agitation against her, alleging the evil effect upon the lower classes of publicity in the case. His motives, however, are not unselfish, since his own name appears, with those of other prominent citizens, upon a list of the lady's visitors. Fortunately, he succeeds in steal-

ing the list, and a police official arrives to upbraid his under-
lings for their excess of zeal which has threatened to compromise, not only honest townsmen, but also a royal personage. The storm blows over after the lady's righteous anger has
been financially assuaged.

Thoma's other comedies, *The Medal*, *Lottchen's Birthday*,
First Class, and *The Local Railway*, are conceived in the same
ironic spirit. The last pokes fun at burghers who have sent
their mayor to intercede with a high official opposed to building a railway they desire. In reporting the interview, the
mayor enlarges upon his heroic conduct in having flouted the
minister, and the burghers organize a parade in honor of their
champion. On the morrow, however, they reflect that he has
really menaced their interests by arousing enmity in high
quarters. When they troop back to assail him as their foe,
he unblushingly retracts his former story, and the curtain
falls upon another procession in his honor. The pettiness of
self-sufficient townsmen is also the theme of Thoma's tragedy,
Magdalena. A country girl astray in the city is sent home by
order of the juvenile court. She arrives in time to receive the
forgiveness of her dying mother; but by the smug neighbors
she is regarded as one accursed. In vain she hopes for happiness with a young farmer who works upon the place; he, too,
is afraid of the Magdalen. The mayor and his friends demand
that she be exiled; and her father, goaded to desperation, stabs
her, and cries to their persecutors, "Now cast us out into
shame!"

Max Dreyer and Otto Ernst are North Germans who have
written plays affected by Ibsen and the naturalists. Both are
careful and humorous observers of the contemporary with a
gift for satire. Dreyer has produced a score of dramas, the best
known being his study of school-life, *The Practice Teacher*,
in which a teacher whose career depends upon catering to
the prejudices of his narrow-minded superiors must either be
crushed by their bigotry or else break the heart of his fond

old mother when turned out of his place. As a student of biology he is unable to recant his conviction that Darwin spoke the truth, but as a cog in the machine of orthodox Christian education he must keep his opinions to himself. Otto Ernst, who, as an instructor in the Hamburg schools, had ample experience on which to draw, followed Dreyer with his *Youth of To-day* and his still more popular *Flachsmann as Educator*, a character sketch of a shallow pedagogue, his servile charges, his self-important colleagues, and one worthy teacher by way of contrast to the rest. Here and in the *Traumulus* of Arno Holz and Oskar Jerschke is nothing of the sentimentalism that made Wilhelm Meyer-Förster's *Old Heidelberg* a favorite with foreign audiences and that gave rise at home to such pieces as Hartleben's *The Green Tree and The Nightingale*, Servaes' *Maiden Ambrosia*, and Roettiger's *Student Love*. Otto Ernst, although best known for his school drama, resorted to the theater to reprove abuses in other fields, directing his *Greatest Sin* against the folly of obedience to convention, and *Justice* against the baneful influence of the scandalous press.

Of all the satirists of the German theater, the chief is Carl Sternheim, born in 1881, a son of a banker in Leipzig. Wherever he has lived—in Berlin, Munich, Brussels, and Switzerland—he has regarded the bourgeois world with cynicism and sought to whip it into a painful perception of its shortcomings. Having written tales, novels, and an eclectic and erotic play *Don Juan*, Sternheim found his true field in the drama of social caricature. He perceived that audiences were foolishly enamored of the new romanticism. Accordingly, in *The Trousers*, he proceeded to give them something different. "In my piece," he writes, "a burgher's wife loses her 'panties' and no one on the stage speaks of anything but that banal event in commonplace German." The occasion of the action is as primitive as that in *Gammer Gurton's Needle*, but the ridiculous scenes that follow serve to expose the frailties of a journalist and a barber fired with love by the lady's misadventure. They reveal, also, the lady's readiness to respond to both or either, and her husband's lapse from morality with her confidante, and his final satisfaction at securing from the journalist a sum sufficient to support his wife's child while he sits in his armchair and reads about the sea serpent. The rollicking caricature is not without a basis of truth in the follies it ascribes to the bourgeoisie. Such follies are laughed at in *The Treasure Chest* when a middle-aged schoolmaster brings home a young second wife and his elderly aunt casts suspicion upon the virtue of the bride. His daughter marries a photographer who has already made love to the bride and earlier to the servant in the house. The schoolmaster, given his aunt's treasure chest to guard, dreams of the wealth he may inherit even while she is dictating a will leaving everything to the Church. These selfish, lustful people, held together by their great expectations of benefits to be conferred by the aunt, are all doomed to disappointment.

In *Burgher Schippel* Sternheim thrusts at the proletarian ne'er-do-well too timid to climb into the bourgeoisie yet succeeding on a fluke. Schippel is asked to take the place in a town quartet left vacant by the death of a singer. As the quartet is competing for a prize, the others cannot afford to be too squeamish. Schippel, seizing his opportunity, bargains with the leader for the hand of the singer's widow, the leader's sister. Since she has already during her brief widowhood succumbed to a prince and needs a husband to conceal her fault, Schippel wins her hand, after having been egged into a duel with another suitor, whom he wounds by sheer accident. Henceforth, though a coward, he is regarded as a hero. What a satire is this upon small-town worthies, with their petty ambitions, loves, and diversions! How glorious is the fate of Schippel, tied at last to the slightly damaged Thekla! "Paul," says Schippel to himself in congratulation, "now you are a burgher!"

In *The Snob* Sternheim returns to the family he had created in his first social satire, *The Trousers*, and follows the rise of Christian Maske, son of that Theodore whose wife by losing her "panties" gained a lover and a child. The self-made Christian has acquired wealth and power. In order that he may owe a debt to no one, he pays off what he calculates is due to his parents and to the woman who has loved and helped him. Then he proceeds to marry for gain the daughter of a count. He impresses her with his greatness, and as a last touch invents a story that will enable him to lay claim to noble blood even though it reflects upon his mother's honor. Only then will the bride sink into his arms, referring to his mother as "that blessed adulteress."

But Christian Maske is not to stop here. In the play *1913* he is shown as Freiherr, a chief industrialist of the country, rearing his children like princes, yet riding for a fall since these children have grown away from him. Phillip-Ernst is intent only upon sport and fashion; Ottilie is spoiled and erotic, philandering with her father's secretary; Sophie, married to a count, is energetic enough yet determined to run her father's business without regard to ethics or quality in striving for mass production. When she contracts to sell a large order of firearms to Protestant Holland, old Maske, the good Catholic, who foresees war for Germany, is overcome by emotion and drops dead. His secretary in the mean time has been won over from Socialism to the side of capital, and, clad in the richest finery, hastily embraces the capitalist's daughter now that she will inherit most of her father's fortune. In conditions like these, Sternheim seems to say, may be found a cause of the disaster soon to overwhelm the Fatherland.

Other satires upon bourgeois life and ideals include *Perleberg*, *The Needle*, *Unchained Contemporaries*, *Berlin or Juste Milieu*, *Libussa*, *The Fossil*, and *The School of Uznach*. By way of variety, Sternheim has dramatized *Manon Lescaut* and also Schiller's translation of Diderot's novel *Jacques the Fatalist*, calling it *The Marquise of Arcis*, and in *Oscar Wilde* he has transferred to the boards pages from the biography of the Irish esthete by Frank Harris, blaming Wilde's misfortunes upon Philistine morality.

In two other plays, *Tabula Rasa* and *The Weakling (Der Nebbich)*, Sternheim continues his war against the middle classes. The former offers a satire on an expert glassblower who distrusts the proposal to provide a library for his fellow workers lest it spread ideas that will upset the established order. As a result of his conservatism, the glassblower is chosen a director of the works, and, assured by a physician that in spite of his fears he still may count on living quarter of a century longer, he resolves to enjoy life as a hero of the bourgeoisie. In *The Weakling* a traveling salesman in love with a little florist has his head turned by a singer and her aristocratic friends, but she grows a tyrant in her determination that he shall be educated to talk of Tagore and the Nibelungenlied and politics. Nevertheless he endures her training and rises to distinction as the consul of a foreign power, the editor of a paper, and the manager of a film manufactory. Sternheim, in short, is a German Molière, somewhat deficient in the Frenchman's breadth of outlook and love of fun for its own sake. In style, Sternheim copies the telegraphic dialogue of Wedekind, dropping out connectives and unnecessary words in order to stress new rhythms. He is not altogether a negative force, for he conceives a regeneration of society as possible when individuals will forsake their selfishness and strive together for the common good. His world, however, is grotesque and his tone sharp and arrogant. Like the expressionists with whom he is often improperly associated, Sternheim represents one line of departure from exactly copying reality. Instead of resorting to romance, to symbolism and the externalization of emotion and ideas through fantasy, he has stylized reality for satiric ends through caricature.

From this review of minor German playwrights mainly realistic, it will be profitable to turn to a consideration of the recoil against realism and toward the romantic, symbolic, and expressionistic. Already, in discussing the work of Hauptmann, we have observed the rise of theatrical realism first fostered by the company of Duke Georg of Saxe-Meiningen and culminating in the naturalism of the Freie Bühne and the Moscow Art Theater. But naturalism could not long endure undiluted. Hauptmann and its other devotees soon reverted to the romantic—at least on occasion—and by degrees there developed a revolt in two fields—in dramatic composition and in stage production.

An early step in the recoil may be noted in the cultivation of dream plays, descending from Hauptmann's *Hannele*, *Schluck and Jau*, and *Elga*. Here may be included pieces like Widmann's *This Side of Good and Evil*, Fulda's *Fool's Paradise*, Bronner's *New Life*, Weil's *Earthly Lights*, Paul's *Devil's Church*, and Schnitzler's *Lady with the Dagger*. Similarly, the *märchen* drama, first cultivated by Holger Drachmann in Denmark and represented by *The Talisman* of Fulda, *The King's Children* of Ernst Rosmer (Elsa Bernstein), and *The Sunken Bell* of Hauptmann, has been developed in Wedekind's *Such is Life*, Lothar's *King Harlequin*, Paul's *The Double Comedy*, Reicke's *The Fair Melusine*, Ricarda Huch's *Dornröschen*, Falke's *Putzi*, Eulenberg's *Knight Bluebeard*, Bonn's *Andalosia*, and Otto Ernst's *Ortrun and Ilsebill*. Of opera librettos in this vein Adelheid Wette's *Hänsel and Gretel* is the best known, with successors in von Wolzogen's *Feuersnot*, Batka's *Cinderella*, and Edmund Frank's *The Stuttgart Dwarf*.

Folk-lore and legend have been felicitously employed as the basis for plays by Friedrich Lienhard, who has produced three dealing with Till Eulenspiegel, and others such as *Münchhausen*, *King Arthur*, *Wieland the Smith*, and a Wartburg trilogy. Wieland, the same character that Scott introduced in *Kenilworth* as Wayland, is treated further in plays by Holger Drachmann, by Eberhard König, by Ernst Hardt, and recently by Hauptmann himself. In the realm of historical drama Ernst von Wildenbruch bears the palm, although most of his work dates from before the beginning of the twentieth century. Except for a few attempts to consider social problems, as in *Master Balzer*, or in his comedy of contemporary life, *The Immortal Felix*, Wildenbruch has devoted himself to reviving a romantic past, especially that of the Hohenzollerns. His masterpiece is the double or triple tragedy *Heinrich and Heinrich's Race* concerned with the opposition between Gregory VII and Henry IV and the eternal conflict of Church and State. His art is virile and imaginative whether he present the Renaissance in *Erasmus*, or the times of Theodoric the Great in *King Laurin*, or those of Henry I in *The German King*.

The neo-romanticists, indeed, are legion. Richard Beer-Hofmann, master of musical verse, turned *The Fatal Dowry* of Massinger and Field into a piece of German brocade in *The Count of Charolais*, and after the War presented, as prologue to a Biblical series, his *Jacob's Dream*. Karl Vollmöller used a tragic ballad as the basis of his *Katharine Countess of Armagnac and her Two Lovers*, and in *The Miracle* expanded Maeterlinck's *Sister Beatrice*. Ernst Hardt, another member of the circle of Stefan George, followed up a Tristan tragedy called *Tantris the Fool* with his *Gudrun*. Eduard Stucken composed *Gawain, Lanval, Launcelot*, and *The Birth of Merlin*, a group of Arthurian plays more poetic than dramatic. Eberhard König revealed his creative power in *Filippo Lippi, Godfather Death, Wieland the Smith, Alcestis* and *Dietrich of Bern*, a trilogy; and Wilhelm von Scholz combined poetry and action in *The Jew of Constance, Meroë*, and *The Race with the Shadow*. Otto Erler won attention with *Czar Peter*, and *Struensee, or The Angel of England*; as did Hans Franck with *Godiva* and *Night of Sacrifice*, the latter an Indian folk tale which involves the problem of chastity. Franz Dülberg, with his *Cardenio* and *King of Fools Kaspar*, proved less stirring than the impassioned Herbert Eulenberg with the high-flavored emotional scenes and characters of his *Anna Walewska*, *Prince Ulrich of Waldeck*, *All for Gold*, and *Belinde*, a German *Enoch Arden*. Eulenberg has written, among other plays, *Münchhausen*, *Half Heroes*, and an adaptation of Shakespeare's *Tempest*. Throughout, he delights in Shakespearean language even when dealing with matters purely modern.

If Eulenberg suffers by his neglect of form for feeling, Paul Ernst, who looked to ancient models, has stressed classic restraint as an essential, declaring in his treatise, *The Way to Form*, that tragedy requires the nice opposition of two conflicting currents, the hero being carried along by one and threatened at the same time with destruction by the other, and the inevitability of the action being rendered clear through the dramatist's paring away all surplusage, reducing the number of his characters, and increasing the element of conflict. In *Demetrios*, *Canossa*, *Brunhild*, *Ninon de Lenclos*, and *The Soul of Prussia*, Ernst has well exemplified such theories. Both classic and realistic materials are dealt with in romantic fashion by Wilhelm Schmidtbonn. Thus, in the four one-act pieces of *Playful Eros* and in *The Wrath of Achilles*, his subjects are classical; in *Mother Landstrasse*, *The Count of Gleichen*, and *Actors*, his subjects are modern and matter-of-fact; and in *The Stricken*, a modern theme receives expressionistic treatment in the presentation of a blinded aviator returning home after the War, enabled to see the sins of thought of his neighbors, although the world is now dark to him outwardly.

Men as diverse as Gustav Renner the Silesian and Joseph Victor Widmann the Swiss have responded to the romantic impulse; the former, like so many others affected by it, proving a perfect eclectic. After writing a Biblical *Ahasuerus*, Renner produced a medieval *Merlin*, a Renaissance *Francesca*, a Greek *Alcestis*, and a bourgeois piece, *Dark Powers*, influenced by the *Mary Magdalene* of Hebbel. More original are the satiric fable plays of Widmann, whose *June Bug Comedy* and *The Saint and the Animals* constitute a cross between the

Chantecler of Rostand and *The Life of Insects* of the brothers Čapek. The June bugs in their subterranean quarters dream hopefully of the realm of light into which ere long they will emerge. But when they rise above ground, it is to find that other animals and men conspire against them, and that even amid the ecstasies of love the most ardent must perish in a rainstorm. A few now hold that God creates but to destroy. Others maintain that those who have been blotted out must have deserved such punishment. All may be consoled to discover that man, looking before and after, suffers greater ills than they, being subject to more devastating feuds and diseases. Similar irony marks *The Saint and the Animals*, a puppet play in seven scenes performed before two candidates for admission into holy orders. A text from the First Chapter of St. Mark suggests the action—"And He was there in the wilderness forty days, tempted of Satan; and was with the wild beasts; and the angels ministered unto Him." Widmann's hero is a Saint who, by means of a magic ring given him by Lilith, can understand the language of the beasts and hear them murmur at the world of pain in which they live. Can a good God permit such evil? Should not the Saint minister to the animals rather than to men? Such questions are propounded by Lilith and by Asasel the spirit of negation, both sent by Satan as tempters. But the Saint remains firm, grieving only that he cannot save man and beast both from suffering and from inflicting suffering. After all, to be guiltless and to be true to oneself can alone afford satisfaction.

Out of this hit-or-miss catalogue of romantic plays and playwrights it is difficult to bring any order. But the tendency of all is clear:—to escape from an exact representation of everyday life and find the thrill of novelty in dealing with dream, legend, history, and symbol—"old, unhappy, far-off things, and battles long ago." A still newer tendency—expressionism—would use the external world merely to suggest and project states of consciousness, the inner world determining the outer. But before considering that, it will be well to say something of the parallel movement in stage production. Here it was Gordon Craig, son of the English actress Ellen Terry, who turned from naturalism and by his theories exerted far-reaching influence upon the Continental theater without ever operating a playhouse of his own. By means of curtains and structures built in, he endeavored to make the scene a pictorial symbol of the mood of the play, "taking us beyond realities," as Arthur Symons has said, replacing "the pattern of the thing itself by the pattern which the thing evokes in the mind, the symbol of the thing." Craig brought his talents to the aid of Otto Brahm in Germany and of the Moscow Art Theater in Russia; and his pupils include Adolph Appia the Swiss, Georg Fuchs the Bavarian, and Max Reinhardt the Austrian. Appia has specialized in shadow and light effects, Fuchs in three-dimensional scenery framed in shadows on the narrow stage of the Munich Art Theater; and Reinhardt through twenty years of experimentation has employed every available resource of production with true imaginative genius.

Even before the turn of the century German theaters had been ready for recoil against naturalism, Maeterlinck and von Hofmannsthal furnishing the text for producers to work upon. In 1898, when *Pelléas and Mélisande* was staged by Martin Zickel, with Reinhardt in the cast, Maximilian Harden announced that for once the work of a poet had been presented and understood. Then Zickel and Paul Martin started a Sezessionsbühne as the first effort of the new romanticism. When the venture failed, its home was turned into the Über-brettl, a small playhouse for the performance of stylized vaudeville after the manner of the Parisian cabarets. This was succeeded by the popular Schall-und-Rauch of similar character, and then by a regular Little Theater. In 1902, after the performance of Wedekind's *Earth Spirit* at the latter, the actor Kayssler wrote to the author: "You have strangled the

naturalistic beast of probability and brought to the stage the
element of play. You will live!''

Max Reinhardt, the Austrian, who had turned from acting
to directing, and had been interested in these various ventures,
took over the New Theater in 1903 and gave *Pelléas and
Mélisande* and *A Midsummer Night's Dream* in the new free
style. Then, in 1905, he succeeded Brahm as director of the
leading Berlin playhouse—the Deutsches Theater—where
he produced more brilliantly *The Merchant of Venice* and von
Hofmannsthal's *Œdipus and the Sphinx*. Having opened the
Kammerspiele next door, a small remodeled dance hall, he
presented in intimate fashion *Ghosts* and several of the plays
of Hauptmann and Wedekind. Thereafter, for two decades, he
dominated production on the German stage. In the handling
of crowds he continued the Meiningen tradition, but for the
most part he drew upon the theory and practice of Craig,
Appia, Fuchs, and the Russians. It was Reinhardt's endeavor
to use the best scenic artists and all the latest devices. These
included the walled horizon, the relief stage, the revolving
stage (earlier introduced at Munich), the magic lantern first
tried by the English painter Hubert Herkomer, and the
Japanese *hanamichi*, or raised entrance platform for actors.
He experimented with every type of background and of lighting, and with the steps and platforms advocated by Craig and
the Russians, and with spectacles indoors and out.

Reinhardt's first move in the direction of the spectacle was
his elaborate performance in 1910 of the *Œdipus* of Sophocles
in the Circus of Schumann. Ten years later he transformed
this Circus into the Grosses Schauspielhaus, roofing it like a
stalactite cavern, arranging seats rising in tiers about a flat
arena for acting, and backing that arena with a low stage
approached by broad steps. He sought to make all those within
the theater feel themselves part of a communal performance,
as in *Sumurun* and *The Miracle*. But the number of pieces
adapted to such production was small, the cost was immense,

the preservation of the truly dramatic amid the spectacular was almost impossible, and the novelty soon wore off. Disheartened, Reinhardt retired to the city of his first love, Salzburg, where he set going the project of a Festspielhaus for the production of drama and opera. Here, with the aid of Richard Strauss and Hugo von Hofmannsthal, he proposed to marry the arts somewhat as Wagner had done at Bayreuth, exalting in particular the spirit of Salzburg's most famous son, Mozart. At the same time, in Vienna, he conducted a very different enterprise in the royal palace, presenting classics in the Redoutensaal with a formal simplicity appropriate to that eighteenth century hall. No régisseur has ever before so thoroughly combined, extended, and mastered all the arts of theatrical production, or done so much to develop and train important actors and producers as Reinhardt. His comrades and pupils have come to rule the Central European stage.

Although Reinhardt has returned from time to time to Berlin for further experiments and has extended his influence by American tours and enterprises, his mantle in Germany has fallen upon the shoulders of Leopold Jessner, who, after training in Hamburg and Königsberg, became director of the Staatstheater in 1919. Jessner has availed himself of most of Reinhardt's methods, but has employed steps and platforms more lavishly and has depended upon colors to imply certain states of mind, and lights of varying intensity and shade to furnish an obligato to the action. These lights he shifts to set off a soliloquy or to emphasize the entrance of a character. When, for example, Othello commits suicide, Jessner dims the lights for a moment and then switches on from the prompter's box a bright shaft against the figure of Iago, whose shadow is thus projected as a blot across the body of his victim, a symbol of the black tragedy he has induced.

Before the War, *Faust* was done as a mystery play, Reinhard Sorge's *The Beggar* was produced with focused lights, and Hamsun's *In the Grip of Life* was rendered in fantastic style. Later, Cubist scenery was provided for Immermann's *Merlin*, and at the Albert Theater in Dresden Hasenclever's *The Son* was given with purely suggestive shifts of scenes. Hasenclever further furnished plays for the first expressionistic theater, The Tribune, established in 1919 at Charlottenburg. Here simplification went so far that there was no curtain between the audience and the actors and no decoration except for the properties on the stage.

The two directors most effective in carrying forward the revolt against realism are Jürgen Fehling and Erwin Piscator. Fehling has produced Ernst Toller's *Masses and Man* at the Volksbühne, departing from the author's own stage directions by using black curtains, flights of steps, and lights focused on central characters. Piscator, in 1926, gave Schiller's *Robbers* in modern dress as a bit of communistic propaganda. Since then he has grown increasingly free in his use of steps and scaffolds and supplementary moving pictures which allow a fluidity to drama that it never knew before. In the *Storm-flood* of Paquet he suggested the crowd in the background by means of films, and in the *Tempest over Gotland* of Ehm Welk he enlarged the rôle of the films and put on this story of a fifteenth century piratical state as though it concerned the Soviet Republic, with characters made up to resemble Lenin and Trotsky. He opened a theater of his own on the Nollendorf Platz with Toller's *Hoppla, We Live!* using films for prologue and the binding between acts, just as Shakespeare, in *Henry V*, used a descriptive and narrative chorus. Moreover, Piscator has resorted to films to translate into visible symbols the sounds made by his characters and even their mental perturbations.

At this point it may be in keeping to refer to two features of the German theater which are especially notable. The first is the rise of the folk stage through the example of a medieval survival like the *Passion Play* of Oberammergau or through the efforts of those interested in local history. Martin Greif, for example, has composed a long line of historical plays ranging through classic and medieval times to the modern. He has grown increasingly nationalistic in his Hohenstaufen trilogy, and, in dramas like *Ludwig the Bavarian* and *Agnes Bernauer, the Angel of Augsburg*, he has fired the popular fancy. For the production of the former, the residents of Kraiburg and its neighborhood erected a special theater, where from 1892 forward the piece has been acted annually. Hans Pöhne, a Viennese dramatist, having campaigned for the establishment of a folk stage, aided the erection of a Volksfestspielhaus at Worms. Scholars earlier and later have fought the same battle. Thus, Hans Herrig awakened interest in a Lutherfestspiel, and in his critical volume, *Luxury Theater and Folk Stage*, contrasted popular with aristocratic drama, as did Ferdinand Frey and R. Gollmer in their *Stage Reform*, and Walter Aszmus in his *Modern Folk Stage Movement*. Peasants regularly give an Andreas Hofer play at Meran, a Wallenstein Festspiel at Eger, and performances of Schiller's *Wilhelm Tell* at Altdorf close to the scene of its action. Most effective of the pure folk stages has been the Harzer Bergtheater. From the Oberammergau celebration have sprung various others like the Höritz Passion Play, the mystery given at Godesberg, and such movements as the amateur performances of religious drama fostered by Dr. Dimmler, a priest of Munich, and by the so-called Christian Drama League. Remotely allied to the folk stages have been such open-air performances as those of von Hartung at Heidelberg Castle.

A second notable feature of the recent German drama, and one of far greater significance, is the rise of the proletarian stage. Back of both phenomena lies the conception of art as something popular rather than aristocratic. The best art, it is argued, should spring from the folk and minister to the folk. But, because the people left to themselves rarely produce anything distinguished, all the emphasis has practically fallen upon the notion of ministering to the people, even to the fourth estate. This attempt to interest the masses in drama is peculiarly characteristic also of the new Russia.

In 1890, shortly after the establishment of the Freie Bühne, Dr. Bruno Wille called a meeting of two thousand workingmen of Berlin to consider founding a Freie Volksbühne. In response to his declaration that "Art should not be the privilege of any social class but should belong to the people," arrangements were made for performances to be given for the benefit of the toilers on Sunday afternoons at an admission of only fifty pfennigs, the seats being distributed by lot. Thus, the plays of well-known writers were rendered available for all. Ibsen's *Pillars of Society*, Sudermann's *Honor*, some of the early dramas of Hauptmann, as well as certain older favorites were so presented. Then, within two years, a Neue Freie Volksbühne was founded in response to the demand by Socialists for pieces more radical. The new society, having given Hauptmann's *Weavers* and Björnson's *Beyond Our Power* in its second part, secured all the Sunday performances and holiday matinees of Reinhardt's theater at a time when he was swinging away from naturalism in his staging of Maeterlinck, von Hofmannsthal, and Wedekind. So the people were initiated into the mysteries of romanticism or incipient expressionism. By 1908 the Volksbühne was leasing, not only evening performances at Reinhardt's Deutsches Theater, but matinees at eleven other playhouses. By 1912 its membership was close upon fifty thousand, and public subscriptions were readily secured for the erection of a building to cost more than a million dollars. Four months after the declaration of war this theater was opened, but it failed to pay until Reinhardt came to the rescue. Running it on the proceeds of half its seats, he presented the other half to members as his rental. At the close of the War, the society reassumed control, with Friedrich Kayssler as director. The number of other theaters from which seats were leased for the membership was augmented, and

Jürgen Fehling and Erwin Piscator succeeded as directors, confirming the radical and expressionistic tendencies of the venture.

In the mean time, in Munich Eugen Felber, after the defeat of the May Revolution, founded a New Stage for the benefit of the workers. In Leipzig Josef von Fielitz followed suit; and in Berlin Karl Heinz Martin put on a mass drama called *Freedom* to express the proletarian spirit. Together with the conservative Bühnenfolksbund, the union of German folk stages formed in 1919 comprises in various parts of the Reich some three hundred theaters and half a million subscribers, many of them good bourgeois citizens. In what other country in the world has interest in the drama ever proved so general? Prophetic indeed was the play performed in the old court theater at Weimar on the evening of the first meeting of the Constituent Assembly of the new German Republic. It was entitled *The Fountain* and came from the pen of Ernst Hardt, who here depicted the guardian of a fountain of healing waters flowing from between the busts of Goethe and Schiller aroused from slumber by a mourning mother and handing to her soldier son a draught of art for the spiritual regeneration of those physically and spiritually crippled by the War.

CHAPTER XIX

THE AUSTRIAN CONTRIBUTION

Schnitzler, Bahr, Schönherr, von Hofmannsthal

OUTSTANDING among Austrian dramatists is Arthur
Schnitzler, born at Vienna in 1862, a practising physician who began to compose for the stage in the early 'nineties.
In his short stories, novels, and plays he has exhibited keen
observation, perfect craftsmanship, and an attitude toward
life half cynical, half sentimental. Men love and die. For
Schnitzler these two facts are of signal importance. But it is
love that chiefly engages his attention, a love sensuous yet
usually refined, a philandering without thought of the morrow,
but charged with fond recollections of the past. The regrets
of love are as enjoyable to Schnitzler as its instant excitements. His people will not be permanently happy, but from
each experience they will extract the most exquisite thrill.
And the knowledge that passion is fleeting renders it more
precious while it endures.

Characteristic among Schnitzler's contributions to the stage
is that early series of seven episodes, paraphrased in English
by Granville Barker as *The Affairs of Anatol*, wherein a light-
hearted worldling, aided by his friend the satirical Max, recalls or indulges in one delicate bit of intrigue after another.
Although at last he will settle down and marry, he cannot
resist bringing home Ilona, a former flame, from whom next
morning he must part as tactfully as possible, leaving Max
to prevail upon the hysterical lady to postpone the revenge
that she threatens. In each of the six other episodes figures
a different charmer, complacent in love and lightly disloyal.

345

Even Anatol will not ask the truth as to Cora's past, though she must surely speak it when hypnotized. If he hesitates to admit his waning affection for Annie, she anticipates his confession by declaring her own preference for another. Inconsistently, he is grieved to learn that it was merely lack of courage which kept Gabrielle from becoming his, and that it was boredom only which sent the married Else to his arms. How ironical that Bianca whom he had pictured as treasuring his memory should not be able even to recall him, or that Emilie should value his gift of a black diamond just for its market price! At best, however, his dream of love is poetic. He would find in the little world, as he calls it, escape from the great world, cherishing some simple girl not too fair, not too clever, but tender, graceful, appealing. As Anatol remarks, "Only in the little world am I beloved, only in the great world am I understood."

The tragedy that may result for the girl in such a case is displayed with delicacy in *The Legacy* and *Light o' Love* (*Liebelei*). The daughter of the poor violinist in the latter has given her heart to the jaunty Fritz; but, for him, she is the diversion of just a few weeks. Indeed, he has sought her on the advice of a friend as a refuge from the dangers of an intrigue with a lady of fashion. When he falls in a duel with the lady's husband, Christiane, in whom he has never confided this other affair, goes forth to die upon his grave. To her, his love had meant everything. "You are free," she had told him; "you can leave me whenever you will. You have promised me nothing, and I have asked for nothing. I have been happy once; I will expect no more of life." Such passionate fidelity contrasts with the easy disloyalty of Fritz, who has sought security in the humble world, where, according to his friend, "there are no great scenes, no dangers, and no tragic developments, where the beginning is beset with no special difficulties and the end with no torments, where the first kiss is received laughingly, and the last parting with gentle emotion." Of course, the fate of Christiane belies this description. Love, for her, is single and tragic. She cannot understand Mizi's question, "Who in May would think of August?" or Theodor's answer, "Truly, eternal love does not last so long." Admirable in this drama is its power of compression and suggestion and its quiet emphasis, with scenes and acts that conclude like a tender caress.

Similarly, tragedy may ensue for the girl if her lover die and leave her to his relatives. Thus, in *The Legacy*, Toni Weber suffers when consigned to the tender mercies of a family well-meaning but outraged by her presence. Her lover's father, mother, former sweetheart, and a suitor for the daughter of the house, all conspire against her. Her child sickens and passes, and Toni departs presumably to take her life. Only her lover's sister has felt her liaison to be as sacred as marriage.

Later, on occasion, Schnitzler was to show free love as something less delicate. Such was the case in his notorious cycle *Reigen*, or *Hands Around*. Though technically of interest as a series of ten duologues between pairs of lovers, one of whom in each group figures in the next, the play by its brutality provoked riots in the theater. Here a courtesan makes love to a soldier, and the soldier to a servant maid; the servant maid makes love to a young gentleman, and the gentleman to a young wife; the wife makes love to her husband, and the husband to a "süsze Mädel"; the "süsze Mädel" makes love to a poet, and the poet to an actress; the actress makes love to a count, and the count to the very courtesan who started the cycle. In this erotic dance of death is depicted the irrationality of animal impulse, its delirious expectancy before satisfaction and its consciousness of defeat and remorse thereafter.

Rather brutal, also, is the love set forth in *The Comedy of Seduction*, which follows the career of a timid youth who develops into a Don Juan, and, after a series of affairs that end badly for his ladies and their husbands, bows to marriage as a necessary reparation. But Schnitzler's distinctive achievement lies in an art more subtle. He paints the perturbations, the ecstasies, the sorrows of a love that comes and goes, seeking without finding a fixed object, fascinated to contemplate its own disloyalties, extracting from passion the sweetness of sentiment.

Often Schnitzler presents single, static situations. So, in *The Companion*, a professor uncovers letters which prove that his dead wife has been untrue and that, further, she has known and accepted the disloyalty of her lover. In *Living Hours*, a man of middle age, learning that his mistress has taken her life for the benefit of her son, challenges the youth to justify her sacrifice by his work as poet. In *The Last Masks*, an invalid while dying plans to humiliate his now famous rival by disclosing the infidelity of the latter's wife, but desists on perceiving that the dead, after all, have nothing to do with the living. In *Literature*, after the quarrel of a poet and his mistress, each has written a novel to pillory the other. But the poet, recognizing the folly of a revenge that will bare their intrigue to the public, destroys his work except for a single copy, and this the lady tosses into the fire. In *Intermezzo*, an orchestra leader, having broken his long alliance with a prima donna, is tempted to renew it, until both realize that the spell of the moment which has again brought them together will quickly pass. So they part, saying, "We were not created with sufficient fidelity to love each other, nor with sufficient strength to preserve our friendship in its purity."

In such plays nothing much happens, and the infidelity at the core of the situation is accepted as inevitable. Since we are but human, let us by all means be indulgent to the failings of others. So, in *The Big Scene*, a wife, discovering that her husband has intrigued with the fiancée of his best friend, would leave him. But, if she does so, he will be too troubled to bear with credit the part of Hamlet in a gala performance. Moreover, though he had promised never to lie again, his most recent lies are truly magnificent. To genius all things must be forgiven.

The same easy indulgence is accorded a wife in *The Festival of Bacchus*. While her husband is away with a fresh fancy in the mountains, she falls in love with a physician at home, and plans to depart with him after they have greeted her returning lord at the station. But the meeting of the three ends unexpectedly, for the wife, on comparing the two men, sends off the physician. As for her husband, he is forgiven and forgives. Why not? He has been writing a play to prove that an occasional romance should not be allowed to disrupt the more serious business of matrimony. In antiquity, once a year, love was free to celebrate its rites in the grove of Bacchus without blame and without afterthought. "There was as little individual responsibility for the experience of that night as there would be for one's dreams." To-day, "Only on occasion in pious souls there is kindled a faint reflection of the marvellous magic which once pervaded the Festival of Bacchus."

Let us enjoy, forgive, and forget. Such is the motto of Schnitzler. So, in *Countess Mizzi*, he introduces figures typical of sophisticated Vienna: a count, who, after twenty years of irregular union with a dancer, surrenders her to his coachman; and the count's daughter, who, pretending ignorance of her father's intrigue, has indulged in several of her own, keeping from him the knowledge that she has borne a son to a prince. The sight of this natural son grown to man's estate so moves her that she drops philandering with her professor of drawing, and surprises the prince and the boy by taking the same train with them for Ostend. There she may even accept the long-standing proposal of marriage of her son's father. Smooth artistry matches the suave immorality. Good art and good form must be preserved even if ethics go hang.

That love and life are but play is the implication of *Paracelsus*, in which the learned physician, in order to be evened with a self-important husband, throws into a trance the wife, who reveals in hypnosis her deeper impulses. What is truth? What is illusion in the human soul? That this soul is a mysterious country with ample room for divergent tendencies is the moral of *The Wide Domain*. Here a husband, suspecting his wife because a pianist has avowedly died out of love for her, goes away with her friend. When the wife, in retaliation, yields to an ensign, her husband shoots her, stung less by jealousy than by resentment at being defeated by youth. Then, bidding farewell to his child and dismissing the girl who would cleave to him, he wanders forth alone, declaring: "There is room for so much in us—love and betrayal, faith and disloyalty, adoration for one and desire for another or for several. We seek to order life as best we can, but this order must be something artistic. The natural is chaos. The soul is a wide domain."

Latterly, in a very light comedy *The Sisters*, Schnitzler describes with similar skepticism one among many gallant adventures of the great Casanova, to whom already the playwright had devoted a story. When the famous lover chances to enter by night the room of the wrong lady, amusing consequences follow, and love itself is revealed as purely subjective. Since the lady who now possesses him, supposes that he is another, that other—her betrothed—is in error to protest, and Casanova himself is as deluded as the lady whom he had thought to embrace.

Seldom with Schnitzler is love unimportant, yet in *Fink and Fliederbusch* attention is fixed rather upon the double personality of a journalist who contributes to both liberal and conservative papers and is forced at last to challenge to a duel his other self. Here we have merely a psychological fantasy. But, even with love as the theme, it is exceptional for Schnitzler to emphasize action. This he does, nevertheless, in several plays. Thus, in *The Path to the Pond*, he seems to assert the primacy of action, for a pacifist chancellor who would save the state from threatened war is defeated by a militant youth, son of a marshal. This youth, moreover, puts to rout as a rival for the chancellor's daughter a passive elderly poet left no other resource but to drown himself. To the strong and the willful accrue all the honors. So, too, in *Gallant Cassian*, a light puppet play accompanied by music, the hero is a soldier who slays his rival in a duel, abducts the lady for whom they have contended, piques her jealousy, and when, in despair, she throws herself from a window, leaps bravely after, but speeds away in pursuit of another charmer.

Active enough, also, is the player in *The Green Cockatoo*, who, in order to thrill the idlers at a Parisian café, bursts in announcing that he has killed the duke for having stolen his bride. When the spectators approve his deed as fully justified, the player perceives that the duke has in fact wronged him, and, as that nobleman chances to enter, leaps upon him, dagger in hand, doing now what before he had merely pretended. Thereupon, the mob, returned from storming the Bastille, hails him as the people's champion. Even in a dream-play like *The Lady with the Dagger*, the inserted vision of past lives is one of action, for the wife and her lover who have planned a farewell meeting behold in their retrospect of a previous incarnation just such a meeting fatally interrupted as now by the lady's husband.

More elaborate as dramas of action are *The Veil of Beatrice* and *Young Medardus*, richly embroidered studies, the first of the Renaissance and the second of Napoleonic times, with intrigue as always at the heart of both. Beatrice slips out from her bridal feast to meet her former lover, a poet, with whom she agrees to die, but when he has swallowed the poison intended for both, she loses courage. Returning to the feast, she is forced to explain the loss of the veil, her bridegroom's present. Its discovery beside her lover's body confirms the duke's suspicion. She has won his forgiveness when she falls stabbed by her outraged brother. Thereupon the duke departs to die in battle, like the poet and the lady, a victim of love.

Young Medardus, too, writhes in the toils of love, fascinated by Princess Hélène of Valois, whom he hates because her royalist father has caused the suicide of Medardus' sister. Having dueled with the lady's betrothed, he finds that he cannot assail Napoleon as he had intended because to do so will be to aid this Valois family in attaining the throne. Yet, having heard that Hélène has become Napoleon's mistress, he is prompted by jealousy to slay the Emperor. While awaiting his chance to do this, he encounters the girl and on impulse turns his weapon against her, only to discover that she too has been plotting Napoleon's destruction and that by killing her he has unwittingly saved his enemy. Since the impetuous weakling will not pledge his word to spare the Emperor, he is shot. Such a melodrama might have been inspired by Sardou. It is well documented without being pedantic in its historical features. The true hero, Napoleon, never appears. The love intrigue, which with Schnitzler tends to become a monotonous constant, is relieved by the play of politics.

Intrigue is again to the fore in *The Call of Life*. Here a girl enamored of a lieutenant would spend a last night with him even though she discovers that he has had an affair with the colonel's wife and beholds that colonel slay his lady and order the lieutenant to efface himself before dawn. Once the colonel's regiment had shown cowardice in the field owing to the bad example of Marie's father, now a whining and tyrannous invalid. The regiment, to repair the blot upon its fame, has vowed to die in battle to the last man. Marie, in resentment at her father and to assure the chance of a final meeting with Max, pours enough sedative into the invalid's sleeping draught to kill him. No one need know, for she is exonerated by a physician, and Max goes from her side to death as one purified by love. Improbable as are the situations and doubtful as is the psychology, one must feel the power of such a scene as that in which Marie, stepping from concealment, confesses that she has seen her rival shot and her lover sentenced to die. That lover questions her.

"You were here?"

She nods.

"You will remain?"

She nods.

"And you know that I must make an end of myself before dawn?"

"I know."

"And you will remain?"

In answer, she clasps his hand, and departs with him beneath the shelter of his cloak.

Twice at least Schnitzler has diverged from his customary path to write dramas of social criticism. In *Fair Game* he proceeds to deal with the point of honor and in *Professor Bernhardi* with racial prejudice. The absurdity of the duel is the theme of the first; yet the duel, after all, is something more civilized, he seems to say, than unregulated violence. A blustering lieutenant, speaking lightly of a soubrette, and being slapped by her lover, retorts with a challenge; but the lover scorns a duel. Why should he slay the lieutenant, or why should the lieutenant slay him? How can his honor be affected by the actions of another? Yet such is the military code that refusal to accept the lieutenant's challenge makes of the challenger an outlaw, who, at last despairing of regaining his professional integrity, shoots down the rationalist in cold blood.

The problem dealt with in *Professor Bernhardi* is less specialized. There Schnitzler, the Jewish physician, speaks from a full heart. The president of a hospital has offended the anti-Semite and clerical party. When the case becomes an issue in parliament, Bernhardi is sent to prison. Though a nun confesses that she had testified falsely against him, he declines to demand a reversal of judgment. Having served his sentence, he will take refuge in some other land where men are free to follow truth.

What has Bernhardi done? He has cheered a dying patient with the belief that her lover, at whose defection she had attempted suicide, is returning to her. He has also begged a priest not to frighten the girl by administering the last sacrament. But since she dies, the incident is exaggerated by his enemies, and he is said to have struck the priest. He can save his neck by appointing to his staff a Catholic notoriously incompetent. When he balks, a cabinet minister, fearing parliamentary opposition, withdraws his protection. The priest is willing to exonerate Bernhardi in private but not in public, lest a sacred cause be jeopardized. Both he and the cabinet minister argue that the individual must be sacrificed for larger issues. It is Bernhardi's doctrine, like Shaw's, that general formulas for conduct are misleading, that each situation should be judged upon its own merits. In attempting to strengthen his case, however, Schnitzler unduly medicates his play. Fourteen of the faculty bear part; and, in spite of the lively dialogue and the skill of the exposition, we miss here the genial art of the smiling Viennese. For once he is writing as bitter a prescription as Brieux.

Finally, it may be noted that the versatile Schnitzler, without descending to propaganda, has shown in *The Lonely Way* that he can be as moral as the English. In unwonted accents he reproves the selfishness which, seizing upon the joy of living, would avoid its responsibilities. "To love means to live for the sake of some one else," declares a poet, who has learned his lesson by harsh experience; and the painter who would claim as his own a son reared by another discovers too late that the boy will cleave not to his parent but to the man who has rendered him a service. In short, blood is not thicker than water, and "the selfish way is the lonely way." It is selfishness that has led Julian the artist to appropriate the sweetheart of his friend and then to desert her in order to preserve his own freedom. It is selfishness that has led him to crush the love-life out of another by refusing to permit her to bear his child. It is selfishness, also, that incites him to reveal to his son the secret of that son's birth in the hope of reclaiming him. But such selfishness is self-defeating.

By contrast with the egotistic artist and poet Schnitzler portrays the poet's generous sweetheart, who drowns herself on perceiving that he cannot love her loyally. Life and beauty both are fleeting. But our past lives may be dimly remembered. Can she not recall how once she danced before the poet as a slave girl in Libya? The poet himself, like Schnitzler, is preoccupied with thoughts of death as well as of love. "Is there ever," he asks, "a blissful moment in any decent man's life when in his innermost soul he can think of aught but death?" Yes, death and love, these for Schnitzler are the two realities.

An artist of the first rank so far as technique is concerned, adept in the analysis of feeling and especially of illicit love and its associated emotions, Schnitzler is usually content to say but one thing. He says it again and again with ingenious variations, adding to the depth of the impression he conveys rather than to its breadth. In mood and manner he is allied with Capus or Bataille in France, though distinctive in breathing the somewhat richer atmosphere of amoral Vienna. But his career as playwright shows little progress. Instead of moving forward, he circles round and round, and he proves, if any proof were needed, that there is no monotony so deadly as that of passion which has become an end in itself.

Of the other Austrian playwrights to be noticed here, Hermann Bahr is a lesser Schnitzler, softening the sharp edges of realism by his scrupulous art; Karl Schönherr is a more stalwart painter of the actual; and Hugo von Hofmannsthal is an expert romanticist. As for Bahr, the eclectic, the list of his published works includes more than eighty titles, for he wrought, not only as playwright, but also as journalist, novelist, and critic, producing in the last-named field the earliest discriminating treatise upon expressionism, a tendency opposed to his own practice. In Berlin and Paris he came under the spell of naturalism, without so far succumbing to it, however, as to surrender his fine sense of form. He was connected with the Freie Bühne and the Deutsches Theater as director; and as playwright he composed pieces of crass observation, like *The Great Sin* and *The Mother*, and suave studies of high society or of theatrical folk, like *The Star* and *The Yellow Nightingale*, the latter raising a laugh at the expense of his countryman Reinhardt. Among his more popular dramas are *The New Men*, *The Domestic Woman*, *Dora*, *Juana*, *Josephine*, *The Athlete*, *Viennese Women*, *The Apostle*, *The Master*, *The Poor Fool*, *Grotesques*, *The Children*, *The Little Dance*, *The Principle*, *The Phantom*, and *The Voice*. It will suffice for our purpose to speak of only two—*The Concert* and *The Mongrel*. The former might have come from the pen of Schnitzler or Molnár. It is as well known on every foreign stage as their best productions. A musical genius with a weakness for returning the affection of his fair pupils craves romantic excitement but needs above all the control, the tact, and the tolerance of his understanding wife. She recognizes in his fiction of a concert engagement at a distance a device to conceal his affair with a youthful charmer. Accompanied by that lady's husband, she pursues, and, by pretending an affair of her own, makes her genius jealous. So she brings him back to the fold, after the four have sought adjustment through a highly amusing second act. Though repentant for the moment, he is ready before the final curtain falls to return the affection of another admiring pupil. One might suppose that this plot were already gray with age, but the humor and humanity of the treatment keep it fresh and blooming. How different in mood is *The Mongrel*, which reveals the soul, not of a favorite of fortune, but of a road-mender, driven distracted on being refused justice when his favorite dog is killed by a forester. The forester he respects as a man of superior station representing vested interests, yet, when a judge imposes on the forester only a small fine, the road-mender rebels. To him the dog, though a mongrel, had meant everything, for his wife is dead, his daughter has disappeared in disgrace, his son has left under a cloud after false imprisonment, and his grandson has proved a half-witted rascal. Rebuked by the forester's daughter for his wordy battle with her father, he starts to strangle her, then desists, shocked at his ingratitude, since she has been kind to his son. After an attempt at flight, he returns to give himself up to justice; but the girl declines to implicate him in the attack. The judge, moreover, turns a deaf ear on his demand for punishment. Surprised by such generosity, the old man recovers his balance, and the girl, hitherto insensible to the judge's suit for her hand, is won over by his intelligent interest in this human mongrel, a lonely, inarticulate, yet somewhat lovable figure.

A much more vigorous realist is Karl Schönherr, the Tyrolese physician, who was born in 1868, practiced for a decade in Vienna, and then withdrew to devote himself to letters. In such plays as *The Carvers* and *Caravan Folk* he has revealed his mastery of the one-act form. The first shows a woodcarver threatened with blood poisoning from a cut in his hand, but refusing to be operated upon after he happens to see his wife embracing in gratitude the man who has given everything to assist his stricken friend. The second piece shows a hungry boy betraying his father to the police when tempted by a loaf of bread, then smitten with remorse and taking his life. Both are remarkable genre pictures, the former of a proud but poverty-stricken family in a cottage, and the latter of ne'er-do-well vagabonds foraging from their house on wheels.

In *Earth* Schönherr enlarges his canvas and brightens its shadows with a boisterous humor not unlike that of the Irishman Synge. A crusty old innkeeper, past seventy, refusing to allow his son, nearing fifty, to marry or to take a man's place at the inn, is warned by the village doctor that he must die. The old fellow, accordingly, orders a coffin to be placed at his bedside, and lies ailing all winter awaiting his end. In the mean time he watches two maids of the inn contending as to which shall capture his son and the inheritance. At length he perceives that the younger has won by guile, and can prove her title to the property by her condition. Already the son is fashioning a cradle to replace the coffin. But, unexpectedly, when spring comes around, the tough old fellow recovers, and, rising from bed, dashes the hopes of the affectionate pair by smashing the coffin into firewood.

With a technique borrowed from Ibsen, *The Children's Tragedy* revamps an earlier play. Both exhibit the evil wrought upon the young by a mother's sin. In *The Family* Fate is all potent, and the mother and her lover are set before us, together with the slaying of the lover by her son whom he had saved from death. In the later and more subtle version, the only characters who appear are the three children, whose lives, as we see, are determined less by Fate than by the actions of their elders already accomplished. On two other occasions Schönherr revised an earlier play. In *The Trenckwalder* he rather spoiled his *Solstice Day* by turning it into a comedy. The first piece ended with a capital scene as the pious mother who had thought to atone for her secret sin by consecrating her son to the priesthood is shocked to learn that he has committed a murder. Then, silently, she extinguishes a taper she has kept always burning before her household shrine and hides her crucifix in the cupboard. Thus the shattering of her hopes is revealed through pantomime. Once more in *Vivat Academia* Schönherr reworks a previous play, *The Struggle*, both dealing with the shady side of medical life. His hero is a student who, failing to pass an examination, declines into chicanery and becomes assistant to a female quack, first cousin to the heroine of Hauptmann's *The Beaver Coat* and *The Conflagration*. Schönherr's pessimism regarding the medical profession deepens in *The Fool's Game of Life* with its hero a surgeon so intent upon science that he comes to consider his fellows only as subjects to be operated on, and, losing humanity, grows embittered and takes poison.

These are minor plays, and so are *The Kingdom*, a folk fairy tale, and *May Dance*, a little tragedy in three scenes which contrasts the Springtime jollity of villagers in the market place with the jealous grief of a girl dying indoors, aware that her lover is dancing outside with a rival. In spite of her foster mother's efforts to make her spend her last moments in prayer, she rises to dance in her room and then falls lifeless. Fuller-bodied is *Frau Suitner* in which the playwright through five acts studies, with an eye on the initial situation of *Rosmersholm*, the psychology of a childless wife determined to die as if by accident that she may yield place to one she has selected to give her husband an heir.

Of broadest scope are two historical plays, *Faith and Fatherland*, dealing with the Counter Reformation, and *Folk in Need*, dealing with the Tyrolese struggle for freedom under Andreas Hofer, whose career is not carried forward to his death at Mantua but concludes in the play with his victory at home. Especially fine here is the character of the innkeeper's wife bereft of husband and sons yet staunch in her stoicism. Better known is *Faith and Fatherland*, a plea for religious toleration which excites sympathy for a family of pious peasants suffering tragic woes as the result of an imperial edict expelling all Protestants from the Austrian Alps. The grandfather hesitates to confess his faith until, with death upon him, he believes it too late for the enemy to tear him from his home. His son, on witnessing the martyrdom of a neighbor's wife, is stirred to declare his religion in spite of the consequences. His own wife, although a Catholic, refuses to desert him and prepares for exile with their boy, but when a fresh edict prohibits a minor from leaving the district with his parents, she perceives that she must remain there with the lad until he comes of age. The boy, discovering that his parents must separate on his account, drowns himself. Thereupon, father and mother, robbed of their child and their home, depart in quest of a land where they may worship God as they see fit. Minor situations strengthen the main story. The husband of the woman martyred for her belief recants his own faith that he may not be driven from her grave. A soldier, forced to be harsh against his will, regrets the misery that he must inflict, and asks why, in the service of the Holy Mother, he must bathe his hands in blood. The hero, having lost his son, is tempted to kill the soldier, but desists on reflecting that Christ would bid him forgive his enemy, and the soldier, touched by such unwonted generosity, breaks his sword in remorse. Fortunately this simple and sincere play, with its plea for freedom of thought and worship, avoids both the sentimental and the abstract.

Most intense and stirring of Schönherr's dramas is *The She-Devil*, developed by only three characters through five acts of increasing tension. A sickly smuggler has advised his robust wife to philander a little with a custom's guard ordered by his superiors to pretend affection for the woman as a means of spying upon her husband. The guard is willing to take so agreeable a method of prosecuting his duty, and the wife, who has mourned her childlessness and her husband's querulous invalidism, falls a ready victim to the soldier she had thought to victimize. When the husband spies upon the pair together, he is gratified to think that she has so adroitly involved his enemy, not realizing that by this time she is more than playing a part. To the guard she admits that the weakling now affects her as might a half-dead fly struggling in a cup of coffee, and she even hints that he be put out of the way. Unexpectedly, however, he wearies of his game of deception. Since his superiors have been warned by the husband that he has failed to report in the case, he must resign and depart. At this threat, the woman's love turns to hate. She will rid herself of both men, setting one against the other, in order to inherit her husband's new house just bought with the profits of smuggling. "Soldier," she reflects, "you were drawn here like a bear to honey. You are good now only to put out of the way as an obstacle. I shall need you for nothing else. And when I have the house in the market place and sit in it as a young widow, then I shall catch for myself such another strong young man. . . . Believe me, I know how to do that now." So she plies the guard with drink, dances with him wildly, and goads him into stabbing her husband when the latter interferes. Throughout, the interactions of these three are managed most cleverly. Although the wife has earlier shown something of tenderness toward her invalid lord, she is at last a very "she-devil."

Whereas Schnitzler, Bahr, and Schönherr represent a realistic strain held well in check by the esthetic sense, Hugo von Hofmannsthal, who died in 1929, represents a deliberately poetic and imaginative recoil against naturalism. Born in Vienna in 1874, he was educated at the university, admired the French symbolists, and Whitman, Wilde, Novalis, Nietzsche, and d'Annunzio, and wrote a lyric play—*Yesterday* —at seventeen. Like Wilde, he argued that the world of art should stand divorced from the world of nature as something ideal and transcendent, that it should be a realm of reasoned dream, concerned with the emotional product of experience rather than with experience itself. So he seeks his themes in fantasy or legend, rejoicing in whatever will afford him satisfactions of sound, color, and form. Although seeming to insist, in his youthful *Death and the Fool*, that an artist may err in forgetting reality, and find only at the moment of his death that he is living, von Hofmannsthal for the most part upholds the cult of estheticism, losing no opportunity to sing its glories, lamenting the loss of the painter Böcklin in *Titian's Death*, and providing splendid examples of an art created for art's sake in the highly decorative and harmonious verse of a dozen dramas short and long. If the first of his more ambitious pieces, *The Marriage of Sobeide* and *The Adventurer and the Singer*, be comparatively unimportant, the later full-length works constitute a noteworthy achievement in a difficult department. Like most contemporary plays in verse, they minimize action, character, and conflict in order to emphasize poetry; their personages deliver rhythmic utterances not to voice some impulsion of the soul but to bless the fleeting moment with beauty. Von Hofmannsthal is as happy to embroider a plot already developed and well known as to invent something fresh. Thus, he alters Thomas Otway's *Venice Preserved*, retelling more ornately that story of the treachery to his plotting friends of Antonio Jaffier, wed to the daughter of the senator against whom their conspiracy is directed. The Austrian modifies the main story, amplifies the diction and the motivation, and substitutes for the hero's suicide, his execution for treason. Thus, too, in *The Death of the Rich Man*, von Hofmannsthal rewrites the English morality play *Everyman*, and in *Dame Kobold* and *The Great Salzburg World Theater* draws upon Calderón.

In turning to classic themes he was inspired by the demand of Paul Schlenther for a free modern rendering of the antique and by the production at the Viennese Burgtheater of the *Orestes* of Æschylus, done into German by Wilamowitz-Möllendorff. As a result, he proceeded to remold and redecorate Greek originals, stressing their barbarity rather than their restraint. The heroine of his *Electra* becomes a mad Mænad, deprived of her rights as woman and consumed with longing to be revenged upon her guilty mother, vainly seeking to inflame her sister to that end, and succeeding with her brother Orestes. After Orestes has slain the sallow and bloated Clytemnestra and struck down Ægisthus, the latter cries, "Does no one hear me?" and Electra, answering, shouts, "Agamemnon hears you!" Then, having put his followers to the sword, she dances in triumph. Here the calm dignity of Sophocles' heroine and her righteous demand for justice is replaced by wild fury. Walter Eaton, when the Austrian play was performed by Mrs. Patrick Campbell in an English version by Arthur Symons, wrote of it: "Pity and fear are not aroused, but curiosity and horror. The emotions are not purged, but scraped, irritated, made to shiver and creep."

With greater inventiveness, the Austrian dramatist, in *Œdipus and the Sphinx*, features the barbaric aspects of the masterpiece of Sophocles, developing that portion of the story which Sophocles but hinted at, namely, the involuntary slaying of Laius by his unrecognized son, Œdipus, and the latter's equally involuntary marriage with his unrecognized mother, Jocasta. In the printed version of the play nearly forty pages are devoted to an expositional dialogue before the entrance of Laius. Then the poet bends his powers to render as plausible as may be the death of Laius and the marriage of the queen. He enlarges the rôle of Creon, her brother, aspirant for the throne, subject to weird seizures and insane controls, and makes of Antiope, the old mother of Laius, a Bacchanalian prophetess mainly responsible for inciting Jocasta to her new and fatal match. Œdipus, whose advent has been foretold in dreams and ecstasies, is hailed as a god, and in the third act climbs to the Sphinx's haunt, and solves her riddle to the despair of the expectant Creon, who has hoped that the creature's scream might be the death wail of the hero. When Œdipus, oppressed by foreboding, expresses a wish to die, Creon is ready to oblige him, but Œdipus wrests the dagger from Creon's hand and refrains from stabbing him only on learning of his relationship to the queen. Then he bids Creon slay him, but invisible powers hold Creon's arm, and, when he tosses the dagger away, a tree upon the cliff where it falls bursts into flame. Jocasta, entering to greet the city's savior, and embraced by him, asks with a shudder, "Ah, what is it that we do?" to which he answers, "The blind deed of the gods." So von Hofmannsthal employs all the claptrap tricks of the romantic drama, effective upon the stage for those who like that sort of thing, but not to be compared with the strength and beauty of Greek tragedy. His personages are creatures of frenzied fears and yearnings subject to a Fate unduly complicated in its workings. The motivation is weak, the treatment Asiatic rather than Hellenic.

Of the brief minor plays of the Austrian romanticist, *The Lady at the Window* may serve as an example. The youthful Madonna Dianora, awaiting on a balcony the coming of her lover who at twilight will steal to her on "footsteps light as the wind in the grass," is surprised by her brutal husband, a captain of mercenaries. Having given her only time for a last prayer, he draws up the silken ladder she had let down for her lover's use and chokes her in its strands. The plot is nothing, but the poetry of its development is rich and rare. Dianora on her balcony has torn the slow hours of a whole day of waiting into shreds. She has dripped the fountain drop on drop through her tresses and dried them languidly. She has watched the birds in the bushes, and travelers and maidens pausing at a well. She has counted and recounted her beads, and tried on her jewels one by one, and drawn from her fingers the rings which she has fancied to be happy naked children released from duty and scampering to a brook to bathe. So her every mood and thought is poetized.

The influence of von Hofmannsthal has been extended by his opera librettos, *The Woman Without a Shadow, Helen, Ariadne at Naxos, The Rose Cavalier*, and a ballet, *The Legend of Joseph*. Richard Strauss wrote the music for these and for *Electra*; Gordon Craig prepared the settings for Otto Brahm's production of *Venice Preserved*, and Reinhardt those for *Everyman*, the collaboration of such artists in production adding to the fame of the poet.

In 1922 von Hofmannsthal, praising the dramas of Eugene O'Neill, remarked that they combine the static and the dynamic. Sardou, Bernstein, Pinero, and Sudermann, he noted as masters of the dynamic, and Hauptmann as master of the

364

static. His own plays, he seemed to imply, would be found
to unite the two elements, nicely balancing action and character. But most have felt that they are static, that he is less
a playwright than a poet, both in his first Mozartian period
marked by the verbal preciosity of Stefan George and in his
later and more robust endeavor to make the past live again.
Indeed, his talents are preëminently pictorial and lyric. In
the Greek plays he abandons the chorus that he may the
better bring out the lyricism of individuals, and for the same
reason he intensifies the emotions of these characters extrava-
gantly. Obsessed by love of beauty, he is a poet of the esoteric,
of art for art's sake.

CHAPTER XX

Irrepressibles of the German Theater

Wedekind and Hasenclever

TO CUT capers in art, to treat with contempt the old, to shatter idols revered,—that is the self-appointed mission of such bad boys of the German theater as Wedekind and Hasenclever. Instead of drawing life as it is, they distort and stylize it, the first preparing the way for expressionism, the second exemplifying that movement. Frank Wedekind, half genius, half charlatan, was the son of a physician who had lived in Turkey and in California. The future dramatist, born at Hanover in 1864, was reared in Switzerland, where he practised journalism and served as publicity agent for a famous table delicacy. Then, attached to a circus, he visited France and England, became secretary to a Danish artist in Berlin, conducted vaudeville and café recitals, wrote for *Simplizissimus* in Munich, joined the theatrical troupe of Dr. Carl Heine of Leipzig, and later that of the Munich Theater, and was imprisoned for *lèse majesté*. He married an actress with whom he presented his own pieces on tour, and died in 1918, recognized as a powerful if eccentric force in German drama.

Wedekind had been influenced by Hauptmann through Karl Henckell in Zürich, and also by the German symbolists whom he read during his stay in London. He gave recitations from the plays of Ibsen, and studied the works of Nietzsche, Stirner, and Strindberg. Thus fortified in radicalism, he aroused the contempt of the conventional and the enthusiasm of those inclined to thumb noses at everything accepted and respectable.

Two early dramatic experiments by Wedekind are well nigh negligible. *The Fast Painter* is an inferior comedy celebrating the success of an artist in winning the hand of a manufacturer's daughter after he has been disdained by her father. The poison he has taken in despair proves harmless; his rival is shown to be a swindler; and his masterpiece is bought by the town gallery. *The World of Youth*, depicting girls in a Swiss boarding-school studying art but thinking only of marriage, and repressed by their teachers, is of interest chiefly as preparing the way for Wedekind's first original work, *The Awakening of Spring*. This "children's tragedy" presents vividly the sexual perturbations of schoolboys and deficiencies in the system of education to which they are submitted. The assertive Melchior and the passive Moritz react diversely to an instinct which their masters and relatives would choke or disguise. They and little Wendla are victims of the conspiracy of silence. Melchior, expelled for endeavoring to instruct his sensitive classmate, unwittingly brings death to him and to the girl. For Moritz, shocked by what he has learned from Melchior and an artist's model, and afraid also of failing in his examinations, takes his life. Wendla, yielding to Melchior but once, is destroyed by her mother's fear of scandal and the bungling of a quack. Then Melchior, sent to a reformatory, escapes, and by night comes upon the graves of his friends. It is Moritz, always fascinated by the story of a headless queen, who now rises as an apparition carrying his head beneath his arm. Descanting upon the joys of the dead, he would lure Melchior, too, into dying. But when a Masked Man interposes and, denouncing the illusions of self-abnegation and conscience, wins Melchior over to faith in life, Moritz confesses his regret at having shot himself, and bids an envious farewell to his assertive comrade. After setting up his cross knocked over by the awkward fellow, he will return to his grave. "When all is tidied," he says, "I'll lie down upon my back and warm myself in putrefaction and laugh." Here are nineteen disconnected scenes and a curious shift at the close from naturalism to symbolism. The effect is startling. It recalls the romantic fictions of Tieck and Novalis, although the author's attack upon false educational ideals allies him somewhat to the dramatists of social criticism.

The suggestion that love is a tyrant, modified here by faith in life if only it be lived daringly, becomes the insistent thesis of *Earth Spirit* and its sequel *The Box of Pandora*. These strange and violent plays are devoted to setting forth the destructive power of sex as incarnated in the unspeakable Lulu, who ruins lover after lover and at last suffers retribution at the hands of a degenerate. In the first piece, Lulu progresses by successive marriages and betrayals. Two of her husbands take their lives on discovering her perfidy, and the third she slays in a scuffle when he has found her intriguing with his son and boasting that she has poisoned that son's mother. The triumph of profane love thus set forth is followed in the second piece by love's defeat. Lulu, seeking refuge in Paris after breaking from prison, is blackmailed by a gambling pimp and by a music-hall acrobat whose death she contrives with the aid of her dissolute foster father. Having fled to London, she walks the streets starving, and, bringing home to her attic Jack the Ripper, she is slashed to death by him in sadistic rage, after vainly defending herself with a splintered bottle.

The only ray to pierce this night of gloom is to be found in the devotion to Lulu of a poor old countess who has sought to protect her. The countess, failing in her attempt at suicide, exclaims, "Only children have reason; men are animals!" Animals, indeed, are all these folk, introduced in a prologue as the wild beasts of a menagerie, among whom Lulu is the beautiful but deadly serpent. Sensational naturalism brightened by an imagination as vivid as that of Strindberg marks these plays, which are brutal, formless, and polyglot, intermingling with their German bad French and worse English as the scenes shift from land to land. In comparison, Tolstoy's *Power of Darkness* and Gorky's *Lower Depths* are pleasant little fairy stories.

Fleshly eroticism more refined is to be found in Wedekind's novel *Mine-Haha*, with its satire upon the education of women, and in the three scenes of his striking play *The Dance of Death*, a study of lust centering about the very pimp who had figured in Lulu's Parisian adventures. This wretch is now visited in his palace of pleasure by an irate social worker, who, through sex repression, has become a reformer. In listening to his self-justification, she perceives how much she has missed of life, and begs him to marry her. But Casti-Piani scoffs at marriage as inimical to the true abandon of love. That abandon Elfriede may witness from concealment in the reunion of a passionate youth and her own servant whom she has come to reclaim. In the interlude of verse that follows, the servant girl, instead of singing the joys of love, speaks only of its anguish. Then Elfriede, intoxicated with masochistic desire to share even such martyrdom, offers herself unconditionally to Casti-Piani. Since now he feels a sudden revulsion at all he has hitherto extolled, he shoots himself, and, in dying, he warns the houris of his establishment that he has deceived them. Lust is horrible, a selfish imperious instinct involving repulsion as well as attraction and a duel to the finish between the sexes.

Such doctrine, derived from Strindberg, finds expression in yet other plays of Wedekind. Usually it is the hero who triumphs in love. Thus, in *The Tenor*, a famous singer thinks only of his career and scorns both the old composer and the women who adore him. What matter if one of these women, as he is about to depart for a performance, should shoot herself because he will not take her along? He must hasten away to win applause in the rôle of Tristan, the great lover. In *The*

Wetterstein Trilogy, each of the three pieces portrays the victory in love of a man over a woman. In the first, the hero forces marriage upon a widow whose husband he has slain. In the second, the hero induces the submission of the woman who hates him; and in the third, the hero incites to suicide a courtesan who has boasted of her powers.

Evidently, Wedekind does not share the shuddering fear felt by Strindberg that the female of the species will ultimately destroy the male, for it is woman again who suffers in the more normal drama *Music.* The talented Klara, seduced by her music master, is taken with her child into his house by his indulgent wife. But Klara is the victim of an insufferable egoist, who bids her remember how much he has done for her art, and warns her to stifle her complaints lest they disturb his creative leisure. When her child dies and she loses her reason, the ruthless artist with a shrug of the shoulders returns to his music.

Another Nietzschean figures in *The Marquis of Keith,* a cheerful scapegrace determined to assert himself over others. Left for dead on a battlefield, and presently defeated in one hope after another, deprived of his sweetheart, his wife, and his friend, he resists the temptation to suicide, steals cash instead from a rival, and makes off, declaring that life is a toboggan slide, and that he is on the way. Still another scapegrace, in *The Love Potion,* is tutor in the family of a Russian count, and, posing as magician, plays upon his master's credulity and by a ruse walks away with the lady that his master would win.

The duel of love is not stressed in these two light dramas, but it reappears in *Simson* and *Franziska,* the latter a parody upon *Faust.* Here the heroine signs a pact with a lover, promising to marry him at the end of two years if, in the mean time, he will aid her to enjoy perfect freedom disguised as a man. Her adventures are grotesque, from that in a Berlin café—a Witches' Kitchen and Auerbach's Cellar combined—

to a far travesty of the Gretchen episode and a vague reflection of Faust's experiences at the court of the Emperor. The second adventure shows her wedded as man to a woman who, on discovering the fraud, commits suicide. The third adventure introduces Franziska taking part in a play got up by a duke whose sweetheart in jealousy stabs herself during the performance. When the period of the pact is concluded and Franziska is claimed by her lover, they are happy, but presently, in the rôle of Helena, she falls enamored of a fellow actor. Her husband, who of course thinks of suicide, is saved from it, and, grown wiser, remains content to watch over her now that an artist, engaged to paint her portrait and that of her child by the actor, succumbs to her spell. We are left to suppose that this female Faust who longed for independence as a man finally accepts fate as a mother, with the Mephisto of her pact becoming her sentimental protector. There is mockery here at the expense of woman, and especially at the author's self. How vain, he seems to say, has been his own yearning to capture satisfaction in feminine arms! How vain to seek in woman fidelity or anything except mother love!

The tortures of passion are set forth more vigorously in Wedekind's *Simson*, a versified rendering of the Biblical story of Samson, designed to expound the workings of "shame and jealousy." Delila, jealous of the rival described to her by Samson, hands him over to be blinded and enslaved, and gives herself to Og of Basan. Though the latter resents her shamelessness, he is willing to profit by it, acting out before the darkened eyes of Samson the excesses of love which that victim describes in song. Then Og, to prove his power, strangles Delila and drinks a health to Samson since now the source of their enmity no longer exists. In maddened resentment, Samson tugs down the pillars of the temple. This study of all that is evil in the effects of passion reflects Wedekind's own bitter experience.

The personal note which is lacking in *Bismarck*, a history

play devoted to the earlier career of the Prussian hero struggling against Austria in the 'sixties, resounds in *Such is Life*, *Oaha*, *Censorship*, and *Heracles*. The last, written in verse, shows the Greek demigod striving in vain to overcome the violence of his nature, slaying the brother of Iole whom he loves, desecrating the shrine at Delphi, resenting his effeminate enslavement to Omphale, striking down the boy who chances to spill wine upon the cloak of Dejaneira, wounding the Centaur Nessos who would carry her off, and, after destroying the vulture of Prometheus, flinging from a cliff the charioteer who, in all innocence, has brought him the poisoned shirt of Nessos sent in revenge. At last, Heracles, to atone for his inability to learn the art of self-control, surrenders Iole to his son, and willingly dies upon a funeral pyre. Just so, Wedekind may be imagined to have suffered from the strains and stresses of his own ill-regulated passions, and to be depicting here symbolically his futile efforts at self-mastery.

More specific in its personal reference is *Oaha*, a comedy making copy out of Wedekind's connection with the satirical journal *Simplizissimus*. It includes, under names easily decipherable, such actual worthies as Albert Langen, Björnson, and Ludwig Thoma, and describes the transfer of the paper from capitalistic to socialistic hands. Very different in its serious attempt at self-justification is *Censorship*, a piece in one act, wherein Wedekind replies to the critics who would condemn his immorality. Walter Buridan, who stands for Wedekind, has sought inspiration in a mistress. But she cannot understand his attempt to create a work that shall unite soul and body. When his tragedy *Pandora* has been prohibited, he protests to the secretary of the king's confessor. Has he ever shown the good as the bad, or the bad as the good? Has he ever misrepresented the consequences of crime? Is he to be held responsible because a neurotic girl, after reading his works, has taken her life? He declares himself to be neither a despiser of men nor a disciple of the doctrine of art for art's sake. He has lived half his days without art, whereas without religion he could not live a moment. He believes in God and immortality. Should he be condemned because he has made reality more real, and has emphasized the ugliness of evil? Such is the author's self-apology. But when Buridan's mistress, who is beauty personified, offers to leap from a balcony and give him back his moral freedom, he restrains her. She knows, however, that her hour is past. Asking with mockery if she shall give his greetings to the girl who had slain herself on reading his works, she springs into space.

So Wedekind reveals his own sense of defeat. Love has eluded him, and his serious purpose in art has been misinterpreted by the public. Two earlier dramas are equally expressive of his sense of disillusion,—*Such is Life* (known also as *King Nicolo*) and *Hidalla*. The first seems an echo of Andreyev's *He Who Gets Slapped*. A monarch, driven forth by a revolution that has set a butcher upon the throne, is supposed to have perished; but, in disguise, he lives as swineherd and then as tailor and is apprehended on being overheard to curse the king who hinders his being a man like other men. He has merely referred to the kingly pride within him which prevents his chastising low-born enemies. But, being unable to explain his meaning without revealing his identity, he is condemned unrecognized to prison. On emerging, he and his daughter join a band of strollers. When at length he admits his kingship, he is hailed as a comedian and accepted by the usurper as court fool. In order that his daughter may marry the usurper's son with whom she is in love, Nicolo endeavors to prove her a princess, but he is now regarded as mad. When he dies, the usurper refuses to investigate Nicolo's story, remarking, "History must never say of me that I made a king my court fool." This story recalls Longfellow's *King Robert of Sicily*, in which a monarch who has abused his office learns humility through suffering and, while an angel rules in his place, serves as court fool. Wedekind calls attention, however, less to the king's earlier guilt than to the world's misunderstanding of his motives.

In *Hidalla*, or *Karl Hetmann, the Pigmy Giant*, Wedekind further suggests the grotesque failure of his own efforts at reform. Hetmann dreams of improving the race by the breeding of those most beautiful and accomplished. But he himself is outwardly ugly, and he falls into the toils of those who are ugly in soul,—a promoter who would make a commercial enterprise out of Hetmann's idealistic endeavor, and a conservative capitalist who opposes the new freedom for women. When the promoter, for the sake of publicity, has incited Hetmann to issue a manifesto that entails police prosecution, it is Hetmann alone who suffers imprisonment. On his release, he continues to challenge what he terms the Feudalism of Love, such medieval superstitions as result in ostracising the woman of easy virtue or the unmarried mother, and in exalting virginity as a prerequisite for wedlock. After the people, at the instigation of the promoter, turn upon Hetmann as a lunatic, he is offered the position of clown in a circus. To quicken laughter, he need merely be himself. Overwhelmed by the failure of others to understand his motives, he takes his life. The beautiful woman who has loved him reproaches the promoter as a rascal, ready even now to exploit the notoriety of his victim. But the promoter blandly offers himself in marriage, saying, "O Fanny, Fanny, a living rascal is worth more to your well-being than the greatest of dead prophets!"

The value of this satiric tragedy is somewhat vitiated by the fantastic character of the reformer and his proposed reform. Hetmann is obviously Wedekind, with all the latter's limitations of sex-obsession and persecution-mania. Neither can quite succeed in awakening our sympathy. But it is worth recording that in Germany no one among the moderns of the theater has excited greater admiration or exerted deeper influence upon a partisan following.

Not the least of the followers of Wedekind is Walter Hasenclever, whose nonchalant and cynical attitude toward life is revealed in the notes he contributed toward a biography in Bartels' *German Poetry of the Present Time*. He writes: "I was born on July 8, 1890, at Aachen, where to-day I still bear an ill name. In the spring of 1908, final school examinations. I went to England and studied at Oxford. There I wrote my first play. The cost of printing it I won at poker. In 1909 I was at Lausanne; then at Leipzig I met the editor of this anthology and was introduced by him into a circle of love and science. Soon I flew higher than my master. I travelled with him in Italy and consulted the physicians. In 1913 appeared *The Youth*; in 1914 at Heyst I completed *The Son*. In the War, I was interpreter, purchaser, and kitchen boy. So *Death and Resurrection* was conceived. In 1919 my friend Ernst Rowohlt printed my play *The Saviour*, suppressed during the War. In the summer of 1919 I began *The Decision*."

Of these plays, *The Son* created the greatest stir in Germany, emphasizing in expressionistic wise the old, old conflict between two generations. A youth, failing in his examinations for entrance to the university, resents his father's tyranny and resolves to commit suicide. He is dissuaded by a friend who urges him to assert himself and to shoot his father, enter upon a life of pleasure, and lead a revolt of all sons against their parents. But this particular father saves his son the trouble of patricide by suffering a stroke of apoplexy.

The son's attitude is revealed when he says: "In the home of the parents begins our first love and first hate. If you have a son, turn him out or die before him, for the day will come when you will be enemies, you and your son, and then God have mercy on him who goes under!" The youthful revolutionists employ as their motto, "Death to the dead!" The son declares: "My father will not permit any one in the world to be my friend. Why does he not speak to me about God? Why does he not speak of women? Why must I read Kant in secret

—Kant who does not even thrill me? And why this scorn of all that is beautiful?" The friend, who would die poetically by drinking poisoned wine from the hand of a mistress, denounces the institution of the family: "Destroy the tyranny of the family, the medieval blood-oath, the witch's paper, the torture room, and the sulphur! Do away with laws! Restore freedom—the highest possession of man."

The instinctive reaction of undisciplined youth against age is presented by Hasenclever without subtlety or evidence of a knowledge of character and through the emptiest of types. That a piece so extravagant as this should have achieved popularity is a commentary on the social ferment in contemporary Germany. It displays the absurd side of a tendency more sanely in evidence in the Youth Movement, which would exalt the rights of the young as opposed to the unfeeling demands of the old.

Having denounced the family, Hasenclever, in *The Saviour* and *Antigone*, denounces the thralldom of the war-making state. In the former play, a poet pleads with a ruler for peace. But although the ruler be sympathetic, he confides control of affairs to a bellicose marshal, who presently demands the life of the poet. In the latter play, the tyrannous state is personified by Creon who rails at Antigone. She has been moved to give her brother burial against the king's wish by a spirit of reverence for all things human, and to the pacifist chorus she utters her condemnation of hate and violence. To the soldiers sent to accord her a living death, she exclaims: "I have softened your hearts! I will hunger for you! I will bleed for you! Only so can good come to pass. The streams are breaking up. Love has conquered. God is merciful to us!" By contrast, Creon is the militaristic tyrant, until, on being shown by Teiresias the mangled victims of the war, he declares, "Freedom is stronger than law and glory!" In the fact that he repents too late and that a rising sweeps him away, critics beheld a forecast of the fate of the Kaiser set forth on the eve of the German debacle.

If this adaptation of Sophocles to modern times be normal enough, abnormal and individual are the cinema-like scenes of *Men*, a rapidly shifting panorama influenced by the work of August Stramm of Berlin, who fell in the War. The hero is a corpse who, rising from his grave at evening, yields his place to a murderer, and, having accepted in a sack the head of the murderer's victim, carries it about on his adventures until he returns to his grave at dawn. Meanwhile, he meets sinners of all degrees, each of whom utters only a word or a phrase. The lady of light virtue cries, "I revenge myself!" the cabaret owner, "Money!" the workers, "Strike!" A girl has betrayed her lover, and both seek the aid of a fortune-teller and a physician. The youth, warned by the physician of his fell disease, appears for a moment as a skeleton, and the girl in horror severs her arteries. When an innocent country lass avows her love for Alexander, the animated corpse, he is moved to open the sack. But the head within looks precisely like his own. "My head!" he exclaims in surprise. "My body!" cries the head in recognition. Of the murderer, Alexander remarks: "He is forgiven! He lies in the grave. . . . I am living for him." But, as one living for a sinner, he must pay the price of sin. So, he is tried and sent to a madhouse, where crawl men in the form of beasts; and then to prison, where, as the stage grows dark, the towers of Heaven appear, and anthems sound. Released mysteriously, he reels back to the graveyard to return the sack to the risen murderer. But the latter, perceiving it to be empty now, cries ecstatically, "I love!" He has evidently been purged of his sin, saved and converted by Alexander, who contentedly resumes his place in the grave.

The discovery of love as the law of life, already declared in *The Saviour* and *Antigone*, strikes Hasenclever as something quite novel. But the only novelty here lies in his peculiar technique. Although this may well have been suggested by the final scene of Wedekind's *Awakening of Spring* and by Andreyev's *Black Maskers*, it is developed into a curious nightmare of incoherent episodes seen by flashes. The stage, like that in such American plays as Lawson's *Roger Bloomer* and O'Neill's *Desire Under the Elms*, is divided into several parts. While the action is taking place in one, the others remain dark. Sound, also, emphasizes the movement. At the beginning and at the end roars a hurricane, and often there are shots and tumults outside. A factory siren summons workers to their toil. The hospital is clamorous with the clatter of falling instruments and the groans of patients, and the prison rings with songs. The dialogue is staccato. Thus a drinker at a table asks with rising inflection, "No ownership any more?" and his companion responds, "Community!"

"No wars?"

"Peace!"

"The future?"

"Shares!"

"Men?"

"Slaves! No ownership any more!"

"Community?"

"No wars!"

"Peace?"

At this juncture, the questioner chances to drop his handkerchief, whereupon the interlocutor, bending as if to pick it up, and remarking, "Your handkerchief!" throttles him. A fine bit of irony!

The play tantalizes by suggesting questions that it fails to answer. Is the hero the murderer's double or his victim? "We are all murderers," he affirms, with something of the faith of Georg Kaiser that each bears a measure of responsibility for the sins of all. The head, on rolling from the sack, declares that the murderer still lives, but Alexander protests that it is he who is living in the murderer's place. How far is this true?

And how did the murderer, after one night in the grave, come to understand that love is a redemptive agency?

Much clearer is the significance of Hasenclever's play, *The Decision*, in which the futility of political revolution is expounded with the same peculiar technique. A revolt has forced the abdication of a prince, who, while biding his time to regain power, serves as a waiter. When struck by a chance shot from the street, he dies after exclaiming, "Fallen on the field of nonsense!" Since a council of officials of the new government can reach no conclusion as to what shall be done, all agree to await the dictum of the press. But the press refuses to do more than ask, "Whither are we steering?" and the conference is broken up by a mob intent upon destroying those who have overthrown the prince. When the leader asserts that he will establish a popular dictatorship, the officials of the previous régime object. "My salary!" exclaims the minister of war. "My reforms!" cries the minister of culture. "Here is the book of punitive laws!" shouts the minister of justice. But the mob, sweeping them away, selects as president a stranger so drugged with sleep that he cannot be wakened. An author, who, because of his treasonable books, had been about to suffer death when the first revolt began, is now shot as a traitor because he refuses to write a poem celebrating the second revolt. As the soldiers who have joined the rising depart amid laughter, a dancing girl runs in to embrace the new president, still asleep, and to help herself to the contents of his pocketbook while she cries, "Long live the republic!"

This play resembles *The Sabine Women* of Andreyev, but it is more violent in irony. It relies for effect upon breathless exclamations and the use of sound as an accompaniment of action. Its personages are types. One of the best is Talmud, "a pusher or shover," who agrees with every party in power, and declares that: "He who to-day is above is to-morrow beneath. Men are of two classes, those deceived and those deceiving." Another type important only for what he says is the

Author, who enunciates Hasenclever's doctrine that men are fools, and that, although the present battle be over, murder will continue. If one system be ruined, men will build upon it another. "What will you build on the ruin? Another and yet the same world. . . . Set up your gallows, string up your systems. Intoxicate yourselves further with freedom and the rights of humanity. Do not forget to destroy those who think differently from you, if there be any such. I go forth to seek a man; perhaps I shall find none but myself."

The most original of Hasenclever's plays is *Beyond*, a drama in five acts kept going by only two characters—a wife whose husband is killed in an explosion, and the husband's friend into whose arms she throws herself on receiving news by telephone of the accident. The piece is made by the inter-position of the dead and unseen husband to prevent the union of his friend and his wife. Their inability to forget him is externalized through suggestion, until the lover, in despair of possessing the lady, stabs her while kissing her, and then, unbinding the bandage of a self-inflicted wound, dies at her side.

Needless to say, only the treatment of this plot is novel. Hasenclever reveals the thoughts and feelings of his pair adroitly, and not by words alone. Doors slam of themselves, suggesting the entrance or exit of the dead husband. As the lovers are about to clasp, a cry fills them with fear. They are startled by lightning and thunder. A lamp is mysteriously extinguished. The fire assumes the shape of a face that van-ishes as the lover thrusts his arm into the flames. At table, a third chair is set for the dead husband, and the lovers address him and listen as if to his answers. When Raul shoots at the empty chair, Jeane cries, "Murderer!"

The scenes are single parts of the same house narrowly focused—a window, a bed, a balcony, a fireplace, a cellar. Says Jeane at the window: "This is my house. This is my window. This is the sky. The sun shines. I know that I live.

I am happy. I am loved. . . . This is my house. This is my window." Here is something of the repetition and ejaculation made popular in the early plays of Maeterlinck. After her husband's death is announced, Jeane asks: "Really dead? Perished? Disappeared? Without greeting? Without farewell? Without me?"

After Raul has slain Jeane, the scene disintegrates. According to the stage directions, "Invisible hands bear away the house. The walls fall noiselessly together; the furnishings sink into the depths; the chandelier sways on high; the window in the background disappears; a gray light surrounds Raul's head. It is as if waves of light were issuing from his forehead." As he lies dying, Raul exclaims: "I see into life! I see into the realm of all things fleeting. For the last time I have been a human being. I am enlightened. I am ready." Although it is difficult to tell for what he may be ready, there is no question as to the startling effect produced by this ejaculatory style. Like other expressionists, Hasenclever conveys verbally and by scenic devices the notion that the external world exists only as a projection of the world that lies within. Time, too, is revealed as only an illusion. The past telescopes into the present. Personality is both single and multiple. "Shadow and illusion," says Raul, "wherever I look. Always only I. Who am I?" It is the same question asked by Alexander in *Men*.

The notion that murder is subjective and that each of us is at heart a murderer haunts the imagination of Hasenclever. After writing *Gobseck*, an adaptation of an episode from Balzac, he produced *Murder*, a piece in two parts, designed to expound his favorite idea. When a rich manufacturer, jealous of his wife, bestows the latter's ring upon a courtesan, he symbolically slays the love of the wife. His perfidy is revealed to her through a lover to whom out of pique she has succumbed, for the lover presents her with the very ring which he has just won at play from the courtesan. The courtesan, having already killed an admirer, shifts the blame for that deed to the manufacturer. He is ready to pay the price for a crime purely mental, but eventually escapes through the self-interested efforts of an anarchist. Much of the play is devoted to satire upon the process of justice. In the thrusts at legal procedure, psycho-analysis, and the sensational press, lies its chief merit; but the action is forced, coincidental, and eccentric.

Both Wedekind and Hasenclever have been called by German critics "bad boys" of the theater. They are certainly fearless and capricious. So bold and bad in the eyes of the respectable bourgeoisie is Hasenclever that during the performance at Frankfort in 1929 of his *Marriages Are Made in Heaven* a clergyman in the audience rose to protest at the impersonation of the Deity in golf clothes, and a crowd in the galleries bombarded those below with tear bombs, and the performance was stopped. Earlier, in more indulgent Berlin, the piece ran for a month unmolested. Later, Berlin accepted nonchalantly his *Napoleon Enters on the Scene*. Here the emperor is reproved as a slayer of men by Landru, the French Bluebeard, slayer of women. Both have come to life in a waxwork show. Landru is content with his estate, but Napoleon, wishing to dominate the world of 1930, goes forth with a bowler hat and the tail coat of Stresemann and the trousers of Mussolini to attend a meeting of the League of Nations. Mistaken for a Bolshevist, he is ridiculed when he offers to head the armies of the United States of Europe. He succeeds, however, in making a conquest of the mistress of an American financier, Mlle. Josephine of the Comédie Française, and with her in a film studio plays the rôle of jealous Emperor so well that he is sent to a madhouse. Thus, disillusioned since the capitalistic state can afford no place for one so romantic, he returns to the wax-works to be greeted with a chuckle by the cynical Landru. Here Hasenclever is almost Shavian. At his worst, he is a sensation monger. At his best, he is a sincere advocate of expressionism.

CHAPTER XXI

EXPRESSIONISM IN THEORY AND PRACTICE

Kornfeld, Wildgans, Kokoschka, Goering, von Unruh, Bronnen, Brecht

THROUGH the plays of Hasenclever just considered rings the voice of expressionism, that type of art already referred to as a final phase in the revolt against naturalism. Such symbolists as Ibsen, Maeterlinck, and Hauptmann led the way to this development, and Strindberg, Andreyev, and Evreinov, among others, showed the possibility of letting states of mind wholly determine representation of the world without. The expressionist is not bent upon depicting objective reality. He wishes only to render an inner significance. So, in Galsworthy's novel *The White Monkey*, an artist explains expressionism by saying, "It means not troubling about the outside except in so far as it expresses the inside." Historically, artists are preoccupied now with outsides and now with insides, the pendulum of their interest swinging from one pole to another. Concern for the world without in all its manifold details results in realism or naturalism. Concern for that world only in so far as its presentation may be made to reflect and reveal the world within results in expressionism. The term is new; the thing is sufficiently old.

A philosophy that may justify expressionism was formulated in the 'nineties by one who never used or heard the word. Oscar Wilde, in writing of art in general, maintained that good art is abstract, ideal, expressive of inner concepts, and that it is not the result of copying nature. "All bad art comes from a return to life and nature," wrote Wilde. "Art begins with abstract decoration, with purely imaginative and pleasurable work dealing with what is unreal and non-existent. This is the first stage. Then Life becomes fascinated with this new wonder and asks to be admitted into the charmed circle. Art takes Life as part of her rough material, recreates it, and refashions it in fresh forms, . . . and keeps between herself and reality the impenetrable barrier of beautiful style, of decorative or ideal treatment. The third stage is when Life gets the upper hand and drives Art out into the wilderness. This is the true decadence, and it is from this that we are now suffering. . . . Art is our spirited protest, our gallant attempt, to teach Nature her proper place."

The term expressionism was first applied to painting. In that field the naturalistic period had attained its climax in impressionism, an endeavor to render faithfully one's individual reaction to a concrete external reality at a particular instant under particular conditions. To a certain observer in a certain light a cow might appear purple or a village to be made of cubic houses and cubic people. It needed but a little daring for the artist to go a step farther and to assert his right to report, not merely his sense impressions induced by some object at a single moment, but his inward vision conveyed through symbols bearing little or no resemblance to anything external.

Soon expressionism appeared in the theater, working in two directions. First, as we have seen, it affected stagecraft through the reforms of Craig, Appia, Fuchs, Reinhardt, Jessner, Fehling, and Piscator. Second, it affected that more fundamental matter, dramatic composition. It was not enough that régisseurs in their scene settings, costumes, and acting should depart from life even when putting on older works originally intended to conform to it. No; playwrights must prepare dramas admitting of production in no other way. In Germany, Wedekind led the movement toward expressionistic composition, and Sorge, Hasenclever, Kaiser, Kokoschka, Von Unruh, Goering, Toller, and a dozen others followed.

To say that the work of an expressionist playwright fails to resemble anything on sea or land is merely to compliment, not to criticize him. He unfolds a story devised to convey some abstract idea, some mood or fancy of his own. He cares nothing for the probability or even the possibility of the events he uses. His plot may therefore be as chaotic or fantastic as the inconsequential turnings of a kaleidoscope. His characters are likely to be figures as symbolic as those of the moralities, types rather than integrated personalities. They bear generic instead of proper names—the son, the father, the maiden, the man in gray. They are puppet-like, mere automata directed from without. To the observer they yield a feeling that all the world is obedient to a process of wire-pulling and mechanization. So Eugene O'Neill, in *The Hairy Ape,* suggests the Sunday procession on Fifth Avenue, not by the representation of real people on a real street, but by means of several manikins with mask-like faces jigging to and fro past a painted curtain. As in primitive art, so in expressionism, figures grotesque, distorted, ideographic, dominate. The effects resemble those produced by the drawings of children or savages. A few lines, angles, planes, steps, scaffolds, screens, and curtains set off by lights and shadows imply all the complexities of natural background, there being no more study of environment than of individual psychology. Since we experience life in snatches rather than in acts nicely arranged, the expressionists exhibit it in many brief, disconnected scenes shifting as shift the pictures of a cinema. In certain plays, like *The Machine Wreckers* of Toller, this multiplication of scenes appears to be a reversion to Elizabethan drama. In others, like Toller's *Masses and Man,* where symbolism rules, the effect is that of a dream; and in many plays of the sort the dream technique prevails. Since speed and the gusto for speed mark the younger generation, action and dialogue become more dynamic. The dialogue is quickened, departing from colloquial speech either toward lyric eloquence or toward a condensation of language that tends to become telegraphic, dispensing with articles, conjunctions, adjectives, and even verbs. The latter style sins shamelessly against the laws of grammar, seeking a lively brevity through explosive apostrophes and exclamations. The former style rises at emotional crises to a lyrical fervor inimical to true drama. In some instances expressionistic plays become mildly operatic, employing recitative and songs. More frequently they rely upon an obligato of sounds beautiful, grim, or harsh as an emotional accompaniment to the action. So O'Neill, our chief American expressionist, has used the beating of a tom-tom in *Emperor Jones* to heighten excitement and to suggest the throbbing in crescendo of the frightened hero's pulse. The point of view of the spectator is often shifted by expressionists from the auditorium to the stage. To this end the old barriers between actor and audience are broken down, as we have remarked in discussing Russian drama. Furthermore, in a play like *The Adding Machine* of Elmer Rice, the spectator, instead of gazing from the outside upon the clerk tempted to commit murder, lives within him, sharing the vertigo of his brainstorm and the explosion of his wrath. When his employer discharges him, the stool whereon he sits revolves faster and faster until he strikes down that employer with a bill file, and the theater lights blaze crimson and every noise-making device crashes loud.

In Germany all the elements of revolt went into expressionism, all the faddist cults in art, all the yearnings after a world posited only by the Ego,—what Thomas Mann has called "the sovereign, explosive, ruthlessly creative edict of the spirit." Since the expressionists tended to be mystics and pacifists, it was not until after the War that they were fully unleashed. A critical literature arose explaining their aims already discussed in periodicals like *Sturm* and *Aktion*. Hermann Bahr, Kasimir Edschmid, and Manfred Schneider, among others, wrote books on the subject. In summarizing their conclusions, an American, Professor Edwin H. Zeydel, has characterized expressionism succinctly, saying: "It denies the world; it boldly maintains that the only true Being is the Ego; it brooks no object at all; . . . It is pacifistic by its nature and humanitarian, . . . Recently, it has become even communistic, yes messianic. It has gone so far as to venture to revolutionize not only art but also mankind, to eradicate from the world the inevitable dualism of subjective and objective by abolishing the latter." In short, says he: "Realism depicts the absolute, objective facts of life; Impressionism portrays life as reflected by the author's mood, by the whims of his fancy and perception, always with a certain dominant objectivity; Expressionism casts aside objective reality in order to describe truth as discerned by the eye of the spirit."

What has been the result? In the long run, eccentricity and decadence, and yet a momentary quickening of art by shifting the axis from outsides to insides, as Galsworthy would say. Both the virtues and the deficiencies of expressionism will be sufficiently evident from the survey of typical plays that follows.

The Beggar of Reinhard Sorge, which was awarded the first Kleist prize in 1912, attracted attention to expressionism. This strange work shows an insane father planning to sail to Mars and begging his son for death. The son would found an experimental theater, but is prevented from realizing his ambition by the madness of his father, the illness of his mother, and his own love affair. Scenes come and go as curtains and screens are withdrawn. The characters are types unnamed. The Form of the Girl and the Form of the Author appear, and three Forms of Inspiration utter antiphonal cries. Outer realities become inner, and inner become outer. Here is lyric yearning, the desire to realize formless feelings through scenes of fantasy. Although of little value in itself, *The Beggar* is historically important as constituting a link between

Strindberg's *To Damascus* or *The Dream Play* and the new expressionistic movement. But Sorge himself did not continue to work this vein. Having been converted to Catholicism, he wrote religious dramas, a mystery called *Metanoeite*, and *King David*, and then died on the field of battle early in the War.

Walter Hasenclever, apt pupil of Strindberg, Wedekind, and Sternheim, succeeded Sorge, as we have seen, and still others followed. August Stramm in his *Powers*, produced in 1921 but written six years earlier, told a story of jealousy and murder in exclamatory style. Hans Johst, in *Young Man*, composed a youth drama that might vie with Hasenclever's *The Son*, and in *The Lonely One*, taking the dramatist Grabbe for hero, affected a lyric eloquence echoing the accents of the old Sturm und Drang. His later plays became less subjective and more natural.

Still louder rings the voice of the Sturm und Drang in the plays of Paul Kornfeld, an erratic, yearning soul whose aspirations for the unattainable, being necessarily met by defeat, induce outcries on the part of his characters against the futility of life. Kornfeld is childlike in his thought and in his art. His thought, indeed, is drowned in formless feeling. His characters act irresponsibly, without reference to natural motives. They enter and leave the scene as the dramatist needs them. To suit his pleasure all the facts of experience are warped. Thus a murderer in prison is allowed freedom to converse with any number of visitors; his jailer and the prosecuting attorney frankly advise his escape; the walls of the jail courtyard are so low and ill-guarded that he has only to vault over them, and, once outside, he is free from pursuit. As to the language of these puppets, they talk in speeches that rise to the pitch of poetical prose and, on occasion, even of verse, speeches unlike those telegraphic exclamations favored by Kokoschka and many others. These are unduly rhetorical, verging upon bombast and bathos.

EXPRESSIONISM IN THEORY AND PRACTICE

In Kornfeld's *The Seduction*, which includes the situation just described, the hero is a sentimental egoist who strangles a bridegroom merely because he finds the sight of such a Philistine offensive. He cannot understand that what he has done is anything out of the ordinary. Sent to prison, he rails at human injustice, but is visited by a girl filled with admiration of his bravery and ready to aid his escape. At first he resists, being happy in his unhappiness; but presently he yields to her soulful seduction—the "seduction" of the title— and accompanies her to an inn where, talking wildly of his love for all the village roisterers, he accepts a lesson in drink. In his muddled mind he cannot understand why the father and the brother of his mistress wish to protect her from him. Presently he is mortally wounded by the brother with a needle dipped in poison, and retorts by inducing the brother to commit suicide. The attempt of his mistress and his mother to save him has failed. The mistress, in order to die with him, imbibes the same poison, and, when he expires and a priest remarks that every day thousands die, the mother exclaims, "But this was my son!" Of all the personages, this mother is the only one clothed in flesh and blood, touching in her devotion to the crazy dreamer. The story is absurdly melodramatic, with its plots and counterplots that would do credit to a penny-dreadful. Wailings and railings against destiny and the misery of the race fill the prolix speeches of the protagonist and his associates. How such a melancholy, ineffective creature could have inspired with love the heroine Ruth and other earlier sweethearts is hard to see. He arouses no sympathy, since his acts are unreasoned and inexplicable. In an appendix addressed to the players Kornfeld declares that whoever would represent death on the stage is not to go to a hospital to learn how to die, nor to a tavern to learn how to feign drunkenness. Let him rather speak and act imaginatively. Let him not imitate any model, but rather abstract the attributes of reality. Let him think of opera, in which the singer, dying, strikes a high C and with the sweetness of his melody expresses more of death than would the exact representation of broken words and stifled breathing.

Kornfeld's *Heaven and Hell* is as arbitrary in its action as *The Seduction*, and its technique is equally peculiar. A count has proved unfaithful to his wife. He loves her but cannot tell her so. When he brings his mistress into the family circle, his wife's dislike of him deepens; but presently she discovers in the mistress a beautiful soul whose whole effort is bent upon reconciling the pair. Wife and mistress embrace in perfect understanding, and presently wife and husband are drawn together and proclaim their rediscovery of love in glowing cadence. But Beata the wife has had a checkered past, one affair causing her rival to hang herself, and the rival's husband to shoot himself. Her own mother is a witch; and her daughter, when Beata asks her for an expression of affection, cries: "Humbug! Let me sleep!" Thereupon, Beata flies into a rage and strangles the girl, even while exclaiming, "Why must I strangle you with my hands instead of holding you in my arms?" If the daughter represents indifference or contempt, Maria, the count's mistress, represents love, and so great now is her love for Beata that she takes this murder upon herself. Her passionate friend Johanna, who has earlier threatened to stab Maria for deserting her, would die with her, and to that end stabs the mother of Beata for having accused Maria of the murder Maria has already confessed.

When all three women are brought to the bar of justice, the court scene becomes fantastic, people standing by to shout their demands for this or that in chorus, and the accused screaming their assertions and denials without order or restraint. Throughout, a mysterious abstract personage, Jacob, plays the part of Mephistopheles, acting as the devilish prompter of murder and suicide, yet declaring himself a mere spectator of the world of evil. He rails at a God who, making men wicked, has given them no power to resist temptation yet induces them to judge one another. "Kill yourselves! Revolt against God!" he cries, whereupon the people stone him. At last, however, after Beata, Maria, and Johanna have been condemned to die, Jacob is so impressed by their faith in immortality, that he too kneels and crosses himself at the command of a priest. Yet, in the Epilogue, we hear him announcing that he is still the Eternal Protest, one who will cry out against the wounds of the world till God either falls from heaven or takes pity on men. But the three women circle above his head as spirits, freed from earthly error, and proclaiming in song that divinity lives in all and that no soul shall be lost. Of the three, only Maria, who has assumed the crime of Beata out of love, would seem to speak with much authority, and she earlier has drowned her own child. The other two have committed even more wanton murders and felt no qualms of conscience. To destroy those who fail to exemplify the law of love appears to be the duty of the loving, but to do this is, paradoxically, to deny that very law. Kornfeld's attitude toward sinners has been compared with that of Dostoyevsky. But his sympathy is merely sentimental. It speaks well for German common sense that the elaborate production of this piece in 1920 at the Deutsches Theater proved a failure.

The later work of Kornfeld need not detain us. His *Eternal Dream* is satirically concerned with a world in which marriage has no sooner been abolished than every one becomes intent upon returning to it. In *Palme, or the Hypochondriac* (*Palme, oder der Gekränkte*) Kornfeld drops the cloak of the revolutionary and turns to burlesque the very sentimentalism of which he had been a foremost exponent. But his comedy of character differs from a hundred others only in being inferior. So the expressionists, out of their province, are likely to make no great showing.

Less eccentric than Kornfeld but equally an expressionist who loves the rhetorical is Anton Wildgans of Vienna, who came up in poverty but derived from his father an ambition for culture. He began by writing verse, and in 1913 presented at the Vienna Volksbühne a one-act poetic piece entitled *Forever and Ever Amen*. Two years later the same theater gave his longer play *Poverty*, which introduces the spectator to a middle-class family destitute in spite of the fact that the father has for thirty years been a faithful post-office employee. He is dying, and his wife, an officer's daughter, who regrets this marriage beneath her and is jealous of her children's love for their father, urges her daughter to make a better match. The daughter borrows money from their student lodger and is even tempted to sell him her honor in order to keep a physician in attendance upon the father. Her brother, discouraged by the family debts, meditates suicide; then, left alone to nurse the dying man, he sleeps as Death personified steals in to engage in a poetic conversation with his victim. When the father is no more, the daughter returns to the student the money she had borrowed, and the undertaker comes to offer his services, which must be secured at the cheapest figure. The mother can only complain that it is too late for amends to be made to her for all she has suffered through her marriage, and the daughter and the son, after a duet concerning poverty, ask if there will ever be a savior to raise the poor from their low estate. As they conclude, heavenly voices fill the room. So prose and poetry, realism and fantasy combine.

The operatic strain dear to Wildgans is continued in *Love*, which treats lyrically the disillusionment that comes in marriage with the lapse of years. A husband on his ninth wedding anniversary seeks solace with a lady of light virtue, leaving his wife in pique to telephone his less prosaic friend to come to her. But neither the wife nor the husband can be unfaithful when brought to the point. In the last act the husband in the moonlight is watching his sleeping wife, who rouses to report a prophetic dream and to declare that for women love should be eternal. Is woman mainly an episode in man's existence? Is monogamous marriage only a law of culture opposed to nature? Such questions agitate the pair, who weep as a mystic orchestra plays and the curtain descends.

In *Dies Irae* there is similarly suggested a domestic problem submitted to half-lyric treatment. The son of a scholar, having with difficulty passed his final examinations, must choose a vocation. But his selfish parents demand that his life shall represent the fulfillment of the desires and ideals of each. The father would have him develop into a man of learning; the mother, who comes of the commercial class, would have him develop into a man of business. "Who desired this child? Not you!" she cries to the father; whereupon he retorts that Hubert inherits from her his disabilities for the intellectual life. So distraught is the boy by the quarrel of the pair that he rejects the love with which little Rose would comfort him, and, writing his school fellow a letter lamenting that he has been born against his father's will, shoots himself. "There—dead!" shrieks the father on finding the body. "Your work!" exclaims the mother. The suggestion that involuntary parenthood is likely to damage the second generation is as clearly an echo of Strindberg as is the duel of sex between the parents. As for the antagonism between youth and age, that is a favorite theme of the newer drama, to be accounted for in part by the rigors of the German educational system and the old subjection of children to parents.

In the dramas of Wildgans thus far considered, at least the basis has been realistic. In *Cain, a Mythical Play* it is legendary and poetic. Here the hero is no natural rebel like Byron's Cain smarting under injustice and questioning the beneficence of God. Instead, he is avarice personified. He envies Abel his flocks, his ability to sing, his place in Eve's affections, and his favor with God. As he dances in triumph after the murder, he boasts that his children shall worship a new god—gold—and inherit the earth. Eve laments the fact that throughout the future brother shall slay brother in imitation of this deed, yet she foresees the birth of a new Abel to teach men the gentler graces—poetry and song. "Always, oh, always again shall Abel be born!" she asserts; but Cain retorts, "And always, always again shall Cain slay Abel." Cain, in short, represents eternal Philistine possessiveness.

On the whole, Wildgans utilizes expressionism in moderation without departing far from reality. But Oskar Kokoschka, a painter turned dramatist, carries expressionism to the limit. This is not the case in his *Orpheus and Eurydice* of 1918, for there he is merely lyrical and pictorial in the Dionysiac style commended by Nietzsche. But in his earlier *Murderer Hope of Women*, *The Burning Thorn Bush*, and especially *Hiob*, he rejoices in wild fantasy. The first of these three, written before the expressionistic fad was even born, forecasts that birth. The scene is a Maeterlinckian tower by night, with a conquering warrior meeting before it the lady of the castle whom he commands to be seized and branded with his mark. She screams, resists, and stabs him, but when he is carried by her maidens behind the grated door of the tower, she assures him through the grille that he will recover and be her husband. When he voices his disdain, she reproaches him for having enthralled her, and sinks lifeless. The man, rising to his full powers once more, tears away the grating and emerges to strike down "like gnats" the terrified warriors and maidens. Flames envelope the tower; the man strides off; and far away a cock crows. As in the darker plays of Strindberg, so here love is a sex duel, and the man who treats woman brutally fascinates her. Woman's only hope of retaining her individual freedom lies in destroying the power that enchants her; yet it is a futile hope, for against the all-conquering male she is helpless.

Love of the same stripe is dealt with symbolically in *The Burning Thorn Bush* where abstract personages utter wild, truncated speeches in short lines of free verse. A woman, gazing from her chamber window in the moonlight, yearns for a lover. The lover approaches, wraps her in a cloth, bids her close her eyes, and turns to depart. Angered at this withdrawal, she rouses against him her drunken suitors by declaring that a werewolf has just dashed forth after devouring her heart. The silhouette of the man in flight appears above a railway bridge over which thunders a train as the man leaps into the water eluding the shots of his pursuers, and a Salvation Army song is heard extolling heavenly love. Again the woman is seen kneeling in the moonlight affirming that she adores the man who hates her, and asking why women should always desire the strange. In a wood she groans as in labor, and old men hunt for the one who has forsaken her. She complains of the fire of passion that devours her, and when the man bids her go free now that he is tired of her, she smites him with a stone she has borne in her bosom, and at the next moment is bending over him in pity. Love for man, in short, torments woman yet drives her on to try to capture him. When man relaxes his devotion, she pursues; and, though she slay him, she would comfort him. The burning thorn bush of the title is love, a fire that consumes the universe composed of the other three Empedoclean elements—water, air, and earth. Here are figures moving blindly in the gloom, emitting incomplete sentences while lights of various colors and intensity are focused sympathetically upon each.

Even more fantastic is *Hiob*. Just as in *Faust*, Mephistopheles emerges from a poodle, so here from a dog emerges a "Rubberman" who inoculates Hiob with erotococcus, causing his head to turn at sight of Anima. With Anima dances Eros. Later, while Anima is making love to the Rubberman behind a lighted window above stairs, Hiob sits below in shadow toying with a skull and crossbones and putting to the mouth of the skull a bottle of poison. When a maiden drums on the skull with the bones, Hiob flings the poison at her testily, and then, alarmed because out of the window above him drop all the garments of Anima and the Rubberman, he telephones for help. He is answered by Adam the Gardener, who runs in to assert that Hiob has been made a fool of by woman and the devil. Anima, as if aware of this revelation of her perfidy, drops like a ripe fruit from the window upon Hiob, who expires as the Rubberman flings out her virtue after her. Then, remarking that Hiob has erred in setting his wife too high, Adam draws across the scene a curtain on which are painted ten mourning figures with an aperture in the face of each through which an actor sticks his own face to utter in quick succession brief speeches as from each mourner. A parrot which has hitherto delivered frequent warnings to Hiob and which Adam recognizes as having warned him also in Paradise while he was eating the apple, suddenly explodes and rises in the shape of a rosy cloud to heaven. Then, as Hiob's head is rolled out from beneath the curtain, Anima bends over it enchanted, and Adam, drawing the body forth and joining it to the head, drops a handful of earth upon the reunited corpse. "But is he really dead?" asks Anima. "No," replies Adam with calm irony, "not really dead,—dead only in his head, in his heart, and in his other parts." Strindberg might have composed this misogynist allegory. Woman, Kokoschka seems to say, is the great foe of man, the more treacherous in that she is elemental and ignorant. Though slaying him by her infidelity, she is surprised at the result.

Expressionism has never gone farther into the realm of fantasy than here. In plays inspired by the War, it is likely to remain at least on speaking terms with reality, although the characters of Goering, von Unruh, Bronnen, and Brecht cry out in a Dionysiac ecstasy of suffering or joy. Goering, who has written *The First*, *The Second*, and *The Saviour*, will be remembered chiefly for *Sea-Battle* and *Scapa Flow*. Both are pacifistic. In the former, sailors in the turret of a battleship during the War reveal their various attitudes to-

ward the conflict with passionate fervor. One is superstitious
and frightened. Another is all impatience to fight. Another
asks whether what the Fatherland requires be necessarily good,
and laments the fact that for years they have been sailing
the seas bringing death to those they meet. "What we are
doing here," he exclaims, "is madness and crime!" Yet, as the
enemy ships are sighted, even he is transformed by the lust
for battle. When an explosion kills a comrade, he shouts,
"Blood, blood! therein alone lies truth!" As the battle rages,
the poor devils exclaim that they are but swine awaiting the
butcher. "Our blood will dye the fishes red. Fatherland, what
more will you do to us?" Thereupon, in a final blast, all are
blown to death. In German, the word *Schlacht* implies not
only *battle* but *slaughter*.

More lyrical and less dramatic is *Scapa Flow*, descriptive
of the sinking of the captured German fleet in a Scottish
harbor. The scene shifts from the flagship of the Germans
to the flagship of the British. The German sailors individually
and in chorus mourn their sore estate, cooped up as in coffins
day after day, far from home and friends. Suppose they
should sink the ships; would it harm or help their country?
Would it be just or unjust?

> "Who would think of it? And who would do it?
> We are already dead.
> Shadows."

On the English fleet the sailors pass the time (somewhat improbably) singing the Prize Song from *The Meistersinger*.
Inwardly they pity their conquered antagonists, overwhelmed
by Fate, waiting desolately on their empty decks. Then the
British utter apprehensive cries as they see a signal of flashing
lights from the enemy flagship. A little German cadet who
has sought to die by plunging into the waves is dragged
aboard dripping only to drop dead. The German admiral is
heard crying:

"My country, my dear country!
Brothers!
I do the secret deed;
In the faith I die!"

His flagship, seen illuminated by a searchlight for just a moment, disappears. British lifeboats are lowered, and he is rescued. On being mildly reproached by the British admiral for having destroyed so much property, he protests that he has but done his duty. When a British sailor calls him "German rascal!" the other British sailors draw apart in horror from their unfeeling comrade, who straightway vows repentance.

"I:
What have I said?
What have I done?
Woe is me!
It was only a word;
I didn't mean it!"

Throughout, there is no conflict between the nominal antagonists. Both are sick and weary of war, equally its victims whether victors or vanquished. Since a struggle is lacking, all that the personages can do is to bleat complaints in ejaculatory style,

"O Fate! O Fatherland! O woe!"

There is no endeavor after realism of character, dialogue, or scene. The scene, indeed, as in most expressionistic plays, is kept almost dark in order to avoid the necessity of any detailed presentation and also to leave each spectator free to imagine what he will.

That Goering possesses no great talent must be evident, but that pacifistic expressionism may be fairly dramatic is proved by the works of Fritz von Unruh. As son of a Prussian general, he received strict military training. But he also studied history and art and tried his hand at poetry. Then, having completed the sketch of an historical drama, *Ferdinand, Prince of Prussia*, he showed it to Reinhardt, who declared it immature, and suggested that he write something closer to his own experience. Von Unruh responded with *Officers*, composed three years before the War. This depicts a clash between an ambitious youth and the discipline imposed upon him by military precedent. Ernst is descended from a line of soldiers and yearns for fame. Delighted at the outbreak of a colonial war, he drinks a toast "To Death!" and sails for Africa aboard a transport. In the field he chafes at the entangling red tape and cuts it all by leading a few brave fellows against a whole squadron. Although he wins a victory, he wins it against the orders of his superiors. He is rebuked by the colonel, his father-in-law, and sent in punishment to a mountain outpost, where, again defying discipline, he achieves a second triumph and dies. Ernst is an individualist who would rely upon his own intelligence as well as upon commands from headquarters. In this respect he differs from the unthinking cavalrymen of *The Charge of the Light Brigade*. Long before, Heinrich von Kleist in *The Prince of Homburg* had argued a similar case from the opposite point of view, approving the condemnation by court-martial of an individualist hero.

Von Unruh, who objects to unintelligent obedience in war, advocates the subordination of the individual to the king in his play disapproved by Reinhardt. Here the weak sovereign, humiliated by Napoleon, is under the domination of ministers who would seek peace at any price in order to enjoy court frivolities. In that court of opportunists only Louis Ferdinand, the king's cousin, stands firm. He loves the beautiful Queen Louise, and longs to assume the crown to save imperiled Prussia, but he nobly declines the proffered support of the army. He will not depose the king, though to do so would profit the State. Having vainly implored the monarch to resist, he marches forth to die in battle rather than prove a rebel.

Obviously, von Unruh is an idealist, whether arguing for self-abnegation, as here, or for individual self-assertion against the rigors of military discipline as in *Officers*. The Great War itself could not shatter that idealism, although it turned him into a pacifist as he beheld the injustice and horrors of carnage. Thus, in *Before the Decision*, written in the Autumn of 1914 and retouched later, he introduced an Uhlan officer—presumably himself—filled with pity as thirteen shifting scenes of warfare unroll before him. Now he is bivouacked with his men outside the enemy's town which is being burnt in reprisal for the shooting of a soldier by civilians. Now he beholds the death from grief of the wife of the burgomaster after her husband, father, and brother have been shot as hostages. Again he sees the body of a gallant youth tossed into a trench grave, hears the reinforcements singing as they advance to fight and fall, and reports to the general the killing of the latter's son,—news accepted stoically, though the general is later seen bending over the grave of his boy. Presently the Uhlan is in the burning town watching army surgeons at work, and then outside it gazing tearfully at abandoned children asleep in a peasant's hut. In the mean time, he has met in the gloom strange visions—Shakespeare who extols the joys of peace and art; Mourning, a dim figure who leads him beneath a ruined church into a burial vault where he encounters the spirit of von Kleist, the dark singer of hate. There he beholds the tombs of the old Hohenzollerns. As the dawn comes up illumining a scene of devastation, soldiers bury a volunteer, the Uhlan's friend, and the Uhlan bids them not despair; these woes will pass; the sun will bring light at last to suffering humanity. The piece is sentimental no doubt, spectacular rather than dramatic, but charged with pathos, and interesting from the point of view of technique. In *Officers*, except for the appearance of Death as a symbolic figure amid the troops on the transport, there was nothing out of the natural order. The characters were individualized, the two best being a Scottish soldier and an easy-going gambler, discharged from the army because of his debts but resuming his commission at the outbreak of hostilities. The Scotchman, secretly in love with the wife of the hero and promising to look after him in the campaign, has received from her three roses which he keeps in his wallet, until his comrades, joking him about them, make him feel that they have been profaned and he tosses them overboard. It is the gambler who spurs the hero on to defy traditional discipline, crying: "To hell with tradition! Here one must stand on one's own feet. To whom are you responsible except your own will, to that spirit which I call might, and you call God?" In *Before the Decision*, however, the characters are but types, and the scenes are dislocated pictures expressionistic in effect.

With *A Race*, written in the field from the Summer of 1915 to the Autumn of 1916, von Unruh's surrender to expressionism is complete; and his mood, as a result of longer contact with the War, has grown black indeed. Nightmare scenes pass in a graveyard where, while a battle rages at a distance, a Mother, aided by her daughter and a young son, has just interred their brother slain in the conflict. No sooner have they placed a rude cross above the dead than two other sons of the Mother are bound by soldiers to either side of the graveyard gate in punishment for misdemeanors. One has proved a coward in the field; the other has been caught mistreating women. He, the eldest of the family, has had his passions unleashed by the War. Dionysiac in his madness, he has done wonders in battle, for which the State would crown his deed; but the same inner drive has forced him to the blind gratification of instinct, for which the State would disgrace him. Drawn now to his own sister, and no longer recognizing any limitations of relationship, he excites in her a similar instinct. Both are victims of the urge toward Chaos, as the Mother represents the urge toward Cosmos, and stands above her children, pitying yet reproving them. When the maddened eldest son released from his bonds tears up the cross from the grave of his fallen brother, he cries to the Mother: "We feed the earth with our bodies. Why did you give us life?" and plunges to death from the graveyard wall, while his sister flees to escape capture by the soldiers intoxicated with victory. The Mother, having sought to bury the body of her suicide son and then struggling against the attempt of the soldiers to dig it up, is overwhelmed and dies. The youngest son, earlier carried off, returns leading a revolt, and unbinds from the gate his coward brother, who all this time has been moaning in fear. As the curtain drops, an officer who is declaiming against the horrors of war, strips off his uniform, crying: "I surrender it. May the sun bleach it!"

Crude and disordered as is this piece, there emerges from it a flaming protest against war. Of the mothers of all nations, the Mother in the play declares, "We will shake this spirit of world destruction out of the dishevelled locks of beautiful life." And her children in turn denounce their father's patriotism, affirming that all he wishes is to march with stay-at-home heroes between kneeling rows of citizens, and to lay his youngest son on the heart of that idol, the Fatherland, saying grandiloquently, "I wish I had more sons to sacrifice." What a selfish, false ideal is this! In vain the Mother protests that mankind is naturally innocent and good. The children can no longer believe her. "You led us astray by making us believe that there was a heaven, with a choir of angels who hovered around the Lord in pious song," they complain. "That may serve to gild the low fear of death; but, for us, all the crowns and embroidered crests and church keys and the splendors of the mass are as nothing. Let us be free from these bonds!" Here von Unruh's bitterness wells up. Instead of the glorification of war in *Officers*, we have violent imprecations against it, and a sense of utter disillusionment. As with expressionism always, no attempt is made to represent reality directly. Dislocated scenes suggest its dynamic essence. These scenes are rendered effective by the use of lights, shadows, and sounds, the sounds varying from the monotonous cries of the coward close at hand to the roaring of the battle that echoes from the valley. In the mist of the churchyard the Mother fancies that she sees a pale child at her breast, and the fallen son as a holy vision of death. The telegraphic dialogue suggests speed and passion.

Much calmer is the sequel to *A Race*, entitled *Platz*, or *Room*, whereby the author would signify the world of organized law. In this work, begun during the War but finished only in 1920, allegory replaces expressionism, as hope replaces despair. Dietrich, who had figured as the youngest son of *A Race*, incarnates that hope. He is admired by two daughters of the sovereign, but both have been ordered by their father to marry others. The pure Irene must wed the commandant Count Gutundblut, and the lustful Hyazinthe must wed the schemer Christlieb Schleich—suitors whose names suggest their characters. Dietrich, imprisoned as a rebel against the state, is clad in the garments of a jester, yet manages to escape with the sovereign's daughters. One of these, the jealous Hyazinthe, causes him to doubt her nobler sister and persuades him to sign a document promising not to revolt. In the mean time, the sovereign, feigning death, has been replaced by an Old Man who plans to dispose of Dietrich in secret. But that hero, repenting of his virtual betrayal of the people, unites with his once coward brother to lead a rebellion for reform. Though at first misunderstood by Irene, he is ultimately reconciled with her—his better nature—and, aided by his sister, will strive to bring in the reign of peace and joy. He is the true idealist to be contrasted with the weak sovereign who feigns death to escape responsibility, the futile Old Man who vainly tries to manage the state, the nationalistic phrase-maker Gutundblut, and the sly courtier Schleich. Through the speeches of Irene and of Dietrich, von Unruh hails the coming of a new era of brotherly love. Whether a third play promised to complete this trilogy will add to von Unruh's reputation is more than doubtful, for *Room* is inferior to *A Race*. In its stress upon symbols and ideas it lacks the emotional quality of its predecessor. It is Apolline rather than Dionysiac art.

But Apolline art is evidently not the forte of von Unruh. When, in *Bonaparte*, written in 1927, he forsakes expressionism and endeavors to compose a drama of character, he produces only a piece of baby make-believe. The action centers about the First Consul's execution of the Duke d'Enghien. Enghien is a boastful aristocrat, proclaiming himself the descendant of forty kings, and Bonaparte is an hysterical blusterer when not a downright clown. As his brother Lucien serves him the imperial crown in a pudding dish at table, Bonaparte apostrophizes it absurdly: "Magnet! My fingers itch after you! By Pharaoh and Alexander! have I a smaller head than those narrow-browed potentates?" For hundreds of lines he raves on, uttering similar fustian. Then he cries: "I must have women; I must have flesh!" No wonder that Josephine remarks, "There are times when I think that he is no human being." Not one of these characters is human, not one draws the breath of life or can awaken any feeling either of sympathy or dislike in the spectators. Here is proof if proof were needed that success in expressionism is no guarantee of success in that good old art which depends upon knowledge of character and careful portraiture of the world as it is. In von Unruh and his puppets there appears something of the madness of Marlowe without Marlowe's poetry.

Two minor exponents of expressionism, Bronnen and Brecht, may be mentioned before passing to the more important men like Kaiser, Toller, and Werfel. Arnolt Bronnen opened his career with *Parricide*, a violent youth drama written in emulation of Hasenclever's *The Son*. The father's death is finally compassed by a boy oppressed by educational tyranny and dominated by the Œdipus complex, which draws him to his mother and makes him jealous of her husband. The play circles round and round this central situation instead of moving forward. Its settings are vague; its characters are abstract; and the dialogue is explosive and repetitious. Similar in theme and technique is *The Birth of Youth*, a bloodless poetic fantasy printed as an appendix to the other piece in Alfred Wolfenstein's Year Book for 1920. *Anarchy in Sillian* presents with fortunate brevity a struggle between two men for one woman; and *Underground Battle* renders hysterically a war scene in a shelter where corpses line the wall or sit at a table as if playing cards, while a lieutenant mad with despair is consoled by a woman disguised as his servant, and cries and drum-fire and the beating of a hammer deafen the ears.

In *Rhenish Rebels* Bronnen makes a more ambitious attempt to dramatize the vain struggle of the Rhineland to break from the Reich at the end of the War; but his work lies in wild disorder, its five acts shifting from city to city, and the political background being left nebulous as the playwright concerns himself with a hero torn between love of his fanatical Rhineland mistress and a fair advocate of imperialism who finally lowers the Rhenish banner and raises that of the Reich. Even the name of the hero—Occc—is absurd. Equally grotesque are Bronnen's comedy *Excesses* and his fantasy *East Pole Quest*, the latter setting forth in successive monologues the madness of those bent on climbing Mount Everest, that same madness which Bronnen presents as controlling Alexander the Great in antiquity. These plays are but movie melodramas, designed to startle and shock, although professing a deeper significance. They represent a waste of creative energy.

More poetic and somewhat less violent are the plays of Bertolt Brecht, another follower of Wedekind and Büchner, who first sought the stage by seeming to exalt a wicked Nietzschean egoist, the hero of his chaotic drama *Baal*. Better still was *Drums in the Night*, which received the Kleist prize in 1922. Here a soldier, believed by his bride to be dead, and returning to claim her, denounces the comrades who would keep him a fighter. Lyrics choke the story, which of course is an old one. In 1924 Brecht revamped *Edward II* of Marlowe as an expressionistic play, and composed an original work, *Thicket*, full of fire yet dispensing with logic and psychology in its fragmentary setting forth of a family drama in the Chinese quarter of Chicago, where lives a Malay from Yokohama who seeks to appropriate the soul of a clerk in a lending library.

Is it necessary to follow farther the vagaries of the extreme expressionists? Surely not! The movement possessed virtue at first; but in its minor manifestations it defies every canon of good art. Those who have profited from the new technique and who stand some chance of being remembered as its exponents are men like Kaiser, Toller, and Werfel, in whom free imagination is a little balanced by reason and the sense of fact. Even the expressionists, in order to remain intelligible, must rely upon a basis of common experience. They must communicate as well as express.

CHAPTER XXII

Expressionism at its Best

Kaiser, Toller, Werfel

INTERESTING, significant, and an original force among modern German playwrights is Georg Kaiser. An idealist of fecund imagination, a Socialist exposing flaws in the present order, an innovator in technique, he creates a new, free drama, designed to make his audiences think. When he is most himself his plots are apologues; his *dramatis personæ* are types; he is more concerned with general problems than with concrete psychology. For him the mind and the spirit are all-important, centers of energy threatened by the machinery of industry, of gold-getting, of warfare. In his most characteristic plays, he sets forth this doctrine schematically through symbols, making no effort to represent life as a copyist, drawing instead mere outline designs stressed and stylized. Although he has responded to the dramatic influence of Strindberg and Wedekind and to the thought of Nietzsche and Schopenhauer, he is more of an optimist than the latter two and more of an expressionist than either of the former.

Born the son of a merchant in Magdeburg in 1878, Georg Kaiser entered business, spent three years in the Argentine, fell ill, returned by way of Spain and Italy, set to writing, and in 1903 produced a tragi-comedy of bourgeois life—*Schoolmaster Kleist*—which gave no hint of his later development. Already he had composed *La Fanciulla* and *Monna Nanna*, privately printed under the title *Hyperion, A Gift to Friends*. In 1908 he married, and soon settled in Weimar. Impoverished by the War, he moved to Erkner near Berlin.

407

Although attacked at first as a radical in the theater, he became the rage and was hailed as a symptom of the time.

Kaiser might have succeeded as a comic dramatist of the old style, but he preferred to experiment in various fresh directions. One vein that he followed is Shavian burlesque. Thus, in *The Jewish Widow* he travesties the Biblical story of Judith and Holofernes, and in *King Cuckold*, the legend of Tristan and Isolde. For him, Judith is only an adventurous girl who regards the youthful Nebuchadnezzar as more desirable than the rough Holofernes. When exalted to the rank of priestess as a reward for cutting off the latter's head, she finds in the high priest a lover still more agreeable. So, again, Kaiser, as the dance fever was at its height, employed the legend of Europa and the bull in a ballet drama to assail the effeminacy of a land disdained by the heroine and her brother. Both, like their father King Agenor, maintain that "The best life is the strong life." In *Alcibiades Saved*, Kaiser contrasts the handsome Greek warrior with the ugly philosopher, who merely happens to effect his rescue when driven to frenzy by pain. For Socrates, having stepped on a cactus thorn, dances about waving his sword so violently that he frightens off the pursuers of the retreating Alcibiades and is awarded the wreath of victory, a hero in spite of himself. The fact that he scorns the reward and hands it to Alcibiades fascinates that soldier. Here is a sage who despises all that men of the world esteem. Fishwives in the market may abuse him as crazy, but Alcibiades' own mistress prefers him. When Alcibiades, moved to contempt of what he has hitherto held sacred, shatters the images of Hermes, it is Socrates who is blamed for corrupting him and condemned to drink hemlock.

From this jocular treatment of legend and history emerge serious meanings, as they do in two later plays with at least a basis of fact. One is *Gilles and Jeanne*, which, like Shaw's *Saint Joan*, rises to tragedy. It sets Joan of Arc over against the sensual marshal of France, Gilles des Rais, who, being rebuffed in his desire to possess her, betrays his innocent victim to condemnation at Rouen, and then, by his continual yearning, is driven to madness, and at last to death, when the saint has reappeared to save his soul that defied salvation in life. The second play is *The Flight to Venice*. This treats as comedy the loves of George Sand and de Musset. The poet flees from the fair novelist who makes copy of the heartache of each of her lovers. She follows, and, when he falls ill, proceeds to captivate before his very eyes the physician who would cure him. What a woman! Let de Musset, however, but induce her to describe to him with eloquence her experiences with this other lover, and her love thus transferred to language will lose its potency, and she will forget the physician in turn. Moreover, she has received from Flaubert a letter begging her to join him in Paris, and that letter is couched in impeccable style. Thus, for her, literature is everything. It swallows up love and life itself.

Such a genial comedy might have come from the pen of Arthur Schnitzler, but Kaiser is earnest enough in *The Burghers of Calais*, his most successful treatment of history. The play is based upon the well-known episode of the six who, in 1347, offered to redeem their city with their lives when Edward III of England threatened to raze it after his victory at Crécy. At first the people would reject the king's proposal, but Eustache de Saint-Pierre shows them their folly and himself volunteers. As others follow suit, two brothers spring forward at the same time and raise the number to seven. Though one be superfluous, none will withdraw. It is Eustache who suggests that they meet at dawn on the morrow at the tolling of a bell, and that then the last of the seven to arrive withdraw. When, at the appointed hour, he fails to appear, he is denounced by the fickle mob as having devised this means of escape. But presently his body is borne in, followed by his blind old father, who explains that, eager to be the first to die for the city, Eustache has already taken his life. As the six, so heartened, turn to march to their doom, word comes that Edward will spare their lives and their city, and is approaching to thank God in their church for the birth of an heir. The body of Eustache, say the people, shall be placed on the highest step of the altar, that "The King of England, when he prays, shall kneel before his conqueror." It is to be observed that Kaiser omits here the chief scene of the ancient chronicle wherein Eustache pleads with the king for mercy, and that he invents the incident of the seventh volunteer. He has further made the harbor works, against the destruction of which the citizens strive, serve as a symbol of the fabric of civilization to be preserved at all costs.

The romantic mood of this play reappears in *Woman's Sacrifice* and in three sketches,—*Juana, Friedrich and Anna,* and *Claudius.* The last shows a knight returned from absence to find his wife disloyal, stabbing her, strangling one who should have guarded her honor, and burning down his castle. *Friedrich and Anna,* by contrast, presents a generous bridegroom refusing to slay his rival who boasts of having earlier possessed the bride. Instead, he invites his rival to supper in recognition of his having so well taught the lady the meaning of passion. *Juana,* best of the group, depicts a wife who, believing her husband to be dead, marries his friend, only to discover that his predecessor still lives. When she further learns that the two men have agreed that whichever she first asks to drink shall accept from her hand a draught secretly poisoned, she drains it herself, in order to preserve a friendship so precious.

Feminine self-abnegation is more fully developed in *Woman's Sacrifice,* with its wife who aids the escape of her husband from a royalist prison by the conventional exchange of garments and taking his place. Having suffered every outrage from her jailers, the countess is turned adrift, and, seeking her husband, finds him comfortably sequestered yet demanding hotly how she managed her release. He even accuses her of having profited from the aid of some amorous friend. "I had no friend, only enemies!" she cries, and confesses the indignities she has suffered for his sake. But, instead of appreciating her sacrifice, he is railing at her as gendarmes come clamoring in quest of him, having released the countess expressly in order to track her to her husband's hiding place. At this new danger, to save him once more, she reassumes his garments. The gendarmes, however, receiving word that Napoleon has broken bounds and is returning from Elba, shoot down the countess and flee. In dying, she stammers to her husband, "You must live—beloved—beyond death—beloved!"

So far, Kaiser appears to be writing in a vein fairly familiar. His characters are drawn in the round, and his plots are those of the older theater. Now he composes a comedy of situation like *The Sorina* or of character like *The Centaur* (or *Constantin Strobel*), laughing at the infatuation of a timid and proper pedant with an ugly servant maid, a satire upon man who resembles the centaur as being both human and bestial. Again he pens a burlesque like *The Spirit of the Antique*, its hero an archeologist intent upon building a perfect mousetrap; or he tosses off comedies like *The Courageous Navigator* and *David and Goliath*, the first turning on the quest for happiness, and the second on the notion that life is an illusion. In more serious mood the dramatist poses a problem of ethics in *The Temptation*, called also *The Mother of God*, asking the question, Has a woman whose husband is physically or morally unfit to give her a child a right to seek it from another for whom she cares nothing?

But Kaiser's distinctive contribution to the stage is contained in his expressionistic plays, those dramas of ideas in which the thought is more important than the picture of reality, and in which, indeed, he sacrifices external probability in order to present plots and personages developed only enough to support a central thesis. Such pieces are abstract, symbolic, and schematic. Scenes follow one another chronicle-wise without the nice organization of the well-made play. The action is carried by personages who are types rather than individuals. No effort is expended in probing for motives or analyzing emotions. Naturalistic details are suppressed. Experience is simply shattered into its elements and then re-shaped in forms strongly stylized to enforce some concept. In *The Conflagration in the Opera House*, in *Literary Trash* (*Kolportage*), and in *Side by Side*, some semblance of reality remains, but it drops away in *From Morn to Midnight*, *The Coral*, the two parts of *Gas*, and *Gats*.

Through his curiously sketchy *Conflagration in the Opera House* Kaiser rebukes feminine faithlessness just as he had extolled feminine fidelity in the fuller-bodied *Woman's Sacrifice*. A nobleman, after a career of worldly pleasure, has married a poor girl and retired with her to his estate in the suburbs of Paris. One night, as he is explaining to an old roué the delights of this simple life, the heavens are illumined by the burning of the opera house. At least, boasts the nobleman, he and his innocent Sylvette are safe. But an usher runs in crying, "She lives!" and the husband thus learns that Sylvette, instead of lying asleep upstairs, has been with her lover at the opera in a box behind drawn curtains. "Yes, I live!" exclaims Sylvette, who has been rescued by the usher. From that moment, however, she no longer exists for her husband. He talks as though she had died in the fire, and, to prove the point, hastens thither, brings back the charred body of the king's mistress, identified by a certain ring, and shows the body to the lover as that of Sylvette. To the hand of the real Sylvette he transfers the ring. She, in despair, returns to the conflagration and dashes into the wreckage to die. A cripple who notes on her finger the ring, claims and secures by virtue of this token the king's reward of a fortune for the recovery of the corpse of his mistress. It is as though by infidelity the personality of the wife as well as her body had

been transferred to another. So, too, a personality is seemingly transferred by means of a trinket in Kaiser's more fantastic *The Coral*.

This drama, written earlier, voices more fully its author's
philosophy. He argues that wealth stifles love, that those
who profit from our capitalistic system are guilty of oppressing the poor, and that each individual is responsible for the
well-being of all. A Billionaire, rising from the depths of
poverty and embittered by his early struggles, would spare
his children the drudgery that he has known. But they refuse
to profit by his ill-earned wealth and, in protest, return to the
proletariat from which he has emerged. It happens that his
secretary so resembles him that the two can be distinguished
apart only by a piece of coral attached to the secretary's
watch-chain. Since this official has led a happy childhood, the
Billionaire would appropriate that childhood by slaying him
and wearing the coral. Accepted by others as the secretary,
he is now suspected and convicted of having shot his master,
in short, of having murdered himself. Thus, the Billionaire
is doubled after the fashion dear to the German romanticists;
one self slays the other. When his son agrees to save him if
he will but resume his place among the workers, he refuses
unless that son resume in turn his life of luxury. Since neither
will yield, the Billionaire dies, clasping the bit of coral which
allows him to escape his own identity and to assume, even
at the price of death, that of the secretary who had known a
happy youth.

Of course, the story is fantastically unreal. The resemblance
of the secretary to his master, the passing of a personality
from one to another as a piece of coral is transferred, the
supposition that by murder the youth of any man can be
appropriated by some one else, such things are the stuff of
fairy tales, although employed to suggest spiritual truths.
The Billionaire has sought to make his secretary a counterpart of his outer semblance, and his son a counterpart, as he

hopes, of his inner self. His conscience is symbolized by a Man in Gray, who, in the first act, begs him to sign a statement that wealth for any single individual constitutes a disgrace. He has refused to accede to this request, declaring that he employs wealth to blot out the memory of his youthful suffering. In the last act, the Man in Gray denounces him as one who has sacrificed all for ease and who now must sacrifice life itself.

As a boy, the Billionaire had agonized in poverty after the disappearance of his father and the suicide of his mother. He had toiled in fear of the machines that threatened to conquer him unless he could conquer them. Since success has crowned his efforts, he would cut off that past, unlike most Americans who would rather glory in having by their own efforts risen from it. The Billionaire will not even come into contact with his workingmen. It is to his secretary that they present their complaints once a month, supposing that they are addressing the master.

But the Socialist son of the Billionaire abhors this attempt to cloak and hide. "I will tear down the veil behind which you are concealed. You know the crime of your wealth; and you only fool yourself with your open Thursdays." The son, hiring out as stoker on a collier, pursued and overtaken by his father on a yacht, explains his own change of heart. "It was as if the scales had suddenly fallen from my eyes. The whole injustice which we are committing became clear to me. We are rich, and these others who stifle in torment and misery are men like us. . . . Here we lie listless in deck chairs and complain of the warmth of the sun. We drink ice-water, and our throats are not choked with coal-dust. There, beneath the soft soles of your white shoes, fever rages, gloom reigns. Tear up this barrier of boards and look down!" As a stoker is brought fainting on deck, the son cries, "You must save him, doctor; otherwise I am his murderer!" The Billionaire's daughter, too, soothing the fever of the stoker, hears the call to become a nurse for the poor. Brother and sister believe, along with Kaiser, that upon each of us weighs a responsibility for the wrongs of the social order.

Kaiser's sympathy with the oppressed and his belief that money is the root of all evil, appear also in *Hell, Way, Earth.* Here an artist is shocked to discover that a lady of fashion prefers jewels for her person to saving the life of his friend. She need merely pay him a pittance for certain pictures, but instead she would lavish the money on gewgaws, and is flattered to think that by refusing to expend so small an amount she can determine a man's very existence. When the artist accuses the lady of murder, he is laughed at. Yet the lawyer who can find no precedent for such a charge will press it if he be paid a sufficient fee. The artist, however, protests that if he had so much he would naturally give it to his starving friend. Perceiving that men are dying for lack of what the gems in a single shop-window would purchase, he resorts to violence against a jeweler, and, for his deed, is sent to prison. Prison is the Hell of the title of the drama. In prison he learns the Way back to Earth, mastering the lesson of love. So he returns to the social world transformed into a beautiful character. He is able now to lead aright the convict who has sought his aid for escape, the harlot who has contemplated suicide, the lawyer who has been bound to the mere letter of the code, and the lady who has valued her jewels above human life. When wealth, vanity, and snobbery disappear, then Heaven may exist upon Earth. The curse of poverty must be abated; an equal distribution of income must be assured. Only so can man's innate goodness assert itself. Especially effective is the scene in the prison yard when to the shout of the convicts, "We are guilty!" the crowd outside responds antiphonally, "We are innocent!" The refrains are then reversed, the prisoners crying, "We are innocent!" and the crowd responding, "We are guilty!"

Kaiser's assault upon wealth in this play and in *The Coral* is directed to single figures elsewhere. Thus, in *David and Goliath* he attacks the capitalist Magnusson, and in *The Courageous Navigator*, an American magnate for whom he has borrowed the name of Joe Jefferson. That assault combines with an attack upon the deadening effects of modern business and industrial routine in *From Morn to Midnight* and the two parts of *Gas*.

The first of these pieces has achieved wide popularity. It renders in snatches episodes of one day in the life of a bank cashier, who, fixed to his desk for decades, is suddenly tempted to break his routine. On the supposition that a fair Italian refused money for a draught at the bank is an adventuress, the cashier leaps to the conclusion that, if he steals a large sum for her, she will reciprocate his kindness with love. But the lady virtuously rebuffs him, and insists that he restore his booty. Already, however, his theft has been discovered. He must flee. "I am on the march," he exclaims; "there is no returning; forward I go!" Launched thus upon his one day of debauch, the erstwhile sober cashier is wholly transformed. He remains unmoved even by the death of his mother. He creates excitement with his gold at a race-track until a more prodigal prince diverts the crowd's attention. He joins the revelers at a masquerade, and, when this gaiety fails to satisfy, he follows a Salvation Army lassie to her headquarters, mounts the bench of penance, and announces his discovery. It is this: "Not with all the money from all the banks of the world can one buy anything of value. One always buys less than he pays for. And the more one pays, the worse is his bargain. Money impairs value. Money hides real worth. Money is the crowning deceit of all!" When the cashier flings away what is left of his booty, his fellow penitents scramble for it. He is gratified that at least the girl he has followed should remain untempted by the gold. But forthwith she opens a door to admit the police, remarking, "This is your man; I have shown him to you; I have earned the reward!" Thus the cashier's one day of freedom is over. "From morn to midnight I have wandered round and round in a circle!" he cries. "Now I see the way out, but where does it lead?" So saying, he shoots himself.

Here are the fragmentary scenes, the symbolic characters, the emphasis upon ideas rather than story, distinctive of expressionism. The play is one of the best of the kind in its simplicity and universality. It exemplifies Kaiser's distrust of money and his tendency to suggest, contrary to the wont of most expressionists, a psychological truth, namely, just what may happen when the soul built up and fortified by routine is suddenly deprived of such support. We think that we would rejoice to escape the round of duties which holds us in our place. Yet to do so would be to disintegrate. Perhaps Kaiser had read Hawthorne's story of the man who, failing for once to go home at night, could never more return there. Again he treats the theme in *Chancellor's Clerk Krehler*. Krehler, like the cashier, flying off at a tangent, is lost. After celebrating the wedding of his daughter, he is given a holiday by his chief. Since this is the first he has enjoyed in years, he is dazed. He can scarcely find his way home. There the furniture has been moved out for the wedding; the place looks strange; and his daughter, who for two decades has been a fixture, is gone. Life seems so changed that Krehler, unsteadied, decides to resign his position. When his wife, protesting, summons his chief, the latter, to deter him, relates the very story of the cashier whose fate is described in *From Morn to Midnight*. In vain his wife objects that they must starve unless he work. His madness grows until, instead of responding with gratitude to his son-in-law's offer of assistance, Krehler thrusts him off a balcony and leaps after to death. Such is the tragedy of one who, rendered an automaton by our industrial system, is suddenly jolted from his usual orbit. Shocked into a desire for freedom and self-assertion, Krehler all at once regards those for whom he has toiled as his enemies. But he lacks the courage of the cashier to live for even one day.

Before discussing *Gas*, that best exemplar of its author's thought and technique, three more recent pieces from his pen may be briefly considered. *Literary Trash* (*Kolportage*) laughs at the theory of a blue-blooded aristocracy by showing a child of noble birth exchanged for a child of the people, brought up in democratic America, and then returned to Europe to confront the proletarian who had been reared in his place as an aristocrat. Ironically, the play is described by Kaiser as written "for the advancement of the education of children." In *Side by Side* he offers a more original satire upon our lack of concern for the welfare of others. What of the social sympathy of which we boast? When a conscientious pawnbroker finds in a coat pledged with him a letter indicating that a girl jilted by her lover is likely to commit suicide, he argues that he must prevent it or become her murderer. But since, in cleaning the coat with benzine, he has smeared off the address of the letter, he is troubled to find the persons concerned. On a chance, he seeks them at a *pension* and a casino. In order to enter the latter where full dress is required, he must don the coat. The police whom he consults laugh at him for his pains and then arrest him for appropriating the property of another. His pawnbroker's license is revoked, and in despair he ends the day by turning on the gas. Meanwhile, the lady whose life he would save has gaily plighted her troth to another; and the man, quite unconcerned, has met a movie actress with whom he has devised a scenario that will bring him fame. How absurd, therefore, is the pawnbroker's interest in the welfare of others! The story is sketched in mere outline, with the language reduced to a series of short, emphatic, telegraphic speeches. In this play and *Literary Trash* may be felt the influence of the satirical Carl Sternheim.

Kaiser is more fully himself in the strange *Noli me tangere*, suggested by his imprisonment in 1922 for alienation of prop-

erty, when, having appropriated an apartment and furnishings
that did not belong to him, he calmly asserted that for one
of his genius in a time of storm and stress any means of preserving life might be justified. The scene is a common
room of a prison. The characters, except for two guards, are
prisoners known only by their numbers. Number 16, seized
on a train for riding without a ticket, explains that it has
been merely mislaid. When, in fact, the ticket turns up, he
offers to exchange garments with Number 15, a poet, that
the latter may escape in his place. But a hungry convict,
Number 5, for a plate of food, betrays Number 16, and then,
recognizing in his features the face of Christ, hangs himself
as a second Judas. There is sympathy here for the victims
of social injustice; but the poet of the play is as naïve about
the reason of his incarceration as was Kaiser himself. Each
must share the guilt of all in a world interdependent in its
parts. In that sense, the Savior bears, indeed, the sins of the
world.

So Kaiser dreams of social solidarity, and is never weary
of asserting faith in the spirit of man as opposed to faith
in mere wealth or machinery. He is an erratic idealist who disdains and condemns the modern industrial order. In the two
parts of *Gas*, his most famous work, he shows that labor as
well as capital is attached to a system which makes of man but
a hand or a foot to operate a machine and deprives him of
his true humanity. The son of the Billionaire who had figured in Kaiser's play *The Coral* is a philanthropist desirous
of sending factory toilers back to the soil to live happily as
roundly developed human beings. Already they have combined
in a strike because he would not dismiss the Engineer in charge
of his work when a great explosion occurred. Yet, given
the all-powerful Gas—symbol of our industrial order—this
explosion was inevitable. The workers have hit upon the Engineer as the scapegoat. In vain the Billionaire's Son points
out that the same thing will occur again with any other Engi-

neer since the fault lies, not in the man, but the system. Then it occurs to him to use their refusal to work in order to check the future manufacture of Gas. He will provide garden plots and cottages for all these folk and teach them to live as independent wholes, no longer the slaves of machinery, mere hands or feet to be pressed on levers. But they scorn his suggestion, as do the Gentlemen in Black, their superintendents. Even the Engineer, believing in the necessity of continuing the manufacture of Gas, will accede to the workers' wishes by withdrawal; and a government commissioner will order the restoration of the plant since armaments depend upon it. In vain the Billionaire's Son protests that it is man alone who counts. The people are ready to stone him in order to get back to work. When he asks where is man, the integrity rather than the fraction, his widowed daughter answers proudly, "I will give him birth."

In the *Second Part* of *Gas* this hope is defeated. With the factory rebuilt, the toilers are turning out an improved product as a means for waging war. The able-bodied have gone to the front; weaklings and children are struggling behind the lines to manufacture this fresh form of energy. Some, however, would cease labor and make friends with their brothers of the attacking army. The Billionaire Worker leads the pacifists; the more potent Engineer leads the militarists. "Let no one resist evil with evil!" cries the former; but the Engineer has discovered a new and deadly poison gas. He and his followers would establish their earthly supremacy by violence. Finally, the Billionaire Worker, in despair of convincing the apostles of force, seizes the little red ball which contains the new energy, and, hurling it among these fanatics, destroys their bodies, as he says, that their souls may live. In vain he has preached the doctrine that God's kingdom is a kingdom of the spirit. How futile is the attempt to enlighten the blind masses so willing to submit to the bondage of industrialism and militarism!

EXPRESSIONISM AT ITS BEST

This play is little more than a skeleton of plot denuded of flesh, a scenario set forth by symbols representing ideas, with its army of Blues defeated by Yellows and its exclamatory choral cries. There is an absence here of the imaginative reality of Čapek's Robots, although, in his *First Part*, Kaiser captures attention by his story and by his fuller verbal expression. The speeches of the opposing leaders as they contend for popular favor are eloquent. To the enslaved toilers, the Engineer declares: "Power, infinite power, throbs in the machines which you set going. . . . You are heroes in soot and sweat. You are heroes at the lever, at the sight-tube, at the switch-block. . . . And even the greatest ordeal of all cannot appal you for long—the explosion." So he encourages them to toil patiently beneath the yoke. But the Billionaire's Son retorts: "Are your thundering trains and vaulting bridges and flying motors sufficient recompense for your fever? You, brother, are more than a hand! You, son, are more than a pair of eyes! You, husband, live longer than one day! You are eternal creatures, perfect from the very beginning! Do not let the days mutilate you, nor dumb mechanical movements of the hand!"

Inferior to both parts of *Gas* is the strange play *Gats*, because the problem it treats is less real. The technique employed remains the same,—a fantastic story told to illustrate a fundamental truth. Men desire children even though misery results from over-population. A Captain has led an expedition to a remote quarter of the world, seeking a paradise for the disinherited and destitute. Proceeding beyond the rest of his party, he has discovered a veritable Eden where love rules since there is no overcrowding or undue competition, owing to the use of a certain powder, "Gats," which, taken in wine, will induce sterility. Abandoning his companions, the delighted Malthusian hastens home to announce to the members of his World Settlement Union this boon which will obviate the necessity of their emigration to another country. But the managers of his enterprise object, since they wish the pleasure of organizing something, and the members of the union, summoned from far and near, object in a theatrically brilliant scene, when, before an arena holding thousands, representatives voice their various protests, answered in turn by the Captain until, the tumult growing, he is shot down by an opponent, and the police open fire upon the crowd. Though the Captain recovers, a law is passed making death the penalty for the use of "Gats," and he is forced to take lodgings in disguise attended only by his fair secretary, who is occupied day and night in preparing clippings for a "History of Human Stupidity" which he now will write. Obliged to offer marriage to the girl by his squeamish landlady, the Captain agrees, but puts into her wine and his own the fatal powder "Gats." She has just assured him that she will bear him a son to restore his faith in mankind. But now she turns upon him in rage, summons in the police, and, while he is being assailed by a mob outside, prepares to depart with one who believes in children and has long sued for her hand. The author's moral could more readily have been conveyed through a commonplace story involving natural characters; but he has preferred to employ the resources of expressionism—an impossible fable, abstract personages, antiphonal songs and speeches, multicolored lights, and the rattle of machine guns. All he really says is that men and women desire children even though they constitute a burden, and that the poor, deprived of other privileges, will at least claim this.

Expressionism is much less in evidence in *Twice Oliver*, which offers a version of the Doppelgänger theme used by Kaiser in *The Conflagration in the Opera House*, *Coral*, and his intimate review *The Two Cravats*. An actor whose vaudeville specialty consists in rapid changes of costume is engaged by a lady to impersonate for an hour each day her lover who has disappeared. When ere long Oliver develops for her the passion that he has hitherto merely feigned, she dismisses him. In the mean time, he has been forced to permit his daughter to become a ballet dancer even though he perceives that the director's interest in her is other than professional. In short, needing to procure money with which to aid his invalid wife, Oliver is goaded into selling his daughter's honor and his own heart. Horrified at what he has done, he seeks to return his gains to both. But the lady rejects the offer, and, when her real lover unexpectedly returns, she takes him for amusement to the theater to behold his other self perform. The actor, now muddled in mind by his trouble, harangues the couple from the stage and then shoots his double. The police regard the case as one of murder prompted by jealousy; but alienists perceive that Oliver thought he was shooting himself, for ever since the deed he has believed himself to be dead. When they rouse him by focusing upon his closed eyes a brilliant light, he assumes that he is in the other world, and confesses to the physician, as to God, his suicide. A final scene that might well have been spared shows him in the asylum confiding to his fellow lunatics that he is in truth the late Czar. Improbable as are the situations, undeveloped as are the characters, and dispersed as are the ten scenes of this play, it is effective in its separate episodes and interesting as showing a stage in the gradual emergence of Kaiser from the spell of expressionism. Here he is moving back toward reality. The second Oliver is not a symbol of some element in the personality of the first; he is a separate person, and the resemblance between the two is purely fortuitous.

How far Kaiser has swung away from expressionism may be seen in *Paper Mill*, a light comedy as French in tone as it is in scene. Perhaps there lingers just a recollection of the Doppelgänger business in the person of a charming girl who comes twice to the same little inn on the Paris-Boulogne line, the first time with a poet and the second time with a critic who is writing the poet's biography, and each time occupies the same balcony room under a different name. Although she endeavors to convince the critic that her visit with him is the first she has made, he grows more and more confident that the summer before, at this very place, she had inspired the play of his friend the poet. The lady, wishing to be rid of the critic, secretly summons the poet, who arrives to claim her and by various amusing ruses frightens each of four witnesses into withdrawing their statements that they have ever seen her before. The critic, too, is glad to withdraw when he learns of the fall from office of her father, a cabinet minister on whose aid he has counted.

Again in a vein quite different from that of his most distinguished work is Kaiser's *October Day*, translated under the title *The Phantom Lover*. His heroine is a naïve and romantic girl, who conceives at sight a passion for a lieutenant quite unconscious of her existence. She has seen him gazing into a shop-window; she has followed him to church and opera; and that night, after dreaming of him, she has chanced to embrace in the dark a butcher's boy stealing to a rendezvous with a scullery-maid. Half in a dream, she has imagined that she was clasping the lieutenant, already far away on a train. Thereafter, she protests that the lieutenant is the father of her child; but the lieutenant, called to account by her uncle, protests his innocence. He is flattered, however, to learn that he has been even the dream lover of such a lady, and offers her marriage. When the butcher's boy seeks to blackmail the uncle, the lieutenant cuts him down. Thus, a play which begins lightly reaches a conclusion half-tragic—at least for the villain. The improbabilities matter little, since attention is focused less on the plot than on the notion that belief determines reality and that the boundary between reality and dream is indefinable. Such a notion reveals the affinity of Kaiser with Pirandello. In structure, his drama has forsaken the rambling arrangement of *From Morn to Midnight* and returned to the coherent unification of the well-made play.

Ernst Toller, who has been called "the most dominant and

flagrant genius hatched by the German revolution," is a Bavarian Jew born in 1893. In a Prussian high school he acquired his dislike of militarism, but, after journeying to Denmark and France and studying at the University of Grenoble, he joined the German colors at the outbreak of the War, inspired by patriotic fervor. More than a year in the field convinced him that the horrors of war can never be justified. Having been invalided home, he studied at Munich and at Heidelberg, and fell in with groups of young idealists determined to end the War and unite the youth of all nations in framing a pact for peace. When the German General Staff objected to the activities of Toller and his friends, he was but fortified in his ambitions. He joined in the strike of the munitions-workers in Munich in 1918, and was held in a military prison. During this period he composed his first play, *Transformation.*

This piece develops symbolically its author's attack upon war and his plea for a world in which righteousness shall prevail. A sculptor, thinking to escape from his personal disillusionment by enlisting in a colonial conflict, is bitterly disappointed. We see him now among soldiers herded on a transport train, now among the wounded on a battlefield, and now on his hospital cot hoping that at least the Fatherland will profit from his sufferings. A surgeon, performing wonders on the wounded, supplies them with artificial limbs and faces fixed like masks, whereupon they dance grotesquely. When Friedrich tells them of Christ the Savior, they retort: "You say He knows of our sufferings? Then He is wicked if He does not deliver us." Presently, Friedrich appears at work upon a statue to symbolize the victory of the Fatherland, pouring into his art the passion that his beloved has scorned. But when he perceives a wretched couple, victims of the War, he asks if any Fatherland be worthy of such a sacrifice, and in answer smashes to bits the statue he was creating.

Dream pictures follow, transformations, which lead Friedrich to resolve upon redeeming the world through love. As a revolutionist, he cries: "You have carved Jesus Christ in wood and nailed Him on a cross because you did not wish to go the way that led Him to redemption. . . . Go to the soldiers and bid them turn their swords to ploughshares. Go to the rich and show them what ash-heaps are their hearts. But be kind to them, for they, too, are weak and erring creatures. . . . March, march to the light of day! . . . Revolution!" That the revolution preached by Toller's hero appears no more practicable than that urged by the poet Shelley matters little. Toller's yearning to overcome hatred and bring in a new era of peace is noble and sincere, and the excellence of his drama lies in its dream-pictures combined in the expressionist manner.

Released from prison, Toller was elected to the Bavarian National Congress, the first German Soviet held in the south. He realized, however, that the time was not ripe for the success of Communism, and saw the revolutionary uprising, which he disapproved, defeated. He was again arrested, and in June, 1919, condemned to imprisonment for five years in the fortress of Niederschönenfeld. While there, he composed among other plays *The Machine Wreckers* and *Masses and Man*. The first presents in many dislocated scenes one phase of the Luddite riots among English workers early in the nineteenth century occasioned by the introduction of steam machinery. In his Prologue, Toller reproduces part of a speech by Lord Byron delivered in Parliament in 1812 on behalf of the Nottinghamshire strikers, and against a bill which would make the destruction of machinery punishable by death. Hauptmann, at the close of *The Weavers*, had intimated that his rebels were about to attack the steam machinery which threatened the livelihood of hand toilers. Toller has developed this notion, but so exaggerates the misery of the poor as to spoil his case by caricature.

A rich manufacturer has installed a steam engine, which,

by performing the work of many men, takes the bread out of their mouths. Women and little children operate the machines. An overseer beats a girl who drowses over her task, and fines the women if they speak or sing. The manufacturer justifies paying children low wages, since to do so rebukes their parents' greed. But he cannot allow them to eat because production would thus be slowed down, and coal would be wasted. Everybody suffers excruciatingly. The manufacturer and his minions are villains unspeakable, and the whole piece is a penny-dreadful, adapted for the new expressionistic stage with some borrowing in technique from the Elizabethan chronicle play.

In *Masses and Man* (*Masse-Mensch*), a far better drama, performed to crowded houses for two seasons in Berlin after its first production in September, 1921, Toller attacked militarism and the slavery imposed upon free souls by our mechanistic civilization. His seven scenes, written in the abstract and symbolical style of the expressionist school, are accompanied and linked together by shifts of light and by incidental music suggestive of the action, present and to come. A woman, though opposed by her husband, allies herself with the workers in protest against a war waged by the State. She and they plan to liberate all who are in servitude in mines and in munition factories. War must cease. But the enthusiasm of the masses flames into frenzy for another war, their own, directed against their oppressor, the State, or Capital. Vainly the woman seeks to dissuade her comrades from this new violence. They turn upon her, declaring that she would spare those of her own class. When their rising is suppressed by the State, they make her their scapegoat, falsely declaring her to have been their leader. Betrayed by those she had sought to save, she is sent to execution.

Although the play might seem to be directed against capitalism, it strikes equally against Communism which would resort to violence, indicating its author's disillusionment with his earlier dream of a Communistic State. Sonia is the individual soul crucified by the masses she would redeem from their faith in force. The world is in misery, Toller would have us see, not merely because of mob rule or State rule, but because both mob and State are inherently selfish and resort to force in imposing their will. Sonia excoriates the State because it oppresses the disinherited. She declares that factories may no longer conquer the souls of men. At the same time, she insists that the Masses should be bound together by love, and she resents their resort to revenge and cruelty. "Guilty are we all!" she cries. "Yes, I am guilty, guilty before mankind." When she is offered a chance to escape on condition that she slay one of her jailers, she refuses to accept at such a price, declaring, "If I took but one human life, I would betray the Masses."

Especially effective are certain scenes in which existence seems to be reduced to mechanic action. Bankers appear trading on the stock exchange, talking in staccato lines of war as their mighty instrument to control kings, ministers, parliaments, and the press, while their dividends roll in, and a recorder chronicles their winnings. When a chorus of lamentations from the Masses is heard, the bankers suggest an entertainment for their benefit and dance a fox-trot to the music of clinking coins. Again, Sonia, the heroine, is seen crouching in an iron-barred cage, about which marches soundlessly a file of prisoners, while the bankers offer her shares in guilt, and gray shadows accuse her of having spilled their blood.

Sonia retains her faith in human nature even to the last, protesting to the priest who pronounces mankind to be evil her belief that "Mankind gropes toward goodness." One circumstance attendant upon her death seems to prove her contention. When she is led out to execution, two hags fall upon the food and clothing she has left, but, at the rattle of the musketry outside, replace their loot, each saying to the other, "Sister, why do we do such things?"

Toller is a voice crying in the wilderness the age-old message of peace on earth, good-will toward men. His sympathy goes out to the victims of an industrial civilization, controlled by capital, and driven to retaliate with violence. Like Sonia, he would find salvation, not in religion, but rather in the essential goodness of humanity itself. Yet, even Toller seems to doubt that humanity can achieve brotherhood unless inspired by the ideals of a power outside itself which makes for righteousness.

In addition to a sonnet sequence, *Poems of a Prisoner*, and two choral works, *Day of the Proletariat* and *Requiem for Brothers who were Shot*, Toller has produced a puppet play, *The Revenge of the Scorned Lover*, drawn from Bandello, and several dramas less effective than *The Machine Wreckers* and *Masses and Man*. One is *Wotan Unbound*, a satire upon militarism and the mischief that can be wrought by patriotic catch-words used by the dull-witted and the evil. Another piece is *Hoppla, We Live!* dedicated to the expressionistic producer Erwin Piscator and of interest as employing in ten interludes moving pictures that show varied scenes from 1919 to 1927, some of them like "Ghandi in India" and "Fighting in China" unrelated to the main action. After his condemnation for taking part in a revolution, Karl Thomas loses his mind and is locked up in a mad house. At the opening of the play he emerges to find a former fellow conspirator now important as a cabinet minister, sneering at the masses and too high and mighty to accord his old friend a position. Karl's sweetheart is dismissed from a job because she has expressed sympathy with strikers, and, when Karl observes the farce of an election which no one takes seriously, he exclaims, "If I'd only remained in the asylum!" The ignorant and vicious try to vote early and often, and the reasons alleged by the intelligent for their choices are absurd. When the cabinet minister has been shot down by a radical student, Karl is apprehended for the deed, and an alienist by psycho-analysis finds complexes in all his protests of innocence. In vain Karl calls for warders to imprison the alienist as crazy; it is Karl that they imprison. Thereupon he hangs himself after declaring: "We speak and do not hear one another. We love and do not know one another. Oh, the madness of the world! . . . Whither? Whither?" It matters little that Toller here turns the Mississippi backward and sideways, making it threaten Chicago with a flood according to a radio report. His real mistake lies in writing a drama so undramatic, one devoid of plot, character, or significant ideas. The personages are types —an alienist, a corrupt financier, a philosopher, a lyric poet devoted to Karl Marx, an oil operator, and a radio man who hears Cairo calling the title of the play: "Hoppla! So this is life!" But the critic is forced to retort that this is not life or anything resembling it.

Bitter, indeed, is Toller's *Hinkemann,* translated into English as *Brokenbrow* and also as *Bloody Laughter.* It was given at Dresden three years before *Hoppla, We Live!* at a performance made memorable by a demonstration of anti-Semitic agitators in the audience. They objected to the fundamental situation of the play as scabrous, for Hinkemann is a good fellow who has been so maimed during his service in the War that he can no longer be a husband to his wife. She feels contempt for his impotency, and a friend makes fun of him to their former comrades. Then this friend and the wife engage in an intrigue. No wonder that Hinkemann suffers in his desolation, unable to satisfy his wife's desires, forced to seek a living by biting live rats in a circus, and deploring man's cruelty toward his fellows and toward animals, a cruelty which turns ugly this beautiful world. How shall beauty be restored? By love. So Hinkemann forgives his enemies, his disloyal friend, his unfaithful wife, and by this Tolstoyan remedy incites her to repent. Yet, in horror at what she has done, she takes her life. Toller may be a Jew by race, but the lesson that he teaches is in accord with Christian doctrine. No doubt his own sufferings have given him a deeper insight into the distress of others. At all events, he is the apostle of a fine humanitarianism. His sympathy extends even to the world of beasts and birds. In *The Swallow Book*, he has collected poems that commemorate the life of the birds that cheered him during his long confinement. In short, he is a Jewish pacifist with the soul of a St. Francis.

Another brilliant Jewish playwright is Franz Werfel. Born at Prague in 1890, he studied there and in Hamburg and issued a series of expressionist lyrics which include *The World Friend*, *We Are*, *One Another*, and *Songs from Three Empires*. Having acted as editorial adviser in Leipzig, he served in the army, and, during the War, rejoined the colors and fought on the Russian and Serbian fronts. Then he withdrew to live in Vienna. In 1918 appeared his translation of *The Trojan Women* of Euripides, and two years later his novel *Not the Murderer but the Murdered is Guilty*. Other volumes of verse, including *Day of Judgment* and *Adjurations*, and a popular biographical novel devoted to the composer Verdi, serve as a complement to his work for the stage. That work comprises a magic trilogy in verse, *Mirror Man*; a dream drama in prose, *Play Yard*; a more realistic tragedy, *Schweiger*; an extravaganza, *Goat Song*; the historical *Juarez and Maximilian*, and the Biblical *Paul Among the Jews*.

Mirror Man is a philosophic fantasy. At thirty, its hero, sated with life, would renounce the world and retire to a mountain monastery. What, asks the monk who receives him, is his attitude toward mundane things? Is he one who sees in outward experience but a reflection of self? or one who sees in self an enemy to be overcome by love for others and for God? or one who, rejecting all phenomena as illusory, would strive to attain the peace of complete renunciation? As Thamal confesses that he belongs to the second class, his leering image grins at him from a mirror, and when in resentment he shoots at it, he releases therefrom his evil genius, or Mirror Man.

This Mephistopheles, delighted to escape, greets Thamal as a god, and reveals to him poor mortals groping with lanterns up a slope, seeking in the gloom for divine aid. Surely, he may prove their savior and guide them to felicity. Thus flattered by the tempter, and withdrawing from the monastery, Thamal proceeds in the second part of the trilogy to lead a life of self-assertion in a fantastic Orient where he slays his father, seduces and then abandons the bride of his friend, yields to the lure of a gipsy dancer, overcomes the king of the serpents, and, having delivered a province, is worshiped as divine. Then, deprived of power by a revolt, he wanders disillusioned, growing smaller, while the evil Mirror Man swells to giant size. Returning to the monastery in the third part, the penitent Thamal is more determined than at first to renounce the passionate confusions of life. He delivers himself to judgment, drinks hemlock in punishment for his sins, and perceives that the mirror no longer reflects his image but is now a window through which he beholds a higher reality. Although he has escaped from the temptations of the Mirror Man, there is a last step which he must take. He must attain "the blissful extinction and self-expiration" of the Hindoo Nirvana. Is this possible? Apparently not, for Werfel remarks that, "It is the tragedy of human life that this duel between the essence ego and mirror ego must remain a draw."

A second fantasy, *Play Yard*, is equally suggestive and obscure. The world constitutes our play yard, and only through loss of personality can we find release from what is futile. The hero, in search of a reality that shall correspond to his vision of truth, finds in a child at play the symbol of his own soul. He would exhibit this mysterious child to other seekers for truth, but, ere he can do so, it is transformed into a waxen puppet. By inference it would seem that only through Buddhistic annihilation, the lapsing of the individual into the all, is there hope for unhappy humanity.

One turns with relief from these nebulous imaginings to

Schweiger, in which the psychology of double personality replaces the maunderings of the mystic. Just after the War, Franz Schweiger (the Silent One) has appeared in an Austrian town, where he lives as watch-maker. His past is unknown; he undertakes a journey unexplained; his wife and neighbors are baffled by the secret of his identity. By degrees, it emerges that the gentle Schweiger is no other than the violent Franz Forster, a scholar, who, during a maniacal seizure, had shot and killed a small boy. Cured by the skill of a psychiatrist, he had lost in the process his Forster personality. When the social democrats, unaware of his past, wish to make him their candidate, his monarchist physician would prevent, and to this end, inducing in the unhappy man a trance, reawakens the memory of his past and impresses him with the folly of his assuming to run for office. The wife, learning from the physician of her husband's earlier madness, and fearing lest the child that she is about to bear may inherit its father's malady, disappears. In the mean time, Schweiger, in his normal second-self, has run mortal risks to save many children in peril on a burning steamer. While smarting under his injuries, he learns that his wife has slain their child, fearing to let it be born. Again madness sweeps upon him, but now, instead of murdering others, he slays himself. Here Werfel, showing real insight in his treatment of the power of hypnotic suggestion and of the phenomena of insanity, continues to conceive of man as the battle-ground of two warring forces. Forster, who slew madly, contrasts with the gentle Schweiger, who risks his life for others; but in this case Dr. Jekyll conquers Mr. Hyde, or at least induces Hyde to efface himself.

More effective than *Schweiger* in its balance between reality and fantasy is *Goat Song,* a drama marked by poetic sweep of action and a picturesque clash of forces. The first act in particular moves toward a stirring climax, and provides a thoroughly artistic exposition. Somewhere beyond the Danube a landowner of the eighteenth century is about to marry his son to the daughter of a neighbor, but, for twenty-three years, he has kept concealed in a stone stable on his estate another son, half goat, half man, never looked at by its horrified parents and tended only by a servant. On the day of Mirko's betrothal, his father will put to death this beast; but the beast escapes, and, falling among revolted vagabonds, is hailed as a demigod. These outcast enemies of property and order are led by a wild-eyed student, who sets up the captured monster as a symbol of the beast within them all, now reawakened. The mob ravishes the land, slays the unfortunate Mirko, and can be stayed by the student only if Mirko's intended bride offer herself to the monster that has been leashed behind the high altar of the church. Stanja agrees, and the love cry of the unseen beast as she submits to its embrace sounds in triumph. That triumph, however, is short-lived, for janissaries come riding to crush the revolt, and in the burning of a forest the monster perishes, leaving his body to be shown as a curiosity. The student leader is to be hanged, but, though order be restored, man is not quite relieved from dread of the beast. For the heroic Stanja announces that she is to bear to the monster a child.

No wonder that the critics have been bewildered by this drama. The New York Theatre Guild, producing the play, announced that, "Beyond all theatrical devices, there are mystical undercurrents, hidden profundities, vague and devastating associations, implied in *Goat Song*, which will elude the spectator as they are unfolded upon the stage, but which, if his heart is open to the author's message, will return to trouble his memory and to prick his thoughts." One critic believes that the monster is the physical in man, the primitive, sylvan, joy-loving nature, rendered evil by the puritanic repression accorded it by the parents. They have been ashamed of the offspring of their natural love, and, by confining the goat-man and regarding him as monstrous, they have made him so.

Hence the warning of the physician that this natural creature has its right to life also. A parallel exists in Calderón's famous drama, *Life's A Dream*, in which a son, destined, according to an oracle, to prove violent toward his parents, is kept by them in solitary confinement and made the very beast that they feared.

In *Juarez and Maximilian* Werfel draws a portrait of the Emperor of Mexico, an incompetent idealist doomed to failure by his own character when brought into conflict with Juarez, who remains potent as incarnating the national spirit, although never brought upon the scene. When Maximilian, sent from Europe to further the ambition of Napoleon III, is cajoled into signing the death warrant of certain civil prisoners, he seals his own fate. It is Carlotta who prevents his return overseas, whither she has sailed to seek aid of Emperor and Pope. As for Maximilian, he knows that he fights for a losing cause, and he goes from his cell to die against the adobe wall of Queretaro, disdaining the means for suicide provided by his physician. The action of the thirteen slow-moving scenes begins with the flight of Juarez, apparently vanquished, and ends with his return when Maximilian is no more. Here, as in his earlier *Visit from Elysium*, Werfel's idealism is evident. It is evident, also, in *Paul Among the Jews*, a sober, solid, somewhat dull play revealing the clash of political and religious forces following the period of Paul's conversion.

Paul, coming to Jerusalem a Christian, visits his old teacher, the patriarch Gamaliel, and seeks out Peter, Barnabas, and James, who can give him at first-hand information as to the crucified Jesus. Imbued with the gospel of love, Paul believes that orthodox Judaism has been transcended by the new faith. Observance of the Jewish law will no longer suffice for salvation. But he must convince of this fact the disciples as well as the Jews. In the mean time, Jewish fanatics have afforded to the Romans a pretext for denying the liberty hitherto accorded them. The Roman governor will proceed to persecute in the name of public safety not only such fanatics but all Jews, alleging against them the disturbances fomented by the Christians. Services must cease in the temple, and the image of the Emperor Caligula must be worshiped as that of a god. The son of the high priest takes his life, distraught by the change in Paul, his former bosom friend. The patriarch Gamaliel, shocked by that change, threatens him as an apostate after defending him against accusers Roman and Jewish, and dies despairing, overwhelmed by the fall of Judaism attacked from within by the followers of Jesus and from without by the minions of Rome. Only Peter finds satisfaction in these distresses since to him they afford infallible witness of the speedy second coming of the Christ.

This piece, however rich in philosophy, lacks a love interest, any strong dramatic appeal, and any evidence of the originality that had marked its author's earlier work. Werfel as a Jew is not greatly concerned with Paul's developing a world religion from a Jewish sect. It is Israel rather than Paul that is here the true protagonist.

Werfel is a prophet, supersensitive to evil, feeling it to be an irrational and malignant power with which only patience, self-abnegation, and divine grace can successfully cope. In the preface to his adaptation of *The Trojan Women* of Euripides, he writes: "The world into which mankind is born is mad. Impulse and accident govern every path, and intelligence, that terrible attribute of man, is asked to stand unshaken before the brutal drama of the elements. . . . There is an essential tragedy in the world, a break, an original sin, wherein all participate, and from which the understanding soul suffers most." In similar vein, the priest of his *Schweiger* declares that there is an absolute, unfathomable Evil, transcending the mere callous gratification of the ego at the expense of others, and he adds that: "The darker, the more insensate Evil is, the greater must be the disposition for Grace in man. And precisely because our epoch is so satanic, it has been divinely appointed, and I am happy to be alive in these times." Such an argument to justify evil seems to echo the medieval notion that the sinner is as necessary to the scheme of salvation as the saint.

Expressionism as a revolt against bourgeois society was threatened from the moment when it became clear that this society had not been affected in its foundations or superstructure by the German disaster. If, at the close of the War, the Reich had gone Bolshevist, expressionism would have flourished as the architectural mode of the new dispensation. But the bourgeoisie lost only its imperial capstone. The middle-class arch and its basis stood firm; already the fantastic fabric of expressionism is crumbling.

CHAPTER XXIII

Hungarian and Czech Innovators

Molnár and the Čapeks

THE only Hungarian dramatist whose plays have been widely produced in other lands is Ferenc Molnár, born in Budapest in 1878, the son of a Jewish merchant. His university studies were pursued at home and in Geneva, and he early attracted attention in the field of journalism by writing satirical sketches and short stories, the latter dealing chiefly with children. Characteristic is such a skit as *Horses' Feathers*, in which small boys discuss death with one of their number mortally ill, and speculate about the plumes worn by undertakers' horses. A play, *Józsi*, in the same vein, paints the picture of a spoiled darling of the newly rich. Somewhat earlier appeared *The Attorney at Law*, a preposterous comedy concerning a burglar so soft-hearted as to steal, expressly that his lawyer may have practice in defending him. After two serious novels, *The History of a Derelict* and *The Hungry City*, Molnár gained more than local reputation with his drama *The Devil*. It was produced in France, England, and America, and made readier the enthusiastic reception accorded *Liliom*, its author's masterpiece. *The Guardsman*, *The Wolf*, and *The Swan* achieved popularity, and during the War Molnár wrote *Fashions for Men*, *White Cloud*, and *Carnival*, as well as a series of descriptive and patriotic articles sent from the battlefront. In the mean time and later, he produced such stories as *Eva*, *A Budapest Girl*, *Andor*, and *The Boys of Paul Street*, a lively juvenile.

Although Molnár could have won his spurs in fiction, he

438

was diverted by the larger rewards of the theater. Out of Hungary, he is known as a dramatist only. He is facile, versatile, romantic, unconcerned with social or political problems. Except in *Liliom* he shows little depth. Proof of his easy superficiality may be found in his treatment of an old idea in *The Devil*. Here he follows Goethe afar off, introducing the Prince of Darkness as a polite go-between in evening dress. When a trustful husband leaves his wife to pose for an artist with whom she has earlier been in love, the Devil emerges from a high-backed chair to incite the artist to resume the old romance. That night he piques the lover's jealousy, making it appear that Olga has come to meet the gentleman Devil clad only in a cloak, "like a classic goddess, like a modern Monna Vanna." When the artist demands that she doff the cloak, the lady proves to be fully dressed; but the trick has served its purpose in awakening Karl's passion. Then the Devil prompts Olga to send Karl a love letter. He seems to comply when she bids him destroy it; but when, vacillating, she wishes it back, he returns it unharmed, declaring that he had burned instead his tailor's bill. As she snatches the letter, and with it goes to give herself to the artist, the Devil, following, listens at the door and rubs his hands in triumph.

All that has happened is little enough. A claptrap Mephistopheles forces together a couple, who, without him, might have remained honest. Olga is happily wed, and the artist is already beloved by two other women. One is a devoted model, who laments that she is like a little railway station at which the mighty train stops only a moment in passing. The Devil is pleasantly humorous. In a different connection he observes that, "If women wrote time-tables, they would tell all the hours at which the trains didn't start, and all the places at which you must not stop to get to your destination." Asked if he be a man of the world, he answers, "Of many worlds"; and he insists that, "The real wife is always the other man's wife," and that, "They may fire cannon out of respect, but pistols?—no!—; that's love every time."

An immense gap separates this play from that which followed. *Liliom* is a masterpiece. It employs what was then the new technique of expressionism to touch the heart and to emphasize a significant idea. The rudest exterior may conceal a tender nature. It is characteristic of human perversity to injure those we love. Molnár, who had married the daughter of a journalist, was divorced by her within two years. In his play he would justify himself against his wife's charge that once he had struck their little girl. His hero is far ruder than he, a bully employed as barker and "bouncer" for a Budapest merry-go-round. Liliom, "the lily," fascinates a little servant maid, who becomes his willing victim, though warned against him by the police. She endures his ill-treatment, does the work that he is too lazy to do, and is content that he exults with new pride when she tells him that she is to make him a father. Thereupon, Liliom rebuffs the flashy proprietress of the merry-go round, who has discharged him in jealousy and would now urge his return. But, to a fresh temptation, he is more open. Needing money for the baby that is coming, he succumbs to the suggestion of a tramp that they rob a factory cashier. "But why use a knife?" asks Liliom. "Only if the cashier wants it," retorts the Swallow. "People are so queer that they refuse to give up their money without dying."

Beneath an archway in a railroad embankment, Liliom, waiting for the cashier, loses at cards his share of the prospective booty, and, as he quarrels with the Swallow, is surprised by his intended victim. The Swallow twists away, but Liliom, though he scales the embankment, is cornered by the police, and stabs himself. Carried dying to Julie, he can do no more than beg her, for the sake of their unborn child, to marry the old carpenter who has offered to make her his bride. Only when Liliom has expired does Julie kneel at his side and speak her mind: "Sleep, Liliom, sleep! . . . You bad, quick-tempered, rough, unhappy, wicked—dear boy;—sleep peacefully, Liliom; they can't understand how I feel. . . . You treated me badly—that was wicked of you—; but sleep peacefully, Liliom! . . . I love you."

At this point, the naturalistic drama turns romantic as two solemn personages lead the dead man out into a serio-comic heaven before the celestial police magistrate. Here suicides are being tried, and each is accorded the privilege of returning to earth to do whatever he had left undone. Liliom declines to return, scoffs at the others, and with chest thrown out marches into the flames to be purged for fifteen years, at the end of which time he will be allowed one day to visit his wife and child.

With the last act, the period of probation is over, and Liliom, come to earth for his one day of grace, stands outside the house of Julie and her daughter. As the little girl turns from him in fear when he declares that her father was a bad man, he calls her back to offer her a star that he has stolen on his way down to earth. At her refusal to kiss him, he slaps her. Then, overcome by shame, he is led away by the celestial policemen, while Julie, summoned by the girl's cry, stares after him, startled by his resemblance to the dead man. The child is perplexed, for the blow that the stranger struck sounded loud yet did not hurt. The mother explains the riddle: "It is possible, dear, that some one may beat you and beat you and beat you,—and not hurt you at all." In short, a steadfast, simple heart like that of Julie cannot feel the blows dealt by the perverse and inexpressive love of one like Liliom.

Note the poetic combination here of realism and idealism, the rough humor, the pathos, the rare character portrayal, and the setting forth of a truth universal. How often, Molnár seems to say, do we injure those we care for, our love by some black magic employing the terms of hate! How impossible, then, to judge of rude and vagabond natures merely by their deeds! The quiet and submissive beauty of Julie's soul contrasts with the violence and obstinacy of Liliom's unmoral personality. In technique the supernatural and the natural mingle perplexingly. Heaven appears as the child-like conception of the untutored hero, but evidently it exists, also, as something outside of his view of it. The final scenes cannot be explained as the vision or dream of any one character. Herein the procedure is that of Wedekind in *The Awakening of Spring*.

Molnár, having sought to propitiate his angry wife in *Liliom*, proceeded in *The Guardsman* and *The Wolf* to dilate upon his affair with Irene Varsanyi. It was for Irene that he had written *The Devil*, wherein he may be seen challenging her to leave her prosaic husband. That husband, the manufacturer Szecsi, soon reclaimed her, and Molnár began to speculate in dramatic wise as to whether it was he or Szecsi for whom she really cared. In *The Guardsman*, he tells the story of an actress yearning for a fresh romance after six months of marriage. Her actor husband, suspecting her, announces that he must leave town to perform at a distance, but plots to return in disguise as a guardsman of the Russian embassy. If she refuse to yield to the guardsman, he will be delighted; if she succumb, he will enjoy in the person of another the love she no longer accords him in his own. When she receives him as the guardsman in her ante-room at the opera, he is torn between jealousy and pride in acting well his assumed rôle. Next day, he returns in his own person and extorts from his wife a half-confession. Then, reassuming his guardsman's costume, he thinks to confound her. But she declares that she has known his identity all along. She had continued to flirt in order to fool him. Is this true? The husband is more perplexed than before. He observes her at the piano playing Chopin with that far look in her eyes, and duplicates the first scene of the play as the curtain falls upon the last. A critic friend can only observe that, after all this pother, the precious pair are just where they were to begin with. The last act here should have been enriched by some further turn of the plot. It is all a bit too thin.

In *The Wolf*, acted in English as *The Phantom Rival*, Molnár shows Irene Varsanyi's husband perturbed by the question as to whether a man to whom she had once given her affections may still hold them. Says Molnár, a woman will revert in longing to her first lover, however happy she may be with her husband, and he adds that the safest cure for such longing is to bring her face to face with that lover. A lawyer of Budapest, by his jealousy, provokes in his wife recollections of one who, years before, had sworn to remain true to her through all vicissitudes. When the very Russian whom the wife had idealized turns up, the husband scoffs at the grandiloquent letter in which the fellow had promised to reappear as a soldier, a statesman, a musician, or even a servant, but, under whatever guise, as her devoted slave. The lady, falling asleep, dreams of her Sascha in each of the rôles suggested by his letter. She sees him at a ball as a dashing colonel, then as a diplomat, then as a baritone in *Don Giovanni*, and finally, to her dismay, as a lackey more sullen than humble. In contrast to the romantic figure cut by Sascha in the first three sections of her dream, is the real Sascha,—only a lawyer's clerk, more intent upon what he can get to eat and drink than upon recalling the dear dead past. His excuses for failing to win honors such as he had foretold are prosaic. He has been kept from the army, for example, by flat feet. At the close of the play, the husband is telling his child the Tale of the Wolf that proved only a bugaboo. For husbands half the danger lies, not in reality, but in the perfervid fancy of their romantic wives. Confront these wives with reality if you would banish your phantom rivals.

There is little novelty in the theme of a royal princess beloved by a man of the people, but Molnár, in *The Swan*, was not so romantic as to show the princess sacrificing her future, or the commoner running dire risks to make her his own.

Instead, he laughs at the struggle of a royal mamma to effect a good match for a dutiful daughter. To this end she has invited to her castle a crown prince. But for four days he has proved only distantly polite. As a last resort, the mother bids Alexandra make the prince jealous by paying marked attention to her brothers' tutor. The tutor, exalted by these unusual signs of favor, grows assertive and insults the royal guest. When the prince threatens him, Alexandra, stepping between them, gives the tutor an impulsive kiss by way of protecting him. Apparently the royal match is ruined. But Alexandra's jovial uncle, a priest, saves the day, explaining to the prince's mother that the girl merely pitied the tutor in his defenceless state. To the girl herself, grown suddenly romantic, he shows how foolish would be her proposal to resign her royal pretensions. Not love but bravado and compassion led her to kiss the tutor. As Alexandra, convinced, upbraids the youth, the penitent prince interposes to protect him, just as she had protected him the night before, and, burlesquing her action, kisses and forgives him. "Alexandra!" he exclaims; "last night you made handsome amends for a blunder of mine. I ask you now to stay at my side through life. And when I am at fault, be always as courageous as you were then." They have not contrived a love match, he admits; but they will attain to something more beautiful still, love that comes after marriage, a "love which comes later and endures longer."

The title of the play is explained in a speech by the prince's mother, who bids Alexandra keep in mind the dignity of her position. "Remember that your sainted father used to call you his swan. Think often what it means to be a swan, gliding proudly, majestically, where the moon gleams on the mirror of the water, gliding always in the purple radiance and never coming ashore. For when a swan walks, my daughter, when she waddles up the bank, then she painfully resembles another bird."

There is a pleasing mixture in this play of the idyllic and

the satiric. The tutor's talk of the stars and of his village and
his sister catches the audience, as does the humorous tolerance
of Father Hyacinth, and the matrimonial anxiety of Beatrice
and her fussy sister, Symphorosa. The dialogue throughout
is sparkling, and the exposition is easily achieved by means
of the bantering gossip of Alexandra's young brothers. The
supper scene is especially admirable in its by-play of *double
entendre*, followed by the insult, the withdrawal of Beatrice,
and the succeeding calm as Father Hyacinth counsels the tutor
and the princess. No sooner has the tutor confessed his love
than a fresh storm breaks with the return of the prince, who
denounces the tutor and provokes the osculatory defence of
Alexandra. After this capital scene leading up to the apparent
wrecking of her royal future, it required real art for the dramatist in the last act to continue without a sense of anti-
climax, uniting the spirited little minx with her indulgent prince.

The Swan was more popular than *Fashions for Men*. Yet
the latter develops an interesting notion, namely, that, in the
long run, generous innocence will conquer guile. With Lowell, Molnár holds to the aphorism, "Be noble, and the noble-
ness which lies in other men, sleeping but never dead, shall
rise in majesty to meet thine own." His hero is what the Germans call a "simple fool,"—an innocent, like Parsifal, without
the medieval trappings. He is proprietor of a fashion-shop.
He will hear no evil, speak no evil, see no evil. He treats his
customers and clerks like friends, and permits his chief salesman to walk away with his wife and fifty thousand kronen.
Thus thrown into the hands of a receiver, Peter quits his shop
to serve as manager on the estate of a count. But good nature
makes him unduly indulgent here to the workmen; and his
virtue leads him to protect that of his former assistant, who
has thought to win wealth by going to the count. So far does
Peter interfere in the count's advances to little Paula that
he is presently sent back to his shop in Budapest on the pre-

text that his salesman has returned the borrowed kronen. Though Peter discovers the ruse, he continues his shop-keeping and wins the affection of Paula, ready now to abandon her scheme of seeking advancement by unworthy dependence. Then the rascal who had robbed Peter of wife and money reappears, down and out, complaining that sympathy for the saintly Peter is so general that no one will give him a job. For once, Peter is inclined to neglect an opportunity to be noble. But Oscar, nothing daunted, takes advantage of a rush of business to step behind the counter and resume his former place, and Paula arrives to take her chair as cashier. She will marry Peter when he has secured a separation from his fugitive wife; but she stipulates that Oscar must go. "Take a dozen pair of socks," says the generous Peter. "I have," retorts Oscar, departing. An amusing minor character here is Philip the drudge, who, although he has witnessed the last act of *Lohengrin* sixteen times, has never been able to leave the shop early enough to behold the entrance of the swan.

Having fallen in love with an opera singer, Sari Fedak, Molnár determined that she should become an ornament of the spoken drama, and for her benefit wrote *Carnival*. This sets forth the situation of a beautiful woman married to an elderly tyrant and living upon a remote country estate where she finds her only amusement in riding horses across foaming floods or jumping them over trains whizzing past through a railway cut. Once a season Camilla comes with her husband to Budapest to be besieged by admirers. These she finds stupid except for one poetical idler, who professes to have loved her with a deep devotion. She wonders if it be real. Then chance puts into her hands a means of testing it. She has picked up unobserved a precious stone lost from the royal coronet, and conceals it, not from avarice, but as a symbol of power. Her lover must share her secret. Her husband will release her from bondage only if thus she threaten his honor. When she offers herself and the green diamond to young Nicholas, he proves wary. Why sacrifice comfort and respectability? Is love worth such a price? How much easier to visit her now and then under cover!

In the mean time, Nicholas has been trailed by an hysterical woman who would countercheck Camilla; and Camilla's husband has grown suspicious of his wife's admirer. That wife, having found her lover wanting in courage to share her guilt, tosses the diamond to one side, puts the police on the track of it, and leaves this one festivity of the season, to return home with her terrible husband. The possibilities of the theme are not fully realized. The situation is superior to the drama. The lady herself is no more capable than her lover of a great sacrifice. Like Molnár she seems to have been just toying with an idea. She found it interesting to test Nicholas; but, had he withstood the test, she would have tossed away the diamond and departed with her gruff old husband just the same.

Although Sari Fedak, thanks to Molnár's play, was transformed from opera singer to actress, she held him at arm's length until, after a tour of America, she consented at least to the ceremony of marriage. No sooner was it performed than she dismissed him that each might continue to live in bachelor freedom. Within six months, Molnár was composing a new play, not for the second Madame Molnár, but for still another actress, Lily Darvas, who figured in *Heavenly and Earthly Love* (adapted from his novel *The Derelict Boat*) as inspiring devotion of the celestial variety. Lily Darvas became the heroine and leading lady, also, of *The Red Mill* and *The Glass Slipper*. When the incensed Sari Fedak, in order to win a triumph over Lily, got Melchior Lengyel to write for her *Antonia*, Molnár retorted by divorcing Sari.

The Red Mill is noteworthy for its elaborate spectacle produced at home under the direction of Ladislas Beötly, and in New York by Belasco, who called the play *Mima*. Like *The Miracle*, it requires a veritable rebuilding of the theater and the use of the auditorium as well as the stage. It repeats the theme of *Liliom*, namely, a faith that beneath the roughest appearance every man is good at heart. Devils are meditating the corruption of a saint. They have constructed in hell a machine designed to make men bad; but, since no good man ever reaches hell, to test it is difficult. The devils find their chance when the soul of a good youth, killed in a traffic jam, takes the wrong ferry across space and blunders into hell. The devils jubilantly thrust him into their machine, but faith and love at last lift his soul from the rollers, for, although he has been on the point of murdering his temptress, Mima, he refuses to bring pain to his old mother. Of this spectacle, Molnár has written: "Every human mood enters into the dramatic action, moods humorous, serious, fantastic in the extreme. The forty scenes are strung together in mutual action, and, while this is a play of hell in hell, it nevertheless is a morality play." One feels that Molnár is on much safer ground when out of the infernal regions, dealing with the rude or polished folk of Budapest. He is truly at home in composing such a trifle as *The Putty Club*, with its recollections of youthful school-days, or a gay and witty piece like *The Play's the Thing*, originally entitled *Play in the Castle*.

In the latter piece, a composer, overhearing through a wall impassioned words poured out to his fiancée, would tear up the score of the opera he is writing for her. But his collaborator conceives the idea of setting all to rights in a truly professional way. During that night, he concocts a little drama in which the phrases overheard are employed in a different situation. Then he forces the repentant lady, a prima donna, and the frightened lover, a baritone, to learn and enact their rôles before the composer, who is now relieved to discover that the night before his fiancée had been only rehearsing for this performance.

Slight as is the fable, it is developed with experienced ease. Sandor, the dramatist, who is Molnár himself, controls and enjoys the action. He finds a wicked pleasure in disciplining the baritone, who, rather than be exposed in a scandal, submits to every indignity. The baritone must copy out the whole text in a day, and learn a part choked with unpronounceable names. He must fall to caressing a "soft, round, fragrant" peach, instead of the lady's shoulder of the night before. His protests, as he steps now and then from the improvised stage, and the comments upon him by the spectators, are as comic as are the maneuvers of the characters at the presentation of the play-within-the-play of *A Midsummer Night's Dream.* The lady, it may be presumed, has learned a lesson; and the composer who had thought to leap from the castle rock accepts Sandor's explanation and retains both her and his illusions.

There is so little doing here that talk and humorous characterization must take the place of action. A comic social secretary and a charming old butler, worthy cousin of Shaw's William the waiter, are amusing additions. The reflections on life that fall from the lips of Sandor are excellent, and the author reflects upon his play as it progresses somewhat after the manner of Pirandello in his *Six Characters* or of Echegaray in his *Great Galeoto.*

As the first act opens, Sandor, musing upon the difficulty of presenting *dramatis personæ*, asks why they may not introduce themselves. As if in answer to his question, he and the others walk to the footlights and explain their identity. Later, Sandor meditates on how a second act should conclude. When his dull collaborator proposes a sentimental ending, it is given, and the curtain starts to descend. At Sandor's objection it lifts. Then the composer substitutes a melodramatic ending, and again the curtain dips. But Sandor cries it up, and himself finishes the scene in sensible fashion. The third act proceeds without further intervention on the part of the characters, affording the audience just the right touch of surprise.

Sometimes with Molnár the gay holiday mood is darkened by cynicism, as in his warning for wives entitled *A Matter of*

Husbands. Here, in a one-act play, when a guileless bride begs the return of her husband, the actress who has stolen him declares that he has sought only to provoke his wife's love through jealousy. That lock of hair which the visitor has found in his possession he must have secured from a hairdresser. Actresses above all are accommodating in consenting to aid husbands in reviving the interest of their wives. "No matter what you may find in his pockets, letters, handkerchiefs, my photograph: no matter what flowers he sends or notes he writes—don't be taken in a second time." As the wife hurries out delighted, the actress calls into her bedroom, saying: "All right, Alfred; you can come in now. She has gone."

Similar cynicism marks *Olympia*, a suave comedy turned into English by Sidney Howard. Here the scene is an Austrian watering place just before the War. Although a princess is charmed by a captain of the hussars, yet, when he presumes to speak to her of honorable love, she disdains him as a man of lower station. Accordingly, he plots revenge, letting it be understood by a colonel of the constabulary that he is in truth an international sharper. The news is passed on to the princess and her foolish mamma, and both are shocked lest they be involved in the scandal of having known one notorious. So ready are they to clear their skirts that the princess will agree to the supposed sharper's proposal that she yield to him for once as the price for his disappearance. Marriage beneath you is one thing; a mere intrigue is another. In any case, we suspect that the lady is not averse to paying in secret, nor is the hussar's bargain entered into purely for revenge.

In *One, Two, Three*, cynicism gives way to good-natured satire as Molnár burlesques the rapidity with which business to-day is transacted, a trick learned, he implies, from the Americans. When a European banker, imbued with the true American spirit, discovers that his house-guest, the daughter of his most important client from the ·States, has just mar-

ried a taxi-driver, he foresees his own downfall as a result of
the wrath of her parents who are due to visit him at any
moment. He cannot break the union, as the pair love each
other; he can only work to elevate the bridegroom to a station
that the American magnate will approve. But to do this he
must act as quickly as the magician who cries, "One, two,
three!" Quite improbably, therefore, the banker proceeds to
turn the chauffeur into a noble and a man of affairs by buying for him the title of an impoverished count and by securing for him a prominent position in the business world through
forcing out the man who has held it. There would be nothing
funny in such an enterprise were it not for the speed with
which it is accomplished, a speed that leaves the characters
and the spectators breathless. A splendid nuptial feast has
been arranged by the banker to astonish the town and, as the
curtain falls, the guests forsake it only in order to meet at
the station and bring back in triumph the American parents.
An inferior dramatist would have thought that he must show
the parents' arrival and their transport of pride at their
daughter's fine match; but Molnár gains a point by leaving
all that to the imagination.

Less successful than *Liliom*, but repeating the mood of
that masterpiece, is *The Glass Slipper*, a study of low life
brightened by the character of its heroine. Irma is the drudge
of a Budapest boarding-house. Endowed with a Barriesque
imagination, she loves in all humility the landlady's star
boarder, a middle-aged cabinet-maker. But the landlady is
determined to marry him. After the wedding, the bride carries
on with a younger lover, and when the groom remains deaf
to the warnings of little Irma, the latter in despair is ready
to throw herself into an evil profession. Caught in a raid upon
the establishment of a Hungarian Mrs. Warren, she is haled
to court. In spite of the circumstances of her arrest, the pure
soul of Irma at last impresses its charm upon the cabinet-
maker. Already he is disillusioned by his abortive marriage

with the vicious landlady. Irma and he will go away together, a strange Cinderella and a stranger prince.

In itself, the story is ugly and improbable. But the heroine redeems it, especially as she is shown in the first act. In setting the table for the cabinet-maker, she kisses the glass from which he will drink and the napkin with which he will wipe his dear mouth. In arranging his room, she sniffs with intoxication his smoking jacket, and caresses his pillow. He is her "beautiful angry aviator" whom she pictures dropping down from the clouds. What if he orders her about in harsh monosyllables? Is he not her Prince Charming? In the later acts, this whimsical, sad, gay child has grown piteous and lovelorn. At last she would drown body and soul in sin as a way of committing suicide. When she is rescued by her adored old cabinet-maker, we wonder if she will find the heaven on earth that she expects. If so, it will be only because, in her dreams, she may wear a glass slipper, and not because of any virtue in the fellow himself. The landlady is admirably drawn,—a wicked shrew secretly yearning to be decent. Once she had loved the cabinet-maker for a week when he was ill; now, after living with him for years, she has betrayed him for a younger man. And yet she knows that the latter is only professing to love her in order to escape paying his board-bill. Here is what Noel Coward has called "heartbreaking beauty" built up from a sordid theme and squalid surroundings. The tenderness and understanding of what is fine in human nature atones in part for the over-emphasized brutality.

On the whole, Molnár is a gifted, facile, highly imaginative writer, apt at transforming his personal experience into effective works of art. Except in *Liliom*, he has shown no special depth of thought, although there, in his conception of a love that is no less love for being cruel and inarticulate, he demonstrates his originality. In that play, also, he has carried forward the new tendency to mingle the naturalistic with the fantastic, just as, in *The Glass Slipper*, he combines crass realism with dreamy idealism, and reveals primitive natures as somehow brightening their clay with a spark of divinity.

The recent Czech drama is known to the world chiefly through a few plays of the brothers Čapek, sons of a village physician of northern Bohemia. Karel, born in 1890, has composed verse, fiction, and critical essays. Josef, born in 1887, has devoted himself principally to painting. Together they have collaborated in such plays as *The Life of Insects* and *Adam the Creator*. Working alone, Karel has achieved his highest success on the stage with *R. U. R.* and *The Makropoulos Affair*. His theatrical career began at twenty-one with *The Robber*, an allegorical presentation of selfish youth arrayed against age. This play, mingling melodrama and farce, was not completed and produced until after the War. Two collections of stories, *The Crucifixion* and *Tales of Distress*, have been followed by fantastic novels in the fashion of the earlier fiction of Wells. *Krakatit* is concerned with the discovery of a new explosive, and *The Absolute at Large* with the manipulation of the internal energy of the atom. In both cases, it is merely the social effect of these physical phenomena that interests the author.

With the appearance of *R. U. R.*, Karel Čapek became a celebrity. Here was a pleasing fantasy to develop a notion implicit in Mrs. Shelley's *Frankenstein*, the peril of man's creating a monster destined eventually to destroy him. To this fable Čapek gives a social application. Rossum's Universal Robots are mechanical workers, the invention of a professor and his son. The professor has sought to prove that God may be dispensed with, and the son has sought to provide a cheap substitute for human labor. With the transfer to Robots of all toil, "everybody will be free from worry and liberated from the degradation of labor," says the manager of the factory that produces Robots. "Everybody will live only to perfect himself." Such is our foolish dream of humanity as inherently noble when relieved from the necessity of toil,—a dream indulged in by Shaw in his *Intelligent Woman's Guide* and by most Utopian philosophers.

As for the Robots, they exemplify industrial efficiency. They are like men but divested of all frills, of all passion or soul or desire to be happy. They feel an interest in nothing; they eat little, do everything, and do it with mechanical precision. But, when a humanitarian lady comes to the island where they are made, and insists that the Robots be given souls, trouble begins. The physiologist of the plant proceeds to provide them with pain-nerves as an automatic protection against damaging themselves. Thereupon, they develop defiance—Robot's cramp—and some are sent to the stamping-mill to be scrapped. Within a decade, however, they have been manufactured so plentifully that man seems only a survival. Governments demand more and still more that armies may be supplied. The manager, foreseeing their revolt, proposes to postpone it by making national Robots of different colors and languages, who, as strangers, will hate and fight one another. But, before he can act, a union of Robots at Havre issues to Robots throughout the world a declaration of war upon man.

Vivid is the scene at the close of the second act when the revolt has spread from Europe to the island, and the last human beings huddle within the factory behind charged wires. As the Robots seize the dynamos and the electric lamps go out, the invaders burst in. "We made their faces too much alike," laments one of the men in dying, " a hundred thousand faces all alike, facing this way. . . . It was a crime to make soldiers of them." To this, the last human survivor adds: "It was a crime to make Robots at all. For our own selfish ends, for profit, for progress, we have destroyed mankind."

So Čapek preaches the folly of regarding work as a curse, exemption from toil as a blessing, and industrial efficiency as an end in itself. If we consider our workingmen as mere machines and strive to make them so, they will some day wreak revenge upon those who thus abuse them. What constitutes civilization is not its machinery, but rather its human values. How absurd the manager's dream—"to turn the whole of mankind into an aristocracy of the world, an aristocracy nourished by milliards of mechanical slaves, but unrestricted, free, consummated in man and perhaps more than man!" The plan has failed, and Alquist, who alone remains alive, suggests why. "There was something good in service and something great in humility; there was a kind of virtue in toil and weariness."

Alquist is retained by the conquering Robots to seek for the lost secret of their manufacture, since without it they will be extinct within a single short generation. But, although his experiments prove vain, two super Robots—a male and a female—have at last evolved souls. They can laugh and weep and love, and each is ready to sacrifice life for the other. So Alquist blesses them, saying: "Go, Adam! Go, Eve! The world is yours!" They will begin afresh, and the race that they breed will perhaps make less of a muddle of life than have men.

This imaginative satire upon the Gradgrind philosophy of industry is Karel Čapek's masterpiece. Even to those who care little for its doctrine, the play remains theatrically effective. Less striking is *The Makropoulos Case*, in which the author deals with problems involved in extending the span of life from seventy to three hundred years, the very theme more profoundly treated by Shaw in *Back to Methuselah*. Whereas Shaw accompanies his fantasy with a scholarly introduction in defence of the Lamarckian theory of evolution, and makes his play illustrate that theory, Čapek is content to proceed as a simple romancer.

The daughter of a Greek physician of the sixteenth century has acquired a fresh lease of life through the action of a drug discovered by her father. His formula, confided to a parchment, has enabled her to live several careers, in each of which she has been a singer and has broken many hearts. Now she must be revivified by use of the formula. But it chances to be in possession of a baron unaware of its value. Emilia's grandson is suing this baron for title to a great estate, a case fought out in the courts by their forbears during more than a century. Emilia, therefore, in approaching the baron, has a double motive. She would make him surrender both the estate and the parchment. Eventually, she agrees to give him herself, and her action leads his son to commit suicide out of jealousy. "But he killed himself for you! Don't you hear?" cries the baron. In reply, she shrugs her shoulders and says, "So many kill themselves." She has lived so long that every aspect of love for her has become a very bore. How can one old as she meet passion with passion? Even the baron, in embracing her, finds no more joy than he would in clasping a corpse.

The complications of the plot are meant only to excite curiosity and lead the spectator by degrees to perceive that Emilia Marty is also Elsa Mueller and Ekaterina Myskin and Eugenia Montez and Ellean MacGregor and Elena Makropoulos, born in 1585. The drama is written, not for the sake of such mystification, but rather to induce consideration of what continued life would mean. Its implications are brought out in the final scene, when the enemies of the heroine, having deprived her of the parchment containing the precious formula, debate the desirability of using it.

A lawyer's clerk advises making the secret public since every one has the same right to life, and since no one, in a bare sixty years, can accomplish much. But, with three hundred years at his disposal, man can spend fifty as child and pupil, fifty in a general broadening of knowledge, a hundred in creative work, and a hundred more in teaching and reviewing with wisdom his achievements. "How valuable human life would be if it lasted for three hundred years!" exclaims the clerk. "There would be no wars. There would be no fear, no selfishness. Every one would be wise and dignified. Give people full human life!"

The lawyer objects that our social system is founded on a life-term comparatively brief, and foresees that no one would be willing to make a contract or stay married for three hundred years. A senile lover of the heroine admits that three hundred years added to his present age might be too much, but advocates the possibility of purchasing leases of life in ten-year periods. A chambermaid thinks that three such life-periods would suffice her. "No longer than that?" she is asked. "No, what would I do then?" The Nietzschean baron would bestow longevity only upon the strong and talented. For him only the best are important; little folk should die. "We should have a dynasty of the strong. . . . Privileged long life, that's the despotism of the select. That's the rule of reason." Another holds that the Makropoulos secret should be confided only to direct descendants of that family, namely, himself and his heirs; but the heroine disillusions the various contenders for the use of long life. She has found that after three centuries nothing matters, experience merely repeats itself. She condemns these youthful beings with their curiosity and faith. Once she too had faith and was happy. Now she knows too much. She has wished to live on only to escape death. So well have her hearers learned her lesson that when she offers each in turn the parchment with its formula for longevity, each declines it, and the girl who takes it does so only to burn it. As she throws the ashes from a window, Emilia, saved from living longer, cries, "The end of immortality!"

With regard to this play, Karel Čapek has explained that the idea came to him before he had written *R. U. R.* and after he had heard of the theories of Professor Micnik to the effect that old age is caused by an auto-intoxicating organism that may be destroyed. Having composed his piece, he was shown a synopsis of Shaw's *Back to Methuselah.* "Mr. Shaw," says he, "believes that it is possible for an ideal community to live several hundred years in a sort of paradise. I think that such a condition is neither ideal nor desirable. Mr. Shaw's play is a classic example of optimism, and my own a hopeless example of pessimism." Presumably, Čapek did not know of Swift's use of the idea in the third part of *Gulliver's Travels*, nor of Tennyson's poem *Tithonus*, which stresses the misery entailed upon the immortal alienated from the fate of humanity as a whole. For Swift, the Struldbrugs illustrate how hideously monotonous life prolonged would become if accompanied by a progressive aging of our faculties. For Shaw, in spite of Čapek's statement, death provides a welcome escape from life, and Adam explains his satisfaction on learning of it. "I am not strong enough," he cries, "to bear eternity!"

The artist, Joseph Čapek, collaborated with his brother Karel in staging effectively the latter's plays, as well as in writing *Adam the Creator* and *The Life of Insects*. The second piece, translated into English as *The World We Live In*, was inspired by the works of the French scientist Jules Fabre. It succeeded through its spectacle as much as through its satire upon human traits and institutions under animal disguise.

A tramp, whose nap has been disturbed by an entomologist pursuing butterflies in a wood, sleeps again and dreams of these insects and of beetles, ants, and moths, his dream being enacted upon the stage. With him we see the butterflies as bright philanderers enjoying the vanity of gossip, love, and poetry. Theirs is the cult of beauty, involving selfishness and jealous spite. They shock the moral tramp, who remarks that man is superior to insects because he cares for family life and knows how to work. But the family life of the insects, now unfolded by beetles, crickets, and flies, shows them to be envious and avaricious. A beetle pair are intent upon rolling up a huge ball of dirt, their lovely capital. While they are gone in search of a hole in which to hide it, a strange beetle rolls it all away. Meantime a cricket, who has brought his bride to live in the house of another snapped up by a bird, finds her slain by a vicious Ichnumon fly. "If you want to keep alive, you've got to fight your way," says the fly. "A strong personality is bound to assert itself." She has fed the female cricket to her larva; but a Parasite, who has apparently sympathized with her, creeps into the nest of the fly and devours her hoard of crickets and her larva, too. Thereupon, the tramp affirms that the trouble with these insects is their failure to work together, by contrast with men who coöperate and give their lives for noble causes.

As if to controvert the tramp's assertion, the industrial state of the ants is next presented, burden-bearers circling round and round as a blind ant counts monotonously, "One, two, three, four!" When an efficiency expert discovers that the work may be speeded up by dropping one number in counting, the toilers quicken their pace to meet competition. What matter if the individual collapse with his load? In the Labor State, designed to promote progress and peace, every movement must be calculated to the nth part of a second. "Work!" cry the engineers; "We are a nation of peace. Peace means work. Work means strength. Strength means war." Then appears an inventor whose enlarged head is ready to burst with a new machine, an expert crusher of lives. Great is science, for it serves the State. There will be war. "Why war?" asks the tramp; and he is told: "Because we have a new war machine. Because we still need a bit of the world. . . . from the birch tree to the pine tree, the road between two blades of grass. . . . a question of prestige and trade and rights of nationality."

When a messenger reports that the Black ants, trespassing upon the frontier of the Yellows, are insulted because asked to withdraw, the Blacks mobilize, and announce that they are fighting for life, liberty, and the interests of civilization. In the name of justice, no quarter must be given to the enemy. A commander, surveying the battle at safe distance, reports that his fifth regiment is destroyed according to plan, and that the sixth must take its place to be destroyed in turn. Let

it be said in the reports, however, that the fifth heroically repelled all attacks and was relieved by the sixth. To a philanthropist collecting funds for the wounded, the tramp hands
his last button torn off as a contribution, but presently he is
disgusted by the vainglorious prayers to their respective gods
of the leaders of both factions.

Finally, in the forest, the tramp observes joyous moths
fluttering for a moment only to fall dead. Here is a Chrysalis,
which has been demanding to be born since the beginning of
the play. Now she rends her husk, leaps forth a full-fledged
moth, and, bidding earth and heaven give ear, offers to proclaim a mystery. But no sooner has she promised to reveal the
world's meaning than she, too, falls dying. The tramp can
only remark: "Poor little mites! all done for! Life's a rapture to them, and death's a rapture." Then he, who in turn
has glimpsed the meaning of the universe and would profit
by it, is overtaken by death. "One's born, and another dies.
No great matter!" remarks a wood-cutter stumbling on the
body.

Although *The Life of Insects* lacks the brilliancy of Rostand's *Chantecler*, it is poetic in conception, powerful in
satire, and altogether significant. How contemptible is the Lil-
liputian world of insects to the man who perceives its pre-
sumptuous folly! How close is the analogy between the insect
world and the world of men! In witnessing this play, you do
not resent the satire as being over-didactic, for the representation is intrinsically interesting. Nevertheless, you cannot
fail to catch the thrusts at greed, lust, family selfishness,
mechanized industry, militarism, worship of the State, and the
futile arrogance of the individual.

It may be assumed that of the two brothers, Josef is less
gifted dramatically in so far as he is the more inclined to deal
with abstractions. Thus, his *Land of Many Names* is a parable
written and produced in expressionistic style to satirize the
selfishness and folly of mankind. A philosopher, a poet, a cap-

italist, and street sweepers, all yearning for the betterment
of the world, rejoice to hear that through a convulsion of
nature a new continent has just arisen in the sea. Forthwith
their city celebrates the event by processions and flags, a
platitudinous speech from the mayor, and an ode from the
poet; and the people of various classes prepare to find in the
Land of Many Names the sort of fulfillment each desires.
Lovers wish to occupy it in solitude; paupers regard it as the
Land of Justice; a stripling will explore it with gun and knife
as a Land of Adventure; a poet will seek it as a Land of
Brotherhood where all are equal; a philosopher thinks of it
as the New Zion: Socialists as the Land of Karl Marx or
Leninia; and a capitalist, Dollarson, will advertise its invest-
ment possibilities to be exploited by his Travel Bureau and
Amalgamated Undertakings. But a rival capitalist, Vandergold, bringing news that other nations will war to gain possession of the new continent, advises instant mobilization, and
to those unable to fight he offers employment in his munition
factories. The war that ensues is suggested by cinema pictures
of shadowy soldiers on the march beneath a star that glows
blood-red, while the troops sing and a woman in black bewails
the death of her son. Then the wounded return to describe
their sufferings, and the lover appears as a ghost to rebuke
his sweetheart for having been false to him while he was fighting at the front. A herald proclaims a victory, although the
Land of the New Life, as Dollarson now calls it, is dubbed
by the soldiers the Land of Dead Armies. Dollarson, pleased
that his rival Vandergold has been torn to pieces by those he
oppressed at home, declares that God Himself will be found
in the Land of the New Life, only first an army of engineers
and officials must be sent there to set up law and authority.
But, at that moment, airplanes come roaring in bringing sad
tidings. The New Continent has subsided as suddenly as it
arose, blighting the hopes of the exploiters, and leaving the
officials and investors to clamor for their salaries and their

shares, while the disillusioned philosopher, on being asked where he is hastening, cries bitterly, "Into the Land of Shadows!"

Such allegory, although inferior to that of *The Life of Insects*, is intelligible enough, but in *Adam the Creator*, written by Josef and Karel Čapek together, it becomes unduly confused, and the surface story ceases to possess any dramatic significance. The play consists of a mixture of long monologues and short staccato dialogue uttered by puppets representing the individual, the mass, poverty, and types of the feminine. At first, the parable is brightened by satirical burlesque, like that in Shaw's *Back to Methuselah* and in Erskine's treatment of Adam, Eve, and Lilith. Ere long, it loses humor and becomes so difficult to follow that only an act of the will can force one through it to the Epilogue. Adam, dissatisfied with the world, resolves to destroy it with his Cannon of Negation. But he is punished for his presumption by God in being forced to try his own hand at creating. Perplexed at first, he exclaims, "Let there be fleas!" and by the same sort of fiat produces successively a superwoman Eve, a warlike superman Miles, a coquette Lilith, and a being made in his own image. This is Alter Ego, who demands and is accorded as wife a changeable new woman. The flirtations and bickerings of the ladies, which promise amusement, are soon superseded by the contentions of Adam, the individualist, and Alter Ego, the collectivist. The latter's wife and Miles the warrior foment their quarrels, which are shared in by the people created by each. In the mean time, from a remnant of clay not used for making the rest of the world, is born Oddly-Come-Short, with his six ragged children, symbolizing poverty or perhaps the poor peasantry. Neither Adam nor Alter Ego will accept responsibility for Oddly's existence, and now those they have actually made, the individualists produced by Adam and the masses produced by Alter Ego, turn upon their creators, since reason has taught them to doubt creation as a myth. In any case, the job has been poorly done, for men are inferior in power to animals or machines. At this juncture, when Adam and Alter Ego have agreed in disgust to wipe out the world they have formed, they are forcibly deterred by Oddly-Come-Short, who, wretched though he be, still clings to life and wields an iron saucepan as his weapon. He even good-naturedly offers to support the two theorists along with his brood. In the Epilogue a priest bids the people pay reverence to their two creators at a temple, but, when that precious pair seek to enter it, they are driven off as loiterers by a conscientious watchman. Adam, who would have dug up his buried Cannon of Negation in order to annihilate the world of his making, finds that it has been fashioned into a bell which in no uncertain tones proclaims the law throughout the land. When God asks him if he will now leave things as they are, he assents, and God retorts, "So will I."

Evidently, the hidden meaning alone can give value to this piece, which in its surface story lacks every vestige of dramatic character or power. But that hidden meaning scarcely warrants the effort necessary to disengage it. Apparently, although the world is bad, we should accept it as it stands. How foolish of man to suppose that he can improve it either in the mass or individually. To destroy by negation is equally foolish. In spite of poverty, the common man wishes to stay alive, and upon him, in the long run, will depend such theorists as Adam and Alter Ego. Even these traditional creators will be overset by reason, and reason itself will tend only to destroy. Some such pessimistic meaning may be detected here. Certainly, reliance upon the masses is shown to be as vain as reliance upon the individual; both the romantic city of Adam's building and the mass-produced and mass-directed city of Alter Ego, resembling Manhattan, go up in flames.

When the drama becomes a thing thus abstract, it ceases to exert any emotional appeal. It may speak to the intellect but not to the feelings. But here what is said to the intellect is of doubtful import and could more effectively be conveyed in narrative satire. *Gulliver's Travels* delivers its message in a story intrinsically entertaining. Here the story is devoid of interest, and the message is by no means clear. If the brothers Čapek would continue to succeed in the theater, they must revert to the methods employed in *The Life of Insects* and *R. U. R.*, pieces that combine story and doctrine with clarity and dramatic effect.

CHAPTER XXIV

The Peninsular Tradition

Echegaray, Pérez Galdós, Guimerá

IN THE Spanish drama of the later nineteenth century the chief figure is José Echegaray. Born in Madrid in 1832, he won honors as a student in a school of engineering, where presently he became professor of mathematics. He published studies in this field and in physics, joined in the founding of a periodical, wrote and spoke in favor of free trade, and for seven years served as minister of education and finance. Having tried his hand surreptitiously at the writing of plays, he achieved a memorable success in 1874 with *The Check Book*, followed immediately by *The Avenger's Wife*. Thereafter, with the facility of invention for which his compatriots are famous, he poured forth a stream of tragedies and comedies, revealing unusual talent in developing theatrical situations and expounding certain ideas.

Echegaray was old-fashioned in some respects, and new-fashioned in others. His stress upon situation, his focusing of interest upon crises in the life of a single character, his fondness for the concept of honor, remind us that he descends from Lope and Calderón. Yet, for him, as for most moderns, honor is subjective and not merely the matter of a code; fate, too, is no longer arbitrary, but rather the result of heredity and environment. He delights to portray high-strung characters, intense hysterical souls, driven by passion or idea. He shows the individual struggling with himself or against social institutions. He loves the moral, the heroic, the perfervid. He is a natural rhetorician, less poetic than theatric.

At his worst, Echegaray sinks to the level of extravagant melodrama; at his best, he rises to the heights with such original creations as *Folly or Saintliness* and *The Great Galeoto*. The influence of Ibsen became apparent in his work during the 'nineties. He returned to politics in 1905, a year after receiving the Nobel prize in literature, along with the Provençal poet Mistral. He died in 1916, everywhere recognized as the dean of Spanish dramatists.

Much that Echegaray has written is sensational and artificial, journeyman's work by a man brought up in the school of Calderón, but lacking his master's romantic finesse. Thus, *The Steps to a Throne* is an historical melodrama which might have come from the pen of Sardou. Teodora is beloved by the tyrant of Pisa, but prefers Roger, who, attempting the tyrant's life, is seized and imprisoned in the famous Tower of Hunger. Later released, and discovering that he is not, as he supposed, of noble blood, he feels that Teodora can no longer care for him, and he even accuses her of having yielded to the tyrant. So angered is the lady at this insult that, accepting the tyrant on the spot, she asks as a boon that her former lover be tortured. After marriage she gloats over reports of the punishment inflicted upon him, but suffers a sudden revulsion of feeling when he bursts in upon her, having been stoned by the populace. Thereupon, in remorse, she slays the tyrant, and sinks into the arms of the man she had never ceased to love.

In the more domestic scenes of *Evil Inheritance*, there is similar violence when Blanca learns that her father had brought disgrace and death to the father of her lover in a quarrel over her mother. How can she marry young Victor? Her brother would duel with Victor, who withdraws at her instance. But when his uncle, taking his place, falls mortally wounded, then Victor, ashamed of having caused that uncle's death, slays Blanca's hot-head brother, a second Romeo killing a second Tybalt. The lovers might now appear to be definitely separated, but their passion is too intense. They embrace and depart to live happy ever after, since love will conquer honor.

In a more subtle play—*The Woman Distraught*—conscience triumphs over love, for Teresina refuses at last to marry the man she adores, after she has drowned, in self-defense, her wicked husband as if by accident. Believing that her father's reputation has been saved only by the action of one who has dueled with her lover, she marries the duelist but soon repents her choice, for he proves to be a wretch who makes her life miserable and attempts to convince the world that she is mentally unbalanced. Once, when she seeks to escape him by flight, her former lover sends her back. Again, that lover duels with her husband and accords him grace only on condition that he desist from his evil schemes against the lady. Teresina, aware that her lord is about to separate her from their son and confine her in an asylum, contrives to overturn a boat and drown him just as, in Calderón's *Secret Vengeance for Secret Injury*, a husband drowned his guilty wife as if by accident. But she cannot join her lover now. "I belong to my crime," she declares, "to my guilt, my remorse. I am going far away, perhaps forever; but I confide to you my son." Surely, the barrier to marriage is less here than it was in *Evil Inheritance*, where love vaults over it lightly; yet these characters are better analyzed, and beneath their rhetoric lies a foundation of psychology.

More purely theatrical is *The Man in Black*, the study of a modern Tartuffe, the middle-aged guardian of a girl who loves an impetuous young sculptor. The Man in Black warns her that the sculptor cares only for her beautiful exterior, not for her soul. But such advice is no more than a maneuver to enable him to keep Eleanor for himself. When piously he visits the sick, he takes her with him among those stricken by smallpox, hoping that, by contracting the disease, she may lose her beauty. By the second act, his diabolical plan has succeeded, and Eleanor retains only a semblance of her former self. When the sculptor, admitted to her darkened room, gradually discovers the contrast between what she now is and what she was as set forth in his bust of her, he rages at the Man in Black who has plotted this dreadful thing, and drives him forth. But Arnold continues to exercise over the girl a baneful influence, urging her now to enter a convent rather than consent to marry the disciple of beauty, one certain to turn from her to some fairer woman. Torn between the two men, Eleanor at length agrees to submit to the advice of the malign Arnold; whereupon Leonardo, threatening never to see her again, rushes from the room, blinds himself with his sculptor's chisel, and staggers back pleading his need of Eleanor to guide and comfort him henceforth. "I am yours to all eternity!" she cries, responding to that need. At the cost of his eyes he has won her. The loss of beauty in Eleanor will no longer offend the worshipper of beauty; he will no longer be tempted by beauty. Only their souls will unite.

The play is half melodrama, half mathematical demonstration of the truth of a formula. But it affords occasion for high-sounding speeches and some tense theatrical scenes. D'Annunzio would have adorned it with gorgeous poetry; Echegaray has decked it out in tinsel rhetoric. Here is the same intensity and overstrain in the characters shown more convincingly in *The Great Galeoto*, in *Folly or Saintliness*, and in *The Son of Don Juan*. The defect of Echegaray's psychology lies in the fact that the motives of his people so often fail to justify their deeds. It is interesting to note that the author has here introduced an idea which Shaw renders humorously in *Candida*, the notion that the way to win a woman's love is to show her your weakness, your need of her. Women will yield to those who require their protection.

The influence of Ibsen appears in *The Son of Don Juan*, which takes over with little modification the situation of *Ghosts* and suggests that to-day the libertine hero of the Spanish legend of Don Juan Tenorio would find his punishment in the operation of a natural law rather than in the supernatural vengeance of an animated statue. The protagonist of Echegaray, in spite of his wicked past, looks to a worthy future for his son. That son shall inherit, he declares, only his own finer aspirations. The boy's mother has sent him to France to escape his father's evil influence. But, like his prototype, Oswald Alving, he is cursed by an insidious disease, the result of his father's excesses. He would shine as a poet, and he would marry the daughter of his father's friend. But Fate interposes in the shape of the law of heredity. Lazarus has returned to Spain distraught in mind. Learning from a physician, consulted as though concerning some hypothetical case, that madness or idiocy awaits him, he resolves to save the girl. So he thrusts her from him at the betrothal ceremony. But later, feeling the need of her, he would marry her whether or no, until her father steps in to prevent the match. As Lazarus in frenzy clings to Carmen, he suffers a collapse, and, like Oswald, asks with pathetic insistence for the sun. Already his mind has given way.

There is here no reproof, as with Ibsen, of the error of the mother in having married such a husband, nor of a conception of marriage which would hold together those unfit for union. Echegaray's only interest consists in condemning by implication the wicked parent whose libertinism, through the law of heredity, has cursed his heir. At the very spot where that heir now loses his mind and begs for the sun, the father had made the same maudlin demand years before on awakening after an orgy. In order to clinch the moral, the dramatist makes his heroine, too, a victim of the same law, her weak lungs the result of her father's early dissipation.

Among the poorer plays of Echegaray are *Mariana* and *The Madman Divine*. The latter, indeed, is strained and overdrawn in situation, impossible in psychology, and written in the flowery language of a penny-dreadful. It shows how low one of talent may stoop in striving for theatrical effect. A girl married at seventeen to a man of seventy and left a widow, is encompassed by scheming relatives who would capture her fortune. Incidentally, they would prevent her marriage to a crazy suitor. This suitor, we are told, is a lawyer, a scholar, a philosopher, a philanthropist, a man, in short, of great intellect, heart, and will. But not a shred of evidence of any such qualities are we shown. Instead, Gabriel talks the veriest nonsense, and "horrifies, allures, and frightens" the little widow. He scolds her for being so unkind as to pluck the garden flowers, yet wishes that he were God to punish evil, God's worst defect being excess of mercy. Having declared himself to be a prophet inspired, Gabriel departs for California, promising to return as a millionaire to marry his Fuensanta within a year. Because he is more perfect than she, he loves her, for only the perfect can really love the imperfect, he explains; God would die for sinful man but not for another god.

By the second act, Gabriel is indeed returning from California immensely wealthy, and Fuensanta has come to love him "with infinite passion" merely on reading his eloquent letters. But now Gabriel conducts himself, on the eve of his wedding, like a lunatic confirmed, announcing to his bride that he is God, felling her uncle who would interpose to protect her, and finally, in order to drive back her relatives, setting fire to the house and clasping the lady in his arms amid the flames which he has kindled. The curtain falls as he cries out that the hour has come for punishment and purification, and that he is no longer Gabriel but a "madman divine." One difficulty here among many lies in the fact that Gabriel is set forth as half crazy from the first. Accordingly, we must sympathize with the scheming relatives, who, for their own ends, would save Fuensanta from him. They may be avaricious, but surely they are right to protect the heiress from marrying such a husband. Had Gabriel been shown as maligned by the relatives, who were wrongly imputing to him an insanity to which they finally drove him, the play might have meant something.

The motives in *Mariana* may be warped and artificial, but the characters at least bear some semblance to human beings, although their actions are determined by an outworn and external ideal of honor. The heroine, on discovering that the man she loves is the son of one who had injured her mother, dismisses him and marries a general twice her age because she knows that with his rigorous military concept of honor he will slay her should she ever be tempted to yield to Daniel. This is precisely what happens. No sooner is the wedding ceremony performed than the impetuous lover climbs to his lady's room where she has begged to be left alone. He extorts from her a confession of her love and of the reason of his jilting, and urges her to flee with him before it is too late. But honor means more to Mariana than love. Feeling herself on the point of yielding, she summons in her avenging bridegroom with the cry, "Your honor calls you!" She admits that she has always loved Daniel. "If you let me go, I shall run away!" she exclaims. "It is now your turn. What will you do?" To this Pablo replies, "What you desired of me!" and fires upon her as she clings to his rival. That rival, after caressing her prostrate form, goes forth to duel with Pablo, with a premonition that he will now join his lady in death.

The situations are theatrically effective, but only a Spanish audience would be likely to sympathize with motives and conduct so perverse. Daniel is in no way at fault for the sin of his father. It may be natural for Mariana to resent for a little the fact that she should have fallen in love with the son of that betrayer of her mother. Yet none save a fanatical devotee of the code of honor would have married a man unloved merely because he was reputed to be a sure avenger of any wrong. Pablo has already slain his first wife for disloyalty, and boasts that, like Calderón's hero, he is "the physician of his own honor." He accepts unmoved Mariana's statement that she cares nothing for him, and will wed him merely as an implacable judge. He shoots her down without a qualm, and, having already dueled once with Daniel, will fight him to the finish. However dramatic the climax and the scene when Mariana first ascertains her lover's identity, the play is unduly drawn out by reason of its indirect exposition. An archeologist and a youth enamored of the scholar's wife are introduced for comic relief, but the comedy passages are only faintly humorous and clog the main action.

Best among the plays of Echegaray are two in which honor is treated more subjectively. These are *Folly or Saintliness* and *The Great Galeoto*. In the former, a sense of honor so delicate that it runs counter to every worldly consideration determines the fate of Don Lorenzo. He is shocked to discover that his old nurse is really his mother, that his supposed mother, in order to secure an inheritance, had passed him off in infancy as her child, that therefore his property and his name are not his own. Accordingly, he declines to sanction the marriage of his daughter to the son of a duchess, although to refuse his consent will wreck that daughter's happiness and perhaps her reason. The duchess, who had consented to the match only to please her son, will still permit it provided that Lorenzo keep silent as to his discovery. He may even confer his property upon the true heirs. But so acute is his sense of honor that he insists upon proclaiming to the world his disgrace. "I must tell the truth, the whole truth, in a loud voice, happen what will," he declares. "I want no half-hearted view of honesty."

When his wife shows him that he will imperil his mother, the nurse, by making her liable to arrest for conspiracy, his continued scruples take on the air of frenzy. Even the dying nurse, who had merely wished to hear him address her as "mother" just once, thinks him mad. To save him, she burns the only evidence of the truth regarding his parentage. When he opens her letter and finds there a blank sheet of paper which she had substituted for the original, the suspicions of his family and of an alienist are confirmed. Harassed at being watched, unable to distinguish right from wrong, Lorenzo acts the madman and turns upon his wife and daughter. When the latter would save him from the keepers who are about to carry him to an asylum, he asks, "What can you do, child, when God Himself has not seen fit to save me?"

In this harsh world, too nice a conscience will make a saint seem a lunatic. Folly or saintliness? Which is the trait of Lorenzo? How slight is the barrier between sanity and insanity! The passion of the honor-loving Lorenzo is admirably set forth. His dilemma, however quixotic, is poignantly perplexing. Indeed, lest the audience fail to note the relationship of this modern idealist to the Knight of La Mancha, Echegaray has shown Lorenzo at the opening of the play reading from Cervantes' novel and extolling the nobility of that famous madman.

Before passing to a discussion of Echegaray's masterpiece, a word may be said of *Always Ridiculous*, which deals with injured honor and presents an appealing hero. The blithe-hearted Eugenio has married the daughter of the man who has reared him, and has supposed her child to be his own. But Teresa had earlier loved his friend Juan, a poetic and romantic painter tied to a bad wife, and little Maria is really the daughter of Juan. To Eugenio the truth is revealed only after seven years. He has fought a duel with a scandalmonger and finds his wife writing a note which runs: "Think of me, think of Maria, think of us both: for me and for your child!" This appeal he interprets as being intended for himself, a plea that he refrain from the duel. As a matter of fact it was written by Teresa to be sent to Juan, who has an appointment to duel with the same adversary. In a fine scene Eugenio discovers the true state of affairs when little Maria, sent to the desk for paper on which to draw, chances to bring back the envelope already addressed by Teresa to Juan. What shall the husband do? For the sake of his wife and his friend he will efface himself. Sealing the letter within its envelope, he hands it to Juan, and then, withdrawing, he shoots himself as if by accident. In dying, he assures his wife of his unwavering love. He may have played a ridiculous rôle in the eyes of the world, but he affirms his continued loyalty to his foster father and to his friend. "I have done my duty to you all— I have loved you all—I have wronged no one—. God help me, lest I look at those two in the pride of my righteousness! Eternal justice—; now it rests with you!"

Here no one is greatly at fault. Teresa would have married Juan in the first place except for the fact that he already had a wife. Having been compromised by Juan, she must quickly find a titular father for her unborn child. She is therefore the readier to yield to her own father's proposal that she marry Eugenio, with whom she has been reared. Juan has broken off his guilty relations with her, and he even agrees never to see her again, though the death of his wife has freed him. Eugenio is a kindly soul, generous to a fault, and never taken seriously by his friends. He may be "always ridiculous," but he is also the most sympathetic of cuckolds.

Best of all the plays of Echegaray and known the world around is *The Great Galeoto*, which suggests, as does Maeterlinck's *Monna Vanna*, that doubt of one's honor may in due course make real the situation which it had merely conjectured. The husband of a young wife has reared in his household a poet. When the gossips of the family begin to talk about the intimacy between the wife and the poet, Don Julian thinks little of it; but, on hearing Teodora defamed in public, he challenges the traducer to a duel. Then, mortally wounded, he is borne to the apartment to which the poet, at the first breath of scandal, has removed. But it chances that Teodora has hastened thither in order to dissuade Ernesto from fighting the same traducer. Her presence in the rooms of her supposed lover, though innocent in itself, seems to confirm the truth of the ugly report. Ernesto rushes forth to lay low in a second duel the antagonist of Julian, and returns successful to protest his innocence. But it is futile for Ernesto and Teodora to explain. Assailed afresh by the dying man's brother, and cursed by Julian with his final breath, they are forced together, whether or no. "What is the use of loyalty?" asks Ernesto. "Why be virtuous when no one will credit our virtue?" Then, turning to Teodora, he cries: "Let no one touch this woman. She is mine! The world has so desired it, and that decision I accept."

In his Prologue, Echegaray has shown Ernesto casting about for the theme of a new play, and catching his suggestion from reading in the *Inferno* the story of Paolo and Francesca, whose perusal of the medieval tale of Launcelot and Guinevere united by Sir Gallehaut—in Italian Galeotto, and in Spanish Galeoto—incited them to yield to love. The go-between, or Galeoto, in his own play shall be the scandal-talking crowd. Admirable in idea, the drama is also theatrically effective, the scene in Ernesto's rooms forecasting that in the rooms of Lord Darlington in Oscar Wilde's *Lady Windermere's Fan*. The characterization is more consistent than usual with Echegaray, and Don Julian, although an intense emotionalist and the victim of a suspicion confirmed by circumstantial evidence, has only a touch of the madness of Don Lorenzo or Don Gabriel. Here beneath the local trappings and the cape and sword dueling appears truth universal, the truth that busy tongues will tend to induce what they profess to condemn.

A great novelist who became also a fair playwright was Benito Pérez Galdós, born in the Canary Islands in 1845. He studied law in Madrid, practiced journalism, and in his middle twenties published his first fiction, *The Fountain of Gold*. Then, influenced by Pereda, he rose to fame as the creator of a monumental group of novels in four series, entitled *National Episodes*, constituting a latter-day epic of the

Spanish peoples, based upon careful study of historical sources. With amazing industry he furnished forty volumes, beginning with *Trafalgar* in 1879. In addition, he wrote romances like *Marianela*, and novels of domestic or religious life like *Doña Perfecta*, *Gloria*, and *The Family of León Roch*. He was liberal and even anti-clerical in spirit. Some of his fictions he adapted for the stage, notably *Reality*, *Doña Perfecta*, and *The Grandfather*. In the 'nineties, he had begun to produce original plays—*The Mad Woman of the House*, *The Beast*, *Gerona*, *The Duchess of San Quintín*, *The Condemned*, and *Will*. In 1901, he stirred all Spain by his attack upon the Church made through *Electra*. His later plays include *Soul and Life*, *Mariucha*, *Barbara*, *Love and Science*, *Celia in the Slums*, *Sor Simona*, *The Rogue Salomón*, and *Santa Juana de Castilla*.

In these works, Galdós leans upon novelistic rather than dramatic technique. He forgets, in large part, the older Spanish stage, and is less interested in what is theatrical than in characterization and ideas. He is a moralist rather than a rhetorician. His qualities may be indicated by a brief resumé of such early plays as *Will*, *The Condemned*, and *The Duchess of San Quintín*, and of such later successes as *Electra* and *The Grandfather*.

An example of middle-class comedy is *Will*, in which the heroine by sheer force of character saves her family from ruin. Her father has suffered his business to decline. Her mother thinks only of the world to come. Her sister dreams only of finery and a piano. Her brother is absorbed in his studies; and even her lover, an artist, despises actual life and the responsibilities of marriage. But, when he loses his fortune, and is tempted to yield to an inherited drive toward suicide, Isadora bucks him up; and she encourages all her family, too, setting them to work, and bringing order and cheerfulness into a discontented household.

In the same vein, Pérez Galdós depicts, in *The Duchess of*

San Quintín, a young widow, who has been impoverished by her profligate husband, and is now offered the opportunity of recuperating financially by marriage with a wealthy widower of middle age. But she prefers to marry for love a youth without family or means. This well-worn plot is somewhat varied by emphasizing the differences in social station of the rivals. It is the dramatist's belief, expressed here and elsewhere, that Spain is to be saved by the new aristocracy of brains and labor. Rosario's dead husband has belonged to the weak old aristocracy of blood. The middle-aged Don César, who sues for her hand, is the son of a sturdy peasant made rich by his thrift. But Don César has not inherited his father's virtues. He is a philanderer, avaricious and ambitious, unable to withstand the prosperity thrust upon him. It is the poetical, romantic, and socialistic Victor, reputed to be his son, who wooes the lady. In spite of the fact that Victor proves to be the natural child of another, and not the heir of Don César, she loves him. He has avowed devotion to the truth at any cost, and it is she who discloses to him the truth that robs him of a father and a fortune. But they will go away to America to seek a career of honest toil. It is this simple life that Pérez Galdós would substitute for the life of useless leisure led by impecunious aristocrats. Most interesting among his characters is the independent Don José, nearly ninety, yet still staunch in mind and body. These self-made men rather than their curmudgeon sons or the corrupt descendants of the titled are the hope of the nation. Although the action here be unduly coincidental and artificial, and the speeches be excessive in length, the play is significant as expressing in winning fashion sound democratic doctrine.

The beginnings of anti-clerical sentiment in Pérez Galdós may be seen in his melodramatic piece *The Condemned.* Here José León, the untamed doer of evil, aspires to the love of Salomé; he is stirred by contact with her virtuous soul. But her conventionally pious uncle, to defend her from committing a mistake, sends her to a convent. When the lover pursues, he is shocked to behold sculptured as a warning upon the gateway the story of a rascal turned penitent on seeing the nun he had sought to abduct transformed into a skeleton. Thereupon, José, confessing a murder he has committed, surrenders to justice, and Salomé, in meditating on his crimes, loses her reason. The implication seems to be that, had José's love for Salomé been allowed to take its natural course without clerical interposition, it would have redeemed him, and the lady might have kept her wits.

It will be observed that Pérez Galdós is something of a propagandist. His *Soul and Life* suggests that the soul can be effective only as the active life becomes its mate, this life being represented by Juan Pablo, and the soul by the Duchess Laura. In *Sor Simona* love is exalted as the basis of peace, and the brotherhood of man is proclaimed. In *Celia in the Slums*, Pepete represents Nietzschean individualism in industry opposed by his noble and socialistic wife Victoria. In *Doña Perfecta* the author's antagonism to what he deems to be clerical prejudice runs to the extreme. It is somewhat sobered, although still obvious, in *Electra*.

This play, however modernistic in its ideas, is sufficiently old-fashioned in technique. It sets forth the folly of forcing upon a free natural spirit the life of the cloister. This it does by describing the trials endured by a girl in love with a scientist, but opposed by her pious friends. When falsely they insinuate that she and her lover are children of the same parents, she is driven to distraction, takes refuge in the convent where her mother had died, and turns for counsel to the spirit of that mother, who had seemed supernaturally to guide her childhood. Electra's prayers are answered. "What you were told," declares the shade of the dead mother, "was an invention, suggested by affection for you, to draw you to our company and the quiet of this holy house. . . . If bridal love and the joys of home invite you, surrender to their sweet

allurements, and do not seek here a sanctity to which you
may not attain. For God is everywhere. . . . Go look for Him
in His world by paths better than those I trod."

So a rational plea for freedom and happiness amid the laity
is corroborated by a ghost. In Spain this message gains force
when communicated by such means. To the Northern mind,
perhaps, in spite of the precedent of warnings from the ghost
to Hamlet, and of similar devices employed by the German
expressionists, the message loses potency when supernaturally
delivered. At least the ghost, we feel, might have been a subjective delusion externalized. As for the human characters,
they are well contrasted. Electra, the pure daughter of an
unmarried mother, long ago repentant and forgiven of heaven,
falls in love with the nephew of her kindly guardians. But the
conservatives who would constrain her to a religious life oppose her match with a scientist, Don Maximo. For three acts
nature struggles against religious convention, and in the
fourth is about to triumph when the obscurantist Don Salvador resorts to a lie, believing that his end justifies this means.
In the fifth act the audience is shown the falsity of Don Salvador's assertion and heavenly proof that Electra is justified
in leaving the convent and throwing in her lot even with a
scientist.

Lovers of symbol have discerned in this play an allegory,
according to which Spain is represented by Electra, for possession of whom the clerical party, or Don Salvador, is contending. Intellectual illumination, or Don Maximo, aided by
commerce, or Don Leonardo Questa, and by the aristocracy,
or the Marquis of Ronda, would save Spain from cloistered
retrogression. Even the dead past would advise for her a life
in the world. Such a message lies implicit in the play. It is
small wonder that ecclesiastical circles objected to its performance, when even in Paris the piece was regarded as a radical manifesto. In justice to Pérez Galdós, it should be noted,
however, that he here makes no attack upon true religion.

Electra had no real vocation for the cloister. If Don Salvador and Doña Evarista are bigots, they are shown to be sincere. The priest is honest with himself when he declares: "My mission in the world is to see that Electra be not lost, and lost she shall not be. Such is the Divine Will of which mine is but the reflection." Surely, Pérez Galdós keeps his own faith in God and in the supernatural.

A more intellectual rebel against convention is the heroine of *Mariucha*, daughter of aristocrats in financial and moral decline. Her mother has turned from earthly concerns to dreams of heaven. Her father, a marquis, has become little better than a spendthrift beggar. Her brother hopes to get on in the world by marrying a rich widow of doubtful antecedents. But Mariucha is self-dependent and attracted to León, a noble youth, saved from punishment for a misdemeanor, repentant and restored to self-respect by hard work. With him she opens a shop, ignoring the foolish scorn of her family that she should stoop so low. Thus, Pérez Galdós again insists upon the need of regeneration for the Spanish aristocrat through toil. Mariucha, like Rosario and Isadora, is something of a new woman—new at least for Spain.

Although in a tragedy like *Barbara* Pérez Galdós seeks to emulate the Greeks by depicting a wife who slays her husband for the sake of a lover, and although he here sets an interesting historical background in Sicily of 1815, such a play is exceptional rather than usual in his theater. More characteristic of his thought and manner is *The Grandfather*. This fine drama emphasizes its author's belief in the duality of the spiritual and material worlds. Honor and love do not depend upon physical inheritance. The girl born of a guilty passion, unsanctified legally, proves to be far nobler than the girl of legitimate birth, who, conventionally, should be her superior. The proud Don Rodrigo has been distressed to learn that one of his supposed granddaughters is not after all the child of his dead son. To discover which is the legitimate grandchild and to erase the blot on the family 'scutcheon by discarding the other, becomes the old man's obsession. Half distraught, he is threatened with confinement in an asylum, with the approval of the selfish Leonora. To his aid comes the unselfish Dorotea, who, if spiritual qualities are derived by inheritance, should be his legitimate granddaughter. Instead, Dorotea turns out to have been the child of dishonor. What shall he do? In his dilemma he puts the case to a wise priest, who has afforded him refuge. And the priest shows him that, although physical qualities may descend from father to child, qualities of soul exist independent of blood inheritance. True honor stands apart from lineage; it is a thing inscrutably subjective. We do not inherit virtue and vice. Dorotea, born out of wedlock, is more honorable than Leonora born within it. So Count Rodrigo perceives that his anxiety to maintain the traditional family honor has been foolish, and with the gentle Dorotea he finds a blessing. "That which is within is that which endures!" he exclaims. "My child, God has brought you to me; love is eternal truth!"

There is just the shadow of Lear upon Count Rodrigo, deprived of his property, misused by his daughter-in-law and his granddaughter, losing his sight, and strained to the verge of madness by ill-treatment and by his doubts as to his son's true heir. A companion figure is the girls' tutor, old Don Pio, deceived by his wife, but a simple-minded idealist. When Count Rodrigo asks, "What do you think of honor, I mean family honor, purity of race, pride of name?" Don Pio replies, "If honor is not virtue, love of one's neighbor, wishing no evil, not even to our enemies,—I don't know what it is." Both Don Pio and the count will find sanctuary with the gentle Dorotea, who has defied her mother in order to become the true child of the count's heart, even though unrelated to him. A love child, she has become the child of his love.

The Catalan drama has been cultivated by a numerous group little known to the world in general. Founded in the 'sixties by Francisco de Sales Vidal and Eduardo Vidal, it was developed by Federico Soler, a watchmaker, who, under the pseudonym of Serafí Pitarra, composed with remarkable fecundity in many genres, but achieved his principal success in the comedy of manners. To the older generation of Catalan dramatists belong Manuel Angelón, Narciso Capmany, José Feliu y Codina, Pedro Antonio Torres, and the accomplished historian of Catalonia and the Troubadours, Victor Balaguer. Later dramatists of the province include Ignacio Iglesias, Adrián Gual, Santiago Rusiñol, and Angel Guimerá. At first, the Catalan drama was given in various Barcelona playhouses, but later it came to be focused in special theaters, the Romea, the Novetats, and the Principal, and it developed its own actors and journalistic critics to reinforce the movement.

Only Angel Guimerá attracted attention outside of the Peninsula. Though born in the Canary Islands in 1847, he came of Catalan stock and spent his life in Barcelona. His earliest ventures were made in the realm of lyric poetry, and it was not until he was thirty-two that he captured the stage with *Gala Placidia*, first of a long line of dramas. Critics have grouped these in four chronological periods. The earliest consists of historical tragedies of love in the romantic epical style influenced by Guimerá's reading of Shakespeare and Hugo. Here belong *Judith de Welp*, *The Son of the King*, *Sea and Heaven*, *King and Monk*, and a religious chronicle in verse, *Jesus of Nazareth*. Typical is *The Dead Soul*, describing a mad monarch's recovery of his reason through the devoted ministrations of his queen, who must defend herself and the state from the intrigues of a wicked bastard. The second group consists of realistic plays of contemporary life dealing with the loves and hates of fishermen, peasants, or folk of the middle class. Here belong such favorites as *Don Powder*, *The Daughter of the Sea*, *Marta of the Lowlands* (*Terra Baixa*), *Aurora*, and *María Rosa*. The third group consists of Guimerá's attempts to follow afar off the northern playwrights—Ibsen,

Björnson, Strindberg, Hauptmann, and Sudermann—resulting for the most part in failure. The best of such pieces are *The Sinner*, *Water Which Flows*, and *La Miralta*, but the Southern playwright proves to be less competent as psychologist than as poet. The fourth group consists of dramas written between 1902 and 1917 which revert to his earliest manner, as witness *The Path of the Sun* and *Andrónica*.

The play last named may be first considered as illustrative of the grandiose manner assumed by Guimerá at his début and reassumed in his final period. It offers a picturesque panorama of imagined history in the style of Sardou. At the close of the Middle Ages the people of Anatolia have risen against their monarch led by Andrónica, a nun who has left her cloister to undertake what she regards as a holy mission. But, on beholding King Nicéforo, she feels drawn to him rather than repelled; and he, in turn, is fired by love of her. In spite of her resolve to prove a champion of the oppressed, she would now save the king from the wrath of his subjects. Back of the revolt against him stand the nobles and an abbot. They are jealous of the power of Andrónica, who is ready to forsake her vows in order to marry the monarch. But the abbot, inspired by an envious favorite of the court, reports to Andrónica that the king intends to do no more than make her his mistress. When she would withdraw to her convent, the people follow to acclaim her, but she dies at the hands of the court favorite. Written in Catalan verse, this romantic and pseudo-historical drama gained currency throughout Spain in the Castilian version of Luis López Ballesteros.

As an example of Guimerá's drama composed under the spell of Northern playwrights may be mentioned *The Sinner*, its heroine a singer and dancer who has won a place in Paris after being secretly beloved by her foster brother at home. Ramón, who had never told her of his passion, had married after her departure the sweet and practical Antonia with whom he lives long in tranquillity. But one day Daniela returns to her village, wearied of the great world, sick in mind and body. On learning that from the first Ramón had cared for her, she upbraids him bitterly. "If I had known fourteen years ago that you loved me!" she exclaims, "how different would have been my destiny! This house and these children would have been mine." But it is not too late. She may still lead Ramón away and seek to repair her failing health and retrieve her lost happiness. Yet the flight of the pair is prevented by a wise little schoolmistress, who had given up her own lover to another woman in order that the latter's reputation might be saved by marriage. Having learned the lesson of renunciation, Monsa can teach it effectively to others. So she touches the heart of Ramón through his little daughter, and dissuades him from leaving his family. As for Daniela, she loses her Bohemian courage and dies repentant. Such an essay in psychology and morality derives from the Scandinavians and the Germans rather than from the author's own countrymen.

More distinguished are his pictures of modern life localized in the province he knows so well. Thus, *Aurora* presents as heroine a factory worker of noble heart who falls in love with a young scientist. He runs the danger of being captured as husband by a designing woman, already attached to another, yet scheming to marry him for the sake of an inheritance. With her selfishness is contrasted the self-abnegation of the girl of the people. *María Rosa* introduces a heroine higher in the social scale whose husband has died in a hospital after his conviction on circumstantial evidence of a crime. But the crime and the evidence have been deftly arranged by the lady's unscrupulous lover who has sought thus to make María Rosa his own. Knowing nothing of the perfidy of Ramón, she is drawn to him yet fears him. When in their first moments together after marriage she learns from his lips that he is indeed responsible for the death of his predecessor, she yields to a frenzy of anger and kills him. This story was later developed to better purpose in *The Road of Evil*, a novel by Grazia Deledda. But Guimerá's play, with its passional crises, pleased even those it shocked.

A more authentic analysis of passion and character makes of *Marta of the Lowlands* its author's masterpiece. This peasant tragedy, called *Terra Baixa* in the original, and *The Wolf* in its first English production, is far and away the best of Catalan dramas. Marta is a wandering beggar girl who has become the mistress of a landed proprietor. When he would marry her off to a mountain goat-herd, in order to take a wealthy wife and regain the favor of an uncle who has disinherited him, Marta objects, for she loves the unworthy Sebastian and would brave imminent scandal in order to remain true to him. But Sebastian, foreseeing even easier access to Marta in the future, forces her to go through the wedding ceremony with the goat-herd. At first she loathes Manelich as a mere stalking-horse; then, being touched by his downright devotion, she refuses to continue her intimacy with Sebastian. Finally, Manelich, learning of her shame through the taunts of others, fights and slays her seducer, and bears her off to the mountains. Here a contrast is drawn between the natural life of the uplands and life grown corrupt in the lowlands, as earlier a contrast had been drawn between the instinctive conscience of Marta emancipated by a new and noble love from her thralldom to the evil Sebastian, and his conscienceless assertion of his rights over her based on wealth and position. Tense are the scenes which lead up to the climax when the goat-herd in describing his victorious battle with a wolf, threatens Sebastian by innuendo, and when Marta, suffering remorse, seeks to draw down upon herself the vengeance of her husband, and he, goaded to fury, wounds her, and then, abashed at what he has done, breathes out his grief and his love. It was with justice that the citizens of Barcelona in May, 1909, united in a public demonstration to hail Guimerá as their ambassador to the world of letters. He and Pérez Galdós and Echegaray best represent the modern Spanish drama as it developed before the advent of Benavente and of the Quintero brothers and Martínez Sierra.

CHAPTER XXV

Spanish Sentimentalists

The Álvarez Quinteros and Martínez Sierra

GENIAL and delightful as writers of comedy are the Quintero brothers, born at Utrera between Seville and Cadiz, Serafín in 1871, and Joaquín two years later. Their boyhood was passed in the capital of Andalusia, where, in their teens, they saw performed their first farce, *Fencing and Love*. Encouraged by its success, the young men went to Madrid, worked in and for the theater, and, after various experiments, won popular approval by another farce, with incidental music, entitled *The Good Spirits*. Thereafter, they produced with apparent ease many delightful airy plays which exhibit life as they have observed it with piquant local color and fine good humor. They are most at home in revealing the manners of the middle or the lower classes and in depicting character. There is nothing profound or unduly subtle about their work. They create the illusion of a world darkened only enough to throw into relief its high lights. For nicely woven plots, they care little. They are content to take the simplest situations, to develop these in one or two acts, and to send their audiences home smiling and confirmed in the belief that a tender heart is the best of human possessions. Even in the three-act form, they remain essentially anecdotal.

The plays of the Álvarez Quinteros bear some resemblance to those of Barrie. Sentiment colors all. The mood of optimism is saddened only by wistful regret. Many of their sketches for the stage remind one also of the short pieces of Lady Gregory. Here are *sainetes* like *The Mad Muse* and *The Happy Nature*, recommending laughter as a cure for every evil. Here are vignettes of humble life like *The Apple of his Eye* and *By Their Words Ye Shall Know Them*. In the last, for example, a stupid shoemaker has won the heart of a vain girl by exclaiming whenever he passes her, "Dumb and blind!" Thereby he implies that it is her beauty which renders him thus mute and inexpressive. But when a neighbor proves to be far more genial and eloquent than the girl had thought him, she sends the poor shoemaker about his business, exclaiming: "Is that all you can say, you clumsy old shoemaker? Yes, dumb and blind! If I have eyes, let me tell you, I don't use them looking at you." In *The Apple of his Eye*, we witness the shrewd bargaining of a donkey-seller who accepts with tears one-tenth of the price he had asked for "the apple of his eye," and then drinks jubilantly over the sale of the beast with a rascal who has negotiated it.

Somewhat more developed is *A Sunny Morning*, in which revives the romance of the past when an elderly couple, once lovers, chance to meet upon a park bench. Failing at first to recognize each other, they begin by quarreling. Then each, perceiving the other's identity, resolves to conceal his own, for time has brought such alterations that the dream of the past is now fairer than reality. Here what counts is the brightness of the dialogue. Doña Laura chides Don Gonzalo for frightening away her birds; and he retorts, alleging his right to sit upon her bench since this is a public park. Then each invents a story to account for his disappearance from the life of the other. When the curtain falls, we know that they will meet on the morrow, and perhaps forget to conceal their identities for the sake of a dear illusion.

Similarly romantic is *The Flower of Life*, translated into English as *The Fountain of Youth*. The daughter of a duke has been worshiped afar by the madcap son of an innkeeper. Cellini is half-rogue, half-poet. Feigning blindness to win Aurea's sympathy, he tells her how as a child at a festival he had kissed the hem of her garment and had yearned to become her hero. Again we see him after fifteen years masquerading as a dashing gallant and threatening to duel with Aurea's dissolute husband in order to punish an insult offered her. She has come to meet him to implore that he will not fight her lord. Although he agrees for love of her to disappear, he blusters when she is gone, declaring that such a promise cannot bind a man of honor. But the duel never comes off. He is only too glad to withdraw; and thirty years later, in the third act, he reappears as a street beggar entertaining Aurea's little grandson by his music. Her husband has long been dead, and she believes that she has prayed his soul into Heaven. "If life be but a dream," she tells Cellini, "our lives have been more dream-like than most." He assures her that each has been the poetry of the other's life,—"The fragrance of the rose that blooms in every heart. Sometimes it is a living flower which, when we gather it, perfumes the corner where we dwell. Sometimes it is only a nodding flower of the imagination, which blossoms just beyond our reach, and, at our approach, eludes us and fades away." Theirs has been a love of the imagination, denied earthly fruition; but they have been happy, and again on the morrow they will meet to stir once more the dead leaves of the past.

Sentiment dominates in the more developed play—*The Happiness of Others*—which bespeaks sympathy for a young physician inspired by the yearning to help his neighbors. He will found an asylum for children, believing that the world can be made better only by shaping through kindness the rising generation. A young woman of wealth enlists in the cause and excites the gratitude and love of the hero; but he is opposed by his former classmate, the cynical José, who has dropped the practice of medicine for employments more profitable, and who defames the reformer. When the reformer saves from death the daughter of the defamer, the latter is stung to remorse, and the play ends agreeably with the marriage of

Doctor Gonzalo and his Gracia. What might have been a story too obvious is relieved by the sparkle of satire.

A typical study of character is afforded by *The Centenarian*, which depicts a grand old man of the provinces who is about to celebrate his hundredth birthday. Life to him has been a long race, made up of successive efforts to attain one goal after another. When he was seventy-six, his neighbors laughed to see him building, not a tomb, but a new house, yet he has enjoyed it for quarter of a century while those who jested at him are dead. He has dreamed of reaching a hundred and of gathering about his knees all his descendants. Now, as he celebrates that event, he enjoys a new dream. "Well, then, hear my dream; I have had sons; I have had grandsons; I have had great-grandsons; and now the notion seizes me to have great-great-grandsons." To that end, Papa Juan will marry off his favorite great-granddaughter to her cousin, his jolly, free-thinking grandson, who has returned from far wanderings to attend the birthday feast. With patriarchal authority, Papa Juan stills the dissension threatened by the resentment of his good and prosperous descendants at the intrusion of the dissolute and poor, and concludes the feast by blessing the happy pair.

Here, the protagonist and the minor characters are picturesquely given. Among them are Papa Juan's elderly daughter, an easy-going soul by contrast with her sour and formal husband, each confident that the other's health is in decline, and a widowed daughter-in-law of the patriarch, so morbidly sensitive as to suppose others of the family to be insulting her at every turn. When one humble relative, a farmer, hesitates to appear among the more elegant folk at the feast, Papa Juan reassures him, declaring that the same sun warms them all.

An example of extravagant comedy is *The Women's Town*, its scene a village in which the women far outnumber the men. No wonder the priest declares that, "Here there is nothing in constant motion except the church bells and the women's tongues." When to his house comes young Adolfo, the ladies spread the rumor that the youth is paying marked attentions to Juanita, and to Juanita they declare that he is madly in love with her. It is the business of Beatrice and Benedict all over. The ladies spy upon the pair and, to bring them together surely, even insinuate that Adolfo has slandered Juanita. Again the pair must meet to explain. Eventually, Adolfo surrenders to the inevitable and is loaned the chief gossip's balcony as a scene for his future lovemaking, and Juanita breaks into verse, aptly comparing man to a vessel under sail, and woman to the wind which propels him where she will. Slight and charming is this piece in two acts, with each detail of the town sketched in delightfully, and the busybody ladies drawn to the life. Chief of them all is Concha Puerto, the invincible matchmaker, "a handsome, meddling, and officious lady who knows everything about everybody."

The protagonist of *Fortunato* is something better than a rogue and something less than a hero. He doesn't mind begging, but, although tempted to steal coins from the cup of a dozing blind man, he relents and puts them back. Then he applies for a job with a woman of character, who proves to be a revolver expert desirous of engaging an assistant to pose as a living target. With shots she will outline his body as he stands against a board. Amaranta boasts that she comes of a noble race ready to die for art. Her dear papa, crossing Niagara on a tight-rope, has fallen into the cataract. Her brother Hannibal has been eaten by his six black panthers; and a younger brother Aristides has perished while fasting in a crystal urn. She will be as fearless as the rest—at the expense of Fortunato.

The rascal who here victimizes an architect from whom Fortunato seeks assistance, finds a counterpart in Felipe, the anti-hero of *The Lady from Alfaqueque* (*La Consulesa*). He practices an easy ruse upon the hospitable by pretending to seek refuge from danger in any likely house where he may feign illness and win sympathetic attention and the leisure to write poetry. He will allay suspicion by presenting his patrons with gifts for which they will receive the bills after he has left. His hostess, on one occasion, the Lady from Alfaqueque, is particularly susceptible, being delighted to dispense charity to anyone hailing from that village. Laughed at by her practical husband, she is first cousin to Galsworthy's sentimentally beneficent Pigeon, an indiscriminate doer of good. Yet she frowns on learning that Felipe has compromised two of the girls she has taken into the house, as well as made love to another girl across the courtyard. He defends himself as a poet, explaining that he has merely taught the ladies what love is, filling their barren lives with dreams, bringing them happiness, however fleeting. He has even persuaded the fair Blanca to marry him after breaking her betrothal to a boor. As for his deceit in gaining entrance to the house, that is justified by the poetry he has composed in praise of Alfaqueque.

More serious than these pleasing trifles in its study of Andalusian life is *La Zagala*, which sets forth the troubles of a widower allured by the dark beauty of a woman come to his household to assist at the marriage of his daughter. The bride and her sister resent his infidelity to the memory of their mother; and an old servant departs rather than see her master degrade himself by paying suit to one of humble station. The conflict between the widower, who is a poet hitherto happy with his garden and his dreams, and his harsh daughters, ends in their forsaking him and driving off "la zagala." Oh, the pity of it! sigh the authors. Why should love be obliged to observe any distinctions of age or station?

Best known of all the plays by the Quinteros is *Malvaloca*, a delicate plea for indulgence toward one guilty of a slip from virtue. In an Andalusian village the cracked convent bell is to be remolded by two brothers. To one, Malvaloca has formerly succumbed, but she has repented. For two years she has not even seen Salvador; then, hearing that he has been injured in his foundry, she comes to inquire after him at the convent where he is convalescent. "I am still his friend," she tells his brother Leonardo. "I have been a tiny bit more; but that is all a thing of the past now." Against him she treasures no resentment; she regards her misfortune sensibly, although because of it she has been abused by her family. She recognizes her folly, admitting, "Sometimes I think there is nothing but heart in my head." Her necklace and money she gives to the nuns for the poor, reflecting that, "Real love is nothing more than sympathy, a sympathy so great that you don't know how to live without the person who gives it to you."

Leonardo, although aware of his brother's former relations with Malvaloca, loves both him and her, and yearns to see the girl forgiven and respected as she deserves. She, caring for him more and more, thinks of leaving him forever, since she perceives that the world will not forget and that her presence may disturb the peace of Salvador and his sister. When the brothers talk of their plan of refashioning the convent bell, Malvaloca bursts into tears, exclaiming, "If I were only made of bronze, like the bell!"

Later, when the bell has been recast, and is ready to peal forth its new brave music, Salvador, in turn, resolves to slip away, lest his presence disturb the felicity of his brother and Malvaloca. They have watched, all of them, the religious procession pass, and Leonardo has kept Malvaloca from following it, barefoot, as a penitent. While they listen to the peal of the recast bell, he tells her that it speaks now to his heart with fresh meaning. "I will also recast your life," he says, "by the warmth of my kisses, by the fire of this wild love of mine, which is as great even as your misfortune." To his entreaty that Malvaloca take up her life with him, she yields, and the bell breaks forth into "a lively, happy song, vibrant with the note of victory, proclaiming to the fields and villages the life that is reborn." So the play closes. Malvaloca may remember Salvador, but she will be faithful to Leonardo. In place of the harsh code of honor so often emphasized in earlier Spanish literature, we find here a tender sympathy that is broadly human, the same indulgence that marks such American plays as *Anna Christie* and *They Knew What They Wanted.*

The Spanish critic, Manuel Bueno, declares of the Quinteros that all Spanish ladies over forty like to regard themselves as mothers to the pair, and that all young folk look upon them as boon comrades. In a given case, everybody thinks that he or she would have said or done just what the characters of these dramatists say and do. Hence they feel themselves to be collaborating with the Quinteros, and are edified without being preached to, and amused without being made to puzzle their heads over problems. Certainly, the Quinteros deserve the recognition they have received. Their work may be sentimental and pretty rather than great, but it satisfies a need of the heart and exhibits the new tendency to make the drama pictorial rather than theatrical.

Equally charming are the plays of another sentimentalist, Gregorio Martínez Sierra. Born at Madrid in 1881, he published at seventeen a prose poem, *The Song of Labor*, with an introduction by Benavente. Similar pieces followed, and short stories, later collected in two volumes,—*Melancholy April* and *The Devil Laughs*. A third collection, called *Evening Sun*, and a novel, *The Humble Truth*, appeared in 1904. Another novel, entitled *Peace*, was later dramatized as *Madrigal*.

In the mean time, Martínez Sierra had made friends with a group of young writers influenced by the modernist movement, due to the reaction following the Spanish-American War. He was inspired by Maeterlinck and by the Fantastic Theater of Benavente to issue in his Dream Theater four little dialogues. He acted also in Benavente's comedy, *A Long Farewell*, at the opening of the Art Theater at Madrid. But it was not until several years later that he became known as a dramatist. This was when he collaborated with his friend, Santiago Rusiñol, in a comedy, *Life and Sweetness*, given at Madrid, and in two comedies in Catalan given at Barcelona. The first of these, *Aucells de pas*, was turned into a Spanish light opera, *The Swallows*.

Having passed through his apprenticeship, Martínez Sierra proceeded to write alone for the stage, beginning with *The Shadow of the Father* and *The Friend of the House*. In 1911, with his *Cradle Song*, he captured general attention. The play was given in other lands. It was followed in 1913 by *The Two Shepherds*. Three years later, the dramatist became director of the Eslava Theater of Madrid, and organized his own stock company. Like other Spaniards, he has shown remarkable fecundity, adapting some fifty foreign plays and writing two score of his own. As editor of the World's Classics in Translation, and as publisher, he has done so much that critics are not to be blamed for remarking the unevenness of his performance. In the drama alone he passes from farce to grand opera, from pantomime and opera bouffe to legitimate comedy. His wife has frequently collaborated with him and confirmed his liberal leanings. Together they have composed such works as *Letters to the Women of Spain* and *Feminism, Femininity, and the Spanish Spirit*.

When at his best, Martínez Sierra breaks with the older artificial drama, writing simply, and allowing his matter to dictate the form. Granville Barker, who edits his plays in English, commends his stark fidelity of vision, his humanity, and effective irony. Many of the pieces are no more than stage anecdotes. Thus, *Love Magic* is a Barriesque trifle in which Columbine seeks aid from a magician to win back the affection of her Pierrot, diverted to nature and poetry. She succeeds by piquing his jealousy, believing that, "The love that has fallen asleep through excess of good fortune is not to be awakened again without the menace of another love which is more passionate and which burns like youth's fire." Harlequin, the philanderer, employed by Columbine to quicken her husband's love, readily transfers his devotion to her maid, and all ends happily, for, says Harlequin, "He who refuses to console himself by the kisses girls will give, for those that he cannot get, is mad entirely."

In *The Romantic Young Lady* (*Sueño de una noche de agosto*), the heroine, bored with life because she cannot seek adventure like her brothers, finds that adventure will seek her when, on a windy night, a straw hat sails in at her casement. The novelist who comes in quest of it writes her a letter of recommendation to be presented in person next day to none other than himself. Though she grows jealous of his apparent devotion to a dancer, the storm passes, for, on the second night, in a dead calm, his straw hat again sails in at the window. This time her vigilant maid in angry response throws out a paper weight which finds its mark. Again the novelist appears, and with a gash in his forehead, to have his wound dressed and to win the hand that dresses it. He proposes while Rosario's old grandmother nods in her chair. When Rosario hesitates to reply to his proposal, her grandmother murmurs, "O my dear child, do say yes or no!" "Weren't you asleep?" demands the girl. "My dear," answers the old lady, "do you suppose that in eighty years I haven't learned when to go asleep and when to wake up again?" Even the maid begs the novelist to remain. "Now don't go away until she has said, yes, or she will cry her heart out and give us a terrible time. For we all love you, all of us, even though it's not my place to tell you so."

Equally artificial but pleasing is *The Lover*, in which Martínez Sierra portrays the romantic devotion of a man of the people for his queen. He is only an oleomargarine maker, but he has sold his factory in order to be able to follow the queen in her travels. He has treasured little mementoes of his divinity, a hairpin, a pair of gloves she has dropped, and a feather blown from her hat. He sleeps in her garden during Summer, and in the house in which she keeps her pet orang-outang in Winter. Wherever she goes, he follows—mad, of course, but flattering the middle-aged lady by his rapt devotion. When he chances to save her from an overturned carriage, and she offers him any boon he may ask, all he requests is a pass over the state railways in order to be able to keep her ever in sight. The queen is delighted by her quixotic admirer. Sighing at this survival of romance, she concludes the piece by saying, "We have been born too late into a world that has grown too old."

What matter that such a play laughs at reality? Martínez Sierra, like other sentimentalists, loves fantasy, and even when intent upon sketching character, he often departs from the real. This is the case in his sketch *Poor John*, its hero one of those lovable folk "as good as God's bread," always in trouble, and lacking the force of will to help himself out of it. The jolly Mariana may get her father to pay off a mortgage that threatens Poor John, but she declines John's proposal of marriage, preferring instead a lively Nietzschean from overseas, on condition that he promise to provide for Poor John. When the latter, in despair, would throw himself into the sea, he only tumbles into a boat, for even in suicide he cannot succeed. At least, says Mariana, he shall act as godfather for the first of her sons. John, however, protests, lest the boy inherit his ill-luck as well as his name. "When things go wrong with him, I don't want to hear you saying forever, 'Poor John, Poor John!'"

Equally light are the comedies *Madame Pepita* and *Wife to a Famous Man*. The hero of the latter is an aviator grown vain because he has won an airplane race. Disdaining the codfish stew of his hardworking wife, he departs in the limousine of a singer. A week later he returns with bandaged head to beg forgiveness. Though his wife knows him for a fraud with his pretended wound, she receives him back, and will continue to keep the house running by taking in washing. "When a

woman truly loves a man," says she, "whether he is a hero or
a scoundrel, she is bound to suffer for it, because it's like this,
ladies and gentlemen, whoever can give the most, has the most
to lose." Yes, says her mother, all women who have husbands
ought to be pitied; but the aviator finds a sympathizer in his
father-in-law, since both, though forgiven their follies, are a
trifle henpecked.

In *Madame Pepita*, there is a closer approach to reality,
although the plot, unduly complicated, counts for little.
Pepita, long ago deceived by a Russian nobleman, has been
forced to earn her living as a dressmaker to the fashionable.
Threatened with falling a victim to the wiles of an impecunious
count when she inherits the Russian's fortune, she is protected by a kindly Academician. Her daughter, proposed to
by the son of the count, is saved for her worthy lover, an
artist, who wins the Prix de Rome. In the end, Pepita falls
in love with her protector, telling him, "You grow fond of a
dog when you live with him." Here the first act is best, and
the last is weakest, its outcome being already too easily foreseen. The count and his son are comic rascals, both claiming a
commission for encouraging an actress to patronize Pepita's
establishment; and the actress herself suggests doubling the
bill to be sent to the count for her wardrobe in order to
share with the dressmaker the excess profits. Not the least
amusing scene is that in which the ingenue daughter passes
on to her mother such bits of her lover's art philosophy as
the fact that some women are built on Gothic lines and some
on Romanesque, and that frocks should be conceived archi-
tecturally.

To balance these flippant comedies of manners, Martínez
Sierra has created plays more serious, such as *Lily among
Thorns*, *Holy Night*, *The Two Shepherds*, *The Kingdom of
God*, and *The Cradle Song*. In the first, there is a touch of
irony as the inmates of a disreputable resort are captivated
by the kindness of a little nun who comes to nurse one of the

frail sisterhood in illness, and rebukes and sends away the gentlemen responsible for the continuance of the shameful establishment. In *Holy Night* we have a modern miracle play that recalls Maeterlinck's *Sister Beatrice* and Lady Gregory's *Travelling Man*. Here the statue of the Virgin steps from her cathedral pedestal, and, accompanied by angels and Saint Francis, goes into the city on Christmas Eve. She is recognized by a female ragpicker and reported by a street boy to the offscourings of humanity in a tavern. It is they rather than the rich who are devoted to Her, they declare, and each offers some excuse to justify his sins. Then, before Her, kneels a priest in disgrace because a woman of the streets whom he benefited was so indiscreet as to kiss him in gratitude. But the sacristan, seeking his statue, asserts that the rabble has taken it away. When assured that the Virgin has come to the poor of her own accord, he cannot understand why She should have deserted the cathedral decked out in festal array. As the Virgin presents the Child to the poor, the disgraced priest tells them: "Christ was born for you. His poverty is your treasury, His law your justice. . . . Let not those who have taken the earth from you, lock also the gate of heaven to you." Then St. Francis bids the sacristan open wide the cathedral doors, adding, "Whoever sincerely seeks the Child and His Mother shall surely find Them."

More fully developed is *The Kingdom of God*, successful in America as played by Ethel Barrymore. It presents three episodes in the career of a beautiful soul who overcomes love of pleasure to dedicate herself to the service of Heaven on earth. As in Barrie's *The Will* and Bennett and Knoblauch's *Milestones*, glimpses of life at far intervals suggest the long lapse of the years. As a girl, having just taken vows in the Order of St. Vincent de Paul, Sister Gracia is visited by her family at the old men's home where she is ministering. Her mother resents her decision to abandon the world; her gay young sister regards it with disdain; but her father understands.

To him she says: "I'm just an ignorant girl. . . . I'm nobody. I've nothing to give away except my happiness. So I want to give that, to those who have none." Among her ancient charges are a complacent drunkard, a rough radical, and a Cuban half-breed touched in mind because his island home has been lost to Spain forever. Gracia assures him that Cuba is safe. It has become a star in the firmament. They will sail away to it when the moon rises. So she humors and controls all the old men, letting them share her romantic fancies. A decade later Sister Gracia is tending the outcasts of a maternity hospital. Among them are various types—the cynical fatalist, the apathetic young mother indifferent to her child, the rustic half-wit back again after another lapse from virtue, the dumb girl fearful lest her baby be taken from her, and the high-strung young miss of good family grown hysterical in her shame. When the physician of the unfortunates proposes marriage to Gracia, whose vows will permit her withdrawal at any time, she can only gasp, "And you talk to me of love—here?"

Then, in the last episode, the Sister, grown old in presiding over the unruly children of an orphanage, quells a riot precipitated by lack of peppers in the soup, calms a small atheist rebel, and settles a dispute between a child and a hunch-backed tailor. To her crucifix she whispers: "Ah, sweet Savior, it's little time we get to talk to each other, You and I. But we're an old couple now." Then, one of her former charges, just become a bull-fighter, returns bringing her as trophy the ear of his first bull; and Sister Gracia, smiling upon him and the rest, bids them repeat after her a pledge to try to build upon earth the kingdom of God. When the little rebel, overcome by her, weeps, she comforts him, saying: "Don't cry, for men don't cry, and they don't complain. They suffer, they work, and hope." If this play be lacking in plot and dramatic conflict, it is none the less charming, its separate scenes linked by a character that grows in nobility.

Again, in *The Two Shepherds* (*Los Pastores*), ecclesiastical life is made agreeably sentimental before a priest and a doctor, shepherds of the village flock, are superseded just because they cannot pass the formal examinations in theology and science set by the new administration. Don Antonio, the good priest, possesses a genius for admonishing the wicked, and showing them the way to repentance. He delights to ask advice of the statue of the Virgin in his garden. True, she never answers, but, "She speaks to the soul, and in our souls we hear her voice." A man forgets all about the sort of things they put in examinations, says he, "after the struggle year in, year out, with these savages for their salvation." A villager adds indignantly: "Why, of course you do. . . . And here's the Virgin, that knows everything, . . . why, they'd stump her with their damned questions." Yet the good father must depart, relegated to a dull chaplaincy in a convent. At least, he can go carrying the gratitude of a pair of lovers, for the mayor's son will be forgiven by his father for having eloped with a girl of lower station, and by this marriage her good name will be restored to her. The new priest to be installed may know all about theology, but what does he know of human nature, he, whose chief ability lies in making flowery speeches? As for the other shepherd, the physician, his fate parallels that of Don Antonio, the priest. What are formal theology and science as compared with leadership and intelligent love?

Best known among the plays of Martínez Sierra is *The Cradle Song*, popularized in America by the acting of Eva Le Gallienne. It is admirable in its analysis of maternal longings that survive even in the cloister. While Dominican nuns are celebrating the saint's day of their mother superior, a new-born infant is brought in, abandoned by a woman of the streets. To the novices the tiny girl is an angel sent by the Lord, and the genial old physician of the convent, agreeing to lend the child his name, assigns her to be nursed and reared by the gardener's wife. Eighteen years pass, and the foundling, about to become a bride, bids farewell to the sisters and the doctor, and leaves her special confidante, Joanna of the Cross, kneeling by her empty chair, broken-hearted.

The life of the convent, with its little hopes and fears and harmless gossip, is set forth delicately. In the first scene, attention is focused upon Joanna of the Cross, who, when the baby is brought in, has been dreaming of how in her village she used to kneel in the brook and wash her small brother's linen. In taking communion, she imagines herself to be receiving our Lord as a child and pressing Him to her heart. In the second scene it is the foundling, now grown to womanhood, who engages our interest. She may have scandalized the older sisters by her worldly happiness, but they love her and approve her marriage to the gardener's son. He promises to answer for the earthly welfare of this flower they have nurtured for the skies. She promises to think of them across the seas. "May you find what you seek in the world, daughter," says the prioress; "for so we hope, and so we pray to God. But if it should not be so, remember, this is your convent." The pathos of the parting is relieved by humor, for the nuns advise the bridegroom what to do for each of the bride's little ailments, and the stern vicaress is heard reproving another sister for having kept a looking-glass with which to flash reflections of the sun about her cell while imagining that they are butter-flies or birds. Here is nothing theatric, nothing even dramatic. All is simple, heartfelt, natural. Such adjectives may best describe the sentimental comedies of Martínez Sierra.

CHAPTER XXVI

The Versatile Benavente

THE most stimulating and artistic of modern Spanish playwrights is Jacinto Benavente y Martínez. His contribution is both varied and original. In it he departs from tradition and expresses himself with refreshing independence. Stirred by the national disaster of the Spanish-American War, he best represents in the theater the impulses of the generation of 1898. Even before that date there was evident in the Peninsula a change in the attitude toward tradition. Admiration for the ideas and technique of Lope de Vega and of Calderón did not flag, but it was perceived that the world had moved since the seventeenth century. Spaniards, accordingly, began looking to more modern writers and to other literatures, not only to Italy and France, but also to Scandinavia, Russia, Germany, and England. Conservatives might assail lovers of the new as deficient in patriotism; but enlightened patriots replied that Spain must know the foreign truth that this truth might make her free.

When the brief conflict with America bereft Spain of the last of her colonies, she was stung into the necessity of consolidating her territory and her people at home, and, at the same time, exposing them to influences that would equip her for competition with a world everywhere changed and in the making. It was seen that the old ideals of pride and honor were insufficient protection. Don Quixote might refuse to put his cardboard helmet to trial lest it fail to serve him; he might substitute faith for experience; but the modern man must rather let faith merely supplement experience, seeking every opportunity of contact with the actual to prove both his armor and his arms. Jacinto Benavente, who appears moderate enough to foreigners, was regarded as a daring progressive in Spain. He was born at Madrid in 1866, the son of a well-known specialist in children's diseases. He studied law at the University, but, on the death of his father, saw life at first hand as impresario of a circus which traveled as far as Russia. He came back to read widely, to write, and to act. He published four short romantic plays in his *Teatro fantástico*, a series of *Women's Letters* revealing a knowledge of feminine psychology, and a volume of poems that were pagan in spirit and richly sensuous. Then he turned to the theater in earnest.

After a slight play—*Thy Brother's House*—he captured attention in 1896 with *People We Know*, a smart satire upon an impoverished aristocrat seeking to fill his pockets by marrying the natural daughter of a parvenu but suffering rebuff from this sister of Ibsen's Nora. Again Benavente flicked the shallow new society in his *Banquet of the Beasts*, reminiscent of *The Vultures* of Becque, *A Bankruptcy* of Björnson, and *The Lion's Share* of de Curel. When a wealthy family meets reverses, those who have appeared to be friends prove to be foes; but the broken financier, heartened by his wife, will begin again, having learned the sweet uses of adversity. There followed two satires upon false ambition—*The Angora Cat*, depicting the folly of an artist tempted to desert his noble sister for the feline aristocrat Silvia whose portrait he paints, and *Lo Cursi*, its title a slang word current in Cadiz as applicable to that which, though middle-class and poor, aspires to be regarded as exquisite. Benavente laughs here at the dandy, who, in attempting to be up-to-date, neglects his fine wife from the country. She in turn, trying to be less bourgeois, piques his jealousy and wins him back when she is threatened by a devil-may-care admirer.

These pieces were composed in the loose and simple technique of the French naturalistic stage, a method Benavente had already applied in *La Farándula* to satirizing life in the provinces. A literary hack grows tired of acting as publicity agent for a politician come from the capital to exploit the town of Moraleda. He laughs at the politician's speechmaking, at his repetition of meaningless phrases which resemble the patter of the old traveling troupe—*La Farándula*. Provincial Moraleda is again the scene in *The Governor's Wife*, the best of such satires; and it figures also in *The Lady of Sorrows*, a late play of more romantic quality.

Within a decade after the performance of his first piece, Benavente had written thirty dramas, and some seventy have now flowed from his pen. He has been an experimenter, indulging in tragedy, farce, bourgeois drama, trifling skits, as well as elaborate studies in symbolism. He has served as director of The National Theater, and he has promoted an Art Theater and a Theater for Children. He has translated or adapted foreign works, notably *Twelfth Night*, *King Lear*, Molière's *Don Juan*, Bulwer's *Richelieu*, plays by Augier and Hervieu, and Hazleton and Benrimo's *Yellow Jacket*. Throughout, he has maintained a happy balance between the idealism of the artist and the common sense of the actor-manager, calling attention to the fact that Shakespeare and Molière were practical men of the theater, and that, with us as with them, good art may be reconciled with good business. He recognizes that audiences, even though unmoral in behavior, are essentially moral in their conception of what should be. He has said that, "One fourth of the morality, rectitude, and sense of justice which an audience brings into the theater would, if left outside, make the world over into a paradise." To foreigners the name of Benavente first became generally known when he was awarded the Nobel Prize for literature in 1920. Since then his plays have received increasing attention abroad.

Because Benavente is versatile or nothing, he shows no dominant style. He can turn with equal facility to peasant tragedy or to child-like fantasy, to satire upon the foibles of provincial or urban life or to a symbolic presentation of the doings of princes on the Riviera. A piquant realist at heart, he is also a master of fantasy, and always an apologist for the good, the beautiful, and the true. He is not concerned with devising ingenious plots, like his Spanish predecessors, or driving home some reform, like the Northern writers for the theater of social criticism. Beneath the surface of the world as it is, he perceives an underlying reality, often opposed to the phenomenal world. In technique he remains serenely free. Now he writes melodrama; now he adapts the Italian *commedia dell'arte*; now he composes a Maeterlinckian fantasy; now he chronicles small happenings among the city poor. The creation or analysis of character is not his only aim, any more than is the weaving of intricate plots. Ideas emerge in some of his plays, but he can scarcely be said to contribute notably to a theater of ideas. Benavente, indeed, is too comprehensive a genius to be confined to any one manner. He cannot be tied to a school, but, attempting pieces in every genre, remains consistent only in laughing always at hypocrisy, sympathizing always with those who truly love and forgive.

For convenience, we may classify Benavente's plays in several groups. There are his airy pieces with a moral; his amusing sketches of reality; his scenes drawn from the real world with satirical intent; his fantasies that signify symbolically more than appears at first blush; a whole series of feministic studies exalting the character of women; and here and there, by exception, a stark presentation of passion.

Of the airy pieces with a moral, *The Magic of an Hour* affords an example. At midnight in a drawing room, two statuettes of porcelain step from their pedestals to discuss love and life, the youth yearning to discover what lies beyond his little world, the maiden holding that the realms outside but duplicate those within. As she speaks of love, he kisses her, striking a chip from her porcelain cheek, and then gallantly pressing his own cheek to hers to conceal the scar ere they stiffen again into images. In the same vein is *The Prince Who*

Learned Everything out of Books, a play composed for the
Children's Theater of Madrid, its hero informed by a good
fairy that although life may not be as enchanting as in the
stories he has read, yet "it is necessary to dream beautiful
things in order to do beautiful things." Somewhat closer to
reality stands *The School of Princesses*, which enunciates the
cheerful doctrine that happiness lies in accepting responsibility. A princess, refusing a royal match designed to benefit the
state, prefers a dashing duke, and relinquishes claim to the
throne in favor of her sister, who will marry the prince. But
when we get what we wish, we no longer wish it, says Benavente. Since the prince proves to be both wise and charming,
and the duke neglects Costanza in suing for popular favor,
she would retract. It is too late, however. She must accept the
duke, or be declared insane.

Far and away the best of Benavente's plays in lighter vein
is *The Bonds of Interest*, a favorite on many stages. Here the
Spaniard makes moral use of the old Italian comedy of masks,
but does so with poetic delicacy, adding to his sweet decoction
something of picaresque spice. Crispin is a rogue who, posing
as servant to his companion Leander, will win for him the hand
of an heiress. To this end he relies upon the aid of an unscrupulous lady who will profit by acting as go-between. But Sylvia's father recognizes in the rogue his former companion of
the convict galleys. Crispin must defend himself and his companion from exposure, and he does so by demonstrating that
it will be to the advantage of all who oppose him to permit
Sylvia and Leander to marry. He has won the girl's pity and
affection for Leander by letting it appear that he has been
beaten by her father's bravos; and he agrees to retire from
the scene as soon as the marriage is arranged. Leander has
risen as Crispin has sunk; and, redeemed by love for Sylvia,
he disputes Crispin's statement that "The ties of love are as
nothing to the bonds of interest." As for Sylvia, she affirms
that, "There is something divine in our lives which will not

end when the farce of life concludes." Obviously, what here interests Benavente is the contrast between body and soul so often set forth in Spanish literature and in the works of the French romanticists down to Rostand. Crispin is that in us which contrives and seeks gain, Leander is that which loves and idealizes. Charming in its fantasy, the comedy lacks dramatic quality in spite of the praise bestowed upon it by the critics. Benavente himself speaks of it as "a little play of puppets, impossible in theme, without any reality at all"; and he adds, with a twinkle in his eye, "The author is aware that so primitive a spectacle is unworthy of the culture of these days."

Nine years later, in 1916, Benavente wrote a sequel called *The Glad and Confident City*. This fantasy is a pessimistic echo of the original, for it shows Leander turned sensualist, intriguing with a dancing girl, and Harlequin now a lazy and cynical poet laureate. Strangely enough, Crispin, the former rogue, has become through his wit ruler of the city, and a moral reformer. In vain he seeks to save the luxurious citizens from the assaults of the Venetians. They surrender without a blow, and although Leander, at last aroused, dies bravely, Crispin and the lover of his daughter must suffer death also. Even if drama be sacrificed here to philosophic allegory, the work was received with enthusiasm, and the author, after its first performance, was borne homeward on the shoulders of the crowd.

It may be something of a relief to turn from imaginative abstractions to Benavente's light sketches of reality such as *Automobile, No Smoking, The Truth,* and *Field of Ermine. No Smoking* is typical of many of its author's briefer plays, a dramatized episode without serious import. There is innocent fun in the spectacle of a talkative woman in a railway compartment, who, by the clatter of her tongue, drives out a fellow passenger, and, supposing that he has departed for good, tosses his luggage from the window. *The Truth* reveals the hesitancy of a girl to profit from her concealment to over-hear what her lover may say of her. After all, what is truth? Men among themselves are not necessarily sincere; they may even pretend to be worse than they are. Truth lives not in words but in the hearts of those who love us. A more serious study of reality is *Field of Ermine*, which recalls *The Grand-father* of Pérez Galdós in exalting character above birth. A boy is adopted by a noblewoman. When she learns that he is not indeed her brother's child, but instead the son of unworthy parents, she disowns him. No sooner has he disappeared than she suffers qualms of conscience. She answers his note asking her to aid him in finding work by begging him to return. She has been wrong to visit upon him the sins of his father and mother.

It will be seen that here an idea emerges, and in the next group of Benavente's plays, ideas dominate in so far as he writes with satirical purpose. His satire, however, is good natured, and there is nothing novel in his contentions in any play. It needs no prophet to tell us that the high cost of living is bound to throttle romance, or that those who attempt to order the loves of others may be evil doers-of-good. Yet Bena-vente's piece of that name holds our interest through its charac-ters. He pokes fun at a marchioness and her women friends who undertake to play providence to their protegées, meddling and muddling with the best of motives. The marchioness marries off a dependent niece to an unattractive widower, and frowns upon her attempt at friendship with his four children. Then she and her *junta* intervene to block the union of a couple in love since childhood. But her jolly brother, who has suffered from the machinations of these evil doers-of-good, aids the pair, and comments on the moral quite in the spirit of the genial *raisonneurs* of Pinero. Throughout, humor of character relieves the threatened didacticism. Especially appealing are the lovers, Jesus and Nativity, so named because it was on

Christmas Day that as babies they were rescued from a shipwreck.

Another *raisonneur*—a physician—philosophizes concerning poverty as the root of all evil—"poverty of blood, poverty of life, poverty of everything." *In the Clouds* depicts the drab existence of a family of the lower middle class in Madrid. A widow with an ailing daughter is dependent upon a son who wishes to marry. She opposes the match, since it will cut off her income and take him away. The girl's mother, too, objects to losing her services, and the girl lacks the courage to accompany her lover overseas. When, still undaunted, he will venture forth alone, the wise old physician approves. Spain has sent her children, he says, "to give life and body to those nations, the daughters of her race; they are to-day her chief, perhaps her only pride. A cradle is more sacred than the grave; the future is greater than the past." The effects of poverty on love are displayed in still other cases. There is Julio's sister, predestined, because dowerless, to be an old maid. There are the contrasted couples, one already married but suffering financial distress, and the other unable to marry even after a seven years' engagement, the lover finding solace "on the side" in affairs with serving maids. There is also the ambitious clerk, aspiring to a rich match, courting each of three sisters impartially, yet forced to marry their maid and to retire to the country to live on the bounty of his uncle, a priest. Such a piece is essentially matter-of-fact, unheroic, ironic, the sort of play that Chekhov in Russia might have written.

Satire is brightened with humor in two other dramas depicting reality, *His Widow's Husband* and *The Governor's Wife*. The latter laughs at the shifts and compromises of politicians and society folk in provincial Moraleda where a *feria* is being held with all the accessories of fireworks, bull-fight, and a play. The conservatives object to the play. The ladies of the church party will prevail upon the governor to forbid its performance. His wife rules the roost, and she is against it. But her lover, the governor's secretary, wishes the play to proceed, for he has discovered in the manager of the traveling troupe his long-lost brother. At the request of the secretary, the wife changes front, and forces her bewildered husband to do the same. By good fortune, at that moment, the Madrid government happens to turn Liberal, and Don Santiago, therefore, is hailed as a patriot, and assured promotion to a governorship of the first class. He who has always feared Madrid is delighted to find himself its servant.

The irony throughout is delicious. Says the governor, "We are in Spain, thank God! and there must be some legal way to break the law." That is what all the inhabitants of Moraleda are engaged in seeking. The leading citizen, Don Baldomero, was once a radical, but is now a bigoted conservative. He has moved to close all the gambling resorts that his own may profit the more. Disturbed because his spoiled daughter, like the governor's wife, is in love with the governor's secretary, he threatens that official in order to drive him from town. But he suffers defeat when the governor's lady and her lover engage a toreador to refer to him slightingly in a speech at the bullfight, and to praise the governor, now turned Liberal. As the crowd shouts against the reactionaries, and the governor reads the telegram announcing his promotion, he says to his secretary, with unconscious irony, "In these days of trial, you have been the real governor, you have taken my place." Thereafter the secretary must always remain at his master's side. When the secretary asks Josefina what he shall do regarding this invitation, she answers from her heart, "Accept!"

Here we seem to live in the town of Moraleda, with its scandals, its hypocrisy, its professed disdain and secret admiration for Madrid. The wit of the dialogue sparkles, and the character types are delightful. They include the rector of the University and his daughters, popularly known as Rhetoric and Poetry; the prudish wife of Baldomero; and the young girl who is preparing to be a nun by sampling life to the full before being shut in the cloister; the toreador, handicapped in reputation by his poor showing at a bull-fight two years before; the mannish daughter of a marquis who raises fancy bulls; and the second secretary of the governor, who, within twenty years, has served seventy-two such officials. These are only a few of the provincial notables.

More evident is the tone of burlesque in that brief but merry comedy, *His Widow's Husband*. Here the widow of a great man, just as a statue is about to be dedicated to his honor, discovers that the dead hero had known all along of her intrigue with his rival, now her second husband. She would like to escape the ceremony, but fears that her absence might be misinterpreted. In attending, she must not appear too sad, lest she seem insincere, nor too happy, lest she appear forgetful of her loss. The society editor of the local paper, who declares that "A woman's position is never so embarrassing as when she is hesitating what to put on," advises that she appear in black and violet in order to attest consideration for the feelings of her two husbands. But the maiden sisters of the illustrious dead are shocked at the nude figures of Truth, Commerce, and Industry sculptured on the pedestal. "I could understand," says one, "why the statue of Truth should be unclothed, but I must say that Commerce and Industry might have worn at least a tunic."

A more serious difficulty arises. A jolly rascal, thinking to profit by the occasion, has issued a biography of the hero containing letters that reveal the scandal concerning his widow. When the bookseller objects to suppressing the edition, the shrewd author, buying it back, sells it again to the second husband at a handsome profit. Even the lady admires his epic impudence. Her present husband grows rueful as he counts up the cost of paying tribute to his distinguished predecessor. "But, are you sorry?" asks his wife. "No, my Carolina," he responds with gallantry; "the glory of being your husband far outweighs the disadvantage of being the husband of his widow."

It need not detract from the originality of Benavente to remark the close parallel in this comedy to the central situation in Pinero's *His House in Order*. There, a park is to be dedicated to the memory of a first wife, and her relatives object to the gift for the park of a drinking fountain bearing nude figures. It is discovered, moreover, through certain letters, that the first wife had been guilty of an intrigue. Surely, these resemblances are not fortuitous. On the other hand, where Pinero supplements satire with a serious discussion of second marriage, Benavente shows himself a humorist as well as a satirist.

Admirers of Benavente are wont to praise his more or less idealistic pieces like *The Fire-Dragon* and *Saturday Night*, perceiving in them underlying significances which escape the more matter-of-fact. *The Fire-Dragon* is a fantasy, comparable to *The White Redeemer* of Hauptmann, but using the Indies instead of Mexico as its locale. When an East Indian realm is invaded by Europeans the Hindoo king accords them welcome, hoping to benefit his people. But the invaders are no sooner granted concessions than they take advantage of the natives, and the king falls a victim to their plots and those of his queen. He is seized during a tiger hunt that his subservient brother may be put in his place, and when, later, this brother is tortured to death by irate subjects, the king, a prisoner, takes his life rather than make his country a vassal of Europe. Benavente has not been unmindful in this dreamy and poetical piece of those ancient works lately adapted for the French stage, *The Clay Cart*, ascribed to King Sudraka, and *The Ring of Sakuntala* of Kalidasa.

Having thus secured romantic idealization by a resort to the remote in space, the playwright turns to the historic past and Queen Elizabeth in *The Vestal of the West*, which might be included among his psychological studies of women. Although Raleigh, Fulke Greville, and other lords and ladies play their part, it is the queen and her love for Essex that chiefly concerns us. In her latter years she yearns toward youth, and, admiring the impulsive Essex, is ready to forgive his every folly so long as he will sacrifice his pride to hers, and ask her pardon. Essex, however, having failed in Ireland and suffered imprisonment in the Tower, proceeds to plot against the queen. When at last he is ready to throw himself upon her mercy, enemies prevent the delivery to her of the ring she had given him as pledge of forgiveness whenever he should send it to her. So he dies, and the queen reflects that the axe of the executioner which slew her mother, Anne Boleyn, has become a weapon in her hands to bring death to those whom she has held most dear. She has been jealous of the exuberant young life in Essex, and of his every thought and ambition that lay beyond her control. But jealousy and pride have destroyed the object of her love. Here the scene of the drama is the soul of the queen; all the historical trappings are but incidental.

The same idealizing process Benavente applies to contemporary reality in *Princess Bebé* and *Saturday Night*, both laid upon the Riviera where blasé nobles are seeking distraction by mingling with the demi-monde. In the former, a princess and a prince, sick of the court, have flown in the face of convention. She has eloped with her husband's secretary; he has married a middle-class actress; and both have been expelled from Suavia by their uncle, the ruler. To the Riviera the rebels come to enjoy their new freedom. But those they have raised from a lower station refuse to drop their new titles. Absurdly, too, they take on moral airs, the actress snubbing the princess because she has eloped, and the secretary-husband of the princess snubbing the prince because he has married beneath him. A count, who entertains them only for the prestige that their presence brings, assumes that, because of Princess Bebé's elopement, he can make love to her; and even his mistress looks askance at her. "How can equality ever be possible in this world?" asks Bebé, "when these puny spirits with their vulgarities remind us, in spite of ourselves, that we are royal?" At length, Stephen and Bebé realize that their turning to these companions has been but a means of escape from the court. They ought to have loved each other, and it is not too late. They will remain together. "Forever?" "Well, at least to-day, to-morrow, a few hours longer. . . . Who can tell? What does it matter? To love is all."

If the meaning of *Princess Bebé* be clear, that of *Saturday Night*, which moves among the same sort of folk, is irritatingly obscure. Called "a novel for the stage," the play unfolds in five "tableaux" for which pose more than forty characters. The heroine is a woman of the people who, in passing from lover to lover, has mounted the social ladder until now she is mistress to a prince. One of her earlier admirers has sculptured her in marble as a beggar, climbing a pedestal of granite to a throne of gilded bronze. Imperia, as he has christened her, is destined at last to mount to an actual throne, but before this can happen she must consider the fate of her daughter. Little Donina, the child of her first lover, is a circus dancer allied with a good-for-nothing clown who would sell her to the dissolute Prince Florencio, a later lover of Imperia. But Donina, in defending herself, stabs him at a low resort; and his gay companions spirit his body away and give out the story that he has committed suicide. By his death and that of an infant heir, Imperia's prince becomes the monarch of Suavia, but refuses to ascend the throne unless she share it. When she hesitates because of her duty to Donina, the latter expires, but not before begging her mother to go rule with the prince. The sculptor, too, bids her, "Fight on and triumph!" Imperia summarizes her philosophy and that of the playwright by saying: "To achieve anything in life, we must subdue reality, and thrust aside its phantoms, which confuse and hem us round, to follow the only reality, the flight of our witches' spirits, as on Saturday Night they turn to their ideal —some toward evil, to be lost in the shadows forever like specters of the night, others toward good, to dwell eternally in it, the children of love and light." In short, let us follow our infallible inner urge.

As a story, the play bewilders. Here are princes who intrigue with a sculptor's model; a model who becomes a queen; her daughter, a circus performer, who slays with impunity the heir to a throne, and then pines to death because deceived by a clown; an Anglo-Italian poet; a crazy old woman once the king's mistress; and a countess fascinated by an elephant-driver and then by a pale Franciscan friar. Unless people and plot possess symbolic significance, the whole thing would seem no better than a nightmare fantasy. As in the symbolic masterpieces of Ibsen, Hauptmann, and Andreyev, the action, which begins on a plane of reality, is perceived ere long to be moving in two worlds. Soon it becomes more essential to discover the secondary than the primary meaning. The sculptor, when asked the significance of his statue, replies: "How can I tell? An artist believes that he speaks through his works, but the works take on form and speech for themselves." So here, all sorts of analogies and symbols emerge, as though in spite of the dramatist's intention. John Garrett Underhill, able translator of Benavente, explains Imperia as meaning ambition or the will, which, drawing near the throne of empire, turns to recover her youth, Donina. In a saturnalia, or Witches' Sabbath,—"her old life dies at the hand of youth, which is itself exhausted by the blow." The sculptor represents her imagination, which had once given her a vision of the ideal. Now, under his tutelage, "she sacrifices her youth, her Donina, who dies immediately; and, by the sacrifice, Imperia achieves for herself character, the mastery of the world and all that is in it, which is the realization of her ideal." But she discovers this ideal to be spiritual rather than material.

Unfortunately, the action of the play scarcely supports

such an interpretation. How can youth be said to slay the old bad life of ambition? How can Imperia, or ambition, be said to sacrifice her youth when, as a matter of fact, Imperia declines to make such a sacrifice of Donina? And how can the death of youth involve the achievement of character or the mastery of the world on the part of ambition? One is reminded of Byron's ejaculation concerning Coleridge, when the latter had been

"Explaining metaphysics to the nation ——,
I wish he would explain his explanation!"

No doubt we may see here a woman's march toward power retarded for the moment by her concern for the fate of her daughter. But does she find her true self in love for a long-neglected child, or in pursuing her way to the throne? She asks the sculptor: "Why do we waste our lives in dreams and ambition? Our true life is the love which springs in our hearts. . . . While my child lives, my place is with her." The sculptor, or Imagination, encourages her to pass beyond that love to attain her ambition. She is still driven on, evidently with the dramatist's approval, to strive for power, the sculptor speaking of "the might of the soul to realize its dream of a throne, where our selfishness, perhaps, is absolute, or our disinterested love." Apparently Benavente would say that the soul must follow its urge for expression through the will, bad or good, as the case may be. Yet the sculptor queries: "What is there in our lives that deserves to endure? Is it what we are, or what we appear to be? the love that was in us once? what we long for and dream? Where are our true selves to be found?" Evidently, he remains as perplexed as Pirandello as to the essence of personality—the true "I"; and this notion Benavente voices more precisely in his play *The Truth*. Philosophically, it may be more appropriate to present no definite conclusion as to the conflict in Imperia's bosom between love for her child and the yearning for power. Dramatically, the piece loses by its confusion of issues and its irrelevant episodes.

If there be any one fixed social attitude on the part of Benavente, it is his attitude toward women. He is essentially a
feminist. Not that he advocates women's rights. Rather, he
shows understanding and admiration of the fair. His earlier
dealings with them in his *Women's Letters* indicate his position. He sympathizes with their aspirations and disap-
pointments. He extols their sacrifices. When husbands prove
unfaithful, he counsels sweet submission, a winning back of the
wayward instead of revolt. Throughout, his women are far
nobler than his men. They are born to suffer and forgive. Of
women who suffer, we have the heroines of *A Lady*, *The Tomb-
stone of Dreams*, and *The Lady of Sorrows*. The last shows a
country girl beloved by an unworthy son of the nobility who
suddenly dies. Although she has scarcely returned his affection, yet to please his parents, and to benefit her own, she
mourns him as though she were his widow, and comes in time
to idealize him. When one to whose honorable love she might
have responded appears, he dare not intrude upon a grief so
ideal.

In *Soul Triumphant*, a wife loses her mind as the result of
grief at the death of her child, but, after five years in an asylum, returns home to find that in the mean time her husband
has sought solace with a mistress, who has borne him another
child. In order that he may be happy, she feigns a recurrence
of madness, deceiving even her physician. But her confessor
recognizes her motive, and warns her that an even greater
sacrifice is possible. "The cross of life is torture indeed if the
soul succumbs to pain, but it becomes a redemption if, when
we are nailed to our cross, the soul through pain rises triumphant." Isabel, though henceforth aloof from her husband, will
remain in his house in order to rear his child by another.

Bernard Shaw's idea of woman as the instinctive pro-
tectress of man appears in Benavente's *Stronger than Love*,
and in his later and inferior work, *The Evil That We Do*. In
the latter, Valentina, rendered unhappy by her jealous lover,

prefers a weak youth who has shown that he needs her. Like Shaw's Candida, she chooses not the stronger but the weaker, yearning to accord him her protection. So, too, in *Stronger than Love*, the heroine turns from the man she adores to find in care for an invalid husband something more potent than love. While visiting Spanish friends on holiday at a Scottish castle, Carmen receives the attentions of the dashing Guillermo and the melancholy Carlos. The former, at the news of her father's bankruptcy and suicide, forsakes her to pay court to the daughter of his wealthy host, and Carmen consents to accept Carlos, whose mother, a duchess, begs her aid for the hypochondriac. Ere long, her martyrdom begins, for Guillermo in spite of his marriage makes advances to her, and her husband, exasperated by his sense of physical disability, becomes insanely jealous. Instead of separating the two, he takes delight in throwing them together that he may spy upon them. But Carmen, although tempted to flee with Guillermo from the reproaches of her husband and his mother, is restrained when Carlos suffers a stroke. She will endure as the slave of the jealous invalid, finding consolation in the maternal instinct which is stronger even than love, for Carlos has become to her as a little child.

Once aspect of woman's sacrifice is her readiness to forgive. Wives in Benavente's theater must be indulgent to light-of-love husbands. Should a wife herself sin, the husband may pardon, but where children are involved the law is inexorable. So, in the play entitled *The Law of the Children*, Paulina, who begs forgiveness of her husband for disloyalty, and would reestablish herself in the eyes of the world, finds it futile. Having once forgotten her duty as a mother, she can never regain that proud office. She departs, declaring, "Divorce is not a law of men; it is a law of the children, and, being of the children, it is a law of God." Men, of course, must be pardoned, and the heroines of *Autumn Roses* and *Señora Ama* are duly indulgent. The latter piece, written in the dialect of Toledo, draws the sympathetic portrait of one who accepts her husband's success with other women as witness to her own powers of fascination; whereas *they* appeal to him one by one for the moment only, *she* has captured him for all time. But the discovery that she is to bear him a child renders her less tender of his disloyalties. Since that child must be able to profit from a good example, she reads her lord a lecture, and wins him back to virtue—for how long?

Once more an all-enduring heroine is exalted in the Isabel of *Autumn Roses*, second wife of a husband incurably polygamous. In years past, he has had an affair with the wife of his business partner, but she, smitten in conscience, has broken it off, and has even confessed it to Isabel at the time of the latter's marriage. When the son of this intrigue bids fair to fall in love with the daughter of the hero's first marriage, Isabel interposes to save the lovers from incest by finding for the girl another husband. But this husband, emulating the devil-may-care conduct of his father-in-law, drives the girl into seeking gallant adventures of her own. Thus the looseness of the older generation breeds looseness in the younger, and to Isabel the misery of her stepdaughter recalls that of her own early married life. Her husband, moreover, has now found a new idol in the scheming bride of an employee come from Paris. When this employee, on being dismissed, would get even by revealing the long-buried intrigue of Gonzalo and Isabel's friend, the patient wife must save that friend by nobly lying, and she must further save her stepdaughter from the wrath of Gonzalo, who illogically would turn her out of the house for following his evil example. As Isabel gently reproves him and inspires his repentance, she gathers "Autumn Roses"—the blossoms of her long and indulgent love.

Women, Benavente seems to say, accomplish most when they forgive. At the same time, Isabel is no Patient Griselda. She can resent ill treatment with spirit, even while displaying her common sense in making the best of a bad matter. She accepts

Gonzalo's protest that he has loved her through all his philandering. The fact that he has caused her pain is nothing. She bids her stepdaughter join her in forgiveness, saying: "Light and thoughtless love, which breathes only illusion and desire, sheds all its flowers in one brief burst of spring; but the love of a wife, love which is holy and true, love which has learned to wait, has other, later flowers,—Autumnal Roses, which are ours. They are not the flowers of love; they are the flowers of duty, watered patiently by tears of resignation, and fragrant of the soul, with the touch of Eternity." What wonder that Gonzalo exclaims: "My wife and saint! On my knees I adore you!" But how long, we ask, will Don Juan remain kneeling?

Woman's willingness to immolate herself on the altar of love is shown in Benavente's early play *Sacrifices*. An opera singer, for the sake of her art, rejects the lover who would interfere with her career, but when he marries her less showy sister, Alma feels that she has given up too much for her art, permitting herself to be deformed by the music master who had adopted them both, as children are sometimes deformed to make them better acrobats. Ricardo, indeed, still loves only Alma; and his sensitive bride, perceiving that fact, drowns herself while apparently seeking to rescue a bird from its youthful tormentors. Alma remarks an analogy here to the torment which she and Ricardo have inflicted upon the innocent Doll. Since the latter has sacrificed herself for love, as Alma had earlier sacrificed herself for art, both Alma and Ricardo feel now that they must sacrifice themselves in turn by separating, for the dead wife and sister still stands between them. In vain she has laid down her life for their union. This drama bears more than a chance resemblance to Maeterlinck's *Aglavaine and Sélysette*, but whereas Maeterlinck conjures up romantic phantoms, Benavente clothes his story with flesh and blood.

Throughout these feminist plays, Benavente exalts love as something unselfish. "The poetry of our lives to-day, which

are barren of swords and lances, and princesses, and troubadours, and Moors, consists in simple duty done and the tasks
of everyday," says one character. "Love is our glory, the
glory of the poor, of the outcast. It is a glory which lies very
near at hand." So, in *The Necklace of Stars*, a poor man,
harassed by the shiftless family of his dead brother living on
the lower floors of his house, escapes from them to the roof,
where, through a telescope, he gazes at the heavens, and forgets the annoyances and limitations of earth. But, perceiving
in the necklace of stars on high a symbol of love, he succeeds
in drawing together by this inspiration his dependents below,
showing them that they must learn the lesson of mutual for-
bearance and devotion. Here may be heard a faint echo of
Andreyev's Russian fantasy *To the Stars*.

Similarly, in *Field of Ermine*, as we have seen, love regen-
erates the heart of a marchioness, who discovers that even
though the boy she has adopted be not the child of her brother,
he may yet be her nephew in affection, one also to whom she
owes a duty. Love, then, for Benavente, is always associated
with duties. Through a character in *Self-Esteem*, he remarks
that: "Love is a mutual work of art, wherein we realize the
thought of him who loves us, and in the object of our love
see our thoughts realized." Another character remarks, "Marriage is not sacred because it is love, but because, from love,
spring duties which sanctify it." Those, accordingly, who seek
to evade these duties, like the hero and the heroine of *The Eyes
of the Dead*, are likely to atone for their sin, each doing justice
on self when smitten in conscience.

The few women, too, who attempt to revolt soon resign
themselves to their destiny. Dominica, in *Señora Ama*, and
Isabel, in *Autumn Roses*, may protest at the treatment accorded by their husbands; but they do not leave home to bear
aloft the banner of feminism. Costanza, in *The School of
Princesses*, may decline to be handed over to Prince Alberto
for reasons of state, but to have accepted life as his queen

would have been her duty. She learns, indeed, that: "Happiness does not exist, but sacrifice does, and sacrifice is the truest of all those phantoms that conceal happiness." Even the Elena of *Princess Bebé*, who does break the shackles of convention, ends by finding that what she mistook for love and rational opposition to a system was merely desire for change. Nené, in *The Manikin*, may resolve to have done with hypocrisy, and lead forth her married lover unafraid. But at length she lacks courage either for this or for stifling her love. She will submit, therefore, to practising the deceits of others, since the world in its exactions proves too strong.

In all these women, even in Nené, passion is but secondary. In one play alone does Benavente show it as the mainspring of vigorous action, and this is his masterpiece, *La Malquerida*, acted in English by Nance O'Neill as *The Passion Flower*. A peasant girl appears to hate her stepfather, resenting the fact that he has captured the heart of her mother and taken the place of her dead father. But her antipathy proves to have been only an instinctive cloak for her love. She is the victim of a Freudian repression. The story hinges upon the fact that Acacia's accepted suitor, on returning home from his betrothal party, is slain from ambush. Her cousin, a jilted rival, is suspected, tried, and acquitted. Still hounded by relatives of the murdered man, he discovers that the deed was done by a servant of Acacia's stepfather. But why? Because the loyal servant has divined and sought to aid his master's love of the girl. Acacia, when questioned by her jealous mother, admits that Esteban has followed her about, eating her up with his eyes; and Esteban finally confesses his infatuation. "I loved you more every·day," he tells Raimunda, "but when I felt her by me, my blood took fire. I could have killed myself and her."

Such madness in one otherwise honorable, Raimunda considers to be the result of her dead husband's prompting. "The dead do not leave us when they die; they are with us day and night; they put thoughts into our minds which are evil and wicked and strange." Acacia, rebuked by Esteban for never having called him "Father," and bidden by her mother to do so, flings her arms about his neck and kisses him wildly. "But you don't call him 'Father!'" cries the mother. Then, protesting because the kiss endures so long, she exclaims: "Let go! let go! Now I see, it was your fault—and I curse you!" Acacia retorts: "Yes, it was! Kill me! He is the only man I ever loved."

To top this surprise comes another. For Esteban, his self-control swept away, declares that he will flee with the girl. When his wife blocks their path, he shoots her down. In dying, she murmurs to Acacia: "This man cannot harm you now! You are saved!" In short, the mother can expire content since her husband dare not marry the daughter of one he has slain.

Although decried as a melodrama, *La Malquerida* is much more. As Ludwig Lewisohn has said, "Benavente turns his melodrama into tragedy by transferring the action from rooms and fields into the souls of people." The actual situation, as in *Rosmersholm*, is artfully concealed until the end. The audience supposes that it is the jilted lover who has slain his successful rival, then that the stepfather is guilty. The latter's struggle against the fascination of Acacia is not revealed until the third act; and, when the servant's guilt becomes clear, Acacia's love for Esteban is still kept obscure, a passion disguised by apparent fear and hatred. As with Ibsen, most of the action occurs offstage, all of it in fact except what is given in the last few minutes—that intense and vivid scene when three souls are suddenly revealed in their ultimate nakedness.

Here, by exception with Benavente, love is a disease, a frenzy, as it is with d'Annunzio; and, moreover, love and hate are coupled as they are with Strindberg. They do not so much alternate as display opposite phases of the same overmastering instinct. According to the servant, an antipathy such as that of Acacia for her stepfather grows always out of a great love;

and Acacia confesses that, as a child, she has resented the sight of her mother hanging on his neck, and has lain awake at night with a knife beneath her pillow, prepared to kill him and "perhaps another." Raimunda is as interesting as Esteban and Acacia. Her life, like theirs, is determined by subconscious impulses. She seeks to repress a sense of guilt at having proved disloyal to her first husband in marrying the second. The originality of this drama may be seen in comparing it with a play from which its central situation seems to have been derived, the *Misteri di dolor* of a Catalan writer, Adrián Gual, where the rivalry between mother and daughter is known from the start, the mother's second husband having been in love with her daughter even before his marriage. Benavente, by concealing this love, even from the girl herself, and then permitting it to appear under the mask of hate until that mask is torn off in the final scene, has rendered the play intellectual in appeal and psychologically significant.

What was said earlier must now be the more evident,—Benavente is so versatile and fecund that he cannot be fitted into any one formula. He has experimented freely in many styles, and in all he has shown himself an expert of unusual skill. He is not a realist, if by that we mean one content simply to set down the outward look of things as he sees them. He is not an idealist, if by that we mean one content to render only some dream, some ideal of what ought to be. He is not a romanticist, if by that we mean one who feels and imagines unrestrainedly and paints in brilliant pigments to satisfy the yearning of his heart. He is not a classicist, if by that we mean one who practices rigorous esthetic self-control, who avoids surplusage, and lays stress upon form, will, and universality. Yet Benavente is a little of all these things. His realism, like that of other Spaniards, is tinged with romance, his classical idealism with a love of local color. When playing the idealist, he attempts to vitalize his symbols. When playing the realist, he does not limit his observation to external ap-

pearance, but seeks to pluck out the heart of the mystery concealed beneath. It is especially in his psychological plays dealing chiefly with women and in those that suggest far more
than they express, that he deserves admiration.

In technique Benavente represents a reaction in the direction of freedom and simplicity. Having abandoned the well-
worn devices of the Spanish stage, and the newer tricks of the
French, he has produced plays loose and fluid in arrangement.
He is not economical in using characters or in getting his story
under way. His people roam about and talk, and there are
more of such people than the action requires. Often they crack
epigrams, and drop smart or proverbial phrases. Only here
and there do they follow the older Spanish fashion of spouting
speeches so long and rhetorical as to seem artificial.

Is Benavente, as Pérez de Ayala asserts, merely a literary
dramatist, maker of "a theater of middle terms, without action
or passion, and therefore without motivation or characters,
and, what is worse, without genuine reality?" Certain plays,
Benavente admits, are better read than seen and heard. Moreover, he confesses the difficulty of embodying through actors
upon a stage the creatures of one's mind. "I have written more
than a thousand parts," he says; "yet of that number I can
recall perhaps five, which, when they stepped upon the stage,
I have recognized as being truly the characters I had conceived. I have not even seen some of my plays." Then he adds,
"The only way in which a play may be appreciated thoroughly is by being read."

Is Benavente unduly subtle? In the main, his dramas are
easy to understand, those that are realistic and satirical no
less than those that develop some idea. But a few admirers profess to have discovered in him the practitioner of a mysterious
and novel art. Thus, Underhill finds the plays "double in
focus, moving upon double planes, poised between the objective and the subjective, between the conscious and the
unconscious and unexplored," and he dilates upon Benavente's

system of "double ententes, previously confined to traffic in contraband wares, transformed into a system of multiple ententes, in which he attempts to realize upon the stage the inarticulate as well as the articulate elements of intellect and character."

Except in a very few dramas, where the method is that of Ibsen and Hauptmann at their symbolic best, it is difficult to perceive in the Spaniard this "double ideation," this "amazing anti-technic." In play after play, the meaning lies quite upon the surface, the characters are the folk of every day, grouped without any deep and mysterious significance. No more than in the dramas of a score of others is there here "an unwritten action which is in constant flux." Yet it is true that at times Benavente can show, not only character in sharp outline, but personality which "invites inference," thus revealing a "rooted antipathy to complete statement, with its inevitable suggestion of finality." It is true that occasionally "he tends away from the plastic toward the insubstantial." Certainly, he likes to suggest a double viewpoint. Thus, *In the Clouds* depicts the poverty that militates against tranquil married life, and, at the same time, the lack of courage to face poverty. *Saturday Night* similarly implies that following the urge to power will afford happiness; but it suggests as well that following the urge to love will do this, and also that obedience to either may lead equally to disaster.

One other point is a bone of contention to the critics. Most are agreed in regarding Benavente as a pessimist. So Walter Starkie finds that even his women seem to have read Schopenhauer and to have concluded that the reason for suffering lies in the nature of the will to live, it being their ideal to resist this instinctive impulse toward life. In such a pleasing trifle as *The Bonds of Interest*, Mr. Starkie perceives a dark shadow, "a sad irony which cannot weep and therefore smiles."

Although Benavente be a master of irony, he is surely not a pessimist expressing "even in his earliest satiric plays the discordant note of bitter disillusion." He is rather a keen observer commenting upon life agreeably and wisely, and imbued with faith in the possibility of making it finer. "I am trying to educate the public and cannot allow it to educate me," he has said; "I am writing for the public, not as it is at present, but as it will be when my object is achieved."

Yet Benavente is not a reformer with a program, although one of his critics—Julio Brouta—perceives in him the spirit of Ibsen. His morality is cheerful, sound, and sensible; it is opposed to stress upon forms, and requires no ardent revolt against established institutions. He is content to flick with his satiric whip those ancient butts of comedy—hypocrisy and vanity—so far as they affect the individual rather than society as a whole. In doing this, he often shows something of the gaiety of Shaw. It is no pessimist who tells us that "The function of the artist is to tranquillize emotion through intelligence; his aim is to bring serenity, not to create a tempest in the mind." It is no pessimist who affirms again and again belief in the nobility of woman and the capacity of man to attain self-control. It is no pessimist who has written: "The government of one's self is a most difficult matter, but once achieved, what splendid liberty!" With jaunty confidence, Benavente declares: "The day that each of us becomes a tyrant over himself, that day will all men become free without revolutions and without laws."

CHAPTER XXVII

Italian Verists *

Giacosa, Verga, Rovetta, Praga, Bracco

THE recent Italian drama grew out of a movement toward realism following the romantic impulse which entered Italy from France. Manzoni and Niccolini had been the standard-bearers of Italian romanticism, reacting against the old classic play, transferring interest from Greek and Roman to medieval and modern subjects, and disdaining restrictions in form. The historical drama flourished during the mid-nineteenth century, with Pietro Cossa as its principal creator. Melodrama was cultivated by Paolo Giacometti, who strove to produce violent effects in the belief that the public wishes above all to be emotionally stirred. In one play, *Civil Death*, Giacometti suggested the need for social reform, and more subtle thesis plays were written by Paolo Ferrari. He was directly influenced by the dramas of Augier and Dumas the younger, whose example was followed by others, including Achille Torelli.

The new realists recognized that the drama must possess a popular appeal, that it must be useful and moral. They determined to make art a faithful transcription of life, something as certain and logical as science. In the end, they reduced their conception of man to that of the animal contending against other animals for food and woman. But the Italians never achieved a drama of social issues at all comparable to the French or the English. With them the institutions of the State

*In this chapter and the next, the author is especially indebted to Lander MacClintock's admirable volume, *The Contemporary Drama of Italy*, 1920, to which the reader is referred for further treatment of the minor playwrights.

and the Church were too firmly established to be questioned. Marriage, which elsewhere was made less rigorous by easy divorce, was maintained in Italy, although methods of going around it to achieve satisfaction in love continued to provide a subject for comedy. There was no special pleading in Italian drama for feminism, socialism, or industrial reform.

Giuseppe Giacosa is the first important realist among the modern Italian playwrights. Born in Piedmont in 1847, he lived chiefly at Turin and Milan, studied law, practiced journalism, wrote fiction, books of travel, and critical articles, but was most successful as a dramatist. In his more than thirty works for the stage he shows the progress of a sane and healthy artist from romanticism to a chastened realism. His first plays, in verse, hark back for their subject matter to medieval times, beginning with the still popular *A Game of Chess* and including *The Triumph of Love*, *Brothers in Arms*, and, best of all, *The Red Count*. *A Game of Chess* might have come from the pen of Alfred de Musset, with its jaunty page who plays chess with the duke's daughter, agreeing to lose his head if he cannot win from her, and to marry her if he can. When he is on the point of forfeiting the game, the lady sets him right, permitting herself to be defeated, and cajoling her noble father into accepting the page as his son-in-law. A contest in wit for the hand of another lady is the basis of *The Triumph of Love*. *Brothers in Arms* and *The Red Count* show conflicts in character against an historical background. The plots of both are complicated, and the language is rhetorical rather than idyllic.

As an admirer of Goldoni, Giacosa cultivated comedy, also, meeting with most success in *The Husband in Love with his Wife* and *Late Repentance*. But he was more and more attracted to the social drama, and after various experiments in this field, he won applause with his *Luisa* and *Unconditional Surrender*, pieces still flavored with romance. The first is a problem play in verse, exalting love as a redeeming influence, a wife laying down her life in order to save her lover from her husband. The second is a comedy of manners which follows a favorite pattern with Giacosa, for it shows a coquette who, after endeavoring to wreck the career of a noble youth, falls in love with her victim and repents.

It was in *Unhappy Love*, however, that Giacosa rose to the full height of his powers, varying the triangular plot with refreshing sobriety, preserving the unities, and avoiding theatrical claptrap. The preoccupied husband who discovers too late the love of his wife for his friend, the wife who is restrained from eloping by the sight of her child's doll, and the lover who betrays his relationship to the wife by refusing her husband's offer of financial aid at a crisis,—these are beings of vitality and of moral stamina. Their tragic emotions lie deep, and no violent scenes are required to reveal them. The conclusion of the piece suggests a possible reconciliation when husband and wife have learned self-control in denying themselves to each other and in laboring to train their child. The lover in this case is tender of conscience, the husband is generous rather than violent, and the wife is too devoted to her child to forsake it. Here is realism at its best, with nothing forced, and an ending, however moral, not too happy.

Giacosa's historical drama, *The Lady of Challant*, written to afford Sarah Bernhardt an opportunity for displaying her powers in the rendering of passion, derives from a story by Bandello, and turns upon the redemption through love of a fallen woman. It was in the playwright's older manner. He returned, however, to the modern world, seeking especially to emulate Ibsen in *Rights of the Soul*. Like *A Doll's House*, the play unfolds with subtlety the relations of a married pair, and pleads for the woman's right to freedom of spirit. A wife who has honorably resisted the attentions of her husband's cousin and thereby induced his suicide, is tortured by her husband's jealousy. It is not enough for him that she has remained loyal in heart and deed; has she remained loyal in thought? Thus the husband would penetrate to the secret places of her soul, forcing her to admit, finally, that she has indeed loved the other man because of his finer nature. It is her husband's brutality, his failure to understand and respect her, that renders their continued union impossible. He has bade her leave him and observed her readiness to depart. Then he suffers a revulsion of feeling and commands her to stay. But, like another Nora, she turns from him in order to preserve intact her integrity of soul.

The later work of Giacosa, who died in 1906, includes librettos for Puccini's operas *La Bohème, Tosca,* and *Madame Butterfly,* written in collaboration with Luigi Illica, and two plays that stress character and minimize the love interest so usual upon the Italian stage. Both are family studies. *The Stronger* treats the same problem as does Barker's *The Voysey Inheritance.* A son learns that his father has been unscrupulous in business. Although his filial devotion never wavers, Silvio must repudiate the paternal dishonesty. He refuses, therefore, to profit by it, and in poverty will begin life anew after condemning the cousin who has weakly condoned such errors. Cesare Nalli, the financier, is an interesting modern type, kind to his family, ruthless to his victims, and self-justified in his doubtful business dealings. "Everything is legitimate that the law cannot reach," is his motto. He is unable to understand the quixotic honesty of his artist son, yet to protect the boy, he is ready to fight the duel with which Silvio threatens his father's detractor. So great is Silvio's love for his father that he laments their disparity of views due to a difference in education. But because their standards of conduct diverge, they can no longer live together.

The best-known play of Giacosa, *As the Leaves,* considers again bourgeois business, and faintly echoes Björnson's *A Bankruptcy.* It presents the condition of an upper-middle-class group unexpectedly exposed to the winds of adversity and fluttering to earth like the leaves of Autumn. Giovanni

Rosani fails in business and with his family moves to Geneva, hoping to redeem the past, but his second wife and his son are irresponsible and gay, the son gambling, and the wife flirting with an artist. Both believe that he has secreted the bulk of his fortune and admire his prudence. His daughter, the sympathetic Nennele, has no such illusions, but is confident that she can earn money to support the others by tutoring. Defeated in this hope by reason of her ignorance, and disheartened at her failure to instill moral strength into these weaklings, she contemplates suicide. But eventually she marries the cousin who has offered the family an asylum, and we are left with the hope that this benefactor may be able, also, to save these others who have been well-nigh ruined through prosperity. "Sweet are the uses of adversity" might have been the motto of this play. Be content with poverty and work, for it is only through these that you can develop character. Giacosa fails to establish our belief that money will inevitably ruin its possessors. Rosani's son and his wife are unnecessarily weak. The son's "exquisite sense of breeding and taste" of which his sister speaks does not prevent his accepting support from an overworked father. He lacks the will to do anything. Giulia might will to do evil, but is restrained by her regard for appearances. Nennele is finely drawn, with her efforts to rouse the family, with her love for her father and at the last for Massimo, whom earlier she had scorned as lacking in cultivation.

It is the merit of Giacosa to have conveyed the sense of life in his plays, creating flesh-and-blood characters who talk simply and effectively and illustrate moral themes. He nowhere assails social institutions, unless it be by implication the institution of marriage when it would destroy the individual soul. Rather, he is intent in his serious plays upon showing the need of restraint, self-sacrifice, and industry. In upholding the bourgeois virtues, he presents a complete contrast to the fiery and individualistic d'Annunzio.

Giovanni Verga, born at Catania in Sicily in 1840, embarked as a romanticist, as did Giacosa, and later became a more rabid realist. He was always, however, fond of melodramatic emotionalism. Art, he held, like other verists, should represent life in its ugliest manifestations. In poetry this attitude had been assumed by Lorenzo Stecchetti, who had issued in his *New Polemic* a manifesto of Verism. Upon the novels of Verga there wrought the influence of Zola. In *The Vanquished*, a fictional trilogy of which only the first two parts were finished, he composed vivid novels of Sicilian life, showing the struggles of those destined to defeat. The first was *The Malavoglia Family* and the second and less powerful was *Master Don Gesualdo*. Having written a volume of short stories, Verga dramatized one of them—*Rustic Chivalry*—for which Mascagni composed his famous music. Here was a youth returned from military service, embittered to discover that his sweetheart had married a carter, then in pique philandering with another girl until won back by the first, whose husband, informed by the second, kills him in a duel of knives. The scene was a village near Verga's birthplace, and the one-act play was a veritable bloody slice of peasant life.

Violent and ugly, too, were the dramas *At the Porter's Lodge*, *The She Wolf*, and *The Wolf Hunt*, all lacking in humor and in appreciation of what is genial and kindly in the Italian nature. *At the Porter's Lodge* shows us a brute making love to a bad woman in the slums of Milan expressly in order to torment her sister, a good girl devoted to him but dying of consumption. *The She Wolf* draws the character of a woman infatuated with a peasant for whose sake she gives up everything, her savings, her daughter, and even her life, after she has schemed to capture him. *The Wolf Hunt* accords a curious twist to the old situation of the jealous husband returning unexpectedly to catch his wife with his rival. For the rival proves so cowardly that the wife in disgust, and to save herself, cries out as though her virtue had been assailed by the fellow, whereupon her watching husband and his friends burst in to shoot the wolf, the poor devil caught in a trap. Less significant were Verga's dramatization of his novel *From Yours to Mine* and his comedy *The Fox Hunt*, developed on a higher social scale.

Gerolamo Rovetta, a thorough man of the world, who took to writing plays out of pique at a rival in love, was born in 1853 and died in 1910. His dramas are of two kinds,—the realistic and ironic, the idealistic and historic. He began in 1877 with *A Flight from the Nest* and *The Wife of Don Giovanni* and a dozen years later entered upon his successful career as realist with *The Trilogy of Dorina*, describing the downfall of a little governess, who, betrayed by a nobleman, becomes a more vicious Becky Sharp. Later, in *The Hubbub*, Rovetta painted the companion picture of a male adventurer. Men, in the opinion of this playwright, are creatures of their physical endowment at birth or of the environment that follows, the criminal being either inwardly sick or forced by outer circumstances into his career. Such is the moral of *The Dishonest*, wherein one who finds that his wife's expensive living has been but the price of her devotion to a lover now dead, seeks to maintain her standard of luxury by theft, in order that the world may not suspect her former source of income. Thus, to obscure knowledge of her crime, he commits another crime—apparently without forfeiting the good will of the audience. But, on being found out, he is obliged to flee, though still adoring his faithless destroyer.

Political revolt is the theme of *Reality* and of *Romanticism*, dramas in contrast, the first treating revolt with cynicism, and the second, with patriotic idealism. *Reality* depicts the futility of such an upheaval in view of the selfishness of the mob which entails disaster upon the few who are animated by noble motives. *Romanticism*, a study of Italian resentment against Austrian domination at the mid-century, follows exciting turns of intrigue in the conspiracy of a young count, who strives for the freedom and unification of his country, and discovers in the wife for whom he had cared little an eager fellow conspirator. No wonder that the play, with its striking situations and its appeal to patriotic fervor, should have won popular favor. It was still faithful to reality in its representation of a period not to be forgotten by Rovetta's countrymen. It indicated fully, however, its author's conversion from his earlier mood of pedestrian realism, employing for relief the melodramatic methods of the French. A less important piece concerned with the struggle against Austria was *The Buffoon King*. In *Molière and his Wife*, Rovetta attempted a character study that reminds one of Donnay's biographical drama concerned with the great Frenchman. Yet, except here and in *Papà Eccellenza*, an Italian *Père Goriot*, with its hero the unwilling victim of a selfish daughter, character was less important to Rovetta than plot and setting. He was never dull, but, save in *Romanticism*, never distinguished.

Marco Praga of Milan, born in 1862, served as a bank-clerk and then turned to literature, the profession of his father. A husband who refuses to obey the old code of honor by slaying his unfaithful wife, is the hero of Praga's first success, a play in one act, *The Friend*. When her lover dies, the lady would retrieve the letters she has written him, but in vain. Her husband gains possession of them, and, learning thus of her infidelity, bids her depart, but uses no violence. In *The Virgins*, a full-length piece which followed three comparative failures—*Giuliana*, *The Spell*, and *Mater Dolorosa*—the playwright drew a family of demi-mondaines, an easy-going mother and three daughters. Only one of the latter possesses any moral scruples. Because she has fallen honestly in love with a certain Dario, she feels that she must confess to him an incident in her past. She has yielded long before to one who would benefit her family. In that affair, she was more sinned against than sinning. It is all over and done with, but after this confession Dario regards her with abhorrence. Then he suggests that, since she is only damaged goods, they limit their relationship to a liaison. When she declines the evil proposal, he turns away, failing to appreciate the beauty of soul that has prompted her refusal to marry him under false pretences. Her sisters offer a conscienceless contrast to the good Paolina as they carry on their intrigues unabashed, seeking only such profit and enjoyment as the moment may afford.

Another important play by Praga is *The Ideal Wife*, an ironic study of feminine disloyalty in the manner of Becque and the French naturalists. Giulia really regards her husband with affection and deceives him comfortably. For his sake and the sake of their children, she is careful to avoid the least breath of scandal; so adroit are she and her lover, a friend of the husband's, that they excite no suspicion. Thus she enjoys playing her double rôle of wife and mistress, and up to the fall of the last curtain she has never allowed either rôle to interfere with the other. In method, both these dramas exemplify the tenets of the Verists. Morality as such is not the playwright's concern. He will tell the truth about his characters impartially. Giulia has learned to adjust her fiery nature to the situation imposed by conventional marriage. Paolina suffers because her nature is too refined to permit of her concealing a past that cuts her off from the future she desires. For such seeming virtue she deserves no particular credit. She is simply born that way, just as her sisters are born to be shameless.

Increasingly, Praga has felt the demands of the box-office, writing in response plays that would please an average audience, and sacrificing thereby something at least of artistic merit. The triangle has continued to be his principal resource in constructing a plot. Occasionally, he seems sincere, as in *The Moral of the Fable*, which exhibits the cynicism of despair and draws a contrast to *The Ideal Wife*. A woman who has succumbed to a lover is ready for his sake to abandon her husband; but, when the lover proves unworthy and withdraws, she is left to stifle her regrets, to return home and wear a galling mask that her lord may never learn of her disloyalty. In *The Crisis*, the wife is more perverse, loving her husband as did Giulia in *The Ideal Wife*, yet feeling that she must test him by sinning with another and then telling him all. In *Ondina*, it is the man who is perverse, for, though he knows his lady to be innocent, a mere rumor regarding her past will separate them, breeding jealousy and social ostracism. So, in *The Doubt*, another lover perversely hesitates as to marrying a sweetheart, lest after he has once possessed her, she cease to interest him. While he vacillates, haunted by this doubt, he is served right by losing her.

Abnormality and violence color *The Enamoured Woman* and *The Heir*, the last seeming an echo of *The Fossils* of de Curel, with a son, as there, making amends by marriage to the girl ruined by his father, a decadent nobleman. Praga's play of the year before, *Alleluja*, showed a husband indulgent to the wife he had found disloyal, but resolved to be severe on later discovering in her daughter an inherited tendency to loose-living. The implication appears to be that unless an erring wife is treated with a heavy hand, the mere force of heredity may corrupt her offspring. It is doubtful, however, that discipline as an acquired characteristic imposed from without would descend from mother to child, although the mother, having learned her lesson, might, of course, pass it on to the child. Praga, indeed, was merely using for dramatic purposes the fresh motif of heredity.

Much more delicate in its psychology and its workmanship than most of the pieces of this author was *The Closed Door*, played by Eleonora Duse in her last days. Here the interest is concentrated in states of soul rather than in outward action. A youth, who has felt unduly constrained at home by the overpowering affection of his mother, desires to join a colonizing expedition to East Africa, but is refused permission until he reveals the fact that he knows he is the child, not of his titular father, but of a friend of the family. Then, with the latter, he departs, understanding and forgiving his mother, but bound to make a new name for himself. Says he: "A closed door confronts me. I must open it. Otherwise I stifle, otherwise I die." The whole interest centers in the mother Bianca, already a stranger to her husband when she bore Giulio, and continuing to live with him only for the sake of the boy. Treated indulgently by this humorous dandy, she has long ago broken off her guilty relations with the lover, ceasing to be a woman in order to become only a mother. She recognizes the justice of her punishment, saying to her son on the eve of his departure for Africa: "It is not because you are going that my heart is broken. It is because I am the reason of your going." She rejects the suggestion that she leave now with her lover to begin life afresh. It is the son that parts them. To him they owe everything. To Decio she says: "You too must put him before me. . . . You must go, and I must stay, —alone." This piece provides an excellent example of how the Italian, objecting to divorce, steers around the obstacle of marriage. A priest in the play even argues that a transformation in marriage may some day occur, since every man is primarily the son of his mother, who alone is sacred. Says the priest, "No child has the right to judge her, to absolve her, or to punish her." Giulio accepts this notion, assuring his mother of his love and of his intention to return ere long to bring her to live with him in the colony. Thus *The Closed Door* expresses a nobility all too rare in the Italian theater, a feeling of the need for expiation and at the same time a generous forgiveness for sin.

Praga's work, however interesting, is lacking in distinction except in its earlier phase. His plots are monotonously based upon the consequences of illicit love. As a realist and as a man of the theater, he inclines to represent human nature in its lower aspects, save in a few notable instances. Those of his characters who are inwardly good are likely to be wronged and unhappy.

For subtlety in technique, for interest in ideas, for breadth and depth of achievement, no Italian playwright excels Roberto Bracco. His best pieces have been produced in many languages. Lacking the sensationalism of d'Annunzio and Sem Benelli, he is well poised, neither unduly elated nor unduly depressed in surveying life. If he offers no remedy for the evils he observes, he awakens sympathy for those who suffer and understanding of those who sin. He is no militant realist, and no shallow romanticist. He combines what is best in both schools, and directs attention not merely to the outward stir of action but to inner conflicts of soul.

Bracco is a Neapolitan, born in 1862. Having served an apprenticeship in the Customs, he became a journalist, and wrote, in addition to critical articles, short plays full of wit. At the time when Northern dramatists were beginning to be interested in feminine freedom, he composed *A Woman*, tracing the career of a courtesan redeemed by her experience of maternity. So far, he was controlled by the romantic tradition of Dumas, but he shows the influence of realism in *Masks*. Here a man, returning from a journey, learns that his wife has committed suicide as a result of her intrigue with his friend and business partner. She has died in despair, not merely because she would have borne him a child, but because she found that he was to marry another. The husband resists the temptation to kill his rival, since to do so would be to expose to the effects of the scandal his own little daughter. Instead, he will force his rival to live a life of smiling deception. "You have betrayed my honor!" he cries; "but the crowd shall never suspect it and trample on my name. Beware how you relax an instant in your part as hypocrite. On with your mask, and forward with the comedy; you are mine to shield myself with as I see fit; you have forged your own chains."

In *The Unfaithful* of the same year, Bracco wrote a realistic comedy that might have come out of Vienna. It concerns a countess who has demanded at marriage that her husband accord her perfect freedom. He has promised to refrain from jealousy whatever she may do. When he finds her visiting the rooms of a dashing lover, he misinterprets her indiscretion, threatens vengeance, but is finally appeased; for she had sought merely to read the libertine a lesson, and she is in fact bored by the suitors whom she had thought so entertaining. This play succeeded in Paris and even in America, where it was acted by Nazimova as *The Countess Coquette*.

The realism of low life rather than high marks *Don Pietro Caruso* and *Lost in Darkness*. The scene of both is Naples, with a background carefully observed and a bit of romance in the foreground by way of contrast. In the first and earlier play, a rascally lawyer who gets on by questionable means as the sycophant of politicians, discovers that one of them, a scion of the nobility, has wronged his daughter. All that the father has done he has stooped to for the welfare of this girl. When the nobleman laughs at the proposal that he make amends by marrying the girl, saying that one does not wed Don Pietro's daughter, the father is overwhelmed with chagrin. He perceives that, much as she loves her seducer, she can receive money from him only in payment for her disgrace. All Don Pietro's chicanery has proved unavailing to bring her happiness, and, since his sole satisfaction in life is gone, he will leave it,—but nonchalantly.

Lost in Darkness shows another original character moving in a low-life milieu. He is the blind fiddler of a café, a dependent relative of the proprietor. Having fallen in love with an outcast girl, he rejoices to hear her declare herself ugly, believing that thus she will be the less tempted to leave him. But Paolina is indeed beautiful and catches the eye of one who can both admire and pay for beauty. It emerges that she is the natural daughter of a duke, who, in dying, would seek her out, but is prevented by his mistress, concerned only with laying her hands on his property. Little Paolina, so nearly rescued from her vagabond life, remains dependent upon her own resources, and is the more readily lured away from her ideal love for the fiddler. She has agreed that should she ever resolve to part from him, she will extinguish the candle that burns before the statue of the Virgin. The last scene shows her furtively blowing out the light, and stealing away as the fiddler plays on. Only later will the blind man know by the lack of warmth from the candle that she has left him forever.

Unhappy and illicit love is the subject of most of Bracco's plays. In *Night of Snow*, *Not even a Kiss*, *The Bitter Fruit*, and *Maternity*, for example, women suffer from the perennial injustice of men, or from their own weakness, or from frustrated ambition. In *The Bitter Fruit*, the heroine agonizes as a result of loving one much younger than herself. In *Maternity*, the heroine, married to an unworthy husband, leaves him for the sake of her unborn child, only to die with that child deliberately. In *Tragedies of the Soul*, a wife, succumbing to a lover for whom she cares little, entails misery upon him, her husband, and herself.

Bracco has written Frenchified comedies of no great moment, such as *Do Not Unto Others*, *The Travel Adventure*, *Photography Without*, *One of the Honest*, and *Concealed Weapons*. In English, *Three* has been produced in an adaptation by Gilbert Cannan, as well as *The End of Love*, a comedy in the mildly cynical style of *The Unfaithful*. More original is *The Triumph*, which smiles at the romantic folly of Platonic love, a dream to appeal to the very young or the sick, but, according to Bracco, destined to melt before the sun of passion. So his Lucio Seppi, conceiving such an airy love for the girl who has tended him in illness, imbues her with his faith that a union higher than that based on sexual attraction is possible. But nature asserts its rights when the pair, invited to the country by a worldly-wise priest, respond to the influence of the summer season, the girl gladly yielding to a painter, and Lucio, though jealous, coming to understand and forgive her because he now thrills at the merely human attraction of the priest's pretty niece.

Once Bracco tried the sociological drama in *The Right to Live*, showing up, without much dramatic success, social inequalities and injustice in the fashion of Hauptmann's *Weavers*. The true Bracco, however, is to be seen rather in such psychological studies as *The Hidden Spring*, *Phantasms*, and *The Little Saint*. The last draws the character of a priest, disappointed in love and withdrawn from the world to a rustic parish, where his natural mysticism has found expression in endeavors to heal the sick as by miracle. The faith of those who believe in him does, indeed, work wonders, and a man cured becomes his devoted servant. When the priest exerts his spiritual powers upon the soul of his former sweetheart's daughter, he feels a faint afterglow of love for the girl, yet is forced with many a secret pang to surrender her in marriage to his easy-going brother. That brother cannot wholly possess his bride so long as she remains beneath the spell of the priest. They will leave, therefore, to live their own lives elsewhere. As they depart, the priest is grief-stricken, and his servant, incensed by such sorrow, pushes the bridegroom over the edge of a precipice. "It was for you, for you!" he exclaims in protest when the priest denounces him as a murderer. The servant, however, has but put into execution a thought in the mind of his master. The agony of that master is therefore the greater. He has turned from love to the religious life and has struggled when love was reborn in his heart, and he has struggled again to be true to his vocation in yielding up the girl to the brother whose loose character he despises. What are all his miracles for others compared to the fruitless miracle of his attempts at self-mastery?

In *The Hidden Spring* (*La piccola fonte*) a poet is absorbed by his writing and unreasonably irritable with his patient wife. He is chafed by her guileless questions and even her humble devotion. "In order to achieve my work," he tells her, "I must concentrate all my thought, all my ideals. I must reject all affections, all silly annoyances." Yet, when Theresa, rebuffed, dashes out of the house into the forest by night, Stephan is frightened. "I am worried because she may be suffering," he admits to his secretary; "I am not so hard as you think, although she is far from indispensable to my life." But the secretary retorts, "The humblest woman may be indispensable to the proudest man." Here is the theme developed by Ibsen in *When We Dead Awaken*, and by Hauptmann in *Lonely Lives*, but Bracco offers an original turn to the action, allowing the negligent husband to make some amends. When Theresa returns from her night in the forest completely distraught, Stephan bestows upon her the attention he had earlier denied and rejects the advances of a princess whom earlier he had encouraged. In vain the princess declares concerning the wife: "She does not want you, nor even recognize you. You were ready to abandon her when she needed you. Why not now, when your presence does not alleviate her suffering?" Stephan remains firm. He finds solace indeed only in the company of his mad Theresa. "I see you," he tells her, "as if you were my soul; I see you so quiet, so quiet—ah! at last I can sleep." But the wife, eluding him, runs to a parapet above the sea, and the play ends as Stephan, aroused to rush after and save her from falling, utters a cry from without. Of the characters, the wife is the chief, a beautiful soul, like Maeterlinck's Sélysette, ready to submit to any indignity so long as she may aid her husband, but exhausted by the overstrain of repression. The husband is the artist wholly consuming the man. Like the hero of d'Annunzio's *Gioconda*, he believes that domestic duties do not exist for one who would consecrate his life to the creation of beauty. But Bracco, unlike d'Annunzio, does not justify his artist. Instead, he shows Stephan to be blinded by the hallucination of his own genius, and in fact cold of heart and calculating. As for the princess Meralda, she figures in the play only to divert from the wife the attention of her husband. She loves flattery and the notice of the great, but she realizes that Stephan demands of her merely an introduction to her circle, and that he fails to give her his deep devotion. His cousin is the most appealing person in the piece, a hunchback of kindly nature, secretly in love with Theresa. When she dies, her passing is conveyed to the audience chiefly through his misery.

If this drama recalls the scholar's neglect of his wife in *Lonely Lives*, Bracco's *Phantasms* faintly echoes the situation in Hauptmann's *Teamster Henschel*. A consumptive professor is dying, tormented by unwarranted jealousy of his young wife. He exacts from her an oath that she will never allow her pity for his pupil to unite them, for he suspects Luciano's love for Julia, and would defeat it even after death. When he passes, Julia opens an asylum for widows who will agree never to remarry, but she finds herself besieged by thoughts of love for Luciano, who, in his despair, has resolved to depart for the African jungles. As his mother pleads with Julia to listen to his suit, the latter gathers courage to refuse, lest she be untrue to her vow. She has been half ready to break it, until, suddenly, she is appalled as if at sight of a specter, and shudders, "I cannot; I cannot." Here the motives, as well as the actions, of husband, wife, and lover are indeed fantastic. The husband's jealousy is purely conjectural and anticipatory. Julia's love for her husband seems unreal, since he has made her miserable by his unjustified suspicion. Luciano's love is fantastic, too, since it thrives in spite of the fact that he has received no word of encouragement from the lady.

Enough has been said, presumably, to indicate the versatility and power of Bracco, who has further experimented with a Sicilian dialect drama, *Consecrated Eyes*, a war piece, *The Cradle*, and two other plays prepared in war time, *The International* and *The Distant Lover*. Upon all his work, Bracco has expended unusual care, writing with a delicacy, a feeling for style, and a knowledge of character that guarantee the survival of his best compositions. He is interested in the psychoses of his people rather than in revolutionary ideas, and yet he has been sufficiently affected by the intellectualist theater of the north to ballast his plays with thought. There is nothing crass, vulgar, violent about Bracco. He is a realist, refined and accomplished, a cultured student of the world without and of the soul within.

CHAPTER XXVIII

D'Annunzio and the Minors

Butti, the Brothers Antona-Traversi, Niccodemi, Testoni, Novelli, Lopez, Gallarati-Scotti, Ludovici, Morselli, Sem Benelli, The Futurists

MASTER of all that is sensuous, emotional, and poetic, Gabriele d'Annunzio was born in 1864 on a yacht in the Adriatic. By race he has variously been described as a Dalmatian or a Hungarian Jew. He lived early in the Abruzzi, then attended school in Tuscany, took up painting, and turned poet under the influence of Carducci. After issuing a first volume of verse, he went to Rome, became the literary lion of the early 'eighties, and published further poems and short stories, one collection of the latter—*Virgin Earth*—depicting Abruzzi peasant life. His first novel, *Pleasure*, developed his ruling idea that the end of human existence is joy, that he who has most intensely experienced pleasure in the widest possible range of satisfactions is the supreme man. By temperament d'Annunzio was a philosophic voluptuary, employing his reason to expose his senses to every gratifying excitation. His imagination was perfervid, his love of beauty profound. He worshiped women, and was worshiped in return, converting many to his comforting doctrine of "purification by pleasure." As a dilettante he was interested in the minor arts from textiles to ceramics and jewelry. As a natural pagan, he was drawn to the culture of the Renaissance and of the Greeks. He was also attracted by the theories of Nietzsche, and dreamed of a world in which he at least might enjoy distinction as an esthetic superman.

Having by the age of twenty-six served his time in the army, d'Annunzio gained a certain strength of fiber hitherto lacking, and supplemented his study of the classics and the early Italians by reading the Russian novelists. He won more than national attention through a series of novels—including *Giovanni Episcopo*, *The Triumph of Death*, *Virgins of the Rocks*, and *The Flame*—and he continued to display his virtuosity in several collections of poems. Essentially a lyric and descriptive genius, he was led only late to the theater, beginning just before the turn of the century with dialogues from the *New Testament*. Herein he praised all that the religious would condemn, emphasizing, for example, the wisdom of the foolish virgins. In two *Dreams of the Seasons—The Dream of a Spring Morning* and *The Dream of an Autumn Sunset*—he set forth in rich colors and by impassioned rhetoric sensational situations. In the first, a crazed wife, whose lover, stabbed by her husband, has died in her arms, imagines the scene as recurring and grows madder still. In the second, the doge's wife, having slain her lord by sorcery in order to wed a lover, finds the latter enamored of a courtesan, and destroys this rival by the same black art she had employed against her husband, the action being merely suggested as the dogaressa raves to her servants and thrusts pins into the waxen image of her victim.

In *The Dead City*, his first full-length drama, d'Annunzio created an atmosphere heavy with the fragrance of morbid passion and of tombs freshly opened. An archeologist, in love with his sister, and delving for the remains of Agamemnon, is infected by the crimes of the ancient house of Atreus and ultimately drowns his sister that she and he may be saved from incest. "Who would have done for her what I have done?" he asks. "I closed her eyelids upon her eyes . . . ah, softer than a flower upon a flower! . . . And every stain is gone out of my soul: I have become pure, quite pure." A second motive to the slaying is confessed by Leonardo. He has drowned his sister that his married friend who has also loved her guiltily may no longer be separated from him by jealousy. "O my brother in life and death, . . . forever reunited to me by this sacrifice that I have made. . . . She is perfect; now she is perfect. Now she can be adored like a divine being." The wife of the friend is a blind girl, supremely unselfish, so much desiring that the husband shall possess Leonardo's sister that she is ready to take her own life to facilitate an amour that will make him happy for the moment. She obviously is a companion character to Maeterlinck's Sélysette,—a quiet, understanding, inexpressive soul. But here the sense of impending doom is deepened.

The artistic credo of d'Annunzio is proclaimed in *Gioconda*, which protests against the common association of art and morality. A sculptor, married to a charming wife, finds inspiration for his work in a beautiful mistress. Distraught by his struggle between duty and desire, he has tried suicide. Nursed back to health by his patient wife, he vows reform, yet can no longer create, and is tempted to revisit his studio where his model has been awaiting him, having kept wet against his return the clay of his unfinished masterpiece. In the meantime, the wife hastens to the studio, lies to Gioconda in declaring that Lucio would turn her out, but when Gioconda, in rage, seeks to overset and destroy the statue, saves it at the cost of her lovely hands—those of Duse, who suggested and played the part. But the wife's sacrifice proves futile, for a final act shows the maimed Silvia deserted by her husband, rallied by a beggar-maid on the loss of her hands, and unable therefore to take the flowers brought by her unsuspecting child. When Silvia affirms the beauty of her love, Lucio replies that his destiny requires him to think only of a beauty of body to be arrested and preserved in marble. "I was born to make statues," he declares. "When a material form has left me with the imprint of beauty, the office assigned me by nature has been fulfilled." Such, too, is the faith of the devoted model, whose features, supposed to be divinely fair, are veiled and thus left to be imagined by the fond fancy of each spectator. Says Gioconda of Lucio's studio: "Household affections have no part here; domestic virtues have no sanctuary here. This is a place outside laws and beyond common rights."

A play which exalts political rather than artistic egotism followed, its scene Papal Rome, its strong and ruthless heroine jilting one lover for another since he promises her greater power. But *Gloria* failed upon the stage, and when printed was dedicated "To the dogs that hissed it." *Francesca da Rimini* was more fortunate. Here, in his first drama after the turn of the century, d'Annunzio richly embroiders the famous episode from the fifth canto of Dante's *Inferno*, using it as an excuse for displaying passion and flamboyant poetry. Francesca, trapped into a marriage of convenience with the lame and ugly Gianciotto, mistakes his handsome brother Paolo for her bridegroom and thereafter loves him absorbingly. She aids him in repelling a siege, and, when peace is won, reads with him the story of Launcelot which prompts them to yield to their desire. Spied upon by a jealous younger brother, one-eyed and malignant, Francesca so rebuffs him that he informs her husband, who thereupon surprises the guilty pair, slays them both—Francesca because she intercepts his thrust at Paolo—and breaks his bloody sword across his knee. This husband, on the whole, is humanized, but the informer Malatestino is a melodramatic villain upon whom falls all the odium, enabling the lovers and even the husband to retain the spectators' sympathy. Every feature of the play is wrought out in elaborate detail. Attention is focused upon what is pictorial and emotional, rather than what is ethical. No greater contrast could be conceived than that between this rococo piece and Maeterlinck's misty *Pelléas and Mélisande* or Stephen Phillips' chaste and delicately chiseled

Paolo and Francesca or the robust and captivating *Francesca da Rimini* of George Boker.

Peasants of the Abruzzi observed by d'Annunzio at first hand are the characters of his powerful tragedy, *The Daughter of Jorio*, perhaps the best of his plays as drama. The superstitious point to Mila di Codra, child of a sorcerer, as being herself a sorceress. Escaping from field hands who have lusted for her in drink, she bursts into the hut of a shepherd about to wed with pagan ceremonies a girl he does not love. Though he starts to drive Mila forth, he succumbs to her spell at one glance, and protects her from her pursuers including his own father. Then, when he has taken her up into the hills, Aligi, to save her from his drunken father who follows, kills the latter in a struggle. As a parricide, Aligi must suffer death, first losing a hand, then being sewn up in a sack along with a wild mastiff, and finally being tossed into deep water. His mother, forgiving his sin, offers him before his execution a draught of forgetfulness to dull his mind. He is already dazed when Mila, distracted, rushes in to declare that it was she who did the murder and then bewitched him into believing himself the slayer. Now, even Aligi, convinced of the truth of her words, curses her, as he sees her dragged forth to be burnt as a witch. Here is brisk action, and a dramaturgic tightening of tension leading to a series of stirring climaxes. The local color is laid on with accurate knowledge of peasant psychology and peasant customs and beliefs. But Mila and Aligi are romantic figures, notwithstanding, living together platonically in their mountain cavern, Mila planning to leave him lest his bride suffer from his defection, and Aligi, who has earlier protected her by laying at the door of his hut a waxen cross that instantly curbs the passion of her pursuers, now wielding upon his imperious father the ax he had been using to carve his vision of Mila's guardian angel. As always with d'Annunzio, the favorite themes are lust and revenge.

So, in *The Light Under the Bushel*, another violent tragedy of the Abruzzi, appears a she-devil to be contrasted with the noble Mila. This is Angizia, daughter of a snake-charmer, who, having found employment in the castle of a decadent nobleman, has caused the death of her master's wife, and proceeds to marry him and poison his son and make love to his brother. The nobleman's daughter, blaming herself for not having saved her mother from the unspeakable Angizia, commits suicide after a novel fashion, plunging her arms into a bag of vipers, part of the stock-in-trade of Angizia's father. In the mean time, the nobleman, rendered frantic by all that his family has endured from the she-devil, slays her, to the delight of the audience.

More than Love, which failed upon the stage, perhaps because the public had come to expect only the sensational from d'Annunzio, was better in dialogue than in plot. It told the story of an explorer embittered to find his discoveries stolen by an impostor. Refused government aid in his desire to return to Africa, he murders a gambler whose ill-gotten gains he will use for a good purpose, like the hero of Dostoyevsky's *Crime and Punishment*. But, being threatened with prosecution, he takes his life, comforted in dying by a mistress who assures him that she is to bear him a child, one to be worthy of its father, this self-justified superman.

Passion is again to the fore in *Fedra* and *The Ship*, the former revamping Euripides, whose Phædra becomes for d'Annunzio a luxury-loving nymphomaniac. Having falsely accused her cold stepson of making advances to her when he has actually rebuffed her, she feels in his ensuing death a certain purification for herself, but is slain by a moon-ray sent by Diana, guardian of the chaste Hippolytus. *The Ship* is all spectacle, a thing of pagan fume and fury, showing the revenge of the imperious Basiliola upon the doge who has blinded and slain her father and her brothers. To accomplish her ends, she comes from the Byzantine camp to Venice, ensnares the doge, secures from him the torture of her enemies, charms them even while shooting them with arrows where they wallow in a trench, and then allures the bishop, the doge's brother, and sets the two to fighting. But when the doge has killed the bishop, he declares that Basiliola shall be nailed as figurehead to the prow of the ship in which he will embark upon a voyage of expiation. As the ship is launched, Basiliola, perceiving that her game is lost, immolates herself upon an altar to naval victory, the people hymning her defeat and that of Byzantium. The period represented is the sixth century, and the scenic panorama is more appropriate to opera than drama, the verse pulsing with fluctuant rhythms in splendid vowel harmonics. It was not long, indeed, before d'Annunzio wrote two librettos for opera, *Parisina*, for the music of Mascagni, and *La Piave*, at the end of the War, for the music of Italo Montemezzi. The former piece, like *Fedra*, tells the story of a woman's love for her stepson, and, like *Francesca da Rimini*, shows that love as mutual and inducing the murder of the lovers by the outraged husband. The Duchess of Ferrara, who has accompanied her stepson Ugo to the shrine at Loreto, nurses him when he is wounded in repulsing the Saracens, and dies with him when her lord wreaks revenge upon them both.

It was natural, too, that d'Annunzio, who had given increasing attention to spectacle, should have attempted the moving picture scenario, accepting the doctrine of Gordon Craig that the stage should emphasize what is plastic, and in *Cabiria* turning the Second Punic War into a splendid show. D'Annunzio has affirmed that he sees in the cinema a new art of enlarged possibilities, thanks to its being no longer bound by the limitations of time and place and also to its supplementing the appeal to the ear by a greatly increased range of appeal to the eye.

In the mean time, just before the War, d'Annunzio had demonstrated his linguistic virtuosity by writing in perfect

French two plays for the actress Ida Rubinstein. Both were couched in free verse. *The Martyrdom of Saint Sebastian*, the first and better of the two, imitates an ancient mystery in the somewhat archaic forms of a foreign tongue, and was aided in production by the designs of Léon Bakst and the incidental music of Claude Debussy. Its subject is the conversion and death of the young Roman archer, friend of Augustus Cæsar, drawn as a superstitious fanatic, converted when the arrow he has shot heavenwards fails to return to earth. His progress is attended by miracles, lilies blossoming from the hot coals over which he walks unharmed. His religious fervor leads him in an ecstasy of passion to destroy the idols of his old faith and to enjoy to the full the thrill of martyrdom as he bids his archers administer to him the sweet balm of death. Here may be noted the influence upon the Italian of French and Belgian mystics.

The second French play of d'Annunzio was *The Pisan Woman*, or *Perfumed Death*, another drama of lust and revenge. Again a father proves the rival of his son for love of a beauty. When the son has been killed by the father, King of Cyprus, the beauty is put to death by order of the jealous queen, and dies a fragrant death, smothered beneath a mountain of roses. In each act, the king dreams of an ideal love, and beholds her now as a beggar girl, now as a slave, now as a courtesan in the guise of a nun, and at last as a dancer in his palace.

Less luxuriantly sensational was a third play in French, the prose *Honeysuckle*, a revenge-tragedy, feverish with suppressed passion. A girl of nineteen, suspecting that her father has been murdered by his friend and physician, now married to her mother, probes the mystery and extorts from the physician a confession of his crime. He alleges that he was justified, since, in slaying his sick friend by an injection of morphia, he but obeyed that friend's sacred injunction. The avenging daughter, however, will accept no such excuse. She endeavors to incite her brother to punish the murderer, whom she also suspects of intriguing with the brother's wife; but, failing here, she nerves her mother to the deed. The physician, protesting that he was but a servant of fate, true to his friend, is stabbed by his wife. He dies after praying to the soul of his victim as one who alone can understand the purity of his motive and his sacrifice. But the girl triumphantly kisses her mother's bloody hand. Setting and atmosphere add to the sense of impending doom in this drama, which echoes *Electra* and *Hamlet*, as to plot, and the tales of Poe and the early plays of Maeterlinck, as to mood and manner.

Although here and elsewhere d'Annunzio's criticism of life is of no value, he is a poet of the first order, and a dramatist of the second or third. It must be conceded that his plays are lacking in variety, harping always upon the same themes, and using the same general incidents and characters over and over. With the single exception of *Gioconda*, they are dramas of emotion rather than ideas, and even *Gioconda* stresses merely the notion that for the artist beauty is an end in itself divorced from morality. Indeed, beauty and feeling constitute d'Annunzio's world. His people are but facets of his own personality. They are abnormal folk dominated by passion, unable to reason, or to defer response to the imperious calls of sense long enough to indulge in wit or humor. They cannot know the genial warmth of friendship or of pity. They are never kind or gentle or devoted. For them the only duty is to follow instinct. Passion thwarted generates jealousy and hate; hence for them revenge is the complement of lust, cruelty of desire.

D'Annunzio is the artist pure and simple, thrilled by lovely forms, by the flow of melodious language, by the ecstasy of high moments. He would render all that is voluptuous in love, sickness, and death. So distinguished is the poetic quality of his work that it will endure in spite of its persistent morbidity. As a playwright d'Annunzio prefers either the static or the spectacular; indeed, his genius is epic and lyrical rather than dramatic. He looks backward rather than forward, disclosing nothing of the new Italy of efficient Fascism. Idolized by his countrymen, especially after the adventure of Fiume, he stands apart in a time of optimistic social coöperation as a reactionary aristocrat, a Byronic individualist, a pagan loving freedom because, like Byron, devoted to it in his personal life.

About such well known writers for the stage as d'Annunzio, Bracco, Praga, and Giacosa may be ranged a group of minors who, for the most part, are realists. Several were influenced, like Praga, by Ibsen. These Southern disciples of the Norwegian are Amalia Rosselli, Teresah Ubertis, and Enrico Butti. So far as ideas are concerned, they lacked the courage or desire to import Ibsen's philosophy. They rather copied his technique. Yet Amalia Rosselli's *The Soul*, which in its central situation recalls Praga's *The Virgins*, faintly echoes *A Doll's House*. It introduces a woman of fine character scorned by a lover who judges her only by externals. He turns from her when, believing that she is in honor bound to tell everything, she reveals to him the fact that once she had yielded to another. Instead of making allowance for her youthful inexperience, he thereupon bestows his heart upon a woman technically chaste but unworthy in mind, only to repent his decision later. Olga is as much of a new woman as the Italians dared to show, upholding feminine rights and feminine education as opposed to the conspiracy of silence in regard to sex. Yet she is not a moral radical. In Signora Rosselli's later play *Illusion* it is a wife who is injured by an unscrupulous lover through no fault of her own. Perceiving that her husband can never forgive and forget, she leaves him for his own good despite her deep devotion. A suggestion of Ibsen's influence is to be found, also, in *The Judge* of Teresah Ubertis, with its introspective hero, who, having refused a bribe to decide a case in favor of a wealthy litigant, awards him the decision in good conscience. As a result he is suspected of dishonesty and even begins to doubt his own motives.

More obviously affected by Ibsen was the conservative reactionary Enrico Annibale Butti, a Milanese, born into easy circumstances in 1868. He studied medicine and law and early took to writing novels which exhibit man as a victim, not only of unintelligent legislation, but of his instincts and his general environment. In 1894, the year after writing his first drama *Bitter Fruit*, Butti produced *Utopia*, a play of ideas to prove that rationalism is bound to fail in a world composed of emotional human beings. The physician who would denounce marriage, the slavery of women, and the coddling of weak and deformed children, discovers that the girl who had seemed to share his theories abstractly, insists upon being legally bound to him. Moreover, she presents him with a child deformed. Instead of destroying it according to the doctrine that he has preached, they will both make it their special care. In the mean time, the physician's eugenic propaganda has been coldly received by the public, and he is forced to recognize the folly of relying upon science as an infallible guide in life.

In *The End of an Ideal*, Butti revealed a similar attitude toward feminism, attacking it as an excuse for mere license. He would answer the contention of Ibsen in *A Doll's House*, and uphold the Latin conception of woman's need for surrender to man as the natural master, protector, provider, and guardian of her honor. Conservative objections to radicalism mark the plays that constitute Butti's trilogy, *The Atheists*. Here, *The Race for Pleasure* shows the futility of selfish individualism in the case of a skeptic made to realize his mistake when his adored mother dies. An agnostic who has retired from the priesthood because he could no longer believe, gives his nickname to the second of the series, entitled *Lucifer*, but his doubts knock the props from beneath his son when the latter's wife falls ill. As she dies, comforted by a churchman, the youth is so impressed by the spectacle that he turns for consolation to the same source, while his agnostic father is left wondering if there be not at least a pragmatic virtue in faith. In *The Tempest*, the third play of the group, Butti pays his respects to the socialists and the revolutionists, those negative forces that would destroy the good old order.

There is admirable character drawing in *Flames in Darkness*, with its hero a gentle priest whose ambitions are rendered frustrate by the misconduct of a sister to whom he sacrifices his life. The more he surrenders for her sake, the worse she behaves. Although he has had a fair chance of becoming a bishop, this family curse prevents his being considered. At length, realizing that he cannot bring the wayward woman to decency amid her old surroundings, he bears her off to a remote village among the hills, resolving to save one soul at least and forget the world. There is unwonted beauty and idealism in the play, combined with careful painting of character and milieu, but there is no note of revolt against the folly of society in condemning the individual for a fault not his. How different is the author's spirit in Galsworthy's *A Bit o' Love*!

The virtue of renunciation is again extolled in *The Invisible Sun*, when a musician displays unusual courage for an artist in warning the wife of another grown infatuated with him to remember her duty to her husband and her child. The vice of idleness, the ungirt loin, is assailed in a closet drama in verse, *The Castle of Dreams*, and the tendency of the nobodies to attack a somebody is set forth satirically in *The Giant and the Pygmies*, wherein a great man's critics make him miserable, and his wife joins forces with one of them. Of Butti's other plays, *In the Land of Fortune* is a melodrama, *The Cuckoo* is a charming light satire, and *Ever Thus* continues his thrusts at the new woman.

Butti died of consumption in 1915, all his literary activity having profited him but little in a financial way. Inspired by the problem dramatists of the North, he had endeavored to make his countrymen think, without unsettling their faith in religion and the established social order. He tried indeed to prove that the new individualism was bound to defeat itself, failing to achieve the happiness which it so frankly makes its goal. Although his sense of the comic was adequate, as witness *All For Nothing*, he won attention chiefly by his dramaturgic talents and his power of pathos.

Two prolific realists are the brothers Antona-Traversi, sons of a Milanese of large property and high station. The elder, Camillo, was born in 1857 and eventually became a professor of literature in Rome and then a man of letters in Paris. He has written more than thirty plays, some of them in French. His principal early success was *The Rozeno Family*, depicting a group of the disreputable in the manner of the French naturalists. He grew more satiric in *The Parasites*, leveling his lance at social climbers and unscrupulous captains of industry. On occasion, he has examined serious problems,—the relation between the faithful and the unbelievers in his brief *Earth or Fire*, and that between spendthrifts and the cautious sons of the middle class in *Dance Macabre*. At other times, he has produced vivid plays of terror and dramas domestic or historical.

Camillo's brother Giannino was four years his junior, a lively person whose excesses caused him to fall out with his father and forced him to write comedies after trying less distinguished expedients to maintain his independence. He excelled in the one-act play, the sort of curtain-raiser so common in Italy, smart, graceful, piquant. In these and in his longer comedies he has dealt with an idle and mildly corrupt high society engaged for the most part in playing the love game. Thus, in *The School of Husbands*, he satirizes those of his own class whose dissipation portends their ultimate destruction. Sometimes he waxes fairly serious in reproving the heartless, as in the ironically entitled *Honest Wife*, a study of chill egotism, or in *The Coquette*, whose heroine at last finds more than her match in a robustious young sculptor, or in *Worldly Charity*, which laughs at those who, merely for selfish reasons, pursue philanthropy. Sometimes, also, as in *The Wedding Journey*, he composes, like his brother, a Grand Guignol drama just to shock. As a rule, however, he writes in lighter vein, endeavoring to revive the tradition of Goldoni. He smiles at folly while reproving it, avoiding the scolding tone of the professional satirist. So, in his first play, *The Morning After*, he permits a lady who is carrying on an intrigue to defend herself from her husband by catching him in a similar attempt at deception. In *The Ascent to Olympus* he laughs good-naturedly at the ambitions of a simple fellow who would ape the manners of the aristocracy, and equally at the aristocrats who accept this social inferior because of his money. In *Martyrs to Work*, the playwright awakens amusement at the expense of those so busy with clubs, committees, and balls that they cannot get the best from marriage. He uses the *raisonneur* of the French stage to state his own views and utter the pronouncements of common sense; and he sprinkles his dialogue with glittering epigrams likely to prove useful to those of his audience who move in that world of fashion which he represents so well.

Another minor playwright is Dario Niccodemi who has won attention by his dramaturgic skill. A number of his pieces have been performed abroad. *Scampolo* has appeared in English as *Remnant*, the story of a pure girl who rises from the Parisian slums to save and marry an artist threatened by her unworthy rival. *Refuge*, which had its first production in French, was acted in English by John Drew as *The Prodigal Husband*; and *The Shadow*, also composed in French, was first performed by Ethel Barrymore in America. Two plays, *The Enemy* and *The Titan*, reflect conditions since the outbreak of the War, the first presenting the reconciliation between a woman and her stepson after her own son dies in action. In English this drama has been produced under the title *Stronger than Love*, with Nance O'Neill in the leading rôle, that of a duchess of the old noblesse of France. Earlier works of Niccodemi include *The Aigrette* and *The Sharks*. It is in *The Refuge*, however, already referred to, that his characteristic qualities are to be seen at their best. An artist who has discovered the infidelity of his wife will be evened with her by making love to another woman. This woman, moreover, is the fiancée of his rival. Thus his revenge will be doubled. But, having succeeded, he is threatened with the loss of the second lady when she learns that what incited his attentions was mere pique. At this juncture, who should step in to save him but his own wife Juliette, assuring the other woman that it is she whom Gerard adores. He has given her a devotion far greater than he ever gave his wife. In recognition of that devotion, Juliette is ready to sacrifice herself by conceding him a divorce that he may marry Dora. She will help him, further, to preserve for a time his mother's illusion that he has been domestically happy. So the wife, though originally guilty in deviating from her duty to her husband, atones for that fault by relinquishing him to the woman upon whom he had at first thought to take revenge. The wife will allow his passion for another full scope, in order, not to free herself, but unselfishly to free him. Here as in his other plays Niccodemi is intent upon a series of episodes that awaken emotion rather than upon a study of vital character.

There is no great novelty in the work of Niccodemi or of Sabatino Lopez, Augusto Novelli, or Alfredo Testoni. The last-named, a resident of Bologna, is gifted with humor, and has written farces and comedies, some of them in Bolognese dialect, and an historical character sketch, *Cardinal Lambertini*, depicting a seventeenth-century churchman engaged in a worldly intrigue. There is excellent fun in the light plotting of *Living Quietly*, which urges in marriage loves for both husband and wife, rather than the introduction of an odd lover for either. Sometimes Testoni is fairly serious, as in *Discipline*, which shows the sufferings in love of a soldier obliged to obey his military superior, who happens to be also his rival. As a rule, however, the dramatist is satisfied merely to provide entertainment, and excels in brief trifles.

Novelli, a journalist and municipal councillor of Florence, depicts the life of the town in many bright comedies, such as *Lippi's Virgins*, *Still Waters*, and *The Changeling*, and in two historical dramas, *The Cupola* and *Canapone*. The first is concerned with the building of the dome of the cathedral in the fifteenth century, and the second with revolt against the Austrians in the mid-nineteenth century. As for Lopez, professor and dramatic critic, born at Leghorn in 1867, he is graver in *The Secret*, *The Good Girl*, and *The Tangle*, the last analyzing the survival of jealousy in the heart of a man who carries over distrust of his deceased wife to distrust of his child. In one play, *The Third Husband*, done in English as *Three for Diana*, Lopez upholds the right of divorce and also the right of remarriage for widows. In *The Beast and the Beauties*, performed in English by Leo Ditrichstein, Lopez paints the portrait of a sensual banker whose ugly face prevents his achieving final success in pursuing the fair. *The Hurricane* he composed in French, and his second play, *By Night*, was acted in that language at Paris by the time that he had won fame at home. Some of his pieces are clever trifles intended for the so-called *Teatri a sezioni*, those theatres specializing in giving a number of short plays in a single night. In his earlier manner, he inclined to be as impersonal and brutal as the Parisian makers of the *comédie rosse*. Later he allowed sentiment to intrude, as in *The Sparrow*, which reveals the grief of a mother forced to leave her baby boy, "the sparrow," with strangers, since she is married already and has a child by her husband. That husband had been absent for a year in America when she fell in love with an aviator presently shot down in the War. At the opening of the little play, his comrade, who had been dropped in the same plane, has come to thank those who had cared for him when he was hurt by the accident, and there he meets for the first time the mother of the babe which he has now adopted. Having told him her story, she refuses his offer to show her the child, since she knows that, having once seen it, she could never relinquish it.

The note of pathos is sounded also in several other Italian pieces. In 1921, on Duse's return to the stage after her long withdrawal, she played not only Ibsen's *Lady from the Sea* and Praga's *Closed Door* but *Thy Will Be Done*, by an unknown dramatist, Tommaso Gallarati-Scotti. This is a peasant drama concerned with the vow of a mother made on condition that her sick child recover. She feels that she has been guilty in loving even at romantic distance a neighbor, and promises the Virgin that, if the child be spared, she will go away on pilgrimage and tear this lover from her heart. Long after, when her boy is grown into a rude fellow like his father, the mother returns just to be near him, but is recognized and railed at by the youth as one who had deserted her home. She accepts his reproach as God's will, and is seen in the epilogue persuading the sacristan of a church to lock her in at twilight, there to die after offering her life to the Virgin that now her son's soul may be saved. "Thy will be done!" are her last words. Duse rendered this character with such rare sympathy that she overcame the protest of her audience at the brutality of the son.

Another pathetic trifle is *L'Eroica* by Cesare Ludovici, in which the mistress of a youth now dead, on coming to his home to bear his child, is scorned by his family. Only two understand,—Leonardo, who declares to the harsh relatives: "She came into our house serenely to offer us a magnificent gift. . . . And you're all against her," and Malvina, who, listening to his playing of Beethoven's *Eroica*, perceives that there is always an injustice involved in one's bringing to birth a life. When the babe is born dead, she declares that, since no one wanted him, he has had the courage to refuse to live. More interesting is Ludovici's *The Idiot*, which upholds the Tolstoyan virtue of non-resistance to evil. Daniel is a Parsifal or "pure fool," a child-like scholar deeply in love with Camilla and undaunted by her frank declaration that she can never for long remain true to him. Even so he will take and trust her, and when, five years later, her former lover reappears to claim her, Daniel leaves the decision to her, saying: "If she does not wish to go, no one can harm me. . . . The only harm would be to have her remain should she wish to leave." At first Camilla responds to his confidence, and then, unlike Ibsen's Lady from the Sea, she departs, and Daniel accepts her choice, sure that some day she will return. To the boasting lover who presently declares her to be happy, he remarks that if she has regretted for a moment all she has left, he should surrender her. Then the lover, surprised by the generous forgiveness accorded him, confesses how he had lured her away by lies, and adds that Camilla in truth hates him now. Daniel merely replies, "Tell her that I am waiting, that all the doors of my house are open to her," and to Maurice he declares with philosophic calm: "I am not a beast offended because another beast has carried off its mate. . . . You have indeed filled my home with sorrow, pain, despair; but you have not offended me. You should be the one who is offended, you who have done this evil deed, and not I who suffer it." Needless to say, such an attitude is distinctly novel in Italy, where "vengeance is mine" saith the injured husband. Daniel is a romantic counterpart to the hero of Molnár's *Fashions for Men*, one whose returning of good for evil is rewarded by winning the wayward. He offers the same test for an unlawful love proposed by Hervieu in *The Awakening*, namely, to submit it to the supposition that the lady or the lover be dead.

Unless in that case life for the survivor be meaningless, such a love is not justified.

Again a moral note is struck in Ludovici's *The Woman of No One*, showing the gradual redemption from sensuous selfishness of a girl who arouses the passion of her brother, then yields to a wastrel lover, and marries him only at her father's instance. After separating from him, she is brought to a sense of responsibility by still another lover, and a worthy one. So changed is she that she dismisses this friend and her brother as well, and will devote herself to the child against whose birth she has fought. She will further summon back the child's father to be her husband indeed. According to her brother, if Fate had not created her his sister she might have proved a lamp on his altar to guide him through life. "But now," he laments, "because of that fact, you will always be the woman of no one; and I—I shall live just to live." Anna, however, proves that she can resist the ordering of Fate, and develop character at least for herself.

The poetic drama has been exemplified by certain plays of Morselli and Sem Benelli and one notable piece in verse by Giovacchino Forzano. This last, entitled *Sly*, derives from the induction to *The Taming of the Shrew*. Whereas Hauptmann in his *Schluck and Jau* makes the situation used by Shakespeare more humorous, Forzano makes it more romantic. A count come to an inn in quest of a fugitive mistress prevails upon her to pose as the wife of a vagabond who, given a sleeping potion, awakens in a palace and is made to believe himself the count in person, recovering from long illness. The novelty here lies in the fact that the vagabond and Dolly fall deeply in love, to the distress of the jealous count, who thereupon exposes his jest and imprisons its victim. Sly, in despair that Dolly should thus have been torn from him after his brief dream of love and beauty, gashes his wrist with a bottle, and too late is found by the weeping girl, who has sought him out to ask his forgiveness for her part in the jest. Though his death be far from inevitable the hero is a figure at once charming and pathetic, so much wittier than the count that he wins the latter's lady, and yet aware of his own unworthiness as a tavern roisterer.

Ercole Luigi Morselli, born at Pesaro in 1882, studied letters and medicine in Florence, traveled about the world, and returned to edit a review and to write ironic fables and several stories and plays. The first of the plays was *Water Upon Fire*, showing the visit to a shepherd's hut of a sailor who captures the heart of a peasant girl ere he leaves for his ship. *Gaston the Animal Tamer* drew a humorous picture of a popular idol brave before his beasts but fearful of a marchioness who makes jealous his sweetheart. In *The Prison* Morselli writes a modern drama, contrasting in its realism with his poetic and symbolic tragedies *Orione* and *Glauco*, the former introducing a demi-god who, wishing to emancipate himself from earthly limitations, would prove his power by destroying a monster, but succumbs to the sting of a little scorpion he has disdained. *Glauco*, which won a government prize in 1919, presents a versified account of the hero's love for Scylla, his quest for fame inspired by the Tritons and Sirens, and his return from far wanderings only to find that Scylla has died. The beauty and simplicity of these plays and the praise of the critic Papini contributed to their success. Two other tragedies, *Daphnis and Chloe* and *Belphagor*, were left by Morselli when he died of consumption in 1921.

Except for d'Annunzio, Morselli's most prominent rival was Sem Benelli, born in 1877 of Jewish stock and early a journalist in Florence. Having failed with a drama in prose, *The Bookworm*, he turned to the poetic play in *The Mask of Brutus*, laid in Florence of the sixteenth century and descriptive of Medicean love, lust, and revenge. This was followed by his well-known masterpiece in the same vein, *The Supper of Pranks*, and by other dramas of historical background. In several, the period represented was the Middle Ages, and in these the romantic conflict centered in the struggle between Christian and pagan ideals. Such was the case in *The Love of the Three Kings*, set to music by Montemezzi, and in the revenge tragedies, *Rosmunda* and *The Marriage of the Centaurs*. Medieval Pisa is the scene of *The Gorgon*, and Renaissance Florence of *The Mantle*. Throughout, Benelli is sensuous, impassioned, and violent. He delights in exposing the stark cruelty of lust and hate, in exciting suspense, and effecting thrilling catastrophes. History provides him with characters and incidents to be shaped to his own imaginative ends. He admits that his fluent verse is the verse of action rather than of song. It is clear, resonant, strongly cadenced.

All the most characteristic qualities of Sem Benelli unite in his *Supper of Pranks*, known in English as *The Jest*. Here a series of highly wrought scenes exhibit the revenge of a constitutional coward upon two brothers who have long bullied him. One he causes to be suspected of madness and then tortured. The other he causes to be slain by the first. The worm who turns thus against his tormentors is a Florentine painter in the days of Lorenzo the Magnificent. As a weakling he has done no more than protest in words when the rough brothers have stolen his mistress and tossed him into the river. At length, offered a banquet to which he may invite any guests of his choice, he selects among others his braggart enemies, and induces the more brutal of the two to tempt his political enemies to a brawl. In the mean time he has spread the report that Neri has lost his mind, and after that wretch is pursued and bound, Giannetto and his mistress mock him as he rages. Neri, confined within a dungeon, is subjected to tortures, physical and mental. One of the women whom he had betrayed advises that he can secure release only by acting as if mad. When, set free, he seeks out Giannetto and Ginevra and thinks to stab the former, he discovers that he has slain his own brother, prevailed upon by the avenger to appear at the same place in disguise. Then, as Neri does in truth go mad, Giannetto, dropping to his knees, recites a prayer of gratitude to the Virgin.

Here the plot and the clash of violent emotions are more important than the study of character. The coward transformed to a devil by the indignities that he has suffered drives directly to his revenge. With a better motive than Iago, he is equally acute and more successful. It might appear that after the scene in the dungeon the play could rise to no higher climax of horror; yet the scene when brother slays brother through error, led to suppose that he is slaying his former victim, is even more intense. These lovers of gross pleasures are men of *virtù*, self-assertors, licentious and brutal. Not the least effective feature of the play is the cynical indifference of Ginevra, bandied from lover to lover and accepting nonchalantly each new master. As for Giannetto, he is interesting in his combination of fear and daring. "All I feel, asleep or waking," he declares, "is a dull ferocity; yet, savage though I be, I am a coward." Later he offers Neri liberty if only that villain will pledge his word never to hurt or frighten him again. He fears to sin, alleging his youth and his desire to be good, and even when Neri has slain his brother by mistake, Giannetto, the devisor of that deed, steps forth and pleads: "O my enemy, I give and take no quarter. Kill me too." Whereas to the foreigner this play is mere melodrama, to the Italian it represents an historical study of a time when men and artists, as Robert Morse Lovett has pointed out, sought "sources of new sensations in subtle compounds of pleasure and fear, . . . and when they had learned to act more lightly and to dare more negligently, to bear themselves more gracefully, to pluck the exquisite moments of life more casually, and to parody the great struggle for the survival of the fittest with a jest, and to make the jest a work of contrived art."

In *Wings*, a later play, Benelli has reverted to prose and wholly altered his manner, writing after some years of silence an analytic and almost static piece. The hero is an ascetic widower who mourns the death of his wife yet succumbs to love for a pupil. Although to her such love is ennobling, to him it signifies weakness, and he even assails his mother as having been in turn a victim of the same unworthy passion. When Marta, his pupil, hears him declare that in yielding to her he had felt himself degraded, she shoots him. But she repents as he dies declaring that he has slain himself. This piece provides an unexpected study by the author of *The Jest* in the dualism of body and soul. Love for Luca has entailed a desecration, whereas for Marta it has meant natural self-expression in accordance with the highest law of her being. Spiritually speaking, no doubt, *Wings* marks an advance on the part of its author, but dramatically it marks also a sharp retrogression.

In the later Italian theater experimentation has been in the air. Let us have a playhouse that shall resemble a temple, says Francesco Scardaoni. Let us have costumes which by their colors shall symbolize the souls of the wearers, says Achille Ricciardi. Let us revolt against worship of the past, says Francesco T. Marinetti, founder of futurism. The manifesto of that eccentric school, printed in the Paris *Figaro* as early as 1909, was never fully confirmed in practice. Marinetti had provoked prosecution by his novel *Mafarka the Futurist*, but the plays he composed to incorporate his theories were poor indeed, as witness the chaotic *King Hubbub* and *Sexual Electricity*. The former, produced by Lugné-Poë in Paris, laid its scene in a fantastic kingdom of Cockayne in the Middle Ages, with a monarch selected because he is the fattest man in his realm, yet destined to die of hunger when the powers of government have been delegated to four of his cooks. After the cooks have been eaten by the starving people, the latter in turn are assailed by a baby vampire.

In spite of such nonsense on the stage, the doctrines of futurism were not without interest. Marinetti urged a complete break with tradition; above all, a departure from the attempt to copy nature. He would substitute for the well-made play a sort of vaudeville performance, a series of unrelated scenes given with abandon to express the full sweep of man's energy and to reveal his determination to conquer by force and to take nothing seriously. So the futurists would jest at life, tearing off all its trappings of respectability. They would obliterate the distinction between the stage and the auditorium; they would play tricks upon the audience, embroiling actors, musicians, and spectators in boisterous fashion. They would mix the solemn and the comic, and substitute for psychology sheer physical madness—fisicofollia. In a manifesto published at Milan in 1915, the innovators professed their desire to create a new theatrical art "in perfect harmony with our vertiginously speedy and laconic futurist sensibility," removing all restrictions upon the genius of the artist, "who must be concerned solely with the creation of synthetic experience of cerebral energy possessing the absolute value of novelty." So the futurists, like the Northern expressionists, sought to exalt speed, brevity, and contempt for observation or the slow processes of logic and reflection.

Of course, such a theater could eventuate in nothing but chaos, its only service consisting in an attempt to break the molds of the old that something new might be achieved. More rational and restrained was the so-called grotesque theater of Luigi Chiarelli, who in one play at least proved fairly successful. This was *The Mask and the Face*, which tells the story of a husband who, according to the familiar tradition of honor, ought to slay his unfaithful wife, but, being a coward, sends her off to seek happiness abroad, and then confesses falsely that he has strangled her and dropped her body into a lake. When the body of another woman happens to be found in that lake, he must pretend that he recognizes it as hers. By a fortunate chance, however, the lawyer summoned to defend him proves to be his unknown rival, informed of the facts in the case and therefore able to procure his acquittal.

The wife, returning in disguise to congratulate her husband upon his escape from conviction, finds that after all she prefers him to the lawyer as a lover; but, since she is now regarded as dead and her husband cannot admit to the police the falsity of his first confession lest he be imprisoned, they are both forced to flee followed by strains of the funeral march played for the lady's defunct self. So Chiarelli laughs at the drama of sentiment, and grows more saturnine in his other pieces, which include *The Silken Ladder*, *Tears and Stars*, *Chimeras*, *The Death of the Lovers*, and *Fireworks*. In all there is a brutal slurring of bourgeois ideals, an ironic and cynical spirit. Men are absurd creatures who as puppets would excite sympathy if they were not so comic.

With the grotesque school of Chiarelli are affiliated several other writers. Luigi Antonelli displays lively imagination in such satires as *The Island of Monkeys*, *The Fable of the Three Magicians*, and *The Man Who Met Himself*. The first suggests that civilization is less to be desired than the freedom of the forest, and the last shows the futility of living life over even though we believe that with a second chance we would act differently. A magic island replaces the magic wood of Barrie's *Dear Brutus*, and the characters perceive themselves as they were a score of years earlier. Ernesto Cavacchioli in his *Bird of Paradise* shows a daughter who becomes the rival of her mother, a situation already employed in Donnay's *The Other Danger*. But here the lover of both is unworthy, and the mother, to prevent the girl's sacrifice, confesses that he has led her to abandon her husband. A Pirandellian character called "He" is introduced to express the thoughts of the audience, to whom he declares: "You give me voice and clothes and human semblance. I think, but I do not exist. The answers which I make to your arguments are formulated by your own imagination."

Still another member of the grotesque school is Rosso di San Secondo. In *What Passion, Ye Marionettes!* a play that might have been written by a German expressionist, the characters are types,—a girl fleeing from her cruel lover, a man clad in mourning because deserted by his wife, and a cynic in gray who drinks poison at a restaurant where all three have been waiting for those they long for. In *The Sleeping Beauty*, the heroine is a lady of light virtue who remains dormant until the desire for motherhood awakens in her breast. Here the author appears in person as a zany who endeavors to force the lady's first lover to make amends by marrying her. In *The Rock and the Monuments* is set forth the ancient conflict between desire and duty, the rock symbolizing instinct and the monuments the result of applying to basic instinct the chisel of the will. It is through the instrumentality of Pirandello, according to his critic and biographer, Walter Starkie, that "the ideas of the grotesque theater, together with those of the futurists, have extended their sphere of influence over Europe, . . . and we are witnessing in every country the death of the bourgeois well-made play, with its vestiges of romanticism, and the rise of a new critical drama which will be an expression of the modern active mentality." Whether Pirandello can justify so large a claim, he certainly exemplifies what is best in the futurist and grotesque schools, and far transcends the narrow limits of both. He is to be associated further with another attempt to displace the banality of the older drama, having organized the art theater movement in Italy. Such art theaters, which served a genuine purpose in Russia, Germany, and England, have accomplished much less in Italy. Although Gordon Craig, the father of modern stagecraft, lives in Florence, he has exerted his principal influence north of the Alps. At Rome, Rudolfo de Angeles has conducted a futurist theater, and Bragaglia has set up a stage of radical tendencies in the newly excavated baths of Septimus Severus. Since 1925, Pirandello also has operated his small Teatro Odescalchi, providing for the intellectual few performances of the best European novelties.

CHAPTER XXIX

The Philosophic Pirandello

IN ITALY the intellectual strain of modern drama is best represented by Luigi Pirandello, born in Sicily at Girgenti in 1867 and the author of several hundred stories, novels, and plays. After studying at Palermo and Rome, Pirandello attended the University of Bonn, and from 1907 to 1923 served in Rome as professor in the Higher Normal School for Women. Comparatively late in life he turned from fiction to the stage at the advice of Marco Praga and the Sicilian playwright, Nino Martoglio. He speedily won attention by dramatizing a number of his tales. He has written some thirty plays, the fame of which has extended from Italy, where they are frequently performed, to Spain, France, England, Germany, and the Americas. Pirandello has traveled abroad to superintend their production, and in Rome since 1925, as we have seen, he has conducted an Art Theater of his own.

During the youth of Pirandello, Italy was conscious of a new life following upon its unification. But enthusiasm waned, and a sense of disillusion succeeded. This skepticism was deepened by the War. It continued in art, although relieved in politics by the vigorous recoil against Communism, under Mussolini, he and the Fascisti looking to the inspiration of Mazzini and professing ideals of class coöperation in place of the Marxian program of class competition. Although the plays of Pirandello never turn upon sociological or political interests, they reflect the skeptical spirit of their author's earlier years. In 1920 he declared: "I think that life is a very sad piece of buffoonery because . . . we need to deceive ourselves constantly by creating a reality (one for each and never the same for all), which from time to time is discovered to be vain and illusory. . . . My art is full of bitter compassion for all who deceive themselves; but this compassion cannot fail to be followed by the cruel derision of destiny which condemns man to deception."

As a youth, Pirandello wrote cheerful poems and sketches. He showed his skill in ironic story-telling in many volumes, where slight incidents served him as an excuse for revealing his gift of subtle analysis. The best known of his seven novels is *The Late Mattia Pascal*, published in 1904, and setting the fashion of the so-called grotesque school in Italy. Through a story diffuse, amusing, and brightly pessimistic we learn how a provincial librarian was enabled by a pretended drowning to escape from one personality to another, leaving behind his debts, his not too virtuous wife, and his disagreeable mother-in-law. On the strength of winnings at Monte Carlo, he builds up a second personality, now in Turin and next in Rome. But, since his second life proves as burdensome as the first, he again feigns death, and returns to his village to find his wife remarried and the mother of another's child. Still unrecognized, he withdraws to write his memoirs in the library and to visit the cemetery now and then to look upon his own tomb. Throughout, Pirandello employs a bantering tone, "jazzing" his tale, as we should say, both by his serio-comic style and by his choice of grotesque incidents. The folk are as whimsical and lopsided as those of Dickens.

Indeed, the whole fiction may be taken as a philosopher's joke seriously meant, a joke intended to indicate that personality is something complex rather than simple. In the preface to a later edition Pirandello remarks that we are all playing under masks "what we would like to be (or what we ought to be); what other people think us to be; while what we really are we do not, up to a certain point, know even ourselves." He adds that "our personality is a fiction (often childishly artificial) which we build up about our real life, or which others build up about us. At any rate, it is a real mechanism in which each deliberately . . . makes a marionette of himself; until at last, in disgust, he sends the whole thing flying with a kick!" This is the author who has written, "Ask the poet what is the saddest sight, and he will reply, 'It is laughter on the face of a man.' Who laughs, does not know."

The dramas of Pirandello are similarly philosophic in considering the limits of personality, of reality and illusion, of madness and sanity. They reveal him as disturbed by the ancient struggle of the Greeks to capture, amid the play of fluid appearance, the permanent. His story, as a rule, is divulged with tantalizing reluctance. Instead of being given at once in rapid exposition, it is presented, now from one angle, now from another. It is as though the nucleus of a play were wound round and round with outer wrappings, and as though the dramatist were uncovering these bit by bit, each different from that above it, and each disclosing another lying deeper still. It is not until a play is concluding that the spectator has penetrated to the core of action. For that reason, he may not for a moment relax attention. To do so would be to lose something essential to the story, which is always changing shape. Moreover, what counts is not the emotion incited by the plot, which may be highly sensational. It is rather the motives of the characters and the author's ideas which stimulate interest. To some, such constant interrogation as to motives and meanings grows wearisome. Yet this art is stimulating to those who think. According to Arthur Livingston, Pirandello exhibits "a certain kindly tolerance" while "stripping reality of the attributes that make it seem to us most real, reducing personality to a fleeting, changing moment in a series of moments, identifying illusion with reality, and vice versa, breaking the individual soul up into many souls, and putting these into conflict one with another." Says Mr. Livingston: "We see before us the process of this disintegration, this dismemberment, this evaporation of personality. We experience, accordingly, a certain weird bewilderment, a certain tense strain, a 'torment of the spirit.' "

Such torment is not induced, however, in the early plays, of which *Sicilian Limes* is the best example. Here, instead, is the story of a simple-hearted Sicilian villager who has traveled to northern Italy just to see the prima donna with whom in old days he had been in love and for whose success he is responsible. He arrives as she is giving a party to her fine new friends. Perceiving that she has forgotten his former kindness and her debt to him, he departs after taking from his satchel the limes which he had brought her all the way from Sicily.

The true Pirandello emerges in *If Not Thus*, later called *The Rights of Others*. Here his diabolical logic finds scope as he exposes the relations of a husband, a wife, and a mistress. The wife, on discovering her lord's alliance with her rival, argues that he should cast in his lot with that rival since the latter has given him a child. As for herself, having been awakened to the situation by her father, she cannot go on wearing a mask of assumed ignorance. But it happens that the man is tired of the other woman and would cleave to his wife. She is willing to forgive and receive him provided that he bring his daughter to become hers. At this suggestion the other woman balks, asserting her rights as mother. But the wife assails her for proposing to hand back the husband without his child. So effective is her strange logic that the play concludes with the real mother weeping over the toys of the child she has surrendered, yet convinced that her claim to it is less than that of the wife.

Such paradoxical relationships are frequently the theme with Pirandello. In *Just Think, Giacomino*, an elderly schoolmaster, planning to marry a young girl, discovers that she is to bear her youthful lover a child. Nothing daunted, the schoolmaster will go on with the match and become a merely titular husband. He will provide a name for the child, a job for its father, protection for its mother, and an inheritance for all three when he dies. As Giacomino, the lover, objects, and threatens to run away, Professor Toti warns him to remain, on pain of being exposed to the village gossips. So, although his action flies in the face of convention, he actually benefits everyone concerned. Let each case be decided upon its merits.

How little the biological paternity of a child really matters is illustrated further in such plays as *The Pleasure of Honesty*, *All for the Best*, and *Grafting*. In the last a wife, after seven years of barren yet happy marriage, chances to be violated by a ruffian. Her husband admits that his honor has not been touched, since the fault was not hers; it is his love rather that has suffered a mortal wound. He would even destroy the child that Laura is now to bear. But a gardener explains that this grafting should not alter the fact that, spiritually at least, the child is Giorgio's; and Laura affirms that maternal love has purified and even heightened her devotion to her husband. "My love has triumphed!" she exclaims, as Giorgio finally consents to accept the child as his own.

Somewhat similar is the situation in *All For the Best*. Here a widower discovers that his supposed daughter is the daughter of his friend and benefactor, a scientist. The world has long suspected the fact and thought him engaged in cloaking the scandal under an assumption of nonchalance. The revelation comes to the shocked Martino when, in a darkened room, the girl, addressing him as father, obviously mistakes him for the scientist. She too recognizes the relationship. What shall Martino do? If he assail his rival before the public, the public will only laugh, having already regarded him as acquiescent for two decades. Perhaps he can force the scientist to deny his paternity, but will the girl be convinced? Or he may expose the fact that the scientist has plagiarized a discovery made by Martino's father-in-law, but will the story be believed? As Martino meditates, his wrath subsides. He concludes to go on as before, but consciously now, for at last he sees himself as others have seen him all along. For the first time, however, the girl, who had held him in contempt, begins to reciprocate his love. The scientist has arranged her marriage with a marquis. She will be happy in her affection for this husband and also for her putative father. "Now my affection for you is true," she says; "there is no deception: my affection and esteem are a reality on which you can live, and this reality will end by imposing itself on all people, even on yourself."

That the father who is not a father may virtually become one is proved more effectively in *The Pleasure of Honesty*. A philosopher fond of experiment deliberately marries a girl to save her from scandal, and proceeds to play his shameful part with such honesty that eventually he wins her from her unworthy lover and makes her child his own. It is in vain that Agata at first objects, and that her married lover tempts his substitute to embezzle certain funds. Baldovino will not touch the money lest he place a stigma upon the child. Then he consents to take it merely to afford the lover the glory of pretending restitution. Next he offers to retain it that Agata may have an excuse for leaving him should she so desire. But, because by this time she loves him truly, he hands the money over to his outwitted rival and will keep the lady and the child. Baldovino is a logician who reasons that he is mere abstract form to hide the action of others. He represents their respectability, their externalized honor. But we tend to become what we profess to be and what others think us. He who was rigorously honest in accepting a position of dishonor has become the honorable husband and father of the part he enacted. Here is a recognition of the power of convention as well as a protest against it. The situation of the lover who thought to procure only a stalking horse is ironic, as is also that of the philosopher who thought merely to perform an objective experiment. Both have been defeated. As for the philosopher, he has become emotionally involved, and in turn he has captured the affections of the lady, who now cleaves to the protector of her child rather than to the child's physical father.

In the same fashion, the play *But It is Not a Serious Affair* shows how a marriage which was entered into experimentally becomes effective through love. Play a part, and you become in time what the part implies. A jolly Mercutio marries as a prank the untidy, draggled drudge of a boarding house and sends her off to the country directly after the ceremony amid the laughter of the boarders,—folk who might have stepped from the pages of Balzac. One of them, an old rustic with a big nose, has already cast sheep's eyes at Gasparina, and, seeking her out after some months, finds her so improved in appearance by her life of healthy leisure that he suggests that she withdraw from her purely formal union with the dandy and marry him instead. She is ready to do so; but the dandy, piqued by this rivalry, and weary of his intrigues in town, proceeds to feel like the loving husband whose rôle he has hitherto taken only in jest. As was the case with Baldovino, he becomes the victim of his own experiment as soon as his affections are engaged. His titular wife, now grown attractive by trying to play her part, finally accepts him as husband in fact as well as in name.

In contrast to these fairly genial studies are three plays of Pirandello's marked by the saturnine cynicism of a Sem Benelli. In *Cap and Bells* a woman, informed by a malicious gossip that her husband is in love with the wife of his clerk, plots revenge. Having got the clerk out of the way for a day, she sends the police to his house to apprehend her husband. But, by having him arrested, she spreads the scandal. When the clerk, returning home, learns what has happened, he assails the jealous Beatrice. All along he had known of his dishonor, but he had constructed a screen to hide it, understanding that it was natural for his young wife to turn from one so old and ugly as himself. Now, however, Beatrice, the informer, must protect him and her husband and her rival from the injury that jealousy would inflict. Let her feign insanity. Only thus will those who have suspected the truth be disarmed. Only thus will the hitherto complacent clerk be relieved of the duty of wreaking vengeance upon his wife and his employer. As Beatrice rages in protest, the clerk smiles, for already she is giving proof of madness. He can discount her charges and her action as the result of insanity.

Each of Us His Own Part (*Il Giuoco delle Parti*) mingles farce and tragedy in the same fashion but presents a vengeance exacted by a husband upon his unfaithful wife. For long he has played the rôle of innocent, but his very indulgence angers her. So one day she flings after him an empty eggshell which chances to attract the attention of certain roisterers. Since they think it intended to provoke a flirtation, they break into the house in quest of the lady. Hastily concealing her lover, she resists the roisterers, and seeks to win credit for herself by summoning aid against them from the neighbors, to whom she declares that they have threatened her honor. Perhaps her husband will be goaded into defending her. To her delight, he responds by consenting to challenge the leader to a duel, but he also insists that Guido, her lover, shall act as second. Since Guido foresees that the inexpert cuckold will be sure to fall, he agrees. But, at the last moment, the wily husband withdraws, thus forcing Guido to take his place according to the Italian code. When the lady complains that her husband has so dishonored himself, he retorts that she is his only dishonor. Then he waxes merry at news that her lover has been slain in his stead, and proceeds to eat breakfast with special gusto. Humorously ironic on the surface, he is all the more dangerous in his revenge, an apparently easy-going gourmand.

Similar cynicism marks *Man, Beast, and Virtue* (acted in English as *Say It With Flowers*), a harsh and ugly play which depicts the flouting by nature of a dull little schoolmaster, who has thought to find romance in an affair with the mother of one of his pupils. She is the wife of a crusty sea captain, who refuses to live with her longer lest she bear him another child. He is absent most of the time on his voyages, and, whenever he returns for a day, he employs every ruse to keep apart from her. The lady, discovering that she is to bear a child to the schoolmaster, appeals to him for aid. He must help induce her husband to bestow his favors once more that he may have cause to believe the child his own. An apothecary assists in the plot by providing a love-excitant. So the schoolmaster, though deeply in love, is forced to mask and defile that love by a trick that will oblige a merely titular husband to become something more.

Philosophic ideas of a different sort emerge in certain other plays of Pirandello. Characteristic is his early piece, *Right You Are* (*If You Think So*), which implies that truth is relative and depends upon the individual mind. Townsfolk gossip because a petty official who lives meanly in a tenement has leased for his mother-in-law an elegant apartment. Why should the wife never call upon Signora Frola? Why should Signora Frola never call upon the wife except to shout up to her lofty tenement from the courtyard? Signora Frola explains to her son-in-law's curious chief that she allows him and her daughter to live their lives apart, believing this to be the best arrangement for young couples. Then Ponza, the son-in-law, explains confidentially that Signora Frola is insane, thinking that his second wife is her daughter, whereas his first wife was that daughter. Next Signora Frola returns to add that it is he who is insane, thinking that his first wife is dead, and being married to her a second time on his release from a sanitarium. Where lies the truth? Who is sane? Who is crazy? When Ponza and Signora Frola are brought face to face and then examined singly, matters grow more confused. Ponza is troubled to hear the lady playing her daughter's favorite music, for she will be agitated by dwelling on her grief over that daughter's death. He declares that he can keep her from realizing her insanity only by making her believe him to be insane. Is Ponza feigning or is he mad? Madmen often show their madness by such feigning. Since an earthquake has destroyed the records of the family, no external proofs are available. Ponza and Signora Frola both protest against the curiosity that would penetrate their defense armor. Then, when a veiled woman is brought in, Ponza calls her by one name, and Signora Frola by another. Which is she, the second wife or the first, or are the two the same? To the audience the veiled lady turns, declaring: "I am the daughter of Signora Frola, and I am the second wife of Signor Ponza. Yes, and for myself I am nobody—no—I am for myself whoever you choose to have me." Then she admonishes against an idle curiosity. "In our lives, as you see, there is something which must remain concealed, otherwise the remedy which our love for each other has found cannot avail." Throughout, the action is commented upon by a cynic, Laudisi, amused by the human animal's tendency to nose into other people's affairs and by the assumption that absolute truth can ever be known. At the close of the first and the second acts he asks the gossips if they still are in quest of the truth. With the fall of the last curtain, he remarks ironically, "Well, and there, my friends, you have the truth, but are you satisfied?"

Double personality is the theme of *Signora Morli One and Two*. The heroine, abandoned by a gay husband who had given her a son, has become the companion of a methodical lawyer, who has given her a daughter. She has almost forgotten her wild days with Morli when he returns from America enriched to reclaim the son, who follows him obediently to Rome. But Morli, wishing the mother also, telegraphs her that the youth is dangerously ill. When she hastens to his side, she discovers the ruse and must listen to Morli's pleading that she recall their feverishly happy days together. Tempted to revert to her earlier self, she realizes that her later, quieter self is the nobler. Moreover, she owes a debt of gratitude to the lawyer Carpani and a duty to his daughter. So she goes back to him, and prevails against his first refusal to receive her. Her second personality, assumed as a mask, has become her truer self.

Somewhat similar is a play of the same year, 1920, entitled *Come prima meglio di prima*, acted three years later in New York as *Floriani's Wife*. Here by contrast it is a woman who has deserted her home. After thirteen years she attempts suicide, is saved, and taken back by her forgiving husband. Their daughter, not dreaming that this is her mother, resents the coming of the intruder until the birth of another child entails an explanation and serves to reunite the family.

The most popular of Pirandello's dramas is *Six Characters in Search of an Author*, developed from an earlier *novella*. A stage manager engaged in rehearsing Pirandello's own play, *Each of Us His Own Part*, is interrupted by six characters who complain that they have been projected by an author, and then left without the opportunity of combining into a finished drama. They beg to be allowed to complete their story through the actors now rehearsing. Then the story is performed, but it emerges only bit by bit, being overlaid by comments from the actors and the manager. Two ideas in particular are set forth. One is the notion that he who creates characters in a play is less real than they, since he may change or die, whereas they remain, still vital and unaltered. The other is the notion that acquiescence in an evil deed will entail evil consequences however long deferred. The fragmentary story of the six characters tantalizes by its obscurity, for it lies in utter disorder, as it might exist in the dramatist's mind before being fully wrought out. The hero has acquiesced in the elopement of his wife with his secretary twenty years ago. The secretary in dying has left to the wife three children. The eldest, grown to womanhood, is encountered at a questionable resort by the hero. Shocked to recognize her as the daughter of his long-lost wife, he seeks to make amends by bringing her and the rest of the family to his home, although his own son looks upon these younger illegitimates as interlopers.

The story of the play-within-the-play is never fully told, because Pirandello is chiefly occupied with the philosophic implications of the situation. He gives reality to the characters and make-believe to the actors. A fictional character, he shows us, is more real than any actual person, for, once established, it cannot change. Though born in the author's mind, it acquires independence, since it can be imagined in circumstances other than those of the author's devising, and it may achieve meaning beyond what the author contemplates. Moreover, characters take the bit in their teeth and run away with an author. "He who has the luck to be born a character can laugh at death. The writer, the instrument of the creation, will die; but his creation does not die."

In such speculations the play-within-the-play is almost forgotten until, at the close of the third act, the mother's little girl is drowned in a fountain, and her brother shoots himself, the two dying as remote victims of the man's original deed in sending his wife off with his secretary. As the father denies that the suicide of the boy is pretense, the manager concludes the performance by exclaiming: "Pretense! Reality! . . . I've lost a whole day over these people, a whole day!"

The personages of the play-within-the-play take form slowly, the mother a poor simple creature, the son by the first alliance contemptuous of his parents and of his half brother and sisters, and the son of the second alliance shocked by his position in reference to the others. Only the father and the stepdaughter are fully developed. The father is self-deluded and self-justified, one who has yielded to the demon of experiment. How could he tell that in prosecuting his secret amours he would encounter the daughter of his former wife? or that she would try to hold him eternally in the stocks for the one fleeting and shameful moment of his career? Others, he is sure, are quite as bad, and, in any case, man succumbs to temptation only to rise from it. The stepdaughter, allured to a life of shame, cynically blames others. "For one who has gone wrong," she declares, "he who was responsible for the first fault is responsible for all that follows. He is responsible for my faults, and was so, even before I was born." We infer that ultimately she departs to follow her own pleasure, leaving together in ironic desolation the original family—father, mother, and son.

Of this play William Archer wrote: "Such stuff has no future. It is freak work of momentary interest, if any;—it had none for me." But the world at large has approved the piece as one of the most brilliant of all modern dramas, a contribution original in technique as in subject matter.

To answer the question what is reality, what is illusion? may involve answering the question what is sanity, what is madness? If the characters who enact a part are more real than he who conceived them, so, too, the madman may lead a life more real than the sane man. Pirandello does not declare this to be the case. He merely suggests the possibility in his challenging drama *Henry IV*.

A nobleman on his way to a masked ball has been unhorsed by the treachery of a rival who stabbed his steed from behind. Knocked insane by the blow, he has imagined himself to be the character he had impersonated, Emperor Henry IV of Germany, humiliated by Pope Gregory VII at Canossa in 1071. For long years his relatives have humored him, hiring attendants to play the part of confidential friends and retainers. Although he has reached the age of fifty, he continues to make up as a youth of twenty-six, since time for him has stopped. Henry's sister, suspecting him of feigning, has in dying exacted from her son the promise to have Henry's case investigated by an alienist. At the opening of the play the alienist has come to Henry's castle accompanied by the woman with whom twenty years earlier he had been infatuated. With them has come also her daughter, now betrothed to Henry's nephew, and her lover who had caused Henry's fall. The physician arranges that he and the others shall take the parts of historical personages of the eleventh century and proposes to administer to the madman a series of shocks that will shatter his dream life and restore him to reason.

But, although the audience does not know it for an act or so, Henry is indeed quite sane. Having recovered his reason earlier, he has chosen to pose as a madman, preferring the life of illusion to that of reality. His is a saturnine humor like that of Hamlet. Having recognized in Donna Matilda the woman who had been false to his memory with his treacherous rival, Belcredi, he delights to make secret thrusts which touch her to the quick. The physician has arranged that she and her daughter shall appear to Henry simultaneously with a view to making him realize the flight of time. As the lights are switched on suddenly when he clasps the daughter in place of the mother, Henry turns to rail at those so insane as to try to trick him. Then he stabs Belcredi. "He is mad!" cry the others, but Belcredi, carried forth to die, declares him to be sane. Sane he is, yet his act done in righteous wrath will compel him henceforth to resume his pretense of insanity. Nay, who knows but he may be insane? Where, indeed, falls the line between what is normal and abnormal, what is real and unreal?

As usual with Pirandello, minor characters hold the boards at first, and the audience remains at cross purposes as to what is happening. Part of the difficulty in apprehending the play arises from its author's reliance upon our knowledge of remote historical personages and the confusion of such personages with those of the present day. It is clear, however, that Henry prefers the fantastic world created by madness to the sensuous world of the present which drives him mad when he meets it face to face.

More recent plays of Pirandello include *Naked*, *The Life*

THE PHILOSOPHIC PIRANDELLO

I Gave Thee, Each in his Own Way, and *Our Lord of the Ship.* The last, a south Italian peasant episode acted at the opening of the author's Art Theater in Rome, is least characteristic. *The Life I Gave Thee* is of interest as transferring the ground of philosophical debate from the relation between illusion and reality, opinion and truth, to that between life and death. How far may people be said to live after death when they are remembered? This question had been asked by Maeterlinck in *The Blue Bird,* where Tyltyl and Mytyl find that those in the Beyond still live whenever thought of. Pirandello draws the portrait of a mother who so passionately loves her son that she will not admit that he is dead. He had returned to her mortally ill after seven years of wandering, and when he expired she puts his room into exactly the condition in which he had originally left it, and sends off the letter he had been writing to his mistress. The latter, knowing nothing of his demise, arrives to tell him that she is to bear him a child, and only by degrees discovers that the journey upon which he has departed is nothing less than the journey of death. The play is made, less by its plot, than by the dialectic of the characters. For the devoted mother the body that is interred is not that of the son who had deserted her seven years before, and even God can take from that son only what God gave him and not the life that was given him by her. He lives for her, moreover, so long as she can maintain in his beloved mistress faith in his continued existence. But her efforts to deceive Lucia as well as herself, in the end prove futile. Lucia, with the birth of her child, will possess an actual remnant of the dead man. But the mother will possess nothing. Indeed, she is beginning to die already inasmuch as so integral a part of herself has disappeared.

A still more recent treatment of the relation between life and death is *Lazzaro,* which, being translated into English by C. K. Scott-Moncrieff, received its first performance on any stage at Huddersfield, England, in July, 1929. A Sicilian gentleman killed by an automobile is revived by a physician engaged on experiments in reanimation. Since, try as he will, the patient recalls nothing of what he has experienced in the other world, he turns skeptic and declares immortality to be an illusion. But this loss of faith in one to whom it had always meant everything entails also a loss of mental balance, and Diego Spina goes mad. Earlier he had driven his wife away because she could not share his orthodoxy and would not approve the religious training he desired for their children. But by leading a simple life among peasants she finds spiritual regeneration. Their son, designed by the father for the priesthood, has lost faith, but, as a result of that father's accident and subsequent resuscitation, he regains it, and restores the madman to mental health by persuading him that the doctor has performed a miracle in accordance with divine laws and that God, in blotting out the recollection of what he saw of the other world, has but wished him to continue to depend upon faith in this. Apparently it has not occurred to Diego Spina that either he had only been in a trance or else that God had purposely shut the door of his memory. Although the spiritual rebirth of the doubter, his wife, and his son be duly noted by Pirandello, he remains too much of a skeptic to allow to the resuscitated even that measure of surety which Eugene O'Neill in *Lazarus Laughed* accords to his Biblical hero.

In *Naked* the playwright shows how a guilty soul will assume robes of virtue, deceiving not only others but itself. The soul is that of a girl who, after attempting suicide, has been brought to the rooms of a novelist. He will use her life story as material for a work of fiction. When he imagines certain incidents and motives that may have led up to her deed, she gladly assents to his explanation, but by degrees she varies her account. Those whom she had implicated when she thought herself dying come to confront her with the truth, and the events and logic of her past change shape as she is stripped naked of her lies. She perplexes the audience by refusing elopement with a man to whom she has already given herself, and by refusing marriage with another, a marriage that will set her straight with the world. Then, sick of her naked and unlovely self, she again takes poison, this time to die, confessing that she had told her story in the first place merely to clothe in a semblance of virtue a life which she could not bear to contemplate in its nakedness.

What has Ersilia done? As governess in the family of the Italian consul at Smyrna, she had once succumbed to her employer. As they embraced, his child, her little charge, was left untended, and had fallen and been killed. Then she had fled to Naples in search of an earlier lover, a naval officer, but finding him about to marry another, she had offered herself to the first passerby, and, being rebuffed, had tried suicide, been rescued, and revived. A melodramatist would have shown the passional crises involved in this ugly story, but Pirandello focuses attention only upon the efforts of the tortured soul to palliate its evil deeds. He would tease us into asking how far Ersilia in her varying confessions merely accepts the motives for her conduct suggested by others, how far she knows herself. The consul and the naval officer both arrive to excuse her, to claim her, and to exculpate themselves. But they catch her in lie after lie. She admits her true reasons only after she has taken the second dose of poison which will now prove fatal. "We all of us want to make a good impression," she explains. "The worse we are and the uglier, the more anxious we are to appear good and beautiful. . . . I wanted at least to be buried in decent clothes, . . . the dress of a bride. . . . with a tear of sympathy from people. . . . But no, not even that have I been allowed to keep! I must die naked. I must die discovered—despised—humiliated—found out. . . . Let me die in silence, naked." The fluid character of reality is commented upon by the novelist, who re-

589

marks, "Facts are what we assume them to be; and then, in their reality, they cease to be facts, and become mere semblances of life which appear in this or that or some other way."

The notion is expanded in *Each in His Own Way*, written, says Pirandello, in less than a month, yet, in his judgment, "more nearly pure art" than his other pieces. An actress of light reputation, on the eve of her wedding to an artist, induces his suicide by giving herself to another. That other is the betrothed of his sister. Friends quarrel as to what can have been Delia's motive in thus flouting the artist and surrendering to Rocca. One declares that she was trying to prove to the artist that she could not marry him since she had been disdained by his mother and sister. Another offers an explanation wholly different. The lady herself, though accepting the first excuse, has earlier protested that she yielded to Rocca simply because she would punish the artist for prizing her, not for herself, but for her beauty. As for Rocca, he declares that he made love to her only to save the artist, his friend, from marrying her, since the artist had dared him to make the lady fall, and had promised to give her up in case she did so. Now Rocca denies that she ever did succumb to him; but presently we find that both Rocca and Delia have been pretending to themselves, for they are madly in love with each other though they have masked and repressed that love, each feigning an interest in saving the artist. Rocca, however, is smitten in conscience at the suicide of his friend. Though he and Delia embrace at meeting, he declares that she must atone with him for what they have done. Her love for him is worth nothing, but what he has suffered on her account gives it value. So he snatches her up, crying that they will drown together in the blood of the dead artist. No wonder that an observer exclaims, "A pair of lunatics!"

Each of the two acts is followed by a choral interlude in which the supposed spectators of the scene come upon the stage, now representing a section of the theater lobby. They comment on the characters. Thus the complex is made more complicated, as the real audience watches a supposed audience, which in turn is supposed to have just watched the play. And that play is supposed to reflect a scandal involving a sculptor and a baron in the supposed audience. They object to having their private affair made public, but in the end proceed to do precisely as have their doubles of the play, and the manager comes forth to apologize that the curtain must be rung down upon the whole thing. At last we understand why the title should read, "A comedy in two or three acts"; the characters have withdrawn after two acts.

The interludes contain amusing self-criticisms, like those introduced by Shaw in the Prologue to *Fanny's First Play*. "You can't make head or tail of the thing," says one critic, and the rest complain of Pirandello's always harping on this "illusion-and-reality" string. Yes, he has taken his plot from the newspapers; he deals with "little problems of philosophy as philosophy is studied by men who are not philosophers"; and "It's as though you were looking into a mirror that had somehow gone crazy." Those favorable to Pirandello ask: "If you want to sleep, why don't you stick to other plays? With them you can just lean back in your seat and take what is sent you across the footlights. But with a comedy of Pirandello's you have to be on your pins." And another remarks of reality, "It's a convention; . . . you think that reality is something fixed, something definite, and you feel as though you were being cheated if someone comes along and shows you that it was all an illusion on your part."

A few words must be said of the one-act plays of Pirandello. Those that are comic, like *Chee-Chee* or *The Jar*, possess no significance beyond the fun in them; and most are lacking in the intellectual subtlety which distinguishes the longer dramas. Already we have seen, in *Sicilian Limes*, the simple treatment of a sentimental situation. As for the later pieces, they stress situations either morbid or whimsical.

In *The Man With a Flower in his Mouth*, the hero, concealing with a blossom the malignant spot upon his lip from which he soon must die, thinks in vain to become disillusioned with life by observing the petty annoyances which passersby in the street must endure. But his wife would have him stay quietly at home and yield to her ministrations. As he wanders about, she dogs his steps. Once she has even scratched her lip and tried to kiss him that she too might die of his disease. In *The House With a Column*, a poor widow explains to a physician why she has had nothing to do with a wealthy son. That son is the child of a bandit, one of a gang implicated in killing her first husband. If now she looks at the youth, she is seized with the same terror she felt when, long ago, she came upon that gang using her husband's head as a football. In *The Doctor's Duty*, a physician saves the life of a man who has attempted suicide after slaying another in self-defense. But the poor devil, on learning that he must wear out the rest of his days in prison, tears open his wound and dies. In *Our Lord of the Ship*, a schoolmaster observes a religious festival that rises into a very orgy, but turns maudlin as the celebrants beat their breasts in contrition and follow the image of their bleeding Christ.

At the Gate is a fanciful "shocker," wherein the soul of a fat man at the entrance to a cemetery is awaiting the coming of his wife whose laughter has driven him mad. Such laughter, he believes, will drive mad her lover as well. Sure enough, in comes the woman with a bullet hole in her breast followed by that lover, who has slain her and then himself. But the woman's only thought now is for her spirit child. As the child appears and then fades away, the woman runs off in pursuit of a living girl who has just passed with her parents. Ironic is *The Imbecile*, in which a dying journalist laughs at the folly of two political enemies who would use him as their tool. Each has suggested that he go kill the other. More humorously original is *By Judgment of the Court*, which depicts the wiles of an honest man forced into fraud when accused of possessing the evil eye. Ruined in business, he must turn his supposed gift to profit. So he sues prominent citizens for slander, knowing that the court, in exonerating them, will attest the reality of his powers. Then he can the more readily levy blackmail, standing before shop windows until he is paid to move on to the windows of some rival concern. While he is explaining his situation to a skeptical judge, a wind chances to blow down a shutter that kills the judge's pet goldfinch. Thereupon the reputed possessor of the evil eye seizes the occasion to boast of his powers. "The wind! the shutter! Nonsense! It was I. You wouldn't believe, so I have given you proof!" Even the judge is convinced.

Can there be any doubt that if Pirandello were to produce nothing more, he would still rank as one of the most distinguished and original of dramatists? According to Giuseppe Prezzolini, he is the first to demonstrate so clearly that men exist in their reciprocal conceptions of one another. "We are nothing more or less than what we seem to be to others—what through the influence of what we seem to be to others we come to seem to ourselves. A person, accordingly, is not one person. He is a hundred thousand different persons, and at the same time nobody. . . . He assumes a different aspect according to the person with whom he has to deal and according to the 'official' character he thinks he represents in life. But, sooner or later, he is bound to discover this situation. Each of us some day 'looks into the mirror,' and the result for us is either consternation or surprise or tragedy or laughter. . . . Pirandello stands in reaction against 'fixed' characters; against people who are, as we say, all of a piece; against a world filled with stiff, unchanging nature." So this amateur philosopher of the stage reacts against the sensuous estheticism of d'Annunzio and the violent melodramatic art of Sem Benelli. Blazing a trail wholly new, he takes his thoughtful way to success, avoiding, not only the drama of social criticism and the emotional drama of tradition, but the fantastic experiments of the futurists.

Pirandello, indeed, is a leader in Italy occupying a place comparable with that of Ibsen in Norway, Strindberg in Sweden, Chekhov in Russia, Hauptmann in Germany, Shaw in England, Molnár in Hungary, the Čapeks in Czecho-Slovakia, Brieux, Rostand, or de Curel in France, and Benavente in Spain. Such names suggest a hundred others. How numerous and how diverse in talent are all those who have wrought at the complex fabric of modern drama! Never before have playwrights in so many different countries at the same time vied with one another in building a structure so intricate and so delightful. Every dramatic genre has been given fair trial; every resource of production has been exploited. Naturalists, propagandists, romanticists, symbolists, and expressionists, all have had their say. If you weary of "the useful theater," you may turn to the dramatized fairy tale; if you weary of romance, you may turn to unflinching portraits of little souls in a mean world; if you weary of bloody slices of life, you may find relief in allegory and scenes suggestive rather than representational. There is no fixed pattern which playwrights agree to follow as once they followed the stereotyped designs of classic tragedy or the machine-made technique of Scribe. Freedom and originality have become the watchwords. The methods of Andreyev differ wholly from those of Björnson, and the methods of Martínez Sierra differ as widely from those of Hervieu. Even the later Hauptmann bears little resemblance to the earlier, for who that is alive and growing would be confined to a single manner? Back of the urge toward experimentation in the theater lies a genuine vitality still unsapped. Unless this be checked as well as diverted in its expression by the cinema, it will create fresh forms in the future. Yet whatever the future bring forth, much that has proved significant during the half century between 1880 and 1930 will survive, bearing witness to a period of dramatic activity extraordinarily rich and varied.

BIBLIOGRAPHY

Although this bibliography is the most complete yet published for so large a number of Continental playwrights, it is selective rather than exhaustive. It lists representative dramas of those whose work is discussed in the foregoing pages. Since the volume is intended primarily for English and American students, play titles are given in English except when untranslatable or differing from the common English rendering. The dates assigned to plays are those of their earliest appearance, whether in print or in production, but it should be remembered that even the most reliable authorities frequently differ on such matters.

In the tables of translations, those of collected plays appear first, followed by those of each individual piece in chronological sequence. Throughout, only the titles of originals are printed in italics in order that these may stand out for readier reference. A few items taken from the volumes of *The Stage Year Books* of London and *The United States Copyright Office Catalogues* are translations of plays merely acted or typed but not printed.

Material for this bibliography has been gleaned from hundreds of sources. The author has drawn upon lists published in his own *Aspects of Modern Drama*, 1914, and *The Contemporary Drama of France*, 1920; and upon such works in English as the following: Norton, Marquand, and Henderson, *The Modern Drama and Opera*, 2 vols., 1911–1915; Ludwig Lewisohn, *The Modern Drama*, 1915; Barrett H. Clark, *Contemporary French Dramatists*, 1916; Lander MacClintock, *The Contemporary Drama of Italy*, 1920; William A. Drake, *Contemporary European Writers*, 1928; Leo Wiener, *The Contemporary Drama of Russia*, 1924; Huntly Carter, *The New Theatre and Cinema of Soviet Russia*, 1924, and *The New Spirit in the Russian Theater*, 1928; B. Q. Morgan, *Bibliography of German Literature in English*, 1922; Angel Flores, *Spanish Literature in English Translation*, a Bibliography, 1926; and Daniel C. Haskell, *Foreign Plays in English in the New York Public Library*, 1920. Use has also been made of play lists published in such collections of translated dramas as T. H. Dickinson, *Chief Contemporary Dramatists*, 1st series, 1915, 2nd series, 1921, 3rd series, 1930; M. J. Moses, *Representative One-Act Plays by Continental Authors*, 1922, and *Representative Continental Dramas*, 1924; and S. M. Tucker, *Modern Continental Plays*, 1929. An especial debt is owed to the best single bibliographical aid in English, *A Study of the Modern Drama*, by Barrett H. Clark, revised and enlarged, 1928. Foreign aids include the following: Wilhelm Kosch, *Das deutsche Theater und drama im 19ten jahrhundert*, 1913, and *Deutsches Literatur-Lexicon*, 2 vols., 1927–1930; Robert F. Arnold, *Das deutsche Drama*, enlarged, 1925; Kürschner's *Deutsche Literatur Kalender*, 1928, and annual volumes earlier; Guido Ruberti, *Il Teatro contemporaneo in Europa*, 3 vols., enlarged, 1928; Attilio Pagliaini, *Catalogo generale della libreria italiana*, 1925; Albert Soubies, *Almanach des spectacles*, 22 vols., 1874–1896; Edmond Stoullig and Édouard Noël, *Les Annales du théâtre et de la musique*, 41 vols., 1876–1918; Lorenz

BIBLIOGRAPHY

and Henri Stein, *Catalogue générale de la librairie française*, 29 vols. to 1928; Juan Hurtado y Jiménez de la Serna and Angel González Palencia, *Historia de la literatura española*, 1921, 1925; Luis Vélez de Guevara, *Bibliografía general española*, 6 vols. to 1928; Antonio Palau y Dulcet, *Manuel del librero hispano-americano*; and the weekly or monthly issues of the *Bibliographie de la France*, *Bibliografía española*, and *Bolletino delle pubblicazione italiane*.

In addition, information has been derived from various histories of literature and from monographs on individual playwrights, a few purely bibliographical, like Ina Ten Eyk Firkins, *Henrik Ibsen, a Bibliography*, 1921, and Rune Zetterlund, *Bibliografiska Anteckningar om August Strindberg*, 1913; but most including such items only as appendices. Not a little supplementary information has been found, also, on the shelves of the Bibliothèque Nationale at Paris, the British Museum at London, and the New York Public Library. Aid in translating foreign play titles has been furnished by my colleagues, Professors Dillwyn Ratcliff, Max Poll, Phillip Ogden, Merton J. Hubert, C. M. Hutchings, and Edwin H. Zeydel.

Much of the credit for the work of investigation and arrangement entailed in preparing these lists is due to Miss Estelle Hunt of the Department of English and Comparative Literature in the University of Cincinnati.

I. FOREIGN PLAYS AND ENGLISH TRANSLATIONS

ÁLVAREZ QUINTERO, SERAFÍN AND JOAQUÍN

(Long as is this list, it is but partial. *El Teatro completo de Álvarez Quintero*, of which 18 vols. were published from 1923 to 1926, will include a total, in 30 vols., of more than 150 plays.)

Fencing and Love, 1888; *Gilito*, 1889; *The Better Half* (*La media naranja —Half Orange*), 1894; *The Old Flute Player*, 1897; *The Window Grating*, 1897; *The Apple of His Eye* (*El Ojito derecho*), 1897; *The Pilgrim*, 1898; *Good Spirits*, 1898; *Intimate Life*, 1898; *Houses of Cards*, 1899; *The Kid* (*El Chiquillo*), 1899; *The Drunkards*, 1899; *Bull-Fighter's Costume* (*El Traje de luces*), 1899; *The Galley Slaves*, 1900; *First Performance* (*El Estreno*), 1900; *The Patio*, 1900; *The Punishment*, 1901; *The Roof*, 1901; *The Nest*, 1901; *Flowers*, 1901; *The Happiness of Others*, 1902; *Compliments*, 1902; *The Arrow Stroke*, 1902; *Fans and Tambourines*, 1902; *Love in the Theater*, 1903; *The Meritorious*, 1903; *The Moorish Queen*, 1903; *The Pretended Seer* (*La Zahorí*), 1903; *The Bargain*, 1904; *The Country Girl* (*La Zagala*), 1904; *Love Which Passes By*, 1904; *The Adventure of the Convicts*, 1905; *The Mad Muse*, 1905; *The Evil of Love*, 1905; *The Pittance*, 1905; *God Will Say*, 1905; *A Sunny Morning*, 1905; *Love in the Dark*, 1906; *The Prodigal Child*, 1906; *Bad Spirits*, 1906; *Torrents of Gold*, 1906; *Morritos*, 1906; *Pepita Reyes*, 1906; *The Happy Nature*, 1907; *The Trick* (*La Zancadida*), 1907; *Fair Lucerito*, 1907; *Life Which Returns*, 1907; *Dear Little Country* (*La Patria chica*), 1907; *The Hidden Path*, 1908; *The Cain Girls* (*Las de Caín*), 1908; *The Bun Makers*, 1908; *The Thousand Marvels*, 1908; *Loves and Amours*, 1908; *Light of the Moon*, 1908; *Miraculous Water*, 1908; *The Farm Yard*, 1909; *Rich Blood*, 1909; *The Centenarian*, 1909; *The Last Chapter*, 1910; *The Flower of Life*, 1910; *Eternal Rhyme*, 1910; *Wounded to Death*, 1910; *Festivals of Love and Poetry*, 1911; *Alone in the World*, 1911;

Malvaloca, 1912; *The House of García*, 1912; *Drama*, 1912; *World, Little World*, 1912; *The Women's Town*, 1912; *Fortunato*, 1913; *Speechless*, 1913; *By Their Words Ye Shall Know Them* (*Hablando se entiende la gente*), 1913; *Nena Teruel*, 1913; *The Lady From Alfáqueque* (*La Consulesa*), 1914; *The Loyal Family* (*Los Leales*), 1914; *El Duque de Él*, 1915; *Of Whom Do You Remind Me?* 1916; *The Backslider* (literally *Little Goat Headed Back to the Mountain*), 1916; *Marianela*, 1916; *Locked Out* (*El Cerrojazo*), 1916; *So History Is Written*, 1917; *The House Opposite*, 1917; *That Which You Wish*, 1917; *Reading and Writing*, 1917; *Eyes of Mourning*, 1917; *The Sensitive Chord*, 1918; *Four Words*, 1918; *The Secret of Confession*, 1918; *The Marchosos*, 1918; *Pedro López*, 1918; *Don Juan, Good Fellow*, 1918; *The Tooth of King Farfán*, 1919; *The Slandered Woman*, 1919; *The World is a Kerchief*, 1920; *Branch of Madness*, 1921; *Haste*, 1921; *The Passion Singer*, 1921; *The Fire*, 1922; *Turns of the World*, 1922; *Brief Quarter of an Hour*, 1922; *Silver Locks*, 1922; *Antón Caballero*, 1922; *The Song Collection*, 1924; *My Brother and I*, 1924; *Tidy Concha*, 1924; *Pepita and Don Juan*, 1925; *The Marriage of Quinita Flores*, 1925; *The Abel Girls* (*Las de Abel*), 1926; *Great Men*, 1926; *Sinful Clay*, 1926; *A Matter of Passing the Time*, 1927; *The Last Rôle*, 1927; *The Mosquitoes*, 1928; *Gossip*, 1928; *A Tale*, 1928; *The Child Restrains Me*, 1929; *Hobgoblins of Seville*, 1929; etc., etc.

IN ENGLISH: Helen and Harley Granville-Barker: Four Plays of the Álvarez Quinteros, 1928; *A Sunny Morning*, tr. as A Bright Morning, by Carlos C. Castillo and E. L. Overman in Poet Lore 27, 1916; tr. as One Autumn Morning, by M. Ashmun, 1917; tr. as A Sunny Morning, by Lucretia X. Floyd, 1920, and in Frank Shay and Pierre Loving, Fifty Contemporary One-Acts Plays, and in James P. Webber and H. H. Webster, One-Act Plays for Secondary Schools, 1923; tr. by Anna S. MacDonald and played, N. Y., 1921; *The Centenarian*, tr. as Papa Juan, or The Centenarian, by Thomas Walsh in Poet Lore 29, 1918; tr. as A Hundred Years Old, by the Barkers in Four Plays; *The Flower of Life*, tr. as The Fountain of Youth, by Samuel N. Baker, 1922; *Malvaloca*, tr. by J. S. Fassett, Jr., 1916, and in T. H. Dickinson, Chief Contemporary Dramatists, 3rd series, 1930; tr. by Beatrice Erskine and played, London, 1925; *The Women's Town*, tr. by C. A. Turrell, in Contemporary Spanish Dramatists, 1919, and played in London, 1923; tr. as The Women Have Their Way, by the Barkers in Four Plays; *Fortunato*, tr. by the Barkers in Four Plays; *The Lady From Alfaqueque* (*La Consulesa*), tr. by the Barkers in Four Plays; *By Their Words Ye Shall Know Them*, tr. by J. G. Underhill in The Drama, 1917, and in M. J. Moses, Representative One-Act Plays by Continental Authors, 1923; *That Which You Wish*, played as Just as You Please, London, 1924.

ANCEY, GEORGES (GEORGES DE CURNIEU)

M. Lamblin, 1888; *The School of Widowers*, 1889; *The Inseparables*, 1889; *Grandmother*, 1890; *The Dupe*, 1891; *The Future*, 1899; *These Messieurs*, 1905.

IN ENGLISH: *M. Lamblin*, tr. in Frank Shay and Pierre Loving, Fifty Contemporary One-Act Plays, 1921; *The Dupe*, tr. by B. H. Clark in Four Plays of the Free Theater, 1915.

BIBLIOGRAPHY

ANDREYEV, LEONID NIKOLAVICH

To the Stars, 1905; *Savva*, 1906; *The Life of Man*, 1906; *King Hunger*, 1907; *The Black Maskers*, 1908; *Days of Our Life*, 1908; *Love of One's Neighbor*, 1908; *The Bat*, 1908; *Anathema*, 1909; *Anfisa*, 1909; *Gaudeamus*, 1910; *The Ocean*, 1911; *The Sabine Women*, 1912; *Professor Storitsyn*, 1912; *Honor*, 1912; *Yekaterina Ivanovna*, 1912; *Thou Shalt Not Kill*, 1913; *Thought*, 1914; *An Incident*, 1914; *The Parrot*, 1914; *King, Law, Liberty*, 1914; *Youth*, 1914; *War's Burden*, 1915; *He Who Gets Slapped*, 1915; *Dear Phantoms*, 1916; *Requiem*, 1917; *The Waltz of the Dogs*, 1922; *Samson in Chains*, 1923.

IN ENGLISH: C. L. Meader and F. N. Scott, Plays by Leonid Andreyeff, 1915; *To the Stars*, tr. by H. Goudiss in Poet Lore 18, 1907; tr. by M. Magnus, 1921; tr. anon., 1921; *Savva*, tr. by Thomas Seltzer, 1914, 1920; *The Life of Man*, tr. by Theresa Malkiel, 1910; tr. by Thomas Seltzer, 1914, and in M. J. Moses, Representative Continental Dramas, 1924; tr. by Meader and Scott in Plays, 1915, and in R. M. Smith, Types of Philosophic Drama, 1928; tr. by C. J. Hogarth, 1915; *King Hunger*, tr. by Eugene M. Kayden in Poet Lore 22, 1911; *Love of One's Neighbor*, tr. by Seltzer, 1914, and in Frank Shay and Pierre Loving, Fifty Contemporary One-Act Plays, 1920; tr. as The Dear Departing, by Julius West, 1916; *The Black Maskers*, tr. in Plays, by Meader and Scott; *Anathema*, tr. by Herman Bernstein, 1910; *The Sabine Women*, tr. as The Pretty Sabine Women, by Seltzer, in Drama 4, 1914; tr. in Plays, by Meader and Scott; *Yekaterina Ivanovna*, tr. by O. F. Murphy, 1922; tr. as Katerina, by Bernstein, 1923, 1924; *An Incident*, tr. by Leo Pasvolsky in Poet Lore 27, 1916, and in Moses, Representative One-Act Plays by Continental Authors, 1922; *King, Law, Liberty*, tr. as The Sorrows of Belgium, by Bernstein, 1915; *He Who Gets Slapped*, tr. as The Knock About, He Who Gets Slapped, by F. Mindell, 1921; tr. as The Painted Laugh, by Khyva St. Albans, and played in London, 1921; tr. as He the One Who Gets Slapped, by Gregory Zilboorg, in The Dial 70, 1921; separately, 1921; and in S. M. Tucker, Modern Continental Plays, 1929; and in T. H. Dickinson, Chief Contemporary Dramatists, 3rd series, 1930; abridged in Burns Mantle, Best Plays of 1921–1922; tr. by Gertrude Schurhoff and Sir Barry Jackson, and played 1926; *The Waltz of the Dogs*, tr. by Bernstein, 1922, and played, N. Y., 1927; *Samson in Chains*, tr. by Bernstein, 1923.

ANSKY, S. A. (SOLOMON RAPPOPORT)

The Dybbuk, 1913–1915.

IN ENGLISH: *The Dybbuk*, tr. by Irving S. Richter, 1926; tr. by H. G. Alsberg and Winifred Katzin, 1926; in Burns Mantle, Best Plays of 1925–1926, and in T. H. Dickinson, Chief Contemporary Dramatists, 3rd series, 1930.

ANTONA-TRAVERSI, CAMILLO

The Rozeno Family, 1891; *Dance Macabre*, 1893; *The Children*, 1894; *Earth or Fire*, 1896; *The Parasites*, 1899; *The French Woman*, 1916; *Don Matteo*, 1917; *Stabat Mater*, 1917; etc., his later plays written for the Grand Guignol in French.

ANTONA-TRAVERSI, GIANNINO

The Morning After, 1890; *Coquette*, 1893; *The School of Husbands*, 1898; *The Ascent to Olympus*, 1899; *Happier Days*, 1902; *The Wedding Journey*, 1903; *The Fidelity of Husbands*, 1904; *Worldly Charity*, 1906; *An Honest Wife*, 1907; *Martyrs to Work*, 1907; *Those Who Pay*, 1908; *The Mother*, 1909; *Flames* (with Pastouchi), 1910; *The Screen*, 1911; *The Great Shadow*, 1914; etc.

ANTONELLI, LUIGI

The House of the Children, 1909; *Moonlight*, 1910; *The Compact*, 1915; *The Man Who Met Himself*, 1918; *The Fable of the Three Magi*, 1919; *Bernardo the Hermit*, 1919; *The Artificial Mountain*, 1920; *The Island of Monkeys*, 1922; *Drama, Comedy, Farce*, 1926; *The Shop of Dreams*, 1927; *I'd Give My Life*, 1929; etc.

ANZENGRUBER, LUDWIG

Temptation, 1865; *The Parson of Kirschfeld*, 1869; *The Farmer Forsworn*, 1871; *The Cross-Markers*, 1872; *Elfriede*, 1873; *The Worm of Conscience*, 1873; *The Daughter of the Usurer*, 1873; *Hand and Heart*, 1875; *The Double Suicide*, 1875; *The Farm Without a Farmer*, 1876; *The Stain*, 1876 (reworked, 1882); *The Fourth Commandment*, 1877; *The Empty Place*, 1877; *Maiden's Wrath*, 1878; *Old Viennese*, 1878; *The Reversed Wooing*, 1878; *The Blow With the Fist*, 1879; *Out of the Usual Track*, 1880; *Brave Folk,* 1880; *Der Sternsteinhof*, 1884; *Heimg'funden*, 1885; *Steel and Stone*, 1887; etc.

IN ENGLISH: *The Farmer Forsworn,* tr. by Adolf Busse in K. Francke and W. G. Howard, German Classics, v. 16, 1913–1914; *The Fourth Commandment*, adapted by A. Sigmann, 1912.

ARTZYBASHEV, MIKHAIL PETROVICH

Jealousy, 1913; *Enemies*, 1913; *The Law of the Savage*, 1913; *War*, 1914.

IN ENGLISH: *Jealousy, Enemies, The Law of the Savage*, in one volume, 1923,—*Jealousy* and *The Law of the Savage*, tr. by Mme. A. Strindberg and W. F. Adams; *Enemies*, tr. by Mme. Strindberg and A. Levitsky; *Jealousy*, tr. by Marjory Meff, 1917; tr. by Wolfgang F. Pauli from the German, 1920; tr. by Fania Mindell, 1921; tr. by Louis Rich, 1921; *Enemies*, tr. as Lovers and Enemies, by Mme. Strindberg, and played in N. Y., 1927; a novel, *The Savage*, tr. by Gilbert Cannan and Mme. Strindberg, 1924; *War*, tr. by Thomas Seltzer in Drama 6, and separately, 1916; tr. by Percy Pinkerton and Ivan Ohzol, 1918.

BAHR, HERMANN

The New Men, 1887; *The Great Sin*, 1889; *The Mother*, 1891; *The Domestic Woman*, 1893; *Dora*, 1893; *From the Suburbs*, 1893; *The Water Sprite*, 1896; *Juana*, 1896; *The Booby*, 1897; *Josephine*, 1898; *The Star*, 1898; *The Athlete*, 1899; *Viennese Women*, 1900; *Der Franzl*, 1900; *The Apostle*, 1901; *Der

BIBLIOGRAPHY

Krampus, 1901; *The Master*, 1903; *Sanna*, 1904; *The Poor Fool*, 1905; *The Deliverers' Club*, 1905; *The Other*, 1905; *The Faun*, 1906; *Grotesques*, 1907; *The Yellow Nightingale*, 1907; *Ring Around (Ringelspiel)*, 1907; *The Concert*, 1909; *The Children*, 1910; *The Little Dance*, 1911; *The Principle*, 1912; *The Phantom*, 1913; *The Complainer*, 1914; *The Jolly Soap Refiner*, 1914; *The Voice*, 1916; *The Moment*, 1917; *The Brute*, 1919; *Indian Summer (Altweibersommer)*, 1924; *The Aunt*, 1926; *Heaven on Earth*, 1928; etc., etc.

IN ENGLISH: *Josephine*, adapted by Washburn Freund and played in N. Y., 1918; *The Master*, adapted by Benjamin Glazer, 1915; *The Poor Fool*, tr. by Mrs. F. E. Washburn-Freund, and played, N. Y., 1917; *The Concert*, adapted by Leo Ditrichstein, 1910, and played, N. Y., 1915; tr. by B. Q. Morgan in T. H. Dickinson, Chief Contemporary Dramatists, 2d series, 1921; *The Voice*, tr. by Joseph B. Rethy, 1919; *The Mongrel*, tr. by Frances C. Fay, 1924; the story adapted by E. L. Rice, in Living Age, 1925; *The Moment*, tr. by Rethy, 1919.

BATAILLE, HENRY

The Fair Leper, 1897; *Thy Blood*, 1897; *The Enchantment*, 1900; *The Masque*, 1902; *Mamma Colibri*, 1903; *The Declaration*, 1903; *The Wedding March*, 1905; *Resurrection* (from Tolstoy), 1902; *Poliche*, 1906; *Woman Unadorned (La Femme nue)*, 1908; *The Scandal*, 1909; *The Dream of an Evening of Love*, 1910; *The Foolish Virgin*, 1910; *The Child of Love*, 1911; *The Torches*, 1912; *The Night Moth (Le Phalène)*, 1913; *The Amazon*, 1916; *Our Image*, 1918; *Love Sisters*, 1919; *The Animator*, 1920; *The Man With a Rose*, 1921; *Tenderness*, 1921; *Possession*, 1922; *Human Flesh*, 1922.

IN ENGLISH: *The Wedding March*, adapted by Charlton Andrews, 1922; *Resurrection*, tr. as The Message, by Michael Morton, 1902; *The Scandal*, adapted by Lady Bell, and played, London, 1922; *The Child of Love*, adapted as The Love Child, by M. Brown, and played, N. Y., 1921; *The Torches*, adapted by Charlton Andrews, and played, N. Y., 1916.

BATKA, RICHARD

Cinderella, 1905.

BAZIN, RENÉ, and HARAUCOURT, EDMOND

The Oberlé Family, 1905.

BECQUE, HENRY

Sardanapalus, an opera, 1867; *The Prodigal Child*, 1869; *Michel Pauper*, 1870; *The Abduction*, 1871; *The Merry-Go-Round (La Navette)*, 1878; *Virtuous Women*, 1880; *The Vultures (Les Corbeaux)*, 1881; *The Parisian Woman*, 1885; *Madeleine*, 1896; *Widowed*, 1897; *A Four-Handed Game (Domino à quatre)*, 1897; *The Departure*, 1897; *An Execution*, 1897; *The Harlequins (Les Polichinelles)*, in fragments from 1888, finished by Henri de Nousanne, 1910.

601

MODERN CONTINENTAL PLAYWRIGHTS

IN ENGLISH: Three Plays by Henry Becque, tr. by Freeman Tilden, 1913; *La Navette*, tr. as The Merry-Go-Round, by Tilden, in Three Plays; tr. as The Shuttle, by L. A. Loiseaux; *The Vultures*, tr. by Tilden, in Three Plays, and in M. J. Moses, Representative Continental Dramas, 1924; tr. as The Crows, in Drama 2, 1912; and abridged in J. A. Pierce, Masterpieces of Modern Drama—Foreign, 1915; *The Parisian Woman*, tr. as The Parisian, by Charles A. Byrne, 1904; tr. as The Woman of Paris, by Tilden, in Three Plays; *Domino à Quatre*, tr. as A Quiet Game, by Sheba Harris, in The Play Book, 1913.

BEER-HOFMANN, RICHARD

The Count of Charolais, 1904; *Jacob's Dream*, 1918; etc.

IN ENGLISH: *Jacob's Dream*, tr. as The Dream of Jacob, by Amelia von Ende, 1927.

BENAVENTE, JACINTO

In the Place of Don Juan, 1892; *The Nest of Another*, 1894; *Well Known Folk*, 1896; *The Husband of La Téllez*, 1897; *La Farándula*, 1897; *The Banquet of the Beasts*, 1898; *Feminist Theater*, 1898; *Tale of Love*, 1899; *Surgical Operation*, 1899; *A Cruel Farewell*, 1899; *The Angora Cat*, 1900; *The Journey for Instruction*, 1900; *For the Wound*, 1900; *Modes*, 1901; *Lo Cursi*, 1901; *Sacrifices*, 1901; *The Governor's Wife*, 1901; *Roman Cousin*, 1901; *Love of Loving*, 1902; *The Husband's Train*, 1902; *Soul Triumphant*, 1902; *The Automobile*, 1902; *Saturday Night*, 1903; *The Favorites*, 1903; *The Perfect Man (El Hombrecito)*, 1903; *Why Women Love*, 1903; *Broad Daylight (Al Natural)*, 1903; *The House of Good Fortune*, 1903; *The Fire Dragon*, 1904; *Princess Bebé*, 1904; *No Smoking*, 1904; *Autumn Roses*, 1905; *Evil Doers of Good*, 1905; *Crickets and Ants*, 1905; *Stronger Than Love*, 1906; *Manon Lescaut*, 1906; *The Owls*, 1907; *Grandmother and Grandchild*, 1907; *The Princess Without Heart*, 1907; *Love Shocked*, 1907; *The Enchanted Cup*, 1907; *The Eyes of the Dead*, 1907; *The Story of Othello*, 1907; *The Smile of Gioconda*, 1907; *The Last Minuet*, 1907; *We Are All One*, 1907; *The Bonds of Interest*, 1907; *Señora Ama*, 1908; *His Widow's Husband*, 1908; *Brute Force*, 1908; *Trifles*, 1908; *Toward the Truth*, 1908; *In the Clouds*, 1909; *The Magic of an Hour*, 1909; *At Close Range*, 1909; *To See What a Man Will Do!* 1909; *The School of Princesses*, 1909; *The Prince Who Learned Everything Out of Books*, 1909; *Earning a Living*, 1909; *The Grandson*, 1910; *The Graveyard of Dreams*, 1911; *The Passion Flower (La Malquerida)*, 1913; *The Necklace of Stars*, 1915; *The Truth*, 1915; *Self-Esteem*, 1915; *Field of Ermine*, 1916; *The Yellow Jacket*, 1916; *The Joyous and Confident City*, 1916; *The Evil that We Do*, 1917; *Young Lions*, 1918; *Mephistophela* (an opera), 1918; *Our Lady of Sorrows (La Immaculada de los Dolores)*, 1918; *The Law of the Children*, 1918; *A Traitor to All, to All Be Ye Loyal*, 1919; *The Vestal of the West*, 1919; *The Honor of Men*, 1919; *Daring*, 1919; *Cinderella*, 1919; *A Lady*, 1919; *A Poor Woman*, 1919; *Beyond Death*, 1922; *Lessons in Love*, 1924; *A Pair of Boots*, 1924; *Doubtful Virtue*, 1924; *The Other Honor*, 1924; *Pinpricks*, 1924; *The Suicide of Lucerito*, 1925; *New Sons-in-Law*, 1925; *The Butterfly that Flew over the Sea*, 1926; *Bright Night*,

BIBLIOGRAPHY

1927; *The Son of Polichinella*, 1927; *Chaste Joseph* (*Pepe Doncel*), 1928; *The Demon Once Was an Angel*, 1928; *Tangled Lives*, 1929; etc.

IN ENGLISH: J. G. Underhill, Plays of Jacinto Benavente, four series, 1917–1924; *In the Place of Don Juan*, tr. in Poet Lore; *The Nest of Another*, tr. as Another's Nest, by M. J. Woodhull, 1922; *The Angora Cat*, adapted by F. de Ros and William Dunn, 1911; *The Governor's Wife*, tr. by Underhill in Poet Lore 29, 1918, and in Plays, 2d series; *Saturday Night*, tr. by Underhill, Poet Lore 29, 1918, and in Plays, 3rd series; *No Smoking*, tr. by Underhill, The Drama 25, 1917, and in Plays, 2d series; *Princess Bebé*, tr. by Underhill in Plays, 2d series; *Autumn Roses*, tr. as Autumnal Roses by Underhill in Plays, 2d series; *Evil Doers of Good*, tr. by Underhill in Plays, 1st series; *The Bonds of Interest*, tr. as Interests Created, by L. J. Rosenberg, 1908; tr. as The Bias of the World, by F. de Ros and Beryl de Zoete, 1913; tr. by Underhill in Drama 20, 1915, and in Plays, 1st series, and in T. H. Dickinson, Chief Contemporary Dramatists, 2d series, 1921, and in M. J. Moses, Representative Continental Dramas, 1924; *His Widow's Husband*, tr. as The Husband of His Widow, by J. A. Herman, 1912; tr. by Underhill in Plays, 1st series, and in Frank Shay and Pierre Loving, Fifty Contemporary One-Act Plays, 1920; *The Magic of an Hour*, tr. by Underhill in Plays, 4th series; tr. as The Enchanted Hour, by Addison McLeod, and played, London, 1926; *In the Clouds*, tr. by Underhill in Plays, 3rd series; *At Close Range*, adapted by J. A. Herman, 1911; *The School of Princesses*, tr. by Underhill in Plays, 4th series; *The Prince Who Learned Everything Out of Books*, tr. by Underhill in Poet Lore 29, 1910, and in Plays, 3rd series; *La Malquerida*, tr. by Underhill in Plays, 1st series, and played as the Passion Flower, N. Y., 1920, and in S. M. Tucker, Modern Continental Plays, 1929; *The Truth*, tr. by Underhill, in Plays, 3rd series; *Field of Ermine*, tr. by Underhill in Plays, 4th series, and played in Syracuse, 1921; *A Lady*, tr. by Underhill in Plays, 4th series; *The Smile of Mona Lisa*, tr. as The Smile of La Gioconda, by J. A. Herman, 1911, and under the original title, 1915; *A Good Marriage*, tr. by M. J. Woodhull, 1922; *The Summer Holidays*, tr. by Addison McLeod, and played, London, 1926.

BENELLI, SEM

Lassalle, 1902; *The Earth*, 1903; *The Bookworm*, 1904; *The Mask of Brutus*, 1908; *The Supper of Pranks* (*The Jest*), 1909; *The Love of the Three Kings*, 1910; *The Mantle*, 1911; *Rosmunda*, 1912; *The Gorgon*, 1913; *The Marriage of the Centaurs*, 1915; *Wings*, 1921; *The Quibble*, 1922; *Holy Springtime*, 1923; *The Amorous Tragedy*, 1925; *The Necklace of Pearls*, 1926; *With the Stars*, 1927; *Orpheus and Proserpina*, 1929.

IN ENGLISH: *The Supper of Pranks*, tr. as The Supper of Scoffers, by A. Sterling, 1910; adapted as The Jest, by C. B. Fernald, 1919, 1920; adapted as The Love Feast, by John Barrymore, 1918; played by him as The Jest, N. Y., 1919; tr. by Edward Sheldon but not published; abbreviated in Burns Mantle, Best Plays of 1919–1920; played, London, in C. B. Fernald's version as The Love Thief, 1921; tr. as A Florentine Wager by Hildegarde D. Lepehne, 1922; transposed into novel form by Marjorie Bowen, 1922; tr. as A

Fool There Was, by J. Pollock, 1923; tr. as The Jesters' Supper, by K. H. B. de Jaffa, 1925; *The Love of the Three Kings*, tr. by R. H. Elkins, 1913; tr. by H. M. Jones, 1923; played, London, 1924; tr. by C. H. Meltzer, 1926, and in T. H. Dickinson, Chief Contemporary Dramatists, 3rd series, 1930.

BERGMAN, HJALMAR

Mary Mother of Jesus, 1905; *Parisina*, 1915; *Marionette Plays*, 1917; *Swedenhielms*, 1925; *Trash*, 1929.

BERGSTRÖM, HJALMAR

Ida's Wedding, 1902; *Lynggaard and Company*, 1905; *Karen Borneman*, 1907; *The Golden Fleece*, 1908; *Ladies' Tea*, 1910; *In the Swim*, 1910; *The Way to God*, 1912; *What People Talk Of*, 1915; *Thora van Deken*, 1915.

IN ENGLISH: *Two Plays by Hjalmar Bergström* (*Lynggaard and Company* and *Karen Borneman*), tr. by Edwin Björkman, 1913; *Ladies' Tea*, tr. as The Birthday Party, by Björkman, 1922, and in M. J. Moses, Representative One-Act Plays by Continental Authors, 1923.

BERNARD, JEAN-JACQUES

The Journey à Deux, 1909; *The Joy of Sacrifice*, 1912; *The House that was Spared*, 1919; *The Fire Slow to Rekindle*, 1921; *Martine*, 1922; *The Invitation to Travel*, 1924; *The Springtime of Others*, 1924; *Denise Marette*, 1925; *The Soul in Distress*, 1926; *The Secret of Arvers*, 1926; *The King of Malousie*, 1928.

IN ENGLISH: *The Fire Slow to Rekindle*, tr. as The Sulky Fire, by J. L. Frith and Marjorie Gabain, and played, London, 1926; *Martine*, tr. by Winifred Katzin, in Eight European Plays, 1927; tr. by Helen Grayson, 1927; *The Invitation to Travel*, tr. as The Years Between, by J. L. Frith, and played, London, 1926; tr. as Glamour, by Katzin, in Eight European Plays.

BERNARD, TRISTAN

The Only Bandit of the Village, 1898; *English As It Is Spoken* (*L'Anglais tel qu'on le parle*), 1899; *The Touring Club Bride*, 1899; *The Mathieu Case*, 1901; *The Gang at Léon*, 1902; *Triplepatte* (with A. Godfernaux), 1905; *The Twins of Brighton*, 1908; *The Ambulant Flirt*, 1908; *The Ardent Artillery-man*, 1910; *The Little Café*, 1911; *The Nocturnal Visitors*, 1912; *The Soubigou Beacons*, 1912; *Jeanne Doré*, 1913; *Prince Charming*, 1914; *The Force of Lying*, 1914; *The Cheap Cravat*, 1919; *The Idea of M. Dumorel*, 1920; *The Blue Ribbon*, 1920; *Embrace Me*, 1923; *She Also*, 1924; etc.

IN ENGLISH: *L'Anglais tel qu'on le parle*, adapted as French Without a Master, by B. H. Clark, 1915; as French as He is Spoke, by Gaston Mayer, 1907; *I'm Going*, tr. by Clark, 1915; *Triplepatte*, adapted as Toddles, by Clyde Fitch, 1906; *The Little Café*, adapted as a musical comedy by C. M. S. McLellan, 1913; *Jeanne Doré*, tr. by Katherine Stewart, 1924.

BIBLIOGRAPHY

BERNÈDE, ARTHUR, and BRUANT, ARISTIDE

French Woman's Heart, 1912.

BERNSTEIN, HENRY

The Market, 1900; *The Detour*, 1902; *Joujou*, 1902; *Brother Jacques* (with Pierre Véber), 1903; *The Fold*, 1904; *The Tempest*, 1905; *The Talon*, 1906; *The Thief*, 1906; *Samson*, 1907; *Israël*, 1908; *After Me*, 1911; *The Assault*, 1912; *The Secret*, 1913; *To the Heights* (*l'Elévation*), 1917; *Judith*, 1922; *The Gallery of Mirrors*, 1926; *Félix*, 1926; *The Poison*, 1927; *Mélo*, 1929.

IN ENGLISH: *The Tempest*, tr. as The Whirlwind, by Mrs. M. S. Wormser, 1906; adapted as The Whirlwind, by Harry Melvill, 1906; played as Baccarat, 1910, and renamed The Whirlwind; *The Talon*, adapted as The Claw, by E. D. Dunn and L. Wolheim, 1920; *The Thief*, adapted by C. Haddon Chambers, 1907; adapted by C. Gordon Lennox, and played, London, 1907; tr. by J. A. Haughton, 1915; abridged in J. A. Pierce, Masterpieces of Modern Drama—Foreign, 1915; *Israël*, adapted by Sidney C. Isaacs, and played, London, 1926; tr. by H. F. Caldwell, 1929; *The Assault*, adapted as The Attack, by George Egerton, and played, N. Y., 1913; *The Secret*, adapted by David Belasco, 1915; *l'Elévation*, tr. as Uplifted, by Angela Thirkell, and played, London, 1923; *Judith*, adapted as The Virgin of Bethulia, by Gladys Unger, 1925.

BISSON, ALEXANDRE

The Deputy from Bombignac, 1884; *My Governess*, 1887; *The Surprises of Divorce* (with Antony Mars), 1888; *The Late Toupinel*, 1890; *The Pont-Biquet Family*, 1892; *The Heroic le Cardunois*, 1894; *M. The Director* (with Carré), 1895; *The Errors of Marriage*, 1896; *The Sleeping Car Conductor*, 1898; *The Joys of Paternity* (with Vast-Ricard), 1902; *The Apache*, 1903; *Yellow Peril* (with Saint Albin), 1906; *Madame X* (*La Femme X——*), 1908; etc., etc.

IN ENGLISH: *A Pleasure Trip*, tr. by Newton Chisnell, 1886; *The Lottery of Love*, adapted by Augustin Daly, 1888; *The Surprises of Divorce*, tr. as The Humors of Divorce, by Frederic Lyster, 1894; *The Late Toupinel*, adapted as The Late Lamented, by Fred Horner, 1891; *M. le Directeur*, adapted as The Chili Widow, by A. Bourchier and Alfred Sutro, 1896; *The Yellow Peril*, adapted as The Grass Widow, a musical comedy, by Channing Pollock and Rennold Wolf, 1919; *Madame X*, adapted by J. M. Raphael, 1909.

BJÖRNSON, BJÖRNSTJERNE

Between the Battles, 1856; *Lame Hulda*, 1858; *King Sverre*, 1861; *Sigurd Slembe*, 1862; *Mary Stuart in Scotland*, 1864; *The Newly Married*, 1868; *Sigurd Jorsalfar*, 1872; *The Editor*, 1874; *A Bankruptcy*, 1875; *The King*, 1877; *Leonarda*, 1879; *The New System*, 1879; *A Gauntlet*, 1883; *Beyond Our Power I*, 1883; *Geography and Love*, 1885; *Beyond Our Power II*, 1895;

MODERN CONTINENTAL PLAYWRIGHTS

Paul Lange and Tora Parsberg, 1898; *Laboremus*, 1901; *At Storhove*, 1902; *Dayland*, 1904; *When the New Wine Blooms*, 1909.

IN ENGLISH: R. F. Sharp, Three Comedies, 1912, and Three Dramas, 1914; Edwin Björkman, Plays, 1st series, 1913; 2d series, 1914; *Sigurd Slembe*, tr. by William M. Payne, 1888, 1910; *Mary Stuart in Scotland*, tr. as Mary Queen of Scots, by August Sahlberg, 1912; *The Newly Married*, tr. by T. Soelfeldt, 1868; tr. by S. and E. Hjerleid, 1870; tr. as The Newly Married Couple, by R. F. Sharp in Three Comedies; tr. as A Lesson in Marriage, by Grace I. Colbron, 1910; *The Editor*, tr. by Sharp in Three Dramas; *A Bankruptcy*, tr. by Sylvester Baxter, 1881; tr. as The Bankrupt, by Sharp in Three Dramas; *The King*, tr. by Sharp in Three Dramas; *Leonarda*, tr. by Payne; tr. by Colbron, 1911; tr. by D. L. Hanson in The Drama 3, 1911; tr. by Sharp in Three Comedies; *The New System*, tr. by Björkman in Plays, 1st series; *A Gauntlet*, tr. by H. L. Braekstad, 1890; tr. as A Glove, by T. Sogard in Poet Lore 4, 1892; tr. by Osman Edwards, 1894, and in The Drama 17, 1903; tr. by Sharp in Three Comedies; tr. by Björkman in Plays, 1st series; *Beyond Our Power I*, tr. as Pastor Sang, by William Wilson, 1893; tr. as Beyond Human Strength, by J. H. Paulding, in Poet Lore 13, 1905; tr. by Björkman in Plays, 1st series, and in S. M. Tucker, Modern Continental Plays, 1929; tr. as Beyond Human Power, by L. M. Hollander, separately, and in T. H. Dickinson, Chief Contemporary Dramatists, 1st series, 1915; abridged in J. A. Pierce, Masterpieces of Modern Drama—Foreign, 1915; *Geography and Love*, tr. as Love and Geography, by Björkman in Plays, 2d series; *Beyond Our Power II*, tr. as Beyond Human Might, by Björkman in Plays, 2d series; *Paul Lange and Tora Parsberg*, tr. by H. L. Braekstad, 1898; *Laboremus*, tr. anonymously, 1901; tr. by Björkman, in Plays, 2d series; *When the New Wine Blooms*, tr. by L. M. Hollander in Poet Lore 22, 1911; tr. as When the Young Vine Blooms, by Avid Paulson, 1915.

BOIS, JULES

The Fury, 1909.

BONN, FERDINAND

Andalosia, 1906.

BORNIER, HENRI DE

Daughter of Roland, 1875.

BOURDET, ÉDOUARD

The Rubicon, 1910; *The Open Cage*, 1912; *The Shepherd's Hour (L'Heure du berger)*, 1922; *The Man Enchained*, 1923; *The Captive (La Prisonnière)*, 1926; *Just Appeared*, 1928; *The Weaker Sex*, 1929.

IN ENGLISH: *The Rubicon*, adapted by Henry Baron, 1922; *The Shepherd's Hour*, tr. as The Happy Hour, by George Middleton, 1923; *The Captive*, tr. by Arthur Hornblow, Jr., 1926.

BIBLIOGRAPHY

BOURGEOIS, EUGÈNE

The Man Who Was Hanged, 1891; *Marriage for Money*, 1893; *The Will*, 1904.

BOURGET, PAUL

A Divorce (with A. Cury), 1908; *The Emigré*, 1908; *A Case of Conscience* (with Serge Basset), 1910; *The Barricade*, 1910; *The Tribune*, 1911; *The Crisis* (with André Beaunier), 1912.

IN ENGLISH: *A Divorce* (the original novel), tr. by E. L. Charlwood, 1904.

BRACCO, ROBERTO

Do Not Unto Others, 1886; *Three (Lui-Lei-Lui)*; *Vice-versa; A Travel Adventure*, 1887; *A Woman*, 1893; *The Unfaithful*, 1894; *Masks*, 1894; *The Triumph*, 1895; *Don Pietro Caruso*, 1895; *The End of Love*, 1896; *Orange Blossoms*, 1898; *Tragedies of the Soul*, 1899; *The Right to Live*, 1900; *One of the Honest*, 1900; *Lost in Darkness*, 1901; *Maternity*, 1903; *Bitter Fruit*, 1904; *Photography Without —*, 1904; *The Little Spring*, 1905; *Night of Snow*, 1905; *Phantasms*, 1906; *Nellina*, 1909; *The Little Saint*, 1909; *The Perfect Love*, 1910; *Not Even a Kiss*, 1912; *Concealed Weapons*, 1913; *The Chatterbox*, 1913; *Three; The International*, 1915; *Consecrated Eyes*, 1916; *The Distant Lover*, 1916; *The Cradle*, 1918; *Crazy Folk (I Pazzi)*, 1922; etc.

IN ENGLISH: *Three*, tr. by Dirce St. Cyr and adapted by Gilbert Cannan, 1914; adapted by W. P. Lipscomb, and played, London, 1921; *The Unfaithful*, tr. by Dirce St. Cyr, and played as The Countess Coquette, 1907; adapted by Gilbert Cannan, and played, London, 1926; *Don Pietro Caruso*, tr. and played, N. Y., 1912; *The End of Love*, adapted and played as I Love You, London, 1913; tr. as The White Fly, by Countess Maria Tomacelli, 1923; adapted by Eduardo Ciannelli, 1925; *Orange Blossoms*, tr. by Dirce St. Cyr, 1908; *One of the Honest*, played as The Honorable Lover, N. Y., 1915; *The Little Spring*, tr. as The Hidden Spring, by Dirce St. Cyr, Poet Lore 18, 1907; *Night of Snow*, tr. as A Snowy Night, by Arthur Livingston in Frank Shay, Twenty-five Short Plays, 1925, and played, N. Y., 1915; *Phantasms*, tr. by Dirce St. Cyr, Poet Lore 19, 1908, and in S. M. Tucker, Modern Continental Plays, 1929; tr. by M. Tracy, 1916; tr. by R. A. Armstrong, 1919; adapted by S. F. Lazarus and Eduardo Ciannelli, 1924.

BRECHT, BERTOLT

Drums in the Night, 1922; *Thicket*, 1922; *Baal*, 1923; *Edward II* (with Lion Feuchtwanger), 1924; *Man is Man*, 1926; *Calcutta* (with Lion Feuchtwanger).

IN ENGLISH: *Calcutta*, adapted by J. V. Reid, 1928.

BRIEUX, EUGÈNE

The Divorce Bureau (with Gaston Salandri), 1880; *Bernard Palissy* (with Salandri), 1880; *Sténio*, 1888; *Artists' Homes*, 1890; *Duramé's Daughter*,

1890; *M. de Réboval*, 1892; *Blanchette*, 1892; *The Nest*, 1893; *Cogwheels*, 1894; *The Blue Rose*, 1895; *Soldier Grandor*, 1895; *The Benefactors*, 1896; *Evasion*, 1896; *The Three Daughters of M. Dupont*, 1897; *The School for Mothers-in-Law* (adapted from *The Nest*), 1898; *Racing Results*, 1898; *The Cradle*, 1898; *The Red Robe*, 1900; *The Substitutes*, 1901; *Damaged Goods* (*Les Avariés*), 1902; *Little Mistress*, 1902; *Maternity*, 1903; *The Fair Deserter* (with Jean Sigaux), 1904; *Armature*, 1905; *The June Bugs*, 1906; *The Frenchwoman*, 1907; *Simone*, 1908; *Suzette*, 1909; *False Gods* (*La Foi*), 1909; *Woman On Her Own* (*La Femme seule*), 1912; *Citizen in the Country* (*Le Bourgeois aux champs*), 1914; *Americans in France* (*Les Américains chez nous*), 1920; *The Attorney*, 1922; *The Child* (*L'Enfant: Pierrette et Galaor*), 1923; *The Lavolette Family*, 1926; *Because I Love You*, 1929.

IN ENGLISH: Mrs. Bernard Shaw, St. John Hankin, and J. Pollock, Three Plays by Brieux, 1911; Frederick Eisemann, Two Plays by Brieux, 1913; Mrs. Bernard Shaw, J. B. Fagan, and A. B. Miall, Three Plays by Brieux, 1916; *Artists' Homes*, tr. as Artists' Families, by B. H. Clark, 1918; *Blanchette*, tr. by Frederick Eisemann in Two Plays; *The Nest* (*La Couvée*), tr. as The School for Mothers-in-Law, by Willard H. Wright, Smart Set, 1913; tr. by Edward Goodman, The International, 1911; *The Benefactors*, tr. as The Philanthropists, by Lucas Malet; *The Evasion*, tr. as The Escape, by Frederick Eisemann in Two Plays; tr. as Prisoners of the Dead, by D. U. Baxter, 1914; *The Three Daughters of M. Dupont*, tr. by St. John Hankin in Three Plays; *The Cradle*, adapted by S. V. Winthrop, 1922; *The Red Robe*, tr. by C. H. Heydemann, 1900; tr. as The Arm of the Law and played, London, 1904; tr. by F. O. Reed in T. H. Dickinson, Chief Contemporary Dramatists, 1st series, 1915; tr. by A. B. Miall in Three Plays; abridged in J. A. Pierce, Masterpieces of Modern Drama—Foreign, 1915; tr. by T. W. Broadhurst, 1916; tr. as The Letter of the Law and as The Law, by Homer St. Gaudens, 1919; *Damaged Goods*, tr. by J. Pollock in Three Plays, and separately, 1912; adapted by G. F. Bragdon and R. Bennett, 1913; *Maternity*, tr. by Mrs. Bernard Shaw, 1907, and (a new version) by J. Pollock in Three Plays; tr. by B. F. Blanchard, 1915; *The Fair Deserter*, tr. as The Deserter, by C. Coste, 1917; *The June Bugs*, tr. under its original title—Les Hannetons— by H. M. Clark, 1907; adapted as Madame Pierre, by A. Hornblow, Jr., 1922; played in English as The Incubus, 1909, and later that year as The Affinity; *False Gods* (*La Foi*), tr. by J. B. Fagan in Three Plays, and in S. M. Tucker, Modern Continental Plays, 1929; *Woman On Her Own* (*La Femme seule*), tr. by Mrs. Bernard Shaw, 1913, and in Three Plays; *The Americans in France*, played in N. Y., 1920; *The Attorney*, tr. as The Advocate, by George Middleton, 1923; played in N. Y. as The Accused.

BRONNEN, ARNOLT

Parricide, 1920; *The Birth of Youth*, 1922; *Excesses*, 1922; *September Story*, 1922; *Anarchy in Sillian*, 1924; *Underground Battle* (*Katalaunische Schlacht*), 1924; *Rhenish Rebels*, 1925; *East Pole Quest*, 1926; *Michael Kohlhaas*, 1929.

BRONNER, FERDINAND

The Wawroch Family, 1899; *New Life*, 1902; *Schmelz the Nibelung*, 1905; *Fatherland*, 1911; *Eighteen Hundred and Forty-Eight*, 1929.

BIBLIOGRAPHY

BUTTI, ENRICO ANNIBALE

Bitter Fruit (with C. Hanau), 1892; *The Vortex*, 1892; *Utopia*, 1894; *The End of an Ideal*, 1898; *The Atheists*, a trilogy including *The Race for Pleasure*, 1900, *Lucifer*, 1900, *The Tempest*, 1901; *The Giant and the Pygmies*, 1903; *Flames in Darkness*, 1904; *All for Nothing*, 1905; *The Cuckoo*, 1907; *The Castle of Dreams*, 1910; *The Twilight of the Lovers* (with Antongini), 1910; *In the Land of Fortune*, 1910; *The Rivals*, 1911; *Ever Thus*, 1911; *The Invisible Sun*, 1912; *The Seduction*, 1913; *The Way of Salvation*, 1913; etc.

IN ENGLISH: *Poetic Intermezzo*, adapted as Her Highness, by A. Hines-Ludovici, 1922; *The Way of Salvation*, adapted as The Wrecked Lover, by the same, 1922.

ČAPEK, KAREL and JOSEF

The Robbers (by Karel), 1920; *R. U. R.* (by Karel), 1921; *The Life of Insects* (by both), 1921; *The Makropoulos Affair* (by Karel), 1922; *The Land of Many Names* (by Josef), 1923; *Loupeznik*, 1926; *Adam the Creator* (by both), 1927.

IN ENGLISH: *R. U. R.*, tr. by Paul Selver (Theatre Guild Version), 1923; tr. by Josef Kalinnov, 1924; in Burns Mantle, Best Plays of 1922–20, in S. M. Tucker, Modern Continental Plays, 1929; and in T. H. Dickinson, Chief Contemporary Dramatists, 3rd series, 1930; *The Life of Insects*, adapted as The Insect, by Owen Davis, 1922, then as The World We Live In; tr. as And So Ad Infinitum, by Selver, 1923; adapted as The Insect Play from Selver's version, by Nigel Playfair and Clifford Box, played, N. Y., 1922, and London, 1923; *The Makropoulos Affair*, tr. as Makropulos, by Grace I. Colbron, 1923; tr. by J. R. Holzinger and M. Arnsteinova, revised by R. C. Burrell, 1924; adapted as The Makropoulos Secret, by R. C. Burrell, 1925; *The Land of Many Names*, tr. by Selver, 1926; *Adam the Creator*, tr. by Dora Round, 1929.

CAPUS, ALFRED

Brignol and his Daughter, 1894; *Rosine*, 1897; *The Little Minxes*, 1897; *Bourgeois Marriage*, 1898; *The Husbands of Léontine*, 1900; *Money or Your Life*, 1900; *The Little Functionary*, 1901; *Luck*, 1901; *The Two Schools*, 1902; *The Châtelaine*, 1902; *The Adversary*, 1903; *Monsieur Piégois*, 1905; *The Passersby*, 1906; *The Wounded Bird*, 1908; *The Two Men*, 1908; *An Angel*, 1909; *The Adventurer*, 1910; *The Favorites*, 1911; *Hélène Ardouin*, 1913; *The Beauty Institute*, 1913; etc., etc.

IN ENGLISH: *Brignol and his Daughter*, tr. by B. H. Clark, 1915; *The Two Schools*, adapted as Better Not Inquire, by Gladys Unger, 1911; *The Wounded Bird*, adapted by F. de Wendt Fenton, 1911; *The Adventurer*, tr. by Benedict Papot, The Drama 4, 1914; *My Tailor*, tr. by Harold Harper in Frank Shay, Plays for Strolling Mummers, 1926; tr. by B. H. Clark in Smart Set, 1918.

609

CAVACCHIOLI, ERNESTO

The Stormy Petrel, 1909; *The Silver Bell*, 1913; *Bird of Paradise*, 1919; *She Who Resembles Thee*, 1919; *The Danse du Ventre*, 1921; *The Camel*, 1923; *Allegory of Spring*, 1923; etc.

CHEKHOV, ANTON PAVLOVICH

On the High Road, 1884; *Ivanov*, 1887; *The Bear*, 1888; *The Tragedian in Spite of Himself*, 1888; *That Worthless Fellow Platonov*, 1889; *The Swan Song*, 1889; *The Proposal*, 1889; *The Wood Demon*, 1889; *The Sea Gull*, 1896; *Uncle Vanya*, 1897; *The Three Sisters*, 1900; *The Jubilee*, 1903; *The Wedding*, 1903; *The Cherry Orchard*, 1904.

IN ENGLISH: George Calderon, Two plays by Tchekhof, 1912; Marian Fell, Plays by Anton Tchekoff, 1st series, 1912; Julius West, Plays by Anton Tchekoff, 2nd series, 1916; Constance Garnett, The Cherry Orchard and Other Plays, 1923; Garnett, Three Sisters and Other Plays, 1924; *On the High Road*, tr. by West in Plays; tr. as On the Highway, by David A. Modell in The Drama 22, 1916, and in Frank Shay, Twenty-five Short Plays, International, 1924; tr. by Garnett in Three Sisters and Other Plays; *Ivanov*, tr. by Fell in Plays, 1912, 1923; tr. by Jenny Covan in O. M. Sayler, The Moscow Art Theatre Series of Russian Plays, 1923; tr. by Garnett in Three Sisters and Other Plays; *The Bear*, tr. by Arthur A. Sykes, 1911; tr. by West in Plays; tr. by Garnett in The Cherry Orchard and Other Plays; tr. as A Bear, by R. T. House, 1904; tr. as The Boor, by B. H. Clark, 1915; tr. as The Boor, by Hilmar Baukhage, 1915, and in Frank Shay and Pierre Loving, Fifty Contemporary One-Act Plays, 1920; tr. as The Boor in B. R. Lewis, Contemporary One-Act Plays, 1923; tr. as The Boor in George A. Goldstone, One-Act Plays, 1926; *The Tragedian in Spite of Himself*, tr. by West in Plays; tr. by Olive F. Murphy in Poet Lore 33, 1922; tr. as An Unwilling Martyr, by Garnett in Three Sisters and Other Plays; *That Worthless Fellow Platonov*, tr. by John Cournos, 1930; *The Swan Song*, tr. by Fell in Plays, and in Alice M. Smith, Short Plays by Representative Authors, 1922; tr. by Garnett in Three Sisters and Other Plays; *The Proposal*, tr. in The International 8, 1914; tr. by West in Plays; tr. by Garnett in The Cherry Orchard and Other Plays; tr. as A Marriage Proposal by W. H. H. Chambers, in The Drama 18, 1903; tr. as A Marriage Proposal, by Hilmar Baukhage and B. H. Clark, 1914, and in C. S. Thomas, The Atlantic Book of Junior Plays, 1924, and in Edwin Van B. Knickerbocker, Twelve Plays, 1924; *The Wood Demon*, tr. by S. S. Koteliansky, 1926; *The Sea Gull*, tr. by George Calderon in Two Plays, and in M. J. Moses, Representative Continental Dramas, 1924; tr. by Fell in Plays; tr. by Fred Eisemann in Poet Lore 24, 1913; tr. by West, 1915; tr. by Garnett in The Cherry Orchard and Other Plays; abridged in J. A. Pierce, Masterpieces of Modern Drama—Foreign, 1915; *Uncle Vanya*, tr. by Fell in Plays; tr. by Frances A. Saphro in Poet Lore 33, 1922; tr. by Garnett in The Cherry Orchard and Other Plays; tr. by Jenny Covan in O. M. Sayler, The Moscow Art Theatre Series of Russian Plays, 1923; *The Three Sisters*, tr. by Julius West in Plays; tr. by Covan in Sayler, The Moscow Art Theatre Series; tr. by Garnett in Three Sisters and Other Plays,

BIBLIOGRAPHY

and in Eva Le Gallienne, Civic Repertory Plays, 1928; *The Jubilee*, tr. by C. E. Bechhofer in Five Russian Plays, 1916; tr. by Olive F. Murphy in Poet Lore 31, 1920; tr. as The Anniversary by West in Plays; tr. as The Anniversary by Garnett in Three Sisters and Other Plays; *The Wedding*, tr. by West in Plays; tr. by C. E. Bechhofer in Five Russian Plays, 1916; tr. by Constance Garnett in Three Sisters and Other Plays; *The Cherry Orchard*, tr. by George Calderon in Two Plays, and in T. H. Dickinson, Chief Contemporary Dramatists, 1st series, 1915; tr. by West in Plays; tr. by Covan separately and in O. M. Sayler, The Moscow Art Theatre Series of Russian Plays, 1923; tr. by Garnett in The Cherry Orchard and Other Plays; tr. by Calderon in S. M. Tucker, Modern Continental Plays, 1929; tr. as The Cherry Garden by M. S. Mandell, 1908.

CHIARELLI, LUIGI

The Mask and the Face, 1915; *The Silken Ladder*, 1917; *Tears and Stars*, 1918; *Chimeras*, 1921; *The Death of the Lovers*, 1923; *Fireworks*, 1923; *Jolly*, 1928; *K 41*, 1929; etc.

IN ENGLISH: *The Mask and the Face*, tr. by Somerset Maugham, 1924; adapted by C. B. Fernald, 1921; *The Death of the Lovers*, adapted as The Lovers' Tragedy, by De Vic Beamish, 1925; *Fireworks*, adapted by Beamish, 1925.

CLAUDEL, PAUL

The Fair Sleeper, 1886, 1890; *Tête d'Or*, 1890, 1894; *The City*, 1890, 1897; *The Maid Violaine*, 1892, 1898; *The Exchange*, 1894; *The Repose of the Seventh Day*, 1894, 1906; *Partage de Midi*, 1900, 1906; *The Hostage*, 1909, 1914; *The Tidings Brought to Mary*, 1910, 1912; *Proteus*, 1914; *Christmas Eve*, 1914, 1915; *Bitter Bread*, 1915; *The Father Humiliated*, 1916; *The Bear and the Moon*, 1917, 1924; *Man and His Wishes*, 1921; *Woman and Her Shadow* (a ballet), 1923; *The Satin Shoe*, 1924.

IN ENGLISH: *Tête d'Or*, tr. by J. S. Newberry, 1919; *The City*, tr. by Newberry, 1920; *The Exchange*, adapted by Rowland Thurman, played, London, 1915; *The Hostage*, tr. by Pierre Chavannes, 1917; *The Tidings Brought to Mary*, tr. by Louise Morgan Sill, 1916, and in S. M. Tucker, Modern Continental Plays, 1929; *Proteus*, tr. by Newberry, 1921.

COOLUS, ROMAIN (RENÉ WEILL)

The Drésile Household, 1893; *Raphaël*, 1896; *The Sick Child*, 1897; *Lysiane*, 1898; *Cœurblette*, 1899; *The Marquis de Carabas*, 1900; *The Lovers of Sazy*, 1901; *Lucette*, 1902; *Antoinette Sabrier*, 1903; *Little Pest*, 1905; *The Cherished Child*, 1906; *Heart to Heart*, 1907; *The Risk*, 1909; *A Woman Passed*, 1910; *The Coast of Love*, 1912; *The Week of Folly*, 1912; *The Eternal Masculine*, 1920; *Love, When You Hold Us*, 1921; *The Ostrich* (with Hennequin), 1922; *The Alarm Clock* (with Hennequin), 1923; *Jim* (with Hennequin), 1924; *The Kisses of Panurge* (with A. Rivoire), 1925; etc.

IN ENGLISH: *The Alarm Clock* (with Hennequin), adapted by Avery Hopwood, and played, N. Y., 1923.

MODERN CONTINENTAL PLAYWRIGHTS

COPPÉE, FRANÇOIS

The Passerby, 1869; *Two Sorrows*, 1870; *The Woman Abandoned*, 1871; *Do What You Should*, 1871; *The Jewels of Deliverance*, 1872; *The Lute Maker of Cremona*, 1876; *The House of Molière*, 1880; *The Treasure*, 1880; *Mme. de Maintenon*, 1881; *Severo Torelli*, 1883; *The Jacobites*, 1885; *Our Father*, 1889; *For the Crown*, 1895; *The Guilty Man*, 1896; etc.

IN ENGLISH: *The Passerby*, tr. by Frederick A. Schwab, 1881; tr. as The Wanderer, by C. Renauld, 1890; tr. by Rathmell Wilson, 1914; tr. by Lucile Dora in Poet Lore 34, 1923; *The Lute Maker of Cremona*, tr. 1892, and in C. S. Thomas, the Atlantic Book of Junior Plays, 1924; tr. as Fennel, by J. K. Jerome; tr. as The Violins of Cremona, by Edgar Scott, 1922; *Our Father*, tr. as Forgiveness, by C. Renauld, 1890; tr. as Pater Noster, by Will Hutchins, 1915; tr. as The Lord's Prayer, by Mary Aldis, 1923, and in J. P. Webber and H. H. Webster, One-Act Plays for Secondary Schools, 1923; *For the Crown*, tr. by Renauld, 1895; tr. by John Davidson, 1896; adapted as opera in The Cross and the Crescent, by Colin McAlpin, 1903; abridged in J. A. Pierce, Masterpieces of Modern Drama—Foreign, 1915; *Militza the Slave*, adapted by T. Delaney, 1911; *The Guilty Man*, adapted by Ruth H. Davis and Charles Klein, 1916.

COURTELINE, GEORGES (GEORGES MOINAUX)

A Serious Client, 1888; *The 8:47 Train*, 1891; *Lidoire*, 1891; *Boubouroche*, 1893; *Ah, Youth!* 1894; *Hortense, to Bed!* 1897; *The Gendarme is Without Pity*, 1899; *Article 330*, 1900; *The Balances*, 1901; *Victories and Conquests*, 1902; *Peace at Home*, 1903; *The Conversion of Alceste*, 1905; *The Lenottes*, 1913; etc., etc.

IN ENGLISH: *Boubouroche*, played, N. Y., 1920; *The Gendarme is Without Pity*, tr. as The Pitiless Policeman, by H. Isabelle Williams in Poet Lore 28, 1917; *Peace at Home*, tr. by F. C. Fay in The International, 1913; tr. by Leroy J. Cook in Poet Lore 29, 1918; *Blank Cartridge*, tr. by Robert W. Sneddon in The International, 1913; *A Private Account*, tr. by E. Goodman and Beatrice Holthoir, 1917; *The Fine System*, played by Olive Wyndham and Jose Ruben, N. Y., 1919.

COUVREUR, ANDRÉ

Higher than Love, 1916.

CROISSET, FRANCIS DE (FRANCIS WIENER)

Chérubin, 1901; *By Virtue*, 1902; *La Passerelle* (with Mme. Fred Gressac), 1902; *The Two Courtesans*, 1902; *Happiness, Ladies!* 1905; *The Good Intention*, 1905; *Paris, New York* (with E. Arène), 1907; *Arsène Lupin* (with Maurice Leblanc), 1909; *The Borrowed Fire* (*Le Feu du Voisin*), 1910; *The Heart Disposes*, 1912; *The Hawk*, 1914; *From One Day to Another*, 1917; *Vineyards of the Lord* (with de Flers), 1923; etc., etc.

BIBLIOGRAPHY

IN ENGLISH: *The March of Time*, adapted by C. Gordon Lennox, 1904; *La Passerelle*, adapted as The Marriage of Kitty, by Lennox, 1909; *Arsène Lupin*, played, London, 1909; *The Hawk*, tr. by Mary J. Taylor, 1914; *The New Secretary*, adapted by Lennox, 1914; *The Return*, adapted by Charlton Andrews, 1922; *The Claw and the Wing* (with Robert de Flers), adapted by Andrews, 1921; *Ciboulette* (with de Flers), adapted as Bluebell, by A. C. O'Dea, 1925.

CUREL, FRANÇOIS DE

The Other Side of a Saint, 1892; *The Fossils*, 1892; *The Fair Guest* (*L'Invitée*), 1893; *Love Adorns* (*L'Amour brode*), 1893; *The Dancer* (*La Figurante*), 1896; *The Lion's Share* (*Le Repas du lion*), 1898; *The New Idol*, 1899; *The Wild Girl*, 1902; *The Beat of the Wing*, 1906; *The Dance Before the Mirror*, 1914; *The Comedy of Genius*, 1918; *The Soul in Madness*, 1920; *The Intoxication of the Sage*, 1922; *Inhuman Land*, 1922; *The Quick and the Dead* (*La Viveuse et le moribond*), 1926; *Mystical Storm*, 1927.

IN ENGLISH: *The Other Side of a Saint*, tr. as A False Saint, by B. H. Clark, 1916; *The Fossils*, tr. by Clark, in Four Plays of the Free Theater, 1915; *The Fair Guest*, adapted as The Guest Wife, by Mary S. C. Holbrook, 1929; *The Lion's Share*, tr. as Lion's Meat, by Mary S. C. Holbrook, 1929; *The Wild Girl*, tr. as The Savage Girl, by Rita Wellman, 1923; *The Beat of the Wing*, tr. by Alice van Kaathoven, Poet Lore 20, 1909; *Inhuman Land*, adapted as No Man's Land, by Ashley Dukes, 1923.

D'AMBRA, LUCIO

Steeple Chase, 1897; *Stagnant Water*, 1897; *Castle of Cards*, 1897; *Fantasy*, 1903; *Bernini*, 1904; *Goffredo Mameli*, 1904; *The Road to Damascus*, 1904; *The Effect of Light*, 1906; *The Garden of Armida*, 1906; *The Quartet*, 1907; *The Guardian Angels*, 1910; *Water, Water, Fire, Fire*, 1910; *The Right and the Left*, 1910; *My Friends of Sans Souci*, 1911; *The Exiles*, 1914; *The Diva of La Scala*, 1915; *The Frontier*, 1916; *The Dead Sentinel*, 1923; *The Grenadier From Pomerania*, 1925; *Red Lantern*, 1925; *The Portrait of a Man*, 1927; *False Fire* (with A. Donnay), 1927; etc.

D'ANNUNZIO, GABRIELE

The Parable of the Foolish Virgins and the Wise Virgins, 1897; *The Dream of a Spring Morning*, 1897; *The Parable of the Rich Man and Poor Lazarus*, 1898; *The Parable of the Prodigal Son*, 1898; *The Dream of an Autumn Sunset*, 1898; *The Dead City*, 1898; *La Gioconda*, 1898; *La Gloria*, 1899; *Francesca da Rimini*, 1902; *The Daughter of Jorio*, 1904; *The Light Under the Bushel*, 1905; *More Than Love*, 1907; *The Ship*, 1908; *Fedra*, 1909; *The Martyrdom of Saint Sebastian* (in French for the music of Claude Debussy), 1910; *The Pisan Woman, or Perfumed Death* (in French), 1911; *The Honeysuckle* (in French), 1913; *Parisina*, 1913, as Ugo and Parisina, 1921 (for the music of Pietro Mascagni); *Cabiria* (a cinema), 1914; *Amaranta*, 1914; *La Piave* (for the music of Italo Montemezzi), 1918.

IN ENGLISH: *The Dream of a Spring Morning*, tr. by Anna Schenck in Poet Lore 14, 1902; tr. by Christopher St. John, 1921; *The Dream of an Autumn*

Sunset, tr. by Schenck in Poet Lore 15, 1904; *The Dead City,* tr. by Arthur Symons, 1900, 1902, in O. M. Sayler, The Eleonora Duse Series of Plays, 1923; tr. by G. Mantellini, 1902; *La Gioconda,* tr. as The Key and the Ring and also as 'Twixt Love and Life, by E. P. King, 1900; tr. by Symons, 1902; in T. H. Dickinson, Chief Contemporary Dramatists, 2d series, 1921; and in Robert M. Smith, Types of Domestic Tragedy, 1928; abridged in J. Pierce, Masterpieces of Modern Drama—Foreign, pt. 2, 1915; *Francesca da Rimini,* tr. by Edward Elsner, 1900; tr. by Symons, 1902; and in S. M. Tucker, Modern Continental Plays, 1929; *The Daughter of Jorio,* tr. by Henry St. Ives, 1906; tr. by C. Porter, P. Isola, and A. Henry in Poet Lore 18, 1907; and separately 1907, 1911, and in Tucker, Modern Continental Plays, 1929; adapted as The Devil's Daughter, by Joseph H. Trant, 1915; *The Ship,* tr. in Poet Lore 19, 1909; tr. by R. H. Elkin, 1919; *Fedra,* tr. as Phaedra, by Sidney Howard, 1920; *The Honeysuckle,* tr. by C. Sartoris and G. Enthoven, 1915, and played, N. Y., 1921.

DELPIT, ALBERT

The Invasion, 1870; *Jean-Nu-Pieds,* 1875; *The Son of Coralie,* 1880; *The Father of Martial,* 1881; *The Maucroix,* 1883; etc.

IN ENGLISH: *Felicia, or Woman's Love,* adapted by A. R. Cazauran, 1881.

DONNAY, MAURICE

They, 1889; *Elsewhere,* 1891; *Phryne,* 1891; *Lysistrata,* 1892; *The Family Boarding-House,* 1894; *A Mad Enterprise,* 1894; *Lovers,* 1895; *The Grief-Stricken Woman (La Douloureuse),* 1897; *The Emancipated Woman,* 1898; *Georgette Lemeunier,* 1898; *The Torreni,* 1899; *Princely Education,* 1900; *The Clearing* (with Lucien Descaves), 1900; *The Seesaw,* 1901; *The Other Danger,* 1902; *The Gimlet,* 1902; *The Return From Jerusalem,* 1903; *The Scaling (L'Escalade),* 1904; *Birds of Passage* (with Lucien Descaves), 1904; *Appearances (Paraître),* 1906; *The Marriage of Telemachus* (with Lemaître), 1910; *Molière's Ménage,* 1912; *Women Scouts (Les Eclaireuses),* 1913; *Impromptu (L'Impromptu du pâquetage),* 1915; *The Theater with the Armies,* 1916; *The Man-Hunt,* 1920; *The Fair One of Anjou* (with André Rivoire), 1922; *The Gesture* (with H. Duvernois), 1924; *Restitution,* 1925; *A Light Man,* 1925; *The Rise of Virginie,* 1929.

IN ENGLISH: B. H. Clark, Three Modern Plays From the French, *Lovers, The Free Woman, They,* 1915; *Lysistrata,* tr. by H. D. Gibbons, 1919; tr. by William A. Drake, 1929; *Lovers,* tr. by B. H. Clark, 1915, and in M. J. Moses, Representative Continental Dramas, 1924; *The Grief-Stricken Woman (La Douloureuse),* tr. by Charles A. Byrne, 1904; *The Emancipated Woman,* tr. as The Free Woman, by Clark, 1915; *The Seesaw,* tr. as See-Saw, by E. Harris and Mason Carnes, 1911; *The Other Danger,* tr. by Charlotte T. David in The Drama 3, 1913, and separately, and in Clark, Three Modern Plays From the French; *The Gimlet,* tr. by Clark, in the Stratford Journal, 1918; *The Return From Jerusalem,* tr. by Owen Johnson, and played, N. Y., 1913; *The Fair One of Anjou* (with André Rivoire), tr. as An Easy Mark, by Robert Lane, 1922.

BIBLIOGRAPHY

DRACHMANN, HOLGER

Once Upon a Time, 1887; *A Thousand and One Nights*, 1889; *Völund the Smith*, 1894; *Renaissance*, 1894; *Honest Fellow*, 1898; *War*, 1898, etc.

IN ENGLISH: *Once Upon a Time*, tr. as There Was Once, by E. Arendrup and W. H. Allderdice, 1909; adapted as The Princess and the Kettle, by G. V. Fisher, 1918; *Renaissance*, tr. by L. M. Hollander in Poet Lore 19, 1908.

DREYER, MAX

Three, 1892; *Winter Sleep*, 1895; *One*, 1896; *Grossmann*, 1897; *Love Dreams*, 1898; *Hans*, 1898; *Among Blond Beasts*, 1898; *The Practice Teacher* (*Der Probe-Kandidat*), 1899; *Steger*, 1900; *The Seventeen Year Old*, 1904; *The Daughter of the Parson of Streladorf*, 1909; *The Valley of Life* (suppressed by the censor during the War); etc.

IN ENGLISH: *The Practice Teacher*, tr. as On Probation, by Mary Harned in Poet Lore 14, 1903.

DÜLBERG, FRANZ

Cardenio, 1912; *King of Fools Kaspar*, 1919; etc.

DUMAS *fils*, ALEXANDRE

(For a complete bibliography, see Henry S. Schwarz, *Alexandre Dumas fils, Dramatist*, 1927.)

The Lady of the Camelias, 1852; *Diane de Lys*, 1853; *The Demi-Monde*, 1855; *The Money Question*, 1857; *The Natural Son*, 1858; *A Prodigal Father*, 1859; *The Friend of Women*, 1864; *The Ideas of Mme. Aubray*, 1867; *The Godchild of Pompignac*, 1869; *A Marriage Visit*, 1871; *The Princess Georges*, 1871; *The Wife of Claude*, 1873; *M. Alphonse*, 1873; *The Fair Stranger*, 1876; *The Danicheffs*, 1876; *Countess Romani*, 1876; *The Princess of Bagdad*, 1881; *Denise*, 1885; *Francillon*, 1887.

IN ENGLISH: *The Lady of the Camelias*, adapted 1852; tr. as The Queen of the Camelias, by J. B. Wright; tr. as Camille, by Matilda Heron, 1856; tr. as Camilla, or The Fate of a Coquette, 1856; tr. as Camille, 1880; edited by Mildred Aldrich, 1907; etc., etc.; *The Demi-Monde*, tr. as The Outer Edge of Society, by B. H. Clark in Brander Matthews, Chief European Dramatists, 1916; *The Money Question*, tr. in Poet Lore 26, 1915; *The Fair Stranger*, tr. as The Foreigner, 1881; *Francillon*, tr. 1887; etc., etc.

ECHEGARAY, JOSÉ

The Check Book, 1874; *The Avenger's Wife*, 1874; *The Last Night*, 1875; *At the Hilt of the Sword*, 1875; *A Sun That Rises and a Sun That Sets*, 1875; *The Gladiator of Ravenna*, 1876; *The Beginning and the End*, 1876; *Folly or Saintliness*, 1877; *The Peacemaker*, 1877; *What Cannot Be Told*, 1877; *Before the Pillar and the Cross*, 1878; *In Pursuit of an Ideal*, 1878; *Sometimes Below*, 1878; *In the Bosom of Death*, 1879; *The Tragic Wedding*, 1879; *The Shoreless Sea*, 1879; *Death on the Lips*, 1880; *The Great Galeoto*, 1881; *Harold the Norman*, 1881; *Two Curious Impertinents*, 1882; *Conflict Between Two Duties*, 1882; *A Miracle in Egypt*, 1883; *In Supposing Evil . . . Will You Guess?* 1884; *The Pest of Otranto*, 1884; *Happy Life, Sad Death*, 1885; *Lysander the Bandit*, 1886; *Evil Race*, 1886; *Two Fanaticisms*, 1887; *Count Lothario*, 1887; *Reality and Delirium*, 1887; *The Son of Steel and the Son of Flesh*, 1888; *The Sublime in the Vulgar*, 1888; *Everlasting Source of Troubles*, 1889; *The Extremists*, 1889; *The Prologue to a Drama*, 1890; *Always Ridiculous*, 1890; *Irene of Otranto*, 1891; *The Embryo Critic*, 1891; *Comedy Without Dénouement*, 1891; *The Son of Don Juan*, 1892; *Sic vos, non vobis*, 1892; *Mariana*, 1892; *The Power of Impotence*, 1893; *At the Sea-Shore*, 1893; *The Enraged Lady*, 1894; *The Cleansing Stain*, 1895; *The First Act of a Drama*, 1895; *The Stigmata*, 1895; *Wild Love*, 1896; *The Street Singer*, 1896; *Calumny as a Chastisement*, 1897; *The Doubt*, 1898; *The Man in Black*, 1898; *The Silence of Death*, 1898; *The Madman Divine*, 1900; *Evil Inheritance*, 1902; *The Steps to a Throne*, 1903; *The Woman Distraught (La Desequilibrada)*, 1903; *Letting Oneself be Dragged Along*, 1905; *Hero and Clown*, 1908.

IN ENGLISH: *Folly or Saintliness*, tr. by Hannah Lynch, 1895; adapted as Madman or Saint, by Benedict Papot, 1907; tr. as Madman or Saint, by Ruth Lansing in Poet Lore 23, 1912; *The Great Galeoto*, tr. by Hannah Lynch, 1895, 1914; tr. by Jacob S. Fassett, Jr., 1914; tr. by Eleanor Bontecou in B. H. Clark, Masterpieces of Modern Spanish Drama, 1922; abridged in J. A. Pierce, The Masterpieces of Modern Drama—Foreign, 1915; adapted and played in N. Y. as Slander and then as The World and his Wife, by C. F. Nirdlinger, 1908, and in M. J. Moses, Representative Continental Dramas, 1924; *The Sublime in the Vulgar*, adapted by Marian Eddy, 1898; *Always Ridiculous*, tr. as Always Ridiculed, Chicago, 1907; tr. by Walter Gilkyson in Poet Lore 27, 1916; *The Son of Don Juan*, tr. by James Graham, 1895, 1911; *Sic vos, non vobis*, adapted as The Little Savage, by J. A. Herman, 1914; *Mariana*, tr. by Graham, 1895; played, N. Y., 1902; tr. by Federico Sardo and Carlos D. Wuppermann, 1909, 1914; *The Cleansing Stain*, tr. by Christopher Sandemann and D. M. Gonzalez, 1917; *The Street Singer*, tr. by J. G. Underhill in The Drama 25, 1917, and in Frank Shay, Twenty-five Short Plays, International, 1924; *The Man in Black*, tr. by Ellen Watson in The Universal Anthology, v. 27, 1899; *The Madman Divine*, tr. by Elizabeth H. West in Poet Lore 19, 1908; tr. as If I Were God, by A. L. Godoy, 1909.

ERCKMANN, ÉMILE, and CHATRIAN, ALEXANDRE

The Polish Jew, 1869; *Friend Fritz*, 1877, etc.

IN ENGLISH: *The Polish Jew*, tr. by H. L. Williams, 1871; adapted as The Bells, by Leopold Lewis, 1874; tr. as Heaven's Vengeance, by J. S. Mackaye and G. Kreisler, 1871; *Friend Fritz (L'Ami Fritz)*, tr. by H. A. Delille, 1877; tr. by N. H. Dole from the adaptation of P. Suardon, 1891; adapted by Stanislaus Stange, 1893; tr. by R. B. Delano and Roxie Odiorne, 1912.

BIBLIOGRAPHY

ERLER, OTTO

Giants, 1901; *Artists of Honor,* 1903; *Czar Peter,* 1905; *The Angel of England* (changed because of the War to *Struensee*), 1916; etc.

ERNST, OTTO (OTTO ERNST' SCHMIDT)

The Greatest Sin, 1895; *Youth of To-Day,* 1900; *Flachsmann as Educator,* 1901; *Justice,* 1902; *Bannermann,* 1905; *Ortrun and Ilsebill,* 1906; etc.

IN ENGLISH: *Flachsmann as Educator,* tr. as Master Flachsmann, by H. M. Beatty, 1909.

ERNST, PAUL

Demetrios, 1905; *Canossa,* 1908; *Brunhild,* 1909; *Ninon de Lenclos,* 1911; *The Soul of Prussia,* 1915; *Manfred and Beatrice,* 1918; etc., etc.

EULENBERG, HERBERT

Münchhausen, 1900; *Passion,* 1901; *Half Heroes,* 1903; *Kassandra,* 1904; *Knight Bluebeard,* 1904; *Prince Ulrich of Waldeck,* 1906; *The Natural Father,* 1907; *Anna Walewska,* 1910; *Samson,* 1910; *All for Love,* 1910; *All for Gold,* 1911; *Belinde,* 1912; *The Barter of Women,* 1914; *The Island,* 1917; *The Night Side,* 1918; *The Crossing,* 1919; *How Might is Right,* 1922; *The Red Moon,* 1925; *What One Does Is Right,* 1926; etc.

EVREINOV, NIKOLAI NIKOLAEVICH

The Rehearsal; Fools as Blind Idols, 1900; *The Foundation of Happiness,* 1902; *Styopik and Manyourotchka,* 1905; *The Beautiful Despot,* 1906; *The Representation of Love,* 1910; *The Theater of the Soul,* 1912; *Grandmother,* 1914; *Plutus; Such a Woman,* 1914; *The Merry Death,* 1914; *The Essential;* etc.

IN ENGLISH: *The Beautiful Despot,* tr. in C. E. Bechhofer, Five Russian Plays, 1916; *The Theater of the Soul,* tr. by Marie Potapenko and Christopher St. John, 1915; in T. H. Dickinson, Chief Contemporary Dramatists, 3rd series, 1930; tr. as Behind the Curtain of the Soul, by Simeon Aller, 1922; tr. as The Back Stage of the Soul, by William A. Drake, 1925; *The Merry Death,* tr. in Bechhofer, Five Russian Plays, and in M. J. Moses, Representative One-Act Plays by Continental Authors, 1923; *The Essential,* tr. as The Most Important Thing, by Evelyn Cohen, 1924; tr. as The Chief Thing, by C. E. Bechhofer, 1923; tr. as The Chief Thing, by Herman Bernstein and Leo Randole (Theatre Guild Version), 1926; *The Radio Kiss,* tr. by Herman Bernstein, 1926; *The Ship of the Saints,* tr. by Herman Bernstein, 1926.

FABRE, EMILE

Like All of Us (Comme ils sont tous), 1894; *Money,* 1895; *The Property of Others (Le Bien d'autrui),* 1897; *The Imperishable,* 1898; *Timon of Athens,* 1899; *Public Life,* 1902; *The Rabbit Hutch (La Rabouilleuse),* 1904; *Gilded*

Stomachs, 1905; *The House of Clay*, 1907; *The Conquerors*, 1908; *César Birotteau*, 1910; *The Locusts* (*Les Sauterelles*), 1911; *A Great Bourgeois*, 1914; *The Storm Beaten House* (*La Maison sous l'orage*), 1920.

IN ENGLISH: *La Rabouilleuse*, adapted as The Honor of the Family, 1908, and as Parasites, by Paul M. Potter, and played under the former title by Otis Skinner, 1926; *The House of Clay*, adapted by Herbert Swears, 1908; tr. by Ysidor Ackenasy and S. E. Ellman, 1909; adapted as The House Builded on the Sands, by Jane G. R. White, 1910; *The Locusts*, tr. by Ada Sterling, 1919.

FARRERE, CLAUDE, and NÉPOTY, LOUIS

Vigil of Arms, 1917.

IN ENGLISH: *Vigil of Arms*, adapted by Michael Morton and played, London, 1919; N. Y., 1921.

FEYDEAU, GEORGES

The Free Exchange Hotel, 1894; *The Lady From Maxim's*, 1899; *The Duchess of the Folies-Bergère*, 1902; *Look Out for Amélie*, 1908; *A Cathartic for Baby* (*On purge Bébé*), 1909; *The Flea in the Ear*, 1910; *But Don't Go About Without Your Clothes* (*Mais n'te promène donc pas toute nue*), 1911; *I Don't Deceive My Husband*, 1915; *A Hundred Millions That Fall*, 1923; etc., etc.

IN ENGLISH: *The Free Exchange Hotel*, adapted as A Night in Paris, played, London, and as The Gay Parisians, played, N. Y., 1896; adapted as a musical play—A Night Out—by George Grossmith and Arthur Miller, London, 1920; *The Flea in the Ear*, adapted as You Never Know, Y'Know, by Martin Henry and Hannaford Bennett, London, 1919; *Breakfast in Bed*, adapted by Willard Mack and H. Booth, 1919.

FINNE, GABRIEL

Owl, 1893.

FITGER, ARTHUR

Albrecht Dürer; Johann Kepler, 1872; *Michelangelo; Adalbert von Bremen*, 1873; *The Witch*, 1876; *By God's Grace*, 1883; *The Roses of Tyburn*, 1888; *San Marco's Daughter*, 1902.

FLERS, ROBERT DE, and CAILLAVET, GASTON-ARMAND DE

The Heart Has Its Reasons, 1902; *The Paths of Virtue*, 1903; *The Angel of the Fireside*, 1905; *Husband's Luck*, 1906; *Miquette and her Mother*, 1906; *Love Watches*, 1907; *The Fan*, 1907; *The King* (with Eugène Arène), 1908; *Buridan's Ass*, 1909; *Papa*, 1910; *The Sacred Wood*, 1910; *Primrose*, 1911; *The Green Coat*, 1912; *Venice*, 1913; *The Beautiful Adventure* (with Etienne Rey), 1913; *Beatrice*, 1913; *Monsieur Brotonneau*, 1914; etc., etc.

BIBLIOGRAPHY

IN ENGLISH: *The Paths of Virtue*, tr., 1903; *Husband's Luck*, adapted as A Lucky Husband, by G. C. Lounsbery, 1906; *Love Watches*, adapted by Gladys Unger, 1908; *The King*, played as The Royal Visitor, N. Y., 1923; *Buridan's Ass*, adapted as Inconstant George, by Unger, 1910; *Papa*, adapted as Dad, by John Kendall, 1911; *The Sacred Wood*, adapted as Decorating Clementine, by Unger, 1910; *Primrose*, adapted by C. Gordon Lennox, 1912; *The Doll Girl*, adapted by Harry B. Smith, 1914; *The Return* (with de Croisset), tr. by Charlton Andrews, 1922; adapted by Arthur Wimperis, 1922; adapted by Avery Hopwood, 1923.

FONSON, FRANZ (JEAN FRANÇOIS)

The Marriage of Mlle. Beulemans (with Fernand Wicheler), 1910; *The Fire of St. John* (with Wicheler), 1912; *Beulemans Marries His Daughter*, an operetta, 1913; *La Kommandantur*, 1915; *The New Poor*, 1916.

IN ENGLISH: *The Marriage of Mlle. Beulemans*, adapted as Little Miss Llewelyn, London, 1912; adapted as Suzanne by C. Haddon Chambers, N. Y., 1910; *La Demoiselle de magasin*, tr. as The Shop Girl, and adapted as Along Came Ruth, by Holman Day, 1914; *La Kommandantur*, tr. by Celia Storm and Ina Cameron, 1915.

FORZANO, GIOVACCHINO

Lodoletta (music by Pietro Mascagni), 1917; *Sister Angelica; Gianni Schicchi*, 1918; *Carnival* (music by Guido Laccetti), 1923; *The Evil Companions* (music by Primo Riccitelli), 1923; *Lorenzino*, 1923; *The Married Lovers* (music by E. Wolf-Ferrari), 1924; *Lilies of Gold*, 1924; *Thien-Hoa* (*Flower of Heaven*), 1924; *The Count of Bréchard*, 1924; *Master Landi*, 1925; *Sly*, 1925 (with music by Wolf-Ferrari), 1927; *Madonna Oretta*, 1926; *The Gift of the Morning*, 1926; *Gigolette*, 1926 (music by Franz Lehár), 1926; *Gutlibi*, 1926; *The Bells of San Lucio*, 1926; *Ginevra of the Almieri*, 1927; *Madame Roland*, 1927; etc.

IN ENGLISH: *Sister Angelica*, tr. by Eduardo Petri, 1918; *The Evil Companions*, tr. by F. H. Martens, 1923; *Thien-Hoa*, tr. by A. Armband and E. Zito, 1925; *The Count of Bréchard*, tr. by Arthur Livingston, 1924; *Sly*, tr. as Christopher Sly, by H. B. Cotterell; *The Bells of San Lucio*, tr. by Ruth E. and Max Sonino, 1929; *Ginevra of the Almieri*, tr. by the same, 1929.

FRANCK, HANS

Godiva, 1919; *Night of Sacrifice*, 1921.

FRANK, EDMUND

The Stuttgart Dwarf, 1906.

FRONDAIE, PIERRE

Montmartre, 1910; *The Woman and the Puppet* (with Pierre Louÿs), 1910; *The Man Who Kills*, 1913; *Blanche Câline*, 1913; *Aphrodite* (from Louÿs), 1914; *Colette Baudoche*, 1915; *The Crime of Sylvestre Bonnard*, 1916; *The*

House Surrounded, 1920; *L'Appassionata*, 1920; *The Battle*, 1921; *The Unsubmissive*, 1922; *The Fair Guardian*, 1923; *The March to Destiny*, 1924; *The Menace*, 1925; *The Reflection*, 1927; etc.

IN ENGLISH: *Montmartre*, tr. by Benjamin Glazer, 1919; *The Woman and the Puppet*, tr. as The Girl and the Puppet, and played, London, 1919; tr. by R. Lane, 1921; *The Man Who Kills*, adapted as The Right to Kill, by Gilbert Cannan and Frances Keyzer, 1915; *Aphrodite*, adapted by George C. Hazleton and "novelized" by William A. Page, 1919; *The House Surrounded*, tr. by G. Glass and P. Duffield, 1920.

FULDA, LUDWIG

Honest Folk (*Die Aufrichtigen*), 1883; *Woman's Right*, 1885; *Beneath Four Eyes* (*Unter Vier Augen*), 1886; *A Meteor*, 1887; *Spring in Winter*, 1887; *The Wild Chase*, 1888; *The Lost Paradise*, 1890; *The Woman Slave*, 1891; *The Wonder Child*, 1892; *The Talisman*, 1892; *The Comrades*, 1894; *Robinson's Island*, 1895; *Miss Widow*, 1895; *The Son of the Caliph*, 1896; *Friends of Youth*, 1897; *Herostrat*, 1898; *The Reckoning*, 1898; *An Affair of Honor*, 1898; *The Land of Cockayne* (*Schlaraffenland*), 1899; *The Twin Sisters*, 1901; *Cold Water*, 1902; *Novella Andrea*, 1903; *Masquerading*, 1904; *The Secret King*, 1906; *The Blockhead*, 1907; *The Dream of the Fortunate*, 1908; *The Example*, 1909; *Master and Servant*, 1910; *The Pirate*, 1911; *Fire Insurance*, 1912; *The Return to Nature*, 1913; *Evening Sun*, 1914; *Pupils of Life*, 1915; *The Lost Daughter*, 1916; *The Correct*, 1917; *The Miraculous Remedy*, 1918; *The Shadow of the Ass*, 1920; *Vulcan*, 1921; *The Beloved*, 1922; *The Rival Candidates*, 1923; *The Fair Débauchée*, 1923; *Film Romanticism*, 1926; *High Sun*, 1927; *The Enchanted Princess*, 1929; etc.

IN ENGLISH: *By Ourselves* (*Unter vier Augen*), tr. by O. Leonard, 1907; tr. by Haya Wally, in Poet Lore 23, 1912; and in Alice M. Smith, Short Plays by Representative Authors, 1920; tr. as Tête-à-Tête, by E. L. Townsend, 1914, and in German Classics, v. 17; *The Lost Paradise*, adapted by Henry C. De Mille, 1897; adapted as Work and Wages, by John A. Fraser, 1898; *Friends of Youth*, tr. by Martin Schuetze; adapted as Our Wives, by Helen Krafft and Frank Mandel, 1911; *The Twin Sisters*, tr. by Louis N. Parker, 1902; *The Blockhead*, tr. by J. L. Jones, 1908; tr. as A Fool and the World, by Grace I. Colbron, 1918; tr. as The Blockhead, by Anna E. Bagstad in Poet Lore 39, 1928; *Moonbeams*, tr. by Arthur H. Schwarz, 1914; *The Cure*, tr. by Mrs. Charles A. Doremus, played, N. Y., 1915.

GALLARATI-SCOTTI, TOMMASO

Thy Will Be Done.

IN ENGLISH: *Thy Will Be Done*, tr. by Valerie Petri in O. M. Sayler, The Eleonora Duse Series of Plays, 1923.

GEIERSTAM, GUSTAV AF

Criminals.

IN ENGLISH: *Criminals*, tr. by Roy W. Swanson in Poet Lore 34, 1923.

BIBLIOGRAPHY

GIACOSA, GIUSEPPE

A Game of Chess, 1871; *An Old Story*, 1871; *To a Dog That Licks Ashes Do Not Confide Flour*, 1871; *Don't Say Flour Unless You Have It in the Sack*, 1871; *The Triumph of Love*, 1872; *Bank Affairs*, 1873; *The Sons of the Marquis Arturo*, 1874; *Sad Doubts*, 1874; *Gallant Intrigues*, 1874; *Nocturnal Surprises*, 1875; *A Candidate*, 1875; *Teresa*, 1875; *Mountain Torrents*, 1876; *At the Piano*, 1877; *The Husband in Love With His Wife*, 1877; *Brothers-in-Arms*, 1877; *The Red Count*, 1880; *Luisa*, 1881; *The Thread*, 1883; *The Siren*, 1883; *Surrender at Discretion*, 1885; *The Honorable Ercole Mallardi*, 1885; *Unhappy Love*, 1888; *The Cat's Claw*, 1888; *The Belated Repentance*, 1888; *The Lady of Challant*, 1890; *Rights of the Soul*, 1894; *La Bohème* (with Luigi Illica), 1896; *La Tosca* (with Illica), 1899; *As The Leaves*, 1900; *Madame Butterfly* (with Illica), 1903; *The Stronger*, 1905.

IN ENGLISH: Edith and Allen Updegraff, Three Plays by Giuseppe Giacosa, 1915; *A Game of Chess*, tr. as The Wager, by B. H. Clark, 1914; *Unhappy Love*, tr. by Albert E. Trombly in Poet Lore 27, 1916; *The Lady of Challant*, played by Bernhardt, N. Y., 1921; *Rights of the Soul*, tr. by F. M. Rankin, and played in England, 1908; tr. by E. F. Davis, 1912; tr. by Isaac Goldberg in Stratford Review, 1918; tr. by Theodora Marcone in Frank Shay and Pierre Loving, Fifty Contemporary One-Act Plays, 1920; tr. as Sacred Ground, by Edith and Allen Updegraff in Three Plays, and in M. J. Moses, Representative One-Act Plays by Continental Authors, 1923; *La Bohème*, tr. by W. Grist and P. Pinkerton, 1898; tr. by Compton Mackenzie, 1929; *Tosca*, tr. by Charles H. Meltzer, 1926; *As the Leaves*, tr. by Donald Robertson, 1908; tr. as Falling Leaves, by Milton Sills, 1908; tr. in The Drama, 1911; tr. as Like Falling Leaves, by Edith and Allen Updegraff in Three Plays, and in Moses, Representative Continental Dramas, 1924; *Madame Butterfly*, tr. by E. H. Elkin, 1905; tr. by Charles H. Meltzer, 1926; *The Stronger*, tr. as The Strongest, by E. F. Davis and M. F. Loyacono, 1911; tr. as The Stronger in The Drama, 1913; tr. by Edith and Allen Updegraff in Three Plays; *Tainted Money*, tr. by Milton Sills, 1908; *Fair Encounter*, tr. by Henry St. Ives, 1906.

GIRAUDOUX, JEAN

Siegfried, 1928, from his novel Siegfried and the Limousin, 1922; *Amphitryon 38*, 1929; etc.

IN ENGLISH: *Siegfried*, played by Eva Le Gallienne, N. Y., 1930.

GOERING, RICHARD

Sea Battle, 1917; *The First*, 1917; *Scapa Flow*, 1919; *The Savior*, 1919; *The Second*, 1919.

GONCOURT, EDMOND DE

Henriette Maréchale, 1865; *The Country in Danger* (with Jules de Goncourt), 1873; etc.

MODERN CONTINENTAL PLAYWRIGHTS

GORKY, MAXIM (ALEXEI MAXIMOVICH PYESHKOV)

The Smug Citizen, 1900; *The Lower Depths*, 1902; *A Country House*, 1903; *Children of the Sun*, 1904; *Vassa Zheleznova*, 1904; *Summer Folk*, 1905; *The Barbarians*, 1906; *The Enemies*, 1906; *The Last*, 1908; *Odd People*, 1910; *The Zykovs*, 1913; *Children*, 1913; *The Judge (The Old Man)*, 1915; *Cain and Artema*, 1921; *The Counterfeit Coin*, 1926.

IN ENGLISH: *The Smug Citizen*, tr. as The Bezsemenoffs, by J. R. Crawford, 1903; tr. by Edwin Hopkins in Poet Lore 17, 1906; *The Lower Depths*, tr. by Hopkins as From the Depths, 1905; as A Night Shelter in Poet Lore 16, 1905; as Submerged, 1915; as A Night's Lodging, 1920; as The Lower Depths in T. H. Dickinson, Chief Contemporary Dramatists, 2d series, 1921; in Robert M. Smith, Types of World Tragedy, 1928, and in S. M. Tucker, Modern Continental Plays, 1929; tr. as In the Depths, by W. H. H. Chambers in The Drama 18, 1906; tr. as The Lower Depths, by Laurence Irving, 1911, and in Plays of To-day and To-morrow, 1912; adapted as A Night's Lodging, by Fania Mindell, 1919; tr. by Jenny Covan in O. M. Sayler, The Moscow Art Theatre Series, 1922; adapted as At the Bottom, by William Laurence, 1930; abridged as The Submerged in J. A. Pierce, The Masterpieces of Modern Drama—Foreign, 1915; *The Children of the Sun*, tr. by Archibald J. Wolfe in Poet Lore 17, 1906; *Summer-folk*, tr. by Aline Delano in Poet Lore 16, 1905; *The Judge*, tr. by M. Zakrevsky and B. H. Clark, 1924.

GREIF, MARTIN

Corfiz Ulfeldt, 1873; *Nero*, 1877; *Marino Faliero*, 1878; *Prince Eugene*, 1880; *Walter's Return Home*, 1880; *Henry the Lion*, 1887; *The Pfalz on the Rhine*, 1889; *Konradin*, 1889; *Ludwig the Bavarian*, 1891; *Francesca da Rimini*, 1892; *Agnes Bernauer, the Angel of Augsburg*, 1894; *Hans Sachs*, 1894; *General York*, 1899.

GUIMERÁ, ANGEL

Gala Placidia, 1879; *Judith de Welp*, 1884; *The Son of the King*, 1886; *Sea and Heaven*, 1888; *The Daughter of the Sea*, 1889; *King and Monk*, 1890; *The Dead Soul*, 1892; *Don Powder (En Pólvora)*, 1893; *Jesus of Nazareth*, 1894; *María Rosa*, 1895; *The Nuns of Saint Aymant*, 1895; *Harvest Home*, 1896; *Marta of the Lowlands (Terra Baixa)*, 1897; *Mossen Janot*, 1898; *The Farce*, 1898; *Arrán de Terra*, 1901; *Aurora*, 1902; *Water Which Flows*, 1902; *The Sinner*, 1902; *The Path of the Sun (El Cami del Sol)*, 1904; *La Miralta*, 1905; *Andrónica*, 1905; *Sol Solet*, 1905; *L'Eloy*, 1906; *The Holy Thorn*, 1907; *The Old Queen*, 1908; *La Aranya*, 1908; *Sanet Trist*, 1910; *Titayna*, 1910; *The Young Queen*, 1911; etc.

IN ENGLISH: *María Rosa*, tr. by Wallace Gillpatrick and Guido Marburg; *Marta of the Lowlands*, tr. by Gillpatrick, 1914; *The Sinner*, tr. by Mariani and V. Ferrau, 1909; tr. as Daniela, by Gillpatrick, 1916; tr. as Daniela, by J. G. Underhill, 1917, and in B. H. Clark, Masterpieces of Modern Spanish Drama, 1922.

BIBLIOGRAPHY

GUITRY, SACHA

The Page, 1902; *Yves the Fool*, 1903; *The Kwtz*, 1905; *Nono*, 1905; *The Cuckold Who Almost Spoiled Everything*, 1905; *With the Zoaques*, 1906; *The Clouds* of Aristophanes, 1906; *A Strange Point of Honor*, 1906; *The Key*, 1907; *An Amorous Misadventure*, 1907; *Little Holland*, 1908; *The Scandal of Monte Carlo; The Mug (Le Mufle)*, 1908; *Like Father, Like Son*, 1908; *After*, 1908; *That Maid Adèle*, 1909; *All Is Saved Except Honor*, 1910; *A Fine Marriage*, 1911; *The Night Watchman (Le Veilleur de nuit)*, 1911; *A Type in the Style of Napoleon*, 1911; *Jean III*, 1912; *The Taking of Berg-op-Zoom*, 1912; *Not Full*, 1912; *The Scottish Pilgrim*, 1914; *Two Covers*, 1914; *A Bad Brunette*, 1915; *Jealousy*, 1915; *Let Us Dream*, 1916; *Jean de la Fontaine*, 1916; *An Evening Alone*, 1917; *With Queen Isabella*, 1917; *The Illusionist*, 1917; *Deburau*, 1918; *Pasteur*, 1919; *The Husband, the Wife, and the Lover*, 1919; *My Father Was Right*, 1919; *Béranger*, 1920; *I Love You*, 1920; *How History Is Written*, 1920; *The Comedian*, 1921; *The Grand Duke*, 1921; *Jacqueline*, 1921; *With Jean de la Fontaine*, 1922; *A Little Hand That Finds Its Place*, 1922; *The White and the Black*, 1922; *One Passes in Eight Days*, 1922; *A Subject For a Novel*, 1923; *Love Masked*, 1923; *A Phenomenon*, 1923; *The Lion and the Hen*, 1923; *The Heart-Breaker*, 1923; *A New Star*, 1924; *One Does Not Play for Amusement*, 1925; *Mozart*, 1925; *Is It a Dream?* 1926; *Désiré*, 1927; *A Miracle*, 1927; *Mariette*, 1928; *Charles Lindbergh*, 1928; *The History of France*, 1929; and various revues written with A. Willemetz.

IN ENGLISH: *Deburau*, tr. by Harley Granville-Barker, 1919, and in Burns Mantle, Best Plays of 1920–1921; *Pasteur*, tr. by Irving H. Brown in T. H. Dickinson, Chief Contemporary Dramatists, 2d series, 1921; adapted by Arthur H. Hornblow, Jr., 1923.

HALBE, MAX

A Self-made Man, 1889; *Free Love*, 1890; *The Ice Drift*, 1892; *Youth*, 1893; *The Traveller to America*, 1894; *The Turn of Life*, 1896; *Mother Earth*, 1897; *The Conqueror*, 1899; *The Homeless Ones*, 1899; *The Millennium*, 1900; *A Meteor*, 1900; *The Rosenhagens*, 1901; *May Day (Walpurgistag)*, 1903; *The Stream*, 1903; *The Island of the Blest*, 1905; *The True Countenance*, 1907; *The Blue Mountains*, 1909; *The Juggler's Ring*, 1912; *Freedom*, 1913; *Castle Zeitvorbei*, 1918; *Hortense Ruland*, 1920; *Kikeriki*, 1921; *The Vision of Adam Thor*, 1926; etc.

IN ENGLISH: *Youth*, tr. by Harry M. Goldberg, 1900; adapted as When Love Is Young, by C. Swickard, 1904; adapted by H. Bernstein, 1908; tr. by Sara T. Barrows, 1916, and played, N. Y., 1919; *Mother Earth*, tr. by Paul H. Grummann, 1914, and in German Classics, v. 20; *The Rosenhagens*, tr. by Grummann, in Poet Lore 21, 1910; *The Stream*, tr. as The River, by Christopher Sandemann, 1913.

HALLSTRÖM, PER

The Count of Antwerp, 1899; *Bianca Capello*, 1900; *A Venetian Comedy*, 1901; *Erotikon*, 1908; *Two Legendary Dramas*, 1908; *Two Saga Dramas*, 1910; *Charles XI*, 1918; *Gustav III*, 1918.

MODERN CONTINENTAL PLAYWRIGHTS

HAMSUN, KNUT

At the Gates of the Kingdom, 1895; *Evening Glow*, 1898; *Munken Vendt*, 1902; *Queen Tamara*, 1903; *In the Grip of Life*, 1910.

IN ENGLISH: *At the Gates of the Kingdom*, played, London, 1922; tr. by Lucille E. Baron-Polianoy, 1926; *Queen Tamara*, tr. by J. Robbins, 1921; *In the Grip of Life*, tr. by Graham and Tristan Rawson, 1924.

HARDT, ERNST

A Dead Time, 1898; *Ninon de l'Enclos*, 1905; *Tantris the Fool*, 1907; *Gudrun*, 1911; *Schirin and Gertraude*, 1913; *King Salomo*, 1915; etc.

IN ENGLISH: *Tantris the Fool*, tr. by W. Nobbe and J. James, 1909; tr. by John Heard as Tristram the Jester in German Classics, v. 20, 1913–1914, and separately, 1913.

HARTLEBEN, OTTO ERICH

Angèle, 1891; *Hanna Jagert*, 1893; *Education for Marriage*, 1893; *The Moral Demand*, 1897; *Departure from the Regiment*, 1898; *The Month of Roses*, 1900; *The Green Tree and the Nightingale*, 1905; etc.

IN ENGLISH: *Hanna Jagert*, tr. by Sarah E. Holmes in Poet Lore 24, 1913; *The Moral Demand*, tr. as The Demands of Society, by Harold Harper in Frank Shay, Fifty More Contemporary One-Act Plays, 1928; *The Month of Roses*, tr. as Love's Carnival by R. Bleichmann, 1904.

HASENCLEVER, WALTER

The Youth, 1913; *The Son*, 1914; *The Savior*, 1915; *Death and Resurrection*, 1916; *Antigone*, 1917; *Men*, 1918; *The Decision*, 1919; *Beyond (Jenseits)*, 1920; *Gobseck*, 1921; *Murder*, 1926; *A Better Master*, 1926; *Marriages Are Made in Heaven*, 1928; *Napoleon Enters on the Scene*, 1930.

IN ENGLISH: *Beyond*, tr. by Rita Matthias, 1924; *Contagion*, in Smart Set, 1918.

HAUPTMANN, CARL

Ephraim's Breite (Ephraim's Daughter Bridget), 1899; *The Mountain Smith*, 1901; *The King's Harp*, 1902; *The Expulsion*, 1905; *Moses*, 1906; *Panspiele*, 1909; *Napoleon Bonaparte*, 1911; *Tall Jule*, 1913; *The Poor Broombinder*, 1913; *War—A Te Deum*, 1914; *From the Great War*, 1915; *Partridges*, 1916; *The Golden Streets*, a Trilogy consisting of *Tobias Buntschuh; Juggler, Death, and Jeweller*; and *Music*, 1916–1919; *The Disloyal Czar*, 1919.

IN ENGLISH: *Ephraim's Breite*, tr. by Mary Harned in Poet Lore 12, 1900; *War, a Te Deum*, tr. by Amelia von Ende in The Drama 6, 1916; *The Dead Are Singing*, tr. by Mary L. Stephenson in Texas Review, Jan., 1916.

BIBLIOGRAPHY

HAUPTMANN, GERHART

Before Sunrise, 1889; *The Festival of Peace*, 1890; *Lonely Lives*, 1891; *Colleague Crampton*, 1892; *The Weavers*, 1893; *The Beaver Coat*, 1893; *The Journey to Heaven of Hannele*, 1893; *Florian Geyer*, 1896; *Helios*, 1896; *The Sunken Bell*, 1896; *Elga*, 1898; *Pastoral*, 1898; *Teamster Henschel*, 1898; *Schluck and Jau*, 1899; *Michael Kramer*, 1900; *The Conflagration (Der rote Hahn)*, 1901; *Poor Heinrich*, 1902; *Rose Bernd*, 1903; *And Pippa Dances*, 1906; *The Maidens of Bischofsberg*, 1907; *Charlemagne's Hostage*, 1908; *Griselda*, 1909; *The Rats*, 1911; *The Flight of Gabriel Schilling*, 1912; *The Commemoration Masque*, 1913; *The Bow of Odysseus*, 1914; *A Winter Ballad*, 1917; *The White Redeemer*, 1920; *Indipohdi*, 1920; *Peter Brauer*, 1921; *Veland*, 1925; *Dorothea Angermann*, 1926.

IN ENGLISH: Ludwig Lewisohn, Dramatic Works of Gerhart Hauptmann, 9 vols., 1921–1929; *Before Sunrise*, tr. by Lewisohn in his v. 1; tr. as Before Dawn, by Leonard Bloomfield in Poet Lore 20, 1909, and separately, 1911; *The Festival of Peace*, tr. as The Reconciliation, by R. T. House in Lewisohn, v. 3, and in Poet Lore 21, 1910, and separately, 1911; tr. as The Coming of Peace, by Janet Achurch and C. E. Wheeler, 1900; *Lonely Lives*, tr. by Mary Morison in Lewisohn, v. 3, and separately, 1898; *Colleague Crampton*, tr. by R. T. House in Lewisohn, v. 3; *The Weavers*, tr. by Morison in Lewisohn, v. 1, and separately, 1911, and in T. H. Dickinson, Chief Contemporary Dramatists, 1st series, 1915, and in K. Francke and W. G. Howard, German Classics, and in Robert M. Smith, Types of World Tragedy, 1928; abridged in J. A. Pierce, The Masterpieces of Modern Drama—Foreign, 1915; *The Beaver Coat*, tr. by Lewisohn in his v. 1; *The Journey to Heaven of Hannele*, tr. as Hannele, by William Archer, 1894; and in The Drama 12, 1906; tr. as Hannele, by C. H. Meltzer, 1908, and as The Assumption of Hannele in Lewisohn, v. 4; tr. as The Assumption of Hannele by G. S. Bryan in Poet Lore 20, 1909; *Florian Geyer*, tr. by B. Q. Morgan in Lewisohn, v. 9; *The Sunken Bell*, tr. by Mary Harned in Poet Lore 10, 1898; tr. by Meltzer, 1899, and in German Classics, v. 18, and in Lewisohn, v. 4, and in M. J. Moses, Representative Continental Dramas, 1924; tr. by F. C. Brown, 1914; *Elga*, tr. by Mary Harned in Poet Lore 17, 1906; tr. by Lewisohn in his v. 7; *Teamster Henschel*, tr. as Fuhrmann Henschel, by Marion A. Redlich, 1910; tr. by Lewisohn in his v. 2; *Schluck and Jau*, tr. by Lewisohn in his v. 5; *Michael Kramer*, tr. by Lewisohn in his v. 3, and in German Classics, v. 18; *The Conflagration (Der rote Hahn)*, tr. by Lewisohn in his v. 1; *Poor Heinrich*, tr. as Henry of Auë, by Lewisohn, in his v. 4; *Rose Bernd*, tr. by Lewisohn, in his v. 2; *And Pippa Dances*, tr. by Mary Harned in Poet Lore 18, 1907, and separately, 1904; tr. by S. T. Barrows in Lewisohn, v. 5; *The Maidens of Bischofsberg*, tr. as The Maidens of the Mount by Lewisohn in his v. 6; *Charlemagne's Hostage*, tr. by Lewisohn in his v. 5; *Griselda*, tr. by Alice Kauser, 1909; tr. by Lewisohn in his v. 6; *The Rats*, tr. by Lewisohn in his v. 2, and in S. M. Tucker, Modern Continental Plays, 1929; *The Flight of Gabriel Schilling*, tr. by Lewisohn in his v. 6; *The Commemoration Masque*, tr. by Lewisohn in his v. 7; *The Bow of Odysseus*, tr. by Lewisohn in his v. 7; *A Winter Ballad*, tr. by Lewisohn in his v. 8; *The White Re-*

deemer, tr. as The White Savior, by Lewisohn in his v. 8; *Indipohdi,* tr. by Lewisohn in his v. 8; *Veland,* tr. by Edwin Muir in Lewisohn, v. 9.

HEDBERG, TOR

Johan Ulfstjerna, 1907; *Borga Gard,* 1915; *Rembrandt's Son,* 1929; etc.

IN ENGLISH: *Johan Ulfstjerna,* tr. by Helga Colquist in Poet Lore 32, 1921; *Borga Gard,* tr. by Colquist in Poet Lore 32, 1921.

HEIBERG, GUNNAR

Aunt Ulrikke, 1884; *King Midas,* 1890; *The Balcony,* 1894; *The Grand Prize,* 1895; *The Council of the People,* 1897; *Harald Svan's Mother,* 1899; *Love Your Neighbor,* 1902; *The Tragedy of Love,* 1904; etc.

IN ENGLISH: *The Balcony,* tr. by E. J. Vickner and Glenn Hughes in Poet Lore 33, 1922; *The Tragedy of Love,* tr. by Edith Björkman in T. H. Dickinson, Chief Contemporary Dramatists, 2d series, 1921.

HEIDENSTAM, VERNER VON

The Birth of God; The Soothsayer.

IN ENGLISH: *The Birth of God,* tr. by Karoline M. Knudsen, 1920; *The Soothsayer,* tr. by Knudsen, 1919.

HENNIQUE, LÉON

Jacques Damour, 1887; *Esther Brandes,* 1887; *The Death of the Duc d'Enghien,* 1888; *Love,* 1890; *The Gold of Others,* 1894; *Two Countries,* 1895; *Queens of Kings,* 1909; etc., etc.

IN ENGLISH: *The Death of the Duc d'Enghien,* tr. by F. C. Evans in Poet Lore 20, 1909.

HERBIER, MARCEL L'

Child of Death, 1917.

HERVIEU, PAUL

No To-morrow, 1890; *Words Remain,* 1892; *The Nippers,* 1895; *The Law of Man,* 1897; *The Enigma,* 1901; *The Torch Race,* 1901; *Théroigne de Méricourt,* 1902; *The Labyrinth,* 1903; *The Awakening,* 1905; *Modestie,* 1908; *Know Thyself,* 1909; *Bagatelle,* 1912; *Destiny Is Master,* 1914.

IN ENGLISH: *The Nippers,* tr. as In Chains by Ysidor Ackenasy in Poet Lore 20, 1909, and as Enchained in The Dramatist, 1910; *The Enigma,* played in English as Caesar's Wife; tr. by Juliet B. Rublee, 1915; *The Torch Race,* tr. as The Trail of the Torch by John Alan Haughton, 1915; abridged in J. A. Pierce, The Masterpieces of Modern Drama—Foreign, 1915; *The Labyrinth,* tr. by B. H. Clark and Lander MacClintock, 1913; *The Awakening,* played in English; *Modestie,* tr. as Modesty by B. H. Clark, 1913; and

BIBLIOGRAPHY

in B. R. Lewis, Contemporary One-Act Plays, 1922; *Know Thyself*, tr. by
B. Cerf in T. H. Dickinson, Chief Contemporary Dramatists, 1st series, 1915.

HEYSE, PAUL

Honor for Honor, 1875; *Count Königsmark*, 1876; *Elfriede*, 1876; *The
Women of Schorndorf*, 1881; *The Right of the Stronger*, 1883; *Among
Brothers*, 1883; *Im Bunde der Dritte*, 1883; *The Transit of Venus*, 1885; *A
First Love*, 1885; *The Most Difficult Duty*, 1888; *A Superfluous Man*, 1889;
World Destruction, 1889; *The Island*, 1895; *Fornarina*, 1895; *The Daughter
of Semiramis*, 1897; *Mary of Magdala*, 1899; *The Veiled Picture of Sais*,
1901; *A Canadian*, 1905; *The Foolish Virgins*, 1905; *King Saul*, 1909; *Mother
and Daughter*, 1909; etc., etc.

IN ENGLISH: *Mary of Magdala*, tr. by A. I. du P. Coleman, 1900; adapted
by Lionel Vale, 1902; tr. by F. Hess, 1903; tr. by William Winter, 1903.

HIRSCHFELD, GEORG

At Home, 1896; *The Mothers*, 1896; *Agnes Jordan*, 1898; *Pauline*, 1899;
The Way Toward the Light, 1902; *Late Spring*, 1906; *Mieze and Maria*, 1907.

IN ENGLISH: *The Mothers*, tr. by Ludwig Lewisohn, 1916.

HOFMANNSTHAL, HUGO VON

Yesterday, 1891; *Titian's Death*, 1892; *Death and the Fool*, 1893; *The Emperor and the Witch*, 1895; *The Mine at Falun*, 1897; *The Little World
Theater*, 1897; *The White Fan*, 1898; *The Lady at the Window*, 1899; *The
Marriage of Sobeide*, 1902; *The Adventurer and the Singer*, 1902; *Electra*,
1904; *Venice Preserved*, 1905; *Oedipus and the Sphinx*, 1906; *The Rose Cavalier*, 1910; *Cristina's Home Coming*, 1910; *Alcestis*, 1911; *Ariadne at Naxos*,
1912; *The Death of the Rich Man* (from *Everyman*), 1912; *The Legend of
Joseph*, 1914; *The Woman Without a Shadow*, 1918; *The Refractory Man*,
1921; *The Great Salzburg World Theater*, 1922; *Dame Kobold*, 1922; *The In-
corruptible Man*, 1923; *The Tower*, 1923; *Helen*, 1924.

IN ENGLISH: *The Death of Titian*, tr. by John Heard, Jr., 1920, and in
German Classics, v. 17, 1913–1914; *Death and the Fool*, tr. by Max Blatt in
Poet Lore 24, 1913; tr. by Elizabeth Walter, 1914; tr. by Heard in German
Classics, v. 17, and in M. J. Moses, Representative One-Act Plays by Con-
tinental Authors, 1923; *The White Fan*, tr. by Maurice Magnus in The Mask,
1909; *The Lady at the Window*, tr. as Madonna Dianora, by Harriet B. Boas,
1916, and in Frank Shay and Pierre Loving, Fifty Contemporary One-Act
Plays, 1920; *The Marriage of Sobeide*, tr. by B. Q. Morgan, in German
Classics, v. 20, and separately, 1924; *The Adventurer and the Singer*, tr. by
H. S. Boas, 1920; *Electra*, tr. by Arthur Symons, 1908, and in T. H. Dickinson, Chief Contemporary Dramatists, 3rd series, 1930; tr. by A. Kalisch, 1908;
tr. by C. T. Mason, 1909; *Venice Preserved*, tr. by Elizabeth Walter, in Poet
Lore 26, 1915; *The Rose Cavalier*, tr. as The Rose Bearer, by A. Kalisch,
1912; *Cristina's Home Coming*, tr. as Cristina's Journey Home, by Roy Temple House in Poet Lore 28, 1917; *Ariadne at Naxos*, tr. by A. Kalisch, 1912;

The Death of the Rich Man (Everyman), tr. by George Sterling and Richard Ordynski, 1912; *Prologue for a Marionette Theater,* tr. by Pierre Loving, 1916, and in Ten-Minute Plays, 1923; *Idyll,* tr. by C. W. Stork in The Drama, 1917.

HOLZ, ARNO

The Selicke Family (with Johannes Schlaf), 1890; *Social Aristocrats,* 1896; *Traumulus* (with Oskar Jerschke), 1904; *Free* (with Jerschke), 1905; *Sun Darkness,* 1908; *Gaudeamus* (with Jerschke), 1908.

HUCH, RICARDA

Dornröschen, 1902.

IBSEN, HENRIK

Catiline, 1850; *The Warrior's Barrow,* 1850; *St. John's Night,* 1853; *Lady Inger of Östraat,* 1855; *The Feast at Solhaug,* 1856; *Olaf Liljekrans,* 1857; *The Vikings in Helgeland,* 1857; *Love's Comedy,* 1862; *The Pretenders,* 1863; *Brand,* 1866; *Peer Gynt,* 1867; *The League of Youth,* 1869; *Emperor and Galilean,* 1873; *The Pillars of Society,* 1877; *A Doll's House,* 1879; *Ghosts,* 1881; *An Enemy of the People,* 1882; *The Wild Duck,* 1884; *Rosmersholm,* 1886; *The Lady from the Sea,* 1888; *Hedda Gabler,* 1890; *The Master Builder,* 1892; *Little Eyolf,* 1894; *John Gabriel Borkman,* 1896; *When We Dead Awaken,* 1899.

IN ENGLISH: William Archer, Henrik Ibsen's Prose Dramas, 5 vols., 1890–1891; Archer, Henrik Ibsen's Works, 11 vols., 1906–1908; Archer, Henrik Ibsen's Collected Works, 12 vols., 1909–1912 (the twelfth, From Ibsen's Workshop, tr. by A. G. Chater); R. F. Sharp, A Doll's House and Two Other Plays, 1910; Sharp, Ghosts and Two Other Plays, 1911; Sharp, The Pretenders and Two Other Plays, 1913; Archer, Ibsen's Collected Works, 13 vols., 1913 (the thirteenth, Gosse's Life of Ibsen); Sharp, Lady Inger of Östraat and Other Plays, 1915; H. L. Mencken, The Master Builder and Other Plays, 1918; Anders Orbeck, Early Plays, 1921; Frank W. Chandler, Plays by Henrik Ibsen, 1927; Havelock Ellis, The Pillars of Society and Other Plays; A Doll's House and Other Plays; The Wild Duck and Other Plays; *Catiline,* tr. by Orbeck, 1921; *The Warrior's Barrow,* tr. as The Hero's Mound, by C. A. Arfwedson and played, London, 1913 (first performance in English); tr. by Orbeck, 1921; *St. John's Night,* played in England, 1921, 1922; *Lady Inger of Östraat,* tr. by Archer, 1890, and in Prose Dramas, v. 3; tr. by Sharp, 1915; *The Feast at Solhaug,* tr. in Archer, Collected Works, v. 1; *Olaf Liljekrans,* tr. by Orbeck, 1921; *The Vikings in Helgeland,* tr. by Archer, 1890; tr. in Archer, Prose Dramas, v. 3; tr. as The Warriors at Helgeland, by Sharp in Ghosts and Two Other Plays; *Love's Comedy,* tr. by C. H. Herford, 1890; tr. in Archer, Works, v. 1; tr. by Sharp in Lady Inger of Östraat and Other Plays; *The Pretenders,* tr. by Archer, 1890, and in Prose Dramas, v. 3, and in Robert M. Smith, Types of Historical Drama, 1928; tr. in the acting version of the Yale Dramatic Association, 1907; tr. by Sharp, 1913; *Brand,* tr. by William Wilson, 1891; tr. by C. H. Herford, 1894; tr. by F. E. Garrett, 1894, 1911; tr. by Herford in Archer, Works, v. 3; tr. by J. M. Olberman,

BIBLIOGRAPHY

1912; tr. by Sharp, 1915; tr. by M. M. Dawson, 1916; *Peer Gynt*, tr. by William and Charles Archer, London, n. d., N. Y., 1923; and in Works, v. 4, in Mansfield acting edition, 1906, 1915; tr. by R. E. Roberts, 1914; tr. by M. M. Dawson, 1916; tr. by Sharp, 1916; *The League of Youth*, tr. by Archer, 1890, and in Prose Dramas, v. 1, and Works, v. 6; tr. as Young Men's League, by Henry Carstarphen, 1900; tr. by Sharp in Lady Inger of Östraat and Other Plays; tr. in The Wild Duck and Other Plays; *Emperor and Galilean*, tr. by Catherine Ray, 1876; tr. by Archer, 1890, 1904, in Prose Dramas, v. 4, and in Works, v. 5; *The Pillars of Society*, tr. as The Pillars of Society or Supports of Society by Mrs. Ric Kiralfy, 1878; tr. by Archer in Prose Dramas, v. 1, in Works, v. 6, and in Ellis, The Pillars of Society and Other Plays; tr. by Sharp in The Pretenders and Two Other Plays; tr. in Mencken, The Master Builder and Other Plays; *A Doll's House*, tr. as Nora by T. Weber, 1880; adapted as The Child Wife by W. M. Lawrence, 1882; tr. as Nora, 1882, and as The Doll's House, 1889, by Henrietta F. Lord; adapted as A Doll Wife, by Edward Holst, 1890; tr. by Archer in Prose Dramas, v. 1, and in Works, v. 7, and in Brander Matthews, The Chief European Dramatists, 1910; adapted by Dorothy Usner, 1907; tr. by Mencken, in The Master Builder and Other Plays; tr. in Sharp, A Doll's House and Two Other Plays; tr. in Chandler, Plays by Henrik Ibsen; tr. in Hubbell and Beaty, Introduction to Drama, 1927; tr. in A Doll's House and Other Plays; *Ghosts*, adapted by W. M. Lawrence, 1882; tr. by Henrietta F. Lord, 1890; tr. by Archer in Prose Dramas, v. 2, and in Works, v. 7, and in O. M. Sayler, The Eleonora Duse Series of Plays, 1923; tr. by Sharp, 1911; tr. in Robert M. Smith, Types of World Tragedy, 1928; tr. by H. F. Lord and Archer in Ellis, The Pillars of Society and Other Plays; tr. in A Doll's House and Other Plays; *An Enemy of the People*, tr. by Archer; tr. by Mrs. E. Marx-Aveling in Prose Dramas, v. 2, and in Works, v. 8; tr. by Sharp in Ghosts and Two Other Plays; tr. in O. M. Sayler, The Moscow Art Theatre Series of Russian Plays, 2d series, 1923; tr. in George R. Coffman, A Book of Modern Plays, 1925; tr. in Stauffer, Progress of Drama Through the Centuries, 1927; tr. as An Enemy of Society by Mrs. E. Marx-Aveling in Ellis, The Pillars of Society and Other Plays; tr. in A Doll's House and Other Plays; *The Wild Duck*, tr. by Mrs. E. Marx-Aveling; tr. by Mrs. F. E. Archer, 1905, in Archer, Prose Dramas, v. 2, and in Archer, Works, v. 8; tr. by Sharp in A Doll's House and Two Other Plays; tr. by Mrs. Archer in Moses, Representative Continental Dramas, 1924; tr. in Chandler, Plays by Henrik Ibsen; tr. in The Wild Duck and Other Plays; *Rosmersholm*, tr. by L. N. Parker, 1889; tr. by Charles Archer in Prose Dramas, v. 5, and in Works, v. 9; tr. by M. Carmichael, 1900; tr. by Sharp in The Pretenders and Two Other Plays; tr. in The Wild Duck and Other Plays; *The Lady from the Sea*, tr. and adapted as The Lady of the Sea, by Edward Holst and Joel Marks, 1889; tr. by Mrs. E. Marx-Aveling, 1890, 1910; tr. by Mrs. F. E. Archer in Prose Dramas, v. 5, and in Works, v. 9; tr. by Sharp in A Doll's House and Two Other Plays; tr. by Mrs. Archer in O. M. Sayler, The Eleonora Duse Series of Plays, 1923; *Hedda Gabler*, tr. by Edmund Gosse, 1891; tr. by Archer in Prose Dramas, v. 5, and in Works, v. 10; tr. by Edmund Gosse and Archer in Collected Works, v. 10; tr. in Mencken, The Master Builder and Other Plays; tr. in Chandler, Plays by Henrik Ibsen; tr. by Julie Le Gallienne and P. Leyssac in Eva Le Gallienne, Civic Repertory Plays, 1928; tr. in Robert

MODERN CONTINENTAL PLAYWRIGHTS

M. Smith, Types of Domestic Tragedy, 1928; *The Master Builder*, tr. by J. W. Arctander, 1893; tr. by Edmund Gosse and Archer, 1893, and in Works, v. 10; tr. in Mencken, The Master Builder and Other Plays; tr. in Chandler, Plays by Henrik Ibsen; *Little Eyolf*, tr. by Archer, 1894, 1895, and in Works, v. 11; tr. by Mencken, 1908; *John Gabriel Borkman*, tr. by Archer, 1897, 1907, and in Works, v. 11; *When We Dead Awaken*, tr. by Archer, 1900, and in Works, v. 11.

IBSEN, SIGURD

Robert Frank, 1914.

IN ENGLISH: *Robert Frank*, tr. by Marcia H. Janson, 1914.

ICRES, FERNAND

Butchers, 1888.

IVANOV, VSEVOLOD

The Armored Train, 1927.

JOHST, HANNS

Straw, 1915; *Young Man*, 1916; *The Lonely One*, 1917; *The King*, 1920; *Prophets*, 1922; *Money Changers and Merchants*, 1923; *The Happy City*, 1925; *Thomas Paine*, 1927; etc.

IN ENGLISH: *The King*, tr. by R. Ivan, 1922.

JULLIEN, JEAN

The Serenade, 1887; *The Day of Reckoning* (*L'Echéance*), 1889; *The Master*, 1890; *The Sea*, 1891; *The Scholar*, 1901; *The Fist*, 1902; *The Miner*, 1903; *Father Basselet*, 1904; *The Oasis*, 1905; *The Rights of the Heart*, 1906; *The Plumes of the Peacock*, 1906.

KAISER, GEORG

Schoolmaster Kleist, 1905; *The Jewish Widow*, 1911; *King Cuckold*, 1913; *The Burghers of Calais*, 1914; *Europa*, 1915; *The Centaur* (*Constantin Strobel*), 1916; *From Morn to Midnight*, 1916; *The Sorina*, 1917; *The Temptation* (*The Mother of God*), 1917; *The Coral*, 1917; *Claudius*, 1918; *Gas—Part I*, 1918; *Woman's Sacrifice* (*Das Frauenopfer*), 1918; *Friedrich and Anna*, 1918; *Juana*, 1918; *Hell, Way, Earth*, 1919; *The Conflagration in the Opera House*, 1919; *Alcibiades Saved*, 1920; *Gas—Part II*, 1920; *David and Goliath* (A reworking of *Citizen Möller*, 1915), 1922; *Chancellor's Clerk Krehler*, 1922; *Noli me tangere*, 1922; *The Protagonist*, 1922; *Gilles and Jeanne*, 1923; *The Spirit of the Antique*, 1923; *Side by Side*, 1923; *The Flight to Venice*, 1923; *Literary Trash* (*Kolportage*), 1924; *The Courageous Navigator*, 1925; *Double Oliver*, 1926; *Paper Mill*, 1927; *The President*, 1927; *The Leatherhead*, 1928; *Gats*, 1928; *October Day*, 1928; *The Two Cravats*, 1929.

BIBLIOGRAPHY

IN ENGLISH: *From Morn to Midnight*, tr. by Irving O. Safir, 1919; tr. by Ashley Dukes in Poet Lore 31, 1920, and separately, 1922, and in T. H. Dickinson, Chief Contemporary Dramatists, 3rd series, 1930; *The Coral*, tr. by Winifred Katzin in S. M. Tucker, Modern Continental Plays, 1929; *Gas— Part I*, tr. by Ashley Dukes, 1923; tr. by Hermann Scheffauer, 1924, and in Tucker, Modern Continental Plays; tr. by George Hexter, 1926; *Juana*, tr. by Geoffrey Dunlop, 1926; *The Conflagration in the Open House*, tr. as The Fire In the Opera House, by Katzin in Eight European Plays, 1927; *Gas— Part II*, tr. by Katzin in Tucker, Modern Continental Plays; *The Flight to Venice*, tr. by Rita Matthias and Pierre Coalfleet, 1923; *Literary Trash (Kolportage)*, tr. as Melodrama, by Hermann Scheffauer, 1927; *Double Oliver*, adapted by Hermann Bernstein, 1928; *October Day*, tr. as The Phantom Lover, by Bernstein and Adolph E. Meyer, 1928.

KAMBAN, GODMUNDUR

Hadda Padda, 1914; *We Murderers*, 1920; etc.

IN ENGLISH: *Hadda Padda*, tr. by Sadie L. Peller, 1917.

KIELLAND, ALEXANDER

On His Way Home, 1882; *All Is Vanity; His Majesty's Bailiff; Three Couples*, 1886; *Betty's Guardian*, 1887; *The Professor*, 1888.

IN ENGLISH: *Three Couples*, tr. by Henry Lindanger in The Drama, 1917.

KIRCHON, V., and OUSPENSKY, A.

Red Rust, 1927.

IN ENGLISH: *Red Rust*, adapted as Rust by Virginia and Frank Vernon, and played in London, 1928; adapted for the N. Y. Theatre Guild, 1930.

KISTEMAECKERS, HENRY

Pierrot in Love, 1890; *Moral of the Century; Nocturnal Idyll*, 1891; *Love in Yellow*, 1892; *Heart Breakers*, 1893; *The Quinquet Household*, 1893; *Marthe*, 1899; *Tooth for Tooth*, 1900; *The Wound*, 1900; *The First Client*, 1902; *Instinct*, 1905; *The Rival*, 1907; *The Merchant of Happiness*, 1910; *The Spy (La Flambée)*, 1912; *The Ambuscade*, 1913; *The Fair Exile*, 1913; *The Occident*, 1913; *An Evening at the Front*, 1918; *The King of the Palaces*, 1919; *She Who Passes (La Passante)*, 1921; *En Bombe*, 1923; *The Wandering Slave*, 1923; *Love*, 1924; *The Night Is Our Own*, 1925.

IN ENGLISH: *Instinct*, adapted by P. Stanlaws, 1912; *The Spy*, tr. as The Turning Point, by Peter Le Marchant, and played, London, 1913, and N. Y., 1914; *The Woman of Bronze* (with Eugène Delard), adapted by Paul Kester, 1919; *Where Poppies Bloom*, adapted by Roi Cooper Megrue, 1918, and played, N. Y., 1919; *Love*, tr. by J. Corpel and George Owen and played, London, 1926; adapted by J. Del Val, 1928.

MODERN CONTINENTAL PLAYWRIGHTS

KOKOSCHKA, OSKAR

The Burning Thorn Bush, 1911; *Murderer Hope of Women*, 1917; *Hiob*, 1917; *Orpheus and Eurydice*, 1918.

KÖNIG, EBERHARD

Filippo Lippi, 1899; *Godfather Death*, 1900; *Clytemnestra*, 1901; *Spring Rain*, 1904; *Master Joseph*, 1906; *Wieland the Smith*, 1906; *King Saul*, 1907; *Alcestis*, 1910; *Don Ferrante*, 1910; *Teukros*, 1915; *Dietrich of Bern, a Trilogy* —1. *Sibich*, 2. *Herrat*, 3. *Rabenschlacht*, 1917–1921.

KORNFELD, PAUL

The Seduction, 1916; *Heaven and Hell*, 1919; *Eternal Dream*, 1922; *Palme, or the Hypochondriac*, 1924; *Sakuntala*, 1925; *Kilian, or the Yellow Rose*, 1926.

KUZMIN, M. A.

The Pentecost at Toledo, 1914.

LAMPEL, PETER MARTIN

Revolt in a House of Correction, 1929.

LANGE, SVEN

A Martyr, 1896; *A Criminal*, 1903; *Samson and Delila*, 1909.

IN ENGLISH: *Samson and Delila*, tr. by Samuel S. Grossman, 1919, and played, N. Y., 1919, London, 1927.

LAVEDAN, HENRI

A Family, 1891; *Prince d'Aurec*, 1892; *The Two Nobilities*, 1894; *Gay Livers (Viveurs!)*, 1895; *Catherine*, 1898; *The New Game*, 1898; *The Old Stager (Le vieux Marcheur)*, 1899; *The Medicis*, 1901; *The Marquis de Priola*, 1902; *Varennes* (with G. Lenôtre), 1904; *The Duel*, 1905; *Sire*, 1909; *The Taste for Vice*, 1911; *To Serve (Servir)*, 1913; *The King's Dog*, 1913; *Pétard*, 1914; *War Dialogues*, 1916; *The Sacrifices* (with Miguel Zamacoïs), 1917; *Enchanted Portraits*, 1918; *Glory*, 1919; *The Immortal*, 1920; *The Fine Story of Geneviève*, 1920; *Monsieur Gastère*, 1927.

IN ENGLISH: *Prince d'Aurec*, tr. by B. H. Clark in Three Modern Plays from the French, 1914, abridged in J. A. Pierce, Masterpieces of Modern Drama—Foreign, 1915; *Catherine*, played in America; *The Duel*, played by Otis Skinner, 1906; *Sire*, adapted by Louis N. Parker, and played, N. Y., 1911; *To Serve*, played as Service, N. Y., 1919; *The King's Dog*, tr. as The King's Favorite, by John Pollock, and played, London, 1921; *Two Husbands*, tr. by R. T. House in Poet Lore 19, 1908; *Sunday on Sunday Goes By*, tr. by Mary Sibyl Holbrook in Poet Lore 27, 1916; *Along the Quays; For Ever and Ever, Where Shall We Go?, The Afternoon Walk, Not at Home*, tr. by

BIBLIOGRAPHY

Sibyl Holbrook in Poet Lore 28, 1917, and in M. J. Moses' Representative One-Act Plays, 1923; *The Age of Folly, In Wedlock, A Friend, Bad News, Distress, Epilogue,* tr. by William V. Silverberg as Their Heart, in Poet Lore 30, 1919; *The Voice of the Earth,* adapted by W. C. Taylor, 1917.

LEMAÎTRE, JULES

The Woman Who Revolted, 1889; *Deputy Leveau,* 1890; *White Marriage,* 1891; *Flipote,* 1893; *The Kings,* 1893; *The Difficult Age,* 1895; *Pardon,* 1895; *The Good Helen* (with Donnay), 1896; *The Eldest,* 1898; *The Studio Assistant (La Massière),* 1905; *Bertrade,* 1905; *Princess of Cleves,* 1908; *The Marriage of Telemachus* (with Donnay), 1910; *Kismet* (from Edward Knoblauch), 1912.

IN ENGLISH: *Deputy Leveau,* adapted as Protection, by C. Renauld, 1890; *White Marriage,* adapted as White Love, by Renauld, 1892; *Pardon,* tr. as Forgiveness, by Frances C. Fay in Poet Lore 24, 1913; tr. as The Pardon, by B. H. Clark in Three Modern Plays From the French, 1914; *The Eldest,* adapted as The Eldest Miss Peterman, by B. B. Vallentine, 1899; *The Studio Assistant,* tr. as Poor Little Thing, by J. K. Jerome, 1915.

LENGYEL, MELCHIOR (MENYHÉRT)

Grateful Posterity, 1907; *Typhoon,* 1909; *The Czarina* (with Lajos Biro), 1913; *The Kingdom of Sancho Panza,* 1919; *Antonia,* 1924; *Maria,* 1925; *The Battle of Waterloo,* 1925; *Seybold,* 1926.

IN ENGLISH: *Typhoon,* adapted by A. Konta and Adrian van Westrum, 1909; tr. by Nyitray, 1910; adapted by George Morehead, 1912; adapted by Una Brinker, 1912; adapted by F. G. Corcoran, 1912; tr. by J. W. McConaughy, 1912; tr. by Laurence Irving, and played, London, 1913; tr. by C. Swickard, 1914; *The Czarina,* adapted by Edward Sheldon and played, N. Y., 1922; *The Kingdom of Sancho Panza,* adapted as The Happy Island, by J. B. Fagan, 1913; adapted by Sidney Howard, 1921; *Antonia,* adapted by Arthur Richman and played, N. Y., 1925; *The Dancer,* adapted by Edward Locke, with L. K. Anspacher and Max Marcin, 1918.

LENORMAND, HENRI RENÉ

White Madness, 1905; *The Possessed,* 1909; *Dust,* 1914; *Time is a Dream,* 1919; *The Failures,* 1920; *Simoom,* 1920; *The Devourer of Dreams,* 1922; *The Red Tooth,* 1922; *Man and his Phantoms,* 1924; *In the Shadow of Evil,* 1924; *The Coward,* 1925; *The Magician Love,* 1926; *Mixture,* 1927; *The Innocent,* 1928; *A Secret Life,* 1929.

IN ENGLISH: D. L. Orna, Three Plays of Lenormand, 1928; *Time is a Dream,* tr. by Winifred Katzin, 1922, and in T. H. Dickinson, Chief Contemporary Dramatists, 3rd series, 1930; *The Failures,* tr. by Katzin, 1923; adapted as Might-Have-Beens, by Rowland Leigh, 1927; *Simoom,* tr. by Madeleine Boyne and John D. O'Neal, 1927; *The Devourer of Dreams,* tr. as The Dream Doctor, by Orna in Three Plays; *Man and His Phantoms,* tr. by Orna in Three Plays; *In the Shadow of Evil,* adapted as Devil's Keep, by

S. Thayer, 1928; *The Coward,* adapted by J. Corpel and Peter Creswell, and played, London, 1926; tr. by Orna in Three Plays.

LEROUX, GASTON, and CAMILLE, LUCIEN

Alsace, 1913.

LIENHARD, FRIEDRICH

Münchhausen, 1900; *King Arthur,* 1900; *Wieland the Smith,* 1905.

LOPEZ, SABATINO

By Night, 1889; *The Secret,* 1892; *Ninetta,* 1892; *Destiny,* 1896; *The Brothers,* 1898; *The Highest Post,* 1900; *The Bearing Point,* 1903; *All Love,* 1903; *Current Morality,* 1904; *The Lady of Others,* 1905; *The Hurricane (Bufere),* 1906; *The Good Girl,* 1908; *The Azure Prince,* 1910; *The Beast and the Beauties,* 1911; *Our Skins,* 1912; *The Third Husband,* 1912; *The Tangle (Il Viluppo),* 1913; *Mario and Maria,* 1915; *October Sun,* 1916; *The Sparrow,* 1918; *Closed,* 1920; *Schicchere is Great,* 1920; *Parodi and Company,* 1920; *Distance,* 1922; *Last of the Gypsies; Signora Rosa,* 1928.

IN ENGLISH: *The Third Husband,* adapted as Three for Diana, by C. B. Fernald, and played, N. Y., 1919; *The Sparrow,* tr. in Isaac Goldberg, Plays of the Italian Theater, 1921.

LOTHAR, RUDOLF

The Lie, 1891; *The Price of Life,* 1893; *The Song of Songs,* 1895; *A Royal Idyll,* 1896; *The Veiled King,* 1897; *King Harlequin,* 1900; *Happiness in Love,* 1903; *Tiefland,* 1904; *The Rose Templar,* 1905; *The Girl in Black,* 1907; *I Love You,* 1910; *Woman's Artifice,* 1916; *The Morning Paper,* 1919; *The Javanese Doll* (with Hans Bachwitz), 1921; *The Werwolf,* 1921; *The Masked Woman,* 1922; *The Beautiful Mélusine,* 1925; *The Republic Commands* (with Fritz Gottwald), 1926; *The Phantom Ship* (with Oscar Ritter), 1926; *The Duchess of Elba* (with Ritter), 1926; *The Night of Three Women* (with Wilhelm Lichtenberg), 1927; *The Lady in the Clouds,* 1928; etc.

IN ENGLISH: *King Harlequin,* adapted as The Harlequin King, by J. Severance, 1906; tr. as King Harlequin, by N. J. Wallerstein, 1924; *Woman's Artifice,* adapted as The Perjurers of Love, by Adolf Philipp, 1920; *The Javanese Doll,* tr. by Karl K. Kerger, 1922; *The Werwolf,* adapted by Gladys Unger and played, N. Y., 1924; *The Masked Woman,* adapted by H. Bernstein, 1928; *The Beautiful Mélusine,* adapted by H. Bernstein, 1928; *The Republic Commands,* tr. as The Command to Love, by H. Bernstein, and played, N. Y., 1926; *The Phantom Ship,* tr. by A. Armband, 1926; tr. by Owen Davis, and played, N. Y., 1926; *The Duchess of Elba,* adapted by Avery Hopwood and played, London, 1927; *The Night of Three Women,* adapted by H. Bernstein, 1929; *Collision* (with Erno Sebesi), tr. by Sidney Howard, 1926.

BIBLIOGRAPHY

LOYSON, PAUL HYACINTHE

The Evangel of Blood, 1902; *The Right of the Virgins*, 1904; *Enemy Souls*, 1907; *The Apostle*, 1911.

IN ENGLISH: *Enemy Souls*, tr. as The War of Souls, by Jane G. R. White and played, N. Y., 1909; *The Apostle*, tr. by F. M. Rankin, 1913; tr. by Barrett H. Clark, 1916.

LUDOVICI, CESARE V.

L'Eroica; The Idiot, 1915; *The Woman of No One*, 1919; *Longsword and the Magician* (*Spadacciola e il Mago*), 1921; *Toby and the Fly*, 1921; *Good News*, 1923; *With Eyes Half Closed*, 1923; *Tales of Good Weather* (*Le Fole del bel tempo*), 1925.

IN ENGLISH: *L'Eroica*, tr. by Petronelle Sombart, 1921, and in Poet Lore 34, 1923; *The Idiot*, tr. by Sombart in Poet Lore 30, 1919; *The Woman of No One*, tr. by Sombart, 1920, and in Poet Lore 32, 1921.

LUNACHARSKY, ANATOLI VASIL'EVICH

The Temptation, 1896; *The King's Barber*, 1906; *The Magi*, 1918; *Vasilisa the Wise*, 1918; *Ivan in Paradise*, 1919; *Steps*, 1919; *Faust and the City*, 1921; *The Chancellor and the Locksmith*, 1921; *The Deliverance of Don Quixote*, 1921; *Oliver Cromwell*, 1921; *Thomas Campanella*, 1921; *The Bear's Wedding*, 1922.

IN ENGLISH: L. A. Magnus and K. Walter: Three Plays of A. V. Lunacharsky (*The Magi, Vasilisa the Wise, Faust and the City*), 1923; *Vasilisa the Wise*, tr. by Magnus separately, 1922; *The Bear Wedding*, adapted by Leon Zamkovoy and Natan Borudin, 1926.

MAETERLINCK, MAURICE

Princess Maleine, 1889; *The Intruder*, 1890; *The Blind*, 1890; *The Seven Princesses*, 1891; *Pelléas and Mélisande*, 1893; *Alladine and Palomides*, 1894; *Home* (*L'Intérieur*), 1894; *The Death of Tintagiles*, 1894; *Aglavaine and Sélysette*, 1896; *Sister Beatrice*, 1900; *Ariane and Blue Beard*, 1901; *Monna Vanna*, 1902; *Joyzelle*, 1903; *The Miracle of Saint Anthony*, 1904; *The Blue Bird*, 1908; *Mary Magdalene*, 1910; *The Betrothal*, 1918; *The Burgomaster of Stilemonde*, 1918; *The Salt of Life* (a sequel to *The Burgomaster*), 1920; *The Power of the Dead*, 1923; *The Cloud that Lifted*, 1923; *Berniquel*, 1923; *Misfortune Passes*, 1926; *Marie-Victoire*, 1927; *Juda de Kerioth*, 1929.

IN ENGLISH: Mary Vielé, The Blind and The Intruder, 1891; Gérard Harry and William Wilson, Princess Maleine and The Intruder, 1892; William Archer and Alfred Sutro, Three Little Dramas for Marionettes, 1899; Bernard Miall, Sister Beatrice and Ardiane and Barbe Bleue, 1902; Richard Hovey, The Plays of Maurice Maeterlinck, 1894–1896, and later; Laurence Alma Tadema, Pelleas and Melisanda and The Sightless, 1913; A Miracle of Saint Anthony and Five Other Plays, 1917; F. M. Atkinson, The Cloud that

Lifted and the Power of the Dead, 1923; *Princess Maleine*, tr. by Richard Hovey in Plays, v. 1; by Gérard Harry and William Wilson, 1892; *The Intruder*, tr. by Hovey in Plays, v. 1, and 1911; tr. by Mary Vielé, 1891; tr. by Gérard Harry and William Wilson, 1892; tr. in A Miracle of Saint Anthony and Five Other Plays; tr. in Frank Shay and Pierre Loving, Fifty Contemporary One-Act Plays, 1920; tr. in Helen L. Cohen, One-Act Plays by Modern Authors, 1921; *The Blind*, tr. by Mary Vielé, 1891; tr. by Hovey in Plays, v. 1, and in M. J. Moses, Representative One-Act Plays, 1923; tr. as The Sightless, by Charlotte Porter and Helen A. Clarke in Poet Lore 4, 1893; tr. by Laurence Alma Tadema, 1913; *The Seven Princesses*, tr. by Hovey in Plays, v. 1; tr. by Porter and Clarke in Poet Lore 6, 1894; tr. by William Metcalfe, 1909; *Pelléas and Mélisande*, tr. by Hovey in Plays, v. 2, and in T. H. Dickinson, Chief Contemporary Dramatists, 1st series, 1915; in A Miracle of Saint Anthony and Five Other Plays; in Robert M. Smith, Types of Romantic Drama, 1928; in S. M. Tucker, Modern Continental Plays, 1929; tr. by Porter and Clarke in Poet Lore 6, 1894; tr. by Erving Winslow, 1894; tr. by C. A. Byrne, for the music of Claude Debussy, 1907; *Alladine and Palomides*, tr. by Hovey in Plays, v. 2; tr. by Porter and Clarke in Poet Lore 7, 1895; tr. by William Archer and Alfred Sutro in Three Little Dramas for Marionettes, 1899, etc.; tr. by R. R. Johnson and N. Erickson, 1899; tr. by Sutro, 1907; and in A Miracle of Saint Anthony and Five Other Plays; *Home* (*L'Intérieur*), tr. by Hovey in Plays, v. 2; tr. as Interior, by Archer and Sutro, in Three Little Dramas for Marionettes; tr. as Interior, by Archer in New Review, 1894; separately in 1908, 1911, 1915, and in Frank Shay, Twenty-five Short Plays, International, 1924; *The Death of Tintagiles*, tr. by Hovey in Plays, v. 2; tr. by Archer and Sutro in Three Little Dramas; tr. by Sutro, 1909, 1911, 1915; tr. in A Miracle of Saint Anthony and Five Other Plays; tr. by Philip Moeller, 1917; tr. in Frank Shay, A Treasury of Plays for Women, 1922; tr. by Paul McPharlin, in A Repertory of Marionette Plays, 1929; *Aglavaine and Sélysette*, tr. by Porter and Clarke in Poet Lore 14, 1903; tr. by Sutro, 1897, 1904, 1908, 1911; *Monna Vanna*, tr. by A. I. du P. Coleman, 1903; tr. by Porter in Poet Lore 15, 1904; tr. by Sutro, 1904, 1907; tr. in M. J. Moses, Representative Continental Dramas, 1924; *Joyzelle*, tr. by Clarence Stratton in Poet Lore 16, 1905; tr. by Alexander Teixeira de Mattos, 1907; *The Miracle of Saint Anthony*, tr. in A Miracle of Saint Anthony and Five Other Plays; tr. by Ralph Roeder and adapted by Philip Moeller, 1916; tr. by de Mattos, 1918; *Ariane and Bluebeard*, tr. as Ardiane and Barbe Bleue, by Bernard Miall, 1901, 1902, 1908; *The Blue Bird*, tr. by de Mattos, 1909, 1910, 1911, with a new act, 1912, 1918, 1923, 1925; tr. by A. H. Sacken as "a lyric comedy," 1919; *Mary Magdalene*, tr. by de Mattos, 1910; *Sister Beatrice*, tr. in The Anglo-Saxon Review, 1900; tr. by Bernard Miall, 1902; tr. by Mrs. C. Wetherill Rice, 1908; *The Betrothal*, tr. by de Mattos, 1918; *The Burgomaster of Stilemonde*, tr. by de Mattos, 1918, and played as A Burgomaster of Belgium, 1919; *The Power of the Dead*, tr. by F. M. Atkinson, 1923; *The Cloud that Lifted*, tr. by Atkinson, 1923.

MAIAKOVSKY, VLADIMIR

Mysteria-Bouffes, 1919; *The Earth Prancing*, 1923; *The Bug*, 1929.

BIBLIOGRAPHY

MARINETTI, FILIPPO TOMMASO

King Hubbub (Il Re Baldoria), 1909; *Sexual Electricity*, 1909; *The Bleeding Mummy; Prisoners; Vulcan; Drumfire*; etc.

IN ENGLISH: *Anti-Neutrality, Simultaneity, Moonlight,* three short plays, tr. by M. Cram in Vanity Fair, April and May, 1919.

MARTÍNEZ SIERRA, GREGORIO

Theater of Dreams (dialogues), 1905; *Life and Sweetness* (with Santiago Rusiñol), 1907; *The Swallows (Aucells de pas)* (with Rusiñol), 1908; *Love Magic,* 1908; *The Shadow of the Father,* 1909; *The Mistress of the House,* 1910; *The Fortune of Isabelita,* 1911; *Lily Among Thorns,* 1911; *The Cradle Song,* 1911; *Spring in Autumn,* 1911; *Poor John,* 1912; *Mamma,* 1912; *The Dance (La Tirana)* (a musical comedy), 1913; *Madame Pepita, 1913; Madrigal,* 1913; *The Shepherds; For Women Only,* 1913; *Youth, Divine Treasure,* 1913; *Wife of the Hero,* 1914; *Passion,* 1914; *The Romantics,* 1914; *Margot* (a lyric comedy), 1914; *The Mournful Palace,* 1914; *The Swallows (Las Golondrinas)* (comic opera based on *Aucells de pas*), 1914; *Dawn,* 1915; *The Kingdom of God,* 1916; *Holy Night (Navidad),* 1916; *Our Hope; Dream of an August Night,* 1918; *Don Juan of Spain,* 1921; *The Tower of Avorio,* 1922; *Cricket on the Hearth,* 1923; *The Tower of Ivory,* 1924; *The Devil's Hour,* 1925; *The Man Who Wanted to Dine* (with J. Abati), 1925; *Modesty* (with F. Sassone), 1925; *Woman,* 1925; *The Daughter of All* (with Jacquetoz), 1925; *Intolerable Mary* (with Honorio Maura), 1926; *The Road to Happiness* (with Eduardo Marquina), 1926; *Let's Be Happy,* 1929; *Triangle,* 1929; etc., etc.

IN ENGLISH: J. G. Underhill, Plays of Gregorio Martínez Sierra, v. 1, 1917, and v. 2, Helen and Harley Granville-Barker, 1922; *The Theater of Dreams,* tr. by A. Sterling, 1918; *Love Magic,* tr. by Underhill in The Drama 25, 1917, and in Plays, v. 1; *Lily Among Thorns,* tr. in T. H. Dickinson, Chief Contemporary Dramatists, 3rd series, 1930; *The Cradle Song,* tr. by Underhill in Poet Lore 28, 1917, and in Plays, v. 1, and in Burns Mantle, Best Plays of 1926–1927; *Poor John,* tr. by Underhill in Plays, v. 1, and in The Drama 10, 1920; *Madame Pepita,* tr. by Underhill in Plays, v. 1; tr. by May Heywood Broun with Underhill, 1921; *The Shepherds,* tr. as The Two Shepherds, by the Granville-Barkers in Plays, v. 2; *The Lover,* tr. by Underhill in Plays, v. 1, and in The Stratford Journal, 1919; tr. in M. J. Moses, Representative One-Act Plays by Continental Authors, 1923; *Wife of the Hero,* tr. as Wife to a Famous Man, by the Granville-Barkers in Plays, v. 2; *The Kingdom of God,* tr. by the Barkers in Plays, v. 2, and in Burns Mantle, Best Plays of 1928–1929; *Nativity,* tr. as Holy Night, by Philip Hereford, 1928; *The Dream of an August Night,* tr. as The Romantic Young Lady, by the Granville-Barkers in Plays, v. 2; *The Mountebanks,* adapted by A. Sterling, 1921; *Idyll,* tr. by Charlotte M. Lewis in Poet Lore 37, 1926; *The Road to Happiness,* played, N. Y., 1927; *The Forgotten Song,* adapted by G. Portnoff, 1928.

MENDÈS, CATULLE

Tabarin's Wife, 1887; *Queen Fiammette*, 1889; *Medea*, 1898; *The Swan*, 1899; *Scarron*, 1905; *Glatigny*, 1906; *The Virgin of Avila*, 1906; *The Empress*, 1909; etc.

IN ENGLISH: *Tabarin's Wife*, tr. by Frank R. Arnold in The International, 1912; adapted as The Mummer's Wife, by F. K. Peile, 1913.

MÉTÉNIER, OSCAR

En Famille, 1887; *The Power of Darkness* (with Pavlovsky from Tolstoy), 1888; *The Casserole*, 1889; *The Gorilla*, 1891; *The Confrontation*, 1892; *Mademoiselle Fifi*, 1896; *He*, 1898; *The Revenge of Dupont d'Anguille*, 1899; etc., etc.

MEYER-FÖRSTER, WILHELM

Old Heidelberg, 1901; etc.

IN ENGLISH: *Old Heidelberg*, tr. by Max Chapelle, 1903; tr. by Catherine Pochin, 1905, 1924; tr. by Rudolf Bleichmann, 1909; tr. as The Student Prince, by Dorothy Donnelly, 1923; tr. as The Student Prince in Old Heidelberg, by Grace B. von Wentzel, 1928.

MEYERHOLD, V.

The Death and Destruction of Europe, 1923 (from a German novel, Trust for the Destruction of Europe, by I. Ehrenburg).

MIRBEAU, OCTAVE

The Epidemic, 1897; *The Bad Shepherds*, 1897; *Old Ménage*, 1901; *The Fair Lover* (*Amante*), 1901; *Scruples*, 1902; *The Portfolio*, 1902; *Business Is Business*, 1903; *The Fireside* (with Thadée Natanson), 1908; etc.

IN ENGLISH: *The Bad Shepherds*, tr. by J. de Susini and C. Byrns, 1897; *Old Ménage*, tr. as An Old Household, by G. B. Munson, 1921; *Scruples*, adapted as A Scrupulous Man, by M. Hecht, 1905; and tr. as Scruples in Pierre Loving, Ten-Minute Plays, 1923; *Business Is Business*, played in America by William H. Crane; abridged in J. A. Pierce, The Masterpieces of Modern Drama—Foreign, 1915.

MOLNAR, FERENC

The Attorney at Law, 1902; *Józsi*, 1904; *The Devil*, 1907; *Liliom*, 1909; *The Guardsman*, 1911; *The Wolf*, 1912; *The Swan*, 1914; *Fashions for Men* (*Uridivat*), 1914; *The White Cloud*, 1916; *Carnival* (*Lent*) (*Farsang*), 1917; *A Prologue to King Lear, Marshal*, and *The Violet*, collected as *Szinhaz*, 1919; *Heavenly and Earthly Love*, 1922; *The Red Mill*, 1923; *The Glass Slipper*, 1924; *Play in the Castle* (*Játek a Kastelyban*), 1924; *Still Life*, 1925;

BIBLIOGRAPHY

The Putty Club; A Matter of Husbands; Riviera, 1925; *The Witch; If Napoleon,* 1927; *Olympia,* 1928; *One, Two, Three,* 1929; *The Good Fairy,* 1930.

IN ENGLISH: Benjamin Glazer, Fashions for Men and The Swan, 1922; Glazer, Husbands and Lovers (nineteen brief pieces), 1924; Louis Rittenberg, The Plays of Ferenc Molnár, 1929; *The Attorney at Law,* tr. as The Lawyer, by George Halász in Plays, 1929; *The Devil,* tr. by Henry Hamilton, 1908; adapted by J. S. Dawley, 1908; adapted by Marie Doran, 1908; adapted by Alexander Konta and W. T. Larned, 1908; adapted as The Cloven Foot and played as The Devil, by Oliver Herford, 1908; and in Plays, 1929; tr. by C. Swickard, 1914; adapted by Ben Sager Dean, 1929; *Liliom,* tr. by Eugene S. Lucas, 1919; in Burns Mantle, Best Plays of 1920–1921; tr. by Benjamin Glazer, 1921, and in S. M. Tucker, Modern Continental Plays, 1929, and in Plays, 1929, and in T. H. Dickinson, Chief Contemporary Dramatists, 3rd series, 1930; adapted as The Daisy by Osmond Shillingford and A. E. Ellis, 1920; adapted as Liliom by the same, 1926; *The Guardsman,* given in London as Playing With Fire, 1911; tr. by Philip Littell, 1913, and played, N. Y.; tr. by Ruth Livingston, 1923; tr. by Grace I. Colbron and Hans Bartsch (Theatre Guild Version), 1924; tr. by Philip Moeller in Plays, 1929; *The Wolf,* adapted and played as The Phantom Rival and The Phantom Lover, by Leo Ditrichstein, 1914; adapted as The Love Letter, a musical comedy, by William L. Baron, 1920; tr. as The Tale of the Wolf, by Melville Baker, in Plays, 1929; *The Swan,* tr. by Benjamin Glazer, 1922, and in Plays, 1929; tr. by Melville Baker, 1923, and in Burns Mantle, Best Plays of 1923–1924; *Fashions for Men,* tr. as Men's Styles, by Irwin C. Safir, 1919; tr. as Fashions for Men, by Glazer, 1922, and in Plays, 1929; *The White Cloud,* tr. by Louis Rittenberg in Plays, 1929; *Lent,* tr. as Carnival, by Elsie Bondy, 1919; tr. by Melville Baker, as Carnival, 1924, and in Plays, 1929; *The Field Marshal* and *Prelude to King Lear,* tr. by Benjamin Glazer, 1924; *A Prologue to King Lear, The Marshal,* and *The Violet,* tr. by Louis Rittenberg, in Plays, 1929; *Heavenly and Earthly Love,* tr. by Glazer in Husbands and Lovers; adapted as Launzi, by Edna St. Vincent Millay, 1923, and as Heavenly and Earthly Love in Plays, 1929; *The Red Mill,* adapted as Mima by David Belasco, 1928, and in Plays, 1929; *The Glass Slipper,* tr. by Irma Szabo, 1925; tr. by F. E. Faragoh, 1925; tr. by Philip Moeller in Plays, 1929; *The Play in the Castle,* adapted as The Play's the Thing, by P. G. Wodehouse, 1927, and in Burns Mantle, Best Plays of 1926–1927, and in Plays, 1929; *A Matter of Husbands,* tr. in Pierre Loving, Ten-Minute Plays, 1923; tr. by Glazer in Husbands and Lovers; tr. as The Actress in Smart Set 33, 1911; *Olympia,* tr. by Sidney Howard, 1928, and in Plays, 1929; *The Host,* tr. by Joseph Szeben in One-Act Plays for Stage and Study, 2nd series, 1925; *Riviera,* tr. by F. E. Faragoh, in The Plays, 1929; *Still Life* and *The Witch,* tr. by S. J. Greenburger, in The Plays; *Lombroso's Monument,* adapted by I. Kaszab, 1910; *The Man in the Cab, A Leave Taking, The Key, Seven O'Clock in the Evening, Two Slaps in the Face, Fledgelings, The Knight of the Blue Chin, A Preliminary Skirmish, Curtain, Lies, A Railroad Adventure, Sacred and Profane Art, The Cab, A Street and Number, Phosphorus, Heavenly and Earthly Love, The Unpardonable Sin, The Kiss,* all tr. by Benjamin Glazer in Husbands and Lovers, 1924; *The Scamp,* tr. by Alexander Konta, 1923.

MODERN CONTINENTAL PLAYWRIGHTS

MORSELLI, ERCOLE LUIGI

Glauco, 1918; *Orione,* 1919; *Water Upon Fire,* 1920; *The Prison,* 1920; *Gastone the Animal Tamer; Daphnis and Chloe,* 1923; *Belphagor,* 1923.

IN ENGLISH: *Glauco,* tr. as Glaucus, by A. Armband and E. Zito, 1922; *Water Upon Fire* and *Gastone the Animal Tamer,* tr. in Isaac Goldberg, Plays of the Italian Theater, 1921.

MOSER, GUSTAV VON

The Easter of Violets, 1876; *The Librarian,* 1878; *The Hypochondriac,* 1878; *War in Peace* (with Franz von Schönthan), 1881; *Reif Reiflingen* (with von Schönthan), 1882; *Military Devotion* (with J. von Trotha), 1893; (22 vols. of comedies dating from 1872 to 1894).

NATHANSEN, HENRI

Within the Walls, 1912.

NICCODEMI, DARIO

Suzeraine, 1908; *The Refuge,* 1909; *The Aigrette,* 1912; *The Sharks,* 1913; *The Shadow,* 1915; *Scampolo,* 1915; *The Enemy,* 1916; *The Titan,* 1916; *The Little Schoolmistress,* 1916; *Pero Pero,* 1918; *Acidalia,* 1918; *The Dawn, the Day, the Night,* 1921; *The Secret House,* 1924; *The Madonna,* 1928; etc. (The first four plays in French, the remainder in Italian.)

IN ENGLISH: *Refuge,* played as The Prodigal Husband, N. Y., 1913; *The Shadow,* tr. by Michael Morton and played, N. Y., 1915, 1923; *Scampolo,* adapted by Morton, and played as Remnant, London, 1917; N. Y., 1919; *The Enemy,* played as Stronger Than Love, N. Y., 1925; *Stolen Fruit,* an adaptation by Gladys Unger, played, N. Y., 1925; *Seeking,* an adaptation by Unger, played, N. Y., 1925; *The Schoolmistress,* an adaptation by Unger, 1925.

NOVELLI, A.

Deputy by Force, 1890; *Lippi's Virgins,* 1891; *The Line Via Reggio to Rome,* 1895; *The Casimir Machine,* 1898; *After,* 1898; *The Sin,* 1899; *The Dead,* 1900; *The Chocolate,* 1901; *Old Heroes,* 1906; etc., and in Florentine dialect *Purgatory, Hell, and Paradise,* 1904; *Still Waters,* 1908; *The Ascension,* 1909; *The Black Beast,* 1909; *Ave Maria,* 1909; *The Cupola,* 1911; *When the Pear is Ripe,* 1912; *The Old Cock,* 1912; *He Who is Cause of His Own Misfortunes,* 1913; *Pollo,* 1914; *Canapone,* 1914; *The Wolf Loses His Hide,* 1915; *From Saying to Doing,* 1916; *Their Prisons,* 1917; etc.

IN ENGLISH: *The Cupola,* adapted by G. C. Speranza, 1915.

OHNET, GEORGES

Marthe, 1877; *The Iron Master,* 1883; *Serge Panine,* 1884; *Lise Fleuron,* 1884; *The Ladies of Croix-Mort,* 1886; *The Countess Sarah,* 1887; *Black and*

BIBLIOGRAPHY

Pink, 1887; *La Grande Marnière,* 1888; *Doctor Rameau,* 1888; *Will,* 1888; *Last Love,* 1890; *Colonel Roquebrune,* 1897.

IN ENGLISH: *The Iron Master,* tr. as The Forge Master, by Carl T. Eben, 1888; tr. as The Iron Manufacturer, by Grace Leslie in The Drama, 1903; *La Grande Marnière,* adapted as Antoinette, by N. Ruthven, 1886.

OSTROVSKY, ALEKSANDR NIKOLAEVICH

(Included here because his last plays fall within our period.)

Poverty is No Vice, 1854; *A Domestic Picture,* 1855; *Incompatibility of Temper,* 1858; *The Ward,* 1859; *The Thunderstorm,* 1860; *We Shall Settle Matters Among Ourselves,* 1861; *Sin and Sorrow Are Common to All,* 1863; *The False Demetrios,* 1867; *Enough Stupidity in Every Man,* 1868; *The Forest,* 1871; *Snegurotchka,* 1873; *Wolves and Sheep,* 1875; *The Last Sacrifice,* 1877; *The Heart is No Stone,* 1879; *Bond-women,* 1880; *Talents and Admirers,* 1882; *Guilty Without Guilt,* 1884; etc.

IN ENGLISH: George R. Noyes, Plays by Alexander Ostrovsky, 1917; *Poverty is No Vice,* tr. as Poverty is No Crime, by Noyes; tr. by Jane W. Robertson, and played, London, 1923; *A Domestic Picture,* tr. by E. L. Voynich in The Humour of Russia, 1895; *Incompatibility of Temper,* tr. by Voynich in the same; *The Ward,* tr. as A Protégée of the Mistress, by Noyes; *The Thunderstorm,* tr. as The Storm, by Constance Garnett, 1899; tr. by Florence Whyte and Noyes, 1927; *We Shall Settle Matters Among Ourselves,* tr. as It's A Family Affair—We'll Settle It Ourselves, by Noyes; tr. by George R. Boxes, and played, London, 1922; *Sin and Sorrow Are Common to All,* tr. by Noyes; *The False Demetrios,* tr. as Russia's Stolen Throne, or The False Dimitri, by A. Cahan, and arranged for the stage by R. Boyarsky, 1888; *Enough Stupidity in Every Man,* tr. as Enough Stupidity in Every Wise Man, by Jenny Covan in O. M. Sayler, Moscow Art Theater Series of Russian Plays, 1923; *The Forest,* tr. by Clara Winslow and Noyes, 1926; *Snegurotchka* (The Snow Maiden), an opera, by F. H. Martens, 1921; adapted by K. and O. Kovalsky and E. Noa, 1926; *Wolves and Sheep,* tr. by Inez Colby and Noyes in Poet Lore 37, 1926; *The Last Sacrifice,* tr. by Eugenia Korvin-Kroukovsky and Noyes in Poet Lore 39, 1928; *Bond-women,* tr. by Schöne C. Kurlandzik and Noyes in Poet Lore 36, 1925; *At the Jolly Spot,* tr. by Jane Campbell and Noyes in Poet Lore 36, 1925.

PAGNOL, MARCEL

Tonton (with Paul Nivoix), 1923; *Straight at the Heart (Un Direct au Cœur)* (with Nivoix), 1924; *Merchants of Glory* (with Nivoix), 1925; *Jazz,* 1926; *Topaze,* 1928; *Marius,* 1929.

IN ENGLISH: *Merchants of Glory,* tr. by Ralph Roeder, and played, N. Y., 1929; *Topaze,* adapted by D. C. Bennett, and played, N. Y., 1930; *Marius,* adapted as Marseilles, by Sidney Howard, and played, N. Y., 1930.

MODERN CONTINENTAL PLAYWRIGHTS

PAILLERON, ÉDOUARD

The Parasite, 1860; *The Wall Between* (*Le Mur mitoyen*), 1860; *The Second Movement*, 1865; *False Ménages*, 1869; *The Spark*, 1879; *The World of Boredom* (*Le Monde où l'on s'ennuie*), 1881; *The Mouse*, 1887; *Cabotins*, 1894; etc.

IN ENGLISH: *The Spark*, tr. by T. R. Sullivan, 1879; adapted as Sparkling, by H. L. Williams, 1882; tr. by H. Goodwin, 1910; tr. by Abbie F. Potts in Poet Lore 38, 1927; *The World of Boredom*, tr. by Martia Leonard and J. T. Grein, 1901; tr. as The Art of Being Bored, by B. H. Clark, 1914; abridged as The Cult of Boredom in J. A. Pierce, Masterpieces of Modern Drama— Foreign, 1915; *Subtleties of Jealousy* (*Coming Events*), tr. by Sidney Rosenfeld, 1898; *The Mouse*, tr. as The Triumph of Youth or The White Mouse, by Donald Robertson, 1907; *Washington*, adapted by Thomas E. White and William H. Fox, 1886; *The Secret of M. Dieudonné*, adapted as Tales Out of School, by M. Freeman, 1901; *The Society Man*, adapted by George Scarborough, 1918.

PAQUET, ALFONS

Stormflood, 1926.

PAUL, ADOLF

King Christian II, 1899; *Harpagos*, 1900; *David and Goliath; The Case of Voltaire; The Tiger*, 1902; *The Comedy of Double Personality*, 1903; *The Devil's Church*, 1905; *Hille Bobbe*, 1906; *The Triumph of the Pompadour,* 1908; *How Sin Came Into the World*, 1909; *Blue Smoke*, 1909; *Unpurchasable*, 1910; *The Language of the Birds*, 1911; *Drones*, 1912; *Lola Montez,* 1917; *The Conscious Somebody*, 1918; *In Behalf of the Right*, 1922.

IN ENGLISH: *The Language of the Birds*, tr. by Arthur Travers-Borgstroem, 2d edition, 1922.

PEREZ, I. L.

A Night in the Old Market, 1923.

PÉREZ GALDÓS, BENITO

Reality, 1892; *Gerona*, 1893; *The Life of the House*, 1893; *The Duchess of San Quintín*, 1894; *The Condemned*, 1894; *Will*, 1895; *Doña Perfecta*, 1896; *The Dragon*, 1896; *Electra*, 1901; *Soul and Life*, 1902; *Mariucha*, 1903; *The Grandfather*, 1904; *Barbara*, 1905; *Love and Science*, 1905; *Pedro Minio,* 1908; *Celia in the Slums* (*Celia en los enfernos*), 1913; *Alcestis*, 1914; *Sister Simona*, 1915; *Reason in Unreason*, 1915; *Miser Solomon*, 1916; *Santa Juana of Castile*, 1918; *Anton Caballero*, 1922.

IN ENGLISH: *The Duchess of San Quintín*, tr. by Philip M. Hayden in Poet Lore 21, 1910, and in B. H. Clark, Masterpieces of Modern Spanish Drama, 1922; *Electra*, tr. by J. de Susini-Etcheverry, 1901; adapted by M. C. Smith,

BIBLIOGRAPHY

1901; adapted as The Nun and the Barbarian, by Osmond S. Herts, 1906; adapted by J. G. Underhill, 1909; tr. in The Drama 2, 1911; tr. in C. A. Turrell, Contemporary Spanish Dramatists, 1919; tr. in S. M. Tucker, Modern Continental Plays, 1929; *The Grandfather*, tr. by Elizabeth Wallace in Poet Lore 21, 1910.

PIRANDELLO, LUIGI

(No two authorities agree on the chronology of Pirandello's earlier plays.)

Scamandra, 1910; *Sicilian Limes*, 1910, 1913; *The Vise*, 1910; *If Not Thus*, 1911 (revised as *The Rights of Others*, 1915); *The Doctor's Duty*, 1911; *Just Think, Giacomino*, 1914, 1916; *The Pleasure of Honesty*, 1914, 1917; *At the Gate* (*All' Uscita*), 1914; *Cap and Bells* (*Il Berretto a Sonagli*), 1915; *Chee-Chee* (*Cecè*), 1915; *The Imbecile*, 1915; *Liolà*, 1916; *Right You Are* (*If You Think So*) [*Così è* (*se vi pare*)], 1916; *Grafting*, 1917; *The Patient*, 1918; *Each of Us His Own Part* (*Il Giuoco delle Parti*), 1918; *But It Is Not a Serious Affair*, 1918; *Man, Beast, and Virtue*, 1919; *All for the Best*, 1920; *Signora Morli, One and Two*, 1920 (revised as *Two in One*, 1922); *As Before and Better* (*Come prima meglio di prima*), 1920; *By Judgment of the Court* (*La Patente*), 1920; *Six Characters in Search of an Author*, 1921; *Henry IV*, 1922; *Naked* (*Vestire gli Ignudi*), 1922; *The Life I Gave Thee*, 1923; *The Man With a Flower in his Mouth*, 1923; *Each in His Own Way*, 1924; *The Consecration of Our Lord of the Ship* (*La Sagra del Signor della Nave*), 1925; *The Jar*, 1925; *The House With a Column* (*L'Altro Figlio*), 1925; *Diana and la Tuda*, 1926; *Friendship of Women*, 1927; *The New Colony*, 1927; *Lazzaro*, 1929.

IN ENGLISH: Arthur Livingston, Three Plays of Pirandello, 1922; Livingston, Each in His Own Way and Two Other Plays, 1923; Livingston, The One-Act Plays of Luigi Pirandello, 1928 (translations by Elisabeth Abbott, Arthur Livingston, and Blanche V. Mitchell); *Sicilian Limes*, tr. by Isaac Goldberg in Plays of the Italian Theatre, 1921; tr. by Elisabeth Abbott in Theatre Arts Magazine, v. 6, 1922; tr. in The One-Act Plays; *The Vise*, tr. by Abbott in The One-Act Plays; *The Doctor's Duty*, tr. by Mitchell in The One-Act Plays; *Just Think, Giacomino*, tr. as Think It Over, Jimmy, by Leo Ongley, 1924; *The Pleasure of Honesty*, tr. in Each in His Own Way and Two Other Plays; *Chee-Chee*, tr. by Abbott in The One-Act Plays; *The Imbecile*, tr. by Mitchell in The One-Act Plays; *Right You Are* (*If You Think So*), tr. in Three Plays; tr. as And That's the Truth, by Livingston, 1925, and acted in N. Y. as Right You Are If You Think You Are; *Man, Beast, and Virtue*, tr. by Alice Rohe, 1923, and as Say It With Flowers, 1926; *As Before and Better* (*Come prima meglio di prima*), adapted as Floriani's Wife by Ann Sprague MacDonald, 1923; *By Judgment of the Court*, tr. as Legal Title by Elisabeth Abbott, 1923, and in The One-Act Plays; *Six Characters in Search of an Author*, tr. by Mrs. A. W. Green, 1922; tr. by Edward Storer in Broom, v. 2 and 3, 1922, and in Three Plays; *Henry IV*, tr. by Storer in Three Plays, and acted as The Living Mask, 1924; *Naked*, tr. by Livingston in Each in His Own Way and Two Other Plays, and in T. H. Dickinson, Chief Contemporary Dramatists, 3rd series, 1930; *The Life I Gave Thee*, tr. as The Life I Gave to Thee (The Mother), by Livingston, 1923; *The Man With a Flower in His Mouth*, tr. by Livingston, 1923; tr. in The One-Act Plays;

Each In His Own Way, tr. by Livingston in Each In His Own Way and Two Other Plays; *Our Lord of the Ship,* tr. in The One-Act Plays; *The Jar,* tr. in The One-Act Plays; *The House With a Column,* tr. in The One-Act Plays; *Lazzaro,* tr. by C. K. Scott-Moncrieff, 1929; *He Didn't Mean It,* tr. by Leo Ongley, 1923; *The Game As He Played It,* tr. by C. K. Scott-Moncrieff, 1927.

PISEMSKY, ALEKSYEY FEOFILAKTOVICH

The Hypochondriac, 1852; *The Division,* 1853; *The Veteran and The Recruit,* 1854; *Bitter Fate,* 1859; *Lieutenant Gladkov,* 1867; *Experienced Falcons,* 1868; *Rapacious Beasts,* 1873; *Baal,* 1873; *Enlightened Times,* 1875; *A Financial Genius,* 1876; *The Last Fledgelings,* 1886; *The Miloslavskis and Naryshkins,* 1886; *The Family Whirlpool,* 1886; *The Fighters and the Temporizers,* 1886; *The Rival Mothers,* 1886.

IN ENGLISH: *Baal,* tr. as The Worshippers of Baal, by F. O. Dempsey, 1928.

PLETNEV, V. F.

Over the Top, 1921; *Lena,* 1921.

PORCHÉ, FRANÇOIS

The Ruffians and Finette (Les Butors et la Finette), 1917; *The Girl With the Rosy Cheeks,* 1919; *The Dauphine,* 1921; *The Knight of Columbus,* 1922; *The Virgin With the Great Heart (Jeanne d'Arc),* 1925.

PORTO-RICHE, GEORGES DE

Vertigo, 1873; *A Drama Under Philip II,* 1875; *The Two Faults,* 1879; *Vanina,* 1879; *The Luck of Françoise,* 1888; *The Unfaithful Woman,* 1890; *The Impassioned Wife (L'Amoureuse),* 1891; *The Past,* 1898; *The Malefilâtres,* 1904; *The Old Man,* 1911; *Zubiri,* 1912; *The Merchant of Prints,* 1918.

IN ENGLISH: *The Luck of Françoise,* tr. as Françoise's Luck, by B. H. Clark in Four Plays of the Free Theater, 1915, and in Frank Shay and Pierre Loving, Fifty Contemporary One-Act Plays, 1920, and in M. J. Moses, Representative One-Act Plays by Continental Authors, 1923; *The Impassioned Wife,* tr. by C. A. Byrne, 1904; adapted as Cupid's Rival, by M. Walsh, 1904; adapted as The Tyranny of Love, by H. A. Baron, 1920; tr. as A Loving Wife, by J. P. W. Crawford in T. H. Dickinson, Chief Contemporary Dramatists, 2d series, 1921; *The Old Man,* adapted as The Old Adam, by E. Goodman, 1921.

POTYEKHIN, A. A.

Men's Judgment is Not God's, 1853; *A Love Marriage,* 1861; *The Cut-Off Piece,* 1865; *Guilty,* 1867; *Knights of Our Time,* 1869; *In Turbid Waters,* 1869; *A Profitable Undertaking,* 1877; *About Money,* 1883; *The Patient* (with V. A. Krylov), 1894; etc.

BIBLIOGRAPHY

PRAGA, MARCO

The Friend, 1886; *Giuliana*, 1888; *The Spell*, 1888; *Mater Dolorosa*, 1888; *The Virgins*, 1889; *The Ideal Wife*, 1890; *The Enamoured Woman*, 1891; *Alleluja*, 1892; *The Heir*, 1893; *The Nun*, 1893; *The Fair Apollo*, 1893; *The Doubt*, 1893; *Ondina*, 1903; *The Moral of the Fable*, 1904; *The Crisis*, 1905; *The Closed Door*, 1913; *The Divorce*, 1915.

IN ENGLISH: *The Ideal Wife*, tr. by Mrs. T. C. Crawford, and played, London, 1913; *The Crisis*, tr. as The Ordeal, by Dirce St. Cyr, 1908; *Born to Sin*, adapted by A. Ludovici, 1921; *The Closed Door*, tr. by Arthur Clyde, 1922; tr. by A. S. MacDonald in O. M. Sayler, The Eleonora Duse Series of Plays, 1923.

RAYNAL, PAUL

The Master of His Heart, 1920; *To the Sun of Instinct; La Francerie; The Apotheosis of Life; The Tomb Beneath the Arc de Triomphe*, 1924.

IN ENGLISH: *The Tomb Beneath the Arc de Triomphe*, tr. as The Unknown Warrior by Cecil Lewis, 1928.

REICKE, GEORGE

The Fair Melusine, 1901.

RENARD, JULES

The Pleasure of Breaking Off, 1898; *Home-made Bread (Le Pain de Ménage)*, 1898; *Carrot Top (Poil de Carotte)*, 1900; *Monsieur Vernet*, 1903; *Eight Days in the Country*, 1906; *The Fair Bigot*, 1909.

IN ENGLISH: *The Pleasure of Breaking Off*, tr. as Good-Bye! by B. H. Clark in Smart Set, 1916; *Home-made Bread*, tr. as Daily Bread, by Vaughan Thomas, 1902; tr. by L. A. Loiseaux, 1917; *Carrot Top*, tr. as Carrots, by Alfred Sutro, 1904.

RENNER, GUSTAV

Ahasuerus, 1904; *Merlin*, 1905; *Alcestis*, 1906; *Francesca da Rimini*, 1909; *Dark Powers*, 1911.

RICHEPIN, JEAN

Bird Lime (La Glu), 1883; *Nana Sahib*, 1883; *Macbeth*, 1884; *The Filibuster*, 1888; *Watch Dog*, 1889; *By the Sword*, 1892; *Towards Joy*, 1894; *Vagabond (Le Chemineau)*, 1897; *Fair Martyr (La Martyre)*, 1898; *Truands*, 1899; *Mademoiselle Napoleon*, 1903; *Miarka*, 1905; *The Du Barry*, 1905; *Don Quixote*, 1905; *Beauty in the Sleeping Wood*, 1908; *The Emerald Way (La Route d'émeraude)*, 1909; *La Beffa*, from *The Jest* of Sem Benelli, 1910; *The Bellringer*, 1913.

MODERN CONTINENTAL PLAYWRIGHTS

IN ENGLISH: *Nana Sahib*, tr. by H. A. D'Arcy and Theodore F. Schatie, 1884; *The Filibuster*, adapted as The Grandsire, by W. Archer Woodhouse, 1889; *Watch Dog*, tr. by C. Renauld, 1890; *Vagabond*, adapted as The Rover, by C. Renauld, 1897; adapted as a lyric opera, by F. H. Martens, 1917; *Mademoiselle Napoléon*, adapted as a musical comedy, by Joseph Herbert, 1903; *Beauty in the Sleeping Wood*, adapted as The Sleeping Beauty, by A. M. Herts, with music by Francis Thomé, 1911.

ROLLAND, ROMAIN

St. Louis, 1897; *Aërt*, 1898; *The Wolves*, 1898; *The Triumph of Reason*, 1899; *Danton*, 1899; *The Fourteenth of July*, 1902; *The Time Will Come*, 1903; *The Montespan*, 1904; *The Three Loving Ladies*, 1904; *Liluli*, 1919; *The Game of Love and Death*, 1925; *Palm Sunday (Pâques-Fleuries)*, 1926; *Shooting Stars (Les Léonides)*, 1928.

IN ENGLISH: B. H. Clark, The Fourteenth of July and Danton, Two Plays of the French Revolution, 1918; Helena Van B. DeKay, Plays of Romain Rolland, The Montespan and Liluli, 1927; *The Wolves*, tr. by B. H. Clark in The Drama, 1918; tr. by H. J. Biberman, 1925; *Danton* and *The Fourteenth of July*, tr. in Two Plays of the French Revolution; *The Montespan*, tr. by DeKay, 1923, and in Plays of Romain Rolland; *Liluli*, tr. by Frans Masereel, 1920; tr. by DeKay in Plays of Romain Rolland; *The Game of Love and Death*, tr. by Eleanor S. Brooks, 1926; *Palm Sunday*, tr. by Eugene Löhrke, 1928; *Shooting Stars*, tr. under the French title, Les Léonides, by Eugene Löhrke, 1929.

ROMAINS, JULES

The Army in the Town, 1911; *Cromedyre-le-Vieil*, 1912; *M. Trouhadec Seized by Dissipation*, 1922; *Amédée and the Gentlemen in Rows*, 1923; *Dr. Knock*, 1924; *The Scintillant Lady*, 1924; *The Marriage of le Trouhadec*, 1925; *Démétrios*, 1925; *The Dictator*, 1926; *Jean le Maufranc*, 1926; *Donogoo*, 1930.

IN ENGLISH: *Amédée and the Gentlemen in Rows*, tr. as Six Gentlemen in a Row by H. Granville-Barker, 1927; *Doctor Knock*, tr. by H. Granville-Barker, 1925.

ROSMER, ERNST (ELSA BERNSTEIN)

We Three, 1889; *Twilight*, 1894; *The King's Children*, (with Humperdinck's music), 1894; *TeDeum*, 1896; *Themistocles*, 1897; *Mother Maria*, 1900; *Johannes Herkner*, 1904; *Nausikaa*, 1906; *Maria Arndt*, 1908; *Achilles*, 1910.

IN ENGLISH: *Twilight*, tr. by Paul H. Grummann in Poet Lore 23, 1912; *The King's Children*, adapted as Kingly Children, a fairy opera, and tr. by C. H. Meltzer, 1910; *Johannes Herkner*, tr. as John Herkner by Mary Harned in Poet Lore 22, 1911.

ROSSELLI, AMALIA

The Soul, 1901; *Illusion*, 1906.

646

BIBLIOGRAPHY

ROSTAND, EDMOND

The Red Glove, 1888; *The Two Pierrots*, 1891; *The Romancers*, 1894; *The Princess Faraway*, 1895; *The Woman of Samaria*, 1897; *Cyrano de Bergerac*, 1897; *The Eaglet* (*L'Aiglon*), 1900; *Chantecler*, 1910; *The Sacred Wood*, 1910; *The Last Night of Don Juan*, 1921.

IN ENGLISH: H. D. Norman, Plays of Edmond Rostand (omitting the first two and the last two), 2 vols., 1921; *The Two Pierrots*, tr. as Weeping Pierrot and Laughing Pierrot, by Amy Lowell, 1914; tr. by Edith Lyttleton, and played, London, 1915; *The Romancers*, tr. by Mary Hendee, 1899; tr. as The Fantasticks, by G. Fleming, 1900; tr. by B. H. Clark, 1915; and in M. M. Smith, Short Plays of Various Types, 1924; tr. by Anna E. Bagstad in Poet Lore 32, 1921; tr. as The Romantics in Plays, v. 1; tr. in George R. Coffman, A Book of Modern Plays, 1925; tr. in George A. Goldstone, One-Act Plays, 1920; *The Princess Faraway*, tr. by Charles Renauld, 1899; adapted as The Lady of Dreams by Louis N. Parker, 1913; tr. by Anna E. Bag stad, 1921; tr. in Plays, v. 1; tr. as The Far Princess, by J. Heard, Jr., 1925; *The Woman of Samaria*, tr. in Plays, v. 1; *Cyrano de Bergerac*, tr. by Gertrude Hall, 1898, and in T. H. Dickinson, Chief Contemporary Dramatists, 2d series, 1921, and in M. J. Moses, Representative Continental Dramas, 1924, and in S. M. Tucker, Modern Continental Plays, 1929; tr. by C. F. Rideal, 1898; tr. by H. T. Kingsbury, 1898; tr. by Charles Renauld, 1898; tr. by George Bertram, 1898; tr. by Helen B. Dole, 1899; and in Robert M. Smith, Types of Romantic Drama, 1928; adapted by Malcolm S. Taylor, 1899; adapted as Cyrano de Bergerac or A Soldier of Fortune, comic opera, by H. B. Smith, 1899; tr. by Gladys Thomas and Mary F. Guillemard, 1900; adapted as an opera by W. J. Henderson, 1913; tr. by Norman in Plays, v. 1; tr. by Brian Hooker, 1923; *The Eaglet*, tr. as L'Aiglon by Louis N. Parker, 1900; tr. by Norman in Plays, v. 2; tr. as L'Aiglon by Basil Davenport, 1927; *Chantecler*, tr. by Hall, 1910; tr. by J. S. Newberry, 1911; tr. by Louis N. Parker, 1911; tr. by Norman in Plays, v. 2; *The Last Night of Don Juan*, tr. by Sidney Howard, 1925; tr. as Don Juan's Last Night, by Julian Leigh, 1925; tr. by T. Lawrason Riggs, 1929.

ROVETTA, GEROLAMO

A Flight From the Nest, 1875; *The Wife of Don Giovanni*, 1877; *The Dream*, 1878; *Blind Anger*, 1878; *Practical Men*, 1879; *The Fair Rogue*, 1882; *Countess Maria*, 1884; *To the City of Rome*, 1888; *The Trilogy of Dorina*, 1889; *The Dishonest*, 1892; *The Hubbub*, 1894; *Reality*, 1895; *Madame Fanny*, 1895; *Beginning of the Century*, 1896; *The Olive Branch*, 1897; *The Poet*, 1897; *The Young Wife*, 1898; *Romanticism*, 1901; *The Buffoon King*, 1904; *The Day of Confirmation*, 1905; *Papa Eccelenza*, 1906; *Molière and His Wife*, 1909; etc.

IN ENGLISH: *Blind Anger*, tr. by E. F. Davis, 1912; *The Trilogy of Dorina*, tr. as Dorina, by Pierre Troubetzkoy, 1919; *Romanticism*, played in English, 1919; *The Rib of Decision*, adapted by Dirce St. Cyr and Witter Bynner, 1908; *Molière and His Wife*, tr. by P. and A. Troubetzkoy, 1920.

MODERN CONTINENTAL PLAYWRIGHTS

SAMAIN, ALBERT

Polyphemus, 1905.

SAN SECONDO, PIER MARIA ROSSO DI

What Passion, Ye Marionettes! 1918; *Bringing the Dawn (Per fare l'Alba),* 1919; *Amara,* 1919; *The Sleeping Beauty,* 1919; *Spring,* 1920; *The Host Desired,* 1921; *Sins of Youth,* 1923; *Rogues and Knives (Lazzarini fra i coltelli),* 1923; *The Dance on One Foot,* 1923; *The Rock and the Monuments,* 1923; *A Matter of Flesh,* 1924; *The Terrestrial Adventure,* 1924; *The Stairs,* 1925; *The Illusion of Days and Nights,* 1926; *The Experiences of Giovanni Arca, Philosopher,* 1926; etc.

IN ENGLISH: *What Passion, Ye Marionettes!* tr. as Puppets and Passions, by Eduardo Cianelli, 1925, and adapted as Puppets of Passion by Cianelli and Ernest Boyd, 1926; *The Sleeping Beauty,* tr. by Alice Rohe, 1923; *The Stairs,* tr. by W. Katzin in Eight European Plays, 1927; adapted by Dario Forza, 1927.

SARDOU, VICTORIEN

The Students' Tavern, 1854; *Figaro's First Weapons,* 1859; *Nervous Folk* (with Barrière), 1859; *M. Garat,* 1860; *Fly Tracks (Les Pattes de Mouche),* 1860; *Strong Women,* 1860; *Our Intimates,* 1861; *The Black Pearl,* 1862; *Numbskulls (Les Ganaches),* 1862; *Les Papillones,* 1862; *Black Devils,* 1863; *Apples of Your Neighbor,* 1864; *The Old Bachelors,* 1865; *The Benoîton Family,* 1865; *Our Good Villagers,* 1866; *The New House,* 1866; *Séraphine,* 1868; *Fatherland (Patrie),* 1869; *Fernande,* 1870; *Rabagas,* 1872; *Andréa,* 1873; *Uncle Sam,* 1873; *The Marvellous Ones,* 1873; *Hatred,* 1874; *Ferréol,* 1875; *Dora* (later *The Spy*), 1877; *The Bourgeois of Pont Arcy,* 1878; *Daniel Rochat,* 1880; *Let Us Divorce* (with de Najac), 1880; *Odette,* 1881; *Fédora,* 1882; *Théodora,* 1884; *Georgette,* 1885; *The Crocodile,* 1886; *La Tosca* (with Illica and Giacosa), 1887; *The Marquise,* 1889; *Cleopatra* (with Emile Moreau), 1890; *Thermidor,* 1891; *Americans Abroad,* 1892; *Madame Sans-Gêne* (with Moreau), 1893; *Gismonda,* 1894; *Marcelle,* 1895; *Don Quixote,* 1895; *Pamela,* 1898; *Robespierre,* 1899; *Dante* (with Moreau), 1903; *The Sorceress,* 1903; *The Trail,* 1906; *The Affair of the Poisons,* 1907; and a score of other plays.

IN ENGLISH: *Fly Tracks (Les Pattes de Mouche),* adapted as A Scrap of Paper, by Frederick Fenn, 1861; adapted as A Scrap of Paper, or The Adventures of a Love Letter, by J. P. Simpson, 1861; *Our Intimates,* tr. as Friends and Foes, by H. Wigan, in Lacy's Acting Edition, v. 54; tr. as Our Friends, by George March in French's Acting Version, v. 115, 1872; tr. as Our Boon Companions, by Frederic Lyster; *Numbskulls (Les Ganaches),* tr. as Progress, by T. W. Robertson in French's Acting Version, v. 133; *The Black Pearl,* tr. by Barrett H. Clark, 1915; *Fatherland (Patrie),* tr. by Clark, 1915; *Fernande,* adapted as Fernando, or Forgive and Forget, by Henry L. Williams, Jr., 1870; adapted by James Schönberg, 1871; *Ferréol,* adapted as Above Suspicion, by William Morpeth, 1911; *Dora,* adapted as Diplomacy,

BIBLIOGRAPHY

by B. C. Stephenson and Clement Scott, 1878; tr. as Diplomates, by H. L. Williams, 1894; *The Bourgeois of Pont Arcy*, tr. as Duty, by James Albery in French's Acting Version, v. 127; *Daniel Rochat*, tr. by J. V. Pritchard, 1880; *Divorçons*, adapted as Let's Get a Divorce, Chicago, 1909; adapted by Margaret Mayo, 1914; adapted as Let Us Divorce, by I. Thompson Buchanan, 1917; *Fédora*, adapted as narrative by Antonio Bracco, 1893; adapted as lyric drama with music by Umberto Giordano, 1896; *Théodora*, novelized, 1888; *La Tosca*, in Italian and English, 1900; "versed" by Walter Howgrave, 1925; tr. by C. H. Meltzer, 1926; *Madame Sans-Gêne*, tr. as Madame Don't Care, by I. G. Reed, Jr., 1895; tr. as Madame Devil-May-Care, by C. H. Meltzer, 1901, 1929; *Robespierre*, adapted and novelized by A. Galdemar, 1899; *Dante*, tr. by Laurence Irving, 1903; tr. by "an Italian student", 1903; *The Sorceress*, tr. by Charles A. Weissert, 1917; adapted as a musical drama by Dillon Shallard, 1919; *Love and Science*, tr. by Henry Bedlow, 1887; *Dolores*, adapted by B. Kiralfy, 1926.

SARMENT, JEAN

The Pasteboard Crown, 1920; *The Shadow Fisher*, 1921; *The Marriage of Hamlet*, 1922; *I Am Too Great For Myself*, 1924; *Madelon*, 1925; *The Most Beautiful Eyes in the World*, 1925; *Have You A Heart?* 1926; *Leopold the Well Beloved*, 1927; *Aboard My Fine Ship*, 1928.

IN ENGLISH: *The Pasteboard Crown*, tr. as The Cardboard Crown by Carrie R. Carns, 1921.

SAVOIR, ALFRED

The Third Cover, 1906; *Before Death*, 1920; *A Woman of Luxury*, 1921; *Banco*, 1922; *The Eighth Wife of Bluebeard*, 1921; *What Woman Wants*, 1924; *The Grand Duchess and the Waiter*, 1924; *The Kreutzer Sonata*, 1924; *The Tamer or English As It Is Eaten (Le Dompteur)*, 1925, after a story by Jacques Théry; *The Christening; The Ballet Dancer of the Gaiety*, 1926; *Passy 0845*, 1928; *The Cocktail*, 1928; *He (Lui)*, 1929.

IN ENGLISH: *The Eighth Wife of Bluebeard*, adapted as Bluebeard's Eighth Wife by Charlton Andrews, 1921, and by A. Wimperis, 1922; *The Grand Duchess and the Waiter*, adapted as The Grand Duchess by Harry Graham, 1925; *The Tamer*, tr. as The Lion Tamer by Winifred Katzin, 1926; adapted as The Lion Tamer by D. Titheradge, 1926; *Banco*, adapted by Clare Kummer, 1922; *The Christening* (with Nozière), adapted by Mark Soliterman and C. J. Teller, 1925.

SCHMIDTBONN, WILHELM

Mother Landstrasse, 1901; *The Golden Door*, 1904; *The Count of Gleichen*, 1908; *The Wrath of Achilles*, 1909; *Help! A Child Has Fallen From Heaven*, 1910; *Playful Eros*, 1911; *The Lost Son*, 1912; *The City of Demoniacs*, 1915; *The Stricken*, 1920; *Actors*, 1921; *Journey to Orplid*, 1922; *Maruf, the Foolish Liar*, 1924; *The Parson of Mainz*, 1927; etc.

IN ENGLISH: *The Lost Son*, adapted as The Wanderer, by Maurice V. Samuels, 1917; *Help*, tr. by A. S. McDonald and J. L. A. Burrell, 1926.

MODERN CONTINENTAL PLAYWRIGHTS

SCHNITZLER, ARTHUR

Anatol, 1893; *The Fairy Tale*, 1894; *Light o' Love* (*Liebelei*), 1895; *Fair Game*, 1896; *The Legacy*, 1898; *The Companion*, 1899; *Paracelsus*, 1899; *The Green Cockatoo*, 1899; *Hands Around* (*Reigen*), 1900; *The Veil of Beatrice*, 1901; *The Lady With the Dagger*, 1902; *Living Hours*, 1902; *The Last Masks*, 1902; *Literature*, 1902; *The Lonely Way*, 1904; *Intermezzo*, 1905; *The Puppet Player*, 1906; *Gallant Cassian*, 1906; *The Call of Life*, 1906; *Countess Mizzi*, 1909; *Young Medardus*, 1910; *The Wide Domain*, 1911; *Professor Bernhardi*, 1912; *The Big Scene*, 1915; *The Hour of Recognition*, 1915; *The Festival of Bacchus*, 1915; *Fink and Fliederbusch*, 1917; *The Sisters*, 1918; *The Comedy of Seduction*, 1924; *The Path to the Pond*, 1926.

IN ENGLISH: Horace B. Samuel, The Green Cockatoo and Other Plays, 1913 and 1914; Edwin Björkman, Three Plays, 1915; Grace I. Colbron, Anatol, Living Hours, The Green Cockatoo, 1917; Pierre Loving, Comedies of Words and Other Plays, 1917; *The Affairs of Anatol*, paraphrased as Anatol by Granville Barker, 1911; tr. as Anatol by Grace I. Colbron; *A Christmas Present* (from The Affairs of Anatol), paraphrased by Barker in The International, v. 4, 1911; *An Episode* (from The Affairs of Anatol), paraphrased by Barker, *ibid.; Questioning the Irrevocable* (from The Affairs of Anatol), tr. by W. H. H. Chambers in The Drama 12, 1903; *A Farewell Supper* (from The Affairs of Anatol), tr. by Edith A. Browne and Mrs. Alix Grein, and played, England, 1908; *The Fairy Tale*, adapted by Mrs. Nina Lewton, 1909; tr. by C. E. Wheeler and Granville Barker, and played, London, 1913; *Light o' Love*, tr. by Colbron, 1907; played as The Reckoning, 1907; tr. by G. Valentine Williams, and played, London, 1909; tr. by B. Q. Morgan in The Drama 7, 1912, and in S. M. Tucker, Modern Continental Plays, 1929; tr. as Playing With Love by P. Morton Shand, 1914; *Fair Game*, tr. as Free Game by P. H. Grummann in Poet Lore 24, 1913; *The Legacy*, tr. by Mary L. Stephenson in Poet Lore 22, 1911; *The Companion*, abridged as The Wife, in Current Literature v. 39, 1905; tr. as The Mate, by Samuel in The Green Cockatoo and Other Plays; tr. as His Helpmeet, by Loving in The International v. 9, 1915; and as His Helpmate, in Comedies of Words and Other Plays; *Paracelsus*, tr. by Samuel in The Green Cockatoo and Other Plays; *The Green Cockatoo*, tr. by Philip Littell and George Rublec, 1910; tr. as The Duke and the Actress, by Hans Weysz in Poet Lore 21, 1910; tr. by Penelope Wheeler, 1913; tr. by Samuel in The Green Cockatoo and Other Plays, and in Francke and Howard, German Classics, v. 20, 1914; tr. by Colbron in Anatol, Living Hours, The Green Cockatoo; *Hands Around* (*Reigen*), tr. by L. D. Edwards and F. L. Glaser, 1920; *The Lady With the Dagger*, tr. by H. T. Porter in Poet Lore 15, 1904; tr. as The Woman With the Dagger, by Samuel in The Fortnightly Review v. 91, 1909; abridged as The Woman With the Dagger, in The International v. 4, 1911; tr. as The Woman With the Dagger, by P. H. Grummann in Poet Lore 24, 1913; tr. by Colbron in Anatol, Living Hours, The Green Cockatoo, and in T. H. Dickinson, Chief Contemporary Dramatists, 2d series, 1921; *Living Hours*, tr. by H. T. Porter in Poet Lore 17, 1906; abridged as Vital Moments by Edward Goodman in The International v. 3, 1910; tr. by P. H. Grummann in Poet Lore 24, 1913; tr. by Porter Davitts in Pierre Loving, Ten-Minute Plays, 1923;

BIBLIOGRAPHY

The Last Masks, tr. by Grummann in Poet Lore 24, 1913; tr. by Colbron in Anatol, Living Hours, The Green Cockatoo; *Literature,* tr. by Elsie Plaut, and played, N. Y., 1908; tr. by Edith A. Browne and Mrs. Alix Grein, and played, England, 1908; adapted as The Literary Sense by Charles H. Genung, 1908; tr. by P. H. Grummann in Poet Lore 24, 1913; tr. by A. I. du P. Coleman in Francke and Howard, German Classics, v. 20; tr. by Loving in The International v. 9, 1915, and in Comedies of Words and Other Plays, and in Shay and Loving, Fifty Contemporary One-Act Plays, 1920; tr. by Colbron in Anatol, Living Hours, The Green Cockatoo; *The Lonely Way,* tr. by Björkman in Three Plays, and in M. J. Moses, Representative Continental Dramas, 1924; *Intermezzo,* tr. by Björkman in Three Plays; *Gallant Cassian,* tr. by Adam L. Gowans, 1914; tr. by M. A. Jagendorf in Poet Lore 33, 1922; *The Call of Life,* tr. by Dorothy Donnelly, 1925; *Countess Mizzie,* tr. as Comtesse Mitzi, by H. A. Hertz, 1914; tr. by Björkman in Three Plays, and in M. J. Moses, Representative One-Act Plays by Continental Authors, 1923; *The Wide Domain,* tr. as The Vast Domain, by Edward Woticky, 1921, and (with A. Caro) in Poet Lore 34, 1923; *Professor Bernhardi,* tr. by Mrs. E. Pohli, 1913; tr. by Hetty Landstone, 1928; *The Big Scene,* tr. by Pierre Loving in Comedies of Words and Other Plays; tr. by C. H. Meltzer, and played, N. Y., 1919; *The Festival of Bacchus,* adapted as The Feast of Bacchus, by H. A. Boas, 1916; tr. by Loving in The International v. 10, 1916, in Comedies of Words and Other Plays, and in Frank Shay, Twenty-five Short Plays, International, 1924; *The Hour of Recognition,* tr. by Loving in The International v. 10, 1916, and in Comedies of Words and Other Plays; *None But the Brave,* tr. by R. L. Simon, 1926; *Genial Remedies,* tr. by William Dunbar, 1920.

SCHOLZ, WILHELM VON

My Prince, 1898; *The Besieged (Besiegte),* 1898; *The Guest,* 1900; *The Jew of Constance,* 1905; *Meroë,* 1906; *The Race With the Shadow,* 1920.

IN ENGLISH: *The Race With the Shadow,* tr. by Graham and Tristan Rawson, 1921.

SCHÖNHERR, KARL

The Carvers, 1895; *Solstice Day,* 1902; *Caravan Folk,* 1904; *The Family,* 1905; *Earth,* 1907; *The Kingdom,* 1908; *Faith and Fatherland,* 1910; *The Trenkwalder,* 1914; *The She-Devil,* 1914; *Folk in Need,* 1915; *Frau Suitner,* 1916; *The Fool's Game of Life (Narrenspiel des Lebens),* 1918; *The Children's Tragedy,* 1919; *The Struggle (Der Kampf),* 1920; *Vivat Academia,* 1922; *May Dance,* 1922; *Hunger Blockade,* 1925; *The Doctor of the Poor,* 1926; *Judas of the Tyrol,* 1927.

IN ENGLISH: *Faith and Fatherland,* tr. as Faith and Fireside by Edmund von Mach in K. Francke and W. G. Howard, German Classics, v. 16, 1913–1914; *The Children's Tragedy,* tr. as Tragic Youth by Amelia von Ende, 1920.

SERVAES, FRANZ

Maiden Ambrosia, 1905.

MODERN CONTINENTAL PLAYWRIGHTS

SIGURJÓNSSON, JÓHANN

Eyvind of the Hills, 1911; *The Hraun Farm*, 1912.

IN ENGLISH: H. K. Schanche, Modern Icelandic Plays, 1916; *Eyvind of the Hills*, tr. as Eyvind of the Mountains by Sir Sydney Olivier, 1915; tr. in Modern Icelandic Plays; tr. in T. H. Dickinson, Chief Contemporary Dramatists, 3d series, 1930; *The Hraun Farm*, tr. in Modern Icelandic Plays, and in Alice M. Smith, Short Plays by Representative Authors, 1922.

SÖDERBERG, HJALMAR

Gertrud, 1906; *The Evening Star*, 1912; *The Hour of Fate*, 1922.

SOLOGUB, FYODOR

The Triumph of Death, 1907; *Liturgy to Me*, 1907; *The Gift of the Wise Bees; To Love; Night Dances*, 1908; *Vanka the Butler and Page Jean*, 1909; *Hostages of Life*, 1916; *A Stone Cast Into Water* (with Chebotarevsky), 1916; *The Rose Design*, 1921; *The Guardian of the Great King*, 1921.

IN ENGLISH: *The Triumph of Death*, tr. by John Cournos in The Drama, 1916; *His Hat and Cane* and *The Serenade*, tr. in Plays for Private Acting.

SORGE, REINHARD

The Beggar, 1912; *Guntwar, the School of a Prophet*, 1914; *Metanoeite* (Three Mysteries), 1915; *King David*, 1916; *Mystic Dialogues*, 1922; *The Victory of the Christ*, 1924 (the last two issued posthumously).

SOULIÉ, MAURICE

1914–1937, 1916.

STERNHEIM, CARL

Don Juan, 1910; *The Trousers (Die Hose)*, 1911; *The Treasure Chest*, 1912; *Burgher Schippel*, 1913; *The Snob*, 1913; *The Candidate*, 1913; *The Needle*, 1915; *1913*, 1915; *Tabula Rasa*, 1916; *Perleberg*, 1917; *Unchained Contemporaries*, 1920; *Berlin, or Juste Milieu*, 1920; *The Marquise of Arcis*, 1920; *Manon Lescaut*, 1921; *Libussa*, 1922; *The Weakling (Der Nebbich)*, 1922; *The Fossil*, 1923; *Oscar Wilde*, 1924; *The School of Uznach*, 1926.

IN ENGLISH: *The Snob*, tr. as A Place in the World, by B. H. Clark and Winifred Katzin in Eight European Plays, 1927.

STRAMM, AUGUST

Rudimentary, 1914; *Powers*, 1915, etc.

IN ENGLISH: *The Bride of the Moor*, tr. by E. J. O'Brien in Poet Lore 25, 1914; *Sancta Susanna (The Song of a May Night)*, tr. by O'Brien in Poet Lore 25, 1914.

BIBLIOGRAPHY

STRINDBERG, AUGUST

The Freethinker, 1869; *Hermione*, 1869; *In Rome*, 1870; *The Outlaw*, 1871; *Master Olof*, 1872; *The Secret of the Guild*, 1880; *The Year 'Forty-Eight*, 1881; *Sir Bengt's Wife*, 1882; *The Journey of Lucky Peter*, 1883; *The Father*, 1887; *Miss Julie*, 1888; *Comrades*, 1888; *Creditors*, 1890; *The Stronger*, 1890; *Pariah*, 1890; *Facing Death*, 1890; *Simoom*, 1890; *The Keys of Heaven*, 1892; *The First Warning*, 1893; *Debit and Credit*, 1893; *Mother-love*, 1893; *The Link*, 1897; *To Damascus I; To Damascus II*, 1898; *There Are Crimes and Crimes*, 1899; *Advent*, 1899; *The Saga of the Folkungs*, 1899; *Gustavus Vasa*, 1899; *Eric XIV*, 1899; *Gustavus Adolphus*, 1900; *The Dance of Death* (2 parts), 1901; *Engelbrecht*, 1901; *Charles XII*, 1901; *Swanwhite*, 1901; *Midsummer*, 1901; *Easter*, 1901; *The Dream Play*, 1902; *The Crown Bride*, 1902; *Christina*, 1903; *Gustavus III*, 1903; *The Nightingale in Wittenberg*, 1903; *To Damascus III*, 1904; *The Thunderstorm*, 1907; *The Burned Lot*, 1907; *The Spook Sonata*, 1907; *The Pelican*, 1907; *The Last Knight*, 1908; *The Slippers of Abu Casem*, 1908; *The Earl of Bjälbo*, 1909; *The National Director*, 1909; *The Great Highway*, 1909; *The Black Glove*, 1909; *The Tooth*, 1909.

IN ENGLISH: Edwin Björkman: Plays, Miss Julia, The Stronger, 1912; Creditors, Pariah, 1912; Edith and Warner Oland, Plays, 3 vols., 1912–1914; Björkman, Plays by August Strindberg, 4 series, 1912–1916; Miss Julie and Other Plays, 1918; H. B. Samuel, Two Plays by August Strindberg, 1914; Easter and Other Plays, Anglo-Swedish Literary Foundation, 1929; *The Outlaw*, tr. by E. and W. Oland in Plays, v. 1; *Master Olof*, tr. by Edwin Björkman, 1915; *The Journey of Lucky Peter*, tr. as Lucky Pehr by Velma S. Howard, 1912; *The Father*, tr. by N. Erichsen, 1899, 1907; tr. by Oland in Plays, v. 1; tr. by Erichsen in T. H. Dickinson, Chief Contemporary Dramatists, 1st series, 1915; tr. in Robert M. Smith, Types of Domestic Tragedy, 1928; *Miss Julie*, tr. as Julie by Arthur Swan in Poet Lore 22, 1911; tr. as Miss Julia by Björkman in Plays: Miss Julia, The Stronger; tr. by Björkman in Plays, series 2; tr. as Countess Julia by Charles Recht, 1912; tr. as Countess Julie by Oland in Plays, v. 1; tr. as Miss Julia by Lucy Carr Shaw and Maurice Elvey, and played, London, 1913; tr. in Miss Julie and Other Plays; *Comrades*, tr. by H. B. Samuel, 1914; tr. by Oland in Plays, v. 2, and in Tucker, Modern Continental Plays, 1929; *Creditors*, tr. as The Creditor by F. J. Ziegler, 1910; tr. as The Creditor by Mary Harned in Poet Lore 22, 1911; tr. by Björkman in Plays: Creditors, Pariah; tr. by Ellie Schleussner, 1913; tr. by Björkman in Plays, series 2; tr. in Miss Julie and Other Plays; tr. as The Creditor in Frank Shay and Pierre Loving, Fifty Contemporary One-Act Plays, 1920; *The Stronger*, tr. by Ziegler in Poet Lore 17, 1906; tr. as The Stronger Woman by Edith A. Browne and Frank Schloesser, 1909, and in Frank Shay, A Treasury of Plays for Women, 1922; tr. by Oland in The International 4, 1911, and in Plays, v. 1; tr. by Björkman in Plays: Miss Julia, The Stronger, and in Plays, series 2; tr. as The Stronger Woman in Miss Julie and Other Plays; tr. by Björkman in B. R. Lewis, Contemporary One-Act Plays, 1922; tr. by Charles Wangel in Pierre Loving, Ten-Minute Plays, 1923; *Pariah*, tr. as The Outcast by Mary Harned in Poet Lore 17, 1906, and 1913; tr. by Oland in Plays, v. 2; tr. by Björkman in Plays: Creditors,

Pariah, and in Plays, series 2; tr. by Samuel in Two Plays; tr. in Miss Julie and Other Plays; *Facing Death*, tr. by Oland in The Dramatist, 1911, and in Plays, v. 2; *Simoom*, tr. by Harned in Poet Lore 17, 1906, and separately, 1913; tr. by Björkman in Smart Set 40, 1913, and in Plays, series 3; tr. by Samuel in Two Plays; tr. in Miss Julie and Other Plays; tr. by Harned in M. J. Moses, Representative One-Act Plays by Continental Authors, 1923; *The First Warning*, tr. by Velma S. Howard, 1907; tr. by Björkman in Plays, series 4; *Debit and Credit*, tr. by Harned in Poet Lore 17, 1906, and separately, 1913; tr. by Björkman in Plays, series 3; *Motherlove*, tr. by F. J. Ziegler, 1910; tr. as Motherly Love in Miss Julie and Other Plays, and in Shay, A Treasury of Plays for Women, 1922; *The Link*, tr. by Björkman in Plays, series 1; *There Are Crimes and Crimes*, tr. by Björkman, 1912, and in Plays, series 2; *Advent*, tr. by Oland in Plays, v. 3; tr. by Björkman in Plays, series 3; tr. by Claud Field, 1914; *Gustavus Vasa*, tr. by Björkman in Plays, series 4; *The Dance of Death*, tr. by Björkman in Plays, series 1; abridged by Henry Stillman, 1920, from Björkman's translation; tr. by C. D. Locock in Easter and Other Plays; *Swanwhite*, tr. by Ziegler, 1909; tr. by Oland in Plays, v. 3; tr. by Björkman in Plays, series 3; *Easter*, tr. by Oland in Plays, v. 2; tr. by Velma S. Howard, 1913; tr. by E. Classen in Easter and Other Plays; *The Dream Play*, tr. by Björkman in Plays, series 1; tr. by C. D. Locock in Easter and Other Plays; *The Crown Bride*, tr. by Björkman in Plays, series 4; *The Thunderstorm*, tr. as The Storm by Oland in Plays, v. 3; tr. by Björkman in Plays, series 3; *The Burned Lot*, tr. as After the Fire by Björkman in Plays, series 3; *The Spook Sonata*, tr. by Björkman in Plays, series 4; tr. as The Ghost Sonata by Erik Palmerstierna and J. B. Fagan in Easter and Other Plays; *The Pelican*, tr. by H. Alin and R. Jamieson, 1929; *The Slippers of Abu Casem*, adapted as The Tulip Slippers by M. Illing, 1906, from translation by M. Herrick; *Lucifer or God?*, tr. by Felix Grendon in The International 3, 1911.

STUCKEN, EDUARD

Gawain, 1902; *Lanval*, 1903; *Lancelot*, 1908; *Astrid*, 1910; *The Birth of Merlin*, 1913; *The Marriage of Adrian Brouwer*, 1914; *Tristram and Ysolt*, 1916; *The White Gods*, 1918; *The Lost Island*, 1922; *Vortigern*, 1923; *The Enchanter Merlin*, 1924.

SUDERMANN, HERMANN

Honor, 1889; *The Destruction of Sodom*, 1891; *Magda*, 1893; *The Battle of the Butterflies*, 1894; *Happiness in a Corner*, 1895; *Morituri, a Trilogy*: *1. Teja; 2. Fritzchen; 3. The Eternal Masculine*, 1896; *Johannes*, 1898; *Three Heron Feathers*, 1899; *The Fires of St. John*, 1900; *The Joy of Living*, 1902; *Storm Brother Socrates*, 1903; *Stone Among Stones*, 1905; *The Flower Boat*, 1906; *Roses: 1. Streaks of Light; 2. Margot; 3. The Last Visit; 4. The Far-Away Princess*, 1907; *The Children of the Strand*, 1910; *The Beggar of Syracuse*, 1911; *A Good Reputation*, 1912; *Claudian's Songs of Praise*, 1914; *The Godless World: 1. The Woman Friend; 2. The Desirable Corner; 3. The Higher Life*, 1915; *The Raschoffs*, 1919; *The Guardian of the Threshold*, 1921; *German Destiny: 1. Holy Time; 2. Sacrifice; 3. Cry of Need*, 1921;

BIBLIOGRAPHY

Like Those Who Dream, 1923; *The Unveiling (Die Denkmalsweihe),* 1923; *The Rabbit Skin Dealer,* 1927.

IN ENGLISH: *Honor,* played in New York, 1905; tr. by Hilmar Baukhage, 1915; *Magda,* tr. by C. E. A. Winslow, 1895; tr. as Casa Paterna by J. A. McGrath, 1896; argument of the play, by E. Beall Ginty, 1896; tr. by Claude Sykes, 1907; tr. by Louis N. Parker; tr. by Count Bonzenta; *The Battle of the Butterflies,* tr. by A. H. Schwarz, 1914; *Happiness in a Corner,* tr. as The Vale of Content by William E. Leonard, 1915, and in T. H. Dickinson, Chief Contemporary Dramatists, 1st series, 1915; *Morituri* (three plays), tr. by Archibald Alexander, 1910; *Morituri: Teja,* tr. as Teias by Mary Harned in Poet Lore 9, 1897, and in M. J. Moses, Representative One-Act Plays by Continental Authors, 1923; *Johannes,* tr. by W. H. and Mary Harned in Poet Lore 11, 1899; tr. as John by N. M. Baumann and G. P. Dingee, 1902; tr. as John the Baptist by Beatrice Marshall, 1908, 1909, and in K. Francke and W. G. Howard, German Classics, v. 17, 1914; abridged as John the Baptist in J. A. Price and Brander Matthews, Masterpieces of Modern Drama, v. 2, 1915; adapted as John the Baptist by Frances Jewett, 1926; *Three Heron Feathers,* tr. by Helen T. Porter in Poet Lore 12, 1900; *The Fires of St. John,* tr. by Charles Swickard, 1904; tr. as Saint John's Fire by Charlotte and H. T. Porter in Poet Lore 15, 1904; tr. as Saint John's Fire by Grace E. Polk, 1905; tr. and adapted as Saint John's Fire by Fernanda Eliscu, 1905; tr. by Swickard in M. J. Moses, Representative Continental Dramas, 1924; *The Joy of Living,* tr. by Edith Wharton, 1902; tr. in M. J. Moses, Representative Continental Dramas, 1924; *The Flower Boat,* adapted as Scherzo by Sidney Howard, 1922; *Roses* (four plays), tr. by Grace Frank, 1909; *Roses: The Far-Away Princess,* tr. by A. Alexander in B. R. Lewis, Contemporary One-Act Plays, 1922, and separately; tr. in W. E. Grady and Paul Klapper, Reading for Appreciation, Bk. 2, 1928; *A Good Reputation,* tr. by Margaret Holz and Olga Marz, 1915; *What Money Cannot Buy,* adapted by M. Magnus, 1906; *On Approval,* dramatized from Das hohe Lied by Alison M. Lederer, 1913; *The Unveiling,* tr. from Die Denkmalweihe by Muriel Hope, 1923.

TESTONI, ALFREDO

Discipline, 1904; *Cardinal Lambertini,* 1906; *Living Quietly,* 1907.

THOMA, LUDWIG

The Medal, 1901; *The Local Railway,* 1902; *Moral,* 1909; *First Class,* 1910; *Lottchen's Birthday,* 1911; *Mary Magdalene,* 1912; *The Nursing Home,* 1913; *The Little Relatives,* 1916; etc.

IN ENGLISH: *Moral,* tr. as Morality by H. Bernstein, 1909; tr. as Champions of Morality by H. A. Hertz and Frederick Whelen, 1910; tr. by Charles Recht, 1916, and in T. H. Dickinson, Chief Contemporary Dramatists, 2d series, 1921.

MODERN CONTINENTAL PLAYWRIGHTS

TOLLER, ERNST

The Transformation, 1919; *Masses and Man (Masse-Mensch),* 1921; *The Machine Wreckers,* 1922; *Wotan Unbound,* 1923; *Hinkemann,* 1923; *The Revenge of the Scorned Lover,* 1925; *Hoppla, We Live!,* 1927.

IN ENGLISH: *Masses and Man,* tr. by Vera Mendel, 1923; tr. by Louis Untermeyer as Mass-Man, 1923, and as Man and the Masses, 1924; *The Machine Wreckers,* tr. by Ashley Dukes, 1923; *Hinkemann,* tr. incompletely as Hobbleman in Germinal, 1923; tr. as Brokenbrow by Mendel, 1924; *Hoppla, We Live!,* tr. as Hoppla! by Hermon Ould, 1928.

TOLSTOY, ALEXEI

Don Juan, 1862; *The Death of Ivan the Terrible,* 1867; *Czar Fyodor Ivanovich,* 1868; *Czar Boris,* 1870.

IN ENGLISH: *The Death of Ivan the Terrible,* tr. by I. Henry Harrison, 1869; tr. by Madame de Meissner, 1900; tr. by Alfred Hayes, 1926; tr. as Ivan the Terrible by Gabriel Pollock and adapted by Stanley Wood, 1926; *Czar Fyodor Ivanovich,* tr. by Madame de Meissner, 1903; tr. by Jenny Covan separately and in O. M. Sayler, The Moscow Art Theatre Series of Russian Plays, 1923; tr. by Alfred Hayes, 1924.

TOLSTOY, LEO

The Power of Darkness, 1886; *The First Distiller,* 1887; *The Fruits of Enlightenment,* 1889; *The Living Corpse,* 1911; *The Light that Shines in Darkness,* 1911; *The Wisdom of Children; The Root of All Evil,* 1912.

IN ENGLISH: Leo Wiener, The Complete Works, 24 vols., 1904–1905; H. Wright, The Man Who Was Dead; The Cause of It All, 1912; Louise and Aylmer Maude, The Plays of Leo Tolstoy, 1914, 1919, 1923; Arthur Hopkins, Redemption and Two Other Plays, 1919; N. H. Dole, Dramatic Works of Lyof N. Tolstoi, 1923; *The Power of Darkness,* tr. as The Dominion of Darkness in Sergel's Columbian Library, 1890; tr. by H. von Hagen, 1902; tr. by Wiener in Complete Works; tr. by Maude in Plays; tr. by Hopkins in Redemption and Two Other Plays; tr. by Dole in Dramatic Works; *The First Distiller,* tr. by Maude in Plays; tr. by Dole in Dramatic Works; *The Fruits of Enlightenment,* tr. 1891; tr. as The Fruits of Culture by George Schumm, 1891; tr. by Wiener in Complete Works; tr. by Maude in Plays; tr. as The Fruits of Culture by Hopkins in Redemption and Two Other Plays; tr. by Dole in Dramatic Works; *The Living Corpse,* tr. by L. Korbin; tr. by André Tridon, 1911; tr. as The Man Who Was Dead by Z. Vengerova and John Pollock, 1912; tr. as The Man Who Was Dead by Wright in The Man Who Was Dead, The Cause of It All; tr. by Anna M. Evarts, 1912, 1919; tr. as The Live Corpse by Maude in Plays; adapted as The Man Who Was Dead by E. Sheldon, 1916; tr. by A. J. Gordin, 1917; tr. by A. Sterling, 1917; tr. as Redemption by Hopkins in Redemption and Two Other Plays; tr. as The Live Corpse by Dole in Dramatic Works; adapted by M. Doran, 1928; adapted as Redemption by August

BIBLIOGRAPHY

Scholz, 1928; tr. as Redemption in Haldeman-Julius Pocket Series; *The Light that Shines in Darkness,* tr. 1911; tr. by Wright in Father Sergius and Other Stories and Plays by Leo Tolstoy, 1912; tr. by Maude in Plays; tr. by Dole in Dramatic Works; *The Wisdom of Children,* tr. by Wright in Father Sergius and Other Stories and Plays by Leo Tolstoy, 1912; tr. by Dole in Dramatic Works; *The Root of All Evil,* tr. as The Cause of It All by Wright in The Man Who Was Dead, The Cause of It All; tr. as The Cause of It All by Maude in Plays; tr. by Dole in Dramatic Works; *Tolstoy,* written by S. Cheney, 1920, based in part on an unfinished autobiographic play of Tolstoy's.

TRARIEUX, GABRIEL

The Hostage, 1907; *The Alibi,* 1908; *The Debt,* 1909; *An Evening,* 1911.

IN ENGLISH: *The Hostage,* adapted as The Shadow of the Surplice by W. H. C. Nation, 1908; *Hypatia,* adapted by F. J. Collins, 1921.

TRETIAKOV, S.

Roar China!, 1926.

IN ENGLISH: *Roar China!,* tr. as Bellow China by Ruth Langner from the German of Leo Lania, 1930; played as Roar China!, N. Y., 1930.

UBERTIS, TERESAII

The Judge, 1903.

UNRUH, FRITZ VON

Officers, 1911; *Louis Ferdinand, Prince of Prussia,* 1913; *Storms,* 1914; *A Race (Ein Geschlecht),* 1918; *Room (Platz),* 1920; *Rosengarten,* 1922; *Heinrich of Andernach,* 1925; *Bonaparte,* 1926.

IN ENGLISH: *Bonaparte,* tr. by Edwin Björkman, 1928.

VERGA, GIOVANNI

Rustic Chivalry, 1884; *At the Porter's Lodge,* 1885; *The She Wolf,* 1896; *The Wolf Hunt,* 1901; *The Fox Hunt,* 1901; *From Yours to Mine,* 1905; *The Fair Sinner,* 1917; etc.

IN ENGLISH: *Rustic Chivalry,* adapted by A. Carrano, 1891; adapted as Cavalleria Rusticana by Michael Orme, 1919, and by Alexander Salvini, 1929; *The Wolf Hunt,* tr. in Isaac Goldberg, Plays of the Italian Theatre, 1921.

VILDRAC, CHARLES

The Steamer "Tenacity", 1920; *The Indigent,* 1922; *The Pilgrim,* 1923; *Michel Auclair,* 1923; *Madame Béliard,* 1925.

IN ENGLISH: *The Steamer "Tenacity",* tr. by John S. Newberry in Poet Lore 32, 1921; adapted as S.S. "Tenacity" by Sidney Howard, 1922; tr. as S.S.

Tenacity by Howard in Tucker, Modern Continental Plays, 1929; tr. as The Steamship Tenacity by Newberry in T. H. Dickinson, Chief Contemporary Dramatists, 3rd series, 1930; The Pilgrim, tr. as The Pilgrimage by Sigourney Thayer, 1925; Michel Auclair, tr. by Sidney Howard, 1925.

VOLLMÖLLER, KARL G.

Katharine Countess of Armagnac and her Two Lovers, 1903; Assüs, Fitne, and Sumurud, 1904; Giulia, 1905; The German Count, 1906; Turandot, Princess of China, 1910; Wieland, 1910, The Miracle, 1912; A Venetian Adventure, 1912; George Dandin, 1912.

IN ENGLISH: The Miracle, played in N. Y., 1924; Turandot, Princess of China, tr. by Jethro Bithell, 1912; A Venetian Adventure, tr. as A Venetian Night, and played in London, 1913; Uncle's Been Dreaming, tr. in W. Katzin, Eight European Plays, 1927.

WEDEKIND, FRANK

The Fast Painter, 1889; The World of Youth, 1890; The Awakening of Spring, 1891; Earth Spirit, 1895; The Love Potion (Fritz Schwigerling), 1899; The Tenor (Der Kammersänger), 1899; The Marquis of Keith, 1900; The Box of Pandora, 1902; Such Is Life (King Nicolo), 1902; Hidalla (Karl Hetmann the Pigmy Giant), 1904; The Dance of Death, 1906; Music, 1908; Censorship, 1908; Oaha, 1908; The Stone of the Wise, 1909; Franziska, 1912; The Wetterstein Trilogy (Schloss Wetterstein): 1. Solid in Every Saddle (1910); 2. Hunted by Every Hound (1910); 3. Washed In All Waters (1910); Simson, 1914; Bismarck, 1915; Heracles, 1917.

IN ENGLISH: Samuel A. Eliot, Jr., Tragedies of Sex, 1923; The Awakening of Spring, tr. by F. J. Ziegler, 1909, 1916; tr. by Eliot in Tragedies of Sex; Earth Spirit, tr. by Eliot, 1915, and in Tragedies of Sex; tr. as The Spirit of Earth by Joseph B. Rethy, 1920; played as The Loves of Lulu, N. Y., 1925; The Tenor, adapted as The Heart of a Tenor by André Tridon in Smart Set, v. 40, 1913; adapted by Tridon and played in N. Y., 1916; tr. as The Court Singer by Albert W. Boesche in K. Francke and W. G. Howard, The German Classics, v. 20, 1914, and in M. J. Moses, Representative One-Act Plays by Continental Authors, 1923; tr. by Tridon in Frank Shay and Pierre Loving, Fifty Contemporary One-Act Plays, 1920; The Marquis of Keith, tr. by Rita Matthias and Pierre Coalfleet, 1924; The Box of Pandora, tr. as Pandora's Box by Eliot, 1914, and in Tragedies of Sex; tr. by Joseph B. Rethy, 1920; Such Is Life, tr. by Ziegler, 1912, and in Tucker, Modern Continental Plays, 1929, and in Dickinson, Chief Contemporary Dramatists, 3rd series, 1930; The Dance of Death, adapted as The Virgin and the White Slaver by André Tridon, The International, 1913; tr. as Damnation! by Eliot in Tragedies of Sex.

WELK, EHM

Tempest over Gotland, 1912; Descent from the Cross, 1926; Knobbe, or the Ghost of Weimar, 1925.

BIBLIOGRAPHY

WERFEL, FRANZ

The Trojan Women, 1915; *Play Yard*, 1920; *Visit from Elysium*, 1920; *Mirror Man*, 1921; *Goat Song*, 1921; *Schweiger*, 1922; *Juarez and Maximilian*, 1924; *Paul Among the Jews*, 1926.

IN ENGLISH: *Goat Song*, tr. by Ruth Langner in Theatre Guild version, 1926; *Schweiger*, tr. by Jack Charash and William A. Drake, 1924; *Juarez and Maximilian*, tr. by Ruth Langner in Theatre Guild version, 1926; *Paul Among the Jews*, tr. by Paul P. Levertoff, 1928.

WETTE, ADELHEID

Hänsel and Gretel, 1894.

IN ENGLISH: *Hänsel and Gretel*, tr. by Constance Bache, 1901; adapted by Norreys J. O'Conor, 1909, 1910.

WIDMANN, JOSEPH VICTOR

The Stolen Veil, 1864; *Iphigenia in Delphi*, 1865; *Orgetorix*, 1867; *Queen of the East*, 1878; *Oenone*, 1879; *Beyond Good and Evil*, 1893; *June Bug Comedy*, 1897; *The Muse of Aretino*, 1902; *The Saint and the Animals*, 1905; etc.

IN ENGLISH: *The Saint and the Animals*, tr. as The Saint and the Beasts by Margarete Münsterberg in K. Francke and W. G. Howard, The German Classics, v. 14, 1914.

WIED, GUSTAV

Four Satyr Plays, 1897; *The Weaker Sex*, 1900; *The Reckoning*, 1902; *Dancing Mice*, 1905; *2 x 2 = 5*, 1906.

IN ENGLISH: *The Reckoning*, tr. as Autumn Fires in Frank Shay and Pierre Loving, Fifty Contemporary One-Act Plays, 1920; *2 x 2 = 5*, tr. as Two and Two Are Five by Frances C. Fay, 1921; tr. by Ernest Boyd and Holger Koppel, 1923, and in Eva Le Gallienne, Civic Repertory Plays, 1928.

WIERS-JENSSEN, HANS

Anne Pedersdotter.

IN ENGLISH: *Anne Pedersdotter*, adapted as The Witch by John Masefield, 1910, 1917.

WILDENBRUCH, ERNST VON

Spartacus, 1873; *The Carolingians*, 1881; *Fathers and Sons*, 1881; *The Mennonite*, 1881; *Harold*, 1882; *Sacrifice for Sacrifice*, 1883; *Christopher Marlowe*, 1884; *Mistress of Her Hand*, 1885; *The New Commandment*, 1886; *The Prince of Verona*, 1886; *The Quitzows*, 1888; *The Field Marshal*, 1890; *The Crested Lark*, 1890; *The New Master*, 1891; *Holy Laughter*, 1891; *Master,*

Balzer, 1892; *The Young Man of Hennersdorf*, 1896; *Heinrich and Heinrich's Race*, 1896; *Stormy Night*, 1898; *The Daughter of Erasmus*, 1900; *King Laurin*, 1902; *The Immortal Felix*, 1904; *The Songs of Euripides*, 1905; *The Gallows Woman*, 1907; *The German King*, 1909.

IN ENGLISH: *Harold*, tr. by Otto Heller and Hugh A. Clarke in Poet Lore 3, 1891, and separately, 1891; *Barseba of Rabenstein*, tr. from Die Rabensteinerin by R. V. Appiano and W. Nobbe, 1909; *Heinrich and Heinrich's Race*, tr. as King Henry, by Robert M. Wernaer in K. Francke and W. G. Howard, The German Classics, v. 17, 1914, and in The Drama 17, 1915; *Bird in the Cage*, adapted by Clyde Fitch.

WILDGANS, ANTON

Forever and Ever Amen, 1913; *Poverty*, 1913; *Love*, 1916; *Dies Irae*, 1918; *Cain a Mythical Play*, 1920.

WOLFF, PIERRE

Those We Respect, 1892; *What One Loves*, 1895; *Fidèle*, 1895; *The Inclination* (*Le Béguin*), 1900; *Rascal Léonce* (*Sacré Léonce*), 1901; *The Secret of Polichinelle*, 1903; *The Brook*, 1907; *The Lily*, 1909; *Forbidden Love*, 1911; *Broken Wings*, 1920.

IN ENGLISH: *The Lily*, adapted by David Belasco, 1909; *Broken Wings*, adapted as There's No Fool, by Stanley Bell, 1926; *The Marionettes*, adapted by Gladys Unger, 1911; *After Love——?*, adapted by A. E. Thomas, 1925; *Embers*, adapted by A. E. Thomas, 1926.

WOLZOGEN, ERNST VON

Children of His Excellency, 1890; *The Rabble*, 1892; *Daniela Weert*, 1894; *Sore Need*, 1896; *An Unwritten Page*, 1896; *The Baths of Lucca* (an opera), 1903; *Colonial Politics*, 1907; *Feuersnot*, 1909; *A Misunderstood Man*, 1909; *The May Bride*, 1909; *Little Woman*, 1916; *The Whip*, 1918; *Faust's Journey to Heaven, or The German Devil*, 1924.

IN ENGLISH: *Feuersnot*, tr. as Feuersnot, The Fire of St. John's Eve, by Charles T. Mason (with music), 1910; adapted as Feuersnot, Beltane Fire, by William Wallace (an opera), 1910.

ZOLA, ÉMILE

The Mysteries of Marseilles (with Marius Roux), 1867; *Thérèse Raquin*, 1873; *The Heirs of Rabourdin*, 1874; *Bouton de Rose*, 1878; *Pot-Bouille* (with William Busnach), 1883; *Renée*, 1887; *Madeleine*, 1889; *The Storm*, 1901.

IN ENGLISH: *Thérèse Raquin*, tr. by A. Teixeira de Mattos, 1891, 1913; tr. by John Stetson, 1892; tr. by E. A. Vizetelly, 1902; tr. as Guilty Love by A. W. Row, 1925; *Renée*, adapted from the novel La Curée, tr. as The Rush for Spoil, by Vizetelly, 1886; *The Heirs of Rabourdin*, tr. by de Mattos, 1894.

II. WORKS OF REFERENCE, CRITICAL AND HISTORICAL

Except in a few cases, limitations of space have prevented the inclusion here of references to articles in periodicals or to chapters in general works, although many of these are of great value.

MODERN EUROPEAN DRAMA IN GENERAL

James Agate, *The Contemporary Theater*, 1923; Charlton Andrews, *The Drama of To-day*, 1913; Robert F. Arnold, *Das moderne Drama*, 1908, *Das deutsche Drama*, 1925; Bruno Busse, *Das Drama*, 4 vols., 2d edit., 1922; Huntly Carter, *The New Spirit in Drama and Art*, 1913, *The New Spirit in the European Theater*, 1925; Frank W. Chandler, *Aspects of Modern Drama*, 1914; Sheldon Cheney, *The Theater*, 1912; *The New Movement in the Theater*, 1914; *Modern Art and the Theater*, 1921; Barrett H. Clark, *The Continental Drama of To-day*, 1914; *A Study of the Drama*, 1925, 1928; T. H. Dickinson, *An Outline of Contemporary Drama*, 1927; F. K. W. Drury, *Viewpoints in Modern Drama*, 1925, Ashley Dukes, *Modern Dramatists*, 1911, *The Youngest Drama*, 1923; *Drama*, 1927; Richard Elsner, *Modern Drama*, 1912; Mrs. Hallie Flanagan, *Shifting Scenes of the Modern European Theatre*, 1928; Isaac Goldberg, *The Drama of Transition*, 1922; Edward Everett Hale, *Dramatists of To-Day*, 1905; Clayton Hamilton, *Conversations on Contemporary Drama*, 1924; Archibald Henderson, *European Dramatists*, 1913; *The Changing Drama*, 1914; Oscar Herrmann, *Living Dramatists*, 1905; Storm Jameson, *Modern Drama in Europe*, 1920; Eleanor Jourdain, *The Drama in Europe*, 1924; Ludwig Lewisohn, *The Modern Drama*, 1915; *The Drama and the Stage*, 1922; Kenneth MacGowan, *The Theatre of To-Morrow*, 1921; Nellie B. Miller, *The Living Drama*, 1924; H. K. Moderwell, *The Theater of To-Day*, 1914; William Lyon Phelps, *The Twentieth Century Theater*, 1918; *Essays on Modern Dramatists* (Maeterlinck, Rostand, etc.), 1926; Guido Ruberti, *Il Teatro contemporaneo in Europa*, 2 vols., 1920-1921, enlarged to 3 vols., 1928; A. Graham Sutton, *Some Contemporary Dramatists*, 1924; Frank Vernon, *The Twentieth Century Theater*, 1924; Stark Young, *The Flower in Drama*, 1923.

THE DRAMA AT LARGE

W. D. Adams, *A Dictionary of the Drama*, 1904; Ramsden Balmforth, *The Ethical and Religious Value of the Drama*, 1925; H. R. Barbor, *The Theater, an Art and an Industry*, 1924; Alfred Bates, J. P. Boyd, and J. P. Lamberton, *The Drama. Its History, Literature, and Influence on Civilization*, 22 vols., 1903-1909; Martha Bellinger, *A Short History of the Drama*, 1927; John Booth, *A Century of Theatrical History* (1816-1916), 1917; Max Burckhardt, *Das Theater*, 1907; R. Clarence, *The Stage Cyclopaedia*, 1909; Christian Gaehde, *Das Theater vom altertum bis zur gegenwart;* Halcott Glover, *Drama and Mankind*, 1923; Charles Hastings, *The Theater, its Development in France and England;* Jay B. Hubbel, *An Introduction to Drama*, 1927; Glenn

MODERN CONTINENTAL PLAYWRIGHTS

Hughes, *The Story of the Theater*, 1928; Smith Ely Jeliffe and Louise Brink, *Psycho-Analysis and the Drama*, 1922; Karl Mantzius, *History of Theatrical Art in Ancient and Modern Times;* Brander Matthews, *A Study of the Drama*, 1910; *Development of the Drama*, 1916; Leo Melitz, *Die Theaterstücke der weltliteratur*, 1904; Allardyce Nicoll, *The Development of the Theater*, 1927; Roland Oliver, *Back Stage, a Story of the Theatre*, 1924; Lucien Solvay, *L'Evolution théâtrale*, 1922; Clarence Stratton, *Theatron*, 1929; Donald Clive Stuart, *The Development of Dramatic Art*, 1928; G. F. Sturges, *The Influence of the Drama*, 1913; Karl Walser, *Das Theater*, 1912; Joseph R. Williams, *Drama, a Guide for Beginners at Criticism*, 1928; Stark Young, *The Theater*, 1927.

MISCELLANEOUS DRAMATIC CRITICISM IN ENGLISH

James Agate, *At Half-Past Eight—Essays of the Theatre*, 1923; *Alarums and Excursions*, 1923; *Playgoing*, 1927; William Archer, *About the Theater*, 1886; *The Theatrical World*, 5 vols., 1894-1898; *Study and Stage*, 1899; *Real Conversations*, 1904; *The Old Drama and the New*, 1923; Herman Bernstein, *With Master Minds*, 1913; Edwin Björkman, *Voices of To-Morrow*, 1913; Ernest Boyd, *Portraits Real and Imaginary*, 1924; Gilbert Cannan, *The Joy of the Theater*, 1913; H. Carter, *The New Spirit in Drama and Art*, 1913; G. K. Chesterton, *Twelve Types*, 1903; *Varied Types*, 1903; Edward A. Choate, *Alarums and Excursions*, 1927; Sir Arthur Quiller Couch, *Adventures in Criticism*, 1896; W. L. Courtney, *Old Saws and Modern Instances*, 1918; Gerald Cumberland, *Set Down in Malice*, 1919; T. H. Dickinson, *The Insurgent Theatre*, 1917; William A. Drake, *Contemporary European Writers*, 1928; F. K. W. Drury, *Viewpoints in Modern Drama*, 1925; Ashley Dukes, *The World to Play With*, 1928; W. P. Eaton, *At the New Theater and Others*, 1910; *Plays and Players*, 1916; Louis William Flaccus, *Artists and Thinkers*, 1916; John Freeman, *The Moderns*, 1916; Edward Garnett, *Friday Nights*, 1922; W. L. George, *Dramatic Actualities*, 1914; Harley Granville-Barker, *The Only Possible Theatre*, 1920; *The Exemplary Theatre*, 1922; J. T. Grein, *Dramatic Criticism*, 1899, 1901, 1904; *Premières of the Year*, 1900; *The World of the Theater*, 1921; W. N. Guthrie, *Modern Poet Prophets*, 1897; Clayton Hamilton, *Seen on the Stage*, 1920; Otto Heller, *Prophets of Dissent* (Maeterlinck, Strindberg, etc.), 1918; Archibald Henderson, *Interpreters of Life*, 1911; P. P. Howe, *Dramatic Portraits*, 1913; Sisley Huddleston, *Those Europeans*, 1924; James Huneker, *Iconoclasts*, 1903; *Egoists*, 1909; *The Pathos of Distance*, 1913; *Ivory Apes and Peacocks*, 1915; *Unicorns*, 1917; *Bedouins*, 1920; H. B. Irving, *The Drama*, 1893; *Occasional Papers*, 1907; Holbrook Jackson, *Romance and Reality*, 1911; Irma Kraft, *Plays, Players, Playhouses*, 1928; Robert Lynd, *Old and New Masters*, 1919; Kenneth MacGowan, *Footlights Across America*, 1929; J. A. Macy, *The Critical Game*, 1922; Allan Monkhouse, *Books and Plays*, 1894; C. E. Montague, *Dramatic Values*, 1911; Edwin Muir, *Latitudes*, 1924; J. M. Murry, *Aspects of Literature*, 1920; George Jean Nathan, *Another Book on the Theater*, 1915; *Comedians All*, 1919; *The Critic and the Drama*, 1922; *The World in False Face*, 1923; *Materia Critica*, 1924; C. F. Nirdlinger, *Masques and Mummers*, 1899; William Rose and J. Isaacs, *Contemporary European Literature*, 1929; Henry Russel, *The Passing Show*, 1926; H. B. Samuel, *Modernities*, 1914; F. E. Schelling, *Appraisements and Asperities*, 1922; Wil-

WORKS OF REFERENCE

liam Sharp, *Studies and Appreciations,* 1912; George Bernard Shaw, *Dramatic Opinions and Essays,* 2 vols., 1907; E. A. Singer, *Modern Thinkers and Present Problems,* 1923; Otis Skinner, *Footlights and Spotlights,* 1924; Edwin E. Slosson, *Major Prophets of To-Day,* 1914; L. C. Strang, *Plays and Players of the Last Quarter Century,* 2 vols., 1903; Arthur Symons, *Plays, Acting, and Music,* 1903; *Studies in Prose and Verse,* 1904; *Figures of Several Centuries,* 1916; *Dramatis Personæ,* 1923; A. Thorold, *Six Masters in Disillusion,* 1909; J. Rankin Towse, *Sixty Years of the Theater,* 1916; C. E. Vaughan, *Types of Tragic Drama,* 1908; H. M. Walbrook, *Nights at the Play,* 1911; A. B. Walkley, *Playhouse Impressions,* 1892; *Frames of Mind,* 1898; *Dramatic Criticism,* 1903; *Drama and Life,* 1907; *Pastiche and Prejudice,* 1921; *More Prejudice,* 1923; William Winter, *The Wallet of Time,* 2 vols., 1913; Alexander Woollcott, *Shouts and Murmurs,* 1922; *Enchanted Aisles,* 1924; Stark Young, *Theater Practice,* 1925; *Glamour, Essays on the Art of the Theater,* 1926.

THEATERS AND CRAFTSMANSHIP

(Works on particular theaters and dramatic companies such as the Moscow Art Theater, the Kamerny, the Moscow Small Theater, The Comédie Française, the Théâtre-Libre, the Vieux Colombier, the Meininger, the Freie Bühne, the Vienna Burgtheater, and the ventures of Reinhardt and his successors are listed here among books on the Russians, the French, and the Germans.)

Charlton Andrews, *The Technique of Playmaking,* 1915; Frank Archer, *How to Write a Good Play,* n.d.; William Archer, *Play-making,* 1912; Émile Augier and Others, *How to Write a Play,* tr. by Dudley Miles, 1916; Stephen F. Austin, *Principles of Drama-Therapy,* 1917; George P. Baker, *Dramatic Technique,* 1919; Sarah Bernhardt, *The Art of the Theater,* 1925; Ferdinand Brunetière, *The Law of the Drama,* 1914; Richard Burton, *How to See a Play,* 1914; Charles H. Caffin, *Appreciation of the Drama;* Sheldon Cheney, *The Art Theater,* 1917; *The Open Air Theater,* 1918; *Modern Art and the Theater,* 1921; Barrett H. Clark, *European Theories of the Drama,* 1921; W. L. Courtney, *The Idea of Tragedy,* 1900; J. Cournos, *Gordon Craig and the Theater of the Future,* 1913; Gordon Craig, *On the Art of the Theater,* 1911; *Towards a New Theater,* 1913; *The Theater—Advancing,* 1919; *Scene,* 1923; *Books and Theaters,* 1925; Ruth C. Dimmick, *Our Theaters To-Day and Yesterday,* 1913; John Drinkwater, *The Art of Theater-going,* 1927; St. John Ervine, *How to Write a Play,* 1928; Willi Flemming, *Das Wesen der schauspielkunst,* 1927; Ferdinand Frey and R. Gollmer, *Stage Reform;* Gustav Freytag, *Die Technik des dramas,* 1872, 1876, tr. by E. J. MacEwan, 1895; R. L. Gannon, *The Technique of the One-Act Play,* 1925; Carl Hagemann, *Moderne Bühnenkunst,* 1916-1918; Bosworth Hallam, *Technique in Dramatic Art,* 1926; Clayton Hamilton, *Theory of the Theater,* 1910; *Studies in Stagecraft,* 1914; *Problems of the Playwright,* 1917; Alfred Hennequin, *The Art of Play-writing,* 1896; Robert Heindl, *Die Theater-Zensur,* 1907; Elizabeth Hunt, *The Play of To-Day,* 1913; Edith Isaacs, *Theater, Essays on the Arts of the Theater,* 1927; B. V. Kazansky, *Method of the Theater,* 1925; E. Kilian, *Aus der Praxis der modernen dramaturgie,* 1909; Friedrich Kranich, *Die moderne Bühnentechnik,* 1928; Roland Lewis, *Technique of the One-Act Play,* 1918; J. Lecomte, *Histoire des théâtres de Paris,*

MODERN CONTINENTAL PLAYWRIGHTS

1905; Kenneth MacGowan and R. E. Jones, *Continental Stagecraft*, 1922; Kenneth MacGowan and Hermann Rosse, *Masks and Demons*, 1923; Percy Mackaye, *The Playhouse and the Play*, 1909; *The Civic Theater*, 1912; *Community Drama*, 1917; T. L. Marble, *How to Appreciate the Drama*, 1914; Brander Matthews, *A Study of the Drama*, 1910; *Principles of Playmaking and Other Discussions of the Drama*, 1919; *Playwrights on Playwriting*, 1923; Allardyce Nicoll, *An Introduction to Dramatic Theory*, 1924; John Palmer, *The Future of the Theater; The Censor and the Theater;* Irving Pichel, *Modern Theaters*, 1925; W. T. Price, *Technique of the Drama*, 1909; *The Analysis of Play Construction and Dramatic Principles*, 1909; Arthur H. Quinn, *The Art of Playwriting*, 1928; Romain Rolland, *The People's Theater*, tr. by Barrett H. Clark, 1918; Francisque Sarcey, *A Theory of the Theater*, tr. by H. H. Hughes, 1916; Hermann Schlag, *Das Drama, wesen, theorie und technik*, 1909; Frank Waugh, *Outdoor Theaters*, 1917; Percival Wilde, *The Craftsmanship of the One-Act Play*, 1923; Adolf Winds, *Die Technik der schauspielkunst*, 1919; Elizabeth Woodbridge, *The Drama, Its Laws and Technique*, 1898.

PLAY PRODUCTION IN GENERAL

(Works on particular experiments in play production are listed here with books on the Russians, the French, and the Germans.)

A. Appia, *Die Musik und die inscenierung*, 1899; Karel Čapek, *How a Play is Produced*, 1928; Sheldon Cheney, *Stage Decoration*, 1928; Allen Crafton, *The Process of Stage Production*, 1926; Gordon Craig, *On the Art of the Theater*, 1911; John Dolman, *The Art of Play Production*, 1928; Alfred von Engel, *Bühnenbeleuchtung*, 1926; Georg Fuchs, *Die Schaubühne der zukunft; Die Revolution des theaters*, 1914; Theodore Fuchs, *Stage Lighting*, 1929; W. B. Gamble, *Development of Scenic Art and Stage Machinery*, 1916, 1928; Firmin Gémier, *Le Théâtre*, 1923; Carl Hagemann, *Moderne Bühnenkunst*, 1916-1918; Glenn Hughes, *The Story of the Theater*, 1928; S. J. Hume and W. R. Fuerst, *XX Century Stage Decoration*, 2 vols., 1929; Theodore Kommisarjevsky, *The Theory of Stanislavsky*, 1919; *Myself and the Theater*, 1930; Kenneth MacGowan, *The Theater of To-morrow*, 1921; Kenneth MacGowan and R. E. Jones, *Continental Stagecraft*, 1922; L. C. Moussière, *La Décoration théâtrale*, 1922; Vladimir Polunin, *The Continental Method of Scene Painting*, 1927; Jacques Rouché, *L'Art théâtral moderne*, new ed., 1924; Albert Rutherston, *Decoration in the Theater*, 1919; Oliver Sayler, *Max Reinhardt and his Theater*, 1924; André Smith, *The Scenewright*, 1926; Milton Smith, *The Book of Play Production*, 1926; Clarence Stratton, *Theatron*, 1929; Alexander Tairov, *Das entfesselte Theater*, 1923; Frank Vernon, *Modern Stage Production*, 1923.

CHAPTER I

(IBSEN)

A. Aall, *Henrik Ibsen als denker und dichter*, 1906; H. Albrecht, *Frauen charaktere in Ibsens dramen*, 1902; A. R. Anderson, *Studies in Ibsen*, 1915; Lou Andreas-Salome, *Ibsens Frauengestalten*, 1907; William Archer, Introductions to his editions of Ibsen; *Prose Dramas*, 5 vols., 1890-1891; *Works*,

664

WORKS OF REFERENCE

11 vols., 1906-1908; *Collected Works*, 12 vols., 1909-1912; E. von Aster, *Ibsen und Strindberg*, 1921; Hermann Bahr, *Ibsen*, 1887; Leo Berg, *Henrik Ibsen*, 1901; W. Berteval, *Le Théâtre d'Ibsen*, 1913; Edwin Björkman, *Ibsen as he Should be Read*, 1907; A. Boccardi, *La Donna nell' opera di H. Ibsen*, 1892; Frederike Boettcher, *La Femme dans le Théâtre d'Ibsen*, 1912; H. H. Boyesen, *A Commentary on the Writings of Henrik Ibsen*, 1895; Otto Brahm, *Henrik Ibsen*, 1887; George Brandes, *Henrik Ibsen*, 2 vols., 1898; *Ibsen*, Björnson, 1899; Brünnings, *Die Frau im drama Ibsens*, 1910; T. M. Campbell, *Hebbel, Ibsen, and the Analytic Exposition;* F. W. Chandler, The Drama of Ideas, in *Aspects of Modern Drama*, 1914; Introduction to *Ibsen's Plays*, 1927; A. G. Chater, *From Ibsen's Workshop*, 1912; René Doumic, *De Scribe à Ibsen*, 1893; A. Dresdner, *Ibsen als Norweger und Europaer*, 1907; A. Ehrhard, *Henrik Ibsen et le théâtre contemporain*, 1892; W. H. Eller, *Ibsen in Germany* (1870-1900), 1918; P. Ernst, *Ibsen*, 1904; Arturo Farinelli, *La Tragedia di Ibsen*, 1923; Ina Ten Eyk Firkins, *Henrik Ibsen, a Bibliography*, 1921; Miriam Franc, *Ibsen in England*, 1919; *Der Grundgedanke in H. Ibsens dichtung*, 1898; Edmund Gosse, *Henrik Ibsen*, 1907; Paul H. Grummann, *Ibsen's Symbolism* in *Univ. of Nebraska Studies*, 1910; *Ibsen in his Maturity* in Poet Lore, 1917-1918; *Henrik Ibsen, an Introduction to his Life and Works*, 1928; M. S. Guhland, *Ibsen's Women*, 1894; Wilhelm Hans, *Schicksal und Wille, . . . Ibsens Weltanschauung*, 1906; *Ibsens Selbstporträt in seinen dramen*, 1911; Otto Harnack, *Essais und Studien zur literaturgeschichte* (Ibsen's social dramas), 1899; A. von Hanstein, *Ibsen als idealist*, 1897; Otto Heller, *Henrik Ibsen, Plays and Problems*, 1912; Sigurd Höst, *Henrik Ibsen*, 1924; Montague Jacobs, *Ibsens Bühnentechnik*, 1920; Henrik Jaeger, *Henrik Ibsen*, 1890; K. N. Janson, *Religious Views of Björnson and Ibsen*, 1911; Ellen Key, *The Torpedo Under the Ark* (Ibsen), 1912; Arne Kildal and L. M. Hollander, *Speeches and New Letters of Henrik Ibsen*, 1910; Ella Kretschmer, *Ibsens Frauengestalten*, 1905; T. Lasius, *Henrik Ibsen*, 1906; Yanko Lavrin, *Ibsen and his Creation*, 1921; Jennette Lee, *The Ibsen Secret*, 1907; G. Leneveu, *Ibsen et Maeterlinck*, 1902; Berthold Litzmann, *Ibsens Dramen* (1877-1900), 1901; Rudolph Lothar, *Henrik Ibsen*, 1902; Ossip D. Lourié, *La Philosophie sociale dans le théâtre d'Ibsen*, 1900; I. K. Lunderberg, *Ibsen in France, Publications of Society For . . . Scandinavian Studies*, 1924; Haldane Macfall, *Ibsen*, 1907; Alfred Markovitz, *Die Weltanschauung Henrik Ibsens*, 1913; E. Mauerhof, *Ibsen der romantiker des verstandes*, 1907; Johannes Mayrhofer, *Henrik Ibsen*, 1911; D. Merejkowski, *The Life Work of Henrik Ibsen*, tr. by G. A. Mounsey, 1915; Montrose J. Moses, *Henrik Ibsen*, 1908; E. Norman, *Henrik Ibsen in seinen gedanken und gestalten*, 1908; H. Plechanow, *Ibsen*, 1909; Emil Reich, *Henrik Ibsens Dramen*, 1910; R. E. Roberts, *Ibsen, a Critical Study*, 1912; E. Russell and P. Cross-Standing, *Ibsen on his Merits*, 1892; Charles Sarolea, *Henrik Ibsen, étude*, 1891; E. H. Schmitt, *Ibsen als psychologischer Sophist*, 1889; *Ibsen als Prophet*, 1908; George Bernard Shaw, *The Quintessence of Ibsenism*, 1891; Philipp Stein, *Henrik Ibsen*, 1901; Albert Wagner, *Henrik Ibsen*, 1907; William Watson, *Excursions in Criticism* (Ibsen), 1893; Herman J. Weigand, *The Modern Ibsen*, 1925; Agnes M. Wergeland, *Leaders in Norway*, 1916; P. H. Wicksteed, *Four Lectures on Henrik Ibsen*, 1892; Josef Wiehr, *Hebbel und Ibsen in ihren anschauungen verglichen*, 1908; Roman Woerner, *Henrik Ibsen*, 2 vols., 1900, 1912; A. E. Zucker, *Ibsen the Master Builder*, 1929.

MODERN CONTINENTAL PLAYWRIGHTS

CHAPTER II

(STRINDBERG)

Fredrik Book, *Sveriges moderna Litteratur*, 1921; Helmont A. W. de Boor, *Schwedische Literatur*, 1924; Axel Brett, *Psychological Abnormalities in August Strindberg*, in Journal of English and Germanic Philology, v. 20, 1921; Frank W. Chandler, The Tyranny of Love, in *Aspects of Modern Drama*, 1914; Carl Enoch W. L. Dahlström, *Strindberg's Dramatic Expressionism*, 1930; E. Diem, *August Strindberg*, 1929; Nils Erdmann, *August Strindberg*, 1924; H. Esswein, *August Strindberg, ein psychologischer versuch*, 1907; *August Strindberg im licht seines lebens und seiner werke*, 1909; Erik Hedén, *Strindberg*, 1921; Martin Lamm, *Strindbergs Dramen*, 1924; A. Liebert, *August Strindberg—seine weltanschauung und seine kunst*, 1924; Lizzy Lind-af-Hageby, *August Strindberg*, 1913, 1928; G. A. Loiseau, *A. Strindberg et son œuvre;* V. J. McGill, *August Strindberg, the Bedevilled Viking*, 1930; C. D. Marcus, *Strindbergs Dramatik*, 1918; Edith and Warner Oland, Introductions to their translations of Strindberg's plays, 1912, 1914; S. Rahmer, *Strindberg, eine pathologische studie*, 1907; C. L. Schleich, *Errinerungen an Strindberg*, 1917; F. W. Schmidt, *Strindberg und seine besten bühnenstücke*, 1922; August Strindberg, *Dramatische Charakteristiken*, tr. into German by Emil Schering, 1914; Vance Thompson, *Strindberg and his Plays*, 1921; C. G. Uddgren, *Strindberg the Man*, 1920; Leopold von Wieser and L. M. W. Kaiserwaldau, *Strindberg*, 1918; Rune Zetterlund, *Bibliografiska anteckningar om August Strindberg*, 1913.

CHAPTER III

(BJÖRNSON AND THE MINOR SCANDINAVIANS)

R. B. Anderson, *Biographical Sketch of Björnson*, in Works, v. 1, 1881-1882; Edwin Björkman, Introductions to his translation of *Björnson's Plays*, 1st series, 1913, 2d series, 1914; Björkman, Introduction to his translation of Hjalmar Bergström's *Lynggaard and Company* and *Karen Borneman*, 1913; H. H. Boyesen, *Essays on Scandinavian Literature*, 1895; George Brandes, *Ibsen, Björnson*, 1899; C. J. B. Burchardt, *Norwegian Life and Literature*, 1920; Christian Collin, *Björnstjerne Björnson*, tr. to German by C. G. Mjöen, 1903; Edmund Gosse, *Northern Studies*, 1890; Illit Grondahl and Ola Raknes, *Chapters in Norwegian Literature*, 1923; Gunnar Heiberg, *The Norwegian Theater;* A. Holitscher, *Lebensgeschichte eines rebellen* (Knut Hamsun), 1921; K. N. Janson, *Religious Views of Björnson and Ibsen*, 1911; John Landquist, *Verner von Heidenstam*, 1909; H. A. Larsen, *Knut Hamsun*, 1922; H. J. Leach, *Scandinavia of the Scandinavians*, 1915; William M. Payne, *Björnson*, 1910; Emil Reich, *Aus Leben und dichtung* (Björnson), 1911; H. K. Schanche, Introduction to *Modern Icelandic Plays* (two by Johann Sigurjonsson), 1916; R. F. Sharp, Introduction to *Three Comedies of Björnson*, 1913; Charles W. Stork, *The Poetry of Verner von Heidenstam*, 1919; Hans Tessmer, *Björnson und 5 seiner besten bühnenstücke;* E. Tissot, *Le Drame norvégien*, 1893; H. G. Topsöe-Jensen, *Scandinavian Literature, From Brandes to Our Day*, 1929; Agnes M. Wergeland, *Leaders in Norway*, 1916.

WORKS OF REFERENCE

CHAPTERS IV TO VIII

(THE RUSSIANS)

Gregoire Alexinsky, *La Russie moderne*, 1912; Anna M. Anitchkoff, *La Pensée russe contemporaine*, 1903; J. Apushkin, *The Kamerny Theater*, 1927; A. Bakshy, *The Path of the Russian Stage*, 1918; *The Theater Unbound*, 1924; Maurice Baring, *Landmarks in Russian Literature*, 1910; C. E. Bechhofer, *Five Russian Plays and One From the Ukranian*, 1917; Alexander Brückner, *Literary History of Russia*, 1908; Huntly Carter, *The New Theater and Cinema of Soviet Russia*, 1924; *The New Spirit in the Russian Theater* (1917-1928), 1928; Arthur Coleman, *Humor in Russian Comedy From Catherine to Gogol*, 1925; Ernest Combes, *Profils et types de la littérature russe*, 1896; Ernest Dupuy, *Great Masters of Russian Literature in the 19th Century*, 1886; Nicolas Efros, *The Moscow Art Theater, 1898-1923*, 1924; V. Filipov, *The Moscow Small Theater*, 1927; A. L. Fovitsky, *The Moscow Art Theater and its Distinguishing Characteristics*, 1922; André Gide, *Dostoyevski*, tr. by Arnold Bennett, 1926; J. T. Gregor and R. Fülöp-Miller, *Das russische Theater;* Isabel Hapgood, *A Survey of Russian Literature*, 1902; C. H. Herford, *A Russian Shakespeare* (Pushkin), 1925; Nadine Jarintzov, *Russian Poets and Poems*, 1917; A. E. Johnson, *The Russian Ballet*, 1913; Theodore Kommisarjevsky, *The Theory of Stanislavsky*, 1919; *Myself and the Theater*, 1930; Prince P. A. Kropotkin, *Russian Literature*, 1905; *Ideals and Realities in Russian Literature*, 1915; Louis Leger, *La Russie intellectuelle*, 1914; Mrs. Rosa Newmarch, *Poetry and Progress in Russia*, 1907; M. J. Olgin, *A Guide to Russian Literature*, 1920; Ivan Panin, *Lectures on Russian Literature*, 1889; Patouillet, *Ostrowsky et son théâtre de mœurs russes*, 1912; Serge Persky, *Contemporary Russian Novelists*, tr. by F. Eisemann, 1913; William Lyon Phelps, *Essays on Russian Novelists*, 1915; Alexander von Reinholdt, *Geschichte der russischen literatur*, 1884-1886; Rothay Reynolds, *My Slav Friends*, 1916; Arthur Ruhl, *White Nights*, 1917; Oliver M. Sayler, *The Russian Theater Under the Revolution*, 1920; *The Russian Theater*, 1922; *Inside the Moscow Art Theater*, 1925; I. Shakhnovski, *A Short History of Russian Literature*, tr. by Serge Tomkeyeff, 1921; Constantin Stanislavsky, *My Life in Art*, 1924; Alexander Tairoff, *Das entfesselte Theater*, 1923; C. E. Turner, *Studies in Russian Literature*, 1882; K. Waliszewski, *A History of Russian Literature*, 1900; Leo Wiener, *The Contemporary Drama of Russia*, 1924; Harold Williams, *Russia of the Russians*, 1914.

W. Allerhand, *Leo Tolstoy als dramatiker*, 1927; F. L. Axelrod, *Tolstois Weltanschauung und ihre entwickelung*, 1902; Paul Birukoff, *Leo Tolstoy, his Life and Work*, 1906; Nathan Haskell Dole, *The Life of Count Lyof N. Tolstoi*, 1911; *The Dramatic Works of Lyof N. Tolstoi*, with Preface, 1923; Friedrich Duesel, *Tolstoy und seine besten bühnenstücke;* Hugh Fausset, *Tolstoy, the Inner Drama;* Edward Garnett, *Tolstoy*, 1914; Maxim Gorky, *Reminiscences of Leo Tolstoy*, tr. by S. S. Koteliansky and Leonard Woolf, 1920; Bolton Hall, *What Tolstoy Taught*, 1911; Yanko Lavrin, *Tolstoy, a Psycho-Analytic Study*, 1924; Aylmer and Louise Maude, *Life of Tolstoy*, 1910; Preface to *The Plays of Leo Tolstoy*, 1919; Aylmer Maude, *Tolstoy and his Problems*, 1904; *Tolstoy as a Dramatist*, in his version of *The Light That Shines in Darkness*, 1912; D. Merejkowski, *Tolstoy as Man and Artist*,

1907; Rapall Noyes, *Tolstoy,* 1918; Romain Rolland, *Tolstoy,* tr. by Bernard Miall, 1911; Edward Steiner, *Tolstoy, the Man and his Message,* 1914; Ilia Tolstoy, *Reminiscences of Tolstoy,* tr. by George Calderon, 1914; Leo Tolstoy, *The Truth About My Father,* 1924; Leo N. Tolstoy, *The Diaries of Leo Tolstoy,* tr. by C. J. Hogarth and A. Sirnis, 1917; *The Journal of Leo Tolstoy,* tr. by Rose Strunsky, 1917.

E. J. Dillon, *Maxim Gorky,* 1902; Friedrich Duesel, *Maxim Gorky and Anton Tchekhov,* 1922; *Gorky und Tchekhov und ihre besten bühnenwerke;* Maxim Gorky, *My Childhood,* 1915; *Reminiscences of My Youth,* tr. by Veronica Dewey, 1924; *My University Days,* 1923; *In the World,* tr. by Mrs. Gertrude M. Foakes, 1917; *Fragments From My Diary,* 1924; Rudolph Meincke, *Maxim Gorki,* 1908; Hans Ostwald, *Maxim Gorky,* 1902; Igino Petrone, *La Visione della vita e l'arte di Massimo Gorki,* 1903; M. de Voguë, *Maxim Gorky, l'œuvre et l'homme,* 1905.

George Calderon, Introduction to *Two Plays by Tchekhof,* 1912; Anton P. Chekhov, *My Life and Other Stories,* tr. by S. S. Koteliansky and Gilbert Cannan, 1920; *Letters of Anton Tchekhoff to his Family and Friends,* tr. by Constance Garnett, 1920; *Letters of Anton Chekhov to Olga Leonardovna Knipper; Letters on the Short Story, the Drama, and Other Literary Topics,* tr. by L. S. Friedland, 1924; Oliver Elton, *Chekhov,* a lecture, 1929; Marian Fell, Introduction to *Plays of Anton Tchekoff,* 1912; William Gerhardi, *Anton Chekhov, a Critical Study,* 1923; Maxim Gorky, A. Kuprin, and I. Bunin, *Reminiscences of Anton Chekhov,* tr. by S. S. Koteliansky and L. Woolf, 1921; S. S. Koteliansky, *Anton Chekhov's Literary and Theatrical Reminiscences,* 1927; Koteliansky and P. Tomlinson, *Life and Letters of A. Tchekhov,* 1925; Robert Lynd, *Old and New Masters* (Chekhov), 1919; J. M. Murry, *Aspects of Literature* (Tchekhof), 1920; C. Nabokoff, *Chekhov and his Plays,* Contemporary Review, 1924; L. Shestov, *Anton Tchekhov and Other Essays,* tr. by S. S. Koteliansky and J. M. Murry, 1916; Constantin Stanislavsky, *My Life in Art,* 1924; Julius West, Introduction to *Plays by Anton Tchekoff,* 2d Series, 1916.

John Cournos, *Feodor Sologub,* in The Drama, 1916; Fyodor Sologub, *Theater of the Single Will;* Nikolai Nikolaevich Evreinov, *An Introduction to Monodrama,* 1909; *Les Novations théâtrales,* 1922; *The Theater for One's Self,* 1915-1917; *The Theater in Life,* tr. by Alexander I. Nazaroff, 1927; V. V. Brusianin, *The Symbolic Drama of Andreyeff;* A. S. Kaun, *Andreyev, a Critical Study,* 1924; C. L. Meader and F. N. Scott, Introduction to *Plays by Leonid Andreyeff,* 1915.

CHAPTERS IX TO XV

(THE FRENCH IN GENERAL)

Paul Abram, *Notes de Critique,* 1913; Paul Acker, *Petites Confessions, visites, et portraits,* 2 vols., 1903-1904; Adolphe Aderer, *Le Théâtre à coté,* 1894; L. Allard, *La Comédie de mœurs en France au 19ième siècle,* 1923; Francisque Armade, *Le Théâtre français des origines à nos jours,* 1909; Max Banner, *Das französische Theater der gegenwart,* 1898; Antoine Benoist, *Essais de critique dramatique,* 1898; *Le Théâtre d'aujourd'hui,* 2 vols., 1911-1912; Adrien Bernheim, *Trente Ans de théâtre,* 3 vols., 1903-1904; Yetta Blaze de Bury, *French Literature of To-Day,* 1898; Léon Blum, *Au Théâtre,* 1908;

WORKS OF REFERENCE

Henry Bordeaux, *Pèlerinages littéraires*, 1907; *La Vie au théâtre*, 3 vols., 1907-1913; Paul Bourget, *Réflexions sur le théâtre*, in *Etudes et portraits*, vol. 1, 1911; *Pages de critique et de doctrine*, 1912; Adolphe Brisson, *Le Théâtre et les mœurs*, 8 vols., 1905-1913; *Le Théâtre*, 1918; Ferdinand Brunetière, *Les Epoques du théâtre français*, 1892; *Essais sur la littérature contemporaine*, 1892; Alfred Capus, *Notre Epoque et le théâtre*, 1906; *Le Théâtre*, 1913; Georges Casella and Ernest Gaubert, *La nouvelle Littérature*, 1906; Frank W. Chandler, *The Contemporary Drama of France*, 1920; Jules Claretie, *Profils de théâtre*, 1902; Barrett H. Clark, *Contemporary French Dramatists*, 1915; Introduction to *Three Modern Plays From the French*, 1914; Introduction to *Four Plays of the Free Theater*, 1914; Introduction to *Four Plays by Emile Augier*, 1915; Francis de Croisset, *Our Puppet Show, Essays in Life and the Drama*, tr. by E. B. Osborn, 1929; J. W. Cunliffe and P. de Bacourt, *French Literature of the Last Half Century*, 1923; René Doumic, *De Scribe à Ibsen*, 1893; *Les Jeunes*, 1896; *Essai sur le théâtre contemporain*, 1897; *Le Théâtre nouveau*, 1908; Mme. A. M. F. Duclaux, *Twentieth Century French Writers*, 1919; J. Ernest Charles, *La Littérature française d'aujourd'hui*, 1902; *Les Samedis littéraires*, 4 vols., 1903-1905; *Le Théâtre des poètes*, 1910; Emile Faguet, *Notes sur le théâtre contemporain*, 7 vols., 1889-1895; *Propos de théâtre*, 4 vols., 1903-1907; *Propos littéraires*, 5 vols., 1902-1910; Augustin Filon, *De Dumas à Rostand*, 1898; tr. as *Modern French Drama*, by J. E. Hogarth, 1898; Paul Flat, *Figures du théâtre contemporain*, 2 vols., 1912-1913; Firmin Gémier, *Le Théâtre*, 1923; Edmund Gosse, *French Profiles*, 1905; A. L. Guérard, *Five Masters of French Romance*, 1916; Jules Guillemot, *L'Evolution de l'idée dramatique . . . de Corneille à Dumas fils*, 1910; Hésoppe, *L'Impuissance du théâtre contemporain*, 1912; S. O. Henry, *French Essays and Profiles*, 1921; Abel Hermant, *Essais de critique*, 1912; René Lalou, *Histoire de la littérature française contemporaine*, 1922, in English, 1924; Gustave Larroumet, *Etudes d'histoire et de critique dramatiques*, 1892; *Nouvelles Etudes*, 1899; *Etudes de critique dramatique*, 1906; J. Lecomte, *Histoire des théâtres de Paris*, 1905; Jules Lemaître, *Les Contemporains*, 7 vols., 1888-1899; *Literary Impressions*, selections from the foregoing tr. by A. W. Evans, 1921; *Impressions de théâtre*, 10 vols., 1888-1898, tr. as *Theatrical Impressions*, by Frederic Whyte, 1924; *Théories et impressions*, 1903; H. Lencou, *Le Théâtre nouveau*, 1896; Charles Lenient, *La Comédie en France au XIXe siècle*, 2 vols., 1898; Cesare Levi, *Autori drammatici francese*, 1923; E. Lintilhac, *Histoire générale du théâtre en France;* P. Lhomme, *La Comédie d'aujourd'hui*, 1898; Emile Mas, *La Comédie Française pendant la guerre*, 1929; Brander Matthews, *French Dramatists of the Nineteenth Century*, 1881, enlarged 1910, 1914; Octave Mirbeau, *Gens de théâtre*, 1924; Daniel Mornet, *Histoire de la littérature et de la pensée française contemporaine*, 1927; Hippolyte Parigot, *Le Théâtre d'hier*, 1893; *Génie et métier*, 1894; Georges Pellissier, *Nouveaux Essais de littérature contemporaine*, 1894; *Le Mouvement littéraire contemporain*, 5th edition, 1915; Louis Petit de Julleville, *Le Théâtre en France*, 1889; Edouard Quet, *La Puissance du théâtre en France*, 1900; P. de Saint-Victor, *Le Théâtre contemporain*, 1889; Francisque Sarcey, *Quarante Ans de théâtre*, 8 vols, 1900-1902; Edouard Schuré, *Précurseurs et révoltés*, 1920; A. Séché and J. Bertaut, *L'Evolution du théâtre contemporain*, 1908; E. Sée, *Le Théâtre français contemporain*, 1928; H. A. Smith, *Main Currents of Modern French Drama*,

1925; Albert-Emile Sorel, *Essais de psychologie dramatique,* 1911; Albert Soubies, *Almanach des spectacles,* 22 vols., 1874-1896; *Le Théâtre en France de 1871 à 1892,* 1893; *La Comédie Française depuis l'époque romantique, 1825-1894,* 1895; Edmond Stoullig and Edouard Noël, *Les Annales du théâtre et de la musique,* 41 vols., 1876-1918; Vance Thompson, *French Portraits,* 1900; Luigi Tonelli, *Lo Spirito francese contemporaneo,* 1917; G. Turquet-Milnes, *Some Modern Belgian Writers,* 1917; *Some Modern French Writers,* 1921; Georges Vitoux, *Le Théâtre de l'avenir,* 1903; Auguste Vitu, *Les Mille et une Nuits du théâtre,* 9 vols., 1884-1893; J.-J. Weiss, *Le Théâtre et les mœurs,* 1889; *Autour de la Comédie Française,* 1892; *Trois Années de théâtre,* 4 vols., 1892-1896; *A Propos de Théâtre,* 1893; *Le Drame historique et le drame passionel,* 1894; *Les Théâtres parisiens,* 1896; Arnold Whitridge, *Critical Ventures in Modern French Literature,* 1924; C. H. C. Wright, *A History of French Literature,* 1912, new ed., 1925.

CHAPTER IX

(The Theatric and the Naturalistic)

Neil C. Arvin, *Eugène Scribe and the French Theater (1815-1860),* 1924; C. J. B. Jacquot, *Scribe,* 1869; Michael Kaufmann, *Zur Technik der komödien von Eugène Scribe,* 1911; Henry Guillard de Champris, *Emile Augier et la comédie sociale,* 1910; Paul Morillot, *Emile Augier,* 1901; Edouard Pailleron, *Emile Augier,* 1889; H. Parigot, *Emile Augier,* 1890; *Le Drame de A. Dumas,* 1899; M. Valentinois, *Emile Augier,* 1897; Jules Claretie, *A. Dumas fils,* 1883; C. M. Noël, *Les Idées sociales dans le théâtre de A. Dumas fils,* 1912; Henry Schwarz, *Alexandre Dumas fils, Dramatist,* 1927; Jerome A. Hart, *Sardou and the Sardou Plays,* 1913; Hugues Rebell, *Victorien Sardou;* Léopold Lacour, *Trois Théâtres* (Augier, Dumas *fils,* Sardou), 1880; H. Behrens, *Francisque Sarceys theaterkritik,* 1911; Pierre Gilbert, *Le Juif dans le théâtre de M. Bernstein, Revue Critique,* 1912.

André Antoine, *Mes Souvenirs sur le Théâtre-Libre,* 1921; A. Arnautovic, *Henry Becque,* 3 vols., 1927; Henry Becque, *Souvenirs d'un auteur dramatique,* 1895; E. Cattier, *Le Naturalisme littéraire,* 1897; Barrett H. Clark, *Introduction to Four Plays of the Free Theater,* 1915; C. S. Darrow, *Realism in Literature and the Drama,* 1899; R. Darzens, *Le Théâtre-libre illustré,* 1890; Eric Dawson, *Henry Becque, sa vie et son théâtre,* 1923; Louis Desprez, *L'Evolution naturaliste,* 1884; Fritz Dubois, *Henry Becque,* 1888; André Fejes, *Le Théâtre naturaliste en France,* 1925; A. Got, *Henry Becque,* 1920; Matthew Josephson, *Zola and his Time,* 1928; Jean Jullien, *Le Théâtre vivant,* 1892; Paul Lenoir, *Histoire du réalisme,* 1887; Edmond Lepelletier, *Emile Zola,* 1907; A. MacDonald, *Emile Zola,* 1901; Pierre Martino, *Le Naturalisme français (1870-1895),* 1923; Guy de Maupassant, *Emile Zola,* 1883; Michel-Delines, *L'Œuvre de Jean Jullien;* Richard Oehlert, *Emile Zola als theater dichter,* 1920; Edmond Sée, *Henry Becque,* 1926; E. A. A. L. Seillière, *Emile Zola,* 1923; Robert H. Sherard, *Emile Zola, a Biographical and Critical Study,* 1903; A. Thalasso, *Le Théâtre-Libre,* 1909; Freeman Tilden, Preface to his translation of Becque's *The Vultures,* etc., 1913; Ernest A. Vizetelly, *With Zola in England,* 1899; *Emile Zola,* 1904; S. M. Waxman, *Antoine and the Théâtre-Libre,* 1926; Emilè Zola, *Nos Auteurs dramatiques,* 1881; *Le Naturalisme au théâtre,* 1881.

WORKS OF REFERENCE

(PLAYWRIGHTS OF THE IRONIC, EROTIC, AND COMIC; MORALISTS AND REFORMERS)

Roger Le Brun, *Maurice Donnay*, 1903; Edouard Quet, *Alfred Capus*, 1904; E. Sansot-Orland, *Jules Lemaître*, 1903; Denys Amiel, *Henry Bataille*, 1909; Henry Bataille, *Écrits sur le théâtre*, 1917; J. B. Besançon, *Essai sur le théâtre de Henry Bataille*, 1928; Paul Blanchart, *Henry Bataille, son œuvre*, 1922; Claude R. Marx, *Georges de Porto-Riche*, 1912; Jules Claretie, *Edouard Pailleron*, 1883; Roger Le Brun, *Georges Courteline*, 1907; Maurice Mignon, *Jules Renard*, 1913.

E. Barberot, *Le Chemin de Damas, critique de Paul Hervieu*, 1901; A. Binet, *Portrait psychologique de Paul Hervieu*, 1914; Joseph de Bonne, *La Pensée de Paul Bourget*, 1913; H. Burckhardt, *Studien zu Paul Hervieu*, 1917; Ernest Dimnet, *Paul Bourget*, 1913; Edmond Estève, *Paul Hervieu*, 1917; Georges Graffe, *Paul Bourget*, 1904; F. Jean-Desthieux, *Paul Bourget*, 1922; Roger Le Brun, *François de Curel*, 1905; Chanoine Le Cigne, *L'Evolution . . . de Paul Bourget*, 1904; Henry Malherbe, *Paul Hervieu*, 1912; R. de Rivasso, *Essai sur l'œuvre de Paul Bourget*, 1914; Tancrède de Visan, *Paul Bourget, sociologue*, 1908.

Ramsden Balmforth, *The Problem Play and its Influence on Modern Thought and Life*, 1928; Antoine Benoist, *Le Théâtre de Brieux*, 1907; A. Bertrand, *Eugène Brieux*, 1910; Frank W. Chandler, The Drama of Social Criticism, in *Aspects of Modern Drama*, 1914; Reformers, in *The Contemporary Drama of France*, 1920; Emma Goldman, *The Social Significance of Modern Drama*, 1914; Henry Arthur Jones, Preface to *The Theater of Ideas*, 1915; Armand Kahn, *Le Théâtre social en France*, 1907; H. L. Le Daum, *The European Problem Play*, in North Dakota Univ. Quarterly, 21, 1911; Emile de Saint-Auban, *L'Idée sociale au théâtre*, 1901; W. H. Scheifley, *Brieux and Contemporary French Society*, 1917; George Bernard Shaw, Preface to *Three Plays by Brieux*, 1911; P. V. Thomas, *The Plays of Eugène Brieux*, 1913; François Veuillot, *Les Prédicateurs de la scène*, 1904; Charles E. Young, *The Marriage Question in Modern French Drama*, 1912.

CHAPTER XIV

(ROMANTICISTS)

Wilhelm Arnold, *Rostands Princesse Lointaine und Samaritaine*, 1901; André Barre, *Le Symbolisme*, 1911; Léon Bazalgette, *Emile Verhaeren*, 1907; J. Bernard, *Savinien de Cyrano et M. Edmond Rostand*, 1903; A. Bertrand, *Catulle Mendès*, 1908; P. Blanchart, *Saint-Georges de Bouhélier*, 1912; Léon Bocquet, *Albert Samain*, 1905; Frank W. Chandler, *Aspects of Modern Drama* (Rostand and Maeterlinck), 1914; A. Daschelet, *Symbolisme et symbolistes*, 1904; G. Duhamel, *Paul Claudel*, 1913; T. S. Eliot, Rostand, in *The Sacred Wood*, 1921; J. Ernest-Charles, *Le Théâtre des poètes (1850-1910)*, 1910; Louis Estève, *De Nietzsche à Bouhélier*, 1912; Maurice Gauchez, *Emile Verhaeren*, 1908; Jules Haraszti, *Edmond Rostand*, 1910; Helmut Hatzfeld, *Paul Claudel und Romain Rolland*, 1921; Louis Haugmard, *Edmond Rostand*, 1910; Maurice Le Blond, *Saint-Georges de Bouhélier*, 1904; M. F. Liberma, *The Story of Chantecler*, 1910; Paul Lombard, *Le Théâtre de Saint-Georges de*

MODERN CONTINENTAL PLAYWRIGHTS

Bouhélier et l'avenir de l'art tragique, 1912; Catulle Mendès, *Le Mouvement poétique française*, 1903; E. Perrin, *L'Introduction à l'œuvre de Paul Claudel*, 1926; Georges Ramaekers, *Emile Verhaeren*, 1900; J. Rictus, *Un Bluff littéraire* (Rostand), 1903; Jean Suberville, *Le Théâtre d'Edmond Rostand*, 1919; Arthur Symons, *The Symbolist Movement in Literature;* Joseph Tonquédec, *L'Œuvre de Paul Claudel*, 1917; Stefan Zweig, *Emile Verhaeren*, 1910, tr. by Jethro Bithell, 1914.

Adolf van Bever, *Maurice Maeterlinck*, 1904; Jethro Bithell, *Life and Writings of Maurice Maeterlinck*, 1913; *Contemporary Belgian Literature*, 1915; Johannes Buschmann, *Maurice Maeterlinck, eine Studie*, 1908; G. K. Chesterton, *Books and Personalities* (Maeterlinck), 1905; Macdonald Clark, *Maurice Maeterlinck, Poet and Philosopher*, 1915; W. L. Courtney, *The Development of Maurice Maeterlinck*, 1904; M. Esch, *L'Œuvre de Maurice Maeterlinck*, 1912; Florence G. Fidler, *The Bird That is Blue, a Study of Maeterlinck's Two Fairy Plays*, 1928; Edward H. Griggs, *Maeterlinck, Poet and Mystic;* Gérard Harry, *Maurice Maeterlinck*, 1909, tr. by Alfred Allinson, 1910; Otto Heller, *The Mysticism of Maeterlinck* (Washington Univ. Studies, v. 2), 1915; E. C. Hills, *Evolution of Maeterlinck's Dramatic Theory*, 1907; Holbrook Jackson, *Maurice Maeterlinck*, 1910; G. Leneveu, *Ibsen et Maeterlinck*, 1902; F. Poppenberg, *Maeterlinck*, 1903; L. Le Sidanier, *Maurice Maeterlinck*, 1928; M. J. Moses, *Maurice Maeterlinck*, 1911; Henry Rose, *Maeterlinck's Symbolism*, 1911; Johannes Schlaf, *Maeterlinck*, 1907; I. Schryver, *Maeterlinck*, 1900; G. F. Sturgis, *The Psychology of Maeterlinck*, 1914; Una Taylor, *Maurice Maeterlinck, a Critical Study*, 1914; Edward Thomas, *Maurice Maeterlinck*, 1911; B. Timmermans, *Evolution de Maeterlinck*, 1912; G. Turquet-Milnes, *Some Modern Belgian Writers*, 1917.

CHAPTER XV

(POST-WAR PLAYWRIGHTS IN FRANCE)

Paul Adam, *La Littérature et la guerre*, 1916; Jean Bonnerot, *Romain Rolland*, 1921; Maurice Bourdet, *Jean Giraudoux*, 1928; Adolphe Brisson, *Le Théâtre pendant la guerre*, 1919; J. Laumonier, *Le Freudisme, Exposé et critique*, 1925; Louis de Monadon, *Le Théâtre de François Porché, Études* t. 174, 1923; John Palmer, *Studies in the Contemporary Theater*, 1927; Jules Romains, *Souvenirs du Vieux Colombier*, 1926; Daniel Rops, *Sur le théâtre de H.-R. Lenormand,—Le Théâtre d'inquiétude, Les Personnages abstraits, L'Utilisation littéraire du Freudisme*, 1926; Albert Schinz, *French Literature of the Great War*, 1920; Edmund Sée, *Les nouveaux Dramaturges*, H.-R. Lenormand, 1928; Paul Seippel, *Romain Rolland*, 1913; A. Tilgher, *La scena e la vita* (on Vildrac), 1923; Jean Vil, *La Littérature de guerre*, 1918; Frank Waldo, *The Art of the Vieux Colombier*, 1918; Stefan Zweig, *Romain Rolland*, tr. by E. and C. Paul, 1921.

CHAPTERS XVI TO XXII

(THE GERMANS AND AUSTRIANS IN GENERAL)

Robert F. Arnold, *Das moderne Drama*, 1908; *Bibliographie der deutschen bühnen seit 1830*, 2d enlarged edit., 1909; *Das deutsche Drama*, greatly amplified, 1925; Julius Bab, *Wege zum drama*, 1906; *Der Wille zum drama*, 1920;

WORKS OF REFERENCE

Neue Kritik der bühne, 1920; *Chronik des deutschen dramas*, 5 vols., 1900-1926; *Schauspiele und schauspielkunst*, 1926; *Das Theater der gegenwart*, 1928; Gerhard Baerg, *The Supernatural in German Drama*, 1923; Hermann Bahr, *Zur Kritik der moderne*, 1890; *Studien zur kritik der moderne*, 1894; *Renaissance*, 1897; *Wiener Theater*, 1899; Adolf Bartels, *Handbuch zur geschichte der deutschen literatur*, 1906; *Die deutsche dichtung der gegenwart*, 1921; Leo Berg, *Zwischen zwei Jahrhunderten*, 1896; *Der Uebermensch in der modernen literatur*, 1897; P. Besson, *Etudes sur le théâtre contemporain en Allemagne*, 1900; Carl Bleibtreu, *Revolution der literatur*, 1885; Otto Brahm, *Kritische schriften über drama und theater;* Hans Brandenburg, *Das neue Theater*, 1926; George Brandes, *Menschen und werke*, 1893, 1900; *Moderne Geister*, 1897; Heinrich Bulthaupt, *Dramaturgie des schauspiels*, 1898-1900, 1902-1905; J. F. Coar, *Studies in German Literature*, 1903; Otto Doell, *Die Entwicklung der form im jüngstdeutschen drama*, 1910; B. Filser, *Das Theater der zukunft*, 1921; Oskar Fischel, *Das moderne Bühnenbild,* 1923; Kuno Francke, *Glimpses of Modern German Culture*, 1898; *German Ideals of To-Day*, 1907; Max Freyhan, *Das Drama der gegenwart*, 1922; Sigismund Friedmann, *Das deutsche Drama des 19 jahrhunderts*, 2 vols., 1900-1903; R. von Gottschall, *Zur Kritik des modernen dramas*, 1900; A. von Haustein, *Das jüngste Deutschland*, 1900; W. Heise, *Das Drama der gegenwart;* Otto Heller, *Studies in Modern German Literature*, 1905; Josef Hofmiller, *Zeitgenossen*, 1910; Karl Holl, *Geschichte des deutschen lustspiels*, 1923; Herbert Ihering, *Der Kampf ums theater*, 1922; Rudolf Kayser, *Das junge deutsche Drama*, 1924; Alfred Kerr, *Das neue Drama*, 1905, 1909; Hermann Kienzl, *Dramen der gegenwart*, 1905; *Die Bühne ein echo der zeit*, 1907; Alfred Klaar, *Probleme der modernen dramatik*, 1921; Camillo von Klenze, *From Goethe to Hauptmann*, 1926; Wilhelm Kosch, *Das deutsche Theater und drama*, 1913; *Deutsches Literatur-Lexicon*, 2 vols., 1927-1930; Max Krell, *Das deutsche Theater der gegenwart*, 1923; Eugen Kühnemann, *Vom Weltreich des deutschen geistes*, 1914; Heinrich Laube, *Theater Kritken und dramaturgische aufsätze*, 1906; Karl Lehmann, *Junge deutsche Dramatiker*, 1923; *Vom Drama unserer zeit*, 1924; O. E. Lessing, *Masters in Modern German Literature*, 1916; Ludwig Lewisohn, *The Modern Drama*, 1915; *The Spirit of Modern German Literature*, 1916; Berthold Litzmann, *Das deutsche Drama*, 1894; Max Lorenz, *Die Literatur am jahrhundertende*, 1900; Rudolph Lothar, *Das Wiener Burgtheater*, 1899; *Das deutsche Drama der gegenwart*, 1905; Pierre Loving, *Revolt in German Drama*, 1925; Max Martersteig, *Das deutsche Theater im 19ten jahrhundert*, 1904; R. M. Meyer and H. Bieber, *Die deutsche Literatur des 19ten und 20ten jahrhunderts*, 1923; Arthur Moeller van den Bruck, *Die moderne Literatur*, 1902; *Die Zeitgenossen*, 1906; H. F. E. Naumann, *Die deutsche Dichtung der gegenwart*, (1885-1923), 1923; Y. Petersen, *Das deutsche national Theater*, 1919; Percival Pollard, *Masks and Minstrels of New Germany*, 1911; Robert Prölsz, *Geschichte der dramatischen literatur und kunst in Deutschland*, 1883; John G. Robertson, *A History of German Literature*, 1902; E. W. E. Roessler, *The Soliloquy in German Drama*, 1915; Carl Roettger, *Zum Drama und theater der zukunft*, 1921; M. J. Rudwin, *An Historical and Bibliographical Survey of the German Religious Drama*, 1924; Hermann Scheffauer, *The New Vision in the German Arts*, 1924; Wilhelm von Scholz, *Deutsche Dramaturgie*, 3 vols., 1912; Heinrich Spiero, *Deutsche Geister*, 1910; Edgar Steiger, *Das*

MODERN CONTINENTAL PLAYWRIGHTS

Werden des neuen dramas, 1898-1903, 1903; Richard Stein, *Literarische Bilder,* 1910; Sublinscki, *Der Bilanz der moderne,* 1904; Calvin Thomas, *A History of German Literature,* 1909; Richard Urban, *Die literarische Gegenwart,* 1908; Karl Westbrecht, *Das deutsche Drama,* 1903; Gustav Wethley, *Dramen der gegenwart,* 1903; W. Widmann, *Theater und revolution,* 1920; Ernst von Wildenbruch, *Das deutsche Drama,* 1906; Georg Witkowski, *The German Drama of the Nineteenth Century,* tr. by L. E. Horning, 1909; Eugen Wolf, *Geschichte der deutschen literatur in der gegenwart,* 1897; Eugen Zabel, *Zur modernen Dramaturgie,* 3 vols., 1903; *Moderne Bühnenkunst.*

CHAPTER XVI

(HEBBEL, NATURALISM, HAUPTMANN)

H. Meyer Benfey, *Hebbels Dramen,* 1913; Thomas M. Campbell, *Life and Works of Friedrich Hebbel,* 1919; Etta Federn, *Friedrich Hebbel,* 1920; Ernest A. Georgy, *Das Tragische bei F. Hebbel,* 1922; M. Grube, *Geschichte der Meininger;* Hermann Krumm, *Friedrich Hebbels Leben und werke;* J. Krumm, *Die Tragödie Hebbels,* 1908; Cort Kuechler, *Friedrich Hebbel,* 1910; Ferdinand Kürnberger, *Friedrich Hebbel als lyriker;* Mrs. C. M. P. Newport, *Woman in the Thought and Work of Friedrich Hebbel,* 1912; T. F. Poppe, *Hebbel und sein drama,* 1900; Carl Strecker, *Friedrich Hebbel und seine besten bühnenwerke,* 1922; E. Tannenbaum, *Friedrich Hebbel und das theater,* 1914; A. von Winterfeld, *Friedrich Hebbel,* 1920.

Julius Bab, *Naturalismus und mystik,* 1923; Hermann Bahr, *Die Ueberwindung des naturalismus,* 1891; Louis Benoist-Hanappier, *Le Drame naturaliste en Allemagne,* 1905; Leo Berg, *Der Naturalismus,* 1892; W. Beyschlag, *Ein Blick in das jugendtsche naturalistische drama,* 1895; Carl Bleibtreu, *Die Verrohung der literatur,* 1903; Otto Brahm, *Kritische Schriften über drama und theater; Briefe und errinerungen,* 1925; M. G. Conradt, *Von Emile Zola bis Gerhart Hauptmann,* 1902; Max Deri, *Naturalismus, idealismus, expressionismus,* 1921; Paul Ernst, *Der Weg zur form,* 1906; A. Fried, *Der Naturalismus,* 1891; K. Goldmann, *Die Sünden des naturalismus,* 1890; M. Günther, *Die soziologischen Grundlagen des naturalistischen drama,* 1912; A. Holz, *Die Kunst, ihr wesen und gesetze,* 1891; *Neue Folge,* 1893; Günther Keil, *Max Kretzer, a Study in German Naturalism,* 1928; Robert Krebs, *Das moderne realistisch-naturalistische Drama,* 1897; O. E. Lessing, *Die neue Form . . . zum verständnis des deutschen naturalismus,* 1910; Riessmann, *Der Naturalismus in der kunst,* 1891; P. Schlenther, *Wozu der Lärm, genesis der Freie Bühne,* 1899; A. R. Schlissmann, *Beiträge zur geschichte und kritik des naturalismus,* 1908; Alfred Stoeckius, *Naturalism in the Recent German Drama,* 1903; C. G. Vollmöller, *Die Sturm und Drang periode und der moderne deutsche realismus,* 1897; Georg Witkowski, *Naturalism in Recent German Drama,* tr. by L. E. Horning, 1909.

Julius Bab, *Gerhart Hauptmann und seine besten bühnenwerke,* 1922; A. Bartels, *Gerhart Hauptmann,* 1897, 1906; P. Besson, *Gerhart Hauptmann,* 1900; Sigmund Bytkowski, *Gerhart Hauptmanns naturalismus und das drama,* 1908; G. Caprin, *La Germania letteraria d'oggi,* 1912; Frank W. Chandler, *The Drama of Naturalism and Hauptmann,* in *Aspects of Modern Drama,* 1914; A. Esprey, *Gerhart Hauptmann und wir Deutschen,* 1916; Paul Fechter, *Gerhart Hauptmann,* 2d edition, 1922; Max Freyhan, *Gerhart Hauptmann,*

1922; K. Haenisch, *Gerhart Hauptmann*, 1922; A. von Hanstein, *Gerhart Hauptmann*, 1898; Georg Hecht, *Gerhart Hauptmann*, 1912; Hans Helmer, *Das Symbolische in Die Versunkene Glocke*, 1897; Christian Herrmann, *Die Weltanschauung Gerhart Hauptmanns in seinen werken*, 1926; Karl Holl, *Gerhart Hauptmann, his Life and his Work*, 1913; C. A. Krause, *Hauptmann's Treatment of Blank Verse*, 1910; E. Langner, *Die Religion Gerhart Hauptmanns*, 1928; Ludwig Lewisohn, Introductions to various plays in *The Dramatic Works of Gerhart Hauptmann*, 9 vols., 1921-1929; C. de Lollis, *Gerhart Hauptmann e l'opera sua letteraria*, 1899; Hans Lorentz, *Der Ideengehalt der Versunkene Glocke*, 1898; P. Mahn, *Hauptmann und der moderne realismus*, 1894; Ludwig Marcuse, *Gerhart Hauptmann und sein werk*, 1922; J. H. Marchan, *Das Mitleid bei Gerhart Hauptmann*, 1919; Hans Rabl, *Die dramatische Handlung in Gerhart Hauptmanns Webern*, 1928; H. Ramiew, *Die Symbolik in Gerhart Hauptmanns märchendrama Die versunkene Glocke;* Julius Röhr, *Gerhart Hauptmanns dramatisches Schaffen*, 1912; Heinrich M. Schaub, *Gerhart Hauptmann*, 1914; Paul Schlenther, *Gerhart Hauptmann, sein lebensgang und seine dichtung*, 1808; *Gerhart Hauptmanns leben und werke* (enlarged by A. Eloesser), 1922; K. W. H. Scholz: *The Art of Translation with Special Reference to . . . Hauptmann and Sudermann;* Kurt Sternberg, *Gerhart Hauptmann*, 1910; Emil Sulger-Gebing, *Gerhart Hauptmann*, 1909; Nesta Thompson, *Naturalism and the Dream Motive in Hauptmann* (Washington Univ. Studies, v. 8), 1920; W. H. F. Trumbauer, *Gerhart Hauptmann and John Galsworthy, a Parallel*, 1917; Franz Vollmers-Schulte, *Gerhart Hauptmann und die sociale frage*, 1923; Oskar Walzel, *Gerhart Hauptmann und der expressionismus*, in Preussische Jahrbücher, 190, 1922; Wilhelm Weygandt, *Abnorme Charakter in der dramatischen literatur*, 1910; Josef Wiehr, *The Naturalistic Plays of Gerhart Hauptmann*, in Journal of English and Germanic Philology, v. 6; U. C. Woerner, *Gerhart Hauptmann*, 1897, 1901.

CHAPTERS XVII TO XX

(SUDERMANN, THE LESSER GERMANS AND THE NEW STAGECRAFT, THE AUSTRIANS, THE IRREPRESSIBLES)

Ida Axelrod, *Hermann Sudermann*, 1907; P. Besson, *Les Romans et les nouvelles de Sudermann;* Kurt Busse, *Hermann Sudermann*, 1927; Theodor H. Kappstein, *Sudermann und seine besten bühnenwerke;* R. A. Hoffmann, *Was hat Sudermann in Johannes gewollt, was erreicht*, 1898; W. Kauwerau, *Hermann Sudermann*, 1897; H. Schoen, *Hermann Sudermann, poète dramatique*, 1904; George Seibel, *Hauptmann and Sudermann;* Heinrich Spiero, *Hermann Sudermann*, 1928; A. Stern, *Sudermann und Hauptmann*, 1925; Hermann Sudermann, *Verrohung in der theater kritik*, 1902.

H. H. Borcherdt, *Carl Hauptmann*, 1911; H. Tessmer, *Carl Hauptmann und seine besten bühnenwerke*, 1922; Cäsar Flaischlen, *Otto Erich Hartleben*, 1896; Gustav Freytag, *Errinerungen aus meiner leben*, 1887, tr. by Katharine Chetwynd, 1890; Paul Heyse, *Jugend errinerungen und bekenntnisse*, 1900; Manfred Georg, *Carl Sternheim und seine besten bühnenwerke*, 1923; Jonas Fraenkel, *J. V. Widmann*, 1919; W. Scheitlin, *J. V. Widmanns Weltanschauung*, 1925; Walther Ziersch, *Ludwig Thoma*, 1928; Ludwig Thoma, *Leute die ich kannte* (Drachmann, Hartleben, Wedekind, etc.), 1923.

MODERN CONTINENTAL PLAYWRIGHTS

On Appia, Fuchs, Reinhardt, Jessner, Piscator, and the new stagecraft see *ante* under Play Production, as well as the following, which necessarily include some titles from that section:

A. Appia, *La Mise-en-scène du drame Wagnérien*, 1895; *Die Musik und die inscenierung*, 1899; Julius Bab, *Das Theater der gegenwart*, 1928; Hermann Bahr, *Wiener Theater*, 1899; Fritz Baumgarten, *Zirkus Reinhardt*, 1920; E. Bergmann, *Der Fall Reinhardt;* Hans Boehm, *Die Wiener Reinhardtbühne im lichtbild*, 1926; Huntly Carter, *Max Reinhardt*, 1914; Sheldon Cheney, *Stage Decoration*, 1928; J. Cournos, *Gordon Craig and the Theater of the Future*, 1913; Gordon Craig, *On the Art of the Theater*, 1911; *Towards a New Theater*, 1913; *The Theater-Advancing*, 1919; *Scene*, 1923; John Dolman, *The Art of Play Production*, 1928; Victor Eckert, *Literatur und theater*, (1) *deutsche theaterkunst*, (2) *die städtische bühne*, 1914; Alfred von Engel, *Bühnenbeleuchtung*, 1926;. M. Epstein, *Max Reinhardt*, 1920; Oscar Fischl, *Das moderne Bühnenbild*, 1918; Georg Fuchs, *Die Schaubühne der zukunft; Die Revolution des theaters*, 1914; Theodore Fuchs, *Stage Lighting*, 1929; M. Grube, *Geschichte der Meininger;* Carl Hagemann, *Moderne Bühnenkunst*, 1916-1918; Heinz Herald, *Max Reinhardt*, 1914; Herald and Ernst Stein, *Das Grosse Schauspielhaus*, 1920; Hans Herrig, *Die Meininger*, 1880; Glenn Hughes, *The Story of the Theater*, 1928; S. J. Hume and W. R. Fuerst, *XX Century Stage Decoration*, 2 vols., 1929; Siegfried Jacobsohn, *Max Reinhardt*, 1910, 1914, 1921; Friedrich Kranich, *Die modernen Bühnentechnik*, 1928; Paul Legband, *Das deutsche Theater in Berlin*, 1909; Siegfried Loewy, *Deutsche Theaterkunst von Goethe bis Reinhardt*, 1923; Rudolph Lothar, *Das Wiener Burgtheater*, 1899; Kenneth MacGowan, *The Theater of To-Morrow*, 1921; MacGowan and R. E. Jones, *Continental Stagecraft*, 1922; Friedrich Michael, *Deutsches Theater*, 1923; Vladimir Polunin, *The Continental Method of Scene Painting*, 1927; Albert Rutherston, *Decoration in the Theater*, 1919; Oliver Sayler, *Max Reinhardt and his Theater*, 1924; Paul Stefan, *Max Reinhardt*, 1923; Andreas Streit, *Das Theater*, 1903; Frank Vernon, *Modern Stage Production*, 1923.

Ludwig Anzengruber, *Beiträge zur selbstbiographie;* A. Bettelheim, *Ludwig Anzengruber*, 1894; Adolf Busse, Preface to his translation of *The Farmer Forsworn*, in K. Francke and W. G. Howard, *German Classics*, v. 16, 1914; Paul Zschorlich, *Anzengruber und seine besten bühnenwerke;* Hermann Bahr, *Wiener Theater*, 1899; Bahr and Hugo von Hofmannsthal, *Theater und kultur*, 1922-1924; Auguste Erhardt, *Grillparzer et le théâtre en Autriche;* R. Lothar, *Das Wiener Burgtheater*, 1899; A. Maderno, *Die deutsch-österreichische Dichtung der gegenwart*, 1920; A. Pollak, *Franz Grillparzer and the Austrian Drama*, 1907; Hermann Kienzl, *Schönherr und 6 seiner besten bühnenwerke;* Richard Sedlmaier, *Schönherr*, 1920; Paul H. Grummann, Introductions to volumes in Vienna Edition of Schnitzler's Works, from 1913; Frank W. Chandler, Schnitzler in *Aspects of Modern Drama*, 1914; Julius Kapp, *Arthur Schnitzler*, 1912; Theodore H. Kappstein, *Arthur Schnitzler und seine besten bühnenwerke*, 1922; Josef Körner, *Arthur Schnitzlers gestalten und probleme*, 1921; Hans Landsberg, *Arthur Schnitzler*, 1904; Theodor Reik, *Arthur Schnitzler*, 1913; Alexander Salkind, *Arthur Schnitzler*, 1907; Richard Specht, *Arthur Schnitzler*, 1922; Mary Macken, *Hermann Bahr*, in *Studies*, Dublin, v. 15, 1926; A. W. Berendsohn, *Der Impressionismus, Hugo von Hofmannsthal*, 1920; Mrs. Patrick Campbell, *My Life and Some Letters*

WORKS OF REFERENCE

(on von Hofmannsthal), 1922; H. M. Elster, *Von Hofmannsthal und 16 seiner besten bühnenwerke;* August Köllmann, *Hugo von Hofmannsthal,* 1907; Philipp Seibert, *Hugo von Hofmannsthal,* in K. Francke and W. G. Howard, *German Classics,* v. 17, 1914; Emil Sulger-Gebing, *Hugo von Hofmannsthal,* 1905.

F. Blei, *Ueber Wedekind, Sternheim, und das theater,* 1915; Frank W. Chandler, Wedekind in *Aspects of Modern Drama,* 1914; P. J. Cremers, *Walter Hasenclever,* 1922; Samuel A. Eliot, Jr., Introduction to Wedekind's *Tragedies of Sex,* 1923; H. M. Elster, *Wedekind und 10 seiner besten bühnenwerke,* 1922; Paul Fechter, *Frank Wedekind,* 1920; Paul Friedrich, *Frank Wedekind,* 1913; Joachim Friedenthal, *Das Wedekindbuch,* 1914; Fritz Hagemann, *Wedekinds Erdgeist und Die Büchse der Pandora,* 1926; Julius Kapp, *Frank Wedekind,* 1909; Hans Kempner, *Frank Wedekind,* 1911; A. Kutscher, *Frank Wedekind,* 1922-1927; K. F. Proost, *Wedekind,* 1928; Raimund Pissin, *Frank Wedekind,* 1905; Ludwig Thoma, *Leute die ich kannte,* 1923; F. J. Ziegler, Introduction to his translation of Wedekind's *The Awakening of Spring,* 1909.

CHAPTERS XXI-XXIII

(EXPRESSIONISTS, MOLNAR, AND THE ČAPEKS)

Hermann Bahr, *Expressionismus,* 1919, tr. by R. T. Gribble, 1925; Bernhard Diebold, *Anarchie im drama,* 1921; *Der Denkspieler Georg Kaiser,* 1924; Anton Dörfler, *Wildgans und seine besten bühnenwerke;* Fritz Droop, *Ernst Toller,* 1922; Kasimir Edschmid, *Ueber den Expressionismus in der literatur und die neue dichtung,* 1919, 1921; Felix Emmel, *Das ekstatische Theater,* 1924; Fritz Engel, *Fritz von Unruh und seine besten bühnenwerke,* 1922; Paul Fechter, *Der Expressionismus,* 1919; Max Freyhan, *Georg Kaisers Werk,* 1926; Wilhelm Geyer, *Fritz von Unruh,* 1924; Edward Goldbeck, *Franz Werfel,* in *Reflex,* 1928; Heinz Jansen, *Der Westfale August Stramm,* in *Westfalische Studien,* 1928; Ernst Jockers, *Franz Werfel als religiöser dichter,* 1927; Hans Knudsen, *Georg Kaiser,* 1929; H. F. Koenigsgarten, *Georg Kaiser mit einer selbstbiographie,* 1928; Walter Küchler, *R. Rolland, H. Barbusse, Fritz von Unruh,* 1919; Ludwig Lewin, *Die Jagd nach dem erlebnis. Ein buch über Georg Kaiser,* 1926; *Das Erlebnis bei Georg Kaiser,* 1929; Arthur Luther, *Franz Werfel und seine besten bühnenwerke,* 1922; Georg Marzynski, *Die Methode des expressionismus,* 1921; Robert Meister, *Fritz von Unruh;* W. Osmankowski, *Georg Kaiser und seine besten bühnenstücke,* 1922; D. R. Pfister, *Expressionism in Art,* tr. from the German, 1922; Camille Poupeye, *Le Théâtre expressioniste,* 1924; Manfred Schneider, *Der Expressionismus im drama,* 1920; Paul Signer, *Ernst Toller,* 1924; Albert Soergel, *Dichtung und dichter der zeit—im banne des expressionismus,* 1925; Richard Specht, *Franz Werfel,* 1926; H. Walden, *Der Expressionismus,* 1919; Paul Westheim, *Oskar Kokoschka,* 1918; Wilhelm Worringer, *Nach-Expressionismus,* 1926.

Louis Brun, *Charles Tchapek,* in *Vie des peuples,* 1923; Jehnek, *La Littérature tcheque contemporaine,* 1912; Hankiss and Juhász, *La Littérature hongroise,* 1930; George Halasz, *Ferenc Molnár, the Man Behind the Monocle,* 1929; Louis Rittenberg, Introduction to *Plays of Ferenc Molnár,* 1929.

MODERN CONTINENTAL PLAYWRIGHTS

Sanz Balza, *La Fuerza bruta, estudio crítico,* 1911; A. J. Bastinos, *Arte dramático español contemporáneo,* 1914; Rudolf Beer, *Spanische Literaturgeschichte,* 1903; Aubrey F. G. Bell, *Contemporary Spanish Literature,* 1925; José Bernat y Durán, *Historia de el teatro español,* 2 vols., 1924; A. González Blanco, *Dramaturgos contemporáneos,* 1917; Manuel Bueno, *Teatro español contemporáneo,* 1909; *Los Dramaturgos españoles contemporáneos;* A. D. Canovas del Castillo, *Le Théâtre espagnol contemporain;* Julio Cejador y Frauca, *Historia de la lengua y literatura castellana (bibliografía de la historia del teatro,* in vol. 2), 14 vols., 1915-1922; Augusto de Lacerda, *Teatro futuro visão de uma nova dramaturgia,* 1924; Barrett H. Clark, Introduction to *Masterpieces of Modern Spanish Drama,* 1917; Francisco Curet, *El Arte dramático en el resurgir de Cataluña,* 1917; P. C. Eguia Ruiz, *Literaturas y literatos, estudios contemporáneos,* 1914; N. D. Escover and F. de P. L. de Vega, *Historia del teatro español,* 2 vols., 1924; J. D. M. Ford, *Main Currents of Spanish Literature,* 1919; Rodríguez Francos, *El Teatro en España,* 2 vols., 1908-1909; A. Gassier, *Le Théâtre espagnol,* 1898; Isaac Goldberg, *The Drama of Transition,* 1922; G. Hubbard, *Histoire de la littérature contemporaine en Espagne;* Juan Hurtado y Jiménez de la Serna, *Historia de la literatura española,* 1921, enlarged, 1925; James Fitzmaurice Kelly, *Bibliographie de l'histoire littéraire espagnole,* 1913; *A New History of Spanish Literature,* new ed., in French, 1913; in English, 1926; in Spanish, with Bibliography, pp. 383-517, 1926; H. Lionne, *Le Théâtre en Espagne et en Portugal,* 1897; Salvador de Madariaga, *The Genius of Spain and Other Essays on Contemporary Literature,* 1923; Manuel Machado, *La Guerra literaria* (1898-1914), 1914; E. Madrazo, *Conferencias dadas en el Ateneo de Madrid;* A. Marichalar, *Contemporary Spanish Literature, Criterion,* 1923; Ernest Mérimée, *Précis d'histoire de la littérature espagnole,* 1908; tr. by S. Griswold Morley, as *A History of Spanish Literature,* 1930; A. Morel-Fatio and A. Rouanel, *Le Théâtre espagnol,* 1900; A. Morel-Fatio, *Bibliographie critique du théâtre espagnol,* 1912; G. T. Northup, *An Introduction to Spanish Literature,* 1925; José León Pagano, *Al través de la España literaria,* 1904; Antonio Palau y Dulcet, *Manuel del librero hispano-americano,* 1926; Emilia Pardo Bazan, *Polémicas y estudios literarios;* R. Pérez de Ayala, *Máscaras,* 1919; Hugo A. Rennert, *The Spanish Stage,* 1909; Cristóbal Rodríguez, *Páginas;* J. Francos Rodríguez, *El Año teatral,* 1908; M. Romera-Navarro, *Historia de la literatura española,* 1928; Salvador Salazar y Roig, *Cursó de historia de la literatura española,* 3 vols., *El Siglo XX,* 1925-1926; José Rogerio Sánchez, *Resumen de historia de la lengua y literatura españolas,* 1918; J. Martínez Ruiz (Azorín), *Clásicos y modernos,* 1913; J. B. Trend, *A Picture of Modern Spain,* 1921; Charles A. Turrell, Introduction to *Contemporary Spanish Dramatists,* 1919; F. Vézinet, *Les Maîtres du roman espagnol contemporain,* 1907; L. Viel Castel, *Essai sur le théâtre espagnol,* 1882; L. A. Warren, *Modern Spanish Literature,* 2 vols., 1929; J. Yxart, *L'Art scénique en Espagne,* 1894-1896.

Mariano Alarcón, *Benavente as an Interpreter of Women,* in *Poet Lore* 29; Jacinto Benavente, *El Teatro del pueblo,* 1909; Julio Brouta, *Spain's Greatest*

Dramatist, in *The Drama,* 1915; Henri de Curzon, *Un Théâtre d'idées en Espagne* (Echegaray), 1912; James Graham, Introductions to *The Son of Don Juan,* by Echegaray, 1895; *Mariana,* by Echegaray, 1895; Harley and Helen Granville-Barker, Introduction to *Four Plays by S. and J. Alvarez Quintero,* 1928; Hannah Lynch, Introduction to her translations of *The Great Galeoto* and *Folly or Saintliness,* by Echegaray, 1895; Gregorio Martínez Sierra, *Un Teatro de arte en España,* 1926; S. Griswold Morley, Introduction to *Doña Clarines* and *Mañana de Sol* of the Quinteros; L. A. del Ohnet and A. G. Carraffa, *Echegaray,* 1912; Federico de Onis, *Jacinto Benavente,* 1923; M. Gil de Oto, *Rasgos de ingenio,* 1921; *El Geni dramátic de Guimerá,* 1924; J. Martínez Ruiz (Azorín), *Los Quinteros y otras páginas,* 1925; José Sánchez, *Estudio crítico acerca de la Malquerida,* 1914; Walter Starkie, *Gregorio Martínez Sierra and the Modern Spanish Drama,* 1924; *Jacinto Benavente,* 1924; J. G. Underhill, *Benavente as a Modern,* in *Poet Lore* 29; Introductions to *Malvaloca* of the Quinteros, tr. by J. S. Fasset, Jr., 1912; *Plays of Jacinto Benavente,* 4 vols., 1917-1924; *Plays of Gregorio Martínez Sierra,* 2 vols., 1923; Joseph Yxart, *Prólech á las poesías de Angel Guimerá,* 2d edit., 1905; *La Escena catalania,* 1906; A. Zacher, *Don José Echegaray der verfasser des Galeoto,* 1892.

CHAPTER XXVII-XXIX

(THE ITALIANS)

A. Andreotti, *Tre Glorie italiane,* 1908; Guillaume Apollinaire, *Le Théâtre italien,* 1910; R. Barbiera, *Polvere di palcoscenico,* 1908; P. Bettoli, *Storia del teatro drammatico italiano,* 1901; A. Boccardi, *Teatro e vita;* G. A. Borgese, *Tempo di edificare,* 1923; A. G. Bragaglia, *La Maschera mobile,* 1926; *Del Teatro teatrale,* 1926; Luigi Capuana, *Il Teatro italiano contemporaneo,* 1872; A. Cippico, *The Romantic Age in Italian Literature,* 1918; Benedetto Croce, *La Letteratura della nuova Italia,* 1915; Lucio d'Ambra, *Le Opere e gli uomini,* 1904; Silvio d'Amico, *Il Teatro dei fantocci,* 1920; D'Ancona and Bacci, *Manuale della letteratura italiana,* 1910; Jean Dornis (Mme. Guillaume Beer), *Le Théâtre italien contemporain,* 1903; V. Ferrari, *La Letteratura italiana moderna e contemporanea,* 1901; M. Ferrigni, *Il Teatro drammatico sperimentale,* 1903-1905; Domenico Flora, *Dal Romanticismo al futurismo,* 1925; P. Gibelli, *Breve Storia del teatro italiano,* 1909; Gino Gori, *Il Teatro contemporaneo,* 1924; P. Gori, *Scenografia,* 1927; Luisa Grapollo, *Autori italiani d'oggi;* J. S. Kennard, *Italian Romance Writers,* 1922; Cesare Levi, *Autori drammatici italiani,* 1922; H. Lyonnet, *Le Théâtre hors de France: Italie,* 1902; Lander MacClintock, *The Contemporary Drama of Italy,* 1920; Addison McLeod, *Plays and Players in Modern Italy,* 1912; D. Mantovani, *La Letteratura contemporanea,* 1903; F. Martini, *Al Teatro,* 1905; Guido Mazzoni, *L'Ottocento,* 1913; Maurice Muret, *La Littérature italienne d'aujourd'hui,* 1906; D. Oliva, *Il Teatro italiano nel 1909,* 1911; R. S. Phelps, *Italian Silhouettes,* 1924; D. Rovito, *Dizionario dei letterati e Italiani contemporanei,* 1907; G. M. Scalinger, *Teatro sociologico,* 1902; Scipio Sighele, *Letteratura tragica,* 1906; Adriano Tilgher, *Voci del tempo,* 1923; *La Scena e la vita,* 1923; *Studi sul teatro contemporaneo,* 1923; Luigi Tonelli, *L'Evoluzione del teatro contemporaneo in Italia,* 1908, 1913; *Il Teatro italiano*

679

MODERN CONTINENTAL PLAYWRIGHTS

dalle origini ai nostri giorni, 1924; B. Villanova d'Ardenghi, *Il Teatro neo-idealistico*, 1908; K. Vossler, *Italienische Literatur der gegenwart*, 1914. Francesco Biondolillo, *Il Teatro di Roberto Bracco*, 1923; Lady Charlotte J. Blennerhasset, *D'Annunzio;* Jeanne Bordeux, *Eleonora Duse, The Story of Her Life*, 1925; G. A. Borgese, *Gabriele d'Annunzio*, 1909; Antonio Bruers, *Gabriele d'Annunzio e il moderno spirito italico*, 1921; Giuseppe Busoli, *Gabriele d'Annunzio*, 1902; L. Capuana, *Per l'Arte*, 1885; *Gli 'Ismi' contemporanei*, 1889; R. Chiti, *I Creatori del teatro futurista*, 1915; A. Donati, *Gabriele d'Annunzio*, 1912; Alfredo Gargiulo, *Gabriele d'Annunzio*, 1912; G. N. Gatti, *Il Teatro di Giuseppe Giacosa*, 1914; Louis Gillet, *Un Humoriste sicilien, Pirandello*, in *Revue des deux mondes*, 1923; Isaac Goldberg, Introduction to *Plays of the Italian Theater*, 1921; *The Drama of Transition*, 1922; E. Gomez de Baquero, *Pirandello y compañia*, 1928; Gino Gori, *Il Grottesco nella arte e nella letteratura*, 1926; Oscar Kuhns, *D'Annunzio in Great Poets of Italy*, 1903; Arthur Livingston, Introductions to his translations of Pirandello—*Three Plays*, 1922; *Each In His Own Way and Two Other Plays*, 1923; *The One-Act Plays*, 1928; J. N. Macdonald, *A Political Escapade, the Story of Fiume and d'Annunzio*, 1921; Roberto Mandel, *Gabriele d'Annunzio*, 1928; F. T. Marinetti, *Le Futurisme*, 1911; *Zang Tumb Tumb!* 1914; *Noi Futuristi*, 1917; *Democrazia futurista*, 1919; *I Manifesti del futurismo*, 1921; F. Martini, *Al Teatro*, 1905; Godfrey W. Masters, *Pirandello, a Study in the Psychology of the Modern Stage*, 1928; V. Morello, *Gabriele d'Annunzio*, 1910; T. Olgiati, *D'Annunzio*, 1916; F. Pala, *Sem Benelli;* E. Palmieri, *Gabriele d'Annunzio*, 1920; P. Parisi, *Roberto Bracco*, 1923; Ferdinando Pasini, *Luigi Pirandello*, 1927; Georges Pellissier, *Sur le Théâtre de Gabriele d'Annunzio*, 1901; Luigi Pirandello, *Pourquoi et comment j'ai écrit Six Personnages en Quête d'Auteur*, 1925; E. Prampolini, *La Scenografia futurista*, 1915; *Rivista d'arte futurista*, 1924; Puttkamer, *Gabriele d'Annunzio*, 1904; G. Rafaelli, *La Tragica e letteraria storia di Francesca da Rimini nella letteratura italiana*, 1916; V. La Rocca, *Sem Benelli*, 1911; Daniel Rops, *Luigi Pirandello*, 1927; L. Russo, *Giovanni Verga*, 1920; Sebastiano Sciuto, *Giuseppe Giacosa e l'opera sua*, 1910; E. Settimelli, *Marinetti, l'uomo e l'artista*, 1921; William Sharp, *Studies and Appreciations* (d'Annunzio), 1912; J. M. Sheehan, *Gabriele d'Annunzio;* Arthur Symons, Introductions to his translations of d'Annunzio's *The Dead City*, 1900; *Gioconda*, 1902; and *Francesca da Rimini*, 1902; and *Studies in Prose and Verse*, 1904; H. D. Sidgwick, *D'Annunzio* in *Essays on Great Writers*, 1903; Luigi Tonelli, *La Tragedia di Gabriele d'Annunzio*, 1915; E. and A. Updegraff, Introduction to their translation of *Three Plays by Giuseppe Giacosa*, 1915.

INDEX

These references do not include the names of plays, translators, editors and critics mentioned only in the Bibliography.

INDEX

INDEX

INDEX

INDEX

INDEX

INDEX

694

INDEX

INDEX

INDEX

INDEX

699

INDEX

INDEX

INDEX

INDEX

INDEX

INDEX

INDEX